6 Class Foundation MATHEMATICS for IIT-JEE/Olympiad

100% useful for Class 6 School Exam

Set of 4 Solved Exercises

→ Exercise 1: FIB, T/F, Matching, VSA, SA and LA Questions

→ Exercise 2: NCERT, Exemplar and HOTS Questions

→ Exercise 3 & 4: MCQs 1 Correct, MCQs $\geq$ 1 Correct, Passage, Assertion-Reason, Multiple Matching and Integer Type Questions

- **Corporate Office :** 45, 2nd Floor, Maharishi Dayanand Marg, Corner Market, Malviya Nagar, New Delhi-110017

  Tel. : 011-49842349 / 49842350

D. P. Gupta
Shikhaa Nagpal

Typeset by Disha DTP Team

Printed at Repro Knowledgecast Limited, Thane

DISHA PUBLICATION

ALL RIGHTS RESERVED

For further information about the books from DISHA,

Log on to **www.dishapublication.com** or email to **info@dishapublication.com**

Contents

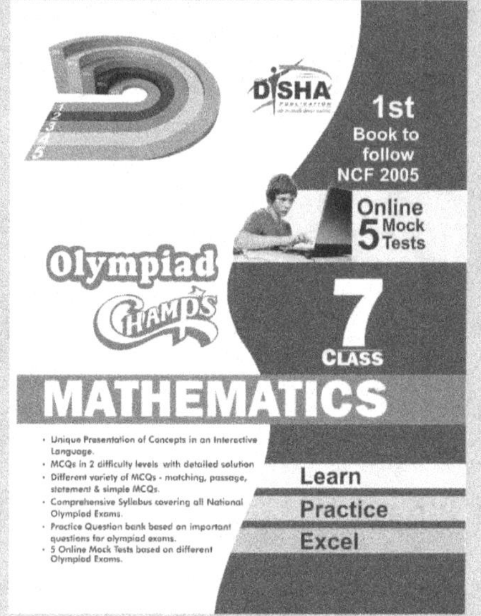

Complete Preparatory Material for all School

Olympiad Exams 7 & 8

Knowing Our Numbers

The method of expressing a number in words is called **numeration**.

While reading numbers, it is always easy to use words instead of reading individual digits.

For example : Instead of reading 5632 as Five, Six, Three, Two, it is easy to read it as "Five thousand six hundred thirty two".

In this section, we shall discuss two commonly used methods of numeration.

(i) Indian system of Numeration.   (ii) International system of Numeration.

Indian System of Numeration

The Indian system of numeration is used in India as well as in Bangladesh, Nepal and Pakistan. In this system, we use ones, tens, hundreds, thousands and then lakhs and crores. The first comma comes after hundreds place the second comma comes two digits later, the third comma comes after another two digits as so on.

The following place value chart is used to write numbers.

Periods →	Crores		Lakhs		Thousands		Ones		
Places →	Ten Crores	Crores	Ten Lakhs	Lakhs	Ten Thousands	Thousands	Hundreds	Tens	Ones
	100000000	10000000	1000000	100000	10000	1000	100	10	1
				5	6	0	3	2	8
		4	1	3	7	2	5	4	6

This place value chart is populary known as **Indian Place Value Chart**.

Reading Numbers

In order to read number in the Indian system of numeration, we group place values into periods. 'Ones', 'thousands' 'lakhs', 'crores', 'Arabs' are periods.

The digits in the same period are read together and the name of the period (except units) is read along with them. Thus, the number 5,43,87,539 is read as 'five crore forty three lakh eighty seven thousand five hundred thirty nine'.

Writing Numbers

Consider the number 'Seven lakh six hundred five'. This number represents a collection of 7 lakhs, no thousands, 6 hundreds, no tens and 5 units. So, it is expressed as

$$7 \ 0 \ 0 \ 6 \ 0 \ 5$$

The expanded form of this number is

$$7 \times 100000 + 0 \times 10000 + 0 \times 1000 + 6 \times 100 + 0 \times 10 + 5 \times 1$$

International System of Numeration

International system is followed by most of the countries of the world. In this system, we use ones, tens, hundreds, thousands, millions and billions.

A number is also split into different groups called periods such as ones, thousands, millions and billions. Given below is the place value chart in the International system.

Periods→	Billions			Millions			Thousands			Ones		
Places →	Hundred Billion	Ten Billion	Billion	Hundred Million	Ten Million	Million	Hundred Thousand	Ten Thousand	Thousand	Hundred	Tens	Ones
	100000000000	10000000000	1000000000	100000000	10000000	1000000	100000	10000	1000	100	10	1
		5	6	4	3	1	0	2	3	7	0	9
				8	9	5	8	8	0	0	6	3

NOTE : The digits in the same period are read together and name of the period (except ones) is read along with them.

Consider the number 456732001

Billions			Millions			Thousands			Ones		
HB	TB	B	HM	TM	M	HTh	TTh	Th	H	T	O
			4	5	6	7	3	2	0	0	1

On inserting the commas after each period, we write the number 456732001 as 456,732,001.

Thus, this number is read as "four hundred fifty six million seven hundred thirty two thousand one".

We may write this number in the expanded form as

$456,732,001 = 4 \times 100,000,000 + 5 \times 10,000,000 + 6 \times 1,000,000 + 7 \times 100,000 + 3 \times 10,000 + 2 \times 1000 + 1 \times 1.$

PLACE VALUE

Place value of a digit in a given number is the value of the digit because of the place or the position of the digit in the number.

For example: Consider the number 6503

        Place value of 3 = 3.

        Place value of 0 = 0, Place value of 5 = 500,

        Place value of 6 = 6000

COMPARISON OF NUMBERS

When the Number of Digits are Different

(i)   Check the number of digits in each number.

(ii) The number having more number of digits is the greater one than the number having less number of digits.

    For example: 12456 > 2345

                1534 < 12345

When the Number of Digits are the Same

(i)   Compare the left most digit of each number.

(ii) The number with the greater left most digit is greater

    For example: 4378 > 2378

(iii) In case, the left most digit is same, compare the next digit of both numbers. The number with the greater digit is greater.

For example: 5765 > 5467

ILLUSTRATION : 1

Which number is greater ?

(i)   64527 or 3482   **(ii)   85893 or 95806**

SOLUTION :

(i)   As we know that the number with more digits is greater.
Therefore, 64527 > 3482

(ii) As we know that if the number of digits in both numerals are equal, then we compare the digits at the extreme left.
Therefore, 95806 > 85893

LARGE NUMBERS

We know that

Greatest single digit number is 9

Greatest two digit number is 99

Greatest three digit number is 999

Greatest four digit number is 9999

If we add 1 to the above numbers, we get

$9 + 1 = 10$ (smallest 2 digit number)

$99 + 1 = 100$ (smallest 3 digit number)

$999 + 1 = 1000$ (smallest 4 digit number)

$9999 + 1 = 10000$ (smallest 5 digit number)

So, from above observation, it is clear that on adding one to the greatest number of any number of digits gives smallest number of next number of digits.

LARGE NUMBERS IN PRACTICE

In our daily life, we have to use different units of measurements to measure different things. For liquid, we use litre or millilitre, for weight, gram or kilogram, for distance, metre or kilometre etc. You may be familiar with most of them. However, let us do a quick revision.

Units of mass	Units of lengths	Units of volume
1 kg = 1,000 g	1 km = 1,000 m	1 k*l* = 1,000 *l*
1 g = 1,000 mg	1 m = 100 cm	1 L = 1,000 m*l*
1 kg = 1,000,000 mg	1 cm = 10 mm	1 k*l* = 1,000,000 m*l*
	1 m = 1,000 mm	

ILLUSTRATION : 2

How many cm makes a km?

SOLUTION :

We know that,   1 km = 1000 m

and   1 m = 100 cm

So,   1 km = 1000 m = 1000 × 100 cm

                  = 1,00,000 cm

Thus 1,00,000 cm makes a km.

ILLUSTRATION : 3

How many mm makes 1 m?

SOLUTION :

We know that, 1 m = 100 cm

and 1 cm = 10 mm

So, 1 m = 100 cm

         = 100 × 10 mm = 1000 mm

Thus 1,000 mm makes a metre.

ILLUSTRATION : 4

A container has a capacity of 500 litres. If the liquid present in it is poured in bottles of capacity 2 L 500 m*l*, how many bottles can be filled?

SOLUTION :

We know that,

1 L = 1000 m*l*

So, 2 L 500 m*l* = 2500 m*l* or 2.5 L

Therefore, number of bottles required to fill 500 litres would be-

$$\frac{500}{2.5} = 200$$

So, 200 bottles are required.

ESTIMATION

Rounding off a Number to the Nearest Ten

(i)   If the one's digit is less than 5, replace it by 0.

    For example: 23 is rounded off as 20

                     284 is rounded off as 280

(ii)   If the one's digit is equal to or more than 5, increase the ten's digit by 1 and replace one's digit by 0.

    For example: 249 is rounded off as 250.

Rounding off a Number to the Nearest Hundred

(i)   If the ten's digit is less than 5, replace the tens and ones digits by 0 only.

    For example: 627 is rounded off as 600.

                     2434 is rounded off as 2400.

(ii)   If the ten's digit is equal to or more than 5, increase hundreds digit by 1 and replace each digit on its right by 0.

    For example: 6587 is rounded off as 6600

                     6557 is rounded off as 6600

Rounding off a Number to the Nearest Thousand

(i)   If the hundreds digit is less than 5, replace the hundreds, tens and ones digit by 0.

    For example: 1482 is rounded off as 1000

                     4341 is rounded off as 4000

(ii)   If the hundreds digit is equal to or more than 5, increase thousands digit by 1 and replace each digit on its right by 0.

    For example: 1877 is rounded off as 2000

                     5936 is rounded off as 6000

ILLUSTRATION : 5

Estimate each of the following by rounding off to nearest thousands.

(i)   9683 + 4815   (ii) 3945 − 1243   (iii) 3042 × 1101

SOLUTION :

(i)   9683 when rounded off   =   10000
     4815 when rounded off   =   + 5000
     Estimated sum   =   15000

(ii)   3945 when rounded off   =   4000
     1243 when rounded off   =   − 1000
     Estimated difference   =   3000

(iii)   3042 when rounded off   =   3000
     1101 when rounded off   =   × 1000
     Estimated product   =   3000000

NOTE : (i) We can estimate the sum and difference of two or more numbers by rounding off the numbers.
(ii) We can estimate the product and quotient of two numbers by rounding off the numbers to the greatest place.

USE OF BRACKETS

Use of brackets help us to calculate in systematic and accurate way. It allows us to avoid confusion in the problems where we need to carry out more than one operations. While using brackets, first turn everything inside the brackets ( ) into a single number and then do the operation outside.

ILLUSTRATION : 6

Is $35 \times (8 + 2)$ is equal to $35 \times 8 + 35 \times 2$.

SOLUTION :

$35 \times (8 + 2) = 35 \times 8 + 35 \times 2$
$35 \times 10 = 280 + 70$
$350 = 350$

ILLUSTRATION : 7

Solve the following with the help of bracket.

(a) 25×23   **(b) 25×98**   **(c) 25×109**

SOLUTION :

(a) $25 \times 23 = 25 \times (20 + 3)$ [Expanding 23 as 20 + 3]
      $= 25 \times 20 + 25 \times 3$
      $= 500 + 75 = 575$

(b) $25 \times 98 = 25 \times (100 - 2)$ [Expanding 98 as 100 − 2]
      $= 25 \times 100 - 25 \times 2$ [98 can also be expand as 90 + 8]
      $= 2500 - 50 = 2450$

(c) $25 \times 109 = 25 \times (100 + 9)$ [Expanding 109 as 100 + 9]
      $= 25 \times 100 + 25 \times 9$
      $= 2500 + 225 = 2725$

ILLUSTRATION : 8

Write the expressions for each of the following by using brackets -
(a) Thirty multiplied by the difference of 35 and 5
(b) Divide the difference of 620 and 80 by 12
(c) Eighty two divided by four times the sum of 5 & 2

SOLUTION :

(a) $30 \times (35 - 5)$ (b) $(620 - 80) \div 12$ (c) $82 \div 4 \times (5 + 2)$

ROMAN NUMERALS

The numerals 0, 1, 2, 3, 4, ..., 9 are used in writing numbers. These numerals are originated in India and the Arabs picked them up and spread to Europe. Therefore, these are called **Hindu-Arabic numerals** system. This is not the only system available. One of the early systems of numeration still in common use today was developed by Romans and is called the **Roman numerals system.**

Roman numerals were developed by the Ancient Romans. We can see them in the numbers on clock faces, number of chapters, denoting ranks in the class, etc.

Unlike the Hindu – Arabic numeral system, Roman numeral system uses 7 basic symbols to represent different numbers. The symbols are as follows :

Roman Numerals	I	V	X	L	C	D	M
Hindu-Arabic Numerals	1	5	10	50	100	500	1000

Using these symbols, we can write any number by following certain rules which are given below.

Rules to form Roman Numbers

Rule 1   Repetition of a symbol in a Roman Numerals means addition.

> **NOTE :** (i)   Only I, X, C, M can be repeated.
> (ii)   V, L and D can never be repeated.
> (iii) No symbol in Roman numerals can be repeated more than 3 times.

For example :
(i)   II = (1 + 1) = 2
(ii) XX = (10 + 10) = 20
(iii) CCC = (100 + 100 + 100) = 300
(iv) MM = (1000 + 1000) = 2000

Rule 2   If a symbol with smaller value is written on the right of a number with greater value, then smaller value is added to the greater value.

For example :
(i)   VI = (5 + 1) = 6
(ii) XV = (10 + 5) = 15
(iii) LX = (50 + 10) = 60
(iv) CL = (100 + 50) = 150

Rule 3   If a symbol with smaller value is written on the left of a number with greater value, then smaller value is subtracted from the greater one.

> **NOTE :** (i)   V, L and D are never subtracted.
> (ii)   I can be subtracted from V and X only
> (iii) X can be subtracted from L and C only
> (iv) C can be subtracted from D and M only.

For example :
(i)   IV = (5 – 1) = 4
(ii) IX = (10 – 1) = 9
(iii) XL = (50 – 10) = 40
(iv) CD = (500 – 100) = 400
(v)   CM = (1000 – 100) = 900

Rule 4   When a smaller numeral is placed between two larger numerals, it is always subtracted from the larger numeral, immediately following it.

For example :
(i)   XIV = 10 + (5 – 1) = 14
(ii) CXIV = 100 + 10 + (5 – 1) = 114

CONCEPT MAP

Comparing Number

- For comparing two numbers, the number having more digits is greater than a number having less digit.
- For comparing two number having same number of digits, compare digits at left most position. In case, they are same, compare next digits and so on.

Indian and International System of Numeration

- In the Indian System of numeration, starting from right, mark periods as Units, Thousands, Lakhs and Crores. The unit period has three places. Remaining periods have two places each.
- In the International System of numeration, starting from right, mark periods as Units, Thousands and Millions. Each period has three places.

Estimation of Numbers

- To estimate or round off a number to the nearest tens, hundreds, thousands ...., etc., we observe the digit at ones, tens, hundreds, ... etc. resp. If this digit is less than 5, then round off the number down wards other wise upwards.

Knowing Our Numbers

Uses of Brackets

- Brackets are used to avoid confusion in the problems having more than one operations. [ ] are known as rectangular brackets. { } are known as curly brackets. ( ) are known as round brackets. ‾ is known as line bracket or vinculum.
- When more than one set of brackets are used in an expressions, we simplify them in the order —, (), {}, and [ ].

Roman Numerals

- There are seven basic symbols used in Roman System for forming different numbers. These are I = 1; V = 5; X = 10; L = 50; C = 100; D = 500; M = 1000

1 2 3 4 5

MISCELLANEOUS
SOLVED EXAMPLES

1. **Which is greater 96580734 or 96721643?**

Sol. Each of the given numbers has 8 digits.
Let us arrange the given numbers in the place-value chart.

C	T–L	L	T–Th	Th	H	T	O
9	6	5	8	0	7	3	4
9	6	7	2	1	6	4	3

At the crores-place both have the same digit, namely 9. At the ten-lakhs place both have the same digit, namely 6. But, at the lakhs place, the first number has 5, while the second has 7. Clearly, 7 > 5. So, the second number is larger. Hence, 96721643 > 96580734.

2. **Write the smallest 4-digit number formed by using the digits 0, 2 and 4 repeating 2 twice.**

Sol. The required number is 2024.

3. **Write the greatest 6-digit number using three different digits.**

Sol. The greatest three different digits are 9, 8 and 7. The required number is possible only when we repeat the largest digit namely 9 four time. Hence, the required number is 999987.

4. **Arrange the following :**
(i) **784, 4597, 2038, 175 in ascending order**
(ii) **1791, 21345, 15788, 47592 in descending order.**

Sol. (i) Here, the greatest number is 4597 and the smallest is 175.
$\therefore$ The ascending order is:
175, 784, 2038, 4597.

(ii) Here, the greatest number is 47592 and the smallest is 1791.
$\therefore$ The descending order is: 47592, 21345, 15788, 1791.

5. **Write the expanded form of each of the following numbers:**
(i) **35827604**   **(ii)** **973468256**

Sol. Putting the given numbers in the place-value chart, we have :

Places $\rightarrow$	TC 100000000	C 10000000	TL 1000000	L 100000	TTh 10000	Th 1000	H 100	T 10	O 1
(i)		3	5	8	2	7	6	0	4
(ii)	9	7	3	4	6	8	2	5	6

In expanded form, we may write them as under :
(i) $3,58,27,604 = (3 \times 10000000) + (5 \times 1000000) + (8 \times 100000) + (2 \times 10000) + (7 \times 1000) + (6 \times 100) + (0 \times 10) + (4 \times 1)$
(ii) $97,34,68,256 = (9 \times 100000000) + (7 \times 10000000) + (3 \times 1000000) + (4 \times 100000) + (6 \times 10000) + (8 \times 1000) + (2 \times 100) + (5 \times 10) + (6 \times 1)$

6. **Rewrite each of the following numbers with proper commas, using international place-value chart:**
(i) **1286475**   **(ii)** **49637582**
Also, write the number name of each in the international system and Indian system.

Sol. Let us arrange the given numerals in an international place-value chart. Then separating the periods, we write them as shown below.

	Millions			Thousands			Ones			
	HM	TM	M	HTh	TTh	Th	H	T	O	
(i)			1	2	8	6	4	7	5	1,286,475
(ii)		4	9	6	3	7	5	8	2	49,637,582
		C	TL	L	TTh	Th	H	T	O	

In the international system, we write them in words as:
(i) One million two hundred eighty-six thousand four hundred seventy-five
(ii) Forty-nine million six hundred thirty-seven thousand five hundred eighty-two
In the Indian system, these numbers are:
(i) Twelve lakh eighty-six thousand four hundred seventy-five
(ii) Four crore ninety-six lakh thirty-seven thousand five hundred eighty-two

7. **Population of Delhi was 1,29,35,297 in 1999. It increased by 45,34,214 in next two years, but 13,29,417 migrated to Bombay and Bangalore. So, What was the population of Delhi in 2001?**

Sol.

Population of Delhi in 1999	=	1,29,35,297
Increase in population	=	+ 45,34,214
Increased population	=	1,74,69,511
Migrated population	=	– 13,29,417
Hence, final population in 2001	=	1,61,40,094

8. **A bus travels a distance of 356 km 500 m daily and for this travelling it consumes 1 *l* of diesel per 15 km. Find**
   (i) how much distance does the bus travel in a month of 30 days?
   (ii) how much diesel does the bus consume in a month?

Sol. (i) In 1 day, the bus travels a distance of 356 km 500 m. In 30 days (1 month), it travels a distance of 356 km 500 m × 30.

$$
\begin{array}{r}
\text{km} \quad \text{m} \\
356 \quad 500 \\
\times \quad\quad 30 \\
\hline
00000 \quad 000 \\
+10695 \quad 000 \\
\hline
10695 \quad 000 \\
\end{array}
$$

Hence, the bus travels a distance of 10695 km in a month.

(ii) The bus consumes 1 *l* of diesel per 15 km. The quantity of diesel consumed by the bus for 10695 km (in 1 month) is given by 10695 ÷ 15

$$
\begin{array}{r}
713 \\
15\overline{)\,10695} \\
\underline{105} \\
19 \\
\underline{-\,15} \\
45 \\
\underline{-\,45} \\
0 \\
\end{array}
$$

Hence, the bus consumes 713 *l* of diesel in a month.

9. **Estimate the following:**
   (i) 283 + 1732   **(ii) 8435 – 597**

Sol. (i) Out of 283 and 1732, the smaller number is 283. Hence, we have to round off both the numbers to the nearest hundred.

$$
\begin{array}{r}
1732 \rightarrow \quad 1700 \\
283 \rightarrow \quad +300 \\
\hline
\text{Estimated value of } 1732 + 283 \quad = \quad 2000 \\
\end{array}
$$

(ii) Out of 8435 and 597, 597 is the smaller number. So, we round off these numbers to the nearest hundred.

$$
\begin{array}{r}
8435 \rightarrow \quad 8400 \\
597 \rightarrow \quad -600 \\
\hline
\text{Estimated value of } 8435 - 597 = \quad 7800 \\
\end{array}
$$

10. **Estimate the following :**
   (i) 87 × 313   **(ii) 9 × 795**
   (iii) 546 ÷ 7   **(iv) 1189 ÷ 56**

Sol. (i)

$$
\begin{array}{r}
313 \rightarrow \quad 300 \\
87 \rightarrow \quad \times 100 \\
\hline
\text{Estimated product of } 87 \times 313 = \quad 30000 \\
\end{array}
$$

(ii)

$$
\begin{array}{r}
795 \rightarrow \quad 800 \\
9 \rightarrow \quad \times 10 \\
\hline
\text{Estimated product of } 9 \times 795 = \quad 8000 \\
\end{array}
$$

(iii) For 546 ÷ 7, we have to round off 546 to the multiple of 7.
Let us say 490 or 560. Since 546 is closer to 560, so 546 should be rounded off to 560.
Now, estimated value of 546 ÷ 7
$$= 560 ÷ 7 = 80$$

(iv) 1189 should be rounded off to 1200 and 56 should be rounded off to 60.
Now, the estimated value of $1189 ÷ 56 = 1200 ÷ 60 = 20$

11. **Simplify each of the following expression :**
   (i) 8 × (3 + 7)   **(ii) (7 – 2) × (12 + 8)**
   (ii) 23 + 9 × (6 – 3) – 20

Sol. (i) $8 × (3 + 7) = 8 × 10 = 80$
(ii) $(7 – 2) × (12 + 8) = 5 × 20 = 100$
(iii) $23 + 9 × (6 – 3) – 20 = 23 + (9 × 3) – 20$
$= 23 + 27 – 20 = 50 – 20 = 30$

12. **Write the following in Hindu-Arabic numerals:**
   (i) LXXXIX   **(ii) CCXXVIII**
   (iii) CDXLVI   **(iv) DCXCVII**
   (vi) MCIX   **(vi) MMMCDVI**

Sol. We have,
(i) $LXXXIX = L + XXX + IX = 50 + 30 + 9 = 89$
(ii) $CCXXVIII = CC + XX + VIII = 200 + 20 + 8 = 228$
(iii) $CDXLVI = CD + XL + VI = 400 + 40 + 6 = 446$
(iv) $DCXCVII = DC + XC + VII = 600 + 90 + 7 = 697$
(v) $MCIX = MC + IX = 1100 + 9 = 1109$
(vi) $MMMCDVI = MMM + CD + VI = 3000 + 400 + 6 = 3,406$

1 EXERCISE

Fill in the Blanks :

DIRECTIONS : *Complete the following statements with an appropriate word / term to be filled in the blank space(s).*

1. 1 crore = _______ million.
2. By reversing the order of digits of the greatest number made by five different non-zero digits, the new number is the _______ number of five digits.
3. By adding 1 to the greatest _________ digit number, we get ten lakh.
4. The number five crore twenty three lakh seventy eight thousand four hundred one can be written, using commas, in the Indian system of Numeration as _______ .
5. In Roman Numeration, the symbol X can be subtracted from _______ and C only.
6. The largest 4-digit number, using any one digit twice, from digits 5, 9, 2 and 6 is _________.
7. The _________ 6-digit number + 1 = 7-digit smallest number.
8. If a symbol is of smaller value is written on the of symbol larger value, then its value is added to the larger numeral.
9. The difference of two place values of 2 in 3230452 is _______.
10. 17819 rounded to nearest hundred is _______.

True / False :

DIRECTIONS : *Read the following statements and write your answer as true or false.*

1. Estimated sum of 7826 and 12469 rounded off to nearest hundreds is 20,300.
2. The largest six digit telephone number that can be formed by using digits 5,3, 4, 7, 0, 8 only once is 875403.
3. The number LIV is greater than LVI.
4. The difference in the face value and the place value of 5 in 85419 is 85414.
5. In Roman numerals V, L and D are never subtracted.

6. The estimated value of 46,530 to the nearest hundred is 46500.
7. 100 lakhs make a million.
8. In Roman numeration, if a symbol is repeated, its value is multiplied as many times as it occurs.
9. The number 81652318 will be read as eighty one crore six lakh fifty two thousand three hundred eighteen.

Match the Columns :

DIRECTIONS : *Each question contains statements given in two columns which have to be matched. Statements (A, B, C, D) in column-I have to be matched with statements (p, q, r, s) in column-II.*

1. Match the following.

Column-I	Column-II
(A) Two hundred thousand	(p) Two crore
(B) Two billion	(q) Twenty lakh
(C) Twenty million	(r) Two hundred crore
(D) Two million	(s) Two lakh

Very Short Answer Questions:

DIRECTIONS : *Give answer in one word or one sentence.*

1. Write the place value of 9 in
   (i) 390345   (ii) 42379502
2. Arrange the following numbers in ascending order : 243795, 51395, 3795, 5343
3. Express the following as Roman numeral :
   (i) 45   (ii) 51
   (iii) 79   (iv) 92
4. Write the following numbers in words:
   (i) 33,06,759   (ii) 6,03,56,034
5. Write each of the following in Hindu-Arabic numeral:
   (i) CLXVI   (ii) CCXXVI
   (iii) CCCXL   (iv) CDXLVI

6. Write the following numbers in expanded form:
   (i) 81, 85, 204
   (ii) 7, 24, 05, 620
7. Write the following numbers in figures:
   (i) Eight-lakh twenty thousand eighty-seven.
   (ii) Thirty-nine lakh forty thousand thirty-eight.
   (iii) Five crore five lakh thirty-six thousand seven.
8. How many mm are there in 1 m?
9. How many cm makes a km?
10. place the commas in each of the following numbers in both Indian and International system of numeration :
    (i) 73325
    (ii) 234637
    (iii) 8089627

Short Answer Questions :

DIRECTIONS : *Give answer in 2-3 sentences.*

1. Give the number name of the following in both the systems of numeration :
   (i) 2856721
   (ii) 7008562
2. Is $45 \times (10 + 3)$ is equal to $45 \times 10 + 45 \times 3$.
3. Write each of the following in Hindu-Arabic numeral :
   (i) XXXIX
   (ii) XCVIII
   (iii) LXXXVII
   (iv) LXIV.
4. Estimate the following:
   (i) $2962 + 4173$
   (ii) $5658 - 2846$
   (iii) 1242×87
   (iv) $4758 \div 26$
5. Express each of the following numbers as a Roman numeral:
   (i) 479
   (ii) 556
   (iii) 625
   (iv) 769
6. Estimate the sum $(274 + 143)$ to the nearest hundred.
7. Estimate the difference $(673 - 258)$ to the nearest hundred.
8. A vessel contains 5 l 625 ml of milk is distributed among some children. If each child gets 125 *ml* of milk, then find the number of children.
9. 2 m 10 cm of cloth is required to stich a shirt. How much cloth will be needed to stich 45 shirts?
10. How many-
    (i) thousands make 1 lakh?
    (ii) lakhs make 1 million?
    (iii) crores make 10 million?
11. Solve the following with the help of brackets:
    (i) 27×105
    (ii) 27×98
    (iii) 27×109

2 EXERCISE

Text-Book Exercise :

1. Population of Sundarnagar was 2,35,471 in the year 1991. In the year 2001 it was found to be increased by 72,958. What was the population of the city in 2001?
2. Shekhar is a famous cricket player. He has so far scored 6,980 runs in test matches. He wishes to complete 10,000 runs. How many more runs does he need?
3. In one state, the number of bicycles sold in the year 2002-2003 was 7,43,000. In the year 2003-2004, the number of bicycles sold was 8,00,100. In which year were more bicycles sold? and how many more?
4. A merchant had ₹ 78,592 with her. She placed an order for purchasing 40 radio sets at ₹ 1,200 each. How much money will remain with her after the purchase?
5. The town newspaper is published every day. One copy has 12 pages. Everyday 11,980 copies are printed. How many total pages are printed everyday?

6. A student multiplied 7236 by 65 instead of multiplying by 56. How much was his answer greater than the correct answer?

7. The number of sheets of paper available for making notebooks is 75,000. Each sheet makes 8 pages of a notebook. Each notebook contains 200 pages. How many notebooks can be made from the paper available?

8. Medicine is packed in boxes, each weighing 4 kg 500 g. How many such boxes can be loaded in a van which can not carry beyond 800 kg?

9. The distance between the school and the house of a student is 1 km 875 m. Everyday she walks both ways. Find the total distance covered by her in six days.

10. A vessel has 4 litres and 500 ml of curd. In how many glasses, each of 25 ml capacity, can it be filled?

11. Give a rough estimate (by rounding off to nearest hundreds) and also a closer estimate (by rounding off to nearest tens):
(i) $439 + 334 + 4,317$
(ii) $1, 08,734 - 47, 599$

12. Estimate the following products using general rule:
(i) 1291×592 (ii) 9250×29

Exemplar Questions :

1. The diameter of Jupiter is 142800000 metres. Insert commas suitably and write the diameter according to International System of Numeration.

2. Radius of the Earth is 6400 km and that of Mars is 4300000 m. Whose radius is bigger and by how much?

3. In 2001, the poplulations of Tripura and Meghalaya were 3,199,203 and 2,318,822, respectively. Write the populations of these two states in words.

4. Chinmay had ₹ 610000. He gave ₹ 87500 to Jyoti, ₹ 126380 to Javed and ₹ 350000 to John. How much money was left with him?

5. A mobile number consists of ten digits. First four digits are 9,9,7 and 9. Make the smallest mobile number by using only one digit twice from 8,3,5,6,0.

6. Find the sum of the greatest and the least six digit mumbers formed by the digits 2,0,4,7,6,5 using each digit only once.

7. The population of a town was 78787 in the year 1991 and 95833 in the year 2001. Estimate the increase in population by rounding off each population to nearest hundreds.

8. A vessel has 13 litres 200 ml of fruit juice. In how many glasses each of capacity 60 ml can it be filled?

9. The population of a town is 450772. In a survey, it was reported that one out of every 14 persons is illiterate. In all how many illiterate persons are there in the town?

10. How many lakhs make five billions?

11. A loading tempo can carry 482 boxes of biscuits weighing 15 kg each, whereas a van can carry 518 boxes each of the same weight. Find the total weight that can be carried by both the vehicles.

12. A box contains 5 strips, each having 12 capsules of 500 mg medicine in each capsule. Find the total weight in grams of medicine in 32 such boxes.

HOTS Questions :

1. Using 6 and 9 equal number of times, form all possible 4-digit numbers. Find the greatest and the smallest number.

2. Ramesh buys 548 chairs and 123 tables for his showroom. If a chair costs ₹ 2470 and a table costs ₹ 5664, find the total money spent by him.

3. The difference between the greatest and smallest numbers which when rounded off to the nearest hundred as 6700, is

4. The difference between the greatest and the smallest numbers which when rounded off to the nearest thousand as 9000, is

5. The difference between the largest three digit number and the largest three digit number with distinct digits is __________.

6. Write the number 2358794031629 in words.

3 EXERCISE

Single Option Correct :

DIRECTIONS : *This section contains multiple choice questions. Each question has 4 choices (a), (b), (c) and (d) out of which ONLY ONE is correct.*

1. Which digit in the number 568731 has a place value of thousands?
   (a) 8   (b) 7
   (c) 6   (d) 5

2. Sum of the greatest 8 digit number and the smallest 9 digit number is
   (a) 19999999   (b) 199999999
   (c) 999999999   (d) 10000999

3. In Indian system of numeration, the number 58695376 is written as
   (a) 58,69,53,76   (b) 58,695,376
   (c) 5,86,95,376   (d) 586,95,376

4. Compare 67389145 and 673891450 using (>, <, =).
   (a) <   (b) >
   (c) =   (d) None

5. Numeral for five hundred three million eight thousand seven hundred two is
   (a) 500380702   (b) 503800702
   (c) 503008702   (d) 503080702

6. 1512 when rounded off to the nearest hundred is
   (a) 1600   (b) 1500
   (c) 1510   (d) None of these

7. The smallest 4-digit number having three different digits is
   (a) 1102   (b) 1012
   (c) 1020   (d) 1002

8. $3 \times 10000 + 7 \times 1000 + 9 \times 100 + 0 \times 10 + 4$ is the same as
   (a) 3794   (b) 37940
   (c) 37904   (d) 379409

9. The smallest 4-digit number formed by using the digits 5, 0, 3, 1 only once contains
   (a) 0 in unit's place.
   (b) 5 in ten's place.
   (c) 3 in ten's place.
   (d) 1 in unit's place.

More Than One Option Correct :

DIRECTIONS : *This section contains multiple choice questions. Each question has 4 choices (a), (b), (c) and (d) out of which ONE or MORE may be correct.*

1. Which of the following Roman symbol can be repeated?
   (a) I   (b) V
   (c) X   (d) C

2. 24×105 is same as
   (a) $(20 + 4) \times 105$ (b) $24 \times (100 + 5)$
   (c) $24 \times (100 - 5)$ (d) None

3. The value of $9307 \times 937 - 9307 \times 837$ is
   (a) 93700   (b) 930700
   (c) 930070   (d) 9307×100

4. The five digit number formed with the digits 7, 5, 3 and 2 using 7 twice is/are
   (a) 75523   (b) 77523
   (c) 77532   (d) 77253

5. Which of the folloiwng Roman numerals is incorrect?
   (a) XC   (b) XD
   (c) DM   (d) VL

6. Which of the following is meaningful?
   (a) VX   (b) XV
   (c) XXV   (d) XXXV

7. Which of the following is meaningful?
   (a) CI   (b) CII
   (c) IC   (d) XC

8. Which of the following is meaningful?
   (a) XIV   (b) XVV
   (c) XIII   (d) XXII

Assertion & Reason :

DIRECTIONS : *Each of these questions contains an Assertion followed by Reason. Read them carefully and answer the question on the basis of following options. You have to select the one that best describes the two statements.*

(a)   If both **Assertion** and **Reason** are correct and reason is the correct explanation of assertion.

(b)   If both **Assertion** and **Reason** are correct but reason is not the correct explanation of assertion.

(c)   If **Assertion** is correct but **Reason** is incorrect.

(d)   If **Assertion** is incorrect but **Reason** is correct.

1.   **Assertion:** After placing commas in the number 56943821 according to international system of numeration, the number is written as 56,943,821.

    Reason: To write a numeral in the Indian system, commas are first put after three digits from the right and then after every two digits.

2.   **Assertion:** Estimated sum of 7004 and 469 is 7500.

    Reason: Estimation is done by rounding off the numbers to the nearest places.

Passage Based Questions :

DIRECTIONS : *Study the given passage(s) and answer the following questions.*

PASSAGE - I

Priya read 38 pages of her storybook on Monday. She read 27 pages more on Tuesday than on Monday. She found that there were still another 220 pages left.

1.   How many pages did Priya read on Tuesday?

    (a) 56   (b) 65

    (c) 55   (d) 66

2.   How many pages were there in the storybook?

    (a) 319   (b) 332

    (c) 323   (d) 285

PASSAGE - II

On Monday, the temperature of Delhi at 10 a.m. was 13°C but by the mid-night, it fell down to 6°C. The temperature of Chennai at 10 a.m. was 18°C but fell down to 10°C by the mid-night.

3.   Which fall is greater?

    (a) Chennai   (b) Delhi

    (c) Both   (d) None of these

4.   On Wednesday the temperature of Delhi at 12 noon was 20°C, decrease by 2°C after every two hours then what will be the temperature of Delhi at 8 p.m on Wednesday.

    (a) 10°C   (b) 20°C

    (c) 12°C   (d) 15°C

Integer Type Questions :

DIRECTIONS : *Answer the following questions. The answer to each of the question is a single digit integer, ranging from 0 to 9.*

1.   The number of zeroes that comes after 1 for 10 millions is

2.   The difference between the greatest and smallest numbers which when rounded off a number to the nearest tens as 540, is

3.   The difference of the smallest three digit number and the largest two digit numbers is

4.   The difference between smallest three digit number having three distinct digits and smallest 3-digit numbers is

5.   The number of 3 digit numbers formed by using digits 3,5,9, taking each digit exactly once, is.

SOLUTIONS

Brief Explanations of Selected Questions

1 EXERCISE

Fill in the Blanks :

1. 10 million
2. smallest
3. 6
4. 5, 23, 78, 401
5. L
6. 9965
7. greatest
8. right
9. 1,99,998
10. 17800

True / False :

1. T   2. F   3. F   4. F   5. T
6. T   7. F   8. F   9. F

Match the Columns :

1. (A) – (s); (B) – (r), (C) – (p), (D) – (q)

Very Short Answer Questions:

1. (i) The place value of 9 in 390345 is 90,000.
   (ii) The place value of 9 in 42379502 is 9,000.
2. Number having more number of digits is greater
   Clearly, $3795 < 5343 < 51395 < 243795$
3. We wirte
   (i) 45 as $40 + 5 = XL + V = XLV$.
   (ii) 51 as $50 + 1 = L + I = LI$.
   (iii) 79 as $50 + 20 + 9 = L + XX + IX = LXXIX$.
   (iv) 92 as $90 + 2 = XC + II = XCII$.
4. (i) $33,06,759 =$ Thirty-three lakh six thousand seven hundred fifty-nine
   (ii) $6,03,56,034 =$ Six crore three lakh fifty six thousand thirty-four
5. We have:
   (i) $CLXVI = 100 + 50 + 10 + (5 + 1) = 166$
   (ii) $CCXXVI = 200 + 20 + (5 + 1) = 226$
   (iii) $CCCXL = 300 + (50 - 10) = 340$
   (iv) $CDXLVI = (500 - 100) + (50 - 10) + (5 + 1) = 446$
6. (i) $81,85,204 = 80,00,000 + 100,000 + 80,000 + 5,000 + 200 + 4$
   (ii) $7,24,05,620 = 7,00,00,000 + 20,00,000 + 4,00,000 + 5,000 + 600 + 20$

7. (i) Eight lakh twenty thousand eighty-seven $= 8,20,087$
   (ii) Thirty-nine lakh forty thousand thirty-eight $= 39,40,038$
   (iii) Five crore five lakh thirty-six thousand seven. $= 5,05,36,007$.
8. We know that
   $1 m = 100 cm$ and $1 cm = 10 mm$
   So, $1 m = 100 cm = 100 \times 10 mm = 1,000 mm$
9. We know that
   $1 km = 1000 m$ and $1 m = 100 cm$
   So, $1 km = 1000 m = 1000 \times 100 cm$
   $= 100000 cm = 1, 00, 000 cm$
   Thus $1,00,000$ cm makes a km.
10. (i) $73, 325$ –   Indian system
    $73, 325$ –   International system
    (ii) $2, 34, 637$ –   Indian system
    $234, 637$ –   International system
    (iii) $80, 89, 627$ – Indian system
    $8,089, 627$ –   International system

Short Answer Questions :

1. (i) Indian System of Numeration
   $28,56,721$ – Twenty eight lakh, fifty six thousand seven hundred twenty one.
   International System of Numeration
   $2,856,721$ – Two million, eight hundred fifty six thousand and seven hundred twenty one.
   (ii) Indian System of Numeration
   $70,08,562$ – Seventy lakh, eight thousand and five hundred sixty two.
   International System of Numeration
   $7,008,562,$ – Seven million, eight thousand and five hundred sixty two.
2. $45 \times (10 + 3) = 45 \times 13 = 585$
   And $45 \times 10 + 45 \times 3$
   $= 450 + 135 = 585$
   Thus, $45 \times (10 + 3) = 45 \times 10 + 45 \times 3$
3. (i) $XXXIX = 10 + 10 + 10 + (10 - 1) = 39$.
   (ii) $XCVIII = (100 - 10) + 5 + 1 + 1 + 1$
   $= 90 + 5 + 3 = 98$.

(iii) LXXXVII $= 50 + 10 + 10 + 10 + 5 + 1 + 1 = 87$.

(iv) LXIV $= 50 + 10 + (5 - 1) = 64$.

4. (i) Rounding off 2962 to the nearest thousand, we get 3000 rounding off 4173 to the nearest thousand, we get 4000

(ii) Rounding off 5658 to nearest thousand, we get 6000

Rounding off 2846 to nearest thousand, we get 3000

∴ Estimated difference $= 6000 - 3000$
$$= 3000.$$

(iii) Rounding off 1242 to nearest hundred we get 1200

Rounding off 87 to ten, we get 90

∴ Estimated product $= 1200 \times 90$
$$= 10800.$$

(iv) Rounding off 4758 to nearest hundred, we get 4800.

Rounding off 26 to nearest 10, we get 30

∴ Estimated quotient

$$
\begin{array}{r}
160 \\
30 \overline{)\ 4800} \\
-30 \\
\hline
180 \\
-180 \\
\hline
00 \\
-00 \\
\hline
0
\end{array}
$$

i.e. $4800 \div 30 = 160$

5. We have:

(i) $479 = 400 + 70 + 9 = $ CDLXXIX

(ii) $556 = 500 + 50 + 6 = $ DLVI

(iii) $625 = 500 + 100 + 20 + 5 = $ DCXXV

(iv) $769 = 500 + 200 + 60 + 9 = $ DCCLXIX

6. 274 estimated to the nearest hundred $= 300$.

143 estimated to the nearest hundred $= 100$.

Hence, the required estimation $= (300 + 100)$
$$= 400.$$

7. 673 estimated to the nearest hundred $= 700$.

258 estimated to the nearest hundred $= 300$.

Hence, the required estimation $= (700 - 300)$
$$= 400.$$

8. Total milk in the vessel $= 5 l + 625$ ml
$$= (5 \times 1000) \text{ ml} + 625 \text{ ml}$$
$$= 5000 \text{ ml} + 625 \text{ ml}$$
$$= 5625 \text{ ml}$$

Milk given to each child $= 125$ ml

∴ Number of children $= 5625 \div 125 = 45$

Thus, 45 children can be given the milk.

9. Length of cloth required for stiching 1 shirt
$$= 2 \text{ m } 10 \text{ cm}$$
$$= (2 \times 100 \text{ cm}) + 10 \text{ cm}$$
$$= 200 \text{ cm} + 10 \text{ cm}$$
$$= 210 \text{ cm}$$

Number of shirts $= 45$

∴ Total cloth required for 45 shirts
$$= 45 \times 210 \text{ cm}$$
$$= 9450 \text{ cm}$$

$$= \frac{9450}{100} \text{ m} = 94 \text{ m } 50 \text{ cm}$$

10. (i) 1 lakh $= 100$ thousands

(ii) 1 million $= 1,000,000$

1 lakh $= 1,00,000$

$1,000,000 \div 1,00,000 = 10$

So 10 lakhs make 1 million.

(iii) 10 million $= 10,000,000$

1 crore $= 1,00,00,000$

$10000000 \div 10000000 = 1$

1 crore will make 1 million.

11. (i) $27 \times 105 = 27 \times (100 + 5)$
$$= 27 \times 100 + 27 \times 5 = 2700 + 135 = 2835$$

(ii) $27 \times 98 = 27 \times (100 - 2)$
$$= 27 \times 100 - 27 \times 2 = 2700 - 54 = 2646$$

(iii) $27 \times 109 = 27 \times (100 + 9)$
$$= 27 \times 100 + 27 \times 9 = 2700 + 243 = 2943$$

2 EXERCISE

Text-Book Exercise :

1. Population of the city in 2001
$$= \text{Population of the city in 1991} + \text{Increase in population}$$
$$= 2,35,471 + 72,958$$

Now,
$$
\begin{array}{r}
235471 \\
+\ 72958 \\
\hline
308429
\end{array}
$$

Population of the city in 2001 was 3,08,429.

2. Runs that he wishes to score $= 10,000$

Runs scored $= 6,980$,

Runs needed $= 10000 - 6980 = 3,020$

3. Clearly, 8,00,100 is more than 7,43,000. So, in that state, more bicycles were sold in the year 2003-2004 than in 2002-2003.

Now, 800100
        $- 743000$
          $\overline{057100}$

57,100 more bicycles were sold in the year 2003-2004.

4. Total money she had $= ₹\ 78,592$
    Cost of 1 radio set $= ₹\ 1,200$
    Cost of 40 radio sets $= ₹\ 1,200 \times 40$
                            $= ₹\ 48,000$
    Money left with her $= ₹\ 78,592 - ₹\ 48,000$
                            $= ₹\ 30,592$

5. Each copy has 12 pages.
    $\therefore$ 11,980 copies will have $12 \times 11,980$ pages.

$$\begin{array}{r} 11980 \\ \times 12 \\ \hline 23960 \\ +119800 \\ \hline 143760 \end{array}$$

    Everyday 1, 43, 760 pages are printed.

6. Student multiplied $= 7236 \times 65$
    He was suppposed to multiply $= 7236 \times 56$
    Difference in answer $= 7236 \times 65$
                            $\qquad - 7236 \times 56$
                            $= 7236 \times (65 - 56)$
                            $= 7236 \times 9 = 65,124$

7. Each sheet makes 8 pages.
    $\therefore$ 75,000 sheets make $8 \times 75, 000$ pages.
    Thus, 6,00,000 pages are available for making notebooks.
    Now, 200 pages make 1 notebook.
    Hence, 6,00,000 pages make $6,00,000 \div 200$ notebooks.
    Thus, 3,000 notebooks can be made.

8. Weight of 1 box $= 4$ kg 500 gm or 4500 gms.
    Maximum weight a van can carry
                $= 800$ kg or 800000 gms
    Number of boxes which can be loaded
                $= 800000 \div 4500$

$$\begin{array}{r} 177 \\ 4500\overline{)800000} \\ \underline{4500} \\ 35000 \\ \underline{31500} \\ 35000 \\ \underline{31500} \\ 3500 \end{array}$$

Thus, the maximum no. of boxes can be loaded $= 177$

9. The distance between school and house
                $= 1$ km 875 m
                $= (1000 + 875)$ m
                $= 1875$ m
    Distance covered by her every day
                $= 2 \times 1875$ m $= 3750$ m
    Distance covered by her in six days
                $= 6 \times 3750$ m $= 22500$ m
                $= 22$ km 500 m.

10. Curd in vessel $= 4$ l 500 ml
                $= 4000$ ml $+ 500$ ml $= 4500$ ml
    Number of glasses that can be filled
                $= \dfrac{4500}{25}$ ml $= 180$ glasses

11. (i) (a) Rough estimate
                $439 + 334 + 4317$
                $= 400 + 300 + 4, 300 = 5000$
         (b) Closer estimate
                $439 + 334 + 4317$
                $= 440 + 330 + 4,320 = 5,090.$
    (ii) (a) Rough estimate
                $1,08,734 - 47,599$
                $= 1,08,700 - 47,600 = 61,100$
         (b) Closer estimate
                $1,08,734 - 47,599$
                $= 1,08,730 - 47,600 = 61,130.$

12. (i) 1291×592
         Estimated product $= 1300 \times 600$
                            $= 7,80,000$
    (ii) 9250×29
         Estimated product $= 9000 \times 30 = 2,70,000$

1. 142,800,000
2. Earth, 2100000 m
3. Tripura-three milllion one hundred ninety-nine thousand, two hundred three
    Meghalaya-Two million three hundred eighteen thousand eight hundred twenty two.
4. $610000 - (87500 + 126380 + 350000)$
    $= 46120$
5. 9979003568
6. $765420 + 204567 = 969987$
7. Population in 1991 $= 78787$ rounded to 78800
    Population in 2001 $= 95833$ rounded to 95800
    $\therefore$ Estimated increase $= 95800 - 78800$
        in popuation $= 17000$

8. $13\,l\ 200\ ml = 13000 + 200 = 13200\ ml$
number of glasses can be filled $= 13200 \div 60$
$ = 220$

9. No of illiterate person $= 450772 \div 14$
$ = 32198$

10. 5 billions $= 5000000000 = 50000 \times 100000$
$ = 50000\ \text{lakhs}$

11. Weight of 1 box $= 15$ kg
Weight of 482 boxes $= 15 \times 482 = 7,230$ kg
Weight of 518 boxes $= 15 \times 518 = 7770$ kg
Total weight, both vehicles can carry
$ = 7230 + 7770 = 15000$ kg

12. Weight of medicine in 1 capsule $= 500$ mg
Weight of medicine in 12 capsules $= 12 \times 500$ mg
$ = 6000$ mg $= 6$ grams
Weight of medicine in 1 strips $= 6$ g
Weight of medicine in 5 strips $= 5 \times 6 = 30$ g
Weight of medicine in 1 box $= 30$ g
Weight of medicine in 32 boxes $= 32 \times 30 = 960$ g

HOTS Questions :

1. The possible numbers are 6699, 6969, 9696, 9966, 6996, 9669.
Smallest number $= 6699$
Greatest number $= 9966$

2. Cost of one chair $= ₹\ 2470$
Cost of 548 chairs $= ₹\ 2470 \times 548$
$ = ₹\ 1353560$
Cost of one table $= ₹\ 5664$
Cost of 123 tables $= ₹\ 5664 \times 123$
$ = ₹\ 696672$
Total money Ramesh spends
$= ₹\ 1353560 + ₹\ 696672$
$= ₹\ 2050232$

3. The greatest number which when rounded off to the nearest hundred as 6700, is 6749
The smallest number which when rounded off to the nearest hundred as 6700 is 6650
∴ The required difference $= 6749 - 6650 = 99$

4. The greatest number which when rounded off to the nearest thousand as 9000 is 9499
The smallest number which when rounded off to the nearest thousand as 9000 is 8500
∴   The required difference $= 9499 - 8500$
$ = 999$

5. The largest three digit number $= 999$
The largest three digit number with distinct digits $= 987$
∴ The required difference $= 999 - 987 = 12$

6. The number contains 13 digits. Starting from the right put commas after every group of 3 digits. Thus, we have 2,358,794,031,629. Stated in words, the number is two trillion three hundred fifty eight billion seven hundred ninety four million thirty one thousand six hundred twenty nine.

3 E X E R C I S E

1. **(a)** Place value of 8 is 8000

2. **(b)** Greatest - 8 digit no. $= 99999999$
Smallest -9 digit no. $= 100000000$
Their sum $= 199999999$

3. **(c)**

4. **(a)** $67389145 < 673891450$
$\phantom{67389145 < 673891450}$ (comparing the numbers)

5. **(c)** 503,008,702

6. **(b)**   **7.** **(d)**   **8.** **(c)**   **9.** **(c)** 1035

More Than One Option Correct :

1. **(a,c,d)**   **2.** **(a,b)**   **3.** **(b,d)**   **4.** **(b,c,d)**
5. **(b,c,d)**   **6.** **(b,c,d)** **7.** **(a,b,d)**
8. **(a,c,d)**

Assertion & Reason :

1. **(b)** 56943821 is written as 56,943,821 according to International place value system.
Assertion: True; Reason : True and is not the correct explanation of the Assertion.

2. **(a)** As 7004 rounds off to 7000 and 469 Rounds off to 500, their estimated sum
$ = 7000 + 500 = 7500$
Assertion: True; Reason: True and is the correct explanation of Assertion.

Passage Based Questions :

1. **(b)** Pages read on Tuesday $= 38 + 27 = 65$

2. **(c)** Total pages $= 38 + 65 + 220 = 323$

3. **(a)** Fall in Delhi's temperature

$\qquad = 13°C - 6°C = 7°C$

Fall in Chennai's temperature

$\qquad = 18° C - 10°C = 8°C$

Clearly, $8°C > 7°C$

Hence, fall in temperature of Chennai is greater.

4. **(c)** From 12 noon to 8 p.m. = 8 hours

Temperature at 8 p.m. $= 20°C - 8°C$

Temperature on Wednesday $= 12°C$.

Integer Type Questions :

1. **(8)**

2. **(9)** $544 - 535 = 9$

3. **(1)** $100 - 99 = 1$

4. **(2)** $102 - 100 = 2$

5. **(6)**

Chapter 2

Whole Numbers

NATURAL NUMBERS

All counting numbers starting from 1 are **natural numbers**.

> **NOTE :** 1. The smallest natural number is 1.
> 2. There is no greatest natural number i.e., there are infinitely many natural numbers.

WHOLE NUMBERS

The natural numbers along with '0(zero)' form whole numbers **Example** - 0, 1, 2, 3, 4, ...
All natural numbers are whole numbers but the converse is not true.

SUCCESSOR AND PREDECESSOR OF WHOLE NUMBERS

Successor

One more than a given number is called as **successor** of the given number. Every whole number has its successor.

Clearly   Successor of 24 is $24 + 1 = 25$
and   Successor of 0 is $0 + 1 = 1$.

Predecessor

One less than a given number is called as **predecessor** of the given number. The whole number 0 does not have any predecessor.

Clearly, predecessor of 30 is $30 - 1 = 29$
and predecessor of 1000 is $1000 - 1 = 999$.

> **NOTE :** Every whole number has a predecessor except '0'. Zero has no predecessor. Since '0' is the smallest whole number.

NUMBER LINE

A straight line, marked with whole numbers at equal distances in ascending order is known as number line.

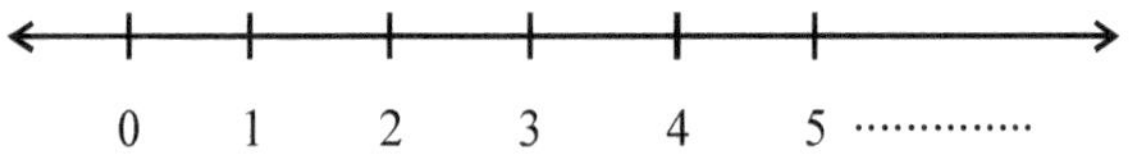

On number line, numbers like 1, 2, 3, 4, ... etc. are marked at equal distances to the right of 0. The distance from one point to next point is taken as one unit.
Look at the position of numbers 3 and 5 in the above figure.
Which one of 3 and 5 is smaller ?
3 lies to the left of 5. Therefore $3 < 5$.

Addition on Number Line

ILLUSTRATION : 1

Find 3 + 2.

SOLUTION :

To add 3 and 2 on the number line, start from 3 and then move 2 points forward (see figure given below).

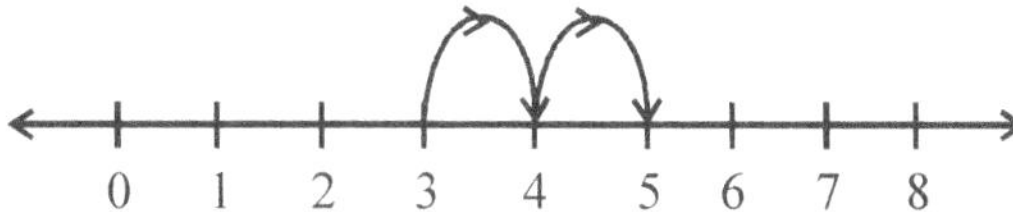

we reach at 5. So, 3 + 2 = 5

Subtraction on Number Line

ILLUSTRATION : 2

Find 6 – 3.

SOLUTION :

To subtract 3 from 6 on the number line, we start from 6 and move 3 points backward (See figure given below)
We reach at 3, so 6 – 3 = 3

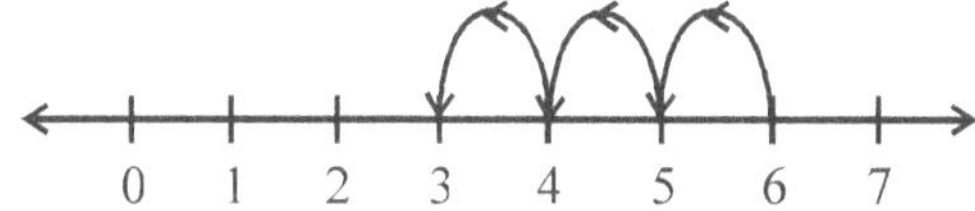

Multiplication on Number Line

ILLUSTRATION : 3

Find 2 × 4.

SOLUTION :

To multiply 2 and 4 on the number line, we start from 0 and move 2 points forward and make 4 such moves (See figure given below). We reach at 8. Hence, 2 × 4 = 8.

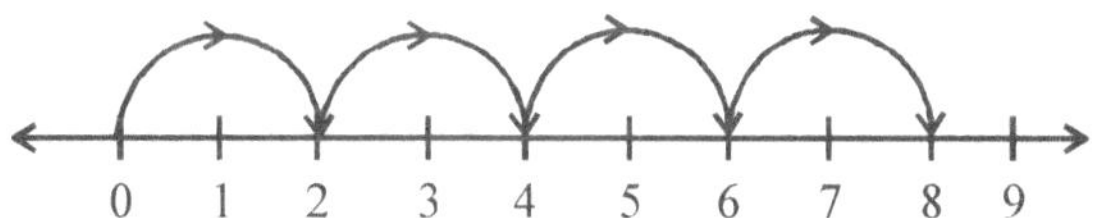

PROPERTIES OF WHOLE NUMBER

Properties of whole numbers make calculations under operations like addition, subtraction, multiplication, division easier. The different types of properties of whole numbers are as follows.

Properties of Addition

(i) Closure Property

When two numbers a and b are added, the result, i.e., $a + b = c$ will also be a whole number. Therefore, whole numbers are closed for addition.

(ii) Commutative Property

If a and b are two whole numbers, then a + b = b + a. In other words, when whole numbers are added, the order does not matter. This property is called **Commutative Property**. **For example**, 11 + 13 = 13 + 11 = 24. So, whole numbers are commutative for addition.

(iii) Associative Property

If a, b and c are three whole numbers, then (a + b) + c = a + (b + c) i.e., the manner of associating numbers does not change the result. This property is called **Associative Property**.

For example : $(2 + 3) + 4 = 2 + (3 + 4) = 9$
So, whole numbers are associative under addition.

(iv) Additive Identity

Additive Identity is a number which when added to any whole number, then the value remains the same. Let a be any whole number, then $0 + a = a + 0 = a$. So, 0 is the additive identity of whole numbers.

Properties of Subtraction

(i) Closure Property

If a and b are two whole numbers such that $a > b$ or $a = b$, then $a - b$ is a whole number. If $a < b$, then $a - b$ is not a whole number.

For example : $8 - 3 = 5$ and $8 - 8 = 0$.   But $8 - 10 = ?$
Therefore, whole numbers are not closed under subtraction.

(ii) Commutative Property

If a and b are two whole numbers, then $a - b$ is not equal to $b - a$. **For example,** $9 - 5 \neq 5 - 9$. So, the subtraction of whole numbers is not commutative.

(iii) Associative Property

If a, b and c are whole numbers, then $(a - b) - c$ is not equal to $a - (b - c)$.
For example : $(12 - 4) - 3 = 8 - 3 = 5$
$12 - (4 - 3) = 12 - 1 = 11$
$\therefore (12 - 4) - 3 \neq 12 (4 - 3)$
So, the subtraction of whole numbers is not associative.

(iv) Property of Zero

If a is any whole number other than zero, then $a - 0 = a$.
For example : $3 - 0 = 3$.

Properties of Multiplication

(i) Closure Property

If a and b are whole numbers, then their product $a \times b = c$ will always be a whole number.
So, whole numbers are closed under multiplication.

(ii) Commutative Property

When two whole numbers, a and b are multiplied in any order, then their product remains the same. This property is called **commutative property. For example,** $2 \times 3 = 3 \times 2 = 6$
So, whole numbers are commutative under multiplication.

(iii) Associative Property

If a, b and c are three whole numbers, then $(a \times b) \times c = a \times (b \times c)$.
For example, $(3 \times 10) \times 4 = 3 \times (10 \times 4) = 120$
So, whole numbers are associative under multiplication.

(iv) Multiplicative Identity

When any whole number a is multiplied by 1, the product is the same number a, i.e., $1 \times a = a \times 1 = a$.
So, 1 is called the multiplicative identity in whole numbers.

(v) Multiplication By Zero

If a is any whole number, then $a \times 0 = 0 \times a = 0$.

(vi) Distributivity of Multiplication Over Addition or Subtraction :

If a, b, c are any three whole numbers, then
(i) $a \times (b + c) = a \times b + a \times c$
(ii) $a \times (b - c) = a \times b - a \times c$

For example : $2 \times (3 + 5) = 2 \times 8 = 16$
or $2 \times 3 + 2 \times 5 = 6 + 10 = 16$
$\therefore$ $2 \times (3 + 5) = 2 \times 3 + 2 \times 5$
again, $15 \times (7 - 3) = 15 \times 4 = 60$
or $15 \times 7 - 15 \times 3 = 105 - 45 = 60$
$\therefore$ $15 \times (7 - 3) = 15 \times 7 - 15 \times 3$
Hence, the multiplication of whole numbers is distributive over addition and subtraction.

ILLUSTRATION : 4

Find the sum of 242, 496 and 758 by using most convenient combination.

SOLUTION :

Using the most convenient grouping
$(242 + 758) + 496 = 1000 + 496$
$= 1496$

ILLUSTRATION : 5

Find the product by suitable rearrangement : $25 \times 60 \times 4 \times 150$.

SOLUTION :

$(25 \times 4) \times (60 \times 150) = 100 \times 9000$
$= 9,00,000$

ILLUSTRATION : 6

Use distributive property to find 394×101.

SOLUTION :

101 may be written as $(100 + 1)$
This gives us $394 \times (100 + 1)$
$= 394 \times 100 + 394 \times 1$ (Distributive property of multiplication over addition).
$= 39400 + 394$
$= 39794$

ILLUSTRATION : 7

Using distributive property, find the value of :
$684 \times 45 + 684 \times 55$.

SOLUTION:

Using distributive property, the above expression may be written as-
$684 \times (45 + 55)$
which equals $684 \times 100 = 68,400$

Properties of Division

Property 1 : If a and b are whole numbers then $a \div b$ may or may not represent a whole number.
For example : $6 \div 3 = 2$ (a whole number)
            $2 \div 9 = 2/9$ (not a whole number)
Therefore, whole numbers are not closed under division.
Property 2 : If a is a whole number, then $a \div 0$ is meaningless.
Property 3 : If a is a non-zero whole number, then $0 \div a = 0$.
For example, $0 \div 4 = 0$.

PATTERNS IN WHOLE NUMBERS

Let us now learn to arrange numbers in elementary shapes made up of dots. We will learn to arrange them in any of the shape given below

(1)   Line   (2)   Rectangle   (3)   Square   (4)   Triangle

Line

All numbers greater than 1 can be arranged in lines - e.g.

No.	Pattern
2	• •
3	• • •
4	• • • •
5	• • • • •

Rectangle

Some numbers can be arranged as rectangles. e.g. No. 6, 8, 10 and 12.

No.	Pattern
6	
8	
10	
12	

Square

Some numbers can be arrange as square 4, 9, 16, 25, 36, 49, etc.

No.	Pattern
4	
9	
16	
25	

Triangle

Some numbers can be arranged like triangles e.g. 3, 6, 10, 15, 21, 28, 36, 45 etc.

No.	Pattern
3.	
6	
10	
15	

OBSERVATION OF PATTERNS

The number pattern can help us to simplify problems. Observe the patterns given below.

Shortcut to Add a Number Closer to 10, 20, 30 or so on

(i) $38 + 9 = 38 + (10 - 1) = (38 + 10) - 1 = 48 - 1 = 47$

(ii) $64 + 18 = 64 + (20 - 2) = (64 + 20) - 2 = 84 - 2 = 82$

(iii) $73 + 27 = 73 + (30 - 3) = (73 + 30) - 3 = 103 - 3 = 100$

Thus, it becomes simple to calculate the sum or the difference of two numbers, when one of the numbers is closer to 10, 20, 30, 40 and so on.

Shortcut to Multiply a Number by 5 or 25 or 125

(i) $38 \times 5 = 38 \times \dfrac{10}{2} = \dfrac{38 \times 10}{2} = \dfrac{380}{2} = 190$

(ii) $38 \times 25 = 38 \times \dfrac{100}{4} = \dfrac{3800}{4} = 950$

Shortcut to Multiply a Number by 9 or 99 or 999

(i) $25 \times 9 = 25 \times (10 - 1) = 25 \times 10 - 25 = 225$

(ii) $25 \times 99 = 25 \times (100 - 1) = 2500 - 25 = 2475$

(iii) $25 \times 999 = 25 \times (1000 - 1) = 25000 - 25 = 24975$

CONCEPT MAP

Successor and Predecessor

- We add 1 to a number to get successor of it and subtract 1 from a number to get its predecessor.
- Every whole number has a successor.
- Every whole number has a predecessor (except 0).

Number Line

- To add on number line, move to the right.
- To subtract on number line, move to the left.
- To multiply on number line, make jumps of equal distance starting from zero.

Properties of Whole Numbers

- Whole numbers are closed under addition and multiplication.
- Whole numbers are not closed under subtraction and division.
- Addition and multiplication both are. commutative for whole numbers.
- Addition and multiplication both are associative for whole numbers.
- Multiplication is distributive over addition and subtraction for whole numbers.

Whole Numbers

(1) (2) (3) (4) (5)

Patterns in Whole Numbers

- We can arrange numbers (greater than 1) in elementary shapes (line, square, rectangle, triangle) using dots.
- Every whole number (greater than 1) can be arranged as a line.
- Some numbers like 4, 9, 16, 25 ..... can be arranged as squares.
- Some numbers like 6, 8, 10 .... can be arranged as rectangles.
- Some numbers like 3, 6, 10, 15 ...... can be arranged as triangles.

Identities for Whole Numbers

- Zero (0) is the identity for addition of whole numbers.
  e.g. $2 + 0 = 0 + 2 = 2$
- 1 is the identity for multiplication of whole numbers
  e.g. $3 \times 1 = 1 \times 3 = 3$

MISCELLANEOUS
SOLVED EXAMPLES

1. Write the successor and predecessor of
(i) 1000   (ii) 1005399   (iii) 999999

Sol. (i) The successor of $1000 = (1000 + 1) = 1001$.
The predecessor of 1000
$= (1000 - 1) = 999$.
(ii) The successor of 1005399
$= (1005399 + 1) = 1005400$
The predecessor of 1005399
$= (1005399 - 1) = 1005398$
(iii) The successor of 999999
$= (999999 + 1) = 1000000$.
The predecessor of 999999
$= (999999 - 1) = 999998$.

2. Find 5 + 4 using number line.

Sol. To add 5 and 4 on the number line, start from 5
and then move 4 points forwards

We reach at 9. Hence, $5 + 4 = 9$

3. Find 7 – 3 using number line.

Sol. To subtract 3 from 7 on the number line, start
from 7 and then move 3 points backwards

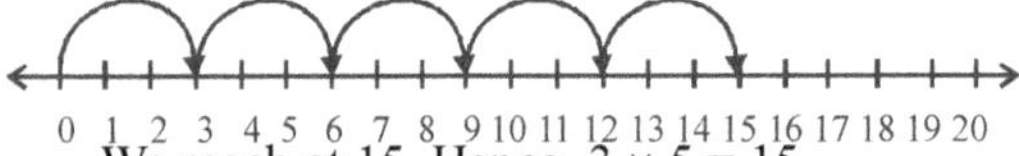

We reach at 4. Hence, $7 - 3 = 4$

4. Find 3 × 5 using number line.

Sol. To multiply 3 and 5 on the number line, we start
from 0 and move 3 points forwards. Now make
5 such moves.

We reach at 15. Hence, $3 \times 5 = 15$

5. Find the sum by suitable rearrangement:
(i)   847 + 306 + 453
(ii)   1852 + 653 + 1648 + 547

Sol. We have:
(i) $847 + 306 + 453 = (847 + 453) + 306$
$= (1300 + 306) = 1606$.
(ii) $1852 + 653 + 1648 + 547 = (1852 + 1648)$
$+ (653 + 547) = (3500 + 1200) = 4700$.

6. Find the product by suitable rearrangement:
(i)   125 × 3958 × 8   (ii) 250 × 7445 × 9 × 8.

Sol. (i) $125 \times 3958 \times 8$
$= (125 \times 8) \times 3958 = 1000 \times 3958 = 3958000$
(ii) $250 \times 7445 \times 9 \times 8$
$= (250 \times 8) \times (7445 \times 9)$
$= 2000 \times 67005 = 1000 \times 2 \times 67005$

$= 1000 \times (67005 \times 2)$
$= 1000 \times 134010 = 134010000$

7. Multiply 3756 × 199 using property.

Sol. We have 3756×199
$= 3756 \times (200 - 1) = 3756 \times 200 - 3756 \times 1$
$= 751200 - 3756 = 747444$

8. Simplify the following: 895 × 27 + 895 × 39 + 895 × 34.

Sol. We have
$895 \times 27 + 895 \times 39 + 895 \times 34$
$= 895 \times (27 + 39 + 34) = 895 \times 100 = 89500$

9. The camp manager ordered 1 samosa and 1 sandwich for each student. If the cost of one samosa is ₹ 6 and one sandwich is ₹ 9, find the total amount spent, if he ordered for 15 student.

Sol. Cost of samosa for 15 students $= 15 \times 6$
Cost of sandwich for 15 students $= 15 \times 9$
Total cost $= ₹ (15 \times 6) + ₹ (15 \times 9)$
$= ₹ (90 + 135) = ₹ 225$

Alternatively :
Total cost of samosa and sandwich for one
student $= ₹ (6 + 9)$
Total cost $= ₹ \{15 \times (6 + 9)\}$
$= ₹ (15 \times 15) = ₹ 225$
Thus, $15 \times (6 + 9) = 15 \times 6 + 15 \times 9$.

10. Find each of the following products:
(i) 30674 × 9 (ii) 4578 × 99 (iii) 23756 × 999

Sol. We have:
(i) $30674 \times 9 = 30674 \times (10 - 1)$
$= (30674 \times 10) - (30674 \times 1)$
$= (306740 - 30674) = 276066$.
(ii) $4578 \times 99 = 4578 \times (100 - 1)$
$= (4578 \times 100) - (4578 \times 1)$
$= (457800 - 4578) = 453222$.
(iii) $23756 \times 999 = 23756 \times (1000 - 1)$
$= (23756 \times 1000) - (23756 \times 1)$
$= (23756000 - 23756) = 23732244$.

11. Study the patterns to fill in the blanks.
$5 \times 11 = 55$
$55 \times 101 = 5555$
$555 \times 1001 = 555555$
$5555 \times 10001 = $ ______
$55555 \times $ ______ $= $ ______

Sol. $5 \times 11 = 55$
$55 \times 101 = 5555$
$555 \times 1001 = 555555$
$5555 \times 10001 = 55555555$
$55555 \times 100001 = 5555555555$

1 EXERCISE

Fill in the Blanks :

DIRECTIONS : *Complete the following statements with an appropriate word / term to be filled in the blank space (s).*

1. The smallest whole number is _______.
2. Successor of 106159 is _______.
3. Predecessor of 100000 is _______.
4. 400 is the predecessor of _______.
5. _______ is the successor of the largest 3 digit number.
6. Whole numbers are closed under _______ and under _______.
7. Multiplication is distributive over _______ and _______ for whole numbers.
8. $1001 \times 2002 = 1001 \times (1001 + $ _______ $)$
9. $2916 \times$ _______ $= 0$
10. $19 \times 12 + 19 = 19 \times (12 + $ _______ $)$
11. $125 + (68 + 17) = (125 + $ _______ $) + 17$
12. $8925 \times 1 = $ _______

True / False :

DIRECTIONS : *Read the following statements and write your answer as true or false.*

1. Successor of a one digit number is always a one digit number.
2. Every whole number has its successor.
3. Every whole number has its predecessor.
4. The smallest 5-digit number is the successor of the largest 4-digit number.
5. 1 is the identity for addition of whole numbers.
6. Any non–zero whole number divided by itself gives the quotient 1.
7. The product of two whole numbers need not be a whole number.
8. There is a whole number which when added to a whole number, gives the number itself.

Match the Columns :

DIRECTIONS : *Each question contains statements given in two columns which have to be matched. Statements (A, B, C, D) in column-I have to be matched with statements (p, q, r, s) in column-II.*

1. Match the Columns.

Column-I	Column-II
(A) $1983 + 647 + 217 + 353 =$	(p) 124384
(B) $736 \times 169 =$	(q) 3200
(C) $569 \times 17 + 569 \times 13 + 569 \times 70 =$	(r) 631000
(D) $631 \times 10 \times 467 - 367 \times 6310 =$	(s) 56900

Very Short Answer Questions :

DIRECTIONS : *Give answer in one word or one sentence.*

1. Write the successor of the following:
   (i) 20199   (ii) 30569
2. Write the predecessor of the following:
   (i) 96   (ii) 98900   (iii) 63520
3. In each of the following pairs of numbers, state which whole number is to the left of the other on the number line. Use appropriate symbol ($>$ or $<$).
   (i) 469, 409   (ii) 3059, 5039
   (iii) 7089, 1023   (iv) 10090, 10009
4. What is the difference between 9 and 0?
5. What is the product of 1 and 9?
6. What is the quotient, when 9 is divided by 9?
7. How many whole numbers are there between 21 and 61?
8. Write down three consecutive whole numbers just preceeding 6510001.
9. Write the whole number whose successor is 475000.
10. Write the whole number whose predecessor is 68999.

11. Write down three consecutive whole numbers succeeding 84998.

Short Answer Questions :

DIRECTIONS : *Give answer in 2-3 sentences.*

1. Find the sum: $(1546 + 498) + 3589$.
Also, find the sum: $1546 + (498 + 3589)$.
Are the two sums equal?
State the property satisfied.

2. Find the sum:
(i) $3678 + 999$ (ii) $34876 + 9999$

3. Verify the associative property of addition and multiplication for the following numbers:
(i) $2, 6, 9$ (ii) $7, 3, 5$

4. Find the sum by suitable rearrangement:
(i) $937 + 908 + 263$
(ii) $2962 + 567 + 1538 + 633$

5. Find the product by suitable rearrangement:
(i) $4 \times 1256 \times 25$
(ii) $5 \times 676 \times 20$
(iii) $125 \times 40 \times 8 \times 25$
(iv) $16 \times 729 \times 625$

6. Using properties of whole numbers simplify the following:
(i) $397 \times 17 + 397 \times 3$
(ii) $54298 \times 93 + 7 \times 54298$
(iii) $81625 \times 169 - 81625 \times 69$
(iv) $3845 \times 5 \times 784 + 769 \times 25 \times 216$

7. Determine the following products by suitable rearrangement:
(i) $8 \times 1250 \times 40 \times 25$
(ii) $250 \times 60 \times 50 \times 8$
(iii) $37256 \times 25 \times 9 \times 40$

8. Using distributivity of multiplication over addition of whole numbers, find each of the following products:
(i) 736×103 (ii) 258×1008

9. Study the patterns to fill in the blanks.
$6 \times 2 - 5 = 7$
$7 \times 3 - 12 = 9$
$8 \times 4 - 21 = 11$
$9 \times \underline{} - 32 = 13$
$10 \times 6 - 45 = \underline{}$

10. Observe the pattern in the following and fill in the blanks:
$9 \times 9 + 7 \qquad = 88$
$98 \times 9 + 6 \qquad = 888$
$987 \times 9 + 5 \qquad = 8888$
$9876 \times 9 + 4 \qquad = \underline{}$
$98765 \times 9 + 3 \qquad = \underline{}$
$987654 \times 9 + 2 \qquad = \underline{}$
$9876543 \times 9 + 1 \qquad = \underline{}$

11. Study the following pattern:
$1 + 3 = 2 \times 2$
$1 + 3 + 5 = 3 \times 3$
$1 + 3 + 5 + 7 = 4 \times 4$
$1 + 3 + 5 + 7 + 9 = 5 \times 5$
By observing the above pattern, find
(i) $1 + 3 + 5 + 7 + 9 + 11$
(ii) $1 + 3 + 5 + 7 + 9 + 11 + 13 + 15$

Long Answer Questions :

DIRECTIONS : *Give answer in four to five sentences.*

1. A school bought 40 tables and 40 chairs. The cost of each table is ₹ 350 and that of each chair is ₹ 225. Find the total money spent by the school.

2. Verify the distributive property for multiplication of the following, where $a = 28$, $b = 15$, $c = 12$.
(i) $a \times (b + c)$ (ii) $a \times (b - c)$,

3. A car moves at a uniform speed of 75 km per hour. How much distance will it cover in 98 hours?

4. If $a = 3$, $b = 5$ and $c = 10$, verify:
(i) $a \times (b + c) = ab + ac$
(ii) $a \times (b - c) = ab - ac$.

2 EXERCISE

1. Find $4 + 5$; $2 + 6$; $3 + 5$ and $1 + 6$ using the number line.

2. Find $8 - 3$; $6 - 2$; $9 - 6$ using the number line.

3. Find 2×6; 3×3; 4×2 using the number line.

4. Write the successor of :
   - (i) 2440701
   - (ii) 100199
   - (iii) 1099999
   - (iv) 2345670

5. Write the predecessor of:
   - (i) 94
   - (ii) 10000
   - (iii) 208090
   - (iv) 7654321

6. Find the value of the following:
   - (i) $297 \times 17 + 297 \times 3$
   - (ii) $54279 \times 92 + 8 \times 54279$
   - (iii) $81265 \times 169 - 81265 \times 69$
   - (iv) $3845 \times 5 \times 782 + 769 \times 25 \times 218$

7. A taxi driver filled his car petrol tank with 40 litres of petrol on Monday. The next day, he filled the tank with 50 litres of petrol. If the petrol costs ₹ 44 per litre, how much did he spend in all on petrol?

8. A vendor supplies 32 litres of milk to a hotel in the morning and 68 litres of milk in the evening. If the milk costs ₹ 15 per litre, how much money is due to the vendor per day?

9. If the product of two whole numbers is zero, can we say that one or both of them will be zero? Justify through examples.

10. If the product of two whole numbers is 1, can we say that one or both of them will be 1? Justify through examples.

1. The product of a non-zero whole number and its successor is always –

2. A whole number is added to 25 and the same number is subtracted from 25. What is the sum of the resulting numbers ?

3. The predecessor of 1 lakh is __________ .

4. The successor of 1 million is __________ .

5. Determine the sum of the four numbers as given below :
   - (i) successor of 32
   - (ii) predecessor of 49
   - (iii) predecessor of the predecessor of 56
   - (iv) successor of the successor of 67

1. Is there any whole number a such that $a \times a = a$ and $a + a = a$?

2. Is there any whole number p such that $p \times p = p$ and $p \div p = p$?

3. Study the following pattern of triangular numbers and extend it to 3 more steps.
   $$8 \times 1 + 1 = 9 = 3 \times 3$$
   $$8 \times 3 + 1 = 25 = 5 \times 5$$
   $$8 \times 6 + 1 = 49 = 7 \times 7$$
   $$8 \times 10 + 1 = 81 = 9 \times 9$$

4. How many 3-digit numbers are there in all?

3 EXERCISE

Single Option Correct :

DIRECTIONS : *This section contains multiple choice questions. Each question has 4 choices (a), (b), (c) and (d) out of which ONLY ONE is correct.*

1. The whole number which does not have a predecessor is
   (a) 100   (b) 0
   (c) 1   (d) 9

2. Successor of every even number is
   (a) even   (b) prime
   (c) odd   (d) None of these

3. $56 (4 + 2) = (56 \times 4) + (56 \times 2)$ is an example of the
   (a) closure property of whole number
   (b) commutative property of whole number
   (c) associative property of whole number
   (d) distributive property of whole number

4. Which of the following is an example of commutative property?
   (a) $21 \times 1 = 21$
   (b) $5 \times (7 + 8) = 5 \times 7 + 5 \times 8$
   (c) $12 + 33 = 33 + 12$
   (d) $13 + 0 = 13$

5. The successor of successor of 99998 is
   __________.
   (a) 100000   (b) 99999
   (c) 99997   (d) 10000

6. $38 + 83 = 83 + 38$ is an example of
   (a) commutative property
   (b) associative property
   (c) closure property
   (d) distributive property

7. The product of successor and predecessor of 999 is
   (a) 999000   (b) 998000
   (c) 989000   (d) 1998

8. Which of the following is not defined ?
   (a) $5 + 0$ (b) $5 - 0$
   (c) 5×0 (d) $5 \div 0$

9. Observe the following sums. Then find the sum of $1 + 3 + 5 + 7 + 9 + ... + 19$?
$$1 = 1 \times 1 = 1$$
$$1 + 3 = 2 \times 2 = 4$$
$$1 + 3 + 5 = 3 \times 3 = 9$$
$$1 + 3 + 5 + 7 = 4 \times 4 = 16$$
$$1 + 3 + 5 + 7 + 9 = 5 \times 5 = 25$$
   (a) 121   (b) 81
   (c) 100   (d) 64

10. Observe the given multiples of 37.
$$37 \times 3 = 111$$
$$37 \times 6 = 222$$
$$37 \times 9 = 333$$
$$37 \times 12 = 444$$
   Find the product of 37×27 ?
   (a) 999.
   (b) Greatest 2 digit number.
   (c) Either A or B.
   (d) Smallest 3-digit number.

More Than One Option Correct :

DIRECTIONS : *This section contains multiple choice questions. Each question has 4 choices (a), (b), (c) and (d) out of which ONE or MORE may be correct.*

1. Which of the following is/are true?
   (a) $(7 + 8) + 9 = 7 + (8 + 9)$
   (b) $(7 \times 8) \times 9 = 7 \times (8 \times 9)$
   (c) $7 + 8 \times 9 = (7 + 8) \times (7 + 9)$
   (d) $7 \times (8 + 9) = (7 \times 8) + (7 \times 9)$

2. Which of the following statements is/are true?
   (a) Both addition and multiplication are associative for whole numbers.
   (b) Zero is the identity for multiplication of whole numbers.
   (c) Addition and multiplication both are commutative for whole numbers.
   (d) Multiplication is distributive over addition for whole numbers.

3. Which of the following statements is/are true?
   (a) $0 + 0 = 0$ (b) $0 - 0 = 0$
   (c) $0 \times 0 = 0$ (d) $0 \div 0 = 0$

4. If a and b are two whole numbers, which of the following is/are whole number.
   (a) $a + b$ (b) $a - b$
   (c) $a \times b$ (d) $2(a + b)$

Assertion & Reason :

DIRECTIONS : *Each of these questions contains an Assertion followed by Reason. Read them carefully and answer the question on the basis of following options. You have to select the one that best describes the two statements.*

(a) If both **Assertion** and **Reason** are correct and **Reason** is the correct explanation of **Assertion**.
(b) If both **Assertion** and **Reason** are correct but **Reason** is not the correct explanation of **Assertion**.
(c) If **Assertion** is correct but **Reason** is incorrect.
(d) If **Assertion** is incorrect but **Reason** is correct.

1. **Assertion :** If a is a whole number then $a + 0 = 0 + a = a$.
   Reason : If a and b are whole numbers then $a + b$ is also a whole number.
2. **Assertion :** If $a = 16$, $b = 12$ then $a \times b = 192$, a whole number.
   Reason : Closure property holds for multiplication of whole numbers.
3. **Assertion :** The value of $78 \times (69 + 22)$ is 7098.
   Reason : If a, b and c are three whole numbers, then $a (b + c) = a \times b + a \times c$

Passage Based Questions :

DIRECTIONS : *Study the given passage(s) and answer the following questions.*

PASSAGE - I

Nilesh consumes a can each of mango juice priced at 50 and lichi juice priced at ₹ 60 everyday.

1. Nilesh spends on lichi juice in five days is
   (a) ₹ 12   (b) ₹ 300
   (c) ₹ 250   (d) ₹ 200

2. Total money spent by Nilesh is 3 days is
   (a) ₹ 300   (b) ₹ 320
   (c) ₹ 330   (d) ₹ 150
3. If Nilesh consumes three cans of mango juice and 2 cans of lichi juice each day, then how much money he will spent in 3 days?
   (a) ₹ 500   (b) ₹ 650
   (c) ₹ 700   (d) ₹ 810

PASSAGE - II

If a, b, c are three whole numbers then $(a + b) + c = a + (b + c)$ and $a \times (b + c) = a \times b + a \times c$

4. Find the value of $546 + (84 + 389)$
   (a) 1917   (b) 2530
   (c) 7990   (d) 1019
5. Find the product of 475×102?
   (a) 10900   (b) 48450
   (c) 12500   (d) 13256
6. State the property used in the following statement.
   $$66 \times 93 + 66 \times 7 = 66 \times (93 + 7)$$
   (a) Commutative property
   (b) Associative property
   (c) Distributive property
   (d) Closure property

Integer Type Questions :

DIRECTIONS : *Answer the following questions. The answer to each of the question is a single digit integer, ranging from 0 to 9.*

1. If $m \div 18 = 0$, then find the value of m.
2. What is the thousands place digit of the successor of 4999?
3. What is the sum of the digits of successor of product of 35×12?
4. Find the difference between the successor and predecessor of 29×46.
5. What is the double of multiplicative identity for whole numbers?

Multiple Matching Question :

DIRECTIONS : *Following question has five statements (A, B, C, D and E) given in Column-I and six statements (p, q, r, s, t, u) in Column-II. Any given statement in Column-I can have correct matching with one or more statement(s) given in Column-II.*

1.

Column-I	Column-II
(A) The difference of two consecutive whole numbers	(p) odd
(B) The product of two non-zero consecutive whole numbers	(q) 0
(C) Quotient when zero is divided by another non-zero whole number	(r) 3
(D) 2 added three times, to the smallest whole number	(s) 1
(E) Smallest odd prime number	(t) 6
	(u) even

SOLUTIONS

Brief Explanations of Selected Questions

1 EXERCISE

Fill in the Blanks :

1. 0
2. 106160
3. 99999
4. 401
5. 1000
6. addition, Multiplication
7. addition, subtraction
8. 1001
9. 0
10. 1
11. 68
12. 8925

True / False :

1. F
2. T
3. F
4. T
5. F
6. T
7. F
8. T

Match the Columns :

1. (A) → (q); (B) → (p); (C) → (s); (D) → (r)
   (A) $1983 + 647 + 217 + 353$
   $= (1983 + 217) + (647 + 353)$
                        (Commutative law)
   $= 2200 + 1000 = 3200$
   (B) $736 \times 169 = 736 \times (170 - 1)$
   $= 736 \times 170 - 736 \times 1$
   $= 125120 - 736 = 124384$
   (C) $569 \times 17 + 569 \times 13 + 569 \times 70$
   $= 569 \times (17 + 13 + 70)$
   $= 569 \times 100 = 56900$
   (D) $631 \times 10 \times 467 - 367 \times 6310$
   $= 6310 \times 467 - 6310 \times 367$
   $= 6310 \times (467 - 367)$
   $= 6310 \times 100 = 631000$

Very Short Answer Questions:

1. (i) 20200   (ii) 30570
2. (i) 95   (ii) 98899
   (iii) 63519
3. (i) $409 < 469$ (ii) $3059 < 5039$
   (iii) $1023 < 7089$ (iv) $10009 < 10090$
4. 9   5. 9   6. 1   7. 39
8. 6510000, 6509999, 6509998
9. 474999

10. 69000
11. 84999, 85000, 85001

Short Answer Questions :

1. 5633; 5633; yes; associative property of addition of whole numbers.
2. We have:
   (i) $3678 + 999 = 3678 + (1000 - 1)$
   $= (3678 + 1000) - 1 = (4678 - 1) = 4677.$
   (ii) $34876 + 9999 = 34876 + (10000 - 1)$
   $= (34876 + 10000) - 1 = (44876 - 1)$
   $= 44875.$
4. (i) $937 + 908 + 263$
   $(937 + 263) + 908$
   $= 1200 + 908$
   $= 2108$
   (ii) $2962 + 567 + 1538 + 633$
   $= (2962 + 1538) + (567 + 633)$
   $= (4500) + (1200)$
   $= 5700$
5. (i) $4 \times 1256 \times 25 = (4 \times 25) \times 1256$
   $= 100 \times 1256 = 125600$
   (ii) $5 \times 676 \times 20$
   $= (5 \times 20) \times 676$
   $= 100 \times 676 = 67600$
   (iii) $125 \times 40 \times 8 \times 25$
   $= (125 \times 8) \times (40 \times 25)$
   $= 1000 \times 1000 = 1000000$
   (iv) $16 \times 729 \times 625$
   $= 729 \times (16 \times 625)$
   $= 729 \times (10000) = 7290000$
6. (i) $397 \times 17 + 397 \times 3$
   $= 397 \times (17 + 3) = 397 \times 20$
   $= 7940$
   (ii) $54298 \times 93 + 7 \times 54298 = 54298 \times (93 + 7)$
                     [Distributive property]
   $= 54298 \times (100) = 5429800$
   (iii) $81625 \times 169 - 81625 \times 69$
   $= 81625 \times (169 - 69)$
                     [Distributive property]
   $= 81625 \times (100) = 8162500$

(iv) $3845 \times 5 \times 784 + 769 \times 25 \times 216$
$= 3845 \times 5 \times 784 + (769 \times 5) \times 5 \times 216$
$= 3845 \times 5 \times 784 + 3845 \times 5 \times 216$
$= 3845 \times 5 \times (784 + 216)$
$= 3845 \times 5 \times (1000)$
$= 19225000$

7. (i) $8 \times 1250 \times 40 \times 25 = (8 \times 1250) \times (40 \times 25)$
$= 10000 \times 1000 = 10000000$
(ii) $250 \times 60 \times 50 \times 8 = (250 \times 8) \times (60 \times 50)$
$= 2000 \times 3000 = 6000000$
(iii) $37256 \times 25 \times 9 \times 40$
$= (37256 \times 9) \times (25 \times 40)$
$= 335304 \times 1000 = 335304000$

8. (i) 736×103
$= 736 \times (100 + 3)$
$= 73600 + 736 \times 3$
$= 73600 + 2208$
$= 75808$
(ii) 258×1008
$= 258 \times (1000 + 8)$
$= 258 \times 1000 + 258 \times 8$
$= 258000 + 2064$
$= 260064$

9. 5, 15

10. $9876 \times 9 + 4 \qquad = 88888$
$98765 \times 9 + 3 \qquad = 888888$
$987654 \times 9 + 2 \qquad = 8888888$
$9876543 \times 9 + 1 \qquad = 88888888$

11. (i) $1 + 3 + 5 + 7 + 9 + 11 = 6 \times 6 = 36$
(ii) $1 + 3 + 5 + 7 + 9 + 11 + 13 + 15$
$= 8 \times 8 = 64$

Long Answer Questions :

1. Cost of a table = ₹ 350
Cost of a chair = ₹ 225
Total cost of a table and a chair = ₹ $(350 + 225)$
∴ The total money spent by school
$= ₹ 40 \times (350 + 225)$
$= 40 \times 575$
$= 40 \times (500 + 75)$
$= 40 \times 500 + 40 \times 75$
$= 20000 + 3000$
$= 23000$

3. Speed of car = 75 km per hour
∴ Distance covered in 98 hours = 75×98 km
$75 \times (100 - 2)$
$= 75 \times 100 - 75 \times 2$
$= 7500 - 150 = 7350$ km

2 EXERCISE

Text-Book Exercise :

1. (i) $4 + 5$

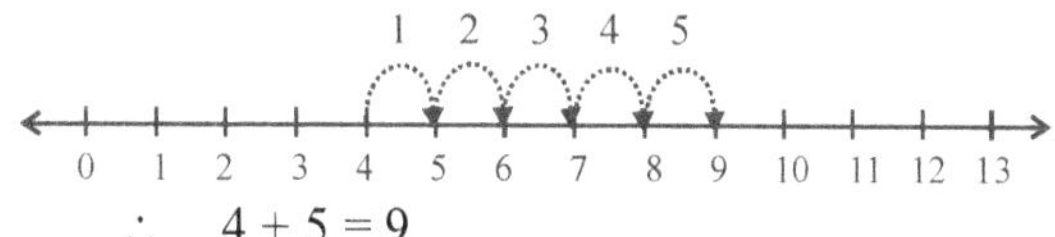

∴ $4 + 5 = 9$
(ii) $2 + 6$

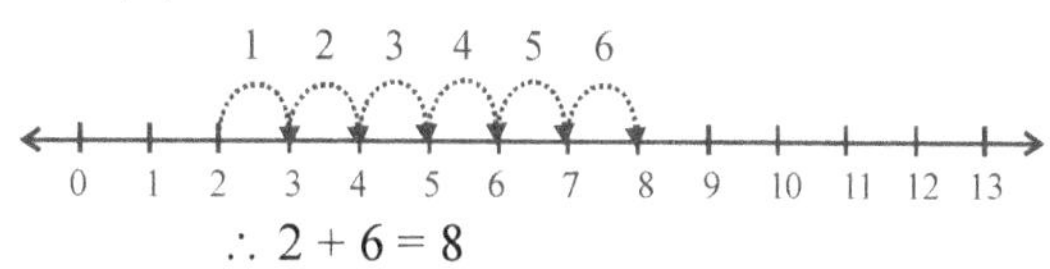

∴ $2 + 6 = 8$
(iii) $3 + 5$

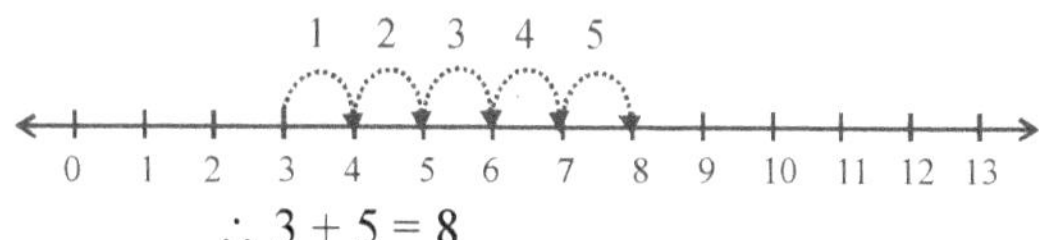

∴ $3 + 5 = 8$
(iv) $1 + 6$

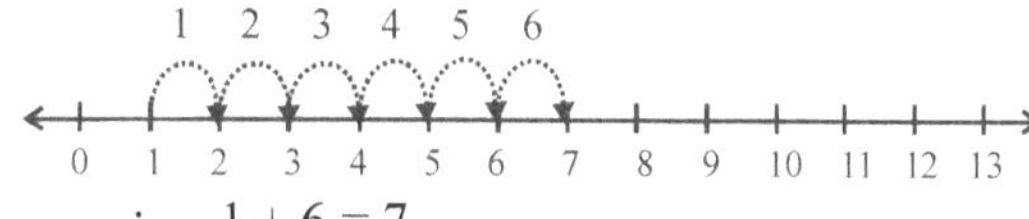

∴ $1 + 6 = 7$

2. (i) $8 - 3$

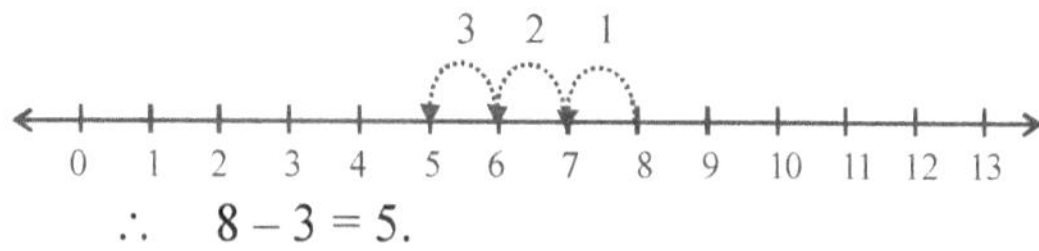

∴ $8 - 3 = 5.$
(ii) $6 - 2$

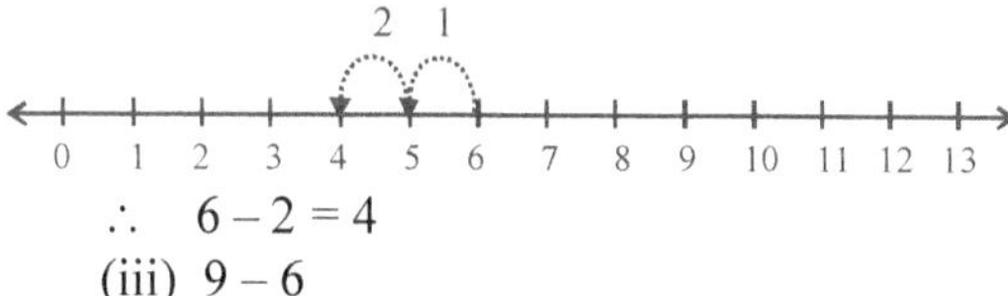

∴ $6 - 2 = 4$
(iii) $9 - 6$

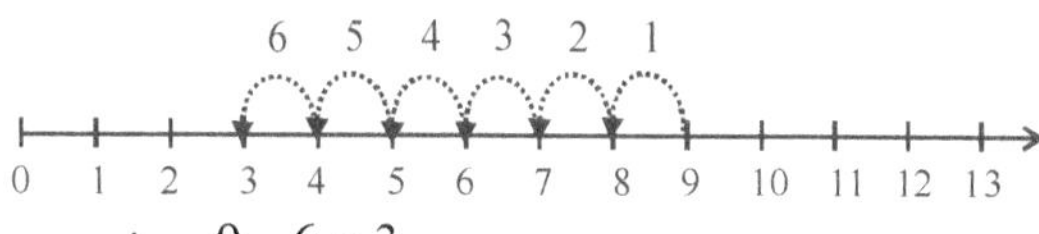

∴ $9 - 6 = 3$

3. (i) 2×6

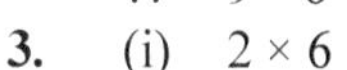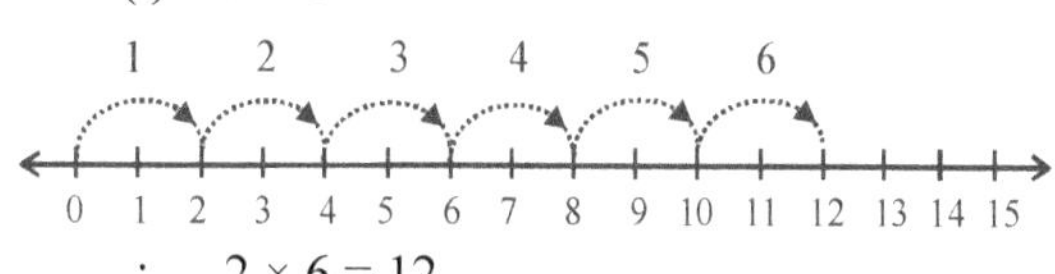

∴ $2 \times 6 = 12$

(ii) 3×3

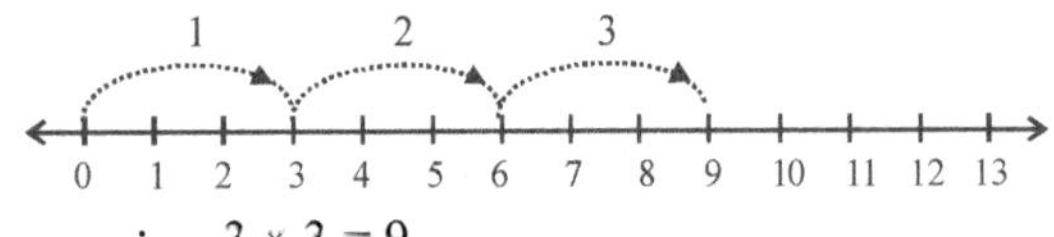

$\therefore \quad 3 \times 3 = 9$

(iii) 4×2

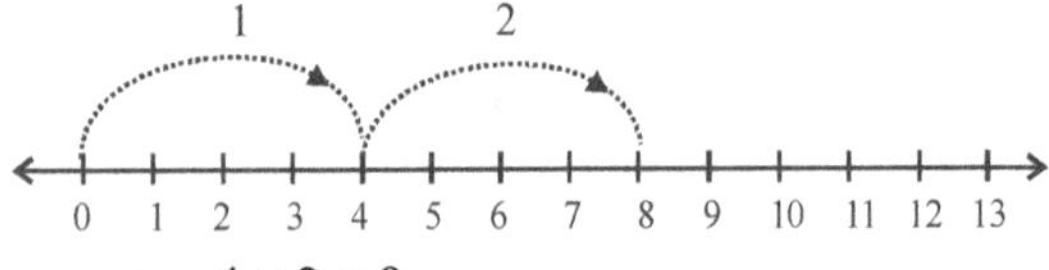

$\therefore \quad 4 \times 2 = 8$

4. | Given Number | Successor |
    |---|---|
    | (i) 2440701 | $2440701 + 1 = 2440702$ |
    | (ii) 100199 | $100199 + 1 = 100200$ |
    | (iii) 1099999 | $1099999 + 1 = 1100000$ |
    | (iv) 2345670 | $2345670 + 1 = 2345671$ |

5. | Given Number | Predeccessor |
    |---|---|
    | (i) 94 | $94 - 1 = 93$ |
    | (ii) 10000 | $10000 - 1 = 9999$ |
    | (iii) 208090 | $208090 - 1 = 208089$ |
    | (iv) 7654321 | $7654321 - 1 = 7654320$ |

6. (i) $297 \times 17 + 297 \times 3$
    $297 \times 17 + 297 \times 3$
    $= 297 \times [17 + 3]$
    $= 297 \times [20]$
    $= 297 \times 20$
    $= 5940$

    (ii) $54279 \times 92 + 8 \times 54279$
    $54279 \times 92 + 8 \times 54279$
    $= 54279 \times [92 + 8]$
    $= 54279 \times 100$
    $= 5427900$

    (iii) $81265 \times 169 - 81265 \times 69$
    $81265 \times 169 - 81265 \times 69$
    $= 81265 \times [169 - 69]$
    $= 81265 \times 100$
    $= 8126500$

    (iv) $3845 \times 5 \times 782 + 769 \times 25 \times 218$
    $3845 \times 5 \times 782 + 769 \times 25 \times 218$
    $= 3845 \times 5 \times 782 + 769 \times 5 \times 5 \times 218$
    $\qquad\qquad\qquad (\because 25 = 5 \times 5)$
    $= 3845 \times 5 \times 782 + (769 \times 5) \times 5 \times 218$
    $= 3845 \times 5 \times 782 + 3845 \times 5 \times 218$
    $= 3845 \times 5 \times [782 + 218]$
    $= 3845 \times 5 \times [1000]$
    $= 19225 \times 1000$
    $= 19225000$

7. Quantity of petrol filled on Monday = 40 litres
    Quantity of petrol filled on the next day = 50 litres
    Per litre cost of petrol = ₹ 44
    $\therefore$ Total cost of petrol for the two days
    $= ₹ 44 \times [40 + 50]$
    $= ₹ [44 \times 50] + ₹ [44 \times 40]$
    $= ₹ 2200 + ₹ 1760$
    $= ₹ 3960$

8. Milk supplied in the morning = 32 litres
    Milk supplied in the evening = 68 litres
    Cost of milk = ₹ 15 per litre
    $\therefore$ Total cost of milk per day $= ₹ 15 \times [32 + 68]$
    $= ₹ 15 \times 100$
    $= ₹ 1500$
    $\therefore$ Money due to the vendor per day = ₹ 1500.

9. We know that the product of any whole number and zero is always zero.
    i.e. $0 \times 0 = 0$
    $1 \times 0 = 0$
    $2 \times 0 = 0$
    $0 \times 3 = 0$, etc.
    Yes, if the product of two whole numbers is zero then one or both of them must be zero.

10. We know that the product of any whole number and 1 is the same whole number.
    i.e. $5 \times 1 = 5$
    $109 \times 1 = 109$
    $1 \times 17 = 17$
    $1 \times 0 = 0$
    $1 \times 1 = 1$
    $\therefore$ The product will be 1, only if both the whole number are 1.

Exemplar Questions :

1. an even number   2. 50   3. 99999
4. 1000001   5. $33 + 48 + 54 + 69 = 204$

Hots Questions :

1. Yes; 0   2. Yes; 1
3. $8 \times 15 + 1 = 121 = 11 \times 11$
    $8 \times 21 + 1 = 169 = 13 \times 13$
    $8 \times 28 + 1 = 225 = 15 \times 15$
4. The largest 3-digit no. = 999
    The largest 2-digit no. = 99
    Hence, the total number of 3-digit numbers
    $= 999 - 99 = 900$

3 E X E R C I S E

Single Option Correct :

1. **(b)** 0
2. **(c)** Odd
3. **(d)** Distributive property of whole numbers
4. **(c)** $12 + 33 = 33 + 12$; It shows commutative property of addition for whole numbers.
5. **(a)** Successor of successor of 99998
$$= 99998 + 1 + 1 = 100,000$$
6. **(a)** (commutative property)
7. **(b)** $1000 \times 998 = 998000$
8. **(d)**
9. **(c)** From 1 to 19 there are 10 odd numbers.
So, $1 + 3 + 5 + 7 + \ldots + 19$
$$= 10 \times 10 = 100$$
10. **(a)** $37 \times 3 = 37 \times (3 \times 1) = 111$
$37 \times 6 = 37 \times (3 \times 2) = 222$
$37 \times 9 = 37 \times (3 \times 3) = 333$
$- - - - - - - - - - - - - - - - - - -$
$- - - - - - - - - - - - - - - - - - -$
$37 \times 27 = 37 \times (3 \times 9) = 999$

More Than One Option Correct :

1. **(a, b, d)** 2. **(a, c, d)** 3. **(a, b, c)** 4. **(a, c, d)**

Assertion & Reason :

1. **(b)** Addition of whole numbers is a closed operation.
Assertion : True; **Reason** : True but **Reason** is not the correct explanation of **Assertion**.
2. **(a)** **Assertion:** True; **Reason** : True and is the correct explanation of **Assertion**.
3. **(a)** **Assertion** : True; **Reason** : True.

Passage Based Questions :

1. **(b)** Money spent on lichi juice in five days
$$= ₹ 60 \times 5 = ₹ 300$$
2. **(c)** Total money spent on both juices in 3 days

$$= ₹ 50 \times 3 + ₹ 60 \times 3$$
$$= 3 \times ₹ (50 + 60)$$
$$[\text{Using distributive property}]$$
$$= 3 \times ₹ (110) = ₹ 330$$
3. **(d)** Amount of money spent in 1 day
$$= ₹ (50 \times 3) + ₹ (60 \times 2)$$
$$= ₹ (150 + 120 = ₹ 270$$
$\therefore$ Amount of money spent in 3 days
$$= ₹ (3 \times 270) = ₹ 810$$
4. **(d)** As $a + (b + c) = (a + b) + c$
We have $546 + (84 + 389)$
$$= (546 + 84) + 389 = 630 + 389 = 1019$$
5. **(b)** 475×102 is written as
$475 \times (100 + 2) = 475 \times 100 + 475 \times 2$
$$[a \times (b + c) = a \times b + a \times c]$$
$47500 + 950 = 48450$
6. **(c)** We have, $66 \times 93 + 66 \times 7 = 66 \times (93 + 7)$
This property is distributive property.

Integer Type Questions :

1. **(0)** Zero when divided by any whole number gives 0.
2. **(5)** The successor of 4999 is $4999 + 1 = 5000$
Thousands place digit of 5000 is 5.
3. **(7)** As we have 35×12
It can written as
$35 \times (10 + 2) = 35 \times 10 + 35 \times 2$
$$[\text{By distributive property}]$$
$= 350 + 70 = 420$
Successor of $420 = 420 + 1 = 421$
Now the sum of digits of 421 is $4 + 2 + 1 = 7$
4. **(2)** We have $29 \times 46 = (30 - 1) \times 46$
$= 30 \times 46 - 1 \times 46$ (by distributive property)
$= 1380 - 46 = 1334$
$\therefore$ Required difference $= 1335 - 1333 = 2$
5. **(2)** Multiplicative identity for whole numbers is 1.
i.e. $1 \times a = a \times 1 = a$, where a is any whole number.
$\therefore$ double of $1 = 2 \times 1 = 2$

Multiple Matching Questions :

1. $(A) \to (s)$, $(B) \to (u)$, $(C) \to (q)$,
$(D) \to (t, u)$, $(E) \to (r)$

Chapter 3

Playing with Numbers

FACTORS

Factors of a number exactly divide that number without leaving any remainder.

A number which divides a given number exactly is called a **factor** of the given number.

Properties of Factors

1. 1 is a factor of every number.
2. A number is a factor of itself.
3. Every factor of a number is either less than or equal to the given number.
4. The smallest factor of a given number is 1 and the greatest factor is the number itself.
5. If a number is divided by any of its factors, the remainder is always zero.
6. Numbers of factors of a given number are finite.

ILLUSTRATION : 1

Find all the factors of 48.

SOLUTION :

$48 = 1 \times 48$; $48 = 2 \times 24$; $48 = 3 \times 16$; $48 = 4 \times 12$; $48 = 6 \times 8$

Thus, 1, 2, 3, 4, 6, 8, 12, 16, 24 and 48 are all the factors of 48.

ILLUSTRATION : 2

Is 15 is a factor of 2255?

SOLUTION :

To check whether 15 is factor of 2255 or not, we divide 2255 by 15 and check if remainder is zero or not.

Since remainder 5 is left. So 15 is not a factor of 2255.

```
        2255 ( 150
15 )    15
        ‾‾‾
        75
        75
        ‾‾
         5
```

MULTIPLES

A **multiple** of a number is a number obtained by multiplying it by a natural number.

Properties of Multiples

1. Every number is a multiple of 1.
2. The smallest multiple of a number is the number itself.
3. We cannot find the greatest multiple of a number.
4. Number of multiples of a number are infinite.

ILLUSTRATION : 3.

Find first 3 multiples of 12.

SOLUTION :

$12 \times 1 = 12$; $12 \times 2 = 24$; $12 \times 3 = 36$

Hence, First three multiples of 12 are 12, 24, 36.

PERFECT NUMBER

A number is called **perfect number** if the sum of all its factor is equal to twice the number.

For example : 6 is a perfect number as 1, 2, 3 and 6 are the factor of 6 and 6 = 1 + 2 + 3 + 6 = 12.

EVEN AND ODD NUMBERS

Even Numbers

Numbers which are multiples of 2 are called **even numbers.** All the even numbers always end with 0, 2, 4, 6, or 8.

Odd Numbers

The numbers which are not multiples of 2. are called **odd numbers**. All odd numbers end with 1, 3, 5, 7 or 9.

PRIME AND COMPOSITE NUMBER

We know that every number has at least two factors, 1 and the number itself. Only 1 is the number which has only one factor i.e. 1. So we can divide the numbers into two groups on the basis of number of factors:

Prime Numbers

Those numbers which have exactly two factors, namely 1 and the number itself are known as **prime numbers.** **For example:** 2, 3, 5, 7, 11, 13, 17, 19, 23 etc. are some prime numbers.

Composite Numbers

Those numbers which have more than two factors are called **composite numbers**. **For example :** 4, 6, 8, 9, 10, 12, 14, etc. are some composite numbers.

Some Important Facts

(i) 1 is neither prime nor composite number.

(ii) 2 is the only even prime number.

(iii) 2 is the smallest prime number.

(iv) 4 is the smallest composite number.

(v) There is no number which has no factor.

Prime Numbers From 1 to 100

A Greek mathematician Eratosthenes found a very simple method for finding the Prime and Composite numbers in third century B.C. This method is called **'Sieve of Erastosthenes'**.

> **NOTE :** A prime number (except 2) cannot have 0, 2, 4, 6, 8 at its ones place.

(i) Prepare a table of natural numbers from 1 to 100.

(ii) Cross out 1 as we know that it is not a prime number.

(iii) Encircle the first and only even prime number i.e. 2 and cross out all its multiples as these are composite numbers.

(iv) Encircle the next uncrossed number i.e. 3 and cross out all its multiples as these are composite numbers.

(v) Continue this process until all the numbers in the list are either encircled or crossed.

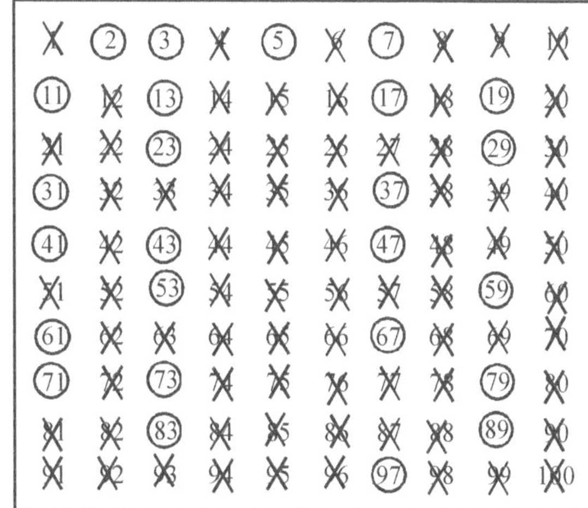

In the table, all the encircled numbers are prime numbers and the crossed numbers are composite numbers.

Twin prime

Two prime numbers having a difference of 2 are known as **twin primes.**

Co-Prime Numbers

The two numbers having only 1 as a common factor are called **co-prime numbers**. (3, 4); (6, 11); (4, 13) etc. are pairs of co-primes.

TEST FOR DIVISIBILITY OF NUMBERS

To check whether a given number is divisible by another number, we need not always carry out entire division. Some simple tests help us to check the divisibility of a number by certain numbers like 2, 3, 4, 5, 6, 7, 8, 9, 10 and 11. Let us learn about these tests.

Number divisible by	Rule	Examples
2	When digit at ones place is 2, 4, 6, 8 or 0	2398 is divisible by 2 as digit at ones place is 8.
3	When the sum of all digits of a number is a multiple of 3.	483 : Sum of digits $= 4 + 8 + 3 = 15$ Since 15 is divisible by 3, So, 483 is divisible by 3.
9	When the sum of all digits of a number is a multiple of 9.	972 : Sum of digits $= 9 + 7 + 2 = 18$ Since 18 is divisible by 9. So, 972 is divisible by 9.
6	A number is divisible by 6 if it is divisible by both 2 and 3.	24 is divisible by 6 because it is divisible by both 2 and 3.
4	When number formed by digits in its ten's and unit's place is divisible by 4.	6984 ends with 84, which is divisible by 4. Therefore 6984 is divisible by 4. 43548 ends with 48, which is divisible by 4. Therefore 43548 is divisible by 4.
8	The number formed by digits in its hundred's ten's and unit's place is divisible by 8.	40512 : 512 is divisible by 8. So, 40512 is divisible by 8
5	The digit at ones place is either	24565 and 5940 are divisible by 5 as they have 0 or 5 at ones place.
10	The digit at ones place is zero.	1890 and 2460 is divisible by 10 as 0 is at ones place.
11	When the difference between the sum of its digits in odd places and sum of digits in even places in either 0 or a multiple of 11	61809 : $6 + 8 + 9 = 23$ (Sum of digits at odd places) $1 + 0 = 1$ (sum of the digits at even places) Difference $= 23 - 1 = 22$, which is a multiple of 11
7	When the difference between twice the digit at ones place and rest of the number is either zero or multiple of 7	357 : $35 - (7 \times 2) = 21$, which is divisible by 7. So, 357 is divisible by 7.

NOTE : If we multiply three consecutive numbers, the product is always divisible by 6.

Some facts about the divisibility rule:
1. If a number is divisible by another number then the first number is divisible by each of the factors of second number.
2. If two numbers are divisible by a number, then their sum is also divisible by that numbers.
3. If two numbers are divisible by a number, then their difference is also divisible by the same number.
4. If a number is divisible by two co-prime numbers then it is divisible by their product also.

PRIME FACTORIZATION

The process of representing a number as product of prime factors is called **prime factorisation** or complete factorisation of the given number.
Prime factorisation can be done by two methods.
1. Factor tree method
2. Division method

Factor Tree Method

Let us factorize 45 using the factor tree method.
In each step of the factor tree, we write the given composite number as the product of its smallest prime factor and another factor until we get all the prime factors. Thus, prime factor of 45 is $5 \times 3 \times 3$.

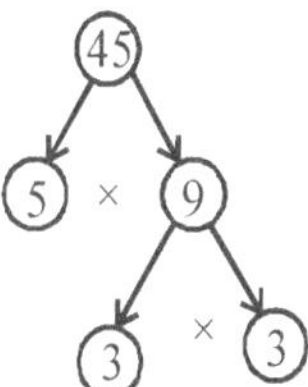

Division Method

Let us find factors of 90 using the division method.
In this method, divide the number by smallest prime number which will exactly divide the number. Continue dividing the quotient by smallest prime number till we get the quotient itself as a prime number.
Thus prime factors of 90 is $2 \times 5 \times 3 \times 3$.

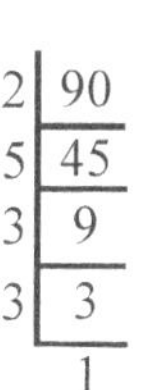

COMMON FACTORS

The factors of two numbers which are common in both the numbers are known as **common factors**.
Consider the numbers 18 and 24.
Factors of 18 = 1, 2, 3, 6, 9, 18
Factors of 24 = 1, 2, 3, 4, 6, 8, 12, 24
Common factors of 18 and 24 = 1, 2, 3, 6
Thus, common factors of 18 and 24 are 1, 2, 3 and 6.

HIGHEST COMMON FACTOR (HCF)

Highest common factor of two or more numbers is the greatest number that divides them exactly.
Consider the numbers 18 and 24.
Factors of 18 are 1, 2, 3, 6, 9, 18
Factors of 24 are 1, 2, 3, 4, 6, 8, 12, 24
Common factors of 18 and 24 are 1, 2, 3, 6.
The smallest common factor is 1.
The highest common factor is 6.
In other words, we can say that HCF of 18 and 24 is 6.
There are two different methods to find HCF of two or more numbers.
(a) Prime factorisation method and   (b) Division method

Prime Factorisation Method

In this method, we get the prime factors of numbers and then determine product of common factors.
For example, to find the HCF of 12 and 28.

$12 = 2 \times 3 \times 2$
$28 = 2 \times 2 \times 7$
HCF of 12 and 28 = $2 \times 2 = 4$

ILLUSTRATION : 4

Find the HCF of 15, 45 and 75.

SOLUTION :

$$15 = 3 \times 5$$
$$45 = 3 \times 3 \times 5$$
$$75 = 3 \times 5 \times 5$$
$$\text{HCF of 15, 45 and 75} = 3 \times 5 = 15$$

NOTE :
  (i)   Two numbers are called co-primes if their HCF is 1.
  (ii) HCF is always smaller than or equal to the smallest of the given numbers.

Division method

There are two division methods for finding out the HCF.
(i)   Common division method
(ii) Long division method

Common division method

To find the HCF by common division method,
Find the smallest common prime factor of the given numbers. Divide all the numbers by it and write the quotients below the numbers. Continue dividing quotient by the smallest common prime factor till there is no common prime factor by which the quotients can be divided. HCF is the product of common prime factors.

For example : Let us find HCF of 12, 16 and 20

$$
\begin{array}{r|l}
2 & 12,\ 16,\ 20 \\ \hline
2 & 6,\ 8,\ 10 \\ \hline
 & 3,\ 4,\ 5
\end{array}
$$

HCF of 12, 16 and 20 = $2 \times 2 = 4$

Long division method

Divide the greater number, by the smaller number. Then divide the divisor by the remainder. Repeat this process till the remainder is 0.
The last divisor is the HCF of the numbers.
To find the HCF of three numbers, first we find the HCF of any two numbers and then find the HCF of the third number and the HCF obtained.

For example : Let us find HCF of 272 and 425 by division method.

$$
\begin{array}{r}
272\overline{)425}\,(1 \\
\underline{272} \\
153\overline{)272}\,(1 \\
\underline{153} \\
119\overline{)153}\,(1 \\
\underline{119} \\
34\overline{)119}\,(3 \\
\underline{102} \\
17\overline{)34}\,(2 \\
\underline{34} \\
0
\end{array}
$$

Hence, HCF of 272 and 425 is 17.

ILLUSTRATION : 5

Find the HCF of 1624, 522 and 1276

SOLUTION :

$$
\begin{array}{r}
522)\overline{1276}(2 \\
\underline{1044} \\
232)\overline{522}(2 \\
\underline{464} \\
58)\overline{232}(4 \\
\underline{232} \\
\overline{0}
\end{array}
\qquad
\begin{array}{r}
58)\overline{1624}(28 \\
\underline{116} \\
464 \\
\underline{464} \\
\overline{0}
\end{array}
$$

So, HCF of 1624, 522 and 1276 is 58.

To find the HCF of four numbers, find the HCF of two numbers, then find the HCF of remaining two numbers. Then find the HCF of already obtained two HCFs. This gives the answer.

PROBLEMS RELATED TO HCF

In this section, we will discuss some applications of H.C.F. in solving some problems.

ILLUSTRATION : 6

Find the largest number which divides 146, 254 and 272 leaving a remainder 2 in each case.

SOLUTION :

Subtract 2 from each number as the numbers thus obtained will be completely divisible by the required number i.e. their HCF.

$$146 - 2 = 144 = 2 \times 2 \times 2 \times 2 \times 3 \times 3$$
$$254 - 2 = 252 = 2 \times 2 \times 3 \times 3 \times 7$$
$$272 - 2 = 270 = 2 \times 3 \times 3 \times 3 \times 5$$

HCF of 144, 252 and 270 = $2 \times 3 \times 3 = 18$

Hence, the required number is 18.

ILLUSTRATION : 7

The length, breadth and height of a room are 1050 cm. 750 cm and 425 cm respectively. Find the length of the longest tape which can measure the three dimensions of the room exactly

SOLUTION :

The longest tape which can measure the given lengths = HCF of 1050 cm, 750 cm and 425 cm.

First we find the HCF of 1050 and 750.

$$
\begin{array}{r}
750)\overline{1050}(1 \\
\underline{750} \\
300)\overline{750}(2 \\
\underline{600} \\
150)\overline{300}(2 \\
\underline{300} \\
\overline{0}
\end{array}
\qquad
\begin{array}{r}
150)\overline{425}(2 \\
\underline{300} \\
125)\overline{150}(1 \\
\underline{125} \\
25)\overline{125}(5 \\
\underline{125} \\
\overline{0}
\end{array}
$$

Hence, the required length of tape is 25 cm.

COMMON MULTIPLES

Common multiples of two or more numbers are the numbers that are multiples of these numbers.

For example : The multiples of 12, 24, 36 are-

Number	Multiples
12	12, 24, 36, 48, 60, 72, 84, 96, 108, 120, 132, 144....
24	24, 48, 72, 96, 120, 144, ...
36	36, 72, 108, 144....

Common multiples of 12, 24 and 36 are 72, 144, ...

LOWEST COMMON MULTIPLE (LCM)

The **lowest common multiple** (LCM) of two numbers is the smallest number that is a multiple of each of the numbers.

For example :

Let us find the LCM of 6 and 12.
(1) Write at least 5-6 multiples of each number.
    Multiples of 6: 6, 12, 18, 24, 30, 36, 42, ...
    Multiples of 12: 12, 24, 36, 48, 60, 72, ...
(2) Identify the numbers that are common in both the numbers. Common multiples of 6 and 12 are:- 12, 24, 36, ...
(3) Take the smallest common multiple which is lowest common multiple.
    Thus, 12 is the smallest common multiple.

NOTE :
1. LCM of two numbers is the greater number of them, if one of the numbers is multiple of the other.
2. LCM of two co-prime numbers is equal to their product. For example: LCM of 3 and 5 is $3 \times 5 = 15$

There are two methods to find LCM :
(a) Prime factorisation method   (b) Division method

Prime factorisation method

In this method, to get the LCM, we find product of all the prime factors with their maximum power.

ILLUSTRATION : 8

Find the LCM of 24 and 36.

SOLUTION :

Prime factorisation of 24 and 36.
$24 = 2 \times 2 \times 2 \times 3$
$36 = 2 \times 2 \times 3 \times 3$
So, LCM of 24 and 36 $= (2 \times 2 \times 2) \times (3 \times 3) = 72$

2	24
2	12
2	6
3	3
	1

2	36
2	18
3	9
3	3
	1

ILLUSTRATION : 9

Find the LCM of 12, 30 and 81.

SOLUTION :

Prime factorisation of 12, 30 and 81.
$12 = 2 \times 2 \times 3$
$30 = 2 \times 3 \times 5$
$81 = 3 \times 3 \times 3 \times 3$
$\therefore$ LCM of 12, 30 and 81
$= (2 \times 2) \times (3 \times 3 \times 3 \times 3) \times 5$
$= 4 \times 81 \times 5 = 1620$

2	12
2	6
3	3
	1

2	30
3	15
5	5
	1

3	81
3	27
3	9
3	3
	1

Division method

In this method, all numbers are written together. They are divided by least prime number that divides one or more of the numbers. Carry forward the number which is not divisible. Repeat the process till they all get divided completely. The product of all prime factors is LCM.

ILLUSTRATION : 10

Find the LCM of 40, 48, 45 by division method.

SOLUTION :

2	40, 48, 45
2	20, 24, 45
2	10, 12, 45
2	5, 6, 45
3	5, 3, 45
3	5, 1, 15
5	5, 1, 5
	1, 1, 1

$\therefore$ LCM of 40, 48 and 45 = $2 \times 2 \times 2 \times 2 \times 3 \times 3 \times 5 = 720$

NOTE : The LCM of numbers is always greater than or equal to the largest number.

PROBLEMS RELATED TO LCM

ILLUSTRATION : 11

Find the smallest number which when divided by 15, 20 and 25 leaves a remainder 5 in each case.

SOLUTION :

The smallest number which when divided by 15, 20 and 25 is their LCM.

5	15, 20, 25
5	3, 4, 5
3	3, 4, 1
2	1, 4, 1
2	1, 2, 1
	1, 1, 1

LCM = $5 \times 5 \times 3 \times 2 \times 2$

$\quad = 300$

Hence, required number = 300 + 5 = 305

Verification: $305 \div 15 \Rightarrow Q = 20, R = 5$

$\qquad\qquad\quad 305 \div 20 \Rightarrow Q = 15, R = 5$

ILLUSTRATION : 12

Three boys step off together from the same place. If their steps measure 36 cm, 48 cm and 54 cm, at what distance from the starting point will they again step off together?

SOLUTION :

To know, at what distance from the starting point will they again step off together, we will calculate the LCM of 36, 48 and 54.

2	36, 48, 54
2	18, 24, 27
2	9, 12, 27
2	9, 6, 27
3	9, 3, 27
3	3, 1, 9
3	1, 1, 3
	1, 1, 1

LCM $= (2 \times 2 \times 2 \times 2) \times (3 \times 3 \times 3)$

$\qquad = 16 \times 27$

$\qquad = 432$ cm

So, they will again step off together at a distance of 432 cm from the starting point.

PROPERTIES OF HCF AND LCM

There are some properties of HCF and LCM of given numbers. These properties are as follows :

(1)   The HCF of given numbers is not greater than any of the numbers.

(2)   The LCM of given number is not less than any of the numbers.

(3)   HCF of two co-prime numbers is 1.

(4)   LCM of two or more prime numbers is their product.

(5)   If a number 'a' is a factor of 'b' then HCF of a and b is 'a' and their LCM is 'b'.

(6)   HCF of two numbers is always a factor of their LCM.

(7)   Product of HCF $\times$ LCM = Product of numbers

$$\text{Also, } \text{LCM} = \frac{\text{Product of the numbers}}{\text{HCF}}$$

$$\text{and } \text{HCF} = \frac{\text{Product of the numbers}}{\text{LCM}}$$

ILLUSTRATION : 13

The HCF of two numbers is 145 and their LCM is 2175. If one of the numbers is 725. Find the other.

SOLUTION :

HCF of two numbers is 145.

LCM of two numbers is 2175

One number = 725

$$\text{So, other number } = \frac{\text{HCF} \times \text{LCM}}{\text{Given number}} = \frac{145 \times 2175}{725} = 435$$

Hence, the other number is 435.

ILLUSTRATION : 14

The LCM of two numbers is 400 and their product is 6400. Find the HCF of the numbers.

SOLUTION :

We know that :

$$\text{HCF} = \frac{\text{Product of the numbers}}{\text{LCM}} = \frac{6400}{400} = 16$$

Hence, the HCF of the numbers is 16.

CONCEPT MAP

Factors and Multiples

- A factor of a number is an exact divisor of that number.
- Every number is a factor of itself.
- 1 is a factor of every number.
- Every factor of a number is less than or equal to the given number.
- A multiple of a number is exactly divisible by the number.
- Every number is a multiple of itself.
  Every multiple of a given number is greater than or equal to that number.

Prime and Composite Numbers

Natural numbers having exact two distinct factors i.e., 1 and the number itself are called prime numbers.

- Natural numbers having more than two factors are called composite numbers.
- Number 1 is neither prime nor composite.
- Every natural number except 1 is either prime or composite.
- There are infinite prime numbers and infinite composite numbers.

(1)   **Playing with Numbers**   **(2)**

(4)   **(3)**

HCF and LCM

- The highest common factor (HCF) of two or more numbers is the greatest number which divides each number exactly.
- The least common multiple (LCM) of two or more numbers is the smallest number which is exactly divisible by each number separately.
- The H.C.F. of two co-prime numbers is 1.
- The L.C.M. of two co-prime numbers is product of the numbers.
- The product of the H.C.F. and the L.C.M. of the two given numbers is equal to the product of those numbers. i.e.,

H.C.F. × L.C.M. =
Product of the given numbers

Tests for divisibility

- If a number is divisible by another number, then it is divisible by each factor of that number.
- If a number is divisible by two co-prime numbers then it is also divisible by their product.
- If two numbers are divisible by a number, then their sum as well as their difference is also divisible by that number.

MISCELLANEOUS
SOLVED EXAMPLES

1. Find the factors of the following:
   (i)   36   (ii)   27   (iii)   18

Sol. (i) $36 =$
$$
\begin{aligned}
&1 \times 36 \\
&2 \times 18 \\
&3 \times 12 \\
&4 \times 9 \\
&6 \times 6
\end{aligned}
$$
Therefore, 1,2,3,4, 6,9,12,18,36 are factors of 36.

   (ii) $27 =$
$$
\begin{aligned}
&1 \times 27 \\
&3 \times 9
\end{aligned}
$$
Therefore, 1,3,9,27 are factors of 27.

   (iii) $18 =$
$$
\begin{aligned}
&1 \times 18 \\
&2 \times 9 \\
&3 \times 6
\end{aligned}
$$
Therefore, 1,2,3,6,9,18 are factors of 18.

2. Find the first three multiples of
   (i)   5   (ii)   14   (iii)   27
   (iv) 89   (v)   101

Sol (i)   The first three multiples of 5: $5 \times 1 = 5$, $5 \times 2 = 10$ and $5 \times 3 = 15$

   (ii)   The first three multiples of 14: $14 \times 1 = 14$, $14 \times 2 = 28$ and $14 \times 3 = 42$

   (iii)   The first three multiples of 27: $27 \times 1 = 27$, $27 \times 2 = 54$ and $27 \times 3 = 81$

   (iv)   The first three nuliples of 89: $89 \times 1 = 89$, $89 \times 2 = 178$ and $89 \times 3 = 267$

   (v)   The first three multiples of 101: $101 \times 1 = 101$, $101 \times 2 = 202$ and $101 \times 3 = 303$

3. Find the prime factorisation of the following numbers:
   (i)   420   (ii)   2574

Sol. (i)   The prime factors of 420:

2	420
2	210
3	105
5	35
	7

$\therefore 420 = 2 \times 2 \times 3 \times 5 \times 7$

(ii) The prime factors of 2574:

2	2574
3	1287
3	429
11	143
	13

$\therefore 2574 = 2 \times 3 \times 3 \times 11 \times 13$

4. Test the divisibility of the following numbers by 11.
   (i)   863423   (ii)   76844

Sol. (i)   Sum of its digits in odd places
   $= (3 + 4 + 6) = 13$
   Sum of its digits in even places
   $= (2 + 3 + 8) = 13$.
   Difference of these sums $= (13 - 13) = 0$, which is divisible by 11.
   Therefore, 863423 is divisible by 11.

   (ii)   Sum of its digits in odd places
   $= (4 + 8 + 7) = 19$.
   Sum of its digits in even places $= (4 + 6) = 10$.
   Difference of these sums $= (19 - 10) = 9$, which is not divisible by 11.
   Therefore, 76844 is not divisible by 11.

5. Find the HCF of 50, 125 and 180.

Sol.
$$
\begin{array}{r}
50\,\overline{)\,125\,}\,2 \\
-100 \\
\hline
25\,\overline{)\,50\,}\,2 \\
-50 \\
\hline
0
\end{array}
$$

$$
\begin{array}{r}
25\,\overline{)\,180\,}\,7 \\
-175 \\
\hline
5\,\overline{)\,25\,}\,5 \\
-25 \\
\hline
0
\end{array}
$$

Hence, HCF of 50, 125 and 180 is 5.

6.   Find the LCM of 16, 28, 40 and 56.

Sol.

2	16,	28,	40,	56
2	8,	14,	20,	28
2	4,	7,	10,	14
7	2,	7,	5,	7
2	2,	1,	5,	1
5	1,	1,	5,	1
	1,	1,	1,	1

The required LCM $= 2 \times 2 \times 2 \times 7 \times 2 \times 5 = 560$.

7.   Find the greatest number which divides the numbers 81, 1411 and 2228 leaving the remainders 7, 5 and 8 respectively.

Sol. Given that 7, 5 and 8 are the remainders when the numbers 81, 1411 and 2228 are divided by the required number. Hence, $81 - 7 = 74$, $1411 - 5 = 1406$ and $2228 - 8 = 2220$ are exactly divisible by the required number. Now, the greatest number which divides the numbers 74, 1406 and 2220 exactly is their H.C.F.

We have,

$$74 \overline{)1406(} 19$$
$$\underline{74}$$
$$666$$
$$\underline{666}$$
$$0$$

∴   H.C.F. of 74 and 1406 is 74. We now find the H.C.F. of 74 and 2220.

$$74 \overline{)2220(} 30$$
$$\underline{222}$$
$$0$$

Hence, the H.C.F. of 74, 1406 and 2220 is 74. Thus, the required greatest number is 74.

8.   Three traffic lights at three different road crossings change after 48 seconds, 72 seconds and 100 seconds respectively. If they all change simultaneously at 8 a.m., at what time will they change again simultaneously?

Sol. Clearly, the time taken for a simultaneous change $= \{$L.C.M. of 48, 72, 100$\}$ seconds.

∴   L.C.M. of 48, 72, 100

$= 2 \times 2 \times 2 \times 2 \times 3 \times 3 \times 5 \times 5 = 3600$.

Time taken for a simultaneous change

$= 3600$ seconds

$$= \left(\frac{3600}{60 \times 60} \right) \text{hour} = 1 \text{ hour}.$$

2	48,	72,	100
2	24,	36,	50
2	12,	18,	25
2	6,	9,	25
3	3,	9,	25
3	1,	3,	25
5	1,	1,	25
5	1,	1,	5
	1,	1,	1

Hence, they will change again simultaneously at 9 a.m.

9.   Find the least number that must be added to 1000 so that the sum is exactly divisible by 16, 64 and 256.

Sol. The required least number, which is divisible by 16, 64 and 256, is also divisible by their LCM.

2	16,	64,	256
2	8,	32,	128
2	4,	16,	64
2	2,	8,	32
2	1,	4,	16
2	1,	2,	8
	1,	1,	4

LCM of 16, 64 and 256 $= 2 \times 2 \times 2 \times 2 \times 2 \times 2 \times 4 = 256$

Now, we divide 1000 by the LCM.

$$256 \overline{)1000(} 3$$
$$\underline{-768}$$
$$232$$

Thus, the least number to be added to 1000 $= 256 - 232 = 24$

10.   The length, breadth and height of a room are 6 m 25 cm, 8 m 75 cm and 5 m 50 cm, respectively. Determine the longest rod which can measure the three dimensions of the room exactly.

Sol. Length of the longest rod in centimetres is the HCF of 625, 875 and 550. We have,

5	625,	875,	550
5	125,	175,	110
	25,	35,	22

So, HCF of 625, 875 and 550 $= 5 \times 5 = 25$.

Hence, the required length of longest rod is 25 cm.

1 EXERCISE

Fill in the Blanks :

DIRECTIONS : *Complete the following statements with an appropriate word / term to be filled in the blank space(s).*

1. A number is a _______ of each of its factor.
2. _______ is a factor of every number.
3. The number of factors of a prime number is _______.
4. A number for which the sum of all its factors is equal to twice the number is called a _______ number.
5. The numbers having more than two factors are called _______ numbers.
6. 2 is the only _______ number which is even.
7. Two numbers having only 1 as a common factor are called _______ numbers.
8. A number is divisible by 5, if it has _______ or _______ in its ones place.
9. If the sum of the digits in a number is a _______ of 3, then the number is divisible by 3.
10. The LCM of two or more given numbers is the lowest of their common _______ .
11. The HCF of two or more given numbers is the highest of their common _______ .

True / False :

DIRECTIONS : *Read the following statements and write your answer as true or false.*

1. If a number exactly divides the sum of three numbers, it must exactly divide the numbers separately.
2. A number is divisible by 6, if the number formed by its last two digits (i.e., ones and tens) is divisible by 6.
3. A number with 4 or more digits is divisible by 8, if the number formed by the last three digits is divisible by 8.
4. The Highest Common Factor of two or more numbers is greater than, their Lowest Common Multiple.
5. LCM of two numbers is 28 and their HCF is 8.
6. Any two consecutive numbers are co-prime.
7. If the HCF of two numbers is one of the numbers, then their LCM is the other number.
8. The LCM of two coprime numbers is equal to the product of the numbers.
9. All numbers which are divisible by 8, must also be divisible by 4.
10. If two numbers are co-primes, at least one of them must be prime.
11. If a number is divisible by 3, it must be divisible by 9.

Match the Columns :

DIRECTIONS : *Each question contains statements given in two columns which have to be matched. Statements (A, B, C, D....) in column-I have to be matched with statements (p, q, r, s....) in column-II.*

1.

	Column-I	Column-II
(A)	The two consecutive prime numbers with difference 2 are called	(p) Perfect number
(B)	The set of natural numbers and 0 is called as	(q) Prime number
(C)	A number other than one which is either divisible by 1 or itself is called a	(r) Whole numbers
(D)	If the sum of all the factors of a number is twice the number, then the number is known as	(s) Twin primes

2.

	Column-I		Column-II
(A)	Smallest odd prime number	(p)	2
(B)	Twin prime with 17	(q)	1
(C)	Only even prime number	(r)	97
(D)	Neither prime nor composite	(s)	3
(E)	The only prime number between 90 and 100	(t)	19

Very Short Answer Questions:

DIRECTIONS : *Give answer in one word or one sentence.*

1. Which of the following are prime numbers?
   (i) 23 (ii) 51 (iii) 37 (iv) 26
2. Find four pairs of co-prime number.
3. Express each of the following numbers as the sum of twin primes:
   (i) 24 (ii) 84
4. Which of the following are composite numbers: 39, 47, 57, 69, 83, 93
5. Which of the following numbers are divisible by 3?
   (i) 57432 (ii) 693503
   (iii) 3002002 (iv) 777771
6. Which of the following numbers are divisible by 9?
   (i) 666657 (ii) 999083
   (iii) 756432 (iv) 876869
7. Write the multiples of 12 lying between 30 and 90.
8. Give three pairs of prime numbers whose difference is 2.
9. Check the divisibility of 1790184 by
   (i) 2 (ii) 3 (iii) 4 (iv) 6
   (v) 8 (vi) 9 (vii) 11
10. Test the divisibility of the following numbers by 8:
    (i) 9364 (ii) 2138
    (iii) 36792 (iv) 901674
    (v) 136976 (vi) 1790184
11. Test the divisibility of the following numbers by 6:
    (i) 2070 (ii) 46523
    (iii) 71232 (iv) 934706
    (v) 251780 (vi) 872536

Short Answer Questions :

DIRECTIONS : *Give answer in 2-3 sentences.*

1. Determine whether 19, 23 and 29 are factors of 2185 or not.
2. Find the common factors of
   (i) 20 and 28 (ii) 56 and 120
   (iii) 15, 25 and 45.
3. Find first three common multiples of
   (i) 6 and 9 (ii) 12 and 18
4. Find the H.C.F. of 616, 644 and 896 by continued division method.
5. Find the H.C.F. of 112, 168 and 420 by prime factorisation method.
6. Find the least number which when divided by 18, 20 and 30 leaves 5 as remainder in each case.
7. 34 divides 35972 exactly. Which two numbers nearest to 35972 are exactly divisible by 34?
8. Reduce $\dfrac{289}{391}$ to the lowest terms.
9. Draw factor tree for each of the following:
   (i) 192 (ii) 456 (iii) 102
10. The HCF and LCM of two numbers are 13 and 1989 respectively. If one of them is 117, find the other.

Long Answer Questions :

DIRECTIONS : *Give answer in four to five sentences.*

1. There are 153 apples and 119 oranges. These fruits are to be arranged in heaps containing the same number of fruits. Find the greatest number of fruits possible in each heap. Also, find the number of heaps formed.
2. Find the least natural number which when divided by 112, 140 and 168 leaves remainder 8 in each case.
3. Find the greatest number that will divide 1025, 1299 and 1575 leaving remainders 5, 7 and 11 respectively.

2 EXERCISE

Text-Book Exercise :

1. What is the sum of any two
   (i) odd numbers?   (ii) even numbers?

2. The numbers 13 and 31 are prime numbers. Both these numbers have same digits 1 and 3. Find such pairs of prime numbers up to 100.

3. Express the following as the sum of two odd primes.
   (i) 44   (ii) 36
   (iii) 24   (iv) 18

4. Write a digit in the blank space of each of the following numbers so that the number formed is divisible by 11:
   (i) 92 ___ 389   (ii) 8 ___ 9484

5. A number is divisible by both 5 and 12. By which other number will that number be always divisible?

6. A number is divisible by 12. By what other numbers will that number be divisible?

7. Renu purchased two bags of fertilisers of weights 75 kg and 69 kg. Find the maximum value of weight which can measure the weight of the fertiliser exact number of times.

8. Three boys step off from the same spot. Their steps measure 63 cm, 70 cm and 77 cm respectively. What is the minimum distance each should cover so that all can cover the distance in complete steps?

9. The traffic lights at three different road crossings change after every 48 seconds, 72 seconds and 108 seconds respectively. If they change simultaneously at 7 a.m, at what time will they change again simultaneously?

10. Three containers contain 403 litres, 434 litres and 465 litres of diesel respectively. Find the maximum capacity of a container that can measure the diesel of three containers exact number of times.

Exemplar Questions :

1. Floor of a room measures 4.5 metres × 3 metres. Find the minimum number of complete square marble slabs of equal size required to cover the entire floor.

2. A merchant has 120 litres of oil of one kind, 180 litres of another kind and 240 litres of a third kind. He wants to sell the oil by filling the three kinds of oil in tins of equal capacity. What should be the greatest capacity of such a tin?

3. Test the divisiblity of following numbers by 11
   (i) 5335   (ii) 9020814

4. Using divisiblity tests, determine which of the following numbers are divisible by 4?
   (i) 4096   (ii) 21084   (iii) 31795012

5. Using divisiblity test. determine which of the following numbers are divisible by 9?
   (i) 672   (ii) 5652

6. Fatima wants to mail three parcels to three village schools. She finds that the postal charges are ₹ 20, ₹ 28 and ₹ 36, respectively. If she wants to buy stamps only of one denomination, what is the greatest denomination of stamps she must buy to mail the three parcels?

7. Three brands A, B and C of biscuits are available in packets of 12, 15 and 21 biscuits respectively. If a shopkeeper wants to buy an equal number of biscuits, of each brand, what is the minimum number of packets of each brand, he should buy?

8. The floor of a room is 8m 96cm long and 6m 72cm broad. Find the minimum number of square tiles of the same size needed to cover the entire floor.

9. In a school library, there are 780 books of English and 364 books of Science. Ms. Yakang, the librarian of the school wants to store these books in shelves such that each shelf should have the same number of books of each subject. What should be the minimum number of books in each shelf?

1. The H.C.F of three numbers is 24. If they are in the ratio 35 : 55 : 77, then find the numbers ?

2. Three sets of English, Hindi and Mathematics books have to be stacked in such a way that all the books are stored topic-wise and the height of each stack is the same. The number of English books is 96, the number of Hindi books is 240 and the number of Mathematics books is 336. Assuming that the books are of the same thickness, determine the number of stacks of English, Hindi and Mathematics books.

3. The circumferences of four wheels are 50 cm, 60 cm, 75 cm and 100 cm. They start moving simultaneously. What least distance should they cover so that each wheel makes a complete number of revolutions?

4. A boy saves ₹ 4.65 daily. Find the least number of days in which he will be able to save an exact number of rupees.

5. Express the following as sum of three odd prime numbers.
   (i) 21   (ii) 31
   (iii) 35   (iv) 61

3 EXERCISE

DIRECTIONS : *This section contains multiple choice questions. Each question has 4 choices (a), (b), (c) and (d) out of which ONLY ONE is correct.*

1. The number which is neither prime nor composite is
   (a) 0   (b) 1
   (c) 2   (d) 5

2. The sum of the prime numbers between 90 and 100 is
   (a) 188   (b) 281
   (c) 376   (d) 97

3. A _______ of a number is an exact divisor of that number.
   (a) multiple   (b) factor
   (c) dividend   (d) None of these

4. In which of the following is the prime factorisation not complete?
   (a) $70 = 2 \times 5 \times 7$
   (b) $28 = 2 \times 2 \times 7$
   (c) $48 = 2 \times 2 \times 2 \times 2 \times 3$
   (d) $108 = 2 \times 2 \times 27$

5. The smallest number which when divided by 4, 6, 10, 15 gives the same remainder 3 is
   (a) 57   (b) 123
   (c) 63   (d) 39

6. The smallest number which when divided by 20, 25, 35 and 40 and leaves a remainder of 14, 19, 29 and 34 respectively is
   (a) 1394   (b) 1404
   (c) 1664   (d) 1406

7. Set of three prime numbers is called a prime triplets, which of the following is a prime triplet?
   (a) (2, 4, 5)   (b) (7, 9, 13)
   (c) (5, 7, 11)   (d) (2, 3, 8)

8. The product of two odd numbers is
   (a) an even number
   (b) an odd number
   (c) cannot be determined
   (d) none of these

9. LCM of two co-prime numbers is their
   (a) sum   (b) difference
   (c) product   (d) quotient

10. Find a number which is a multiple of all the numbers from 1 to 10?
    (a) 5040   (b) 1260
    (c) 720   (d) 1440

More Than One Option Correct :

DIRECTIONS : *This section contains multiple choice questions. Each question has 4 choices (a), (b), (c) and (d) out of which ONE or MORE may be correct.*

1. Which of the following statement is/are false?
   (a) 1 is the smallest prime number
   (b) Every prime number is an odd number
   (c) The sum of two prime numbers is always a prime number
   (d) None of these

2. A number is always divisible by 90 if
   (a) it is divisible by both 2 and 45
   (b) it is divisible by both 5 and 18
   (c) it is divisible by both 9 and 10
   (d) it is divisible by both 6 and 15

3. Which of the following statements is/are true?
   (a) The HCF of two distinct prime numbers is 1.
   (b) The HCF of two co prime numbers is 1.
   (c) The HCF of two consecutive even numbers is 2.
   (d) The HCF of an even and an odd number is even.

4. Choose the co-prime numbers from the following pairs.
   (a) 7 and 63   (b) 36 and 25
   (c) 35 and 18   (d) 63 and 81

5. Which of the following numbers is/are prime?
   (a) 161   (b) 137
   (c) 127   (d) 353

6. Which of the following number is a multiple of 19?
   (a) 114   (b) 95
   (c) 171   (d) 369

Assertion & Reason :

DIRECTIONS : *Each of these questions contains an Assertion followed by Reason. Read them carefully and answer the question on the basis of following options. You have to select the one that best describes the two statements.*

(a) If both **Assertion** and **Reason** are correct and reason is the correct explanation of assertion.

(b) If both **Assertion** and **Reason** are correct but reason is not the correct explanation of assertion.

(c) If **Assertion** is correct but **Reason** is incorrect.

(d) If **Assertion** is incorrect but **Reason** is correct.

1. **Assertion :** If 25 and 95 is divisible by 5, then, their sum $25 + 95 = 120$, is divisible by 5.
   Reason : If a number is a factor of two given numbers, then it is the factor of their sum.

2. **Assertion :** 17 and 19 are two prime numbers. LCM of 17 and 19 is 323.
   Reason : The LCM of two prime numbers is always their product.

3. **Assertion :** 9 is smallest even composite number.
   Reason : Composite number need not be even.

Passage Based Questions :

DIRECTIONS : *Study the given passage(s) and answer the following questions.*

PASSAGE-I

At an International Airport, planes take off from four different runways at 4, 8, 12 and 15 minutes interval. At 9 a.m., planes took off from all the four runways simultaneously but Reema has missed her flight due to traffic jam.

1. When will four planes take off together again?
   (a) 11 : 00 a.m.   (b) 10 : 00 a.m.
   (c) 12 : 00 noon   (d) 11 : 30 a.m.

2. If Reema reaches airport at 9:30 a.m. then how much time she has to wait for the next flight?
   (a) 1 hour   (b) 1 hour 30 minutes
   (c) 30 minutes   (d) 2 hour

PASSAGE-II

If a is a factor of both b and c, then a is a factor of $(b - c)$ and $(b + c)$.

3. If 64 and 48 are divisible by 4 then what is the difference of the given numbers so that it is divisible by 4?
   (a) 12   (b) 18
   (c) 20   (d) 16

4. If the value of $a = 6$, $b = 2$ then what is the value of c so that a is a factor of $b + c$?
   (a) 3   (b) 5
   (c) 10   (d) 7

5. What is the product of sum and difference of the two numbers 625 and 500 so that it becomes a multiple of 25?
(a) 1125   (b) 140625
(c) 125   (d) 31250

Integer Type Questions :

DIRECTIONS : *Answer the following questions. The answer to each of the question is a single digit integer, ranging from 0 to 9.*

1. What least value should be given to* so that the number 653*47 is divisible by 11 ?
2. What is the GCD of 12, 18, 21?
3. If the nth multiple of 5 is 25. Find the value of n.
4. What is the common prime factor of 6 and 21?
5. Find the greatest number which will divide the greatest 4-digit number and the greatest 5-digit number exactly.

Multiple Matching Question :

DIRECTIONS: *Following question has six statements (A, B, C, D, E and F) given in Column-I and six statements (p, q, r, s, t, u) in Column-II. Any given statement in Column-I can have correct matching with one or more statement(s) given in Column-II.*

1.
(A) 42	(p) A perfect number
(B) 15	(q) Fifth multiple of 5
(C) 8	(r) Factor of every number
(D) 6	(s) A multiple of 7
(E) 1	(t) A multiple of 3
(F) 25	(u) Factor of 24

SOLUTIONS

Brief Explanations of Selected Questions

1 EXERCISE

Fill in the Blanks :

1. multiple
2. 1
3. 2
4. perfect
5. composite
6. prime
7. co-prime
8. 0, 5
9. multiple
10. multiple
11. factors

True / False :

1. F
2. F
3. T
4. F
5. F
6. T
7. T
8. T
9. T
10. F
11. F

Match the Columns :

1. (A) → (s); (B) → (r); (C) → (q); (D) → (p)
2. (A) → (s); (B) → (t); (C) → (p); (D) → (q); (E) → (r)

Very Short Answer Questions:

1. (i) $23 = 1 \times 23$
   Hence, 23 is a prime number.
   (ii) $51 = 1 \times 51$ or 3×17
   Hence, 51 is not a prime number.
   (iii) $37 = 1 \times 37$
   Hence, 37 is a prime number.
   (iv) $26 = 1 \times 26$ or 2×13
   Hence, 26 is not a prime number.
2. (3, 5), (4, 9), (7, 10) and (31, 65)
3. (i) $11 + 13$ (ii) $41 + 43$
4. Composite numbers: 39, 57, 69, 93.
5. (i), (iv)
6. (i), (iii)
7. 36, 48, 60, 72, 84
8. (3, 5); (5, 7) ; (11, 13)
9. (i) 1790184 : Digit at ones places is 4. So, it is divisible by 2.
   (ii) 1790184 : $1 + 7 + 9 + 0 + 1 + 8 + 4 = 30$, 30 is a multiple of 3. So, it is divisible by 3.
   (iii) 1790184 : 84 is divisible by 4. So, 1790184 is divisible by 4.
   (iv) 1790184 is divisible by 2 and 3. So, it is divisible by 6 also.
   (v) 1790184 : 184 is divisible by 8. So, 1790184 is divisible by 8.
   (vi) 1790184 : $1 + 7 + 9 + 0 + 1 + 8 + 4 = 30$. 30 is not a multiple of 9. Hence, 1790184 is not divisible by 9.
   (vii) 1790184 : $1 + 9 + 1 + 4 = 15$
   $7 + 0 + 8 = 15$
   $15 - 15 = 0$
   So, 1790184 is divisible by 11.
10. (iii) 36792, (v) 136976, (vi) 1790184 are divisible by 8.
11. (i) 2070, (iii) 71232 are divisible by 6.

Short Answer Questions :

1. We divide 2185 by 19. Then, quotient = 115, remainder = 0
   Hence, 19 is a factor of 2185.
   Now, we divide 2185 by 23. Then, quotient = 95, remainder = 0
   Hence, 23 is a factor of 2185.
   We divide 2185 by 29.
   Then quotient = 75, Remainder = 10. Hence, 29 is not a factor of 2185.
2. (i) Factors of 20 are 1, 2, 4, 5, 10, 20
   Factors of 28 are 1, 2, 4, 7, 14, 28
   Cammon factors of 20 and 28 are 1, 2 and 4.
   (ii) Factors of 56 are 1, 2, 4, 7, 8, 14, 28, 56
   Factors of 120 are 1, 2, 3, 4, 5, 6, 8, 10, 12, 15, 20, 24, 30, 40, 60, 120
   Common factors of 56 and 120 are 1,2,4,8.
   (iii) Factors of 15 are 1, 3, 5, 15
   Factors of 25 are 1, 5, 25
   Factors of 45 are 1, 3, 5, 9, 15, 45
   Common factors of 15, 25 and 45 are 1 and 5.
3. (i) Multiples of 6 are 6, 12, 18, 24, 30, 36, 42, 48, 54, 60, 66, 72,....
   Multiples of 9 are 9, 18, 27, 36, 45, 54, 63, 72, 90,....
   Common multiples are 18, 36, 54, 72,....
   First three common multiples are 18, 36 and 54.

(ii) Multiples of 12 are 12, 24, 36, 48, 60, 72, 84, 96, 108, 120, 132, 144,....
Multiples of 18 are 18, 36, 54, 72, 90, 108, 126, 144,....
First three common multiples are 36, 72, 108, 144,....

4. We first find the H.C.F. of 616 and 644 as follows:

$\therefore$ The required H.C.F. of the given three numbers is 28.

5. By prime factorisation, we get:

2	112
2	56
2	28
2	14
7	7
	1

2	168
2	84
2	42
3	21
7	7
	1

2	420
2	210
3	105
5	35
7	7
	1

$\therefore$ $112 = 2 \times 2 \times 2 \times 2 \times 7;$
$168 = 2 \times 2 \times 2 \times 3 \times 7;$
$420 = 2 \times 2 \times 3 \times 5 \times 7.$
$\therefore$ H.C.F. of given numbers = $(2 \times 2 \times 7) = 28.$

6. Required number = {L.C.M. (18, 20, 30)} + 5.

2	18, 20, 30
3	9, 10, 15
5	3, 10, 5
	3, 2, 1

$\therefore$ L.C.M. = $(2 \times 3 \times 5 \times 3 \times 2) = 180.$

Hence, the required number = $(180 + 5) = 185.$

7. Since, 34 divides 35972

Then, $35972 - 34$, i.e. 35938 and $35972 + 34$, i.e. 36006 are two numbers which are exactly divisible by 34.

8. We find the HCF of 289 and 391 as under:

Hence, the HCF of 289 and 391 is 17.

$$\frac{289}{391} = \frac{289 \div 17}{391 \div 17} = \frac{17}{23}.$$

9. (i)

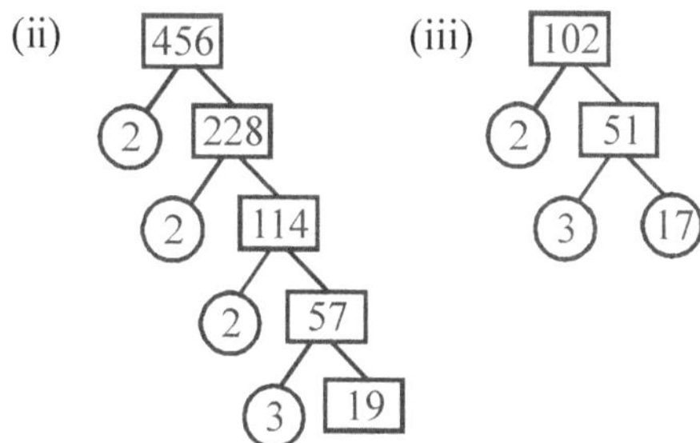

(ii) 456 ... (iii) 102 ...

10. Required number = $\dfrac{\text{HCF} \times \text{LCM}}{\text{One number}}$

$$= \frac{13 \times 1989}{117} = 221$$

Long Answer Questions :

1. The required number is the H.C.F. of 153 and 119.

   By long division method, we have

$$
\begin{array}{r}
119\overline{)153}\,(1 \\
\underline{119} \\
34\overline{)119}\,(3 \\
\underline{102} \\
17\overline{)34}\,(2 \\
\underline{34} \\
\times
\end{array}
$$

   H.C.F. of 153 and 119 is 17.

   Hence, the greatest number of fruits in each heap is 17.

$$
\text{Number of heaps} = \left(\dfrac{153}{17} + \dfrac{119}{17}\right)
$$

$$
= (9 + 7) = 16.
$$

2. To find the LCM of 112, 140 and 168, we have

2	112	140	168
2	56	70	84
2	28	35	42
7	14	35	21
	2	5	3

$$
\therefore \quad \text{LCM} = 2 \times 2 \times 2 \times 7 \times 2 \times 5 \times 3 = 1680.
$$

   Since, 1680 is the smallest natural number which when divided by the given numbers, will leave a remainder 0 in each case.

   Therefore, the required number must be 8 more than their LCM.

   Hence, the required least number = $1680 + 8 = 1688$.

3. The required number will divide the following numbers exactly.

$$
1025 - 5 = 1020
$$
$$
1299 - 7 = 1292
$$
$$
1575 - 11 = 1564
$$

   The required number is the HCF of 1020, 1292 and 1564.

$$
\begin{array}{r}
1020\overline{)1292}\,(1 \\
\underline{-\,1020} \\
272\overline{)1020}\,(3 \\
\underline{-\,816} \\
204\overline{)272}\,(1 \\
\underline{-\,204} \\
68\overline{)204}\,(3 \\
\underline{-\,204} \\
0
\end{array}
$$

$$
\begin{array}{r}
68\,\overline{)1564}\,(23 \\
\underline{-\,136} \\
204 \\
\underline{-\,204} \\
0
\end{array}
$$

Thus, the required number is 68.

$\boxed{2}$ E X E R C I S E

Text-Book Exercise :

1. (i) The sum of any two odd numbers is even.
   (ii) The sum of any two even numbers is even.

2. The required pair of prime numbers are:
   (17 and 71); (37 and 73) and (79 and 97).

3. (i) 44
   $44 = 13 + 31$ or $44 = 3 + 41$
   or $44 = 7 + 37$
   (ii) 36
   $36 = 5 + 31$ or $36 = 23 + 13$
   or $36 = 17 + 19$
   (iii) 24
   $24 = 11 + 13$ or $24 = 5 + 19$
   or $24 = 7 + 17$
   (iv) 18
   $18 = 7 + 11$ or $18 = 5 + 13$

4. (i) 92 ___ 389
   We have:
   Sum of the digits at odd places
   $= 9 + 3 + 2 = 14$
   Sum of digits at even places
   $= 8 + [\text{Missing digit}] + 9$
   $= [\text{Missing digit}] + 17$
   Difference of these sums
   $= [\text{Missing digit}] + 17 - 14$
   $= [\text{Missing digit}] + 3$

∴ For the given number to be divisible by 11
[Missing digit] + 3 = 11
Missing digit = 11 – 3 = 8
Thus, the number is 928389.

(ii) 8 ___ 9484
Sum of the digits at odd places
= 4 + 4 + [Missing digit]
= [Missing digit] + 8
Sum of the digits at even places =
8 + 9 + 8 = 25
Difference of these sums = 25 – [(Missing digit) + 8]
= 25 – Missing digit – 8
= 17 – Missing digit
For the given number to be divisible by 11, 17 – Missing digit = 11
i.e., Missing digit = 17 – 11 = 6
∴ The given number is 869484.

5. The given number will be divisible by the product of 5 and 12.
The number will be divisible by 5 × 12 or 60.

6. The number divisible by 12 will also be divisible by the factors of 12.
Factors of 12 are 1, 2, 3, 4, 6 and 12.
∴ The number will be divisible by 1, 2, 3, 4 and 6.

7. To find the H.C.F. of the two given weights of fertiliser bags.

3	69		3	75
23	23		5	25
	1			5

69 = 3 × 23
75 = 3 × 5 × 5
H.C.F. = 3.
Hence, 3 kg is the required weight which can measure 69 kg and 75 kg exact number of times.

8. We need to calculate L.C.M. of 63 cm, 70 cm and 77 cm.
We will use division method to find L.C.M.

7	63, 70, 77
	9, 10, 11

L.C.M. (63, 70, 77) = 7 × 9 × 10 × 11 = 6930 cm.
∴ 6930 cm is the required minimum distance.

9. We will calculate L.C.M. of 48, 72 and 108 seconds.

2	48, 72, 108
2	24, 36, 54
2	12, 18, 27
3	6, 9, 27
3	2, 3, 9
	2, 1, 3

L.C.M. of (48, 72, 108)
= 2 × 2 × 2 × 2 × 3 × 3 × 3 = 432 sec.
Traffic lights will change simultaneously after 432 sec. or 7 min. 12 sec.
∴ The traffic light will change at 7 : 07 : 12 a.m.

10. We find H.C.F. using long division method

$$403 \overline{)434} (1$$
$$\underline{403}$$
$$31\overline{)403} (13$$
$$\underline{31}$$
$$93$$
$$\underline{93}$$
$$×$$

$$31\overline{)465} (15$$
$$\underline{31}$$
$$155$$
$$\underline{155}$$
$$×$$

H.C.F. of (403, 434, 465) = 31.
Hence, the maximum capacity of a container is 31 litres.

Exemplar Questions :

1. To find the minimum number of square slabs to cover the floor, we have to find the greatest size of each such slab. For this purpose, we have to find the HCF of 450 and 300.
(Since 4.5 m = 450 cm and 3m = 300 cm)
Now, HCF of 450 and 300 = 150
So, the required size of the slab must be 150cm × 150cm.
Hence, the number of slabs required

$$= \frac{\text{Area of the floor}}{\text{Area of one slab}} = \frac{450 \times 300}{150 \times 150} = 6$$

2. Let us first find the H.C.F. of 120, 180, and 240

$$120 \overline{)180} (1$$
$$\underline{120}$$
$$60 \overline{)120} (2$$
$$\underline{120}$$
$$×$$

$$60 \overline{)240} (4$$
$$\underline{240}$$
$$×$$

∴ H.C.F. is 60.
Hence, greatest capacity of tin is 60 *l*.

3. (i)   Sum of digits at odd places = $5 + 3 = 8$

Sum of digits at even places = $3 + 5 = 8$

Their difference = $8 - 8 = 0$, which is divisible by 11.

$\therefore$ 5335 is divisible by 11.

(ii)   Sum of digits at odd places = $4 + 8 + 2 + 9$ $= 23$

Sum of digits at even places = $1 + 0 + 0 = 1$

Their difference = $23 - 1 = 22$, which is divisible by 11.

$\therefore$ 9020814 is divisible by 11.

4. (i)   Number formed by last two digits of 4096 is 96, which is divisible by 4.

$\therefore$ 4096 is divisible by 4.

(ii)   Number formed by last two digits of 21084 is 84, which is divisible by 4.

$\therefore$ 21084 is divisible by 4.

(iii)   Number formed by last two digits of 31795012 is 12, which is divisible by 4.

$\therefore$ 31795012 is divisible by 4.

5. (i)   Sum of digits = $6 + 7 + 2 = 15$, which is not divisible by 9.

$\therefore$ 672 is not divisible by 9.

(ii)   Sum of digits = $5 + 6 + 5 + 2 = 18$, which is divisible by 9.

$\therefore$ 5652 is divisible by 9.

6. To find H.C.F. of 20, 28 and 36

```
   20) 28 (1            4) 36 (9
       20                  36
      ——————               ——
     8) 20 (2              ×
        16
      ————————
       4) 8 (2
          8
         ———
          ×
```

Hence, H.C.F. of 20, 28 and 36 is 4.

$\therefore$ The greatest denomination of stamps must be ₹ 4.

7. A shopkeeper has three brands A, B and C of biscuits are available in packets of 12, 15 and 21 biscuits respectively.

Also, a shopkeeper wants to buy equal number of biscuits of each brand for that we need to find the LCM of 12, 15 and 21.

```
2 | 12, 15, 21
2 |  6, 15, 21
3 |  3, 15, 21
5 |  1,  5,  7
7 |  1,  1,  7
  |  1,  1,  1
```

$\therefore$ The LCM of 12, 15 and 21

$= 2 \times 2 \times 3 \times 5 \times 7 = 420$

Thus, the required number of packets of

brand A $= \dfrac{420}{12} = 35$, brand B $= \dfrac{420}{15} = 28$ and

brand C $= \dfrac{420}{21} = 20$

8. Length = 8 m 96 cm = 896 cm

Breadth = 6m 72 cm = 672 cm

Side of square tile = H.C.F. of 896 and 672

```
   672) 896 (1
       672
      —————————
     224) 672 (3
          672
         ———
          ×
         ———
```

= 224 cm.

$\therefore$ The number of square tiles

$$= \dfrac{896 \times 672}{224 \times 224} = 12$$

9. Number of English books = 780

Number of Science books = 364

Number of books in each shelf = H.C.F. of 364 and 780

```
   364) 780 (2
       728
      —————————
        52 ) 364 (7
             364
            ———
             ×
            ———
```

Hence, the number of books in each shelf should be 52.

HOTS Questions :

1. Let the numbers be $35x$, $55x$ and $77x$

$35x = 5 \times 7 \times x$, $55x = 5 \times 11 \times x$,

$77x = 7 \times 11 \times x$

$\therefore$ H.C.F = 24 = x
$\therefore$ Numbers are $35 \times 24, 55 \times 24, 77 \times 24$
    i.e. 840, 1320, 1848

2. In order to arrange the books as required, we have to find the largest number that divides 96,240 and 336 exactly. We find the H.C.F. of 96, 240 and 336 as under.

2	96,	240,	336
2	48,	120,	168
2	24,	60,	84
2	12,	30,	42
3	6,	15,	21
	2,	5,	7

Thus, H.C.F. of 96, 240 and 336
$= 2 \times 2 \times 2 \times 2 \times 3 = 48$.
Hence, there must be 48 books in each stack.
Now,
No. of stacks of English books

$= \dfrac{\text{No. of English Books}}{\text{No. of books in each stack}} = \dfrac{96}{48} = 2$

No. of stacks of Hindi books

$= \dfrac{\text{No. of Hindi Books}}{\text{No. of books in each stack}} = \dfrac{240}{48} = 5$

And,
No. of stacks of Mathematics books

$= \dfrac{\text{No. of Mathematics Books}}{\text{No. of books in each stack}} = \dfrac{336}{48} = 7$

3. Required least distance = L.C.M. of 50, 60, 75 and 100

5	50,	60,	75,	100
5	10,	12,	15,	20
2	2,	12,	3,	4
2	1,	6,	3,	2
3	1,	3,	3,	1
	1,	1,	1,	1

$\therefore$ LCM of 50, 60, 75 and 100
    $= 5 \times 5 \times 2 \times 2 \times 3 = 300$
Thus, all the wheels will make complete revolutions after covering 300 cm i.e. 3m distance.

4. The number of rupees will always be a multiple of 100 paise,

According to the question ₹ 4.65 = 465 paise. Hence, saved money will be a multiple of 465 paise.

$\therefore$ LCM of 100 and 465 is as follows:

5	100	465
	20	93

$\therefore$ LCM = $5 \times 20 \times 93 = 9300$
$\therefore$ The boy have to save 9300 paise.

$\therefore$ The required no. of days $= \dfrac{9300}{465} = 20$ days.

5. (i) $21 = 3 + 5 + 13$
   (ii) $31 = 3 + 5 + 23$
   (iii) $35 = 5 + 7 + 23$
   (iv) $61 = 7 + 13 + 41$

3 EXERCISE

1. **(b)**

2. **(d)**   The prime numbers between 90 and 100 is only 97.

3. **(b)**   factor

4. **(d)**   Complete prime factorisation is
    $108 = 2 \times 2 \times 3 \times 3 \times 3$

5. **(c)**

2	4,	6,	10,	15
5	2,	3,	5,	15
3	2,	3,	1,	3
	2,	1,	1,	1

$\therefore$ LCM of 4, 6, 10, 15 $= 2 \times 5 \times 3 \times 2 = 60$
$\therefore$ Required number = $60 + 3 = 63$.

6. **(a)**

5	20,	25,	35,	40
2	4,	5,	7,	8
2	2,	5,	7,	4
	1,	5,	7,	2

$\therefore$ L.C.M. $= 5 \times 2 \times 2 \times 5 \times 7 \times 2 = 1400$
Now, $20 - 14 = 25 - 19 = 35 - 29$
    $= 40 - 34 = 6$
$\therefore$ required number = LCM $- 6$
    $= 1400 - 6 = 1394$.

7. **(c)**   (5, 7, 11) is a prime triplet

8. **(b)** $\because 3 \times 3 = 9; 5 \times 7 = 35$

9. **(c)**

10. **(a)** Required number
$$= 7 \times 8 \times 9 \times 10 = 5040$$

More Than One Option Correct :

1. **(a, b, c)**

2. **(a, b, c)** $\therefore$ If a number is divisible by 'a' and 'b', where 'a' & 'b' are co-primes, then that number is divisible by 'ab'.

3. **(a, b, c)**

4. **(b, c)** (36 and 25) and (35 and 18)

5. **(b, c, d)** 161 is not a prime number as it is divisible by 7 and rest of the options are prime numbers.

6. **(a, b, c)** 369 is not a multiple of 19.

Assertion & Reason :

1. **(a)** As 25 and 95 is divisible by 5.
Then their sum, $25 + 95 = 120$ is divisible by 5, as number ends with 0.
Assertion: True; Reason: True and Reason is the correct explanation of Assertion.

2. **(a)** As $17 \times 19 = 323$
Assertion: True; Reason: True and Reason is the correct explanation of Assertion.

3. **(d)** As 9 is an odd number and it is the smallest odd composite number.
Assertion: False; Reason: True.

Passage Based Questions :

1. **(a)** L.C.M. of 4, 8, 12 and 15

2	4, 8, 12, 15
2	2, 4, 6, 15
2	1, 2, 3, 15
3	1, 1, 3, 15
5	1, 1, 1, 5
	1, 1, 1, 1

L.C.M. $= 2 \times 2 \times 2 \times 3 \times 5 = 120$
Thus, four planes take off together again after 120 minute i.e. after 2 hour. i.e. 11 a.m.

2. **(b)** 11 : 00 a.m. $-$ 9 : 30 a.m. = 1 hour 30 min

3. **(d)** If 64 and 48 is divisible by 4, then $64 - 48 = 16$, which is divisible by 4.

4. **(c)** If $a = 6$, $b = 2$, then c should have the minimum value so that sum will be multiple of 6.
$\therefore$ $c = 10$
and $b + c = 10 + 2 = 12$ and 6 is a factor of 12.

5. **(b)** Given, 25 is factor of 625 and 500.
$\therefore$ $625 + 500 = 1125$ is also a multiple of 25 and $625 - 500 = 125$ is a multiple of 25.
$\therefore$ Their product $= 1125 \times 125 = 140625$ and 25 is a factor of 140625.

Integer Type Questions :

1. **(1)** If we put 1 in place of * then that number will be divisible by 11.

2. **(3)** Factors of $12 = 3 \times 2 \times 2$
Factors of $18 = 2 \times 3 \times 3$
Factors of $21 = 3 \times 7$
Common factor $= 3$
$\therefore$ GCD of 12, 18, 21 is 3

3. **(5)** As $25 = 5 \times n$
$$\Rightarrow \quad n = \frac{25}{5} = 5$$

4. **(3)** Prime factors of $6 = 2 \times 3$
Prime factors of $21 = 3 \times 7$
Common prime factor of 6 and $21 = 3$

5. **(9)**

Multiple Matching Question :

1. (A) $\rightarrow$ (s, t); (B) $\rightarrow$ (t); (C) $\rightarrow$ (u);
(D) $\rightarrow$ (p, t, u); (E) $\rightarrow$ (r, u); (F) $\rightarrow$ (q)

POINT

A **point** determines a location. A point has no dimensions i.e. no length, breadth or height. It also does not have size.

For example:

(i)   The sharpened end of a pencil.

(ii)   Tip of a needle.

A point is named by a capital letter of English alphabet such as P, Q, R etc.

LINE

A **line** is a straight path that extends indefinitely in both directions. It has no end points.

For example : The line is named as $\overleftrightarrow{AB}$ and read as line AB.

A line passing through two points P and Q is denoted by $\overleftrightarrow{PQ}$ or $\overleftrightarrow{QP}$. We may also represent a line by small letter l, m, n etc.

LINE SEGMENT

A **line segment** is a portion of a line with two fixed end points. It has a definite length.

This is a line segment named as $\overline{AB}$ and read as line segment AB.

RAY

A **ray** is a part of a line that extends indefinitely in one direction from a given point.

Here, $\overrightarrow{AB}$ is a ray.

Distinction between line segment, line and ray

S. No.	Line segment	Line	Ray
(i)	It has a definite length.	It does not have a definite length.	It does not have a definite length.
(ii)	It has two end points.	It has no end points.	It has one end point.
(iii)	It can be drawn on paper.	It can not be drawn on paper. We can simply represent it by a diagram.	It can not be drawn on paper. We can simply represent it by a diagram.
(iv)	$\overline{AB}$ is a line segment.	$\overleftrightarrow{AB}$ is a line.	$\overrightarrow{AB}$ is a ray.
(v)	$\overline{AB}$ and $\overline{BA}$ represent the same line segment.	$\overleftrightarrow{AB}$ and $\overleftrightarrow{BA}$ represent the same line.	$\overrightarrow{AB}$ and $\overrightarrow{BA}$ represent two different rays.

INTERSECTING LINES

If two lines meet each other at a point P, then they are called **intersecting lines** and point P is called the **point of intersection**. Here, AB and CD are intersecting lines and O is the point of intersection.

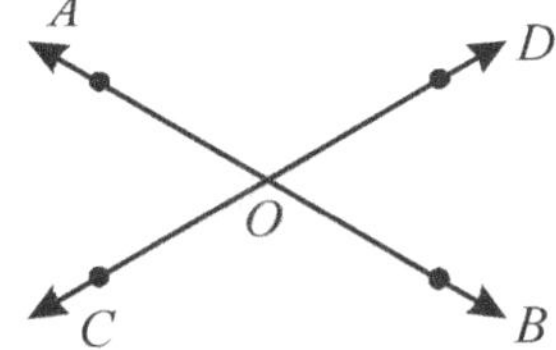

For example : crossing roads, the multiplication sign (×), two adjacent edges of notebook, etc. are the examples of the intersecting lines.

PARALLEL LINES

If two lines do not intersect each other, even if extended in both directions and they have no point in common, then they are called **parallel lines. For example**, rail lines, the opposite edges of a ruler etc.

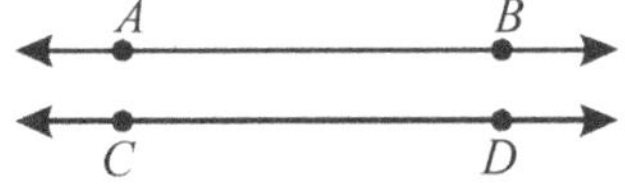

Here, AB is parallel to CD.

CONCURRENT LINES

If three or more lines pass through a point, then they are called **concurrent lines** and the point through which these lines pass is called **point of concurrence**. Here, lines l, m, n and p pass through a point O. Thus, l, m, n and p are concurrent lines and point O is the point of concurrence.

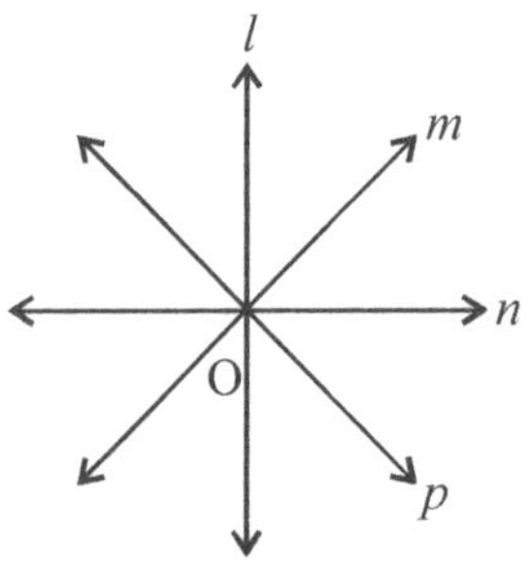

ILLUSTRATION : 1

From the given figure, write
(i)   Lines intersecting at A
(ii) Lines intersecting at B.
(iii) Concurrent lines and their point of concurrence.

SOLUTION :

(i)   Lines l, q and r intersect at A.
(ii) Lines m, p and r intersect at B.
(iii) Lines l, q and r are concurrent at A and lines m, p and r are concurrent at B.

COLLINEAR AND NON-COLLINEAR POINTS

If three or more points in a plane lie on the same line, then they are said to be **collinear**.

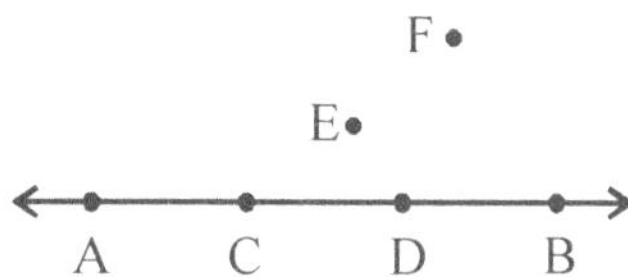

In above figure, the points A, B, C, D, E and F are collinear.

If three or more points do not lie on the same line, then they are said to be **non-collinear**.

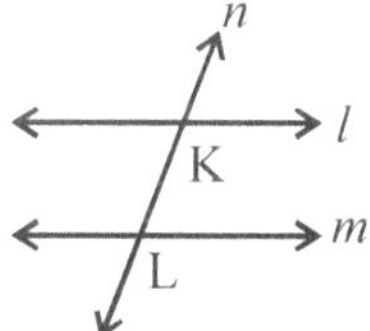

In above figure, points A, B, C, D, E and F are non-collinear.

ILLUSTRATION : 2

From the figure given below, name the :
(i)   pairs of parallel lines
(ii) points of intersection

SOLUTION :

(i)   Pairs of parallel lines are *l* and m.   (ii)   Points of intersection are K and L.

CURVES

A curve is a figure drawn without lifting the pencil. Thus, the pictures that are the results of doodling are called **curves**.

Generally, the word 'curve' means not straight. In mathematics a curve can be straight.

A curve which does not cross itself is called a **simple curve**. Figures (i), (ii) and (iii) are simple curves.

(i)

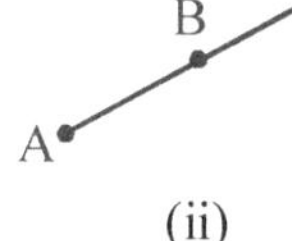

(ii)

(iii)

(iv)

Types of curves

There are two types of curves : (i) Open Curve and (ii) Closed curve

Open Curve

The curves that do not begin and end at the same point are called **open curves**.

Closed Curve

The curves which begin and end at the same point are called **closed curves**.

POLYGONS

A closed figure made up entirely of line segments is known as **polygon**. A polygon means having many sides: (poly means many, gons means sides). Given below are some examples of polygons.

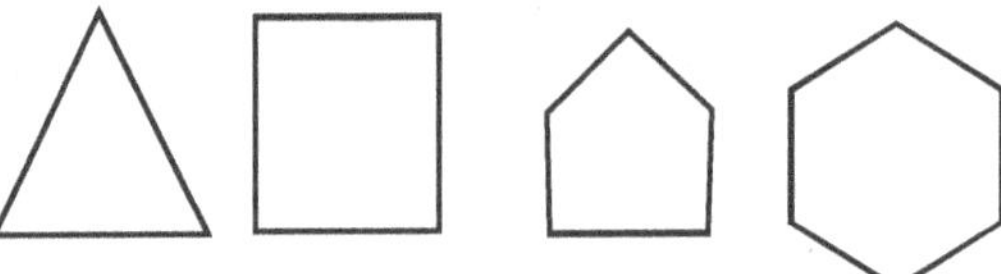

Sides

The line segments which form a polygon are called its **sides.**

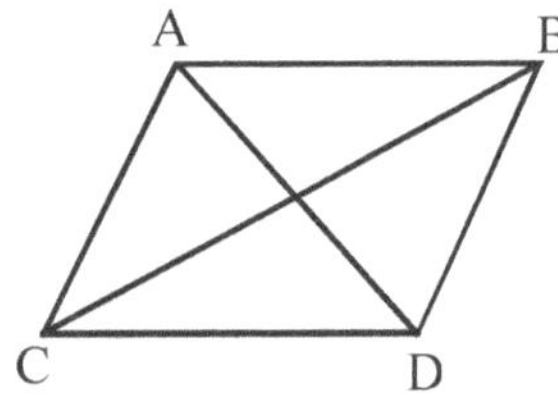

$\overline{AB}$, $\overline{BD}$, $\overline{DC}$ and $\overline{CA}$ are the sides of the polygon ABCD.

Vertices

The meeting point of a pair of sides is known as **vertex**. In polygon ABCD, A, B, C, D are **vertices**.
Two sides which have common vertex are known as **adjacent sides.**
In polygon ABDC, AB and BD, BD and DC, DC and CA, CA and AB are adjacent sides.

NOTE : A polygon is named by its vertices written in order.

Adjacent Vertices

The end points of a side of a polygon are known as **adjacent vertices.**
In polygon ABDC, A and B, B and D, D and C and C and A are the adjacent vertices.

Diagonals

The line segment formed by joining non-adjacent vertices is called the **diagonal** of the polygon.
Line segment AD and BC are the diagonals of the polygon ABDC.

ANGLES

An **angle** is formed when two rays start from a common point.
The two rays forming an angle is known as sides or **arms** of the angle and the common point of the rays is called the **vertex** of the angle.

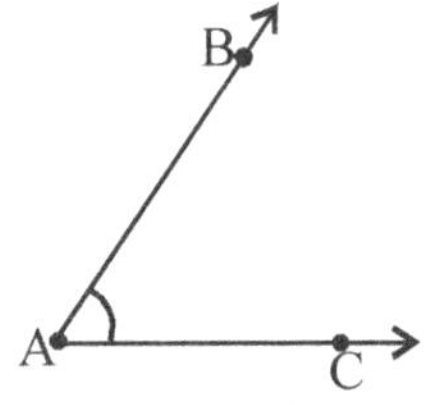

In the given figure, $\overrightarrow{AB}$ and $\overrightarrow{AC}$ are two arms and A is the vertex.

Naming an Angle

We use symbol '$\angle$' to denote an angle. We name an angle in three different ways.

(i)   The name of an angle can be written using the letter at the vertex of the angle. **For example**, the angle given in the adjoining figure can be named as $\angle Q$.

(ii) We can name an angle using three capital letters. The vertex is written in the middle. **For example**, the given angle can be named as $\angle PQR$.

(iii) We can also name an angle by placing any number (1, 2, 3 ... etc.) or a small letter (a, b, c ... etc.) at the vertex in the interior of the angle. So, the angle given can be named as $\angle a$.

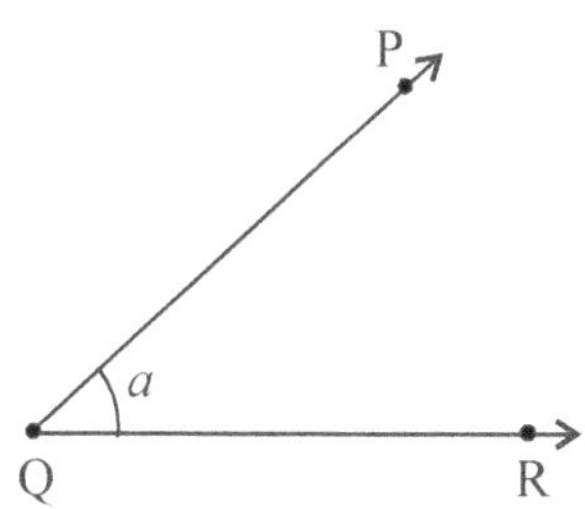

Interior, exterior and boundary of an angle

An angle such as $\angle BAC$ as shown below consists of 3 parts :

(i)   The part consisting of all those points which lie between the arms of the angle is called the **interior of the angle.**

(ii) The part consisting of all those points which lie outside the arms of the angle is called the **exterior of the angle**.

(iii) The part consisting of all those points which lie on the arms of the angle is called the **boundary of the angle**.

In the given figure, points D, E and F lie in the interior while points K, L M and N lie in the exterior of $\angle BAC$. Points A, C, G and B lie on the boundary of $\angle BAC$.

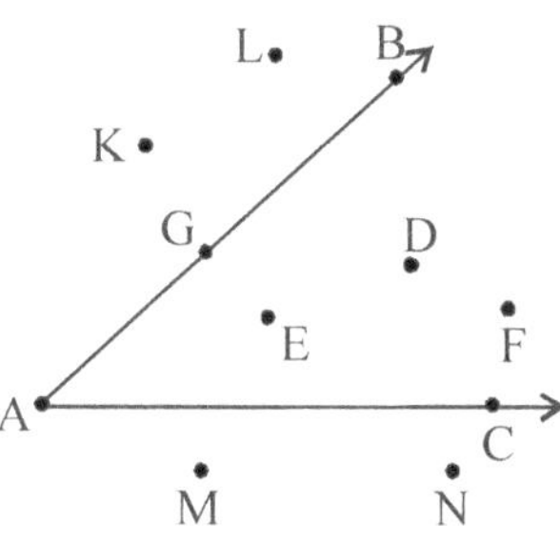

TRIANGLES

A polygon with three sides is known as triangle. It is denoted by the symbol 'Δ'. A triangle has three sides, three vertices and three angles.

Here, $\overline{AB}, \overline{BC}$ and $\overline{CA}$ are the three sides ΔABC. A, B and C are the three vertices. $\angle A$, $\angle B$ and $\angle C$ are the three angles.

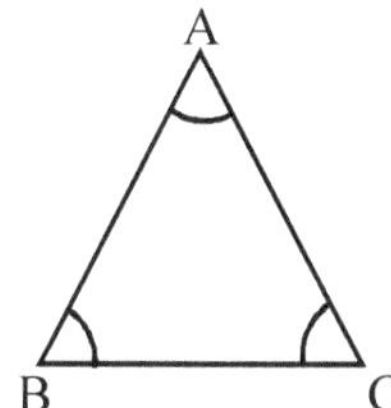

Interior, exterior and boundary of a Triangle

When we draw a ΔPQR, then it divides a plane into three parts :

(i)   The part of the plane enclosed by the triangle is called the **interior** of the triangle. In the given figure, points L, M and N are in the interior of ΔPQR.

(ii) The part of the plane not enclosed by the triangle is called the **exterior** of the triangle. In the given figure, points A, T and S are in the exterior of ΔPQR.

(iii) The part of the plane made by the points that lie on the triangle is called the boundary of the triangle. In the given figure, points P, C, Q, R and B are on the boundary of ΔPQR.

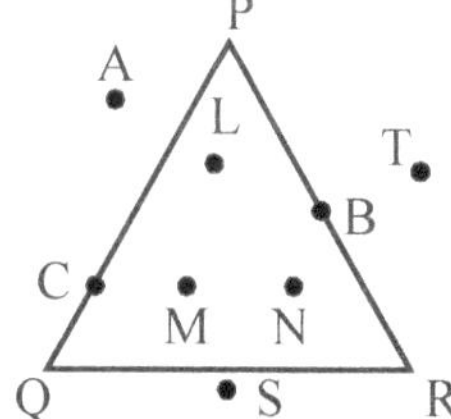

NOTE: A triangle is a polygon with least number of sides.

QUADRILATERALS

A polygon with four sides is known as **quadrilateral**. A quadrilateral has four vertices, four sides and two diagonals.

In a quadrilateral ABCD, A, B,C and D are vertices. AB, BC, CD and DA are sides of the quadrilateral. $\angle ABC$, $\angle BCD$, $\angle ADC$ and $\angle BAD$ are angles of the quadrilateral. AC and BD are diagonals.

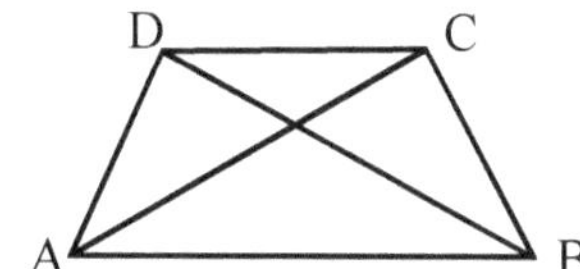

Adjacent sides

Two sides of a quadrilateral having a common vertex are called its **adjacent sides**.

Thus AB, BC; BC, CD; CD, DA and DA, AB are four pairs of adjacent sides of the quadrilateral ABCD.

Opposite sides

Two sides of a quadrilateral are called its **opposite sides**, if they do not have a common end point. AB and CD, AD and BC are two pairs of opposite sides of quadrilateral ABCD.

Adjacent angles

Two angles of a quadrilateral having a common side are called its **adjacent angles**.
Thus $\angle A$, $\angle B$; $\angle B$, $\angle C$; $\angle C$, $\angle D$ and $\angle D$, $\angle A$ are four pairs of adjacent angles of a quadrilateral ABCD.

Opposite angles

Two angles of a quadrilateral which are not adjacent angles are known as **opposite angles**.
Thus $\angle A$, $\angle C$ and $\angle B$, $\angle D$ are two pairs of opposite angles of the quadrilateral ABCD.

Regular Polygon

A polygon is called regular if all its sides and angles are equal e.g. square, equilateral triangle, etc.

CIRCLE

A circle is a simple closed curve, all the points of which are at the same distance from a given fixed point. They remain constant.
For example : shapes of wheels, coins etc.

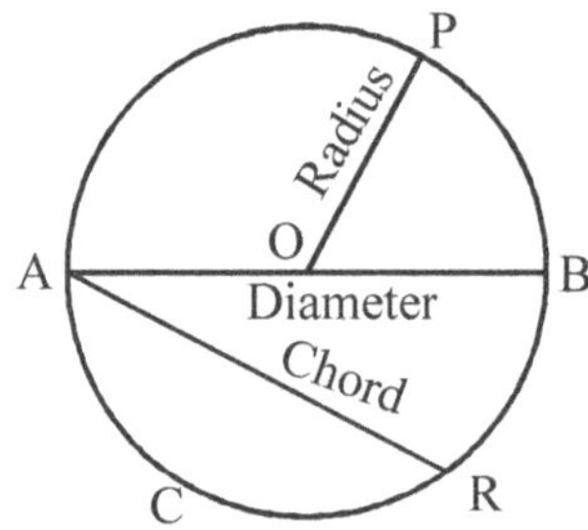

Parts of a Circle

Centre
The fixed point in the plane which is equidistant from every point on the boundary of the circle is called **centre**. In the adjoining figure, O is the centre of the circle.

Radius

The fixed distance between the centre and any point on the circle is called **radius**. In the figure, $\overline{OP}$ is a radius.

Chord

A line segment joining any two points on the circle is called a **chord** of the circle. In the figure, $\overline{AR}$ is a chord.

Diameter

A chord that passes through the centre of a circle is called **diameter** of the circle. In the figure, $\overline{AB}$ is a diameter. The length of a diameter = $2 \times$ radius. In a circle, diameter is the longest chord.

Circumference
The distance around a circle is called the **circumference**. Circumference of a circle is the perimeter of that circle.

Arc

A part of a circumference is called an **arc**. In the above figure, the curve line AR is an arc of the circle. It is written as $\overset{\frown}{AR}$. A chord of a circle divides it into two parts. The smaller part the minor arc and the greater part is the major arc of the circle. Here, $\overset{\frown}{ACR}$ is the minor arc and $\overset{\frown}{APR}$ is the major arc.

Segment

The region of circle enclosed by an arc and its correponding chord is called a **segment**.
The segment formed by a minor arc and its corresponding chord is called a **minor segment**.
The segment formed by a major arc and its corresponding chord is called a **major segment**.

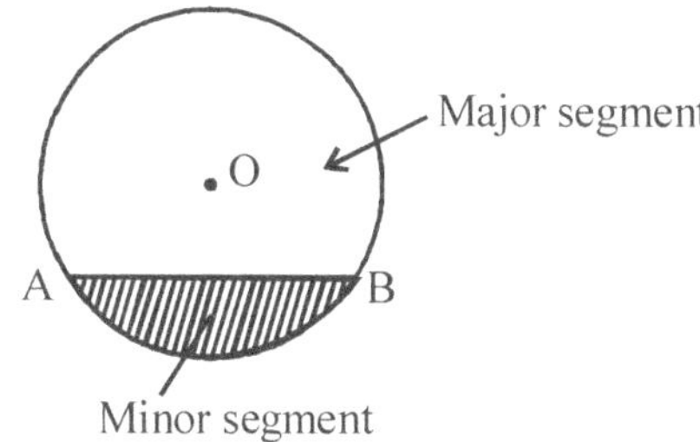

Sector

The region of circle enclosed by an arc and two radii of a circle is called **sector**. In the adjoining figure, shaded area covered by AOB is sector of the circle.

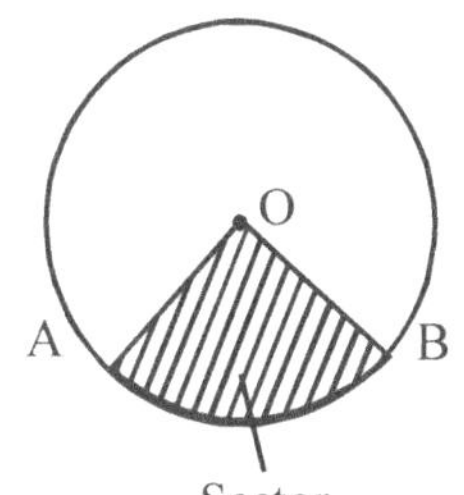

Concentric circles

Two or more circles with the same centre and different radii are called concentric circles.

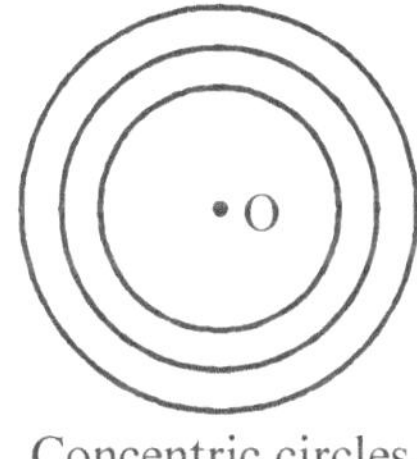

Concentric circles

CONCEPT MAP

Points line, ray and line segment

- A point determines a location. It does not have length, breadth and thickness. It is denoted by capital letter.
- A line segment is the shortest distance between two points.
- A line is obtained by extending line segment in both directions indefinitely.
- A ray is a portion of line starting at a point and extending in one direction endlessly.

Polygon

- A drawing (straight or non-straight) drawn without lifting the pencil is called a curve.
- A simple curve does not cross itself.
- If the ends of a curve are joined, then it is called a closed curve.
- If the ends of a curve are not joined, then it is called an open curve.
- A closed curve made up of line segments is called a polygon. These line segments are the sides of the polygon.

Basic Geometrical Ideas

(1) **(2)** **(3)** **(4)**

Angles, triangles and quadrilaterals

- Two rays with a common initial point form an angle.
- A three-sided polygon is called a triangle.
- A four sided polygon is called a quadrilateral.

Circle and its Parts

- A circle is a simple closed curve such that all its points are at the same distance from a fixed point.
- The fixed point is the centre and the fixed distance is the radius.
- The distance around the circle is the circum ferences.
- A line segment joining the two points on a circle is called chord of a circle.
- A chord passing through the centre of a circle is called diameter of the circle.
- The region in the interior of a circle enclosed by an arc and a pair of radii is called sector.
- The region in the interior of a circle enclosed by an arc and a chord is called segment.

MISCELLANEOUS

SOLVED EXAMPLES

1. **In the given figure, state the total number of distinct lines and name them. Also, answer the following questions:**
   (i) **What is the total number of points of intersection of all pairs of lines? Name them.**
   (ii) **Name any four points which are collinear.**
   (iii) **Name any three points which are non-collinear.**
   (iv) **Name any three lines which are non-concurrent.**
   (v) **Do you find any three lines which are concurrent?**

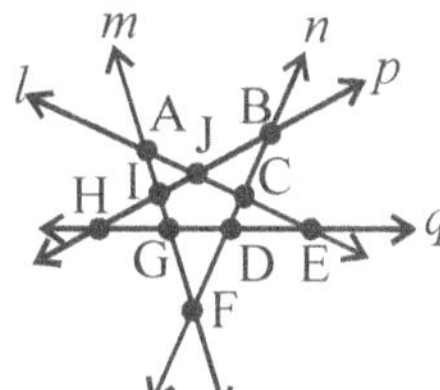

Sol. There are five distinct lines. l, m, n, p and q are the lines in the figure.
   (i) There are 10 points of intersection of all pairs of lines, which are A, B, C, D, E, F, G, H, I and J.
   (ii) A, I, G, F [other possible points are H, G, D, E; F, D, C, B, etc.]
   (iii) A, I, H [other possible points are A, J, B; B, C, E; G, D, F, etc.]
   (iv) l, m, n [other possible lines are l, m, p; m, n, p etc.]
   (v) No

2. **In the following figure, write :**
   (i) **all pairs of parallel lines**
   (ii) **lines whose point of intersection is I**
   (iii) **lines whose point of intersection is D**
   (iv) **lines whose point of intersection is E**

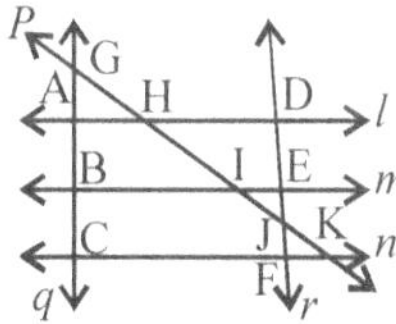

   (v) **lines whose point of intersection is A**

Sol. (i) In the given figure, all pairs of parallel lines are l, m; m, n; l, n, i.e., $l \parallel m$; $m \parallel n$; $l \parallel n$
   (ii) m, p (iii) l, r (iv) m, r (v) l, q

3. **In the given figure, name :**
   (i) **Sides**
   (ii) **Vertices**
   (iii) **Pairs of adjacent sides**
   (iv) **Diagonals**
   (v) **The polygon**

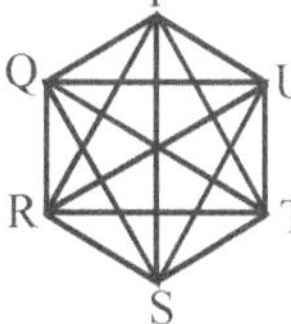

Sol. (i) PQ, QR, RS, ST, TU, UP
   (ii) P, Q, R, S, T, U
   (iii) PQ and QR, QR and RS, RS and ST, ST and TU, TU and UP, UP and PQ
   (iv) PR, PS, PT QU, QT, QS, RT, SU, UR
   (v) Hexagon

4. **From the figure, list the points which are:**
   (i) **in the interior of ∠MPT**
   (ii) **in the exterior of ∠MPT, and**
   (iii) **lie on ∠MPT.**

Sol. (i) The points in the interior of ∠MPT are G and S
   (ii) The points in the exterior of ∠MPT are R and N
   (iii) The points lie on ∠MPT are M, T and P

5. **In the given figure, name the points that lie**
   (i) **on the boundary of △PQR.**
   (ii) **in the interior of △PQR.**
   (iii) **in the exterior of △PQR.**

Sol. (i) P, A, M, Q, L, R, T, N
   (ii) F, S, U   (iii) G, H, O

6. **In the adjacent figure, name:**
   (i) **its diagonals,**
   (ii) **two pairs of opposite sides,**
   (iii) **two pairs of opposite angles,**
   (iv) **two pairs of adjacent sides,**
   (v) **two pairs of adjacent angles.**

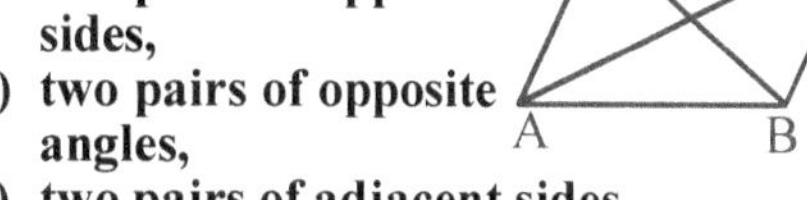

Sol. (i) AC, BD
   (ii) (AB, DC) and (AD, BC)
   (iii) (∠A, ∠C)(∠B, ∠D)
   (iv) (AB, BC), (AD, DC) (v) (∠A, ∠B)(∠B, ∠C)

7. **See the adjoining figure and name the following :**
   (i) **Centre of the circle**
   (ii) **Radii of circle**
   (iii) **Diameter of circle**
   (iv) **A chord** (v) **A sector**

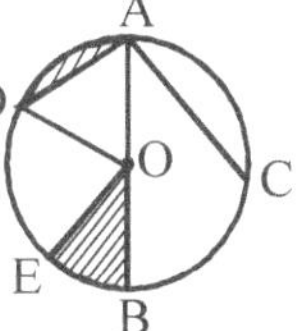

Sol. (i) O
   (ii) OA, OB, OE, OD
   (iii) AB
   (iv) AD
   (v) EOB

1 EXERCISE

Fill in the Blanks :

DIRECTIONS : *Complete the following statements with an appropriate word / term to be filled in the blank space(s).*

1. A line segment has a _______ length, which can be measured.
2. A line segment extended endlessly in one direction is called a _______ .
3. An _______ number of lines can be drawn passing through a given point.
4. A figure which begins and ends at the same point is called _______ figure.
5. A _______ is a simple closed figure formed by more than two line segments.
6. Two rays forming an angle are known as _______ .
7. The point where two adjacent edges meet is known as _______ .
8. The distance around a circle is called as _______ .
9. Diameter of a circle is the _______ chord.
10. A quadrilateral is _______ sided polygon.

True / False :

DIRECTIONS : *Read the following statements and write your answer as true or false.*

1. The ray $\overrightarrow{AB}$ is same as the ray $\overrightarrow{BA}$
2. Two points A and B in a plane determine a unique line segment
3. An unlimited numbers of line can be drawn to pass through a given point.
4. The region inside the curve is known as exterior of the curve.
5. The meeting point of two sides of polygon is known as adjacent sides.
6. Any angle have three arms.
7. The diameter of a circle is always greater than its radius.
8. The region enclosed by a chord and an arc is called a segment.
9. Every chord of a circle is also its diameter.
10. All the diameters of a circle are equal.

Match the Columns :

DIRECTIONS : *Each question contains statements given in two columns which have to be matched. Statements (A, B, C, D, E) in column-I have to be matched with statements (p, q, r, s. t) in column-II.*

1. Match the following :

Column-I	Column-II
(A) A stretched thread	(p) Rays
(B) Opposite edge of table	(q) Point
(C) Scissors	(r) Parallel lines
(D) Tip of compass needle	(s) Intersecting lines
(E) Beam of light	(t) Line segment

Very Short Answer Questions:

DIRECTIONS : *Give answer in one word or one sentence.*

1. Name all the line segments in each of the following figures.

(i) 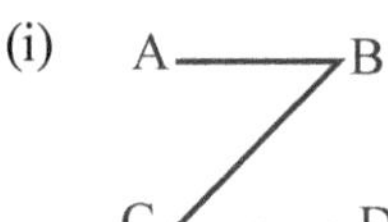

(ii) 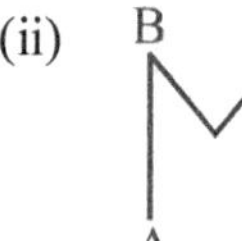

(iii) 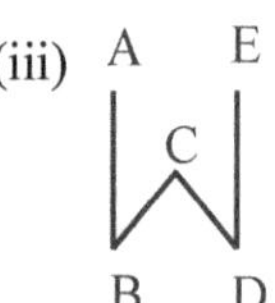

(iv) 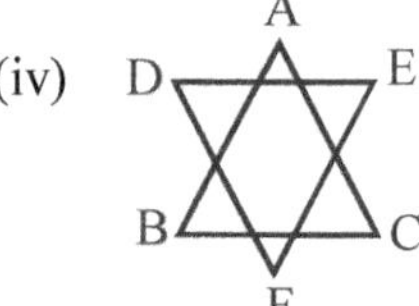

2. From the given figure, name.

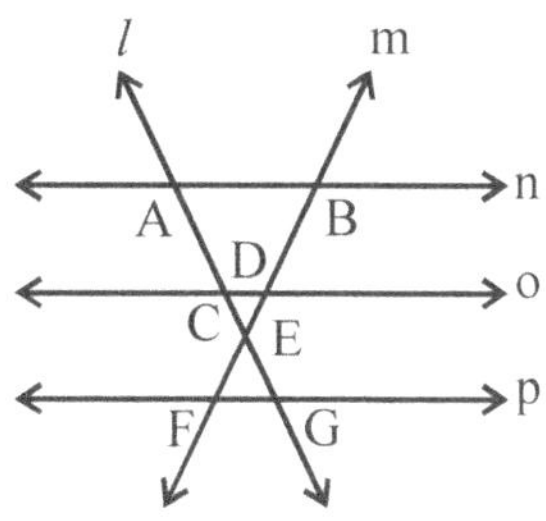

(i) All pairs of parallel lines.

(ii) All pairs of intersecting lines.

(iii) Lines whose point of intersection is D.

(iv) Point of intersection of lines l and m.

(v) Point of intersection of lines m and p.

(vi) Any two sets of collinear points.

3. Which of the following are simple closed curves?

　(i)　　　(ii)　　　(iii)　　　(iv)

4. Identify the polygons:

　(i)　　(ii)　　(iii)　　(iv)　　(v)

5. In the following figure, one of the line segment (either AD or BF) is not a diagonal. Which one? Give reason?

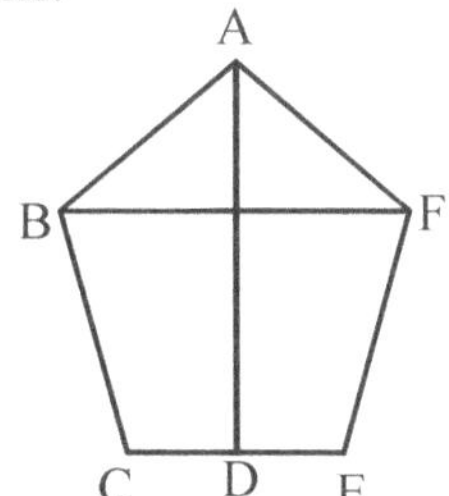

6. Name all the angles in the following figures :

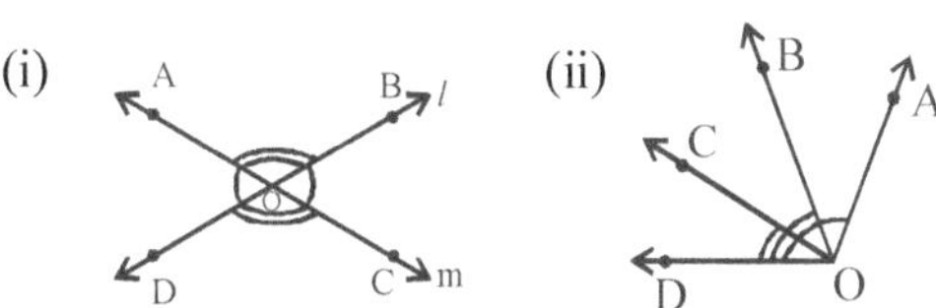

(i)　　　　　　　　(ii)

7. In the following figure, name the points that lie
(i) In the interior of ∠XYZ
(ii) In the exterior of ∠XYZ
(iii) On ∠XYZ

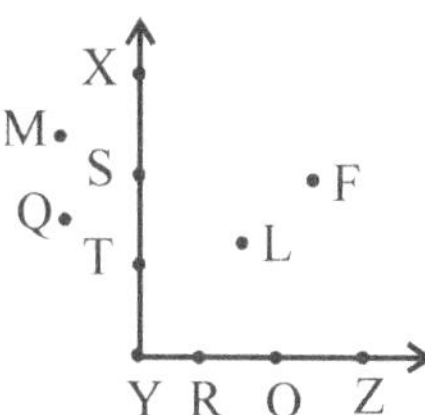

DIRECTIONS : *Give answer in 2-3 sentences.*

1. From the given figure, write the concurrent lines and their point of concurrence.

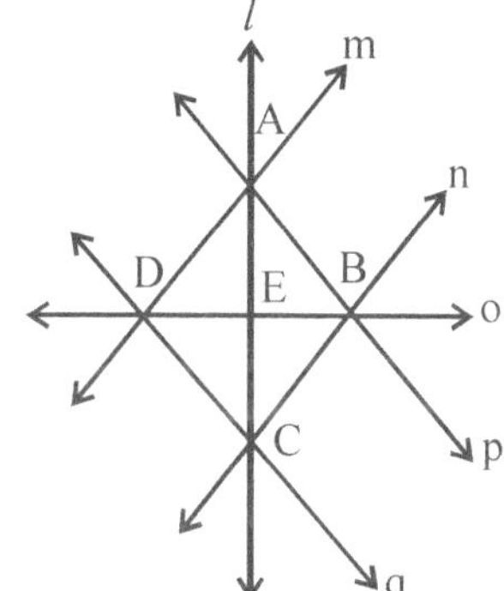

2. Name the vertex and the arms of the following angles. Also, name the angles.

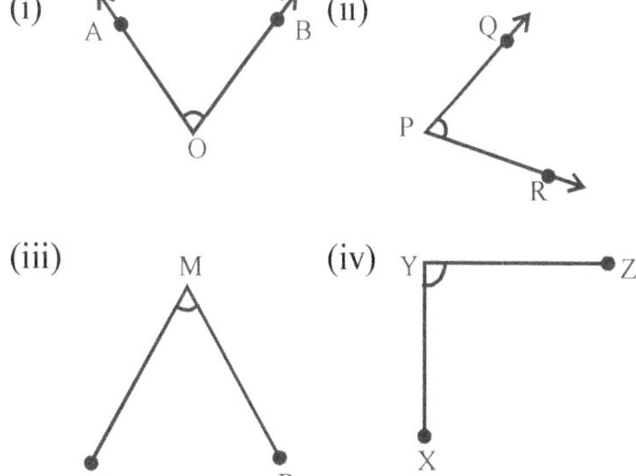

(i)　　　　　　(ii)

(iii)　　　　　(iv)

3. In the given circle, name the following:
   (i) Three radii
   (ii) Three chords
   (iii) A diameter
   (iv) A triangle that has the centre of the circle as vertex.

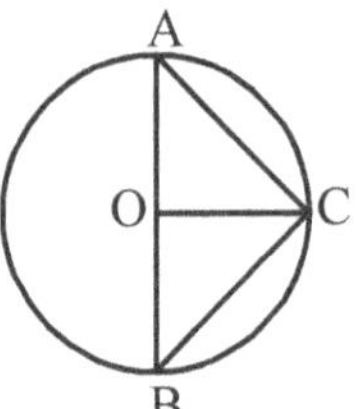

4. In the adjoining figure, name :
   (i) the pairs of adjacent sides
   (ii) the pairs of opposite sides
   (iii) the pairs of adjacent angles
   (iv) the pairs of opposite angles

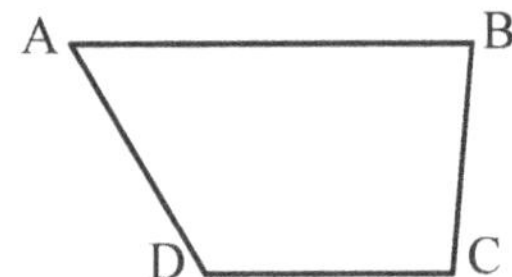

5. In the given figure, name :
   (i) all the angles
   (ii) all the triangles
   (iii) all the line segments

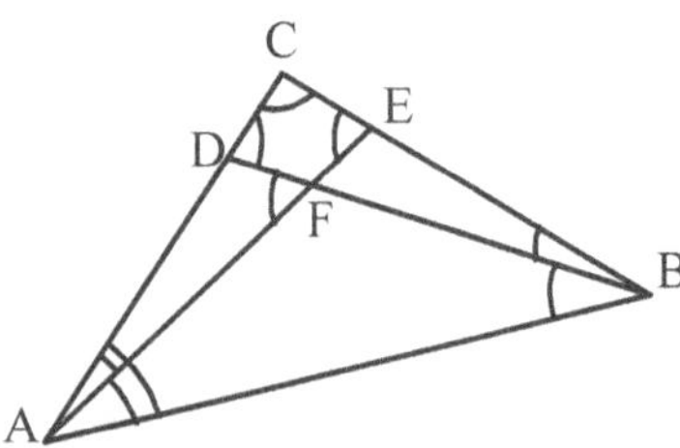

6. In the adjoining figure, name
   (i) four line segments;
   (ii) four rays;
   (iii) two non-intersecting line segments.

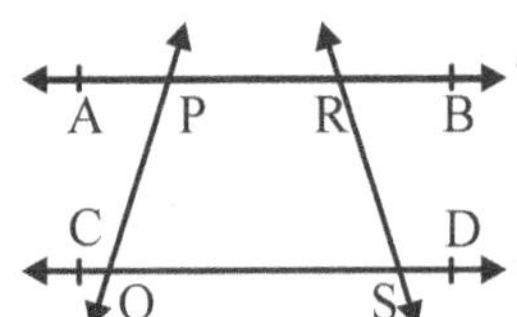

7. In the adjoining figure, write another name for :
   (i) $\angle 1$ (ii) $\angle 2$ (iii) $\angle 3$

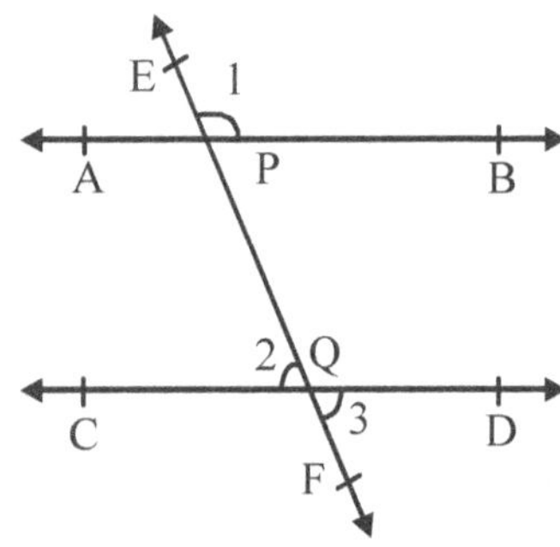

Long Answer Questions :

DIRECTIONS : *Give answer in four to five sentences.*

1. For the given quadrilateral ABCD, name:
   (i) all the vertices
   (ii) all the sides
   (iii) all the angles
   (iv) all the triangles
   (v) side opposite to BC
   (vi) sides adjacent to AD
   (vii) diagonal joining the vertices other than A and C.
   (viii) point which is in the interior of the quadrilateral ABCD.
   (ix) angles adjacent to $\angle$B.

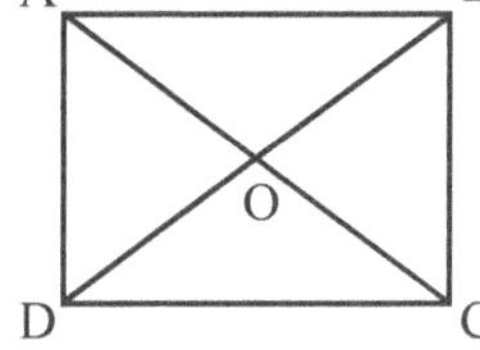

2. Draw a circle and mark:
   (i) a centre
   (ii) a radius
   (iii) a diameter
   (iv) a chord
   (v) any point in its interior
   (vi) any point on its exterior
   (vii) any point on the boundary of the circle
   (viii) a segment
   (ix) a sector
   (x) an arc

3. In the given figure, find the triangles that have
   (i) P as the vertex
   (ii) D as the vertex
   (iii) E as the vertex
   (iv) R as the vertex

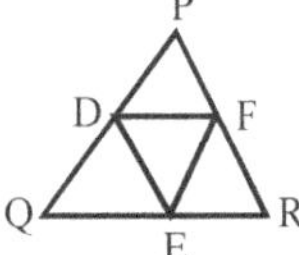

2 EXERCISE

1. Use the figure to name :
   (i)   Five points
   (ii) a line
   (iii) Four rays
   (iv) Five line segments

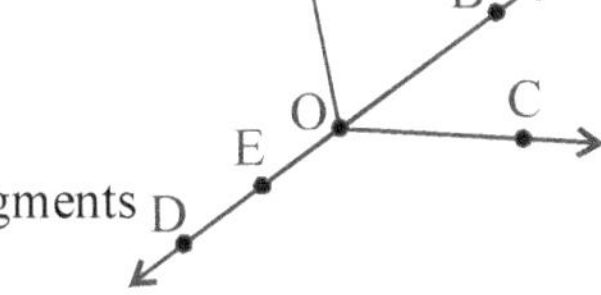

2. Consider the following figure of line $\overleftrightarrow{MN}$. Say whether following statements are true or false in context of the given figure.

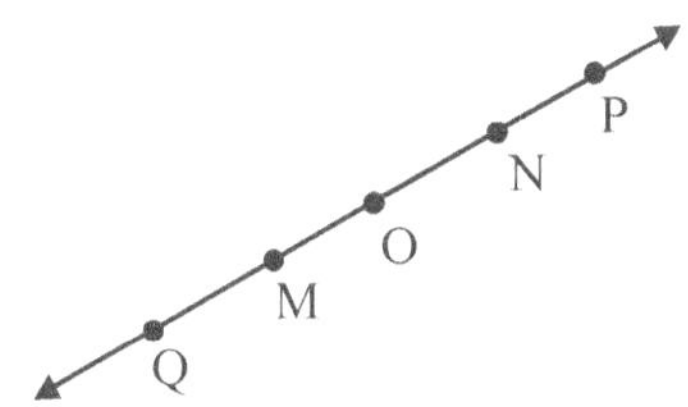

   (i)   Q, M, O, N, P are points on the line $\overleftrightarrow{MN}$.

   (ii) M, O, N are points on a line segment $\overline{MN}$.

   (iii) M and N are end points of line segment $\overline{MN}$.

   (iv) O and N are end points of line segment $\overline{OP}$.

   (v) M is one of the end points of line segment $\overline{QO}$.

   (vi) M is a point on ray $\overrightarrow{OP}$.

   (vii) Ray $\overrightarrow{OP}$ is different from ray $\overrightarrow{QP}$.

   (viii)Ray $\overrightarrow{OP}$ is same as ray $\overrightarrow{OM}$.

   (ix) Ray $\overrightarrow{OM}$ is not opposite to ray $\overrightarrow{OP}$.

   (x) O is not an initial point of $\overrightarrow{OP}$.

   (xi) N is the initial point of $\overrightarrow{NP}$ and $\overrightarrow{NM}$.

3. Draw rough diagrams of two angles such that they have
   (i)   One point in common
   (ii) Two points in common
   (iii) Three points in common
   (iv) Four points in common
   (v) One ray in common.

4. Draw a rough sketch of a quadrilateral PQRS. Draw its diagonals. Name them. Is the meeting point of the diagonal in the interior or exterior of the quadrilateral?

5. From the figure identify
   (i)   the centre of circle
   (ii) three radii
   (iii) a diameter
   (iv) a chord
   (v) two points in the interior
   (vi) a points in the exterior
   (vii) a sector

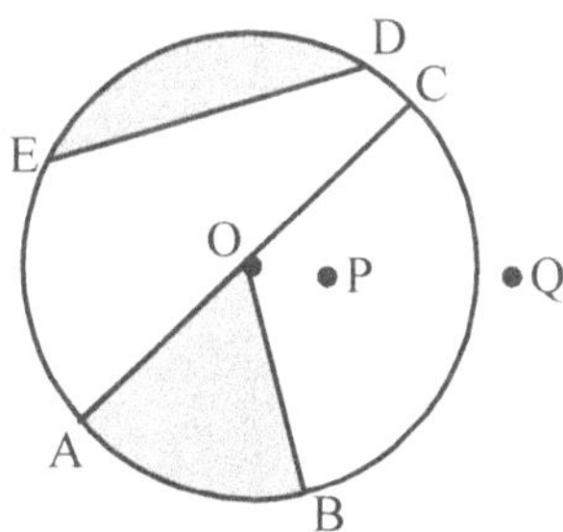

6. Name the angles in the given figure.

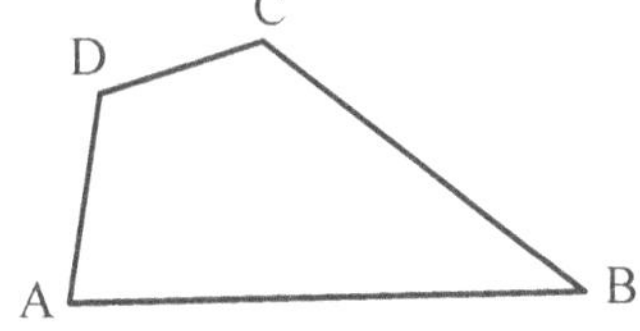

Exemplar Questions :

1. The number of common points in the two angles marked in figure is __________ .

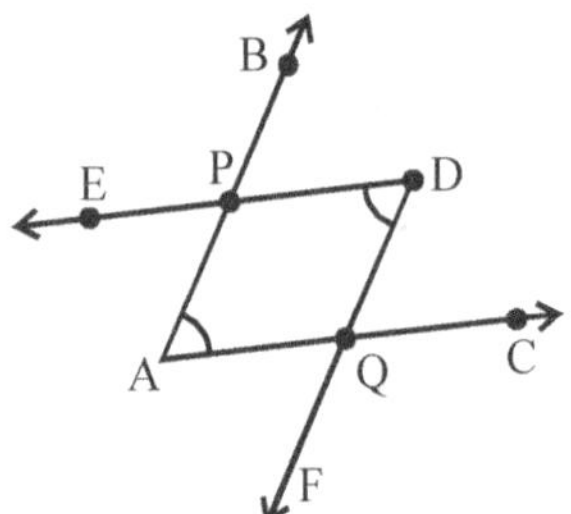

2. The number of common points in the two angles marked in figure is __________ .

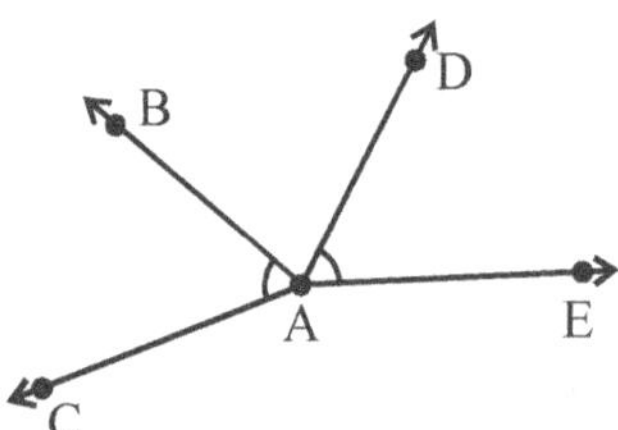

3. Name the vertices and the line segments in the given figure.

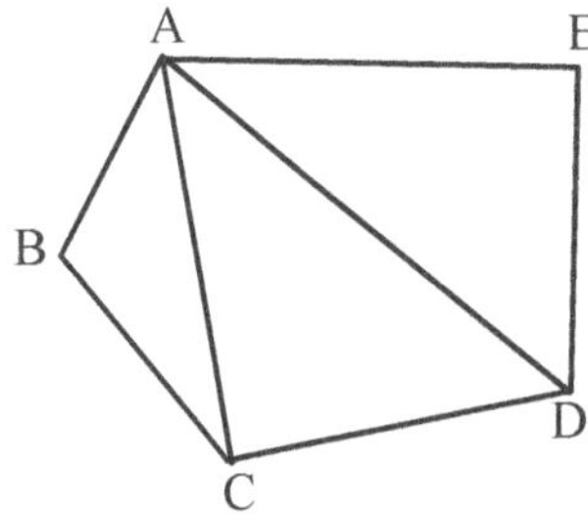

4. Name the following angles of the figure using three letters:

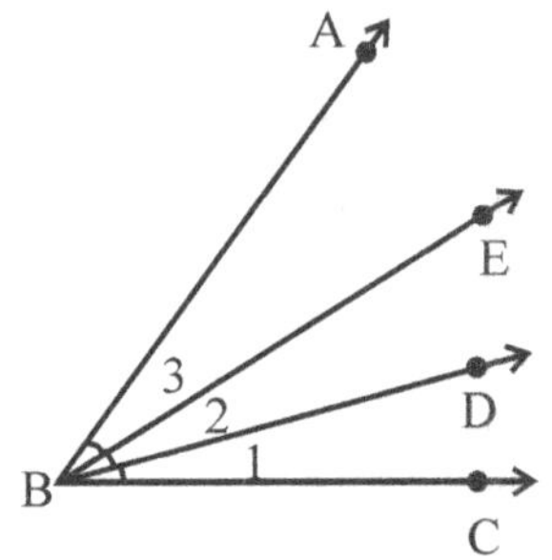

(i) $\angle 1$ (ii) $\angle 2$
(iii) $\angle 3$ (iv) $\angle 1 + \angle 2$
(v) $\angle 2 + \angle 3$ (vi) $\angle 1 + \angle 2 + \angle 3$
(vii) $\angle CBA - \angle 1$

5. Name the points and then the line segments in each of the following figures.

(i)

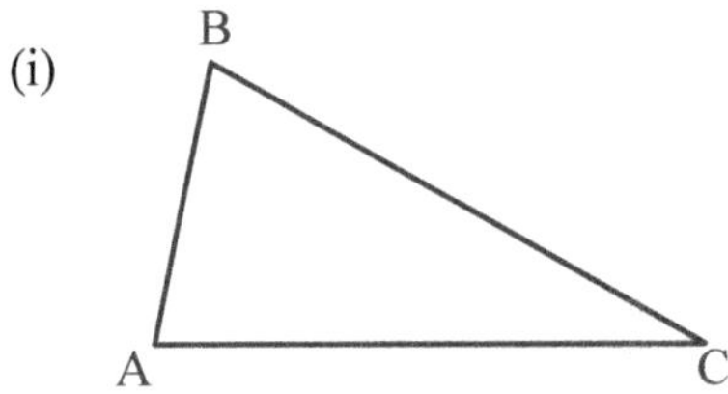

(ii)

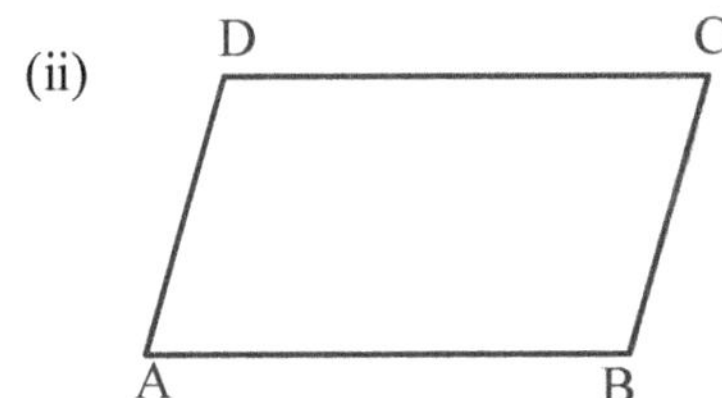

(iii)

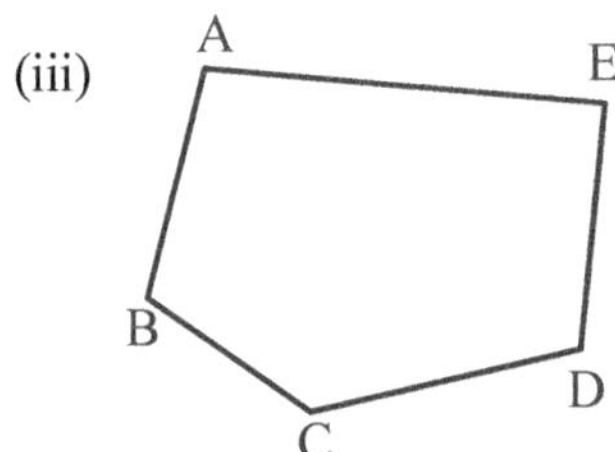

(iv) 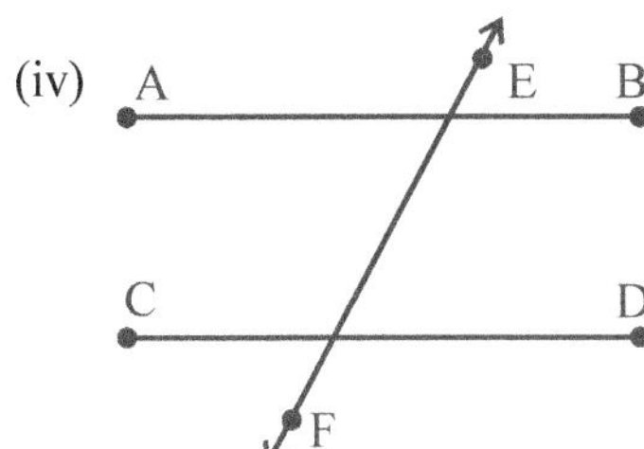

6. Will the measure of ∠ABC and of ∠CBD make measure of ∠ABD in figure ?

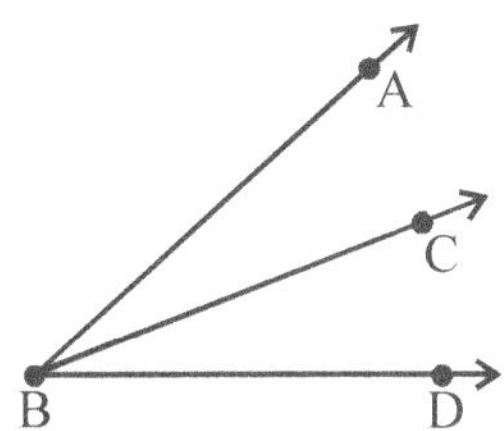

7. Will the lengths of line segment AB and line segment BC make the length of line segment AC in figure ?

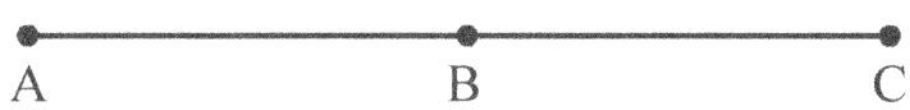

8. What is common in the following figures (i) and (ii).

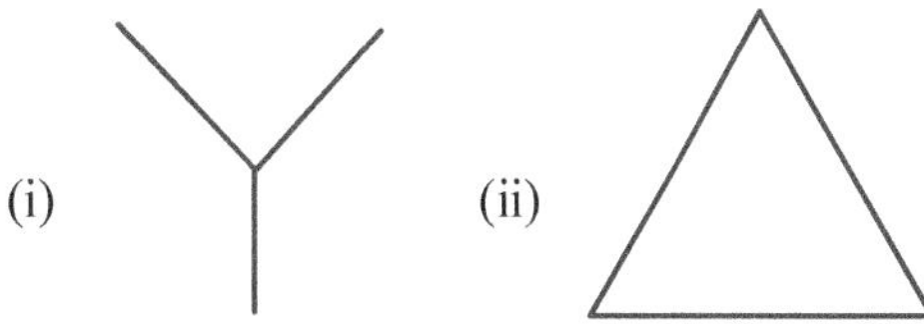

(i)   (ii)

Is fig (i) that of triangle ? if not, why?

3 EXERCISE

Single Option Correct :

DIRECTIONS : *This section contains multiple choice questions. Each question has 4 choices (a), (b), (c) and (d) out of which ONLY ONE is correct.*

1. The number of angles in the figure is

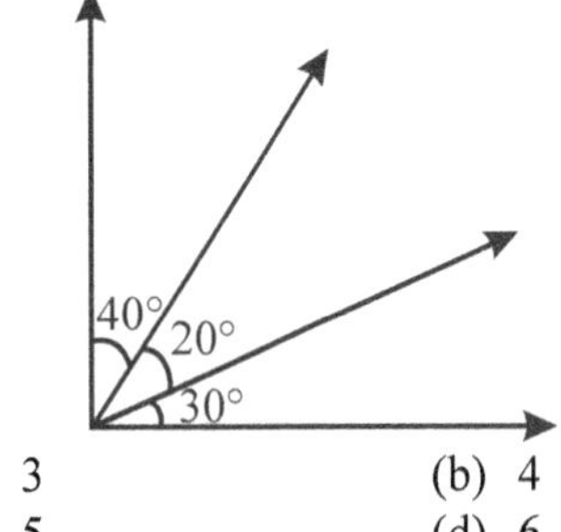

(a) 3   (b) 4
(c) 5   (d) 6

2. Three or more lines are said to be concurrent if they pass through the
(a) same line   (b) same point
(c) same plane   (d) none

3. Three or more points in a plane are said to be collinear if they lie on the
(a) same plane   (b) same line
(c) different lines   (d) none

4. When two lines are parallel the distance between them is
(a) always equal   (b) not equal
(c) increases   (d) none

5. The region bounded by chord and its minor arc is called
(a) minor segment   (b) minor arc
(c) major segment   (d) semicircle

6. A chord which passes through the centre is called
(a) radius   (b) diameter
(c) arc   (d) none

7. Number of rays that can be drawn from a given point is
(a) 2   (b) 5
(c) 8   (d) infinite

8. The number of diagonals in a septagon is
(a) 21   (b) 42
(c) 7   (d) 14

9. Region inside the boundary of curve is-
(a) interior   (b) exterior
(c) both (a) and (b)   (d) None of these

10. The end points of a side of polygon are-
(a) adjacent vertices
(b) adjacent sides
(c) adjacent angles
(d) None of these

11. A polygon is a _______ made up of line segments.
(a) open curve
(b) close curve
(c) both (a) and (b)
(d) None of these

12. A part of a circle enclosed by an arc and two radii is
(a) segment   (b) sector
(c) diameter   (d) radius

13. The infinite number of lines that can pass through a given point are called.
(a) Concurrent lines
(b) Parallel lines
(c) Perpendicular lines
(d) None of these

More Than One Option Correct :

DIRECTIONS : *This section contains multiple choice questions. Each question has 4 choices (a), (b), (c) and (d) out of which ONE or MORE may be correct.*

1. Which of the following are quadrilaterals? :

(a)    (b) 

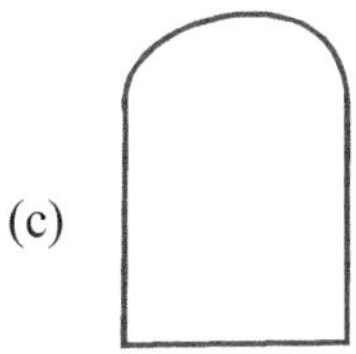
(c)

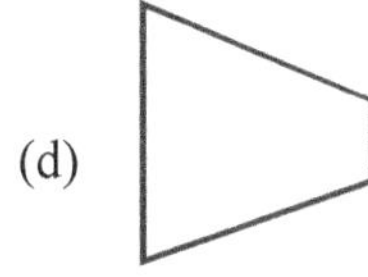
(d)

2. Which of the following is/are incorrect?
(a) A diagonal of a quadrilateral is a line segment joining any two vertices of the quadrilateral.
(b) The sides that have a common vertex are called the adjacent sides.
(c) The part of the plane that is not enclosed by the quadrilateral is known as the exterior of the quadrilateral.
(d) The quadrilateral region consists of the exterior and the boundary of the quadrilateral.

3. Which of the following is/are correct?
(a) The diameter of a circle is always greater than its radius.
(b) The line segments drawn from the centre of a circle to any point on its boundary are always equal.
(c) The centre of a circle may be present on the exterior of the circle.
(d) Every chord of a circle is also its diameter.

4. Region of a polygon includes
(a) Interior (b) Exterior
(c) Boundary (d) All of these

5. Name the shaded part.
(a) Semi-circle (b) Segment
(c) Sector (d) None of these

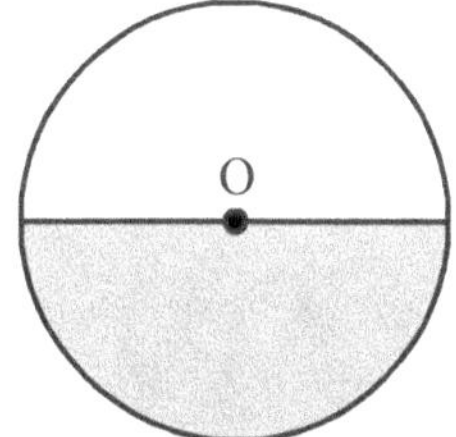

DIRECTIONS : *Each of these questions contains an Assertion followed by Reason. Read them carefully and answer the question on the basis of following options. You have to select the one that best describes the two statements.*

(a) If both **Assertion** and **Reason** are correct and Reason is the correct explanation of **Assertion**.
(b) If both **Assertion** and **Reason** are correct but reason is not the correct explanation of **Assertion**.
(c) If **Assertion** is correct but **Reason** is incorrect.
(d) If **Assertion** is incorrrect but **Reason** is correct.

1. **Assertion :** AB and CD are the adjacent sides of quadrilateral ABCD
Reason : Adjacent sides are any two sides with a common end point.

2. **Assertion :** A triangle has 3 sides, 2 angles and 1 diagonal.
Reason : A triangle is a polygon made up of 3 line segments.

DIRECTIONS : *Study the given passage(s) and answer the following questions.*

PASSAGE–I

A polygon is entirely made up of straight lines only. A octagon ABCDEFGH is an eight sided polygon.

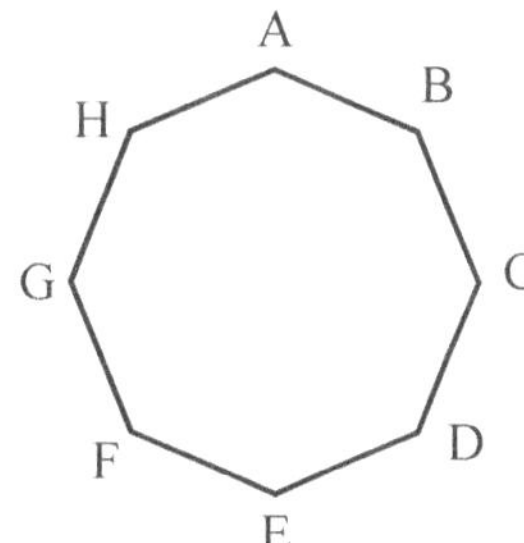

1. How many sides are there in the octagon?
(a) 7 (b) 8
(c) 9 (d) 5

2. How many angles are there in the octagon?
(a) 5 (b) 6
(c) 7 (d) 8

3. How many diagonals are there in the octagon?
(a) 20 (b) 18
(c) 15 (d) 10

Integer Type Questions :

DIRECTIONS : *Answer the following questions. The answer to each of the question is a single digit integer, ranging from 0 to 9.*

1. Count the number of lines in following figure.

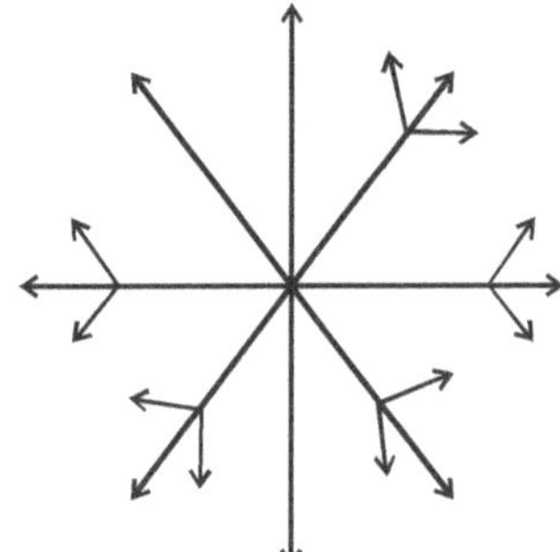

2. If radius OP = 5cm in the figure, then find the length of OR.

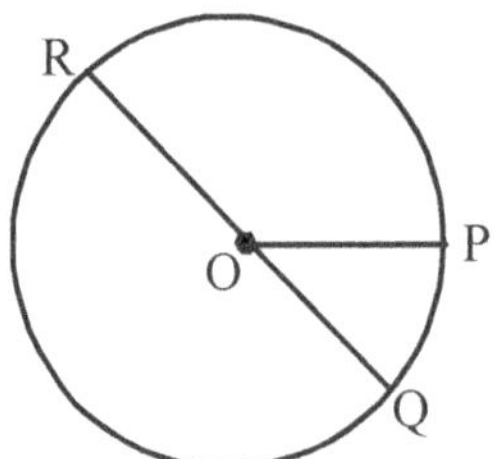

3. How many pairs sides are there in a heptagon?
4. How many pairs of intersecting lines are there ?

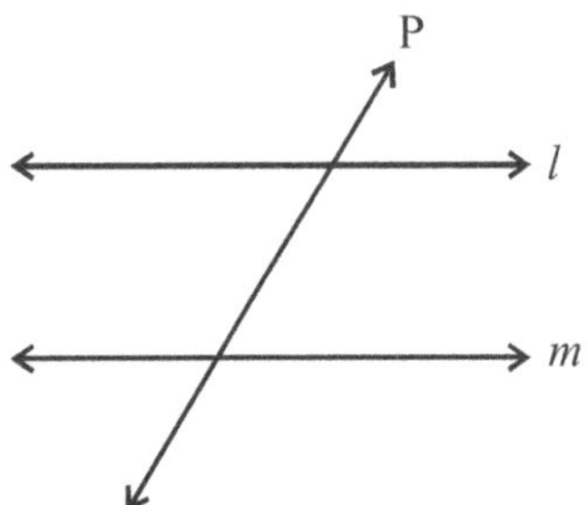

5. How many minimum sides are required to make a polygon?

Multiple Matching Question :

DIRECTIONS : *Following question has four statements (A, B, C and D) given in Column-I and five statements (p, q, r, s, t) in Column-II. Any given statement in Column-I can have correct matching with one or more statement(s) given in Column-II.*

1. Study the given figure and match the following:

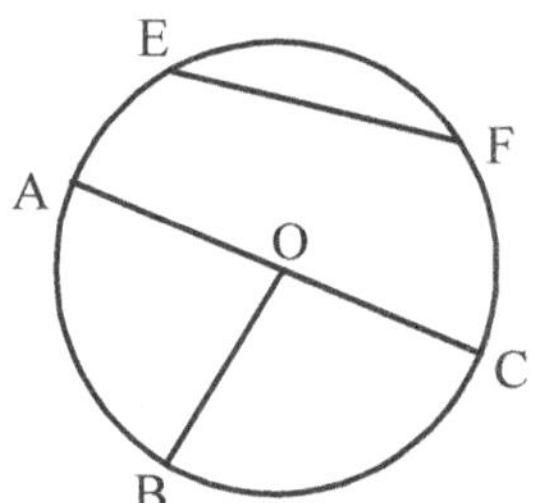

	Column I		**Column II**
(A)	OA	(*p*)	Sector
(B)	EF	(*q*)	Diameter
(C)	$\overline{AC}$	(*r*)	2 × OC
(D)	AOB	(*s*)	Radius
		(*t*)	Chord

SOLUTIONS

1 EXERCISE

Fill in the Blanks :

1. definite
2. ray
3. infinite
4. closed
5. polygon
6. arm / sides
7. vertex
8. circumference
9. longest
10. four

True / False :

1. False
2. True
3. True
4. False, interior
5. False
6. False
7. True
8. True
9. False
10. True

Match the Columns :

1. (A) → (t); (B) → (r); (C) → (s); (D) → (q); (E) → (p)

Very Short Answer Questions:

1. (i) AB, BC, CD
   (ii) AB, BC, CD, DE
   (iii) AB, BC, CD, DE
   (iv) AB, BC, AC, DE, DF, EF
2. (i) n, o; o, p; n, p
   (ii) l, n; l, o; l, p; m, n; m, o; m, p; l, m
   (iii) m, o
   (iv) E
   (v) F
   (vi) B D E F; A C E G
3. (iii), (iv)
4. (i) Yes   (ii) Yes
   (iii) No   (iv) Yes
   (v) No
5. AD because diagonal is obtained by joining two opposite vertices of a polygon while in the given figure D is not a vertex.
6. (i) ∠AOB, ∠BOC, ∠DOC, ∠AOD
   (ii) ∠DOC, ∠COA, ∠DOB, ∠BOA, ∠AOD, ∠BOC
7. (i) Points L and F
   (ii) Points M and Q
   (iii) Points S, T, R & O

Short Answer Questions :

1. l, m, p concurrent at A
   n, o, p concurrent at B
   q, l, n concurrent at C
   m, o, q concurrent at D
2. (i) Vertex is O, arms are OA and OB and angle is ∠AOB.
   (ii) Vertex is P, arms are PQ and PR and angle is ∠QPR
   (iii) Vertex is M, arms are MN and MR and angle is ∠NMR
   (iv) Vertex is Y, arms are YX and YZ and angle is ∠XYZ.
3. (i) Three radii : $\overline{OA}$, $\overline{OB}$, $\overline{OC}$
   (ii) Three chords : $\overline{AC}$, $\overline{BC}$, $\overline{AB}$
   (iii) Diameter : $\overline{AB}$
   (iv) A triangle that has the centre of the circle as vertex is ΔAOC or ΔBOC.
4. (i) AB, BC; BC, CD; CD, AD; AD, AB
   (ii) AB, DC; AD, BC
   (iii) ∠A, ∠B; ∠B, ∠C; ∠C, ∠D; ∠D, ∠A
   (iv) ∠A, ∠C; ∠B, ∠D
5. (i) ∠ACE, ∠CAE, ∠AEC, ∠CDB, ∠DBC, ∠EAB, ∠CBA, ∠CAB, ∠DBA, ∠AFB, ∠DFA, ∠EFB, ∠FEB, ∠FDA, ∠DFE
   (ii) ΔFDA, ΔFEB, ΔAFB, ΔCDB, ΔACE, ΔADB, ΔEAB, ΔCAB
   (iii) $\overline{AC}$, $\overline{DC}$, $\overline{AD}$, $\overline{AB}$, $\overline{BC}$, $\overline{BE}$, $\overline{EC}$, $\overline{AE}$, $\overline{AF}$, $\overline{EF}$, $\overline{BF}$, $\overline{FD}$
6. (i) $\overline{PR}$, $\overline{PQ}$, $\overline{RS}$, $\overline{QS}$
   (ii) $\overrightarrow{PA}$, $\overrightarrow{QC}$, $\overrightarrow{RB}$, $\overrightarrow{SD}$
   (iii) $\overline{PR}$ and $\overline{QS}$
7. (i) ∠EPB   (ii) ∠PQC   (iii) ∠FQD

Long Answer Questions :

1. (i) A, B, C and D
    (ii) AB, BC, CD and DA
    (iii) ∠ABC, ∠BCD, ∠CDA, ∠DAB, ∠ABO, ∠OBC, ∠BCO, ∠OCD, ∠CDO, ∠ODA, ∠DAO, ∠OAB, ∠AOB, ∠BOC, ∠COD and ∠DOA
    (iv) ΔAOB, ΔBOC, ΔCOD, ΔDOA, ΔABC, ΔADC, ΔABD and ΔBCD
    (v) AD
    (vi) AB and DC
    (vii) BD
    (viii) O
    (ix) ∠C and ∠A

2. Do it yourself.

3. (i) ΔPDF, ΔPQR
    (ii) ΔDEF, ΔDQE, ΔPDF
    (iii) ΔEFD, ΔEFR, ΔEDQ
    (iv) ΔREF, ΔPQR

2 EXERCISE

Text-Book Exercise :

1. (i) O, B, C, D, E
    (ii) $\overleftrightarrow{DB}$
    (iii) $\overrightarrow{OB}, \overrightarrow{OC}, \overrightarrow{OE}, \overrightarrow{OD}$
    (iv) $\overline{OB}, \overline{OC}, \overline{OE}, \overline{OD}, \overline{ED}$

2. (i) True (ii) True (iii) True
    (iv) False (v) False (vi) False
    (vii) True (viii) False (ix) False
    (x) False (xi) True.

3. (i)

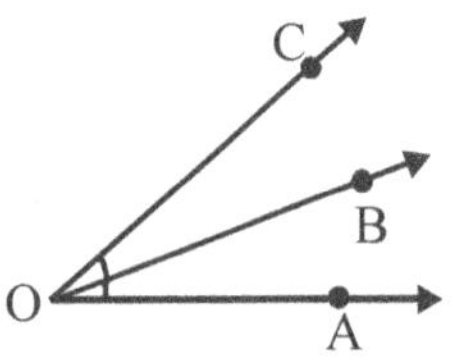

∠AOB and ∠BOC have one point O in common.

    (ii) ∠AOB and ∠OBC have two points O and B in common.

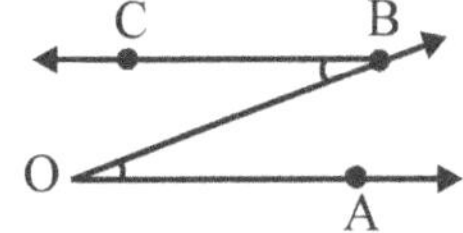

(iii) ∠BAE and ∠BDE have three points B, C and E in common.

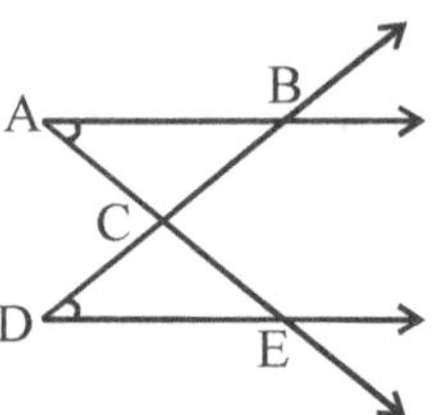

(iv) ∠FBE and ∠ADF have four points A, F, C and E in common.

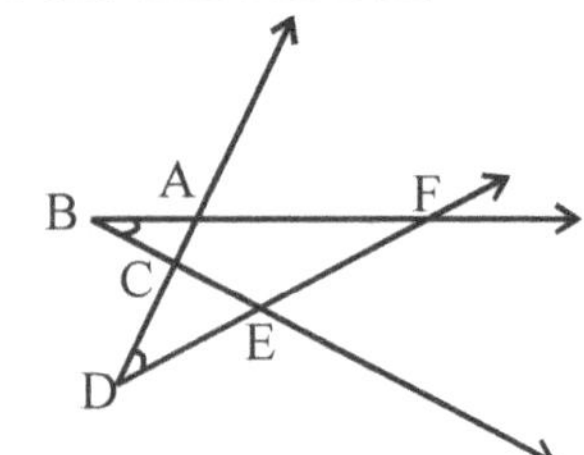

(v)

∠AOB and ∠BOC have one ray $\overrightarrow{OB}$ in common.

4.

The meeting point O of the diagonals PR and QS of the quadrilateral PQRS is in the interior of the quadrilateral PQRS.

5. (i) O is the centre of the circle
    (ii) $\overline{OA}, \overline{OB}, \overline{OC}$ are three radii of the circle
    (iii) $\overline{AC}$ is a diameter of the circle
    (iv) $\overline{ED}$ is a chord of the circle
    (v) O and P are two points in the interior

(vi) Q is a point in the exterior
(vii) OAB (shaded portion) is a sector of the circle.

6. ∠A or ∠DAB ; ∠B or ∠ABC ; ∠C or ∠BCD ; ∠D or ∠CDA.

Exemplar Questions :

1. Two
2. One
3. Vertices – A, B, C, D and E;
    line segments – AB, AC, AD, AE, BC, CD, DE
4. (i) ∠CBD, (ii) ∠DBE, (iii) ∠EBA, (iv) ∠CBE,
    (v) ∠DBA, (vi) ∠CBA,(vii) ∠DBA
5. (i)   A, B, C, AB, BC, AC
    (ii) A, B, C, D, AB, BC, CD, DA
    (iii) A, B, C, D, E, AB, BC, CD, DE, EA
    (iv) A, B, C, D, E, F, AB, CD, EF
6. Yes
7. Yes
8. Both figures have 3 line segments.
    No. it is not a closed figure.

3 EXERCISE

Single Option Correct :

1. (d)   2. (b)   3. (b)   4. (a)
5. (a) Minor segment (chord & minor arc)
6. (b) Diameter is the longest chord which passes through the centre of the circle.

7. (d)   8. (d)   9. (a)   10. (a)
11. (b)   12. (b)   13. (a)

More Than One Option Correct :

1. (a, d)   2. (a, d)
3. (a, b)   4. (a, c)
5. (b, c)

Assertion & Reason :

1. (d) AB and CD are the opposite sides of quadrilateral ABCD
         Assertion : False, Reason : True.
2. (d) Assertion : False, Reason : True.
         A triangle has three sides, three angles and no diagonal.

Passage Based Questions :

1. (b) 8   2. (d) 8
3. (a) 20

Integer Type Questions :

1. (4)
2. (5) Since O is the centre of the circle.
         ∴ OP = OR = 5cm
3. (7) Heptagon is a seven sided polygon.
4. (2) ℓ and p; m and p
5. (3)

Multiple Matching Question :

1. (A) → (s); (B) → (t); (C) → (q, r, t); (D) → (p)

Chapter 5

Understanding Elementary Shapes

MEASURING AND COMPARING LINE SEGMENTS

A line segment is a part of a line with two end points. Adjoining figure of line segment have two end points A and B

1. The measure of line segment is known as **length**.
2. A line segment has a fixed length but no breadth or thickness.
3. The fixed length of line segment makes its measurement and comparison possible.

Comparing Line Segments

We can compare two or more line segments by following methods.

I. By observation :

Line segments can be compared by just observing them visually.

In the adjacent figure, $\overline{AB}$ is shorter than $\overline{CD}$.

It is clear by observation. But comparison of $\overline{PQ}$ and $\overline{XY}$ is not clear by observation. We need some accurate methods for comparison.

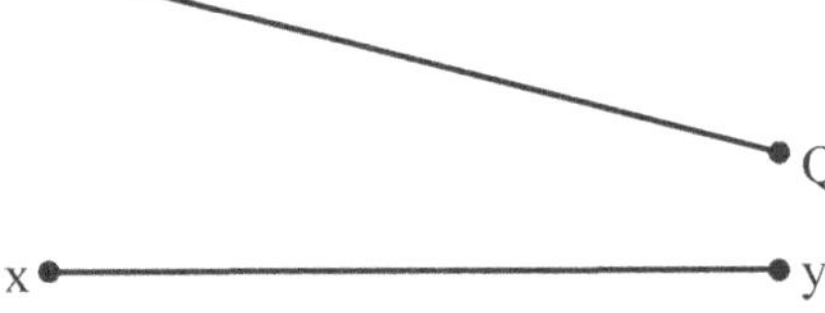

II. By tracing

If there are two line segments $\overline{AB}$ and $\overline{CD}$.

Trace $\overline{AB}$ on a tracing paper and place it on $\overline{CD}$ in such a way that the point A coincides with point C. By doing so, There can be three possibilities :

(i) 

B is between C and D. So, it is clear that $\overline{AB} < \overline{CD}$

(ii)

B is exactly on D. So, it is clear that $\overline{AB} = \overline{CD}$

(iii)

B is beyond D. So, it is clear that $\overline{AB} > \overline{CD}$

III. Using a divider

Let us compare the two line segments $\overline{AB}$ and $\overline{CD}$, using a divider.

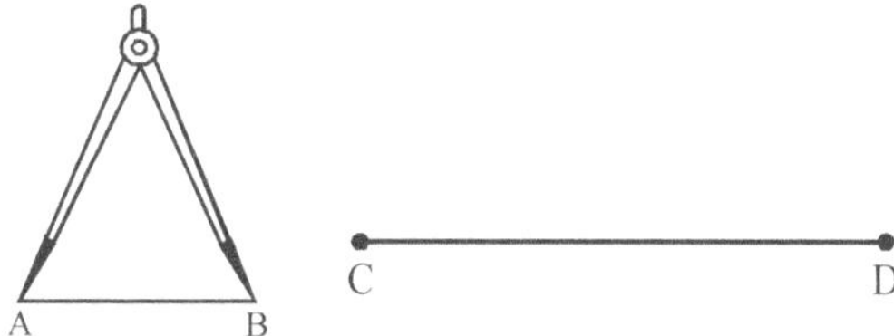

Place the end point of one arm of divider at A and open the other arm so that it coincides with B. Now without disturbing the both arms of divider, place one end point of the pair of divider on end point C of the other line segment CD and let the other end point of the pair of divider rest on the line segment CD as shown in the figure.

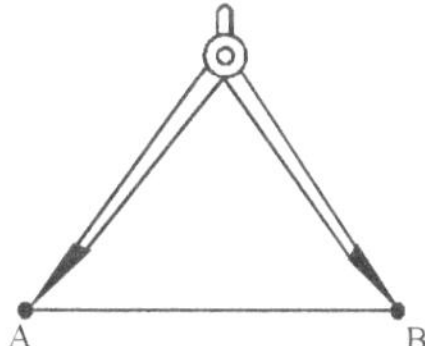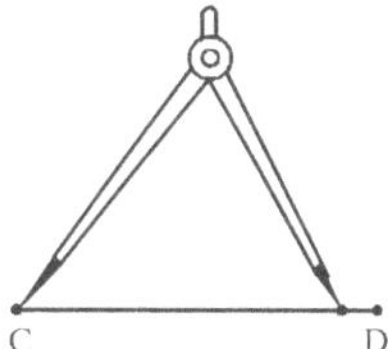

We see that this end point of divider falls before the other end point D.

$\therefore$ $\overline{AB}$ is shorter than $\overline{CD}$.

If the end point of the divider falls beyond the point D, then AB is longer than CD.

But this method is not useful when, we want to know by how much a line segment is longer or shorter than the other. So let us learn to measure the lengths of the line segments.

Measurement of a Line Segment

For measuring the actual length of a line segment, we use a ruler or a scale. A ruler has centimetres marks along one edge and inches marks along the other edge.

The standard unit of measurement of length is metre. A metre is divided into 100 equal parts and each part is called a **centimetre**. Each centimetre is further divided into 10 equal parts and each part is known as **millimetre**.

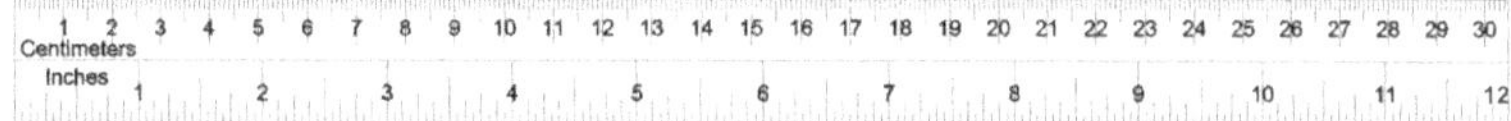

To measure any line segment $\overline{AB}$, keep the ruler in such a way that point A of the line segment coincides with the '0' mark on ruler . Now, read the mark on the ruler that coincides with B. Here, we see that the 3.5 centimetre mark coincides with the end point B. Thus, the length of the line segment AB is 3.5 cm or $\overline{AB}$ = 3.5 cm.

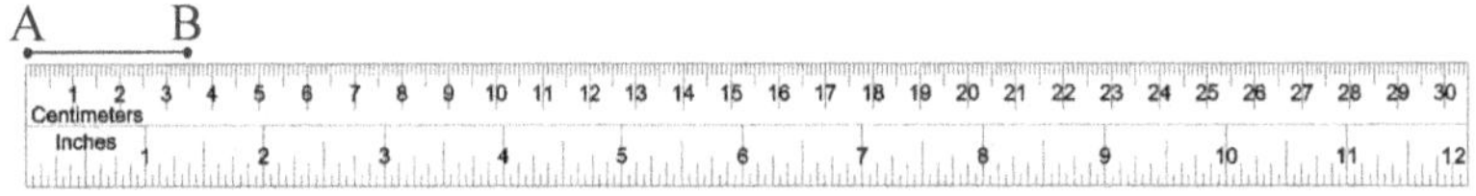

ANGLES

The hands of a clock or two arms of a divider are joined together at a common point. They are inclined towards each other. We say that these arms form an angle at common point.

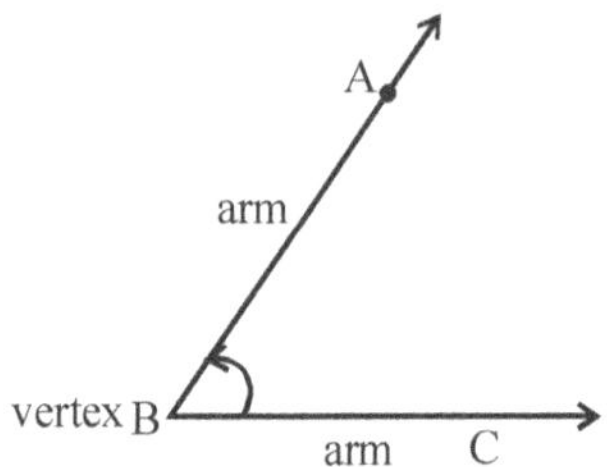

An angle can be defined as - "Figure formed by two rays with the same starting point. The common point is called the vertex of the angle while the rays forming the angle are its arms." Here, ∠ABC can also be written as ∠B. Vertex is B and BA and BC are arms.

DIRECTIONS AND ANGLES

We have heard of directions in Geography.
We know, there are four main directions North (N), South (S), East (E) and West (W).
South is opposite to north and West is opposite to east.

Right Angle

Suppose you stand facing North and are asked to face upto the East,

then you will turn $\dfrac{1}{4}$ th clockwise or one right angle.

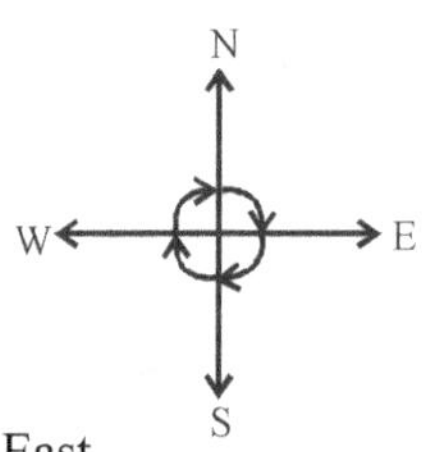

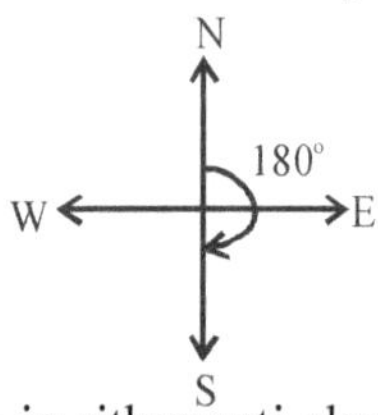

Straight Angle

Suppose you stand facing North and are asked to face upto the South in

clockwise manner, then you will turn $\dfrac{1}{2}$ th clockwise or one straight angle.

Complete Angle

Suppose you stand facing North and are asked to turn towards the same direction in either anti-clockwise or clockwise manner then you will take a full turn (i.e. 4 right angles) either clockwise or anti-clockwise manner.

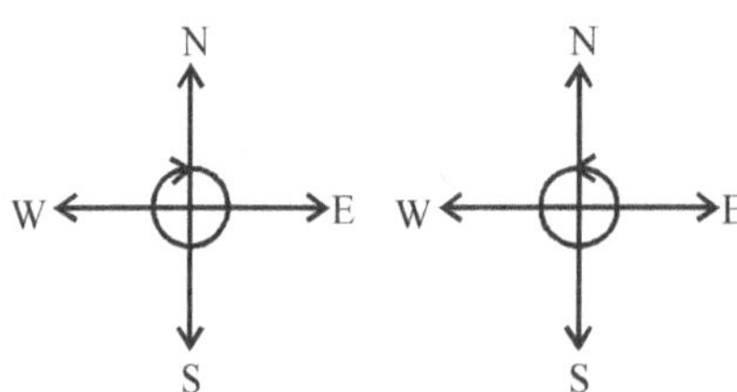

ACUTE, OBTUSE AND REFLEX ANGLE

Acute Angle - If the measure of an angle is smaller than 90°, then it is called as acute angle.

Obtuse Angle - An angle whose measure is greater than 90° and smaller than 180° is called as obtuse angle.

Reflex Angle - An angle having its measure greater than 180° and smaller than 360° is called as reflex angle.

ILLUSTRATION : 1

Which direction will you face, if you are

(i)   facing north and making $\dfrac{1}{2}$ revolution clockwise.

(ii) facing north and making $\dfrac{1}{4}$ revolution clockwise.

(iv) facing east and making $\dfrac{3}{4}$ revolution clockwise.

SOLUTION :

(i)   Half-revolution means 180° turn clockwise
      from north, so it will take you in south direction.

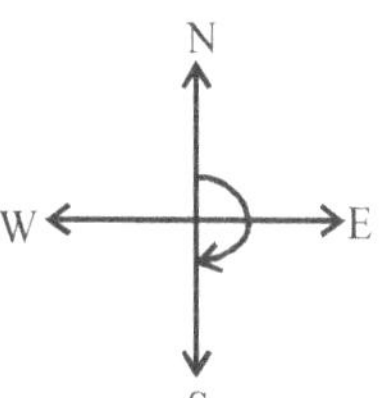

(ii) One-fourth revolution means 90° turn clockwise
      from north, so it will take you in east direction.

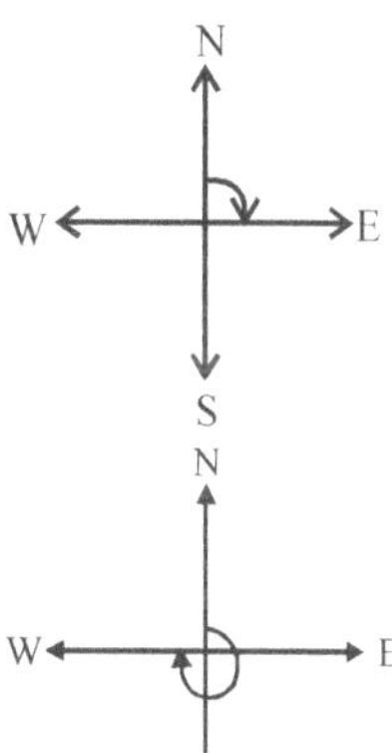

(iii) Three fourth revolution means 270° revolution
      clockwise from north, so it will take you in west direction.

MEASURING OF AN ANGLE

An angle can be measured by using a semi-circular device known as protractor. It is used for constructing angles also. It has two scales- outer scale and inner scale. Each scale begins with 0° and ends at 180°. There are 180° small equal divisions each denoting 1°. The line segment between 0° and 180° is known as baseline. The mid-point of the baseline is known as centre of the protractor.

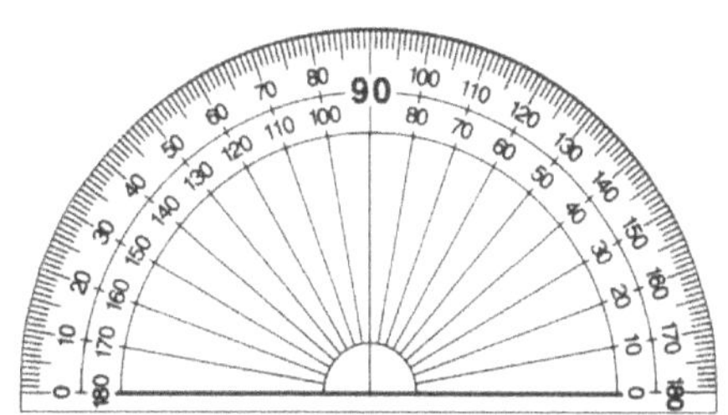

How to measure an angle

Let us measure an angle ABC with a protractor.

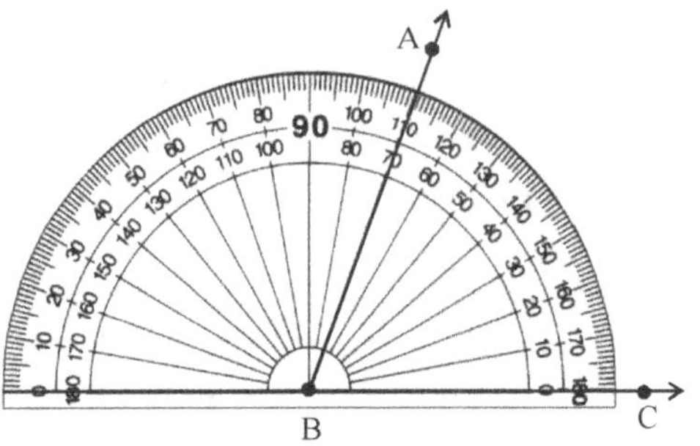

1. Place the centre of the protractor on the vertex of ∠ABC. i.e., B. Adjust the protractor in such a way that its baseline coincides with BC.
2. Now observe, in which direction the arm AB points. Another arm BC points to 0° on the inner scale.
3. Now, read the mark pointed by AB on the inner scale. This shows the degrees of angle ABC.

Here arm AB points to 70° protractor is used to measure an acute angle (0° to 90°) and an obtuse angle (90° to 180°) because its marked from 0° to 180°.

How to measure reflex angle

Let us consider a reflex angle of 210° i.e. ∠MNO.

To measure the reflex angle MNO extend the arm MN to P, to form a straight angle MNP i.e., 180°. Then measure the ∠PNO i.e., 30° so

$$\angle MNO = \angle MNP + \angle PNO$$
$$= 180° + 30°$$
$$= 210°$$

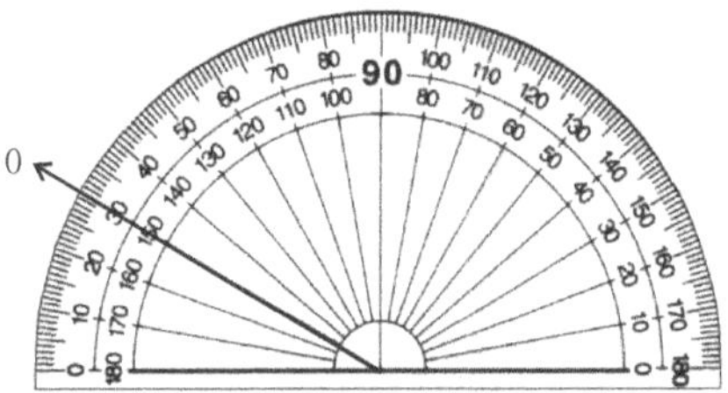

NOTE:	1.	The base line points to 0° towards right : read the inner scale for another arm.
	2.	The base line points to 0° towards left : read the outer scale for another arm

PERPENDICULAR LINES

If two lines intersect each other at a right angle, then the lines are called perpendicular lines. In the figure, WX is perpendicular to line YZ. It is written as WX ⊥ YZ.

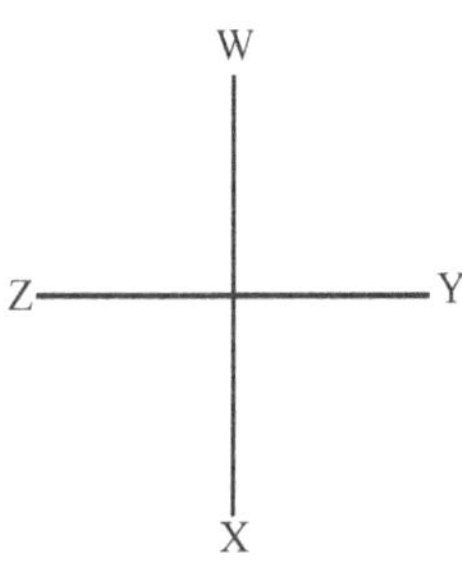

TRIANGLE : A THREE SIDED POLYGON

A triangle is a 3-sided polygon. It has three sides and three angles.

Classification of triangle

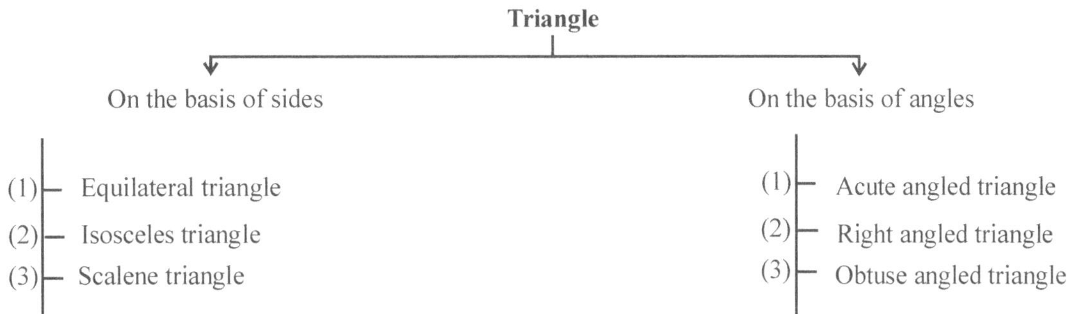

I.   On the basis of sides :

S. No.	Name	Property	Figure
(1)	Equilateral triangle	A triangle in which all three sides are equal in length is called equilateral triangle.	
(2)	Isosceles triangle	A triangle in which two sides are equal in length is called isosceles triangle.	
(3)	Scalene triangle	A triangle in which all the sides are different in length is called scalene triangle.	

II.   On the basis of angles :

S. No.	Name	Property	Specific property	Figure
(1)	Acute angled triangle	A triangle in which all three angles are acute angles i.e. less than 90° is called an acute angled triangle or an acute triangle.	It may be equilateral, isosceles or scalene triangle.	
(2)	Right angled triangle	A triangle in which one of the angle is a right angle i.e. 90° is called right angled triangle.	It can only be isosceles or scalene.	
(3)	Obtuse angled triangle	A triangle in which one of the angle is obtuse angle i.e. more than 90° is called as obtuse angled triangle.	It can only be isosceles or scalene.	

NOTE: Equilateral triangle is also called as equiangular triangle as each of its angle is 60º.

QUADRILATERAL

A quadrilateral is a polygon made up of four line segments. It has four sides, four vertices, four angles and two diagonals. Quadrilaterals can be classified as rectangle, parallelogram, square, rhombus and trapezium. Let us study them one by one.

(a) Rectangle

A rectangle is a quadrilateral with all its angles are right angle.

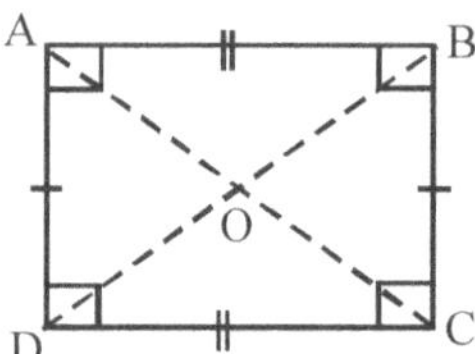

Properties:

(i)　Each angle is 90° i.e., $\angle A = \angle B = \angle C = \angle D = 90°$

(ii)　Opposite sides are parallel and equal.

(iii)　Both the diagonals are equal and bisect each other
　　　i.e. $AC = BD$, $AO = OC$ and $DO = OB$

(b) Parallelogram

A parallelogram is a quadrilateral whose each pair of opposite sides are equal and parallel.

In parallelogram ABCD,

$AB = CD$　and　$AD = BC$

$AB \parallel DC$　and　$AD \parallel BC$

Properties:

(1)　Opposite sides are equal and parallel. i.e.
　　　$AB = CD$　　　　　　　　$AD = BC$
　　　$AB \parallel DC$　　　　　　　$AD \parallel BC$

(2)　Opposite angles are equal.

(3)　Diagonals bisect each other but not equal.

(c) Rhombus

A rhombus is a parallelogram whose all four sides are equal.

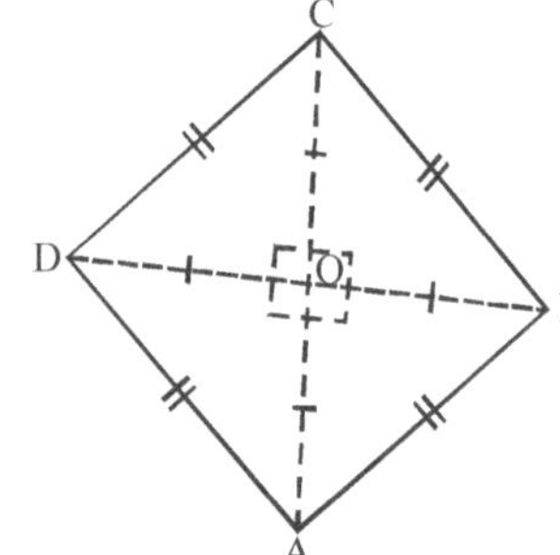

Properties:

(1)　All sides are equal in length i.e. $AB = BC = CD = DA$

(2)　Opposite sides are parallel i.e. $AD \parallel BC$ and $DC \parallel AB$

(3)　Opposite angles are equal i.e. $\angle D = \angle B$ and $\angle A = \angle C$

(4)　The diagonals bisect each other at right angles but not equal.

(d) Square

A square is a rhombus with all its angles as right angles.

Properties:

(1)　All sides are equal in length i.e. $AB = BC = CD = DA$

(2)　Opposite sides are parallel i.e. $BA \parallel CD$, $BC \parallel AD$.

(3)　Each angle measure 90°.

(4)　Both the diagonals are equal in length and bisect each other at right angles $BD = AC$.

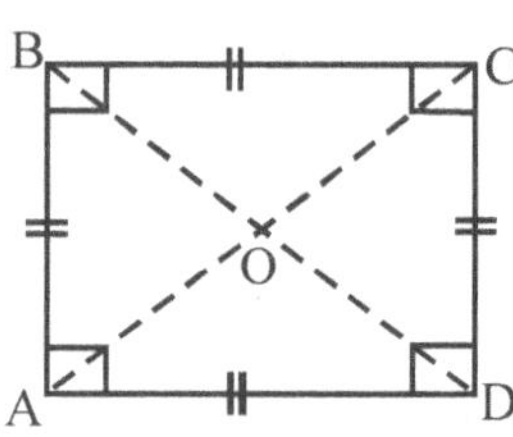

(e) Trapezium

A trapezium is a quadrilateral with only one pair of opposite sides parallel but the other pair of opposite sides are non parallel. Thus,
In the given trapezium ABCD, AB || CD.

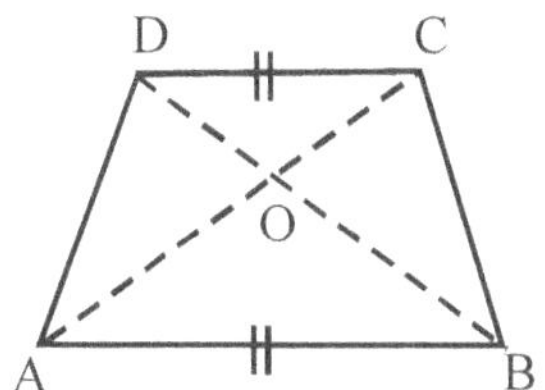

(f) Kite

A kite is a quadrilateral with two pairs of adjacent sides equal but opposite sides are not equal i.e. AB = AD and BC = CD
In a Kite diagonal intersect each other at right angles.

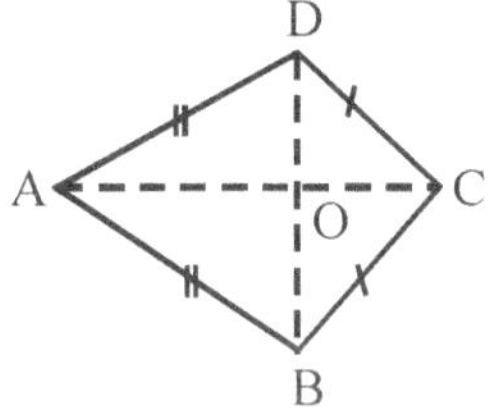

NOTE: All the properties of parallelogram are followed by a rectangle, square and rhombus. since, they all are parallelogram.

POLYGONS

The closed figures made up of three or more line segments are called polygons. Each line segment of a polygon is called as side.

Classification of Polygons

Polygons are classified on the basis of number of their sides.

Figure	No. of sides	Name
	3	Triangle
	4	Quadrilateral
	5	Pentagon
	6	Hexagon
	7	Heptagon
	8	Octagon
	9	Nanogon
	10	Decagon

REGULAR AND IRREGULAR POLYGONS

A regular polygon has all sides of same length and all angles of the same measure whereas an irregular polygon has sides of different lengths and angles of different measures.

S. No.	Polygon name	Regular polygons	Irregular polygons
(1)	Triangle		
(2)	Quadrilateral		
(3)	Pentagon		
(4)	Hexagon		
(5)	Septagon (Heptagon)		
(6)	Octagon		
(7)	Nanogon		
(8)	Decagon		

THREE DIMENSIONAL SHAPE

You have learnt about flat shapes which are also known as two dimensional shapes. Now, you will learn about solid shapes or three dimensional shapes. The objects around us are made up of various mathematical shapes like chalk box a cube/cuboid, a matchbox is cuboid, ice-cream cone is a cone, ball is a sphere, dice is a cube etc. All are these three dimensional shapes.

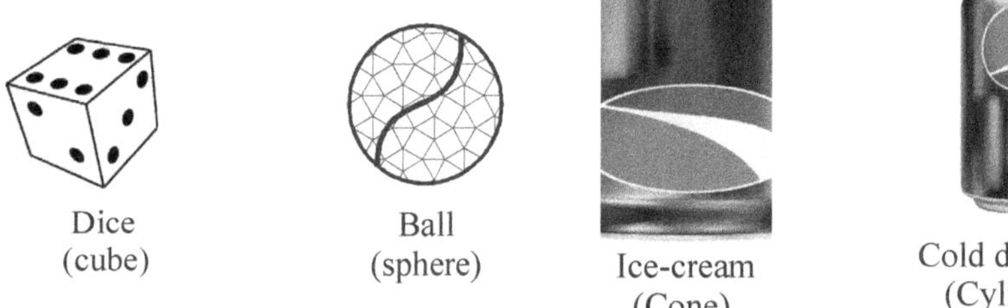

Dice
(cube)

Ball
(sphere)

Ice-cream
(Cone)

Cold drink can
(Cylinder)

The surface of the solid shape is known as **face**
The line where two faces meet is called an **edge**
The point where three edges meet is called a **corner** or **a vertex**.

S.No.	Shape	Name	Faces	Edges	Vertex
(1)	Cuboid	Cuboid	6	12	8
(2)	Cube	Cube	6	12	8
(3)	Cylinder	Cylinder	2	2 (Circular edges)	0
(4)	Cone	Cone	2	1	1
(5)	Sphere	Sphere	1	0	0
(6)	Triangular prism	Triangular prism	5	9	6

CONCEPT MAP

Understanding Elementary Shapes

1. Types of Angles

- If the measure of an angle is smaller than a right angle, then it is known as an acute angle.
- An angle measuring greater than right angle and less than a straight angle is known as obtuse angle.
- An angle having its measure greater than a straight angle is called a reflex angle.

2. Triangles

- Triangles can be classified based on their angles and sides.
- A triangle having each of its angle acute is called an acute angled triangle.
- A triangle having one of its angle obtuse is called an obtuse angled triangle.
- A triangle having one of its angle right is called a right angled triangle.
- A triangle having all its sides equal is called an equilateral.
- A triangle having two sides equal is called an isosceles triangle.
- A triangle having all its sides unequal is called a scalene triangle.

5. 3-D shapes

- Solid shapes around us are known as 3-dimensional shapes. Each of its surface is called face.
- Two face meet at a line segment which is called an edge.
- The meeting point of three edges is called a vertex.

4. Polygons

- Polygons can be named based on the sides.
- A polygon bounded by 3 sides is called a triangle.
- A polygon bounded by 4 side is called a quadrilateral.
- A polygon bounded by 5 sides is called a pentagon.

3. Quadrilateral

- Quadrilaterals can be classified based on their properties.
- A quadrilateral in which one pair of opposite sides are parallel is called trapezium.
- A quadrilateral with each pair of opposite sides parallel is called a parallelogram.
- A parallelogram with all its sides equal is called a rhombus.
- A parallelogram with each angle as right angle is called a rectangle.
- A rectangle with all its side equal is called square.

MISCELLANEOUS SOLVED EXAMPLES

1. **Through what angle does the minute-hand of a clock rotate in 25 minutes.?**

Sol. We know that the minute-hand of a clock rotates through 360° in 60 minutes.

∴ In 60 minutes, it rotates through 360°.

In 1 minute, it rotates through $\left(\dfrac{360°}{60}\right) = 6°$

In 25 minutes, it rotates through $(6 \times 25)° = 150°$. Hence, the required angle is 150°.

2. **Find the angle measure between the hands of the clock in each figure. Also write it in term of a revolution.**

 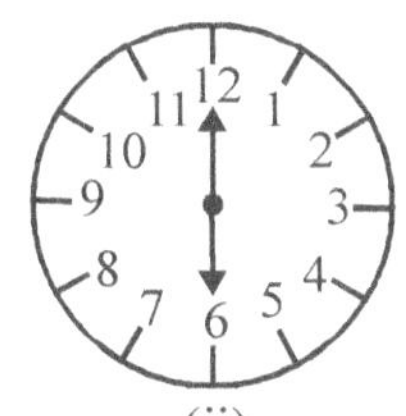

(i)   (ii)

Sol. (i) Angle formed is of 90° or 1/4 of a revolution.

(ii) Angle formed is of 180° or 1/2 of a revolution.

3. **A boy is standing facing towards the East. Find the kind of angle if he moves.**

(i) **Clockwise from East to South-West**

(ii) **Anticlockwise from East to South-East**

Sol. (i) Obtuse angle

(ii) Reflex angle

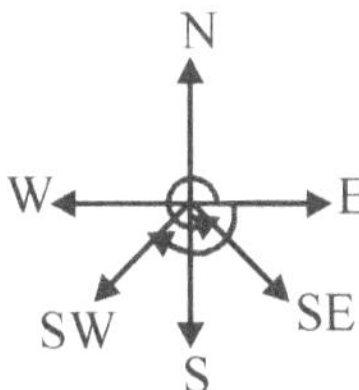

4. **The lengths of three sides of a triangle are given below. Identify the type of triangle on the basis of sides in each case giving reasons:**

(i) **5 cm, 8. 9 cm and 7.8 cm**

(ii) **7 cm, 4 cm and 4 cm**

(iii) **10 cm, 10 cm and 10 cm**

Sol. (i) It is a scalene triangle, since the lengths of its three sides are different.

(ii) It is an isosceles triangle, since two of its sides are equal to each other, each being equal to 4 cm.

(iii) It is an equilateral triangle, since all the three sides are equal to each other, each being equal to 10 cm.

5. **The three angles of a triangle are given below. Identify the type of triangle on the basis of angles in each case giving reasons:**

(i) **60°, 60° and 60°** (ii) **75°, 15° and 90°**

(iii) **130°, 20° and 30°** (iv) **45°, 95° and 40°**

Sol. (i) It is an acute-angled triangle, since each angle is acute, i.e. less than 90°.

(ii) It is a right-angled triangle, since one of the angles is 90°, *i.e.* a right angle.

(iii) It is an obtuse-angled triangle, since one of the angles, viz. 130° is an obtuse angle, *i.e.* greater than 90°.

(iv) It is an obtuse-angled triangle, since one of the angles, viz. 95° is an obtuse angle, *i.e.* greater than 90°.

6. **Classify the following polygons according to the number of sides:**

(i) 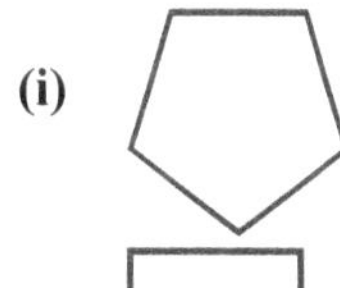 (ii) 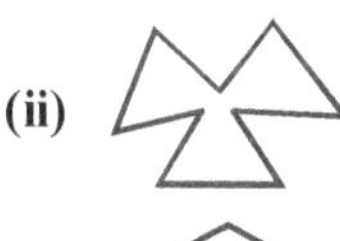

(iii) 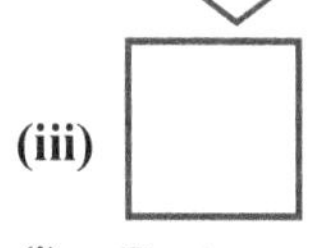 (iv) 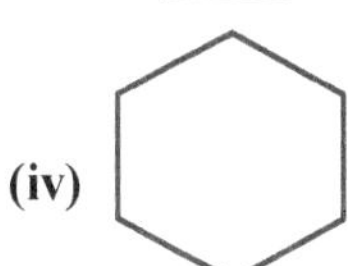

Sol. (i) Pentagon (ii) Nonagon

(iii) Quadrilateral (iv) Hexagon

7. **In the following figure of a cuboid, write all its:**

(i) **surfaces**

(ii) **edges**

(iii) **corners/ vertices**

Sol. (i) Surfaces : ABCG, AFEG, GCDE, BCDI, ABIF, FIDE.

(ii) Edges : AB, BC, CD, DE, EF, AF, AG, GC, FI, BI, DI, EG

(iii) Vertices : A, B, C, D, E, F, G, I.

1 EXERCISE

Fill in the Blanks :

DIRECTIONS : *Complete the following statements with an appropriate word / term to be filled in the blank space(s).*

1. A straight angle is made by two _________.
2. One complete angle measures to _________ complete revolution of hands of clock.
3. A reflex angle measure more than _________ but less than _________
4. Perpendicular lines are at _________ angle.
5. Opposite sides of square are _________ and _________.
6. Diagonals of rhombus _________ each other at right angle.
7. In rectangle, diagonals are _________.
8. Regular polygon have all sides _________ and all angles _________.
9. Sphere has only _________ curved surface and no _________ and _________ .
10. In an isosceles triangle, _____ angles are equal.

True / False :

DIRECTIONS : *Read the following statements and write your answer as true or false.*

1. One complete angle is equal to one complete revolution.
2. The standard unit of measuring an angle is degree.
3. The sum of two straight angle is reflex angle.
4. Every rectangle is a parallelogram.
5. Every rhombus is a parallelogram.
6. Every parallelogram is a square.
7. Road roller is an example of a cylinder.
8. Pyramid with rectangular base is also known as rectangular prism.
9. Coin is an example of sphere.
10. Square is a regular polygon.

Match the Columns :

DIRECTIONS : *Each question contains statements given in two columns which have to be matched. Statements (A, B, C, D, E) in column-I have to be matched with statements (p, q, r, s, t) in column-II.*

1.

	Column-I	Column-II
(A)	North to east clockwise	(p) Straight angle
(B)	North to south clockwise	(q) Right angle
(C)	North to west clockwise	(r) Obtuse angle
(D)	North to south-east clockwise	(s) Acute angle
(E)	North to north-east clockwise	(t) Reflex angle

Very Short Answer Questions:

DIRECTIONS : *Give answer in one word or one sentence.*

1. Measure the line segment using a ruler and a divider and write their lengths.

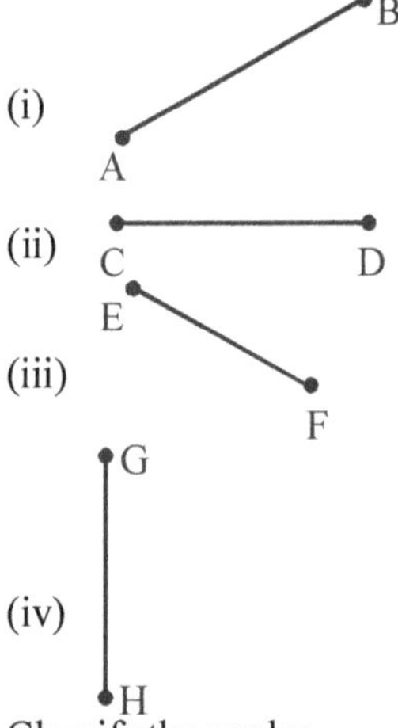

(i)

(ii)

(iii)

(iv)

2. Classify the angles.
   (i)   200°
   (ii) 35°
   (iii) 90°
   (iv) 125°
   (v)   280°
   (vi) 360°

3. How many degrees are there in

(i) $1\frac{1}{2}$ right angles? (ii) $\frac{1}{4}$ right angle?

(iii) $\frac{1}{2}$ straight angle? (iv) $\frac{1}{2}$ complete angle?

(v) $\frac{6}{9}$ right angle?

4. What part of a revolution does Rohan turn through if he is facing?
   (i) North and turn clockwise, to face east.
   (ii) West and turn clockwise, to face east.
   (iii) East and turn clockwise, all the way around back to east?

5. Radha and Geeta start from a common point O. Radha moves in the north direction and Geeta moves in the east direction. Draw their paths and name them as N and E, respectively. What kind of angle is formed between their paths?

6. What kind of angles are these?

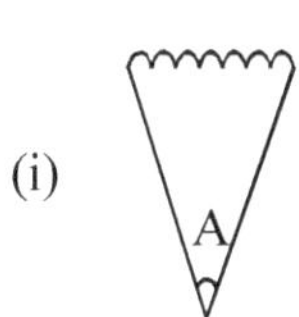

(i)   (ii)

7. Write the name of lines perpendicular to line segment XY.

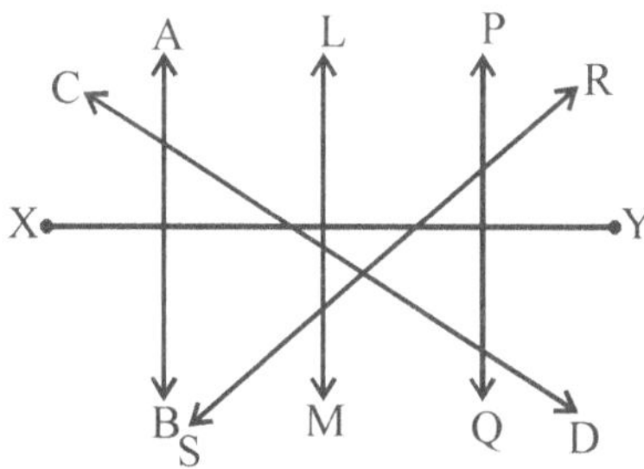

8. Name each of the following shapes-

(i) 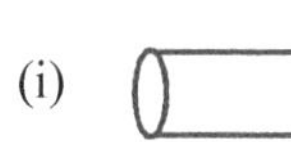   (ii) 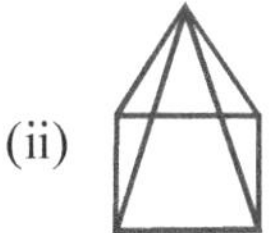

(iii) 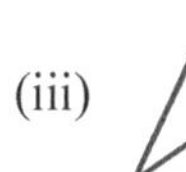   (iv) 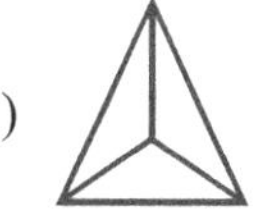

(v)    (vi) 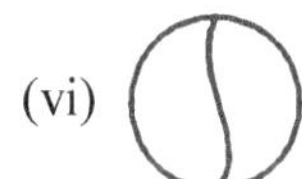

DIRECTIONS : *Give answer in 2-3 sentences.*

1. Look at the following triangles and complete the table:

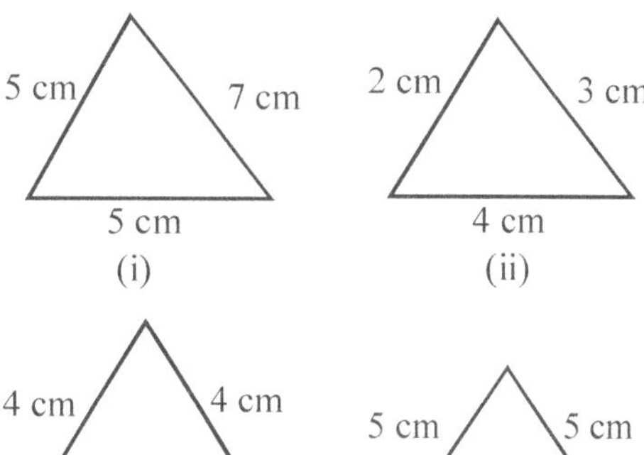

Triangle	No. of equal sides	Type of triangles
(i)		
(ii)		
(iii)		
(iv)		

2. Name the type of triangle.
   (i) In $\triangle ABC$, AB = 5 cm, BC = 4 cm and AC = 3 cm
   (ii) In $\triangle PQR$, PQ = 10 cm, QR = 10 cm and PR = 6.5 cm
   (iii) In $\triangle DEF$, $\angle D = 90°$
   (iv) In $\triangle XYZ$, $\angle X = 30°$, $\angle Y = 80°$ and $\angle Z = 70°$
   (v) In $\triangle CDE$, $\angle C = 40°$, $\angle D = 40°$ and $\angle E = 100°$
   (vi) In $\triangle LMN$, $\angle L = 90°$ and $\angle M = \angle N$

3. Classify the following shapes on the basis of their shapes-

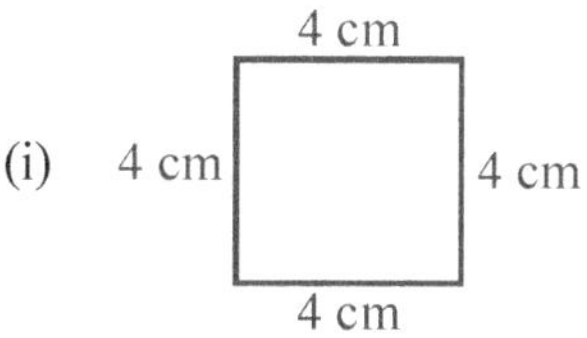

(ii) 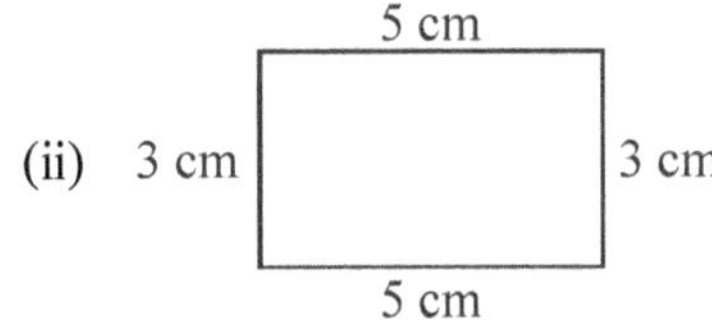

(iii) 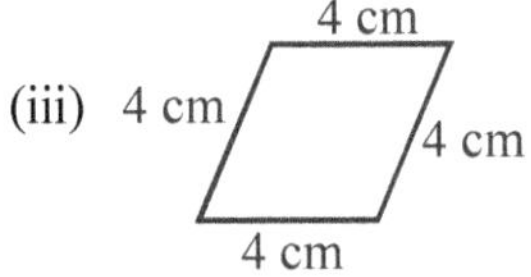

(iv) 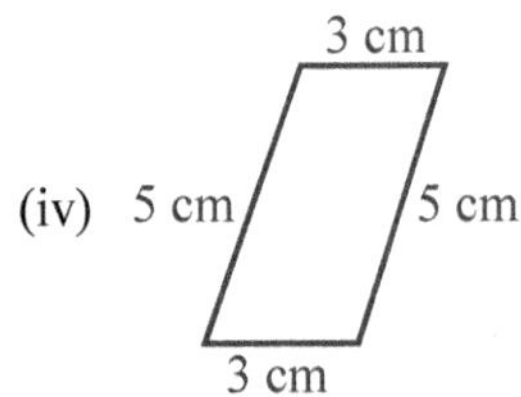

(ii) 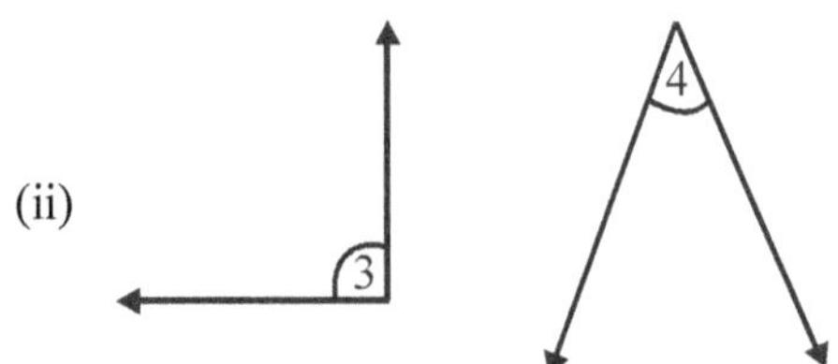

(iii)

(iv) 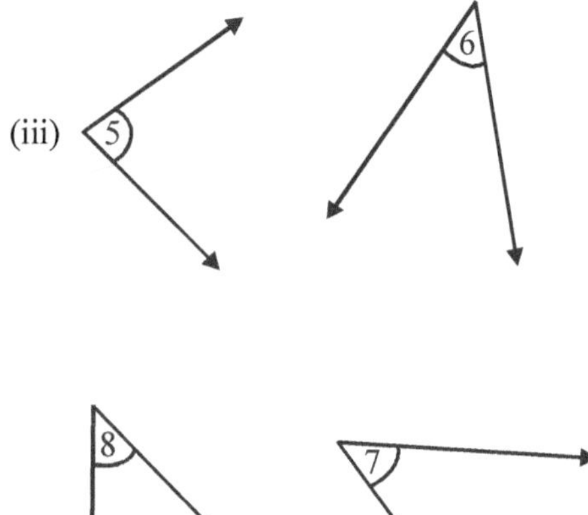

4. ABCD is a rectangle as shown below. Fill in the blanks:

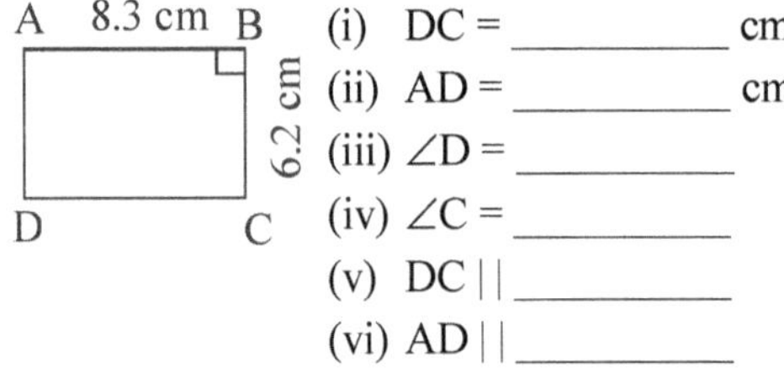

(i) DC = _________ cm

(ii) AD = _________ cm

(iii) ∠D = _________

(iv) ∠C = _________

(v) DC || _________

(vi) AD || _________

5. By measuring each angle by a protractor, determine which angle is greater in each of the following pairs of angles:

(i) 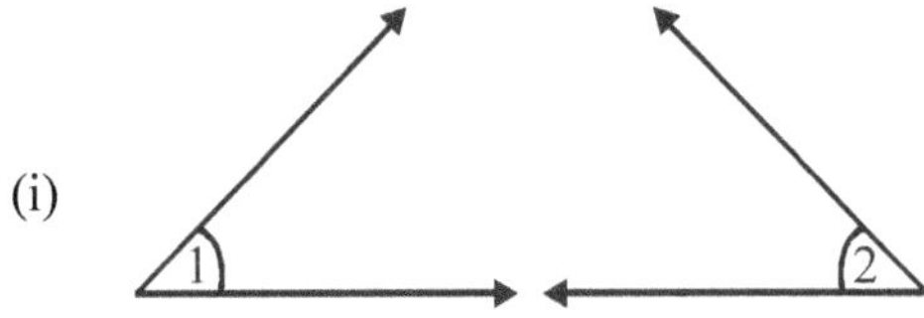

6. Classify the triangles as scalene, equilateral or isosceles in each of the following cases when their sides are given below:

(i)   1.2 cm, 3.5 cm and 2.7 cm

(ii)   8.5 cm, 7 cm and 8.5 cm

(iii) 13 cm, 24 cm and 30 cm

(iv) 100 cm, 100 cm and 100 cm

(v)   5.9 cm, 5 cm and 5.9 cm

(vi) 22 cm, 23 cm and 30 cm

Long Answer Questions :

DIRECTIONS : *Give answer in four to five sentences.*

1.   Complete the following:

Quadrilateral	Opposite sides		All sides Equal	Opposite Angles Equal	Diagonals	
	Parallel	Equal			Equal	Perpendicular
Parallelogram	Yes	Yes	No	Yes	No	No
Rectangle			No			
Square						Yes
Rhombus				Yes		
Trapezium		No				

2.   Fill in the table.

S. No.	Shape	Number of flat faces	Number of corners	Number of edges
(i)	Cuboid			
(ii)	Cube			
(iii)	Cylinder			
(iv)	Cone			
(v)	Sphere			
(vi)	Triangular prism			
(vii)	Square Pyramid			
(viii)	Tetrahedron			

2 EXERCISE

Text-Book Exercise :

1. If A, B, C are three points on a line such that AB = 5 cm, BC = 3 cm and AC = 8 cm, which one of them lies between the other two?

2. If B is the mid point of $\overline{AC}$ and C is the mid point of $\overline{BD}$, where A, B, C, D lie on a straight line, say why AB = CD?

3. Where will the hour hand of a clock stop if it starts
(i) from 6 and turns through 1 right angle?
(ii) from 8 and turns through 2 right angles?
(iii) from 10 and turns through 3 right angles?

4. Measure the angles given below using the protractor and write down the measure.

(i) 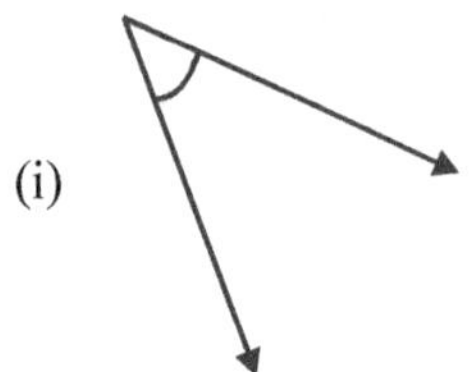

(ii) 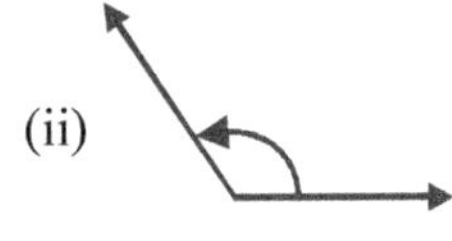

(iii) 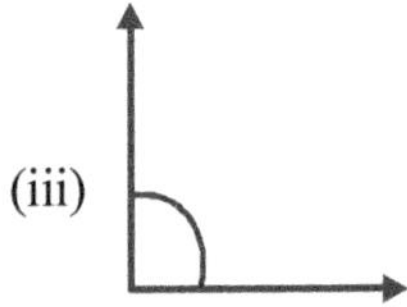

5. Find the measure of the angle shown in each figure. (First estimate with your eyes and then find the actual measure with a protractor).

(i) 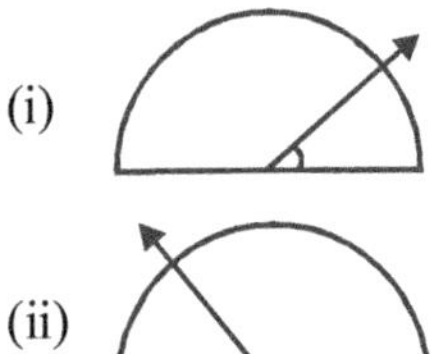

(ii)

(iii) 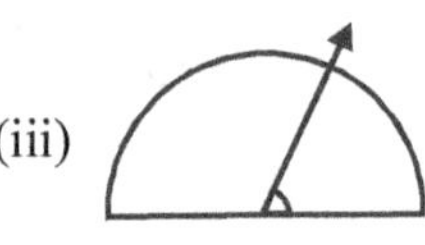

(iv) 

6. Measure and classify each angle:

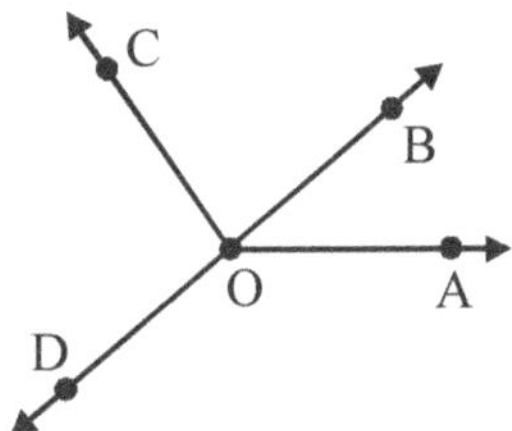

Angle	Measure	Type
∠AOB		
∠AOC		
∠BOC		
∠DOC		
∠DOA		
∠DOB		

7. Which of the following are models for perpendicular lines:
(i) The adjacent edges of a table top.
(ii) The lines of a railway track.
(iii) The line segments forming the letter 'L'.
(iv) The letter V.

8. Study the diagram. The line *l* is perpendicular to line *m*
(i) Is CE = EG?

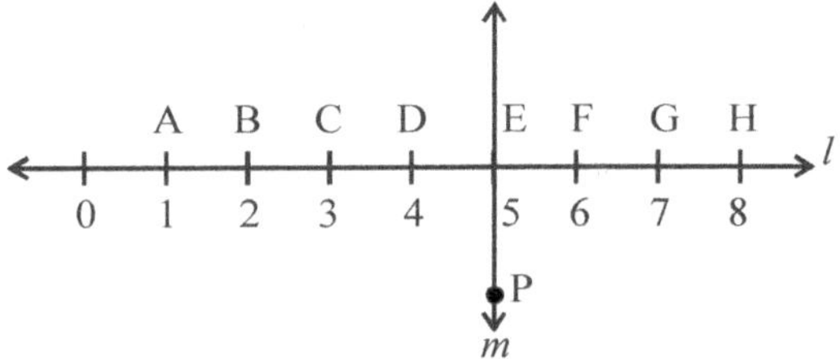

   (ii) Does PE bisect CG?

   (iii) Identify any two line segments for which PE is the perpendicular bisector.

   (iv) Are these true?

      (a) AC > FG

      (b) CD = GH

      (c) BC < EH

9. Name the type of following triangles:

   (i) Triangle with lengths of sides 7 cm, 8 cm and 9 cm.

   (ii) $\triangle$ABC with AB = 8.7 cm, AC = 7 cm and BC = 6 cm.

   (iii) $\triangle$PQR such that PQ = QR = PR = 5 cm.

   (iv) $\triangle$DEF with m $\angle$D = 90°

   (v) $\triangle$XYZ with m $\angle$Y = 90° and XY = YZ.

   (vi) $\triangle$LMN with m $\angle$L = 30°, m $\angle$M = 70° and m$\angle$N = 80°.

10. Given reason for the following:

   (i) A square can be thought of as a special rectangle.

   (ii) A rectangle can be thought of as a special parallelogram.

   (iii) A square can be thought of as a special rhombus.

   (iv) Squares, rectangles, parallelograms are all quadrilaterals.

   (v) Square is also parallelogram.

11. Draw a rough sketch of a regular hexagon. Connecting any three of its vertices, draw a triangle. Identify the type of the triangle you have drawn.

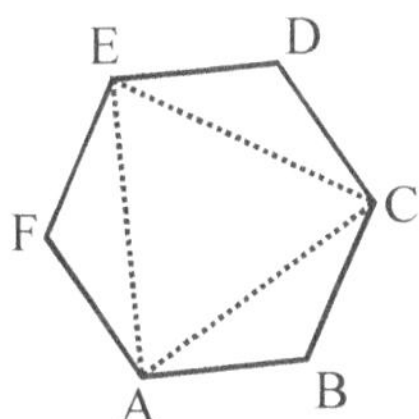

Exemplar Questions :

1. In figure PQ $\perp$ AB and PO = OQ. Is PQ the perpendicular bisector of line segment AB? Why or why not?

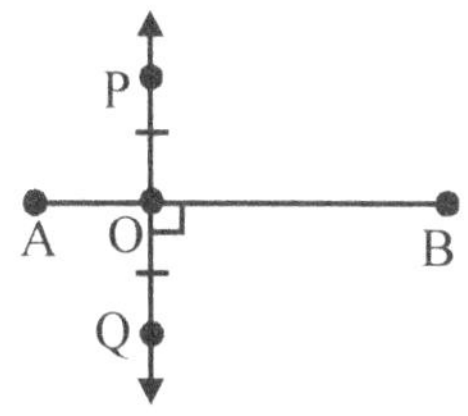

2. In figure if AC $\perp$ BD, then name all the right angles.

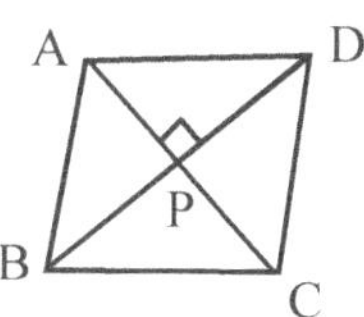

3. Write the measure of smaller angle formed by the hour and the minute hands of a clock at 7 O' clock. Also, write the measure of the other angle and also state what types of angles these are.

4. In figure, points A, B, C, D and E are collinear such that AB = BC = CD = DE. Then

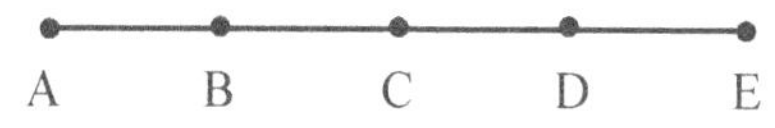

   (i) AD = AB + _____

   (ii) AD = AC + _____

   (iii) mid point of AE is _____

   (iv) mid point of CE is _____

   (v) AE = _____ × AB.

5. In figure

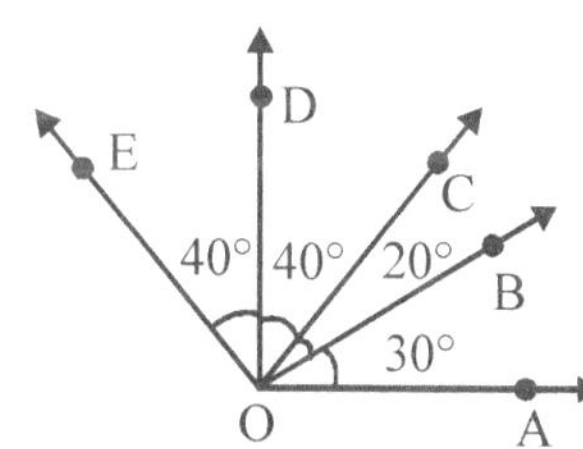

   (i) $\angle$AOD is a/an _____ angle

   (ii) $\angle$COA is a/an _____ angle

   (iii) $\angle$AOE is a/an _____ angle

6. In which of the following figures,

   (i) perpendicular bisector is shown?

   (ii) bisector is shown?

   (iii) only bisector is shown?

   (iv) only perpendicular is shown?

(a) 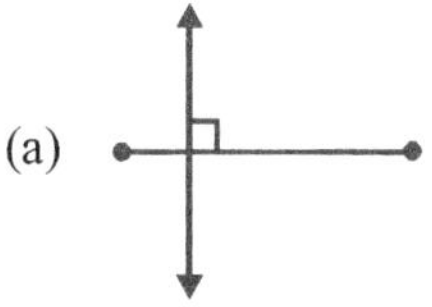

(b) 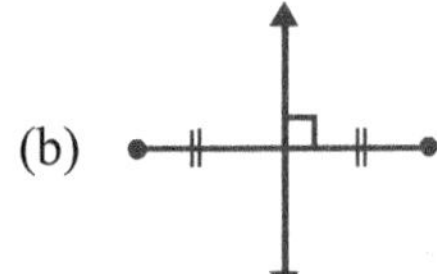

(c) 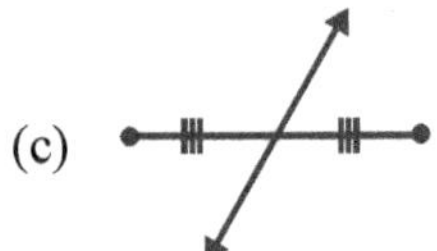

7.   In figure,

A   C   B

(i)   is AC + CB = AB?
(ii)   is AB + AC = CB?
(iii) is AB + BC = CA?

8.   What conclusion can be drawn from each part of figure if
(i)   DB is the bisector of ∠ADC?

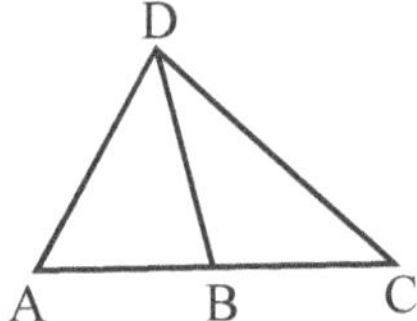

(ii) BD bisects ∠ABC?

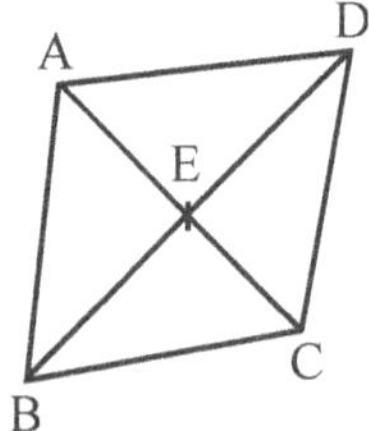

(iii) DC is the bisector of ∠ADB, CA ⊥ DA and CB ⊥ DB?

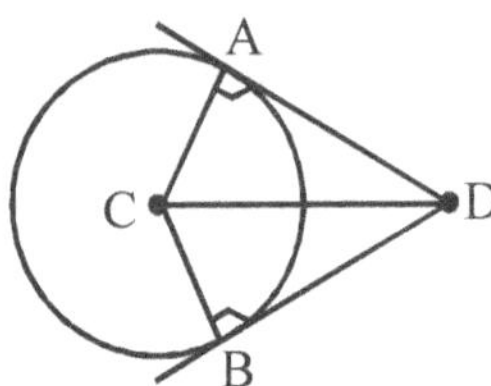

9.   An angle is said to be trisected, if it is divided into three equal parts. If in figure ∠BAC = ∠CAD = ∠DAE, how many trisectors are there for ∠BAE?

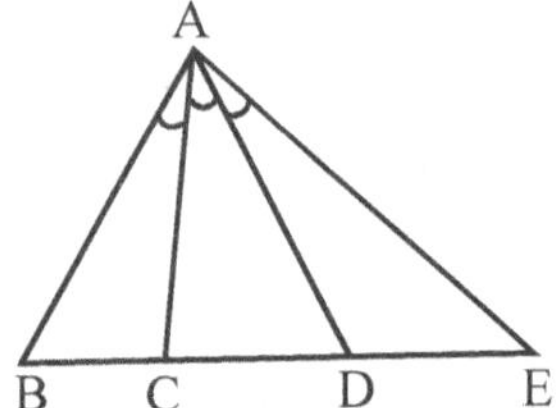

10.   Can we have two acute angles whose sum is
(i)   an acute angle? Why or why not?
(ii)   a right angle? Why or why not?
(iii) an obtuse angle? Why or why not?
(iv) a straight angle? Why or why not?
(v)   a reflex angle? Why or why not?

11.   Can we have two obtuse angles whose sum is
(i)   a reflex angle? Why or why not?
(ii)   a complete angle? Why or why not?

HOTS Questions :

1.   Which two solid shapes have been combined to form this solid shape?

2.   Which solid has sum of faces and vertices as 10?

3.   Give an example of each category from the figure given here.

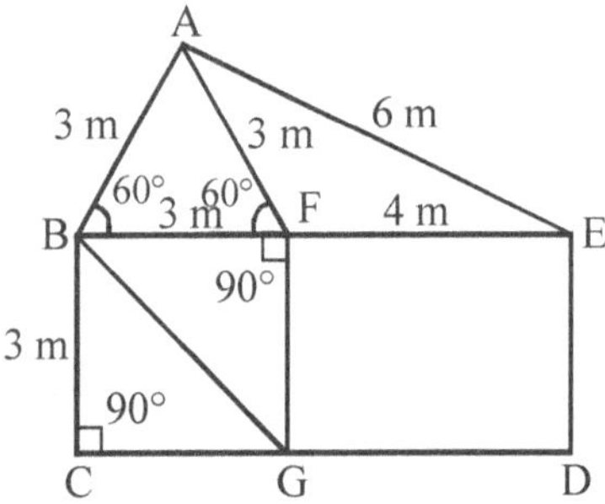

(i)   An equilateral triangle   △ABF
(ii)   A scalene triangle   _______
(iii) An acute-angled triangle   _______
(iv) A right-angled triangle _______
(v)   An obtuse-angled triangle _______
(vi) An isosceles triangle   _______

3 EXERCISE

Single Option Correct :

DIRECTIONS : *This section contains multiple choice questions. Each question has 4 choices (a), (b), (c) and (d) out of which ONLY ONE is correct.*

1. A quadrilateral is a rhombus but not a square if
   (a) its diagonals do not bisect each other
   (b) its diagonals are not perpendicular
   (c) opposite angles are not equal
   (d) the length of diagonals are not equal

2. In a square ABCD, the diagonals bisect at O. Then triangle AOB is.
   (a) an equilateral triangle.
   (b) an isosceles but not a right angled triangle.
   (c) a right angled but not an isosceles triangle.
   (d) an isosceles right angled triangle.

3. A meter is divided into 100 equal parts known as
   (a) centimetres   (b) decimetres
   (c) millimetres   (d) None of these

4. If initial and final position of ray forming an angle is in same direction after making a complete rotation then angle formed is a
   (a) zero angle   (b) complete angle
   (c) right angle   (d) straight angle

5. If a boy turns 270° clockwise from north then he will finally facing towards.
   (a) North   (b) South
   (c) East   (d) West

6. Irregular polygon has-
   (a) all sides of equal length
   (b) all angles of equal measure
   (c) All sides and angle of difference measure
   (d) None of these

7. A nanogon has
   (a) 6 sides   (b) 7 sides
   (c) 8 sides   (d) 9 sides

8. Cylinder has-
   (a) no edges   (b) 2 edges
   (c) 1 edge   (d) None of these

More Than One Option Correct :

DIRECTIONS : *This section contains multiple choice questions. Each question has 4 choices (a), (b), (c) and (d) out of which ONE or MORE may be correct.*

1. If the sum of two angles is greater than 180°, then which of the following is possible for the two angles?
   (a) One obtuse angle and one acute angle.
   (b) One reflex angle and one acute angle.
   (c) Two obtuse angles.
   (d) Two right angles.

2. Which of the following statement (s) is/are true?
   (a) A parallelogram in which two adjacent angles are equal is a rectangle.
   (b) A quadrilateral in which both pairs of opposite angles are equal is parallelogram.
   (c) In a parallelogram the number of acute angles is zero (or) two.
   (d) None of these

3. Which of the following statement (s) is/are false?
   (a) In a trapezium the diagonals bisect each other.
   (b) In a rectangle diagonals intersect at right angles.
   (c) The diagonals of a rhombus are equal.
   (d) None of these.

4. Which of the following properties are not true for a parallelogram?
   (a) Its diagonals are equal.
   (b) Its diagonals are perpendicular to each other.
   (c) The diagonals bisects each other
   (d) None of these

5. Which of the following statements is/are true?
(a) Every parallelogram is a quadrilateral
(b) Every rectangle is a parallelogram
(c) Every rhombus is a parallelogram
(d) Every trapezium is a parallelogram

Assertion & Reason :

DIRECTIONS : *Each of these questions contains an Assertion followed by Reason. Read them carefully and answer the question on the basis of following options. You have to select the one that best describes the two statements.*

(a) If both **Assertion** and **Reason** are **correct** and Reason is the **correct explanation** of Assertion.

(b) If both **Assertion** and **Reason** are correct, but Reason is **not the correct explanation** of Assertion.

(c) If **Assertion** is **correct** but **Reason** is **incorrect**.

(d) If **Assertion** is **incorrect** but **Reason** is **correct**.

1. **Assertion:** A rhombus is a polygon.
Reason: A polygon is a closed figure with more than three sides.

2. **Assertion :** Rectangle is not a parallelogram
Reason: The opposite sides of a rectangle are parallel.

3. **Assertion:** A football has a shape of a sphere.
Reason: A ball-like shape is called a sphere.

Passage Based Questions :

DIRECTIONS : *Study the given passage(s) and answer the following questions.*

PASSAGE-I
Faces : The flat surface of any solid is called face.
Edges : Line segments where two faces meet is called an edge.
Vertices : Corners of the solid are its vertices

1. Find the number of faces, edges and vertices respectively of rectangular prism.
(a) 6, 12, 10   (b) 6, 8, 10
(c) 4, 6, 8   (d) 6, 12, 8

2. Find the number of faces and edges respectively of tetrahedron.
(a) 4, 4   (b) 4, 6
(c) 6, 4   (d) 6, 8

3. Find the number of edges and vertices respectively of octahedron.
(a) 12, 6   (b) 6, 12
(c) 8, 12   (d) 12, 8

Integer Type Questions :

DIRECTIONS : *Answer the following questions. The answer to each of the question is a single digit integer, ranging from 0 to 9.*

1. The number of obtuse angles in the figure is

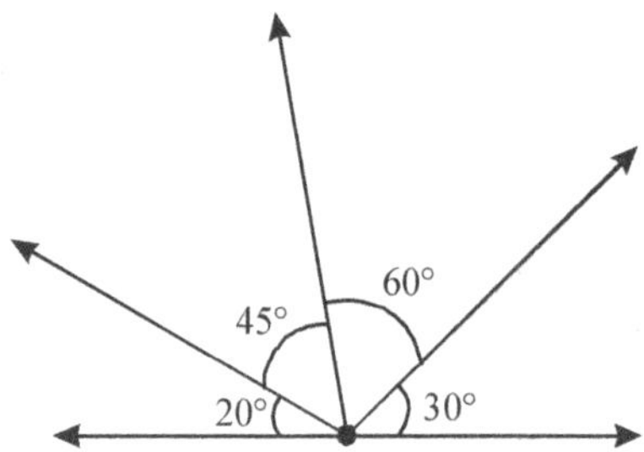

2. In fig. $AB = BC$ and $AD = BD = DC$.
The number of isoscles triangles in the figure is

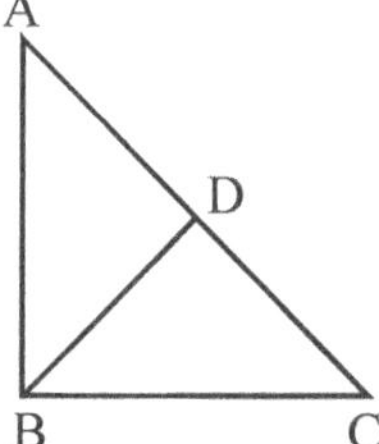

3. Number of line segments used in the figure of a tetrahedron is

4. Number of line segments possible with three collinear points is

5. The number of diagonals of a triangle is

Multiple Matching Question :

DIRECTIONS : *Following question has four statements (A, B, C and D, E) given in Column-I and five statements (p, q, r, s, t) in Column-II. Any given statement in Column-I can have correct matching with one or more statement(s) given in Column-II.*

1.   Match the following

	Column-I		**Column-II**
(A)	All sides are equal	(p)	Parallelogram
(B)	Diagonals bisect each other	(q)	Square
(C)	Only opposite angles are equal	(r)	Kite
(D)	Diagonals are perpendicular to each other	(s)	Rectangle
(E)	Each angle is a right angle	(t)	Rhombus

SOLUTIONS

Brief Explanations of Selected Questions

1 EXERCISE

Fill in the Blanks :

1. right angle
2. one
3. 180°, 360°
4. 90°
5. equal and parallel
6. bisect
7. equal
8. equal, equal
9. One, edge, vertex
10. Two

True / False :

1. True
2. True
3. False
4. True
5. True
6. False
7. True
8. False
9. False
10. True

Match the Columns :

1. (A) → (q); (B) → (p); (C) → (t); (D) → (r); (E) → (s)

Very Short Answer Questions:

1. (i) AB = 2.5 cm
   (ii) CD = 2.3 cm
   (iii) EF = 1.8 cm
   (iv) GH = 2.1 cm
2. (i) Reflex
   (ii) Acute
   (iii) Right
   (iv) Obtuse
   (v) Reflex
   (vi) Complete
3. (i) 135°
   (ii) $22\frac{1}{2}^{\circ}$
   (iii) 90°
   (iv) 180°
   (v) 60°

4. (i) $\frac{1}{4}$ (ii) $\frac{1}{2}$ (iii) 1
5. 90°
6. (i) Acute (ii) Obtuse
7. AB, LM, PQ
8. (i) Cylinder
   (ii) Square pyramid
   (iii) Triangular pyramid
   (iv) Cuboid
   (v) Cone
   (vi) Sphere

Short Answer Questions :

1. (i) 2, Isosceles triangle
   (ii) No, Scalene triangle
   (iii) 2, Isosceles triangle
   (iv) 3, Equilateral triangle
2. (i) Scalene triangle
   (ii) Isosceles triangle
   (iii) Right angled triangle
   (iv) Acute angled triangle
   (v) Obtuse angled triangle
   (vi) Isosceles right angled triangle
3. (i) Square (ii) Rectangle
   (iii) Rhombus (iv) Parallelogram
4. (i) 8.3 cm (ii) 6.2 cm
   (iii) 90° (iv) 90°
   (v) AB (vi) BC
5. (i) $\angle 2 = \angle 1$ (ii) $\angle 3 > \angle 4$
   (iii) $\angle 5 > \angle 6$ (iv) $\angle 8 < \angle 7$
6. (i) Scalene triangle
   (ii) Isosceles triangle
   (iii) Scalene triangle
   (iv) Equilateral triangle
   (v) Isosceles triangle
   (vi) Scalene triangle.

Long Answer Questions :

1.

Quadrilateral	Opposite sides		All sides Equal	Opposite Angles Equal	Diagonals	
	Parallel	Equal			Equal	Perpendicular
Parallelogram	Yes	Yes	No	Yes	No	No
Rectangle	Yes	Yes	No	Yes	Yes	No
Square	Yes	Yes	Yes	Yes	Yes	Yes
Rhombus	Yes	Yes	Yes	Yes	No	Yes
Trapezium	1 pair	No	No	No	No	No

2.

S. No.	Shape	Number of flat faces	Number of corners	Number of edges
(i)	Cuboid	6	8	12
(ii)	Cube	6	8	12
(iii)	Cylinder	2	0	2 (Curved edges)
(iv)	Cone	1	1	1 (Curved edge)
(v)	Sphere	0	0	0
(vi)	Triangular prism	5	6	9
(vii)	Square Pyramid	5	5	8
(viii)	Tetrahedron	4	4	6

2 EXERCISE

Text-Book Exercise :

1. $\because$ AB = 5 cm, BC = 3 cm
But AC = 8 cm
$\therefore$ AB + BC = 5 cm + 3 cm = 8 cm
$\therefore$ The point B lies between A and C.

2.

A   B   C   D

Since, B is the mid point of AC
AB = BC ...... (i)
Similarly
BC = CD ...... (ii)
From (i) and (ii)
We have AB = CD.

3. (i) Starting from 6 and turning through 1 right angle, The hour hand will reach at 9.

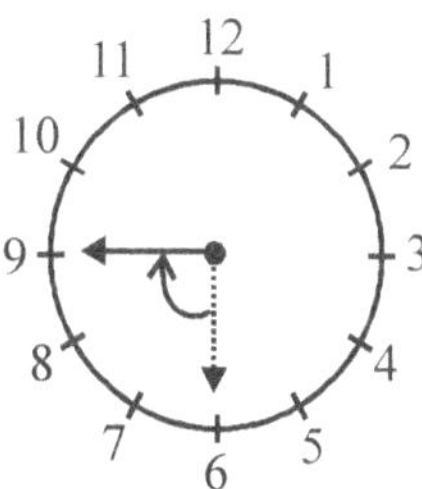

(ii) Starting from 8 and turning through 2 right angles, the hour hand will reach at 2.

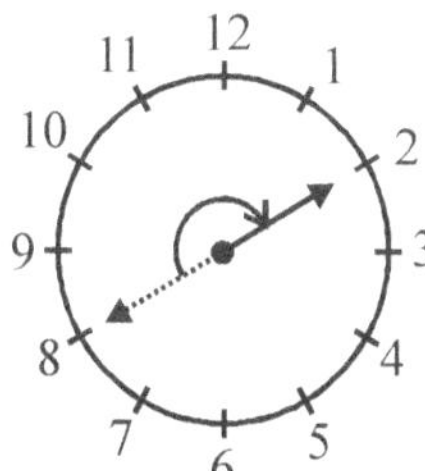

(iii) Starting from 10 and turning through 3 right angles, the hour hand will reach at 7.

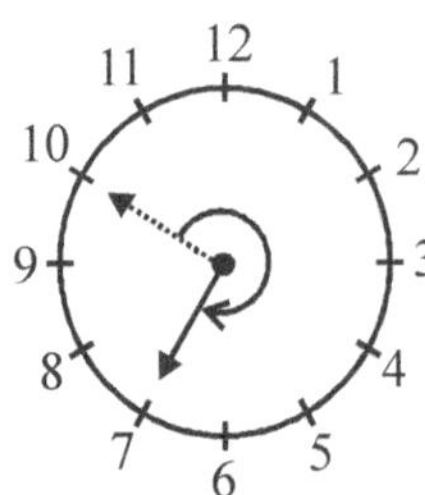

4. (i) 45° (ii) 125° (iii) 90°
5. (i) 40° (ii) 130°
(iii) 65° (iv) 135°

6.

Angle	Measure	Type
∠AOB	40°	Acute angle
∠AOC	125°	Obtuse angle
∠BOC	85°	Acute angle
∠DOC	95°	Obtuse angle
∠DOA	140°	Obtuse angle
∠DOB	180°	Straight angle

7. (i) Yes, (ii) No,
(iii) Yes (iv) No
8. (i) EC = 2 units, EG = 2 units
∴ CE = EG
(ii) Yes, PE bisects CG
(iii) $\overline{BH}$ and $\overline{DF}$
(iv) (a) Yes (b) Yes (c) Yes
9. (i) The triangle is a scalene triangle.
(ii) ΔABC is a scalene triangle.
(iii) ΔPQR is an equilateral triangle.
(iv) ΔDEF is a right angled triangle.
(v) ΔXYZ is an isosceles right angled triangle.
(vi) ΔLMN is an acute angled triangle.
10. (i) A square can be considered a rectangle having all of its sides equal.
(ii) A rectangle can be considered a parallelogram having each of its angles equal to 90°.
(ii) A square can be considered a rhombus having each angle equal to right angle.
(iv) Quadrilateral is a polygon having four sides. Squares, rectangles, parallelograms are four-sided polygons.
(v) The opposite sides of a square are parallel, therefore a square is also a parallelogram.

11. ABCDEF is a regular hexagon.
Joining its alternate vertices A, C and E we get ΔACE, which is a regular triangle.
Thus, the triangle so formed is an equilateral triangle.

1. PQ is not the perpendicular bisector of line segment AB, because AO ≠ BO.[Note: AB is the perpendicular bisector of line segment PQ].
2. There are four right angles. ∠APD, ∠APB, ∠BPC and ∠CPD.
3. Measure of the required angle = 30° × 5° = 150°
Measure of the other angle = 360° − 150° = 210°
Angle of measure 150° is an obtuse angle and that of 210° is a reflex angle.
4. (i) BD (ii) CD (iii) C
(iv) D (v) 4
5. (i) Right (ii) acute
(iii) obtuse
6. (i) (b) (ii) (b) and (c)
(iii) (c) (iv) (a)
7. (i) Yes (ii) No
(iii) No
8. (i) ∠ADB = ∠CDB (ii) ∠ABD = ∠CBD
(iii) ∠ADC = ∠BDC, ∠CAD = 90°, ∠CBD = 90°
9. Two, AC and AD
10. (i) Yes. The sum of two acute angles may be less than a right angle.
(ii) Yes. The sum of two acute angles may be equal to a right angle.
(iii) Yes. The sum of two acute angles may be more than a right angle.
(iv) No. The sum of two acute angles is always less than 180°.
(v) No. The sum of two acute angles is always less than 180°.
11. (i) Yes. The sum of two obtuse angles is always greater than 180°.
(ii) No. The sum of two obtuse angles is always greater than 180°, but less than 360°.

1. A rectangular pyramid and a cuboid.
2. Square pyramid
3. (i) Δ ABF (ii) Δ AFE
(iii) Δ ABF (iv) Δ BCG
(v) Δ AFE (vi) Δ BFG

3 EXERCISE

Single Option Correct :

1. **(d)**
2. **(d)** Since diagonals of a square are equal and bisect at right angles
3. **(a)** 4. **(b)** 5. **(d)** 6. **(c)** 7. **(d)**
8. **(b)**

More Than One Option Correct :

1. **(a, b, c)**
2. **(a, b, c)**
3. **(a, b, c)**
4. **(a, b)**
5. **(a, b, c)** Every trapezium is not a parallelogram.

Assertion & Reason :

1. **(c)** A polygon is a closed figure with three and more than three sides.
   Assertion: True, **Reason**: False
2. **(d)** Opposite side of a rectangle are parallel, so it is a parallelogram.
   Assertion: False, **Reason**: True
3. **(a)** **Assertion**: True, **Reason**: True and Reason is correct explanation of Assertion.

Passage Based Questions :

1. **(d)**
2. **(b)**
3. **(a)**

Integer Type Questions :

1. **(3)** 2. **(3)** 3. **(6)** 4. **(3)**
5. **(0)**

Multiple Matching Question :

1. (A) → (q, t); (B) → (p, q, s, t); (C) → (p, t); (D) → (q, r, t); (E) → (q, s)

Chapter 6

Integers

INTEGERS

We know that 1, 2, 3, 4 ...... are natural numbers and when we include 0 (zero) to the collection of natural numbers we get whole numbers. Now, if negative numbers are included to whole numbers, we get a new set of numbers called integers.

Integers 1, 2, 3, 4 ...... are known as positive integers, while integers $-1, -2, -3, -4,$ ...... are known as negative integers. 0 is neither negative nor positive integer.

REPRESENTATION OF INTEGERS ON NUMBER LINE

Draw a line and mark a point on it as 0. Now, mark some points at equal distances on the right and left of 0.
The points to the right of zero represent positive integers. Mark them as $+1, +2, +3,$ .... or simply as 1, 2, 3, ... etc
The points to the left of zero represent negative integers. Mark them as $-1, -2, -3,$ ....
The points marked as -1 and $+1$ are equidistant from 0 but are in opposite direction. Similarly, the points marked as 2 and -2 are equidistant from 0 but are in opposite direction.

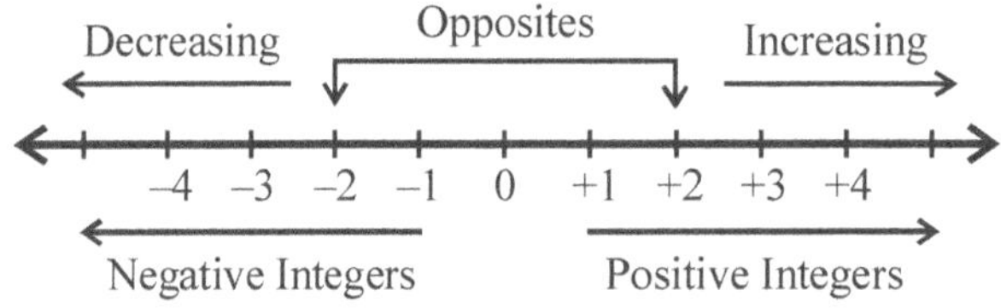

ABSOLUTE VALUE OF AN INTEGER

The absolute value of an integer is its numerical value regardless of its sign. Absolute value of an integer is written by drawing two vertical lines on either side of the integer.

For example: Absolute value of $+2 = |+2| = 2$

Absolute value of $-6 = |-6| = 6$

ORDERING OF INTEGERS

Any number lying on the right of the number line is greater than any other number lying on its left and the number lying on the left is smaller than that on the right.

Some Important facts

1. Every positive integer is greater than every negative integer. e.g. $6 > -1$.
2. Zero is less than every positive integer e.g. $0 < 3$.
3. Zero is greater than every negative integer e.g. $0 > -3$.
4. Every integer has its successor as well as predecessor.
5. Greater the integer the lesser is its opposite, e.g. $5 > 3$ but $-5 < -3$.

> **NOTE:** The smallest positive integer is 1 and the greatest negative integer is –1.

ADDITION OF INTEGERS ON NUMBER LINE

We have learnt how to add two whole numbers on the number line. We shall extend the same method for addition of integers on number line. When we add a positive integer we move to the right and when we add a negative integer we move to the left on the number line.

For example: adding – 2 to a number means moving 2 steps to the left of the number.

adding + 2 to a number means moving 2 steps to the right of the number.

ILLUSTRATION : 1

Add + 5 and – 4 on the number line.

SOLUTION :

On the number line we start from 0 and move 5 steps to the right to reach a point A. Now, starting from A, move 4 steps to the left to reach a point B as shown below :

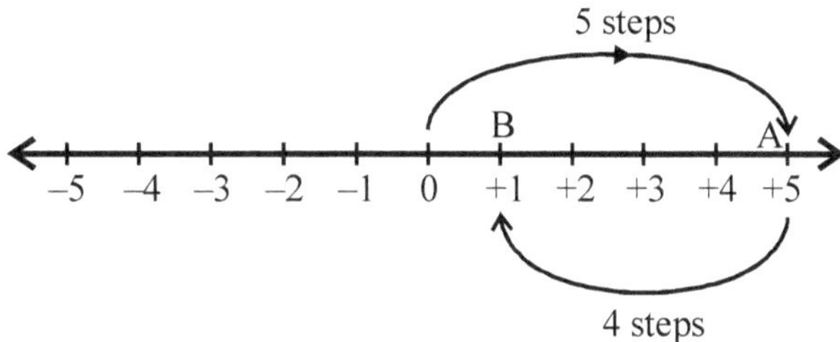

and B represents the integer 1.

$\therefore \quad 5 + (– 4) = 1$

ILLUSTRATION : 2

Add + 3 and – 7 on the number line.

SOLUTION :

On the number line, we start from 0 and move 3 steps to the right to reach point A. Now starting from A, move 8 steps to the left to reach a point B as shown below:

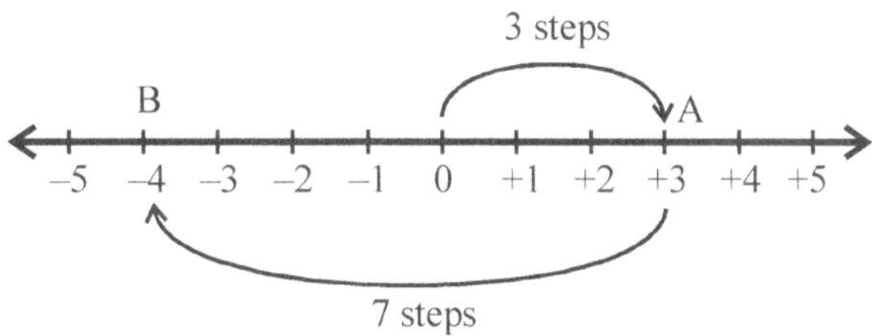

Here, B represents – 7.

$\therefore \quad + 3 + (– 7) = – 4$

ADDITION OF INTEGERS

Rules for addition of integers

Rule I : Adding integers with like signs :

> For adding integers with like signs (both positive or both negative), we add their numerical values, and place the common sign before the sum.

For example :(i) $(+2) + (+10) = (+12)$ (ii) $(-3) + (-7) = (-10)$

Rule II : Adding integers with unlike signs :

> For adding integers of unlike signs, we find the difference of their numerical values and give the result the sign of the integer with the greater numerical value.

For example : (i) $(+13) + (-8) = (+5)$ (ii) $(+5) + (-18) = (-13)$

ILLUSTRATION : 3

Add the following:

(i) $20 + (-8)$ (ii) $(-70) + (-55)$

SOLUTION :

(i) Since the integers have unlike signs, we shall subtract their absolute values and give the sum (+)ve sign.

$$20 + (-8) = 12$$

(ii) Since, integers have like signs, add the absolute values and give the sum the same sign.

$$= (-70) + (-55) = -125$$

Additive identity

When 0 is added to any integer, the result is the integer itself. So, 0 is called the additive identity of integers.

e.g.

(i) $7 + 0 = 7$ (ii) $0 + (-3) = -3$

Additive inverse

If we add the negative of a number to the number itself, the result is 0. The number and its negative are called the additive inverse of each other. **For example:**

(i) $2 + (-2) = 0$ (ii) $4 + (-4) = 0$

In the above examples, 2 and (-2), 4 and (-4) are the additive inverse of each other.

> **NOTE :** Additive inverse of 0 is 0.

SUBTRACTION OF INTEGERS ON NUMBER LINE

We know that subtraction is the inverse of addition. For example, to subtract 3 from 8 is same as to find a number which is added to 3 and gives 8.

i.e. $8 - 3 = 5 \Rightarrow 3 + 5 = 8$

Let us use the number line. To subtract 3 from 8, we start from position of 8, and come back 3 steps and reach at 5.

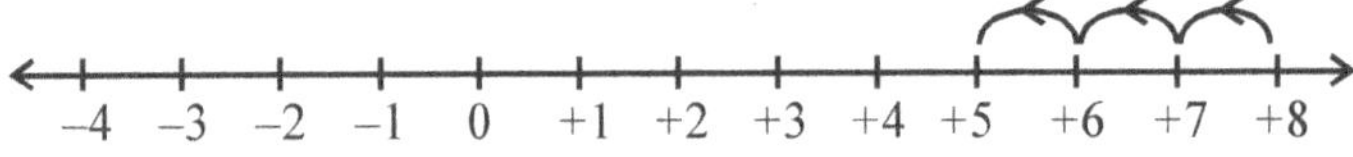

ILLUSTRATION : 4

Use number line to find $7 - (-4)$.

SOLUTION :

$$7 - (-4) = 7 + \text{(additive inverse of } -4)$$
$$= 7 + 4$$

On number line, starting from O move 7 steps to the right to reach +7 and then move 4 steps to the right to reach +11 as shown below.

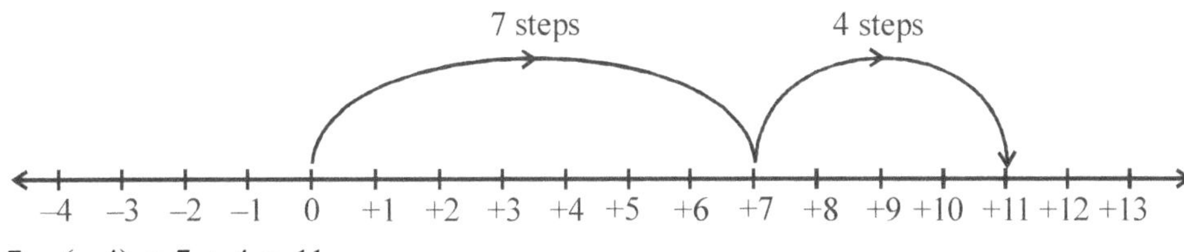

$\therefore 7 - (- 4) = 7 + 4 = 11$

SUBTRACTION OF INTEGERS

Rule for subtraction of integers

To subtract one integer from another, we add the additive inverse of the integer that to be subtracted to the other integer.

In other words, for nay two integers a and b,

$a - b = a + $ (*additive inverse of b*)

ILLUSTRATION : 5

Subtract :

(i) – 4 from 2   **(ii) 5 from – 3**   **(iii)   – 4 from 3**   **(iv)   20 from 35**

SOLUTION :

(i) – 4 from 2
$2 - (- 4) = 2 + $ (additive inverse of –4) $ = 2 + (+ 4) = 6$

(ii) 5 from – 3
$- 3 - (5) = -3 + $ (additive inverse of 5) $ = - 3 + (- 5) = - 8$

(iii) – 4 from – 3
$- 4 - (- 3) = - 4 + $ (additive inverse of – 3) $ = - 4 + (+ 3) = - 1$

(iv) 20 from 35
$35 - 20 = 35 + $ (additive inverse of 20) $ = 35 + (- 20) = 15$

CONCEPT MAP

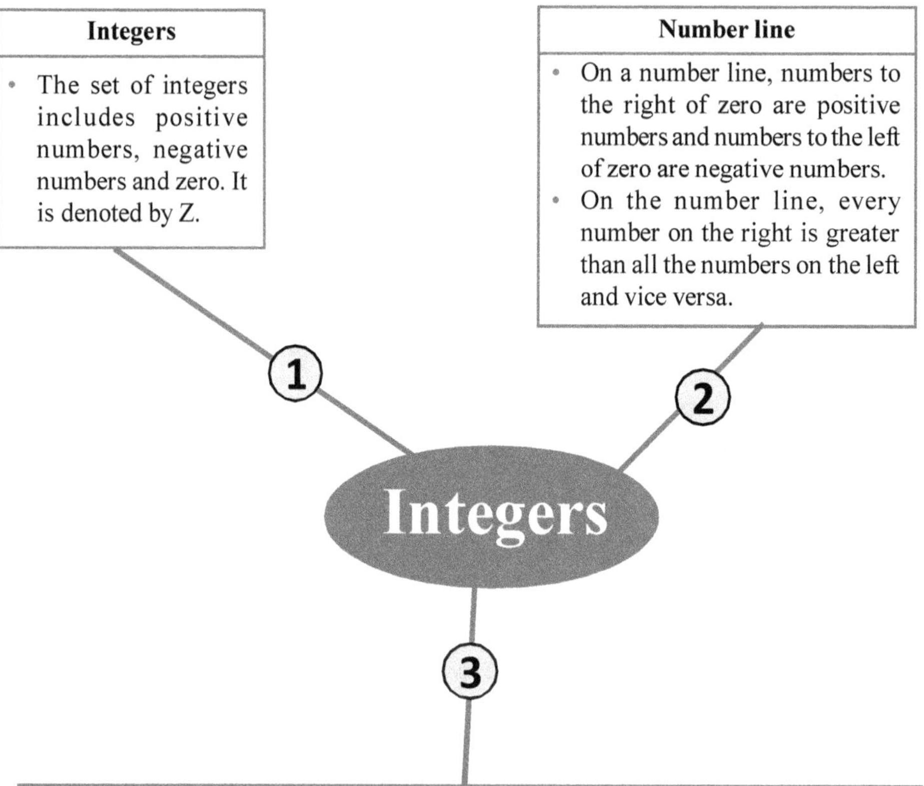

Operations on integers

- For adding two integers of same sign, we add their numerical value and put the same sign before the sum.
- When we add two positive integers, we get a positive integer.
  e.g. $(+5) + (+3) = +8$
- When we add two negative integers, we get a negative integer.
  e.g. $(-4) + (-3) = -7$
- For adding two integers of unlike sign, we subtract their numerical value and put the sign of the integer of greater numerical value. e.g. $(+5) + (-2) = +3$, $(-6) + (+1) = -5$
- If the sum of two integers is 0, then they are additive inverse of each other.
- The subtraction of an integer is same as addition of its additive inverse.

MISCELLANEOUS
SOLVED EXAMPLES

1. **Using the number line, write the integer which is :**
   (i) 4 more than 3 **(ii)** 5 less than 2
   (iii) 8 more than –9 **(iv)** 4 less than –3

Sol. **(i)** We want to obtain integer 4 more than 3. So, we start from 3 and proceed 4 units to the right to obtain 7

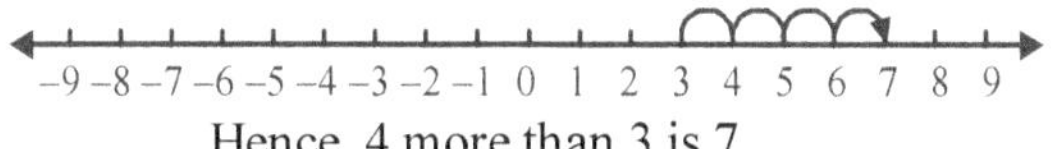

   Hence, 4 more than 3 is 7.

   (ii) Here we want to know the integer 5 less than 2. So, we start from 2 and proceed 5 units to the left of it to obtain –3

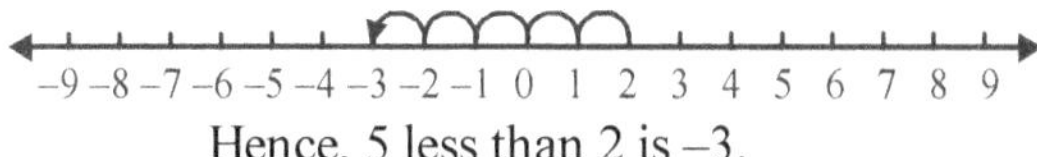

   Hence, 5 less than 2 is –3.

   (iii) Here we want to know the integer 8 more than –9. So, we start from –9 on the number line and move through 8 units to the right of it to obtain –1

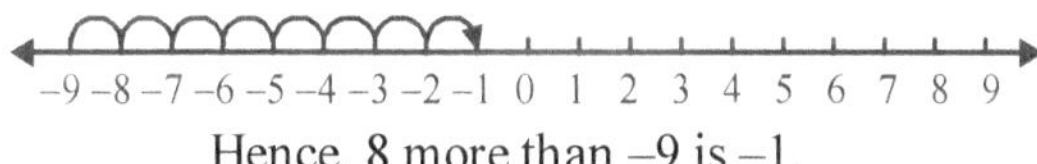

   Hence, 8 more than –9 is –1.

   (iv) Here we want to know the integer 4 less than –3. So, we start from –3 on the number line and move through 4 units to the left of it to obtain –7

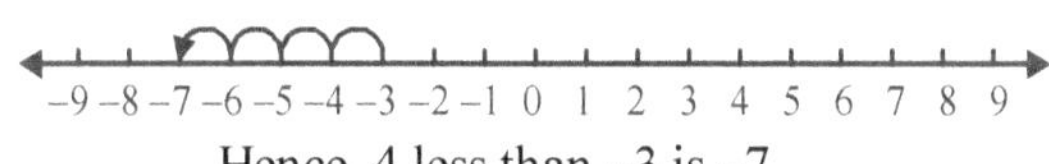

   Hence, 4 less than –3 is –7.

2. **Arrange the following numbers**
   0, –3, 5, –7, 1, –2
   (i) in increasing order
   (ii) in decreasing order

Sol. **(i)** On number line, a number on the right is greater than a number on the left.
   The numbers in increasing order (starting from the smallest) are :
   –7, –3, –2, 0, 1, 5.

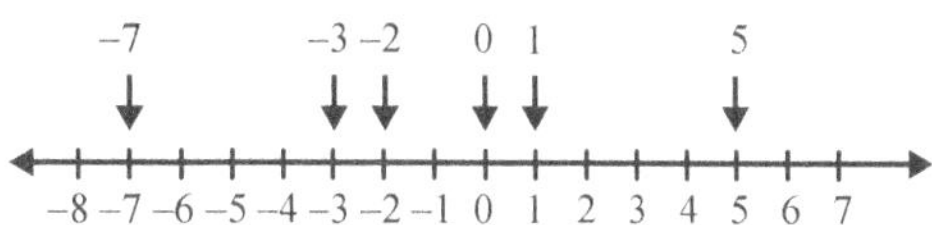

   (ii) The numbers in decreasing order (starting from the largest) are :
   5, 1, 0, –2, –3, –7

3. **Evaluate :**
   (i) $|-8|+|12|$ **(ii)** $|-9|+|-13|$
   (ii) $|-10|-|4|$ **(iv)** $|-17|-|-12|$

Sol. Clearly, we have
   (i) $|-8|+|12| = 8 + 12 = 20$
   (ii) $|-9|+|-13| = 9 + 13 = 22$
   (iii) $|-10|-|4| = 10 - 4 = 6$
   (iv) $|-17|-|-12| = 17 - 12 = 5.$

4. **Use number line to find (–3) + (+4).**

Sol. Starting from 0 on the number line move 3 steps to the left and from there move 4 steps to the right to reach (+1), as shown below.

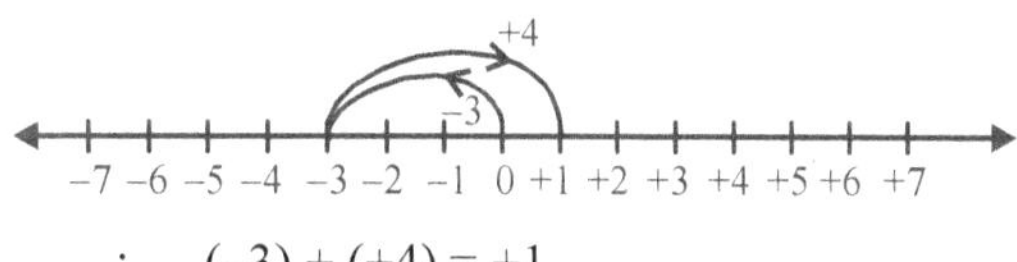

   $\therefore$ $(-3) + (+4) = +1$

5. **Use number line to find (–3) + (–2).**

Sol. Starting from 0 on the number line move 3 steps to the left and from there move 2 steps to the left to reach (–5), as shown below.

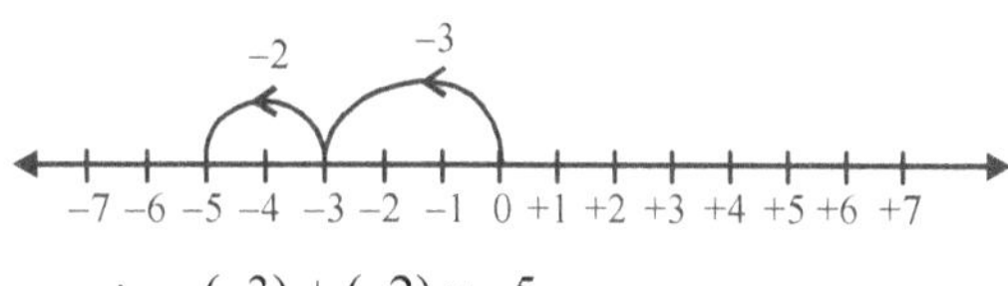

   $\therefore$ $(-3) + (-2) = -5$

6. **Find the sum of the following :**
   (i) 2 and 5 **(ii)** –3 and –4
   (iii) –8 and 5 **(iv)** 5 and –2

Sol. **(i)** Here, 2 and 5 are both positive.
   Therefore, the sum $= + (|2|+|5|) = +7 = 7.$

(ii) Here, –3 and –4 are both negative.

Therefore, the sum $= - (\,|\,3\,|+|\,4\,|\,) = -7$.

(iii) Here, – 8 is negative and 5 is positive and $|-8\,|>|\,5\,|$.

Therefore, the sum $= - (\,|-8\,|-|\,5\,|)$

$= - (8 - 5) = -3$

(iv) Here, 5 is positive and –2 is negative and $|\,5|>|-2\,|$.

Therefore, the sum $= + (\,|\,5|-|\,2\,|\,)$

$= + (5 - 2) = +3$

7. **Use number line to find (+4) – (–3).**

Sol. We have :

$(+4) - (-3) = (+4) + (\text{additive inverse of } -3)$

$= (+4) + (+3)$

Starting from 0 on the number line move 4 steps to the right to reach +4 and then move 3 steps to the right to reach +7, as shown below.

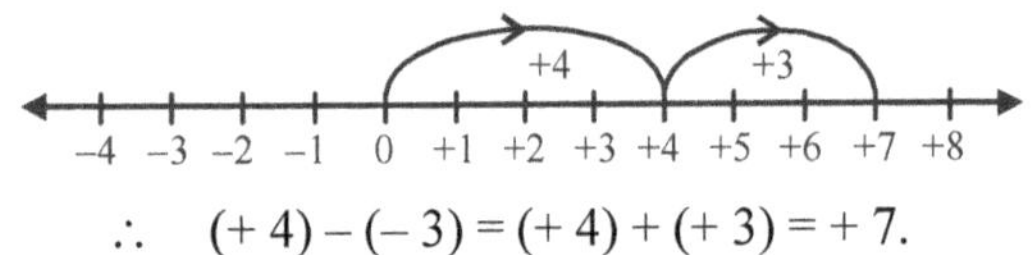

$\therefore \quad (+4) - (-3) = (+4) + (+3) = +7.$

8. **Use number line to find (–3) – (–5).**

Sol. We have,

$(-3) - (-5) = (-3) + (\text{additive invese of } -5)$

$= (-3) + (+5).$

Starting from 0 on the number line move 3 steps

to the left to reach (–3) and from there move 5 steps to the right to reach (+2), as shown below.

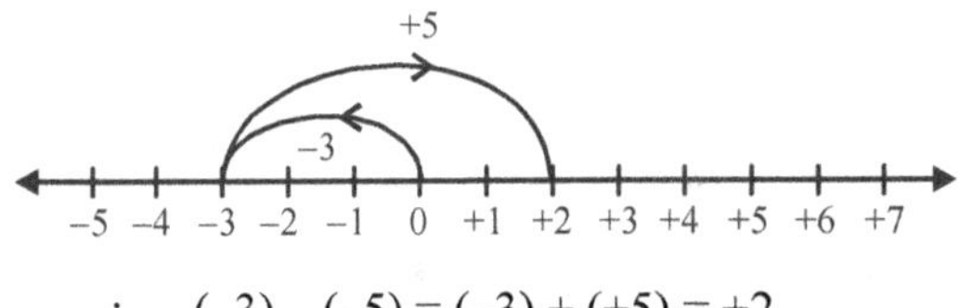

$\therefore \quad (-3) - (-5) = (-3) + (+5) = +2.$

9. **Subtract the sum of 998 and –486 from the sum of –290 and 732.**

Sol Sum of 998 and –486 is $998 + (-486)$

$= (998 - 486) = 512$

Sum of –290 and –732 is $-290 + 732$

$= 732 - 290 = 442.$

Now, $442 - 512 = 442 + (-512) = -70.$

[We subtract 442 from 512 and give minus sign to the result]

10. **Subtract –5 from 7. Subtract 7 from –5. Are the two results the same?**

Sol. $7 - (-5) = 7 + 5 = 12$,

$-5 - 7 = -5 + (-7) = -12$

So, the two results are not the same.

11. **Find the sum of –8, 23, –32, –17 and –63.**

Sol. $(-8) + 23 + (-32) + (-17) + (-63)$

$= [(-8) + 23] + (-32) + [(-17) + (-63)]$

$= [15 + (-32)] + (-80) = (-17) + (-80) = -97.$

1 EXERCISE

Fill in the Blanks :

DIRECTIONS : *Complete the following statements with an appropriate word / term to be filled in the blank space(s).*

1. The largest negative integer is ______.
2. The smallest positive integer is ______.
3. The two integers, which are at the same distance from 0 on the opposite directions, are called __________ of each other.
4. $(-11) + (-2) + (-1) =$ ______.
5. ______ $+ (-11) + 111 = 130$
6. $(-80) + 0 + (-90) =$ ______.
7. ______ $-3456 = -8910$
8. The number of integers lying between -5 and 5 is ______.
9. On the number line, 10 is to the ______ of zero.
10. The additive inverse of -1 is ______.
11. To subtract 7 from 13 we add ______ to 13.
12. To subtract -4 from 15 we add 4 to ______.

True / False :

DIRECTIONS : *Read the following statements and write your answer as true or false.*

1. $(-12) + 16 = (-16) + 12$
2. The sum of an integer and its negative is zero.
3. The sum of two negative integer is always negative integer.
4. $|-6| < |-2|$
5. The sum of all the integers between -5 and -1 is -6.
6. The successor of the integer 1 is 0.
7. The sum of any two negative integers is always greater than both the integers.
8. All integers are whole numbers.
9. Zero is less then every positive integer.
10. The sum of three different integers can never be zero.

11. The difference between an integer and its additive inverse is always even.

Match the Columns :

DIRECTIONS : *Each question contains statements given in two columns which have to be matched. Statements (A, B, C, D) in column-I have to be matched with statements (p, q, r, s) in column-II.*

1. If an operation * for two integers 'a' and 'b' mean that $a * b = a + b + (-2)$, then match the following

Column-I	Column-II
(A) $2 * (-6)$	(p) -1
(B) $(-4) * (-7)$	(q) 5
(C) $(-2) * 3$	(r) -6
(D) $3 * 4$	(s) -13

Very Short Answer Questions :

DIRECTIONS : *Give answer in one word or one sentence.*

1. Which number is greater in each of the following ?
   (i) $-15, -6$ (ii) $20, -20$
   (iii) $0, -3$ (iv) $-6, 0$
2. Using the number line, write the integer which is :
   (i) 3 more than 5   (ii) 6 more than -6
   (iii) 2 more than -4 (iv) 5 less than 2
3. Find the value of
   (i) $|-9|$ (ii) $-|-3|$
   (iii) $|0|$ (iv) $8 - |-7|$
4. Find an integer a such that :
   (i) $a + 3 = 0$ (ii) $5 + a = 0$
   (iii) $a + (-6) = 0$
5. Subtract :
   (i) 20 from -32 (ii) -15 from 38
   (iii) -16 from -28 (iv) 220 from 0
   (v) -341 from -249

6. Fill in the blanks with > or < sign.

(i) $(-7) + (-6)$ ☐ $(-7) - (-6)$

(ii) $(-23) - (-17)$ ☐ $(-33) + (-27)$

(iii) $(38) - (-10)$ ☐ $63 + (-18)$

7. The sum of two integers is –396. If one of them is 64, determine the other.

8. Write all integers between
(i) – 2 and 3 (ii) – 4 and 2.

9. Show that the additive inverse of +3 is –3 on the number line.

10. A submarine was situated 800 feet below the sea level. If it rises by 250 feet, what is its new position?

11. Solve.

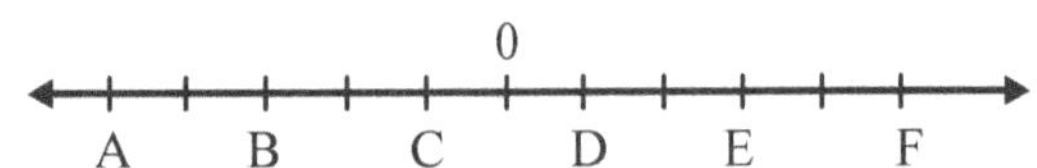

(i)   If point B is – 3, then which point is + 3?
(ii)   Write the value of points from 'A' to 'F'.

Short Answer Questions :

DIRECTIONS : *Give answer in 2-3 sentences.*

1. Write the following integers in decreasing order :
(i)   0, – 3, – 9, 7, 23
(ii)   – 300, 200, 300, 241
(iii) – 26, – 15, 0, 52, – 29
(iv) 55, – 20, – 52, – 7

2. Write the following integers in increasing order :
(i)   – 16, 0, 16, – 2, – 81
(ii)   – 71, – 23, 36, 0, – 10
(iii) – 503, – 363, 15, 17
(iv) – 100, – 8, 0, 12, – ₹23, – 1

3. Add the integers on number line.
(i)   4 + (– 6)   (ii)   (– 3) + 8
(iii) (– 2) + (– 5)   (iv) 6 + (– 6)

4. Find the additive inverse of :
(i)   – 63   (ii)   123
(iii) 0   (iv) 1000
(v)   3985

5. Write the successor and predecessor of the following :
(i)   – 34   (ii)   38
(iii) – 125   (iv) – 490

6. Add – 24 to the difference of – 8 and – 78.

7. The sum of two integers is – 30. If one of them is – 100, find the other.

8. Find the value :
(i)   25 – (– 15)
(ii)   (– 28) – 32 + 6
(iii) 4 – (– 9) + 7 – (– 3)
(iv) 2 – 3 + 4 – 5 + 6 – 7 + (– 10) + 10
(v)   1 + (– 3) + 5 + (– 7) + 9 + (– 11) + 13 + (– 15)

9. On a particular day, the temperature at Dehradun at 10 a.m, was 20°C but by midnight, it fell down to 11°C. The temperature at Bangaluru at 10 a.m. on the same day was 30°C but fell down to 18°C by the midnight. Which fall is greater?

10. Subtract the sum of –1050 and –750 from 400.

11. A point A is on a mountain which is 3786 m above sea-level and a point B is in a mine which is 894 m below sea-level. What is the vertical distance between A and B?

12. Evaluate each of the folowing :
(i) $|8 - 17|$
(ii) $|-14| + |5|$
(iii) $|-9| + |-6|$
(iv) $|-23| - |-12|$
(v) $|-8| - |-10| + |-6|$
(vi) $-|-5| + |-6| - |-1|$

13. Amit deposited ₹ 2350 in his account on Monday and then withdrew ₹ 800 on Tuesday. The next day he again deposited ₹ 1560. What was his balance on Wednesday?

2 EXERCISE

Text-Book Exercise :

1. In each of the following pairs, which number is to the right of the other on the number line?
   (i)   2, 9
   (ii) $-3, -8$
   (iii) $0, -1$
   (iv) $-11, 10$
   (v) $-6, 6$
   (vi) $1, -100$

2. Draw a number line and answer the following:
   (i)   Which number will we reach if we move 4 numbers to the right of -2.
   (ii) Which number will we reach if we move 5 numbers to the left of 1.
   (iii) If we are at -8 on the number line, in which direction should we move to reach -13?
   (iv) If we are at -6 on the number line, in which direction should we move to reach -1?

3. Find the solution of the following without using number line:
   (i) $(+7) + (-11)$
   (ii) $(-13) + (+10)$
   (iii) $(-7) + (+9)$
   (iv) $(+10) + (-5)$

4. Use number line and add the following integers :
   (i) $(-1) + (-2) + (-3)$
   (ii) $(-2) + 8 + (-4)$

5. Find the sum of :
   (i) -312, 39 and 192
   (ii) -50, -200 and 300.

6. Find the value of:
   (i) $(-7) + (-9) + 4 + 16$
   (ii) $(37) + (-2) + (-65) + (-8)$.

7. Subtract :
   (i) $(-15) - (-18)$
   (ii) $(-20) - (13)$
   (iii) $23 - (-12)$
   (iv) $(-32) - (-40)$

8. Find the value of :
   (i) $(-7) - 8 - (-25)$
   (ii) $(-13) + 32 - 8 - 1$
   (iii) $(-7) + (-8) + (-90)$
   (iv) $50 - (-40) - (-2)$

Exemplar Questions :

1. Calculate:
   $1 - 2 + 3 - 4 + 5 - 6 + 7 - 8 + 9 - 10$

2. Write the digits 0, 1, 2, 3, 4, 5, 6, 7, 8 and 9 in this order and insert ' + 'or '–' between them to get the result
   (i)   5
   (ii) -3

3. Write five distinct integers whose sum is 5.

4. Find the value of successor of the predecessor of -50.

5. Write the opposite of each of the following:
   (i)   Decrease in size
   (ii)   Failure
   (iii) Profit of Rs. 10
   (iv)   1000 A.D.
   (v)   Rise in water level
   (vi)   60 km south
   (vii) 10 m above the danger mark of river Ganga
   (viii) 20 m below the danger mark of the river Brahmaputra
   (ix)   Winning by a margin of 2000 votes
   (x)   Depositing Rs. 100 in the Bank account
   (xi)   20° C rise in temperature.

6. Temperature of a place at 12:00 noon was $+5°C$. Temperature increased by 3°C in first hour and decreased by 1°C in the second hour. What was the temperature at 2:00 pm?

7. Write the digits 0, 1, 2, 3, ..., 9 in this order and insert '+' or '–' between them to get the result 3.

8. Write the integer which is 4 more than its additive inverse.

9. Write two integers whose sum is less than both the integers.

10. Observe the following:
    $1 + 2 - 3 + 4 + 5 - 6 - 7 + 8 - 9 = -5$
    Change one '–' sign as '+' sign to get the sum 9.

11. Write two integers whose sum is 6 and difference is also 6.

12. Write five integers which are less than -100 but greater than -150.

HOTS Questions :

1. Find the sum: $5 + (-5) + 5 + (-5) + ...$
   (i)   If the number of terms is 40.
   (ii) If the number of terms is 45.

2. Write four pairs of integers which are at the same distance from 2 on the number line.

3. Write two distinct integers whose sum is equal to one of the integers.

3 EXERCISE

Single Option Correct :

DIRECTIONS : *This section contains multiple choice questions. Each question has 4 choices (a), (b), (c) and (d) out of which ONLY ONE is correct.*

1. Write the integer which has been represented on number line given below?

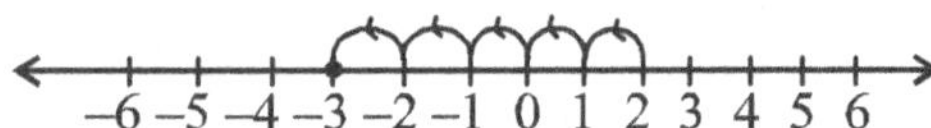

   (a) 5 more than 3   (b) 4 more than 2

   (c) 5 more than 4   (d) 5 less than 2

2. Absolute value of –58 is

   (a) +58   (b) –58

   (c) 58   (d) 0

3. Negative of a negative integer is

   (a) negative   (b) zero

   (c) positive   (d) none

4. Temperature at the foot of a mountain is +5°C. It fell down by 10°C at the top of the mountain. The temperature recorded on the top is

   (a) +15°C   (b) –15°C

   (c) +5°C   (d) –5°C

5. The additive inverse of a negative integer

   (a) is always negative.

   (b) is always positive.

   (c) is the same integer.

   (d) zero.

6. Which is the greatest number of the following:
   –8, –250, –600, –3, –99, –130

   (a) –600   (b) –8

   (c) –3   (d) –250

7. Find the difference between the smallest and the largest number of the following:
   –68, 32, –32, 0, –3

   (a) 68   (b) 100

   (c) 36   (d) 65

8. $|-138| - |-243| = ?$

   (a) 105   (b) 381

   (c) –381   (d) –105

9. If p and q are two integers such that p is predecessor of q, find the value of p – q.

   (a) 1   (b) –1

   (c) 0   (d) None of these

10. Which of the following shows the maximum rise in temperature?

    (a) 0°C to 10°C   (b) –4°C to 8°C

    (c) –15°C to –8°C   (d) –7°C to 0°C

11. The successor of – 11 is ?

    (a) – 9   (b) – 10

    (c) – 12   (d) 0

12. The sum of a number and its additive inverse is :

    (a) 1   (b) – 1

    (c) 0   (d) Number itself

13. The sum of two integers is 10. If one of them is – 3, then the other is :

    (a) 14   (b) 13

    (c) 12   (d) 15

14. What should be subtracted from 4 to get – 6 ?

    (a) 6   (b) 10

    (c) – 4   (d) 0

More Than One Option Correct :

DIRECTIONS : *This section contains multiple choice questions. Each question has 4 choices (a), (b), (c) and (d) out of which ONE or MORE may be correct.*

1. Sania and Trapi visited Leh and Tawang respectively during winter. Sania reported that she had experienced –4°C on Sunday, while Trapi reported that she had experienced –2°C on that day. On that Sunday

   (a) Leh was cooler than Tawang

   (b) Leh was hotter than Tawang

   (c) Leh was as cool as Tawang

   (d) Tawang was hotter than Leh.

2. Which expression has a value less than -3?
 (a) $4 + (-9)$
 (b) $3 + (-8) + 1$
 (c) $-10 + 8$
 (d) $-1 + (-5) + 2$

3. Which of the following represents positive integer?
 (a) $25°$ C above freezing point
 (b) 2 km below sea-level
 (c) A deposit of ₹ 2589
 (d) Gain of ₹ 1987

4. Which of the following statements is/are true?
 (a) $5128 - (-2459) > (-687) - (-1040)$
 (b) $-584 - (-347) < 960 - (-728)$
 (c) $6250 + (-3012) > 6240 - (-271)$
 (d) $-888 + (3002) > 1001 - (-13)$

5. Which sum is negative?
 (a) $-38 + (-24)$
 (b) $-61 + 43$
 (c) $-53 + 72$
 (d) $-25 + 0$

Assertion & Reason :

DIRECTIONS : *Each of these questions contains an Assertion followed by Reason. Read them carefully and answer the question on the basis of following options. You have to select the one that best describes the two statements.*

(a) If both **Assertion** and **Reason** are true and reason is the correct explanation of assertion .
(b) If both **Assertion** and **Reason** are true but **Reason** is not the correct explanation of **Assertion**.
(c) If **Assertion** is true but **Reason** is false.
(d) If **Assertion** is false but **Reason** is true.

1. **Assertion:** The number 749 is greater than -749.
 Reason: Every positive integer is to the right of every negative integer on the number line.

2. **Assertion:** $(-986) + (-493) + (-545)$ is greater than $(-126) + (-234) + 2$.
 Reason: Greater the number, the lesser is its opposite.

Passage Based Questions :

DIRECTIONS : *Study the given passage(s) and answer the following questions.*

PASSAGE-I

Read the information given below and answer the questions that follows.

In Dheeraj's house, there are stairs for going up to the terrace and for going down to the Godown. Consider the number of stairs going up as positive integer, the number of stairs going down as negative integer, and the number representing ground floor as zero.

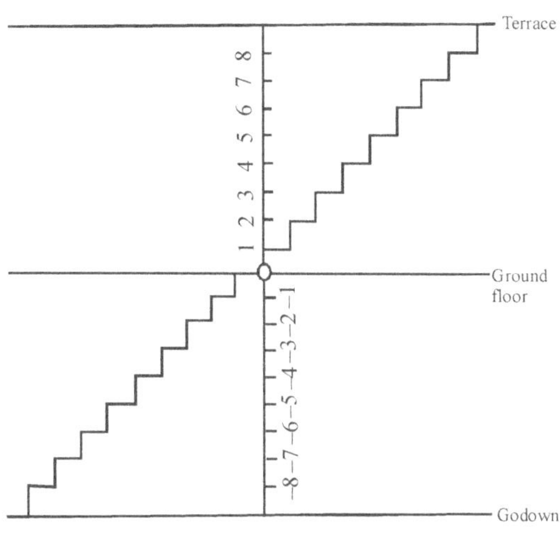

1. When Dheeraj will go 5 steps up from the ground floor and then further goes 3 steps up. At which step will he finally reach?
 (a) 8th step up
 (b) 2nd step up
 (c) 8th step down
 (d) 2nd step down

2. When he will go 6 steps down from the ground floor and then further goes 2 steps down. At which step will he finally reach?
 (a) 4 steps up
 (b) 4 steps down
 (c) 8 steps up
 (d) 8 steps down

3. When he will go 7 steps up from the ground floor and then further goes 10 steps down. At which step will he reach finally?
 (a) 3 steps up
 (b) 17 steps up
 (c) 17 steps down
 (d) 3 steps down

PASSAGE-II

During a week in the month of December, Shimla recorded the following temperatures:

$$-3°C, -6°C, 2°C, 1°C, -4°C, 0°C \text{ and } 9°C.$$

4. The difference between the highest and lowest temperature during the week was
   (a) 11°C (b) 15°C
   (c) 13°C (d) 10°C

5. The 10°C above freezing point is
   (a) 100°C (b) 10°C
   (c) 0°C (d) – 100°C

6. The ascending order of the given temperatures is
   (a) – 3°C, – 6°C, 2°C, 1°C, – 4°C, 0°C, 9°C
   (b) 9°C, 2°C, 1°C, 0°C, – 3°C, – 4°C, – 6°C
   (c) – 6°C, – 4°C, – 3°C, 0°C, 1°C, 2°C, 9°C
   (d) None of these

Integer Type Questions :

DIRECTIONS : *Answer the following questions. The answer to each of the question is a single digit integer, ranging from 0 to 9.*

1. One day on a hill, the temperature at 8 p.m. was 2°C but at mid-night it fell down to – 3°C. By how many degrees did the temperature fall?

2. Find the value of $– 12 – [(– 15) + (– 2) – 3]$.

3. Find the value of $1 – 2 + 3 – 4 + 5$.

4. $(– 22) + 21 + (– 22) + 21 + \ldots\ldots$ 20 terms is $– 2k$. Find the value of k.

5. If Δ is an operation on integers such that $a \Delta b = a – b – 2$, for all integers a, b. Then, $7 \Delta (– 4) =$

6. The value of $38 – (– 25) – 58 + (– 15) + 23 – (– 8)$ is $3k$. Find the value of k.

Multiple Matching Question :

DIRECTIONS : *Following question has four statements (A, B, C and D) given in Column-I and five statements (p, q, r, s, t) in Column-II. Any given statement in Column-I can have correct matching with one or more statement(s) given in Column-II.*

1. Match the following:

   Column-I
   (A) $(– 516) + \{(– 327) – (– 925)\} =$
   (B) $– 45632 – (– 35632) =$
   (C) $\{– 380 – (675)\} – \{865 + (– 493)\} =$
   (D) $\{– 340 – (– 170)\} – \{(– 45) – 83\} =$

   Column-II
   (p) – 10000
   (q) – 42
   (r) 82
   (s) – 1427
   (t) 100 – 18

SOLUTIONS

Brief Explanations of Selected Questions

1 EXERCISE

Fill in the Blanks :

1. -1	**2.** 1	**3.** (i) opposites	
4. -14	**5.** 30	**6.** -170	
7. -5454	**8.** 9	**9.** right	
10. 1	**11.** -7	**12.** 15	

True / False :

1. F	**2.** T	**3.** T	**4.** F	**5.** F
6. F	**7.** F	**8.** F	**9.** T	**10.** F
11. T				

Match the Columns :

1. (A) → (r); (B) → (s); (C) → (p); (D) → (q)
(A) $2 * (-6) = 2 + (-6) + (-2) = -6$
(B) $(-4) * (-7) = -4 - 7 + (-2) = -13$
(C) $(-2) * 3 = (-2) + 3 + (-2) = -1$
(D) $3 * 4 = 3 + 4 + (-2) = 5$

Very Short Answer Questions:

1. (i) -6 (ii) 20
(iii) 0   (iv) 0

2. (i) 8   (ii) 0
(iii) -2 (iv) -3

3. (i) 9   (ii) -3
(iii) 0   (iv) 1

4. (i) -3 (ii) -5
(iii) 6

5. (i) -52 (ii) 53
(iii) -12 (iv) -220
(v) 92

6. (i) $<$ (ii) $>$
(iii) $>$

7. Other integer = Sum – Given integer
$= (-396) - 64 = (-396) + (-64)$
$= -460$

8.
```
←─┼──┼──┼──┼──┼──┼──┼──┼──┼─→
  -4  -3  -2  -1   0   1   2   3   4
```

(i) The integers between -2 and 3 are $-1, 0, 1, 2$
(ii) The integers between -4 and 2 are $-3, -2, -1, 0, 1$

9.

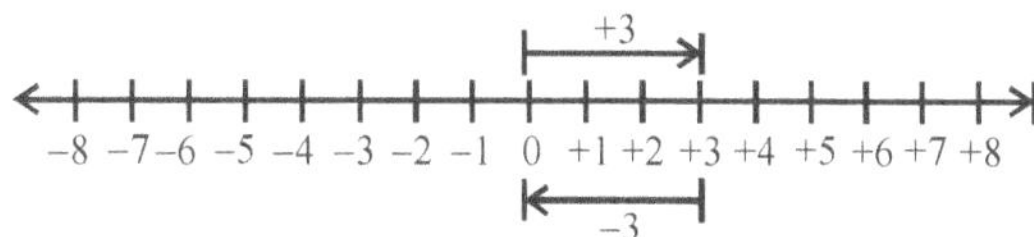

Thus, we have shown the additive inverse of $+3$ is -3 on the above number line.

10. 550 feet below sea level

11. (i) E
(ii) $A = -5, B = -3, C = -1, D = 1, E = 3, F = 5$

Short Answer Questions :

1. (i) $23 > 7 > 0 > -3 > -9$
(ii) $300 > 241 > 200 > -300$
(iii) $52 > 0 > -15 > -26 > -29$
(iv) $55 > - > -20 > -52$

2. (i) $-81 < -16 < -2 < 0 < 16$
(ii) $-71 < -23 < -10 < 0 < 36$
(iii) $-503 < -363 < 15 < 17$
(iv) $-100 < -23 < -8 < -1 < 0 < 12$

3. (i) -2 (ii) $+5$
(iii) -7 (iv) 0

4. (i) 63   (ii) -123
(iii) 0   (iv) -1000
(v) -3985

5. (i) $-33, -35$ (ii) 39, 37
(iii) $-124, -126$ (iv) $-489, -491$

6. 46

7. 70

8. (i) 40   (ii) -54
(iii) 23   (iv) -3
(v) -8

9. Fall in temperature at Dehradun
$= 20°C - 11°C = 9°C.$
Fall in temperature at Bangaluru
$= 30°C - 18°C = 12°C.$
So the fall in temperature at Bangaluru is greater and it is $12°C.$

10. 2200

11. Let us consider a point O at the sea level.
Then, height OA = + 3786 m;
height OB = – 894 m
Distance between A and B

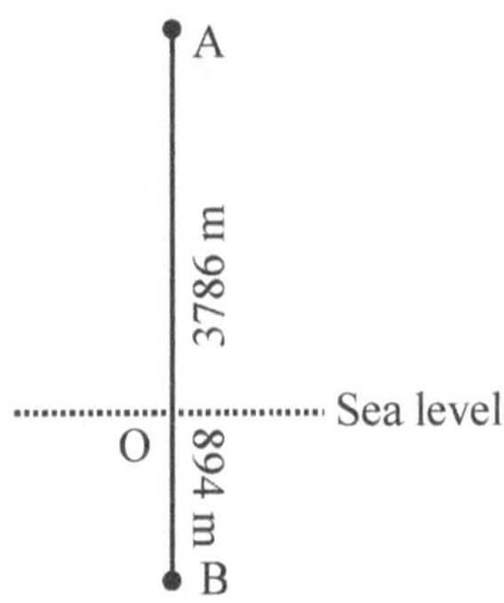

$$= |OA| + |OB|$$
$$= \{|+3786| + |-894|\} \text{ m}$$
$$= (3786 + 894) \text{ m} = 4680 \text{ m}$$

12. (i) 9   (ii) 19   (iii) 15

     (iv) 11   (v) 4   (vi) 0

13. ₹ 3110

2 EXERCISE

Text-Book Exercise :

1. (i) The number 9 is to the right of the number 2.

     (ii) The number –3 is to the right of the number – 8.

     (iii) The number 0 is to the right of the number – 1.

     (iv) The number 10 is to the right of the number – 11.

     (v) The number 6 is to the right of the number – 6.

     (vi) The number 1 is to the right of the number – 100.

2. (i) We will reach the number 2.

     (ii) We will reach the number – 4.

     (iii) We should move in the left direction.

     (iv) We should move in the right direction.

3. (i) $(+7) + (-11)$

     (ii) $(-13) + (+10)$

     (iii) $(-7) + (+9)$

     (iv) $(+10) + (-5)$

4. (i) $(-1) + (-2) + (-3)$

First we move 1 step to the left of 0 reaching –1, then from this point we move 2 steps to the left to reach –3 and finally from –3, we move 3 steps to the left. We reach the point –6.

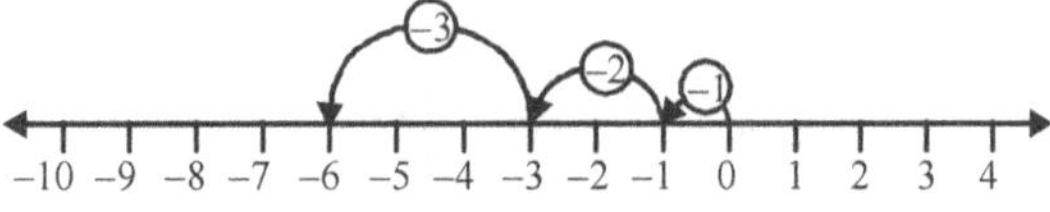

Thus, $(-1) + (-2) + (-3) = -6$

(ii) $(-2) + 8 + (-4)$

First we move 2 steps to the left of 0 reaching –2, then from this point we move 8 steps to the right to reach + 6 and finally from + 6 we move 4 steps to the left. We reach the point 2.

Thus, $(-2) + 8 + (-4) = 2$.

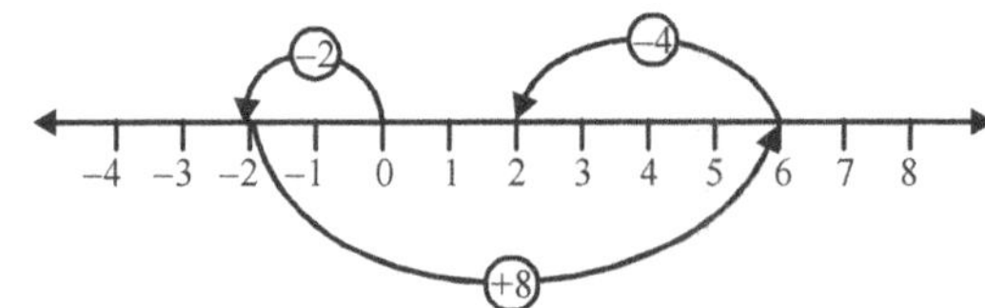

5. (i) $(-312) + (39) + (192)$
$$= (-312) + (231) = (-81)$$

     (ii) $(-50) + (-200) + (300)$
$$= (-250) + (300) = 50$$

6. (i) $(-7) + (-9) + 4 + 16$
$$= (-16) + 20 = 4$$

     (ii) $(37) + (-2) + (-65) + (-8)$
$$= (37) + (-75)$$
$$= -38.$$

7. (i) $(-15) - (-18)$
$$= (-15) + (\text{additive inverse of} -18)$$
$$= (-15) + (18) = 3$$

     (ii) $(-20) - (13)$
$$= (-20) + (\text{additive inverse of } 13)$$
$$= (-20) + (-13) = -33$$

     (iii) $23 - (-12)$
$$= 23 + (\text{additive inverse of} - 12)$$
$$= 23 + 12 = 35$$

     (iv) $(-32) - (-40)$
$$= (-32) + (\text{additive inverse of} -40)$$
$$= (-32) + (+40) = 8$$

8. (i) $(-7) - 8 - (-25)$
$$= (-7) + (\text{additive inverse of } 8) - (-25)$$
$$= (-7) + (-8) - (-25)$$
$$= -15 - (-25)$$

$$= -15 + \text{(additive inverse of } -25)$$
$$= -15 + (+25)$$
$$= 10$$

(ii) $(-13) + 32 - 8 - 1$
$$= (-13) + 32 - 9$$
$$= (-13) + 23$$
$$= 10$$

(iii) $(-7) + (-8) + (-90)$
$$= (-15) + (-90)$$
$$= -105$$

(iv) $50 - (-40) - (-2)$
$$= 50 + (40) - (-2)$$
$$= 90 - (-2)$$
$$= 90 + 2 = 92$$

Exemplar Questions :

1. $1 - 2 + 3 - 4 + 5 - 6 + 7 - 8 + 9 - 10$
$$= (1 + 3 + 5 + 7 + 9) - (2 + 4 + 6 + 8 + 10)$$
$$= 25 - 30$$
$$= -5.$$

2. (i) $0 + 1 - 2 + 3 - 4 + 5 - 6 + 7 - 8 + 9 = 5$
 (ii) $0 - 1 - 2 + 3 + 4 - 5 + 6 - 7 + 8 - 9 = -3$

3. $5 + [2 + (-2)] + [3 + (-3)] = 5.$
   Thus, the required five integers are 5, 2, –2, 3, –3
   There can be many combinations of five integers, such as 5, 3, –3, 6, –6 or 4, 2, 3, –3, –1 etc., whose sum is 5.

4. Successor of (predecessor of – 50)
   = Successor of (– 51)
   = – 50

5. (i) Increase in size
   (ii) Success
   (iii) Loss of Rs. 10
   (iv) 1000 B. C.
   (v) Fall in water level
   (vi) 60 km North
   (vii) 10m below the danger mark of river Ganga.
   (viii)20m above the danger mark of river Brahmaputra.
   (ix) Losing by a margin of 2000 votes.
   (x) Withdrawing Rs 100 from the Bank account
   (xi) 20ºC fall in temperature.

6. Temperature at 12 : 00 noon $= + 5°C$
   Increase in temperature in first hour $= 3°C$
   Decrease in temperature in second hour $= 1°C$

$\therefore$ Temperature at 2 : 00 pm
$$= 5°C + 3°C - 1°C = 7°C$$

7. $0 - 1 - 2 - 3 - 4 - 5 - 6 + 7 + 8 + 9 = 3$
8. 2
9. $(-5) + (-4) = -9$ which is less than -5 and -4. (any two negative integers can be taken)
10. $1 + 2 - 3 + 4 + 5 - 6 + 7 + 8 - 9 = 9$
11. 6 and 0 as $6 + 0 = 6$ and $6 - 0 = 6.$
12. $-140, -130, -120, -110, -101$ (there can be many answers).

HOTS Questions :

1. (i) 0   (ii) 5
2. $(1, 3), (0, 4), (-1, 5), (-2, 6)$
3. 2, 0 (any two integers with one of them as 0).

3 EXERCISE

Single Option Correct :

1. (d) Since moving 5 steps left from 2.
   $\therefore$ 5 less than 2.
2. (c) Absolute value of a number is its numerical value without any sign.
3. (c) Positive
4. (d) $+5°C + (-10°C) = -5°C$
5. (b)
6. (c)
7. (b) The smallest and largest number are – 68 and 32 respectively.
   Their difference $= 32 - (-68)$
   $$= 32 + 68 = 100$$
8. (d) $|-138| = 138$

   $|-243| = 243$

   $|-138| - |-243| = 138 - 243 = -105$
9. (b) Since P is predecessor of q, p comes before q.
   $\therefore p - q = -1$
10. (b) $8°C - (-4°C) = 128$
    Which is maximum rise.
11. (b)   12. (c)   13. (b)   14. (b)

More Than One Option Correct :

1. **(a, d)**
2. **(a, b, d)**
   (a) $4 + (-9) = -5$ (b) $3 + (-8) + = -4$
   (c) $-10 + 8 = -2$ (d) $-1 + (-5) + 2 = -4$
3. **(a, c, d)** Only 2 km below sea-level represents negative integer
4. **(a, b, d)**
   (a) $5128 - (-2459) = 5128 + (2459) = 7587$
   $(-687) - (-1040) = (-687) + (1040) = 353$
   $\because \quad 7587 > 353$
   $\therefore \quad 5128 - (-2459) > (-687) - (-1040)$
   (b) $-584 - (-347) = (-584) + (+347) = -237$
   $960 - (-728) = 960 + (728) = 1688$
   $\because \quad -237 < 1688$
   $\therefore \quad -584 - (347) < 960 - (-728)$
   (c) $6250 + (-3012) = 3238$
   $6240 - (-271) = 6240 + (271) = 6511$
   $\because \quad 3238 < 6511$
   $\therefore \quad 6250 + (-3012) < 6240 - (-271)$
   (d) $-888 + (3002) = 2114$
   $1001 - (-13) = 1001 + (13) = 1014$
   $\because \quad 2114 > 1014$
   $\therefore \quad -888 + (3002) > 1001 - (-13)$
5. **(a, b, d)**
   (a) $-38 + (-24) = -62$, which is a negative integer.
   (b) $-61 + 43 = -18$, which is a negative integer.
   (c) $-53 + 72 = 19$, which is a positive integer.
   (d) $-25 + 0 = -25$, which is a negative integer.

Assertion & Reason :

1. **(b)** $749 > -749$, as positive integer is always greater than negative integer.
   Assertion: True; **Reason:** True but **Reason** in not the correct explanation of **Assertion**.
2. **(d)** As $(-986) + (-493) + (-545) = -2024$
   And, $(-126) + (-234) + 2 = -358$
   Also, $-2024 < -358$
   Assertion: False; **Reason:** True.

Passage Based Questions :

1. **(a)** $(5) + (+3) = +8$
2. **(d)** $(-6) - 2 = -8$ i.e. 8 steps down.
3. **(d)** $(+7) - 10 = -3$ i.e. 3 steps down
4. **(b)** The highest temperature was $9°C$. The lowest temperature was $-6°C$. Their difference
   $= (9 - (-6))°C = (9 + 6)°C$
   $= 15°C$
5. **(b)** $10°C$ above freezing point is $10°C$.
6. **(c)**

Integer Type Questions :

1. **(5)** Fall in temperature $= 2 - (-3)°C = 5°C$
2. **(8)** $-12 - [(-15) + (-2) - 3]$
   $= -12 - (-20) = -12 + 20 = 8.$
3. **(3)** $1 - 2 + 3 - 4 + 5 = 3$
4. **(5)** $(-22) + 21 + (-22) + 21 + \ldots\ldots$ 20 terms
   $= -10$
   $= -2 \times 5$
   $\Rightarrow \quad k = 5$
5. **(9)** $7 \, \Delta \, (-4) = 7 - (-4) - 2 = 11 - 2 = 9$
6. **(7)** $38 - (-25) - 58 + (-15) + 23 - (-8)$
   $= 63 - 73 + 31$
   $= -10 + 31$
   $= 21 = 3 \times 7 \Rightarrow k = 7$

Multiple Matching Question :

1. **(A) → (r, t); (B) → (p); (C) → (s); (D) → (q)**
   (A) $(-516) + \{(-327) - (-925)\}$
   $= (-516) + \{(-327) + (925)\}$
   $= (-516) + (598) = 82$
   (B) $-45632 - (-35632) = -45632 + 35632$
   $= -10000$
   (C) $\{-380 - (675)\} - \{865 + (-493)\}$
   $= (-1055) - (372)$
   $= -1427$
   (D) $\{-340 - (-170)\} - \{(-45) - 83\}$
   $= \{-340 + (170)\} - \{(-45) + (-83)\}$
   $= (-170) + (128) = -42$

Chapter 7

Fractions

FRACTION

A fraction represents a part of a whole or of a group.
Let us divide a circle into four equal parts by drawing two diameters of the circle.
Then shade two parts.

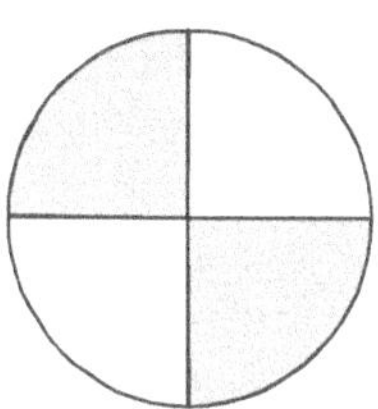

Two parts shaded

Thus, fraction of shaded part $= \dfrac{\text{shaded parts}}{\text{total no. of parts}} = \dfrac{2}{4}$ (read as 'two by four')

In a fraction, number above the line is called numerator and number below the line is known as denominator.

or $\qquad$ fraction $= \dfrac{\text{numerator}}{\text{denominator}}$

For example : Suppose a month has 30 days in which we have to represent 10 days as fraction. So,

$$\text{fraction} = \dfrac{\text{No. of required days}}{\text{Total no. of days}} = \dfrac{10}{30} = \dfrac{1}{3}$$

So, 10 days are $\dfrac{1}{3}$ rd part of a month, where 1 is the numerator and 3 is the denominator.

Let us take another example

For example : Suppose 9 balls to be distributed equally among 3 friends, then let's find the fraction of balls each will get.
We will divide the balls into 3 equal parts as shown in the figure.

$\therefore$ Each will get $= \dfrac{3}{9}$ or $\dfrac{1}{3}$

ILLUSTRATION : 1

(i) $\quad \dfrac{1}{6}$ **of 30 hours** $\qquad\qquad$ (ii) $\dfrac{1}{8}$ **of 168 m**

SOLUTION :

(i) We have, $\dfrac{1}{6}$ of 30 hours $= \dfrac{1}{6} \times 30 = 5$ hours   (ii) We have, $\dfrac{1}{8}$ of 168 m $= \dfrac{1}{8} \times 168 = 21$ m.

Types of Fractions

There are different types of fractions. Let us learn about them.

Proper fraction

A fraction whose numerator is less than its denominator is called a proper fraction. A proper fraction is always

less than a whole, e.g. $\dfrac{5}{7}, \dfrac{3}{8}, \dfrac{2}{5}$ etc.

Improper fraction

A fraction whose numerator is greater than or equal to its denominator is called an improper fraction. An

improper fraction is always equal to or greater than a whole, e.g. $\dfrac{4}{3}, \dfrac{5}{2}, \dfrac{8}{5}$ etc.

Unit fraction

Fractions with numerator 1 are called unit fractions, e.g. $\dfrac{1}{4}, \dfrac{1}{7}, \dfrac{1}{9}$ etc.

Mixed fraction

A combination of a whole and a proper fraction is called a mixed fraction, e.g. $5\dfrac{1}{3}, \ 2\dfrac{2}{5}, \ 7\dfrac{9}{11}$ etc.

REPRESENTATION OF FRACTION ON NUMBERS LINE

We have learnt the representation of integers $-4, -3, -2, -1, 0, 1, 2, 3, ...$ etc. on number line. We will now learn the representation of fractions on number line.

Representation of proper fraction

Consider various proper fractions namely $\dfrac{1}{2}, \dfrac{2}{3}, \dfrac{3}{4} ....$ etc.

Each of them is greater than zero but less than 1, so each one of them lies between 0 and 1. Now, draw

a number line and mark two points on it and name them as 0 and 1. To show $\dfrac{3}{4}$ on number line, we divide

the gap between 0 and 1 into as many parts as the denominator of the fraction i.e., 4 and move as many steps forward as the numerator of the fraction i.e., 3.

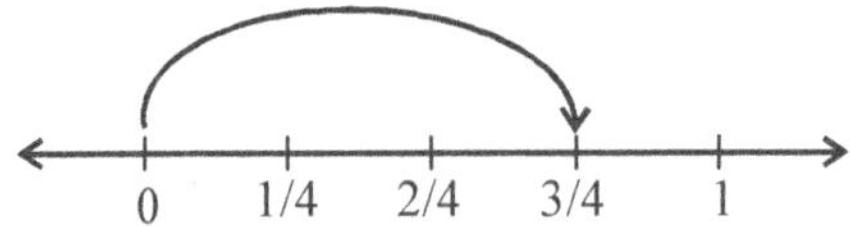

ILLUSTRATION : 2

Represent $\dfrac{2}{5}$ on number line.

SOLUTION :

Draw a line and mark two points 0 and 1 on it. Denominator = 5
So, divide the gap between 0 and 1 into five equal parts. Numerator = 2.
So, move 2 steps forward from 0.

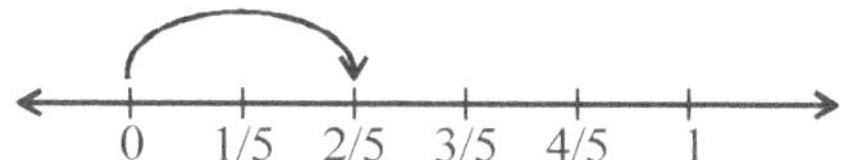

Representation of mixed and improper fraction on number line

Let us represents $1\dfrac{4}{5}$ on the number line. We know that $1\dfrac{4}{5}$ lies between 1 and 2.

Divide the gap between 1 and 2 into 5 equal parts and move 4 steps forward.

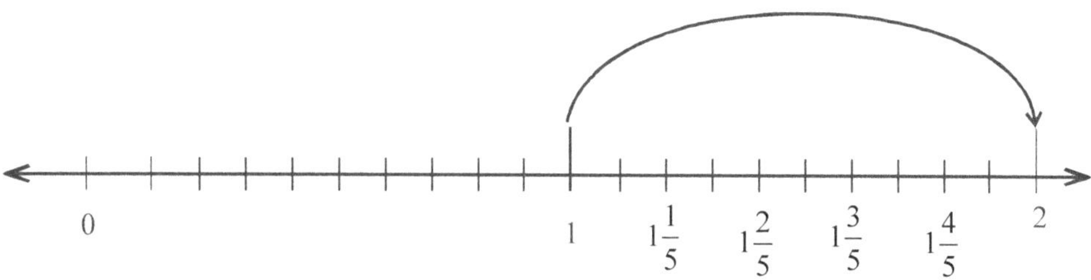

Similarly, an improper fraction can be represented on the number line by converting it into a mixed fraction.

EQUIVALENT FRACTIONS

Equivalent fractions are the fractions which represent the same value. They represent the same part of a whole.
To find equivalent fractions of any given fraction :
(i)   We may multiply both the numerator and the denominator of the given fraction by the same number.
(ii)   We may divide both the numerator and the denominator of the given fraction by the same number.

ILLUSTRATION : 3

Find two fractions equivalent to $\dfrac{5}{7}$.

SOLUTION :

$$\frac{5}{7} = \frac{5}{7} \times \frac{2}{2} = \frac{10}{14}; \qquad \frac{5}{7} = \frac{5}{7} \times \frac{3}{3} = \frac{15}{21}$$

ILLUSTRATION : 4

Find the equivalent fraction of $\dfrac{12}{20}$ having 5 as the denominator.

SOLUTION :

$$\frac{12}{20} = \frac{\square}{5}$$

In order to get 5 as denominator, we divide 20 by 4. We also divide 12 by 4 to get numerator of the resultant fraction.

Thus, $\quad \dfrac{12}{20} = \dfrac{12 \div 4}{20 \div 4} = \dfrac{\boxed{3}}{5}$

FRACTION TO THE LOWEST TERMS

A fraction is said to be in its lowest terms or simplest form or irreducible if there is no common factor, other than 1 between its numerator and denominator.

ILLUSTRATION : 5

Reduce $\dfrac{114}{513}$ into lowest terms :

SOLUTION :

The given fraction is $\dfrac{114}{513}$.

First, we find the H.C.F of 114 and 513.

$$
\begin{array}{r}
114\overline{)513}(4 \\
456 \\
\hline
57\overline{)114}(2 \\
114 \\
\hline
\times \\
\hline
\end{array}
$$

$\therefore \quad$ H.C.F. of 114 and 513 is 57.

So, we divide the numerator and denominator of the given fraction by 57.

$$\therefore \quad \frac{114}{513} = \frac{114 \div 57}{513 \div 57} = \frac{2}{9}.$$

Hence, the given fraction in its simplest form is $\dfrac{2}{9}$.

LIKE AND UNLIKE FRACTIONS

Fractions with same denominators are called like fractions.

For example :

$\dfrac{5}{15}, \dfrac{3}{15}, \dfrac{17}{15}$ and $\dfrac{31}{15}$ are unlike fractions.

The fractions with different denominators are called unlike fractions

For example : $\dfrac{2}{7}, \dfrac{9}{11}, \dfrac{3}{13}$ and $\dfrac{39}{46}$ are unlike fractions.

COMPARISON OF FRACTIONS

Comparison of Like Fractions

When we compare two fractions having same denominator, then the fraction with greater numerator will be greater.

For example : $\quad \dfrac{7}{15} > \dfrac{4}{15}$

Comparison of unlike fractions.

Unlike fractions can be compared by any of the following two methods :

1. By converting them into like fractions :

To compare unlike fractions, we first convert them into like fractions by obtaining their equivalent fraction with a denominator which is LCM of the denominators of both the fractions.

e.g. $\dfrac{3}{5}$ and $\dfrac{2}{7}$ can be compared by converting them into like fractions having their denominator equal to LCM

of 5 and 7.

L.C.M. of (5, 7) = 35

$$\dfrac{3\times7}{5\times7}=\dfrac{21}{35} \text{ and } \dfrac{2\times5}{7\times5}=\dfrac{10}{35} \qquad \text{Now,} \qquad \dfrac{21}{35}>\dfrac{10}{35} \qquad \therefore \qquad \dfrac{3}{5}>\dfrac{2}{7}$$

2. Cross multiplication method :

To compare any two fractions such as $\dfrac{a}{b}$ and $\dfrac{c}{d}$, we cross multiply as shown below.

$$\dfrac{a}{b}\diagdown\dfrac{c}{d}$$

Thus, the cross products are ad and bc.

(a) If $ad > cd$ then $\dfrac{a}{b}>\dfrac{c}{d}$ (b) If $ad < cd$ then $\dfrac{a}{b}<\dfrac{c}{d}$ (c) If $ad = cb$ then $\dfrac{a}{b}=\dfrac{c}{d}$

NOTE: When two fractions have same numerator, but different denominators, then the fraction with smaller denominator is greater. **For example :** $\dfrac{5}{7}>\dfrac{5}{9}$

ILLUSTRATION : 6

Compare :   (a) $\dfrac{11}{5}$ and $\dfrac{13}{3}$ (b) $\dfrac{1}{2}$ and $\dfrac{3}{7}$

SOLUTION :

(a) $\dfrac{11}{5}$ and $\dfrac{13}{3}$

By Cross multiplication, we see that

$$\dfrac{11}{5}\diagdown\dfrac{13}{3}$$

$\Rightarrow 33 < 65$

So $\dfrac{11}{5}<\dfrac{13}{3}$

(b) $\dfrac{1}{2}$ and $\dfrac{3}{7}$

$$\dfrac{1}{2}\diagdown\dfrac{3}{7}$$

$1 \times 7 > 3 \times 2 \Rightarrow 7 > 6$

So, $\dfrac{1}{2}>\dfrac{3}{7}$

ILLUSTRATION : 7

Arrange the following fractions in ascending order :

$$\frac{4}{6}, \frac{3}{8}, \frac{7}{12}, \frac{3}{16}$$

SOLUTION :

Change all these fractions into like fractions by finding their equivalent fractions.
LCM of 6, 8, 12 and 16 is 48.
Converting each fraction into a fraction with denominator 48

$$\frac{4\times8}{6\times8}, \frac{3\times6}{8\times6}, \frac{7\times4}{12\times4}, \frac{3\times3}{16\times3} \qquad \text{or} \qquad \frac{32}{48}, \frac{18}{48}, \frac{28}{48}, \frac{9}{48}$$

Now, arrange the fractions in ascending order

$$\frac{9}{48} < \frac{18}{48} < \frac{28}{48} < \frac{32}{48} \qquad \therefore \qquad \frac{3}{16} < \frac{3}{8} < \frac{7}{12} < \frac{4}{6}$$

ADDITION AND SUBTRACTION OF FRACTIONS

Addition and subtractions of like fractions

The sum (or difference) of two or more like fractions can be obtained as follows:
Step I : Add (or subtract) the numerators
Step II : Write the common denominator
StepIII : Write the fraction as

$$= \frac{\text{Sum (or difference) of numerators}}{\text{Common denominator}}$$

ILLUSTRATION : 8

Add : $\dfrac{3}{11} + \dfrac{2}{11}$

SOLUTION :

$$\frac{3}{11} + \frac{2}{11} = \frac{5}{11}$$

ILLUSTRATION : 9

Subtract : $\dfrac{6}{14} - \dfrac{3}{14}$

SOLUTION :

$$\frac{6}{14} - \frac{3}{14} = \frac{3}{14}$$

Addition and subtraction of unlike fractions

To add or subtract unlike fractions, we first convert unlike fractions into equivalent like fractions and then add or subtract as we do with like fractions.

ILLUSTRATION : 10

Add $\dfrac{2}{5}$ and $\dfrac{3}{7}$

SOLUTION :

LCM of 5 and 7 is 35.

Converting $\dfrac{2}{5}$ and $\dfrac{3}{7}$ into like fractions, we have $\dfrac{2\times7}{5\times7}$ and $\dfrac{3\times5}{7\times5}$ or $\dfrac{14}{35}$ and $\dfrac{15}{35}$

Now, $\dfrac{2}{5}+\dfrac{3}{7}=\dfrac{14}{35}+\dfrac{15}{35}=\dfrac{29}{35}$

Short method :

$$\frac{2}{5}+\frac{3}{7}=\frac{2\times7+3\times5}{5\times7}=\frac{14+15}{35}=\frac{29}{35}$$

ILLUSTRATION : 11

Subtract $\dfrac{4}{9}$ from $\dfrac{3}{5}$

SOLUTION :

Converting $\dfrac{4}{9}$ and $\dfrac{3}{5}$ into like fractions, we have

$$\frac{3\times9}{5\times9}\text{ and }\frac{4\times5}{9\times5}\qquad\text{or}\qquad\frac{27}{45}\text{ and }\frac{20}{45}$$

Now, $\dfrac{3}{5}-\dfrac{4}{9}=\dfrac{27}{45}-\dfrac{20}{45}=\dfrac{7}{45}$

ILLUSTRATION : 12

Simplify :

(i) $\quad 1\dfrac{3}{7}+2\dfrac{1}{5}$ $\qquad\qquad$ (ii) $\quad \dfrac{17}{3}-2\dfrac{1}{4}$

SOLUTION :

(i) $\quad 1\dfrac{3}{7}+2\dfrac{1}{5}$

$$=\frac{10}{7}+\frac{11}{5}=\frac{10\times5}{7\times5}+\frac{11\times7}{5\times7}$$

$$=\frac{50}{35}+\frac{77}{35}=\frac{127}{35}=3\frac{22}{35}$$

(ii) $\quad \dfrac{17}{3}-2\dfrac{1}{4}$

$$=\frac{17}{3}-\frac{9}{4}=\frac{17\times4}{3\times4}-\frac{9\times3}{4\times3}$$

$$=\frac{68}{12}-\frac{27}{12}=\frac{41}{12}\text{ or }3\frac{5}{12}$$

CONCEPT MAP

Fraction

- A number representing a part of a whole is called a fraction. The whole may be a single object or a group of objects.
- A fraction is written as $\dfrac{a}{b}$ where a is the numerator and b is the denominator.
- A fraction whose numerator is less than its denominator is called proper fraction. e.g. $\dfrac{2}{3}, \dfrac{9}{13}, \dfrac{6}{17}$ etc.
- A fraction in which the numerator is greater than or equal to the denominator is called improper fraction. e.g. $\dfrac{5}{3}, \dfrac{12}{7}, \dfrac{83}{9}$
- A fraction written as a combination of a whole and a part is called mixed fraction. e.g. $2\dfrac{1}{3}, 4\dfrac{2}{5}, 1\dfrac{2}{3}$ etc.

Equivalent Fractions

- To find an equivalent fraction of a given fraction, we multiply or divide both the numerator and denominator of it by the same number.

Comparison of Fractions

- When two like fractions are compared then the fraction with the greater numerator will be the greater fraction.
- When two unlike fractions are compared then first convert the two fractions into like fractions and then compare.

Fractions

Like and Unlike Fraction

- Two or more fractions having the same denominator are called like fractions.
- Two or more fractions having different denominators are called unlike fractions.

Addition and subtraction of fractions

- To find the sum of two like fractions, we add the numerators and retain the common denominator.
- To find the difference of two like fractions, we subtract the smaller numerator from the bigger numerator and retain the common denominator.
- To add or subtract unlike fractions, we first convert them into equivalent fraction having the same denominator. Then proceed as addition and subtraction of like fractions.

MISCELLANEOUS
SOLVED EXAMPLES

1. Show $\dfrac{0}{7}$ and $\dfrac{3}{7}$ on number line.

Sol. Since $\dfrac{0}{7}$ and $\dfrac{3}{7}$ are less than 1, hence divide the portion of number line between 0 and 1 into 7 (denominator) equal parts.

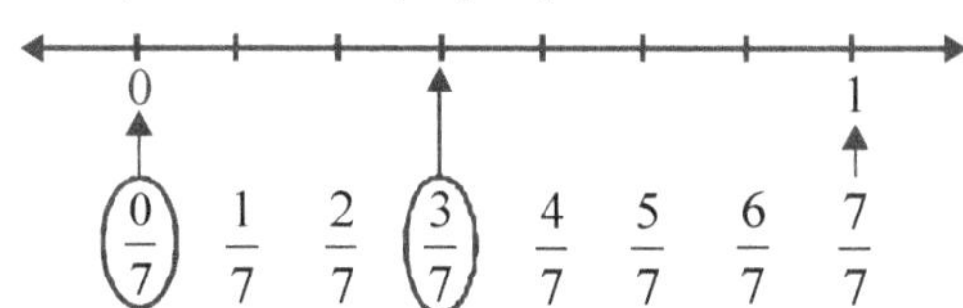

2. Represent $\dfrac{13}{5}$ on the number line.

Sol. $\dfrac{13}{5}$ can be written as $2\dfrac{3}{5}$.

Let us divide the line segment on the number line between 2 and 3 in 5 parts.

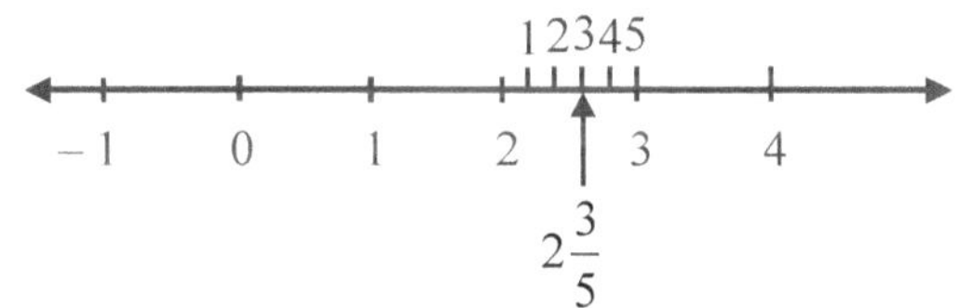

Thus, the point shown on the number line represents $2\dfrac{3}{5}$ or $\dfrac{13}{5}$.

3. Write an equivalent fraction of:

(i) $\dfrac{3}{4}$ with numerator 24.

(ii) $\dfrac{2}{7}$ with denominator 35.

Sol. **(i)** Let $\dfrac{3}{4} = \dfrac{24}{\boxed{?}}$

To get 24 in the numerator, we multiply 3 by 8.

∴ We multiply the denominator also by 8.

∴ $\dfrac{3}{4} = \dfrac{3 \times 8}{4 \times 8} = \dfrac{24}{32}$.

Hence, $\dfrac{3}{4}$ and $\dfrac{24}{32}$ are equivalent fractions.

(ii) Let $\dfrac{2}{7} = \dfrac{\boxed{?}}{35}$.

To get 35 in the denominator, we multiply 7 by 5.

∴ We multiply the numerator also by 5.

∴ $\dfrac{2}{7} = \dfrac{2 \times 5}{7 \times 5} = \dfrac{10}{35}$.

Hence, $\dfrac{2}{7}$ and $\dfrac{10}{35}$ are equivalent fractions.

4. Are the following fractions equivalent ?

(i) $\dfrac{5}{6}$ and $\dfrac{20}{24}$ **(ii)** $\dfrac{3}{8}$ and $\dfrac{6}{18}$

Sol. **(i)** Cross products of $\dfrac{5}{6}$ and $\dfrac{20}{24}$:

$$\dfrac{5}{6} \bowtie \dfrac{20}{24}$$

$5 \times 24 = 120;\ 6 \times 20 = 120$

Thus, $\dfrac{5}{6}$ and $\dfrac{20}{24}$ are equivalent fractions.

(ii) Cross products of $\dfrac{3}{8}$ and $\dfrac{6}{18}$:

$$\dfrac{3}{8} \bowtie \dfrac{6}{18}$$

$3 \times 18 = 54;\ 8 \times 6 = 48$

Thus, $\dfrac{3}{8}$ and $\dfrac{6}{18}$ are not equivalent fractions.

5. Compare :

(a) $\dfrac{2}{7}$ and $\dfrac{3}{4}$ **(b)** $\dfrac{5}{9}$ and $\dfrac{2}{3}$

Sol. (a) By cross multiplication, we see that

$$\frac{2}{7} \diagdown \frac{3}{4} \Rightarrow 2 \times 4 \text{ and } 3 \times 7$$

or 8 and 21
Since 8 < 21

So, $\dfrac{2}{7} < \dfrac{3}{4}$.

(b) On cross multiplying, we get

$$\frac{5}{9} \diagdown \frac{2}{3}$$

5 × 3 and 2 × 9
or 15 and 18
Since, 15 < 18

So, $\dfrac{5}{9} < \dfrac{2}{3}$.

6. Find the sum : $\dfrac{5}{12} + \dfrac{9}{16} + \dfrac{17}{24}$.

Sol.

$$
\begin{array}{r|lll}
4 & 12, & 16, & 24 \\ \hline
3 & 3, & 4, & 6 \\ \hline
2 & 1, & 4, & 2 \\ \hline
& 1, & 2, & 1
\end{array}
$$

L.C.M of 12, 16, 24 = 4 × 3 × 2 × 2 = 48.

$$\therefore \quad \frac{5}{12} + \frac{9}{16} + \frac{17}{24} = \frac{5 \times 4 + 9 \times 3 + 17 \times 2}{48}$$

$$= \frac{20 + 27 + 34}{48}$$

$$= \frac{\overset{27}{\cancel{81}}}{\underset{16}{\cancel{48}}} = \frac{27}{16} = 1\frac{11}{16}.$$

7. Subtract $4\dfrac{5}{9}$ **from** $7\dfrac{1}{6}$**.**

Sol. We have,

$$7\frac{1}{6} - 4\frac{5}{9} = \frac{43}{6} - \frac{41}{9}$$

L.C.M. of 6 and 9 = 18

$$= \frac{43 \times 3 - 41 \times 2}{18} = \frac{129 - 82}{18} = \frac{47}{18} = 2\frac{11}{18}.$$

8. Reshma bought $5\dfrac{1}{2}$ **of ribbon from the market. She cut off a** $2\dfrac{3}{4}$ **m piece of ribbon from it and gave it to Sushima. What length of ribbon is left with her?**

Sol. Total length of the ribbon = $5\dfrac{1}{2}$ m

Length of piece, given to Sushima = $2\dfrac{3}{4}$ m

∴ Length of ribbon left with Reshma

$$= 5\frac{1}{2}\,\text{m} - 2\frac{3}{4}\,\text{m}$$

$$= \frac{11}{2}\,\text{m} - \frac{11}{4}\,\text{m} = \frac{(11 \times 2) - 11}{4}$$

$$= \frac{22 - 11}{4}\,\text{m} = \frac{11}{4}\,\text{m} = 2\frac{3}{4}\,\text{m}$$

Thus, the length of ribbon left with Reshma is $2\dfrac{3}{4}$ m.

9. A farmer grows wheat in $\dfrac{2}{3}$ **of the field and vegetables in** $\dfrac{1}{4}$ **of the field. What part of the field is used for growing wheat and vegetables both?**

Sol. The part used for growing both wheat and vegetables is $\dfrac{2}{3} + \dfrac{1}{4}$.

LCM of 3 and 4 is 12.

So, $\dfrac{2}{3} + \dfrac{1}{4} = \dfrac{2 \times 4}{3 \times 4} + \dfrac{1 \times 3}{4 \times 3} = \dfrac{8}{12} + \dfrac{3}{12} = \dfrac{11}{12}$

Thus, the farmer used $\dfrac{11}{12}$ of his field for growing both wheat and vegetables.

1 EXERCISE

Fill in the Blanks :

DIRECTIONS : *Complete the following statements with an appropriate word / term to be filled in the blank space(s).*

1. A number representing a part of a _______ is called a fraction.

2. A fraction with denominator greater than the numerator is called a _______ fraction.

3. Fractions with the same denominator are called _______ fractions.

4. $13\dfrac{5}{18}$ is a _______ fraction.

5. The fraction $\dfrac{17}{34}$ in simplest form is _______.

6. $\dfrac{18}{135}$ and $\dfrac{90}{675}$ are proper, unlike and _______ fractions.

7. In addition / subtraction of unlike fractions _______ of denominators is required.

8. In addition / subtraction of mixed fractions first we have to convert the mixed fractions into _______

9. To reduce a fraction to its lowest terms, we divide the numerator and denominator of the given fraction by their _______.

10. Two or more fractions representing the same part of a whole are called _______ fractions.

True / False :

DIRECTIONS : *Read the following statements and write your answer as true or false.*

1. Fraction $\dfrac{18}{39}$ is in its lowest form.

2. Fractions $\dfrac{15}{39}$ and $\dfrac{45}{117}$ are equivalent fractions.

3. The result obtained by subtracting a fraction from another fraction is necessarily a fraction.

4. $3\dfrac{1}{3} > \dfrac{33}{10}$.

5. $8 - 1\dfrac{5}{6} = 7\dfrac{1}{6}$.

6. $\dfrac{1}{2}, \dfrac{1}{3}$ and $\dfrac{1}{4}$ are like fractions.

7. $\dfrac{3}{5}$ lies between 3 and 5.

8. Among $\dfrac{1}{2}, \dfrac{1}{3}, \dfrac{3}{4}, \dfrac{4}{3}$ the largest fraction is $\dfrac{4}{3}$.

Match the Columns :

DIRECTIONS : *Each question contains statements given in two columns which have to be matched. Statements (A, B, C, D, E) in column-I have to be matched with statements (p, q, r, s, t) in column-II.*

1. Match the following columns

Column- I	Column-II
(A) $2\dfrac{1}{5} + 3\dfrac{1}{5}$	(p) $\dfrac{37}{36}$
(B) $\dfrac{13}{15} - \dfrac{3}{15}$	(q) 3
(C) $\dfrac{7}{12} + \dfrac{4}{9}$	(r) $5\dfrac{2}{5}$
(D) $5\dfrac{1}{3} - 2\dfrac{1}{3}$	(s) $\dfrac{7}{6}$
(E) $2\dfrac{1}{2} - 1\dfrac{1}{3}$	(t) $\dfrac{2}{3}$

Very Short Answer Questions:

DIRECTIONS : *Give answer in one word or one sentence.*

1. Identify proper, improper and mixed fractions

   (i) $\dfrac{2}{5}$ (ii) $\dfrac{3}{2}$ (iii) $\dfrac{2}{4}$

   (iv) $1\dfrac{2}{5}$ (v) $3\dfrac{7}{9}$ (vi) $\dfrac{7}{5}$

   (vii) $\dfrac{11}{11}$ (viii) $\dfrac{3}{18}$

2. Express the following as mixed fraction.

   (i) $\dfrac{77}{6}$ (ii) $\dfrac{20}{3}$ (iii) $\dfrac{80}{7}$

   (iv) $\dfrac{26}{3}$ (v) $\dfrac{53}{12}$ (vi) $\dfrac{33}{5}$

3. Express the following as improper fraction.

   (i) $2\dfrac{1}{3}$ (ii) $2\dfrac{4}{5}$ (iii) $19\dfrac{4}{5}$

   (iv) $16\dfrac{2}{3}$ (v) $10\dfrac{3}{5}$ (vi) $14\dfrac{1}{7}$

4. Write a fraction equivalent to

   (i) $\dfrac{4}{8}$ with numerator 8

   (ii) $\dfrac{1}{2}$ with numerator 8

   (iii) $\dfrac{5}{7}$ with numerator 35

   (iv) $\dfrac{15}{75}$ with denominator 25

   (v) $\dfrac{20}{150}$ with denominator 75

5. Check if the given fractions are equivalent.

   (i) $\dfrac{2}{3}, \dfrac{5}{9}$ (ii) $\dfrac{7}{5}, \dfrac{35}{25}$

   (iii) $\dfrac{6}{17}, \dfrac{12}{51}$ (iv) $\dfrac{2}{5}, \dfrac{14}{35}$

6. Reduce the following fractions into their simplest form

   (i) $\dfrac{13}{65}$ (ii) $\dfrac{16}{80}$ (iii) $\dfrac{68}{72}$

   (iv) $\dfrac{36}{63}$ (v) $\dfrac{46}{76}$

7. Fill in the blanks with symbols =, > or <

   (i) $\dfrac{2}{5} \square \dfrac{6}{5}$ (ii) $\dfrac{11}{5} \square 4\dfrac{1}{3}$

   (iii) $\dfrac{2}{7} \square \dfrac{3}{4}$ (iv) $\dfrac{2}{5} \square \dfrac{1}{4}$

8. Find $\dfrac{5}{8}$ of 32.

9. What fraction of an hour is 24 minutes?

Short Answer Questions :

DIRECTIONS : *Give answer in 2-3 sentences.*

1. Add the following and reduce it to lowest term

   (i) $\dfrac{5}{2} + \dfrac{7}{3}$ (ii) $3\dfrac{1}{3} + 4\dfrac{3}{5}$

   (iii) $\dfrac{5}{8} + \dfrac{1}{4}$ (iv) $3 + \dfrac{2}{11}$

   (v) $\dfrac{1}{2} + \dfrac{1}{4} + 1\dfrac{1}{3}$

2. Find the difference and reduce it to lowest form

   (i) $6 - \dfrac{3}{5}$ (ii) $2\dfrac{3}{8} - 1\dfrac{3}{16}$

   (iii) $\dfrac{7}{12} - \dfrac{1}{6}$ (iv) $6\dfrac{3}{4} - 2\dfrac{1}{5}$

   (v) $\dfrac{7}{12} - \dfrac{4}{15}$

3. Show $\dfrac{3}{5}$ on a number line.

4. Raju read 30 pages of a book containing 150 pages. Geeta read $\dfrac{3}{5}$ of the same book. Who read less ?

5. Show $\dfrac{1}{10}, \dfrac{0}{10}, \dfrac{5}{10}$ and $\dfrac{10}{10}$ an a number line.

6. Mr. Singh bought one dozen eggs. He has used $\dfrac{1}{3}$ rd of eggs. How many eggs are left?

7. Find three equivalent fractions of the following.

(i) $\dfrac{2}{5}$ (ii) $\dfrac{1}{8}$

(iii) $\dfrac{3}{7}$ (iv) $\dfrac{4}{5}$

8. Write a fraction equivalent to $\dfrac{5}{8}$ with denominator 56.

9. Write a fraction equivalent to $\dfrac{36}{63}$ with numerator 4.

Long Answer Questions :

DIRECTIONS : *Give answer in four to five sentences.*

1. Ira read 25 pages of a 100 page book. Ritu read 40 pages of a 160 page book and Divya read 30 pages of a 120 page book. What fraction of books did each read? Have they read the same fraction of their books?

2. Arrange the following in descending order:

(i) $\dfrac{11}{24}, \dfrac{7}{16}, \dfrac{5}{6}, \dfrac{3}{8}$ (ii) $\dfrac{3}{8}, \dfrac{1}{9}, \dfrac{1}{5}$

3. The sum of two fractions is $14\dfrac{5}{12}$. If one of them is $7\dfrac{2}{3}$, find the other.

4. Three boxes weight $9\dfrac{1}{2}$ kg, $14\dfrac{1}{5}$ kg and $18\dfrac{3}{4}$ kg respectively. A porter carriers all the three boxes. What is the total weight carried by the porter?

5. Simplify : $6\dfrac{1}{6} - 5\dfrac{1}{5} + 3\dfrac{1}{3}$

6. Subtract the sum of $3\dfrac{5}{9}$ and $3\dfrac{1}{3}$ from the sum of $5\dfrac{5}{6}$ and $4\dfrac{1}{9}$.

2 EXERCISE

Text-Book Exercise :

1. What fraction of a day is 8 hours ?
2. What fraction of an hour is 40 minutes?
3. Write the natural numbers from 102 to 113. What fraction of them are prime numbers?
4. Write five improper fractions with denominator 7.
5. Check whether the given fractions are equivalent :

(i) $\dfrac{5}{9}, \dfrac{30}{54}$ (ii) $\dfrac{3}{10}, \dfrac{12}{50}$ (iii) $\dfrac{7}{13}, \dfrac{5}{11}$

6. Ramesh had 20 pencils, Sheelu had 50 pencils and Jamaal had 80 pencils. After 4 months, Ramesh used up 10 pencils, Sheelu used up 25 pencils and Jamaal used up 40 pencils. What fraction did each use up? Check if each has used up an equal fraction of her/his pencils ?

7. The following fractions represent just three different numbers. Separate them into three groups of equivalent fractions, by changing each one to its simplest form.

(i) $\dfrac{2}{12}$ (ii) $\dfrac{3}{15}$

(iii) $\dfrac{8}{50}$ (iv) $\dfrac{16}{100}$

(v) $\dfrac{10}{60}$ (vi) $\dfrac{15}{75}$

(vii) $\dfrac{12}{60}$ (viii) $\dfrac{16}{96}$

(ix) $\dfrac{12}{75}$ (x) $\dfrac{12}{72}$

(xi) $\dfrac{3}{18}$ (xii) $\dfrac{4}{25}$.

8. In a class A of 25 students, 20 passed in first class; in another class B of 30 students, 24 passed in first class. In which class were there more number of students getting first class?

9. Sohan was putting covers on his note books. He put one fourth of the covers on Monday. He put another one fourth on Tuesday and the remaining on Wednesday. What fraction of the covers did he put on Wednesday?

10. Fill in the missing fractions :

(i) $\dfrac{7}{10} - \square = \dfrac{3}{10}$ (ii) $\square - \dfrac{3}{21} = \dfrac{5}{21}$

(iii) $\square - \dfrac{3}{6} = \dfrac{3}{6}$ (iv) $\square + \dfrac{5}{27} = \dfrac{12}{27}$

11. Nandini's house is $\dfrac{9}{10}$ km from her school. She walked some distance and then took a bus for $\dfrac{1}{2}$ km to reach the school. How far did she walk ?

12. Asha and Samuel have bookshelves of the same size. Asha's shelf is $\dfrac{5}{6}$ th full of book and Samuel's shelf is $\dfrac{2}{5}$ th full. Whose bookshelf is more full? By what fraction?

Exemplar Questions :

1. A rectangle is divided into certain number of equal parts. If 16 of the parts so formed represent the fraction $\dfrac{1}{4}$, find the number of parts in which the rectangle has been divided.

2. Mr. Rajan got a job at the age of 24 years and he got retired from the job at the age of 60 years. What fraction of his age till retirement was he in the job?

3. The food we eat remains in the stomach for a maximum of 4 hours. For what fraction of a day, does it remain there?

4. Roma gave a wooden board of length $150\dfrac{1}{4}$ cm to a carpenter for making a shelf. The Carpenter sawed off a piece of $40\dfrac{1}{5}$ cm from it. What is the length of the remaining piece?

5. Nasir travelled $3\dfrac{1}{2}$ km in a bus and then walked $1\dfrac{1}{8}$ km to reach a town. How much did he travel to reach the town?

6. Neelam's father needs $1\dfrac{3}{4}$ m of cloth for the skirt of Neelam's new dress and $\dfrac{1}{2}$ m for the scarf. How much cloth must he buy in all?

7. Write the fraction representing the total number of natural numbers in the collection of numbers $-3, -2, -1, 0\ 1, 2, 3$. What fraction will it be for whole numbers? What fraction will it be for integers?

8. Write a pair of fractions whose sum is $\dfrac{7}{11}$ and difference is $\dfrac{2}{11}$.

9. What fraction of a straight angle is a right angle?

10. What is wrong in the following additions?

(i)
$$\begin{aligned} 8\dfrac{1}{2} &= 8\dfrac{2}{4} \\ +\ \ 4\dfrac{1}{4} &= 4\dfrac{1}{4} \\ \hline &= 12\dfrac{3}{8} \\ \hline \end{aligned}$$

(ii)
$$\begin{aligned} 6\dfrac{1}{2}& \\ +\ \ 2\dfrac{1}{4}& \\ \hline = 8\dfrac{2}{6} &= 8\dfrac{1}{3} \\ \hline \end{aligned}$$

HOTS Questions :

1. Angela is making pancakes. The recipe calls for 1 cup of milk. She pours in $\dfrac{1}{3}$ cup of milk. How much more milk does she need to add?

2. Marty is helping to make costumes for the class play. One costume needs $\dfrac{3}{4}$ yard of fabric Marty has two pieces of fabric. One is $\dfrac{1}{4}$ yard and one is $\dfrac{3}{8}$ yard. Does he have enough?

3. $\dfrac{4}{7}$ of a pole is in the mud. When $\dfrac{1}{3}$ of it is pulled out, a 8 m long piece of the pole still remains in the mud. What is the full length of the pole?

3 EXERCISE

Single Option Correct :

DIRECTIONS : *This section contains multiple choice questions. Each question has 4 choices (a), (b), (c) and (d) out of which ONLY ONE is correct.*

1. Which fraction does not belong to the group:

$$\dfrac{18}{45}, \dfrac{10}{15}, \dfrac{12}{30}, \dfrac{14}{35}, \dfrac{24}{60}$$

(a) $\dfrac{18}{45}$ (b) $\dfrac{14}{35}$

(c) $\dfrac{10}{15}$ (d) $\dfrac{12}{30}$

2. Which of the following fraction is the largest?

(a) $\dfrac{29}{30}$ (b) $\dfrac{29}{23}$

(c) $\dfrac{29}{27}$ (d) $\dfrac{29}{25}$

3. Insert the correct number in the box:

$$\dfrac{28}{35} = \dfrac{\Box}{30}$$

(a) 24 (b) 23
(c) 20 (d) 7

4. Which of the following fractions will be in middle if the given fractions are arranged in the descending order of their values ?

$$\dfrac{9}{17}, \dfrac{13}{26}, \dfrac{7}{15}, \dfrac{5}{8}, \dfrac{3}{7}$$

(a) $\dfrac{7}{15}$ (b) $\dfrac{9}{17}$

(c) $\dfrac{13}{26}$ (d) $\dfrac{5}{8}$

5. Which of the following fractions is the smallest?

(a) $\dfrac{13}{15}$ (b) $\dfrac{15}{17}$

(c) $\dfrac{8}{19}$ (d) $\dfrac{11}{24}$

6. A proper fraction is always
(a) less than 1 (b) Greater than 1
(c) Equal to 1 (d) None

7. An improper fraction is always
(a) less than 1 (b) Greater than 1
(c) Equal to zero (d) None

8. If $\dfrac{45}{60}$ is equivalent to $\dfrac{3}{x}$ then the value of x is
(a) 4 (b) 5
(c) 6 (d) 20

9. Which of the following are like fractions?

(a) $\dfrac{2}{3}, \dfrac{3}{4}, \dfrac{4}{5}, \dfrac{5}{6}$ (b) $\dfrac{2}{5}, \dfrac{2}{7}, \dfrac{2}{9}, \dfrac{2}{11}$

(c) $\dfrac{1}{8}, \dfrac{3}{8}, \dfrac{5}{8}, \dfrac{7}{8}$ (d) none of these

10. Which of the following fraction is the greatest of all?

$$\frac{7}{8}, \frac{6}{7}, \frac{4}{5}, \frac{5}{6}$$

(a) $\dfrac{6}{7}$　　　　　(b) $\dfrac{4}{5}$

(c) $\dfrac{5}{6}$　　　　　(d) $\dfrac{7}{8}$

11. A fraction equivalent to $\dfrac{2}{3}$ is

(a) $\dfrac{2+3}{3+3}$　　　　(b) $\dfrac{2-1}{3-1}$

(c) $\dfrac{2\times5}{3\times5}$　　　　(d) $\dfrac{2+5}{3+5}$

More Than One Option Correct :

DIRECTIONS : *This section contains multiple choice questions. Each question has 4 choices (a),* (b), (c) and (d) out of which *ONE or MORE may be correct.*

1. The fractions are equal to $\dfrac{4}{5}$ are

(a) $\dfrac{40}{50}$　　　　(b) $\dfrac{12}{15}$

(c) $\dfrac{16}{20}$　　　　(d) $\dfrac{9}{15}$

2. Mixed numbers always represent a
(a) fraction
(b) Proper fraction
(c) Improper fraction
(d) Unit fraction

3. Which of the following is/are not the equivalent fraction of $\dfrac{2}{7}$?

(a) $\dfrac{35}{10}$　　　　(b) $\dfrac{10}{35}$

(c) $\dfrac{6}{28}$　　　　(d) $\dfrac{10}{70}$

4. Which of the following fractions are not in their simplest form?

(a) $\dfrac{35}{49}$　　　　(b) $\dfrac{45}{81}$

(c) $\dfrac{46}{64}$　　　　(d) $\dfrac{13}{84}$

5. Which of the following is in the lowest form?

(a) $\dfrac{7}{5}$　　　　　(b) $\dfrac{15}{20}$

(c) $\dfrac{13}{33}$　　　　(d) $\dfrac{27}{28}$

Assertion & Reason :

DIRECTIONS : *Each of these questions contains an Assertion followed by Reason. Read them carefully and answer the question on the basis of following options. You have to select the one that best describes the two statements.*

(a) If both **Assertion** and **Reason** are correct and **Reason** is the **correct explanation** of **Assertion**.
(b) If both **Assertion** and **Reason** are correct but **Reason** is **not the correct explanation** of **Assertion**.
(c) If **Assertion** is correct but **Reason** is incorrect,
(d) If **Assertion** is incorrect but **Reason** is correct.

1. **Assertion :** $\dfrac{7}{10}$ and $\dfrac{9}{13}$ are equivalent fractions.

Reason : If $ad = bc$, then $\dfrac{a}{b}$ and $\dfrac{c}{d}$ are equivalent fractions.

2. **Assertion :** Simplifying $\dfrac{6}{8} - \dfrac{5}{12}$ we get $\dfrac{1}{3}$.

Reason : Difference of like fractions

$$= \frac{\text{difference of numerator}}{\text{common denominator}}$$

3. **Assertion :** $\dfrac{2}{7}$ lies between 0 and 1.

Reason : All proper fractions are less than 1.

Passage Based Questions :

DIRECTIONS : *Study the given passage(s) and answer the following questions.*

PASSAGE-I

My elder sister divided a watermelon into 18 parts. I ate 7 out of them. My friend ate 4.

1. How much did we eat ?

 (a) $\dfrac{7}{18}$ (b) $\dfrac{12}{18}$

 (c) $\dfrac{11}{18}$ (d) $\dfrac{9}{18}$

2. How much more of watermelon did I eat as compared to my friend ?

 (a) $\dfrac{3}{18}$ (b) $\dfrac{5}{18}$

 (c) $\dfrac{4}{18}$ (d) $\dfrac{7}{18}$

3. What amount of watermelon remained?

 (a) $\dfrac{5}{18}$ (b) $\dfrac{4}{18}$

 (c) $\dfrac{7}{18}$ (d) $\dfrac{3}{18}$

PASSAGE-II

Akshara walked for $\dfrac{10}{20}$ km on Monday, $\dfrac{15}{20}$ km on Tuesday and $\dfrac{13}{20}$ km on Friday.

4. How much did she walk on three days?

 (a) $2\dfrac{18}{20}$ km   (b) $\dfrac{9}{10}$ km

 (c) $1\dfrac{9}{10}$ km   (d) $1\dfrac{8}{20}$ km

5. How much more did she walk on Tuesday than on Monday?

 (a) $\dfrac{15}{20}$ km   (b) $\dfrac{1}{4}$ km

 (c) $\dfrac{3}{20}$ km   (d) $\dfrac{5}{10}$ km

6. On which day did she walk longer?
 (a) Monday   (b) Tuesday
 (c) Wednesday   (d) Friday

Integer Type Questions :

DIRECTIONS : *Answer the following questions. The answer to each of the question is a single digit integer, ranging from 0 to 9.*

1. How many one-eighths do you have when you subtract $\dfrac{1}{8}$ from $\dfrac{6}{8}$?

2. What is the missing number in $\dfrac{3}{10} = \dfrac{\square}{20}$?

3. Find the missing digit :

$$\dfrac{\square}{8} + \dfrac{1}{3} = \dfrac{17}{24}$$

4. What is the value of $\dfrac{2}{3} + \dfrac{4}{5} + \dfrac{4}{3} + \dfrac{1}{5}$?

5. Evaluate : $8 \times \left(\dfrac{4}{8} + \dfrac{1}{2} \right)$

6. What is the difference between $\dfrac{9}{4}$ and $\dfrac{1}{4}$?

Multiple Matching Question :

DIRECTIONS : *Following question has four statements (A, B, C and D) given in Column-I and five statements (p, q, r, s, t) in Column-II. Any given statement in Column-I can have correct matching with one or more statement(s) given in Column-II.*

1. Match the following.

Column-I Figure	Column-II Fraction for shaded part
(A) 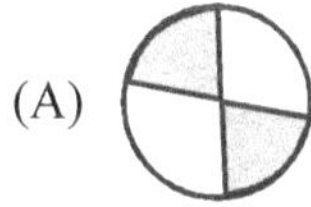	(p) $\dfrac{2}{9} + \dfrac{1}{9}$
(B) 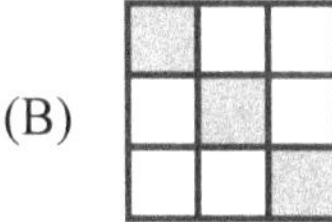	(q) $\dfrac{6}{8} - \dfrac{1}{8}$
(C) 	(r) $1 - \dfrac{3}{8}$
(D) 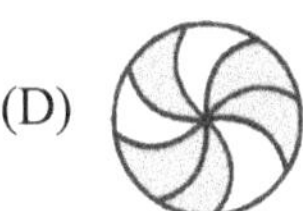	(s) $\dfrac{5}{4} - \dfrac{3}{4}$
	(t) $\dfrac{14}{9} - \dfrac{11}{9}$

SOLUTIONS

1 EXERCISE

Fill in the Blanks :

1. whole
2. proper
3. like
4. mixed
5. $\dfrac{1}{2}$
6. equivalent
7. LCM
8. improper fractions
9. HCF
10. equivalent

True / False :

1. F
2. T
3. F
4. T
5. F
6. F
7. F
8. T

Match the Columns :

1. (A) → (r); (B) → (t); (C) → (p); (D) → (q); (E) → (s)

Very Short Answer Questions:

1. (i) Proper   (ii) Improper
   (iii) Proper   (iv) Mixed
   (v) Mixed   (vi) Improper
   (vii) Improper   (viii) Proper

2. (i) $12\dfrac{5}{6}$ (ii) $6\dfrac{2}{3}$ (iii) $11\dfrac{3}{7}$
   (iv) $8\dfrac{2}{3}$ (v) $4\dfrac{5}{12}$ (vi) $6\dfrac{3}{5}$

3. (i) $\dfrac{7}{3}$ (ii) $\dfrac{14}{5}$ (iii) $\dfrac{99}{5}$
   (vi) $\dfrac{50}{3}$ (iv) $\dfrac{53}{5}$ (vi) $\dfrac{99}{7}$

4. (i) $\dfrac{8}{16}$ (ii) $\dfrac{8}{16}$ (iii) $\dfrac{35}{49}$

(iv) $\dfrac{5}{25}$ (v) $\dfrac{10}{75}$

5. (i) No   (ii) Yes   (iii) No
   (iv) Yes

6. (i) $\dfrac{1}{5}$ (ii) $\dfrac{1}{5}$ (iii) $\dfrac{17}{18}$
   (iv) $\dfrac{4}{7}$ (v) $\dfrac{23}{38}$

7. (i) <   (ii) <   (iii) <   (iv) >

8. $\dfrac{5}{8}$ of $32 = \left(\dfrac{5}{\cancel{8}_1} \times \dfrac{\cancel{32}^4}{1}\right) = \dfrac{20}{1} = 20$.

9. $\dfrac{24}{60} = \dfrac{2}{5}$

Short Answer Questions :

1. (i) $4\dfrac{5}{6}$ (ii) $7\dfrac{14}{15}$ (iii) $\dfrac{7}{8}$ (iv) $3\dfrac{2}{11}$
   (v) $2\dfrac{1}{12}$

2. (i) $5\dfrac{2}{5}$ (ii) $1\dfrac{3}{16}$ (iii) $\dfrac{5}{12}$ (iv) $4\dfrac{11}{20}$
   (v) $\dfrac{19}{60}$

3. We divide the length between 0 and 1 on a number line into 5 equal parts. The point A represents $\dfrac{3}{5}$.

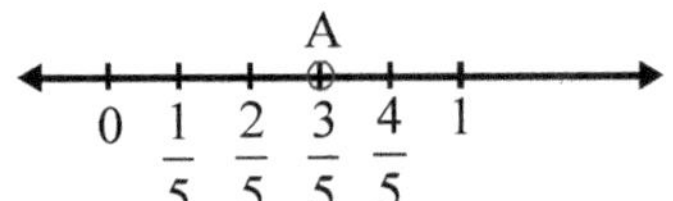

4. Raju

5. We draw a number line. Divide the length between 0 and 1 into 10 equal parts.

The point B represents $\dfrac{1}{10}$.

The point A represents $\dfrac{0}{10}$.

The point C represents $\dfrac{5}{10}$.

The point D represents $\dfrac{10}{10}$.

6. Number of eggs used = $\dfrac{1}{3}$ of 12 = 4

Number of eggs left = 12 − 4 = 8

7. (i) $\dfrac{2}{5} = \dfrac{2 \times 3}{5 \times 3} = \dfrac{6}{15}$

$\dfrac{2}{5} = \dfrac{2 \times 4}{5 \times 4} = \dfrac{8}{20}$

$\dfrac{2}{5} = \dfrac{2 \times 5}{5 \times 5} = \dfrac{10}{25}$

(ii) $\dfrac{1}{8} = \dfrac{1 \times 2}{8 \times 2} = \dfrac{2}{16}$

$\dfrac{1}{8} = \dfrac{1 \times 3}{8 \times 3} = \dfrac{3}{24}$

$\dfrac{1}{8} = \dfrac{1 \times 4}{8 \times 4} = \dfrac{4}{32}$

(iii) $\dfrac{3}{7} = \dfrac{3 \times 4}{7 \times 4} = \dfrac{12}{28}$

$\dfrac{3}{7} = \dfrac{3 \times 5}{7 \times 5} = \dfrac{15}{35}$

$\dfrac{3}{7} = \dfrac{3 \times 6}{7 \times 6} = \dfrac{18}{42}$

(iv) $\dfrac{4}{5} = \dfrac{4 \times 3}{5 \times 3} = \dfrac{12}{15}$

$\dfrac{4}{5} = \dfrac{4 \times 5}{5 \times 5} = \dfrac{20}{25}$

$\dfrac{4}{5} = \dfrac{4 \times 8}{5 \times 8} = \dfrac{32}{40}$

8. Let $\dfrac{5}{8} = \dfrac{\square}{56}$

Clearly, 56 = (8 × 7).

So, we multiply the numerator also by 7.

$\therefore \quad \dfrac{5}{8} = \dfrac{5 \times 7}{8 \times 7} = \dfrac{35}{56}$.

Hence, the required fraction is $\dfrac{35}{56}$.

9. Let $\dfrac{36}{63} = \dfrac{4}{\square}$.

Clearly, 4 = 36 ÷ 9.

So, we divide the denominator also by 9.

$\therefore \quad \dfrac{36}{63} = \dfrac{36 \div 9}{63 \div 9} = \dfrac{4}{7}$.

Hence, the required fraction is $\dfrac{4}{7}$.

Long Answer Questions :

1. Part of book Ira read = $\dfrac{25}{100} = \dfrac{1}{4}$

Part of book Ritu read = $\dfrac{40}{160} = \dfrac{1}{4}$

Part of book Divya read = $\dfrac{30}{120} = \dfrac{1}{4}$

Yes, Each of them read $\dfrac{1}{4}$ of the book.

2. (i) L.C.M of 24, 16, 6 and 8
= 2 × 2 × 2 × 2 × 3 = 48

2	24,	16,	6,	8
2	12,	8,	3,	4
2	6,	4,	3,	2
2	3,	2,	3,	1
3	3,	1,	3,	1
	1,	1,	1,	1

$\therefore \quad \dfrac{11}{24} = \dfrac{11 \times 2}{24 \times 2} = \dfrac{22}{48}$

$\dfrac{7}{16} = \dfrac{7 \times 3}{16 \times 3} = \dfrac{21}{48}$

$$\frac{5}{6} = \frac{5 \times 8}{6 \times 8} = \frac{40}{48}$$

$$\frac{3}{8} = \frac{3 \times 6}{8 \times 6} = \frac{18}{48}$$

Now, $\dfrac{40}{48} > \dfrac{22}{48} > \dfrac{21}{48} > \dfrac{18}{48}$

$\therefore \quad \dfrac{5}{6}, \dfrac{11}{24}, \dfrac{7}{16}, \dfrac{3}{8}$

(ii) L.C.M of 8, 9, and 5

$= 2 \times 2 \times 2 \times 3 \times 3 \times 5 = 360$

2	8,	9,	5
2	4,	9,	5
2	2,	9,	5
3	1,	9,	5
3	1,	3,	5
5	1,	1,	5
	1,	1,	1

$\therefore \quad \dfrac{3}{8} = \dfrac{3 \times 45}{8 \times 45} = \dfrac{135}{360}$

$$\frac{1}{9} = \frac{1 \times 40}{9 \times 40} = \frac{40}{360}$$

$$\frac{1}{5} = \frac{1 \times 72}{5 \times 72} = \frac{72}{360}$$

Now $\dfrac{135}{360} > \dfrac{72}{360} > \dfrac{40}{360}$

$\therefore \quad \dfrac{3}{8} > \dfrac{1}{5} > \dfrac{1}{9}$

3. The other fraction $= 14\dfrac{5}{12} - 7\dfrac{2}{3}$

$$= \frac{173}{12} - \frac{23}{3}$$

2	12,	3
2	6,	3
3	3,	3
	1,	1

L.C.M of 12 and 3 is 12

$$= \frac{173}{12} - \frac{23 \times 4}{12}$$

$$= \frac{173}{12} - \frac{92}{12}$$

$$= \frac{173 - 92}{12} = \frac{81}{12} = \frac{27}{4} = 6\frac{3}{4}$$

4. Total weight $= \left(9\dfrac{1}{2} + 14\dfrac{1}{5} + 18\dfrac{3}{4}\right)$ kg

2	2,	5,	4
2	1,	5,	2
5	1,	5,	1
	1,	1,	1

L.C.M. of 2, 5 and 4 $= 20$

$$= \frac{19}{2} + \frac{71}{5} + \frac{75}{4}$$

$$= \frac{190 + 284 + 375}{20}$$

$$= \frac{849}{20} = 42\frac{9}{20} \text{ kg}$$

5. $6\dfrac{1}{6} - 5\dfrac{1}{5} + 3\dfrac{1}{3}$

2	6, 5, 3
3	3, 5, 3
5	1, 5, 1
	1, 1, 1

L.C.M of 6, 5 and 3 $= 30$

$$= \frac{37}{6} - \frac{26}{5} + \frac{10}{3}$$

$$= \frac{185 - 156 + 100}{30}$$

$$= \frac{129}{30} = 4\frac{9}{30}$$

6. The sum of $3\dfrac{5}{9}$ and $3\dfrac{1}{3} = 3\dfrac{5}{9} + 3\dfrac{1}{3}$

$$= \frac{32}{9} + \frac{10}{3} = \frac{32 + 30}{9} = \frac{62}{9}$$

The sum of $5\dfrac{5}{6}$ and $4\dfrac{1}{9}$

$$= 5\frac{5}{6} + 4\frac{1}{9}$$

$$= \frac{35}{6} + \frac{37}{9} = \frac{105 + 74}{18} = \frac{179}{18}$$

Now Subtract $\dfrac{62}{9}$ from $\dfrac{179}{18}$

$$\dfrac{179}{18} - \dfrac{62}{9} = \dfrac{179-124}{18} = \dfrac{55}{18} = 3\dfrac{1}{18}$$

2 EXERCISE

Text-Book Exercise :

1. 1 day = 24 hours

$\therefore$ Required fraction $= \dfrac{8}{24} = \dfrac{1}{3}$

2. 1 hour = 60 minutes

$\therefore$ Required fraction $= \dfrac{40}{60} = \dfrac{2}{3}$

3. The natural numbers from 102 to 113 are
102, 103, 104, 105, 106, 107, 108, 109, 110,
111, 112, and 113
Total number of natural numbers = 12
Out of these, the prime numbers are 103, 107,
109, 113.
Total number of these prime numbers = 4

$\therefore$ Required fraction $= \dfrac{4}{12} = \dfrac{1}{3}$.

4. Required fractions are $\dfrac{18}{7}, \dfrac{19}{7}, \dfrac{10}{7}, \dfrac{11}{7}$ and $\dfrac{12}{7}$.

5. (i) $\dfrac{5}{9}, \dfrac{30}{54}$

$5 \times 54 = 270$
$9 \times 30 = 270$
$\because 5 \times 54 = 9 \times 30$

$\therefore$ The given fractions $\dfrac{5}{9}$ and $\dfrac{30}{54}$ are

equivalent.

(ii) $\dfrac{3}{10}, \dfrac{12}{50}$

$3 \times 50 = 150$
$10 \times 12 = 120$
$\because 150 \neq 120$
$\therefore 3 \times 50 \neq 10 \times 12$

$\therefore$ The given fractions $\dfrac{3}{10}$ and $\dfrac{12}{50}$ are not

equivalent.

(iii) $\dfrac{7}{13}, \dfrac{5}{11}$

$7 \times 11 = 77$
$13 \times 5 = 65$
$\because 77 \neq 65$
$\therefore 7 \times 11 \neq 13 \times 5$

$\therefore$ The given fractions $\dfrac{7}{15}$ and $\dfrac{5}{11}$ are

not equivalent.

6. Number of pencils Ramesh had = 20
Number of pencils used by him = 10

$\therefore$ Required fraction $= \dfrac{10}{20} = \dfrac{10 \div 10}{20 \div 10} = \dfrac{1}{2}$.

Number of pencils Sheelu had = 50
Number of pencils used by her = 25

$\therefore$ Required fraction $= \dfrac{25}{50} = \dfrac{25 \div 25}{50 \div 25} = \dfrac{1}{2}$.

Number of pencils Jamaal had = 80
Number of pencils used by him = 40

$\therefore$ Required fraction $= \dfrac{40}{80} = \dfrac{40 \div 40}{80 \div 40} = \dfrac{1}{2}$.

Yes! each has used up an equal fraction of
their pencils.

7. (i) $\dfrac{2}{12} = \dfrac{2 \div 2}{12 \div 2} = \dfrac{1}{6}$

(ii) $\dfrac{3}{15} = \dfrac{3 \div 3}{15 \div 3} = \dfrac{1}{5}$

(iii) $\dfrac{8}{50} = \dfrac{8 \div 2}{50 \div 2} = \dfrac{4}{25}$

(iv) $\dfrac{16}{100} = \dfrac{16 \div 4}{100 \div 4} = \dfrac{4}{25}$

(v) $\dfrac{10}{60} = \dfrac{10 \div 10}{60 \div 10} = \dfrac{1}{6}$

(vi) $\dfrac{15}{75} = \dfrac{15 \div 15}{75 \div 15} = \dfrac{1}{5}$

(vii) $\dfrac{12}{60} = \dfrac{12 \div 12}{60 \div 12} = \dfrac{1}{5}$

(viii) $\dfrac{16}{96} = \dfrac{16 \div 16}{96 \div 16} = \dfrac{1}{6}$

(ix) $\dfrac{12}{75} = \dfrac{12 \div 3}{75 \div 3} = \dfrac{4}{25}$

(x) $\dfrac{12}{72} = \dfrac{12 \div 12}{72 \div 12} = \dfrac{1}{6}$

(xi) $\dfrac{3}{18} = \dfrac{3 \div 3}{18 \div 3} = \dfrac{1}{6}$

(xii) $\dfrac{4}{25} = \dfrac{4}{25}$

Thus, $\dfrac{2}{12} = \dfrac{10}{60} = \dfrac{16}{96} = \dfrac{12}{72} = \dfrac{3}{18} \left(= \dfrac{1}{6} \text{ each} \right)$;

$\dfrac{3}{15} = \dfrac{15}{75} = \dfrac{12}{60} \left(= \dfrac{1}{5}\text{each} \right)$;

$\dfrac{8}{50} = \dfrac{16}{100} = \dfrac{12}{75} = \dfrac{4}{25} \left(= \dfrac{4}{25} \right)$ each.

8. $\dfrac{20}{25} = \dfrac{20 \div 5}{25 \div 5} = \dfrac{4}{5}$

$\dfrac{24}{30} = \dfrac{24 \div 6}{30 \div 6} = \dfrac{4}{5}$

Hence, in both the classes the same fraction $\left(\dfrac{4}{5} \right)$ of total students got first class.

9. $\dfrac{1}{4} + \dfrac{1}{4} = \dfrac{1+1}{4} = \dfrac{2}{4} = \dfrac{1}{2}$

$1 - \dfrac{1}{2} = \dfrac{2}{2} - \dfrac{1}{2} = \dfrac{2-1}{2} = \dfrac{1}{2}$

Hence, he put $\dfrac{1}{2}$ fraction of the covers on Wednesday.

10. (i) $\dfrac{7}{10} - \square = \dfrac{3}{10}$

$\Rightarrow \square = \dfrac{7}{10} - \dfrac{3}{10} = \dfrac{7-3}{10} = \dfrac{4}{10} = \dfrac{2}{5}$

(ii) $\square - \dfrac{3}{21} = \dfrac{5}{21}$

$\Rightarrow \square = \dfrac{3}{21} + \dfrac{5}{21} = \dfrac{3+5}{21} = \dfrac{8}{21}$

(iii) $\square - \dfrac{3}{6} = \dfrac{3}{6}$

$\Rightarrow \square = \dfrac{3}{6} + \dfrac{3}{6} = \dfrac{3+3}{6} = \dfrac{6}{6} = 1$

(iv) $\square + \dfrac{5}{27} = \dfrac{12}{27}$

$\Rightarrow \square = \dfrac{12}{27} - \dfrac{5}{27}$

$\Rightarrow \square = \dfrac{12-5}{27} = \dfrac{7}{27}$

11. Distance of Nandini's house from school

$= \dfrac{9}{10}$ km

Distance travelled by bus $= \dfrac{1}{2}$ km

$\therefore$ Distance walked by Nandini

$= \dfrac{9}{10} \text{ km} - \dfrac{1}{2} \text{ km} = \left(\dfrac{9}{10} - \dfrac{1}{2} \right) \text{ km}$

$= \left(\dfrac{9}{10} - \dfrac{1 \times 5}{2 \times 5} \right) \text{ km}$

$= \left(\dfrac{9}{10} - \dfrac{5}{10} \right) \text{ km} = \dfrac{9-5}{10} \text{ km}$

$= \dfrac{4}{10} \text{ km} = \dfrac{2}{5}\text{km.}$

12. L.C.M. $(6, 5) = 30$

$\dfrac{5}{6} = \dfrac{5 \times 5}{6 \times 5} = \dfrac{25}{30}$

$\dfrac{2}{5} = \dfrac{2 \times 6}{5 \times 6} = \dfrac{12}{30}$

$\because \quad 25 > 12 \quad \therefore \quad \dfrac{25}{30} > \dfrac{12}{30}$

$\therefore$ Asha's book self is more full by fraction

$$\frac{25}{30} - \frac{12}{30}$$

$$= \frac{25 - 12}{30} = \frac{13}{30}$$

Exemplar Questions

1. $\frac{1}{4}$ of whole = 16 parts

$\therefore$ Whole = 4 × 16 parts = 64 parts.

2. Number of years in job = 60 − 24 = 36 years

His age = 60 years

$\therefore$ Fraction of his age in the job = $\frac{36}{60} = \frac{3}{5}$

3. The required fraction = $\frac{4}{24} = \frac{1}{6}$

4. The length of remaining piece = $150\frac{1}{4} - 40\frac{1}{5}$

$$= \frac{601}{4} - \frac{201}{5}$$

$$= \frac{3005 - 804}{20} = \frac{2201}{20} = 110\frac{1}{20} \text{ cm}$$

5. Total distance travelled = $3\frac{1}{2} + 1\frac{1}{8}$

$$= \frac{7}{2} + \frac{9}{8} = \frac{28 + 9}{8}$$

$$= \frac{37}{8} = 4\frac{5}{8} \text{ km}$$

6. Total length of cloth = $1\frac{3}{4} + \frac{1}{2} = \frac{7}{4} + \frac{1}{2}$

$$= \frac{7 + 2}{4} = \frac{9}{4} = 2\frac{1}{4} \text{ m}$$

7. Fraction for natural numbers = $\frac{3}{7}$

Fraction for whole numbers = $\frac{4}{7}$

Fraction for integers = $\frac{7}{7} = 1$

8. $\frac{7 \times 2}{11 \times 2} = \frac{14}{22}$ and $\frac{2 \times 2}{11 \times 2} = \frac{4}{22}$

$\therefore$ 9 and 5 are two nos. whose sum is 14 and difference is 4.

Hence $\frac{9}{22}$ and $\frac{5}{22}$ are the required fractions

9. Right Angle = 90°

and Straight angle = 180°

$\therefore$ The required fraction = $\frac{90}{180} = \frac{1}{2}$

10. (i) Equal denominators too have been added.

(ii) Numerators and denominators have been added.

HOTS Questions :

1. Milk needed to add = $1 - \frac{1}{3} = \frac{3 - 1}{3} = \frac{2}{3}$ cup

She need $\frac{2}{3}$ cup of milk.

2. Total length of fabric = $\frac{1}{4} + \frac{3}{8} = \frac{2 + 3}{8} = \frac{5}{8}$ yard

Fabric needed for one costume = $\frac{3}{4}$ yard

Let us compare $\frac{5}{8}$ and $\frac{3}{4}$

5 × 4 = 20 and 8 × 3 = 24

$\therefore$ 20 < 24

$\therefore \frac{5}{8} < \frac{3}{4}$

Hence, Marty does not have enough fabric.

3. Part of the pole in the mud = $\frac{4}{7}$

Part of the pole pulled out of mud

$$= \frac{1}{3} \text{ of } \frac{4}{7} = \frac{4}{21}$$

Part of the pole still in the mud = $\left[\frac{4}{7} - \frac{4}{21}\right] = \frac{8}{21}$

$\therefore \frac{8}{21}$ of the full length = 8 m

$\therefore$ Full length = $\left[8 \times \frac{21}{8}\right]$ m = 21 m.

3 E X E R C I S E

Single Option Correct :

1. **(c)** We write all fraction in reduced form and then find the odd-one.

$$\frac{18}{45} = \frac{9 \times 2}{9 \times 5} = \frac{2}{5} \qquad \frac{10}{15} = \frac{2 \times 5}{3 \times 5} = \frac{2}{3}$$

$$\frac{12}{30} = \frac{2 \times 6}{5 \times 6} = \frac{2}{5} \qquad \frac{14}{35} = \frac{7 \times 2}{7 \times 5} = \frac{2}{5}$$

$$\frac{24}{60} = \frac{12 \times 2}{12 \times 5} = \frac{2}{5}$$

Clearly $\frac{10}{15}$ does not belong to the group.

2. **(b)** $\therefore$ All fractions are having same numerator. So, the fraction having smallest denominator is the largest.

Hence, $\frac{29}{23}$ is the largest.

3. **(a)** $\dfrac{28}{35} = \dfrac{7 \times 4}{7 \times 5} = \dfrac{4}{5} = \dfrac{4 \times 6}{5 \times 6} = \dfrac{24}{30}$

$\therefore \boxed{}$ should be replaced by 24.

4. **(c)** $\dfrac{13}{26}$

5. **(d)** The smallest fraction is $\dfrac{11}{24}$.

6. (a) **7.** (b) **8.** (a) **9.** (c) **10.**(d)
11. (c)

More Than One Option Correct :

1. **(a, b, c)**
2. **(a, c)**
3. **(a, c, d)**
4. **(a, b, c)**

$\dfrac{13}{84}$ is in its simplest form, because

HCF (13, 84) = 1

5. **(a, c, d)**

In $\dfrac{7}{5}$, the common factor of 7 and 5 is 1.

In $\dfrac{15}{20}$, the common factor of 15 and 20 is 5.

In $\dfrac{13}{33}$, the common factor of 13 and 33 is 1.

In $\dfrac{27}{28}$, the common factor of 27 and 28 is 1.

Assertion & Reason :

1. **(d)** : Cross multiplication of $\dfrac{7}{10}$ and $\dfrac{9}{13}$

$\Rightarrow 91 \neq 90$.
Assertion : False, **Reason :** True

2. **(b)** $\dfrac{6}{8} - \dfrac{5}{12} = \dfrac{18}{24} - \dfrac{10}{24} = \dfrac{8}{24} = \dfrac{1}{3}$

Assertion : True, **Reason :** True but Reason is not the correct explanation of Assertion.

3. **(a)** $0 < \dfrac{2}{7} < 1$.

Assertion : True, **Reason :** True and Reason is the correct explanation of Assertion.

Passage Based Questions :

1. **(c)** The fractions of watermelon eaten by me and my friend $= \dfrac{7}{18} + \dfrac{4}{18} = \dfrac{11}{18}$

2. **(a)** Portion of watermelon which I ate more in comparison to my friend

$= \dfrac{7}{18} - \dfrac{4}{18} = \dfrac{7-4}{18} = \dfrac{3}{18}$

3. **(c)** Portion of watermelon remained

$= 1 - \left(\dfrac{7}{18} + \dfrac{4}{18}\right)$

$= \dfrac{18 - (7+4)}{18} = \dfrac{18 - 11}{18} = \dfrac{7}{18}$

4. (c) On three days, she walked

$$= \left(\frac{10}{20} + \frac{15}{20} + \frac{13}{20} \right) \text{km}$$

$$= \frac{10+15+13}{20} = \frac{38}{20} = \frac{19}{10} = 1\frac{9}{10} \text{ km}$$

5. (b) Walking excess on Tuesday by

$$\frac{15}{20} - \frac{10}{20} = \frac{5}{20} = \frac{1}{4} \text{ km}$$

6. (b) As $\dfrac{15}{20} > \dfrac{13}{20} > \dfrac{10}{20}$

$\therefore$ She walked longer on Tuesday.

Integer Type Questions :

1. (5) $\dfrac{6}{8} - \dfrac{1}{8} = \dfrac{6-1}{8} = \dfrac{5}{8}$

$\therefore$ 5 one-eighths are there

2. (6) As $20 \div 10 = 2$

Equivalent fraction of $\dfrac{3}{20} = \dfrac{3 \times 2}{10 \times 2} = \dfrac{6}{20}$

$\therefore$ The missing number is 6.

3. (3) We have, $\dfrac{\square}{8} + \dfrac{1}{3} = \dfrac{17}{24}$

Subtracting $\dfrac{1}{3}$ from both sides

$$\frac{\square}{8} + \frac{1}{3} - \frac{1}{3} = \frac{17}{24} - \frac{1}{3}$$

$$\Rightarrow \frac{\square}{8} = \frac{17}{24} - \frac{1}{3} = \frac{17}{24} - \frac{8}{24} = \frac{9}{24}$$

$$\Rightarrow \frac{\square}{8} = \frac{3}{8}$$

$\therefore$ Missing number $= 3$.

4. (3) $\dfrac{2}{3} + \dfrac{4}{5} + \dfrac{4}{3} + \dfrac{1}{5} = \dfrac{2 \times 5 + 4 \times 3 + 4 \times 5 + 1 \times 3}{15}$

$$\frac{10}{15} + \frac{12}{15} + \frac{20}{15} + \frac{3}{15}$$

$$\frac{10+12+20+3}{15} = \frac{45}{15} = 3$$

5. (8) $8 \times \left(\dfrac{4}{8} + \dfrac{1}{2} \right) = 8 \times \left(\dfrac{4}{8} + \dfrac{4}{8} \right)$

$$= 8 \times \left(\frac{4+4}{8} \right)$$

$$= 8 \times \left(\frac{8}{8} \right) = 8 \times 1 = 8$$

6. (2) The difference between $\dfrac{9}{4}$ and $\dfrac{1}{4}$ is

$$\frac{9-1}{4} = \frac{8}{4} = 2$$

Multiple Matching Questions :

1. (A) $\rightarrow$ (s), (B) $\rightarrow$ (p, t); (C) $\rightarrow$ (q); (D) $\rightarrow$ (r)

(A) represents $\dfrac{2}{4}$ shaded fraction which is

equal to $\dfrac{5}{4} - \dfrac{3}{4} = \dfrac{2}{4}$

(B) represents $\dfrac{3}{9}$ shaded fraction which is

equal to $\dfrac{2}{9} + \dfrac{1}{9} = \dfrac{3}{9}$ and $\dfrac{14}{9} - \dfrac{11}{9} = \dfrac{3}{9}$

(C) represents $\dfrac{5}{8}$ which is equal to

$$\frac{6}{8} - \frac{1}{8} = \frac{5}{8}$$

(D) represents $\dfrac{5}{8}$ which is equal to $1 - \dfrac{3}{8}$

$$= \frac{8}{8} - \frac{3}{8} = \frac{5}{8}$$

Chapter 8

Decimals

READING A DECIMAL NUMBER

A decimal number has two parts – whole number part and decimal part. These two parts are separated by a dot (.) called as decimal point. The digits lying to the left of decimal is its whole part and the digits lying to the right of decimal is its decimal part. **For example :**

$$42 \ . \ 67$$

Whole part | Decimal part

Decimal point

We read it as 'Forty two point six seven'.

DECIMAL FRACTIONS

The fractions in which the denominators are 10, 100, 1000 etc. are known as **decimal fractions. For example,**
$\dfrac{3}{10}, \dfrac{75}{100}, \dfrac{236}{1000}$ etc.

PLACE VALUE OF DECIMAL NUMBERS

The positions to the right of the decimal point are called the decimal places; the 1st, the 2nd, the 3rd, and so on.

Each decimal digit occupies a decimal place.

Let us see the different decimal places in the following number.

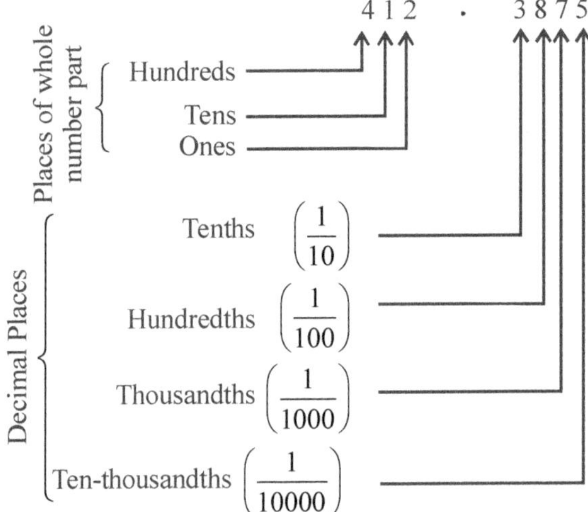

In the whole number part, if we move right to left by 1 place, the value of a digit decreases by 10 times for each place.

In the decimal part, if we move left to right by 1 place, the value of a digit decrease by $\dfrac{1}{10}$ for each place.

∴ Place value of each of the digit in the number 412.3875 is as follows.

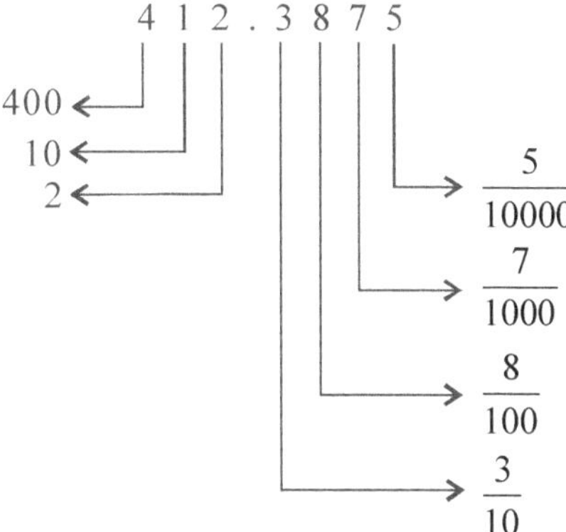

Tenths Place

The digit at the 1st decimal place shows the number of Tenths. If we move one place to the right of ones place, the value becomes $\dfrac{1}{10}$ of the digit and this place is known as tenths place.

For example : Place value of 3 in 412.3875 is 3 tenths or $\dfrac{3}{10}$.

Hundredths Place

The 2nd decimal place shows the number of Hundredths. If we move one place to the right of tenths place, the place value becomes $\dfrac{1}{100}$ of the digit and this place is known as Hundredths place.

For example : Place value of 8 in 412.3875 is 8 hundredths or $\dfrac{8}{100}$.

Thousandths Place

The 3rd decimal place shows the number of Thousandths. If we move one place to the right of hundredths place, the place value becomes $\dfrac{1}{1000}$ of the digit and this place is known as Thousandths place.

For example : Place value of 7 in 412.3875 is 7 thousandths or $\dfrac{7}{1000}$.

Expanded Forms

Writing the place values of each digit of a given number as sum is the expanded form of that number.

For example : $412.3875 = 400 + 10 + 2 + \dfrac{3}{10} + \dfrac{8}{100} + \dfrac{7}{1000} + \dfrac{5}{10000}$

The above number can also be expanded using decimal as :
$$400 + 10 + 2 + 0.3 + 0.08 + 0.007 + 0.0005$$

ILLUSTRATION : 1

Write the following decimals in place value chart.
(i)   529.16   (ii)   16.53   (iii)   8.921   (iv)   0.755   (v)   26.035

SOLUTION :

S. No.		Thousands	Hundreds	Tens	Ones	Decimal	Tenths	Hundredths	Thousandths
(i)	529.16		5	2	9		1	6	
(ii)	16.53			1	6		5	3	
(iii)	8.921				8	.	9	2	1
(iv)	0.755						7	5	5
(v)	26.035			2	6		0	3	5

REPRESENTATION OF DECIMALS ON THE NUMBER LINE

Let us represent 4.2 on the number line

Clearly, 4.2 lies between 4 and 5. Take a magnified look of the line segment between 4 and 5 and divide it into 10 equal parts and mark each point of division between 4 and 5 as shown in the Fig. (ii).

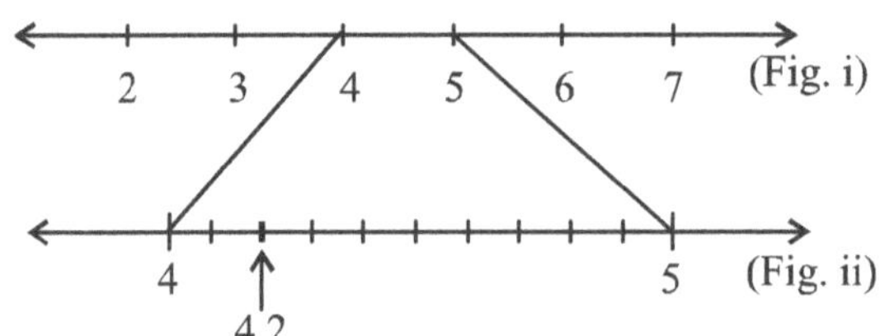

We can see in Fig. (ii), 4.2 is represented by the second mark of division after 4 in between 4 and 5.

ILLUSTRATION : 2

Write the decimal and fractional expansion of the following :
(a)   38.02   (b)   183.048   (c)   3.678

SOLUTION :

Decimal expansion

(a) $38.02 = 30 + 8 + 0.0 + 0.02$

(b) $183.048 = 100 + 80 + 3 + 0.0 + 0.04 + 0.008$

(c) $3.678 = 3 + 0.6 + 0.07 + 0.008$

Fractional expansion

(a) $38.02 = 30 + 8 + \dfrac{0}{10} + \dfrac{2}{100}$

(b) $183.048 = 100 + 80 + 3 + \dfrac{0}{10} + \dfrac{4}{100} + \dfrac{8}{1000}$

(c) $3.678 = 3 + \dfrac{6}{10} + \dfrac{7}{100} + \dfrac{8}{1000}$

CONVERSION BETWEEN DECIMALS AND FRACTIONS

Fractions as decimals

To express given fraction into decimals, we follow the following steps:
Case I: Fractions whose denominators are of 10, 100, 1000 etc.

Step (i)   Count the number of zeros in denominator.

Step (ii)   Place the decimal point in numerator so that the number of digits on right of decimal point becomes equal to the number of zeros in denominator.

Step (iii)   In case the number of digits in numerator is less than the number of zeros in denominator, we place zero just right to decimal.

For example : In $\dfrac{14}{1000}$, number of zeros in denominator is 3

So, $\dfrac{14}{1000} = 0.014$

Case II: Fractions whose denominators are not 10, 100, 1000 etc.

Divide the numerator by the denominator and write the quotient in decimal form.

Decimals as Fraction

To express the given decimals into fraction, we follow the following steps:

Step (i)   Write the decimal without the decimal point as the numerator of the fraction.

Step (ii)   Write the denominator of the fraction by inserting as many zeros on the right of 1 as the number of decimal places in the given decimals.

Step (iii)   Simplify the fraction and write the fraction in the lowest form.

For example: Let us express 0.038 as fraction

$$0.038 = \dfrac{38}{1000} = \dfrac{19}{500}.$$

ILLUSTRATION : 3

Convert the following fractions into decimals.

(i) $\dfrac{35}{100}$ (ii) $11\dfrac{2}{100}$ (iii) $\dfrac{3}{8}$ (iv) $8\dfrac{1}{5}$

SOLUTION :

(i) $\dfrac{35}{100} = 0.35$

(ii) $11\dfrac{2}{100} = 11 + \dfrac{2}{100} = 11.02$

(iii) $\dfrac{3}{8} = \dfrac{3 \times 125}{8 \times 125} = \dfrac{375}{1000} = 0.375$

(iv) $8\dfrac{1}{5} = 8 + \dfrac{1}{5} = 8 + \dfrac{1 \times 2}{5 \times 2} = 8 + \dfrac{2}{10} = 8 + 0.2 = 8.2$

LIKE AND UNLIKE DECIMALS

The decimals having the same number of decimal places are called **like decimals**.

For example: 0.25, 1.37, 15.14 and 13.86, are like decimals. All have two decimal places.

The decimals having different number of decimal places are called **unlike decimals**.

For example: 0.6, 0.34 and 1.386 are unlike decimals. They have different number of decimals places.

Conversion of unlike decimals into like decimals

To convert unlike decimals into like decimals, we put extra zeros to the extreme right of decimal part to make number of digits equal after decimal.

For example: Let us convert 7, 5.3, 9.21 and 8.406 into like decimal.

Here, the maximum number of decimal places is 3.

Now, convert all decimals into like decimals by putting extra zeros to the extreme right of the decimal part.

$$7 = 7.000, \ 5.3 = 5.300, \ 9.21 = 9.210$$

NOTE: Adding extra zeros to the right of a decimal does not change its value i.e. $0.96 = 0.96000$

COMPARISON OF DECIMALS

To compare two decimals we should follow the following steps:

Step 1 : Compare the whole number part, the decimals having greater whole part is greater.

Step 2 : If the whole number parts are equal, then compare the tenth digits. The decimal number with greater tenth digit is greater.

Step 3 : If the tenths digit are equal, then compare the hundredths digit. The decimal number having greater hundredths digit is greater and so on.

For example: Let us compare 4.397 and 4.391

Compare the whole parts of both the numbers. But, whole parts are same.

Now, compare tenths digits. But tenths are also same.

So, compare hundredths digits. These are also same.

Now, compare thousandths digits. Clearly, 7 thousandths > 1 thousandth

So,   4.397 > 4.391

USE OF DECIMALS IN DAILY LIFE

Concept of decimal is very useful in our daily life. Some examples are as follows:

Money

We know that, 100 paise = ₹1

Therefore, $1\,\text{paisa} = ₹\dfrac{1}{100} = ₹\,0.01$

So, $45\,\text{paise} = ₹\dfrac{45}{100} = ₹\,0.45$

Length

We know that,

$$1\,\text{km} = 1000\,\text{m} \Rightarrow 1\,\text{m} = \dfrac{1}{1000}\,\text{km}$$

Similarly, $1\text{m} = 100\,\text{cm} \Rightarrow 1\,\text{cm} = \dfrac{1}{100}\,\text{m}$

For example : $7\,\text{m} = \dfrac{7}{1000}\,\text{km} = 0.007\,\text{km}$

Weight

We know that,

$$1\,\text{kg} = 1000\,\text{g} \Rightarrow 1\,\text{g} = \dfrac{1}{1000}\,\text{kg} = 0.001\,\text{kg}$$

Similarly, $1\,\text{g} = 1000\,\text{mg} \Rightarrow 1\,\text{mg} = \dfrac{1}{1000}\,\text{g} = 0.001\,\text{g}$

For example : $7\text{g} = \dfrac{7}{1000}\,\text{kg} = 0.007\,\text{kg}$

OPERATIONS OF DECIMALS

Addition of decimals

Step (i) Convert the given decimals to like decimals.

Step (ii) Write the decimals in columns with the decimal points directly below each other so that tenths come under tenths hundredths come under hundredths and so on.

Step (iii) Add as we add whole numbers, starting from right.

Step (iv) Place the decimal point in the answer directly below the other decimal points.

For Example: Add 12.73, 4.7, 1.074

$$
\begin{array}{r}
12.730 \\
+\ \ 4.700 \\
+\ \ 1.074 \\
\hline
18.504 \\
\hline
\end{array}
$$

ILLUSTRATION : 4

Raja spent ₹ 35.70 for Mathematics book and ₹ 42.50 for science book. Find the total amount he spent.

SOLUTION :

Cost of mathematics book = ₹ 35.70

Cost of science book   = ₹ 42.50

Total cost   = ₹ 35.70

$$
\begin{array}{r}
+\ 42.50 \\
\hline
₹\ 78.20 \\
\hline
\end{array}
$$

Total amount spent by Raja is ₹ 78.20.

Subtraction of Decimals

We may follow the following steps to subtract a decimal number from another decimal number.

Step (i) Convert the given decimals to like decimals.

Step (ii) Write the decimals in columns with decimal points directly below each other.

Step (iii) Subtract as we subtract whole numbers starting from right.

Step (iv) Place the decimal point in the difference directly below the other decimal points.

For example: Subtract 10.205 from 20.05

$$
\begin{array}{r}
20.050 \\
-\ 10.250 \\
\hline
9.800 \\
\hline
\end{array}
$$

CONCEPT MAP

Decimals

Decimal Number

- When a whole is divided into 10 equal parts, then each part is one-tenth $\left(\dfrac{1}{10}\right)$ of a unit. In decimal notation it can be written as 0.1.
- The decimal point always lies between units place and the tenths place.
- The number before the decimal point is called the whole part and the number after the decimal point is called the fractional part or decimal part.

Like Decimals

- Decimal numbers having same number of decimal places are called like decimals.

Addition and Subtraction of Decimals

- To add decimal numbers, place them one below the other such that the decimal points are in a vertical line. Then add hundredths, tenths, ones and so on. Put the decimal point in the sum vertically below the other decimal points.
- To subtract decimals, arrange them as did in case of addition. Then subtract hundredths from hundredths, tenths from tenths ones from ones and so on.

Note: If decimals are unlike decimals, then first convert them into like decimals before subtracting.

Use of Decimals

- 1 paisa = Re 0.01
- 1 cm = 0.01 m
- 1 mm = 0.1 cm
- 1 m = 0.001 km
- 1g = 0.001 kg

Comparison of Decimals

- To compare two decimals, compare their whole parts. Decimal having greater whole part is greater.
- If whole part are equal, then compare tenths part. If tenths parts are also equal, then compare hundredths part and so on.

MISCELLANEOUS
SOLVED EXAMPLES

1. Write 357.248 in expanded form (Using Place Value Chart).

Sol.

Places	Thousands	Hundreds	Tens	Ones	Decimal	Tenths	Hundredths	Thousandths
Number		3	5	7	•	2	4	8

Thus, the expanded form of 357.248 is given by

$$357.248 = 3 \times 100 + 5 \times 10 + 7 \times 1 + \frac{2}{10} + \frac{4}{100} + \frac{8}{1000}$$

2. Write each of the following as a decimal number:

(i) $90 + 5 + \dfrac{6}{10} + \dfrac{3}{100}$.

(ii) $400 + 8 + \dfrac{5}{10} + \dfrac{7}{100} + \dfrac{1}{1000}$.

Sol. We have:

(i) $90 + 5 + \dfrac{6}{10} + \dfrac{3}{100} = 95.63$

(ii) $400 + 8 + \dfrac{5}{10} + \dfrac{7}{100} + \dfrac{1}{1000} = 408.571$

3. Write the given decimals as fractions in lowest form.

(a) 0.29   (b) 2.08

(c) 148.32   (d) 200.812

Sol. (a) $0.29 = \dfrac{29}{100}$.

(b) $2.08 = \dfrac{208}{100} = \dfrac{104}{50} = \dfrac{52}{25}$.

(c) $148.32 = \dfrac{14832}{100} = \dfrac{7416}{50} = \dfrac{3708}{25}$

(d) $200.812 = \dfrac{200812}{1000} = \dfrac{100406}{500} = \dfrac{50203}{250}$.

4. Convert following fraction into decimal:

(i) $\dfrac{21}{8}$ (ii) $5\dfrac{3}{8}$

Sol. (i)
```
     2.625
8 ) 21.000
   -16
    50
   -48
    20
   -16
    40
   -40
     0
```

Hence, $\dfrac{21}{8} = 2.625$

(ii)
```
      .375
8 ) 3.000
   -24
    60
   -56
    40
   -40
     0
```

$5\dfrac{3}{8} = 5.375$

Hence, $5\dfrac{3}{8} = 5.375$.

5. Express the following fractions as decimals:

(i) $7\dfrac{1}{2}$ (ii) $9\dfrac{1}{4}$ (iii) $12\dfrac{1}{8}$

Sol. (i) $7\dfrac{1}{2} = 7 + \dfrac{1}{2} = 7 + \dfrac{5 \times 1}{5 \times 2} = 7 + \dfrac{5}{10} = 7 + 0.5 = 7.5$

(ii) $9\dfrac{1}{4} = 9 + \dfrac{1}{4} = 9 + \dfrac{25 \times 1}{25 \times 4} = 9 + \dfrac{25}{100}$

$= 9 + 0.25 = 9.25$

(iii) $12\dfrac{1}{8} = 12 + \dfrac{1}{8} = 12 + \dfrac{125 \times 1}{125 \times 8}$

$= 12 + \dfrac{125}{1000} = 12 + 0.125 = 12.125$

6. Compare the following pairs of decimal numbers:
    (i) 2.735 and 3.1   **(ii)** 37.765 and 37.699
    (iii) 157.99 and 157.989
    (iv) 2.3456815 and 2.3456807

Sol. **(i)**

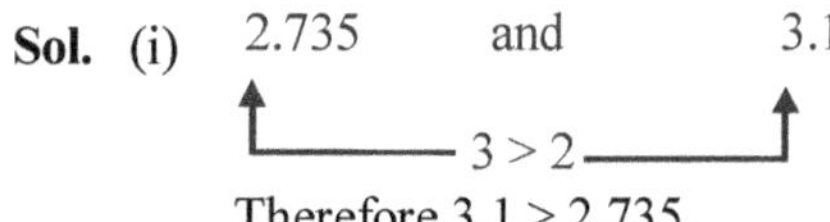

Therefore $3.1 > 2.735$.

(ii)

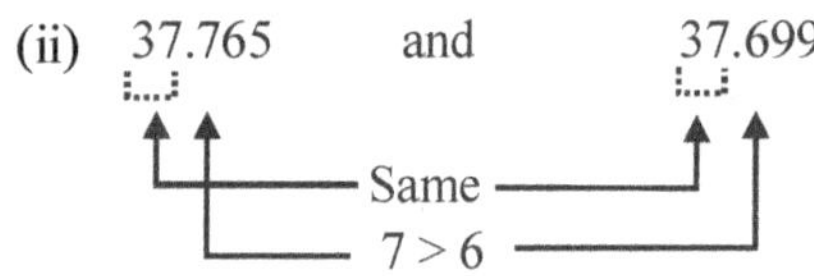

Therefore $37.765 > 37.699$.

(iii)

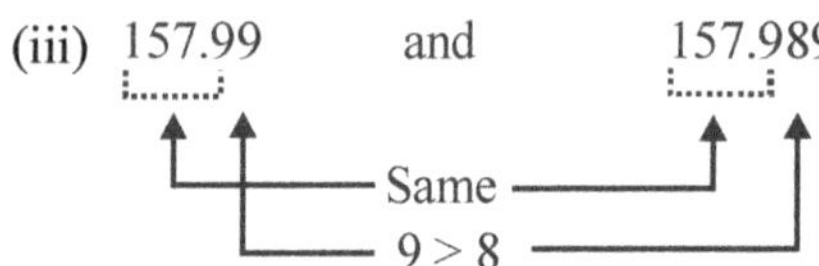

Therefore $157.99 > 157.989$.

(iv)

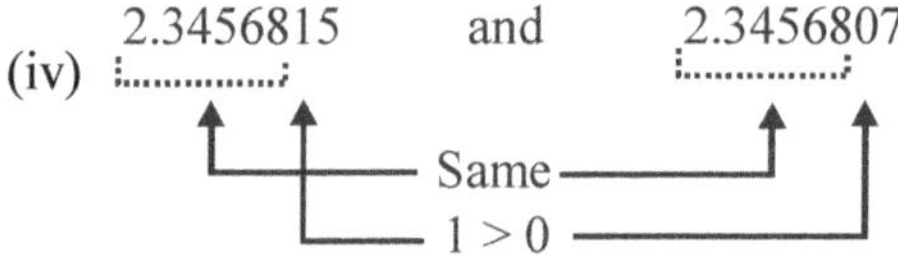

Therefore $2.3456815 > 2.3456807$.

7. **Express in kilograms, using decimals:**
    (i) 5 kg 35 g   **(ii)** 78 g

Sol. (i) $5 \text{ kg } 35 \text{ kg} = 5 \text{ kg} + 35 \text{ kg} = 5 \text{ kg} + \dfrac{35}{1000} \text{ kg}$
           $= 5 \text{ kg} + 0.035 \text{ kg} = 5.035 \text{ kg}.$

(ii) $78 \text{ g} = \dfrac{78}{1000} \text{ kg} = 0.078 \text{ kg}.$

8. **Express in kilometres, using decimals:**
    (i) 9 km 46 m   **(ii)** 56 m

Sol. (i) $9 \text{ km } 46 \text{ m} = 9 \text{ km} + 46 \text{ m}$

$= 9 \text{ km} + \dfrac{46}{1000} \text{ km} = 9 \text{ km} + 0.046 \text{ km} = 9.046 \text{ km}$

(ii) $56 \text{ m} = \dfrac{56}{1000} \text{ km} = 0.056 \text{ km}$

9. **Express in rupees, using decimals:**
    (i) ₹ 6 and 9 paise   **(ii)** 38 paise

Sol. (i) ₹ 6 and 9 paise $= ₹ 6 + ₹ \dfrac{9}{100}$
          $= ₹ 6 + ₹ 0.09 = ₹ 6.09.$

(ii) 38 paise $= ₹ \dfrac{38}{100} = ₹ 0.38.$

10. **Tarun cycled from his house to the post office, from the post office to the market from the market to the temple and from the temple he cycled back to his home. Find the total distance covered by him.**

Cycled	Distance
(i) Tarun's house - Post office	3.750 km
(ii) Post office - Market	0.674 km
(iii) Market - Temple	0.845 km
(iv) Temple - House	2.493 km

Sol.

Total distance covered $= (3.750 + 0.674 + 0.845 + 2.493) \text{ km}$

$$
\begin{array}{r}
3.750 \text{ km} \\
0.674 \text{ km} \\
0.845 \text{ km} \\
+\ 2.493 \text{ km} \\
\hline
7.762 \text{ km} \\
\hline
\end{array}
$$

Therefore, the total distance covered by Tarun is 7.762 km.

11. **The total weight of three parcels is 48.057 kg. If two of them weigh 12.64 kg and 18.57 kg, find the weight of the third parcel.**

Sol. Weight of one parcel $= 12.64 \text{ kg}$
Weight of second parcel $= 18.57 \text{ kg}$
Total weight of two parcels $= (12.64 + 18.57) \text{ kg}$
Total weight of two parcels $= 31.21 \text{ kg}$
Total weight of three parcels $= 48.057 \text{ kg}$
The weight of the third parcel is 16.847 kg.

12. **Simplify : 48.6 – 23.48 + 108.57 – 78.9.**

Sol. Writing each of the given numbers with two decimal places, we get:
Given expression
$= 48.60 - 23.48 + 108.57 - 78.90.$
$= (48.60 + 108.57) - (23.48 + 78.90)$

$$
\begin{array}{r}
48.60 \\
+\ 108.57 \\
\hline
157.17 \\
\end{array}
\qquad \text{and} \qquad
\begin{array}{r}
23.48 \\
+\ 78.90 \\
\hline
102.38 \\
\end{array}
$$

Given expression $= 157.17 - 102.38 = 54.79$

Hence, $48.6 - 23.48 + 108.57 - 78.9 = 54.79.$

$$
\begin{array}{r}
157.17 \\
-\ 102.38 \\
\hline
54.79 \\
\hline
\end{array}
$$

1 EXERCISE

Fill in the Blanks :

DIRECTIONS : *Complete the following statements with an appropriate word / term to be filled in the blank space(s).*

1. $9 + \dfrac{2}{10} + \dfrac{6}{100}$ is equal to the decimal number _______.

2. Decimal 16.25 is equal to the fraction _______.

3. Fraction $\dfrac{7}{25}$ is equal to the decimal number _______.

4. $4.55 + 9.73 =$ _______.
5. $8.76 - 2.68 =$ _______.
6. 3 Hundredths + 3 tenths = _______.
7. $1\ m =$ _______ km
8. $7\ kg\ 15\ g =$ _______ kg.
9. $2\ l\ 5\ ml =$ _______ l.
10. $2\ m\ 5\ cm =$ _______ m.

True / False :

DIRECTIONS : *Read the following statements and write your answer as true or false.*

1. The place value of a digit at the tenths place is 10 times the same digit at the ones place.

2. The place value of a digit at the hundredths place is $\dfrac{1}{10}$ times the same digit at the tenths place.

3. In the decimal form, fraction $\dfrac{25}{8} = 3.125$.

4. The decimal $23.2 = 23\dfrac{2}{3}$.

5. $3.03 + 0.016 = 3.019$
6. $42.28 - 3.19 = 39.09$
7. $19.25 < 19.053$
8. $13.730 = 13.73$
9. $3.02 < 3.2.$

10. 2.3, 3.41, 4.53, 5.61 are examples of like decimals.

Match the Columns :

DIRECTIONS : *Each question contains statements given in two columns which have to be matched. Statements (A, B, C, D) in column-I have to be matched with statements (p, q, r, s) in column-II.*

1.

	Column-I		Column-II
(A)	The sum of 1.8, 16.3 and 72.985 is	(p)	14.091
(B)	The value of $27.091 - 32.05 + 19.05$ is	(q)	13.063
(C)	Sum of 0.5, 12.56 and 0.003 is	(r)	19.754
(D)	When we add the decimal forms of fraction $\dfrac{7}{100}, \dfrac{124}{1000}$ and $\dfrac{1956}{100}$, the result is	(s)	91.085

Very Short Answer Questions:

DIRECTIONS : *Give answer in one word or one sentence.*

1. Find the place value of underlined digits.
   (i) 960.83$\underline{4}$ (ii) 225.$\underline{7}$75
   (iii) 26.0$\underline{5}$ (iv) 679.8$\underline{9}$7

2. Write the fractional expansion of the following.
   (i) 5.68   (ii) 34.03
   (iii) 732.6   (iv) 53.003
   (v) 0.89

3. Represent the following decimals on number line.
   (i) 0.5   (ii) 0.8   (iii) 1.3
   (iv) 1.9   (v) 2.4   (vi) 2.7

4. Identify the groups of like decimals.
   (i)   0.23   1.28   27.69   638.54
   (ii) 0.10   2.0   38.512   263.1
   (iii) 0.4   0.04   0.004   0.40
   (iv) 26.8   26.9   26.1   26.7
   (v)   0.323   2.198   24.600   841.201

5. Convert each group into like decimal.
   (i)   3.6   4.38   9.008
   (ii) 0.4   2.10   3.86
   (iii) 81.29   17.9   0.6

6. Which is greater ?
   (i)   0.5 or 0.05   (ii) 0.9 or 0.90
   (iii) 2 or 0.02   (iv) 8.00 or 8.0
   (v)   1.01 or 1.1   (vi) 3.20 or 3.02

7. Arrange the following decimal number in ascending order :
   (i)   0.4   0.52   0.81   0.43
   (ii) 0.9   1.32   5.62   2.183
   (iii) 4.83   4.80   14.6   14.63
   (iv) 17.341   205.03   17.211   205.1
   (v)   332.192   82.61   332.446   76.5

8. Arrange the decimals in decending order :
   (i)   7.9,   79.9,   79.09,   7.6
   (ii) 15.88,   158.8,   15.80,   15
   (iii) 0.63,   0.6,   0.68,   0.601
   (iv) 19.25,   0.38,   1.108,   0.235

9. Convert as required:

S.No.	Unit	Required unit
(i)	50 rupees 5 paise	______ rupees
(ii)	20 cm 1 mm	______ cm
(iii)	45 m 82 cm	______ m
(iv)	5454 m	______ km
(v)	3 kg 92 g	______ kg
(vi)	21 rupees 12 paise	______ rupees
(vii)	11 cm 21 mm	______ cm
(viii)	1.42 m	______ m ______ cm
(ix)	3km 60m	______ km
(x)	0.52 kg	______ g

10. Write each of the following decimals in figures:
   (i)   Seventy three point eight four.
   (ii) Three hundred forty six point zero nine five.
   (iii) Five hundred eight point two six.
   (iv) Nineteen point six one eight.
   (v)   Zero point seven nine three.
   (vi) Ten point zero zero seven.

DIRECTIONS : *Give answer in 2-3 sentences.*

1. Convert each of the following fractions into a decimal:
   (i) $\dfrac{7}{20}$ (ii) $\dfrac{9}{25}$
   (iii) $\dfrac{8}{125}$ (iv) $\dfrac{121}{250}$

2. Convert the following decimal number into fraction:
   (i)   6.75   (ii) 924.275

3. Add 65.251, 32.72, 4.9 and 22.64

4. Add: 27.8, 46, 175.09 and 685.7

5. Subtract 28.65 from 73.

6. What is to be added to 74.5 to get 91?

7. What is to be subtracted from 7.3 to get 0.862?

8. Arrange the following weights in ascending order:
   500 g, 2 kg, 1.99 kg, 9999 mg

9. By how much is 4 m greater than 298 cm? Give your answer in m.

10. Find the sum of 7m, 4 cm and 94 mm in metres.

DIRECTIONS : *Give answer in four to five sentences.*

1. Ramesh purchased a book, a pen and a notebook for ₹ 165.35, ₹ 72 and ₹ 14.85 respectively. How much money will he have to pay to the shopkeeper for these items?

2. Abhishek had ₹ 7.45. He bought toffees for ₹ 5.30. Find the balance amount left with Abhishek.

3. Simplify: $53.5 - 34.68 + 64.75 - 28.9$

4. A piece of 15.34 m long string is cut into two pieces. If the length of one piece is 8.26 m, find the length of the other piece.

5. Anshika bought vegetable weighing 17 kg. Out of this, 5 kg 500 g is onions, 7.2 kg is potatoes, 3.5 kg is tomatoes and rest is cauliflower. Find the weight of cauliflower?

6. Gopal travelled 125.5 km by bus, 14.25 km by pony and the rest of distance to Kedarnath on foot. If he covered a total distance of 150 km, how much did he travel on foot?

2 EXERCISE

Text-Book Exercise :

1. Can you now write the following as decimals?

	Hundreds	Tens	Ones	Tenths
	(100)	(10)	(1)	$\left(\dfrac{1}{10}\right)$
(i)	5	3	8	1
(ii)	2	7	3	4

2. Write the following decimals in the place value table.
   (i) 19.4   (ii) 0.3

3. Write each of the following as decimals:

   (i) $\dfrac{5}{10}$ (ii) $3 + \dfrac{7}{10}$

   (iii) $200 + 60 + 5 + \dfrac{1}{10}$ (iv) $\dfrac{88}{10}$

   (v) $4\dfrac{2}{10}$

4. (i) The length of Ramesh's notebook is 9 cm 5mm. What will be its length in cm?
   (ii) The length of a young gram plant is 65 mm. Express its length in cm.

5. Between which two whole numbers on the number line are the given numbers lie? Which of these whole numbers is nearer the number?

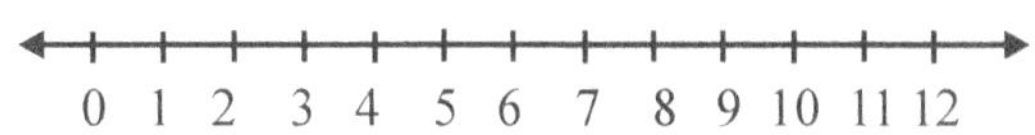

   (i)   0.8   (ii) 5.1
   (iii) 2.6   (iv) 6.4
   (v)   9.1   (vi) 4.9

6. Write as fractions in lowest terms.
   (i)   0.60   (ii) 0.05
   (iii) 0.18   (iv) 0.125
   (v)   0.066

7. (i) Write 2 rupees 5 paise and 2 rupees 50 paise in decimals?
   (ii) Write 20 rupees 7 paise and 21 rupees 75 paise in decimals?

8. Can you now write 52 m as 'km' using decimals? How will you write 340 m as 'km' using decimals? How will you write 2008 m in 'km'?

9. Sunita travelled 15 km 268 m by bus, 7 km 7 m by car and 500 m on foot in order to reach her school. How far is her school from her residence?

10. Namita travels 20 km 50 m every day. Out of this she travels 10 km 200 m by bus the rest by auto. How much distance does she travel by auto?

Exemplar Questions :

1. Arrange 12.142, 12.124, 12.104, 12.401 and 12.214 in ascending order.

2. Express $3\dfrac{2}{5}$ as a decimal.

3. Express 0.041 as a fraction.

4. Express 6.03 as a mixed fraction.

5. Convert 5201 g to kg.

6. Convert 2009 paise to rupees and express the result as a mixed fraction.

7. Convert 1537 cm to m and express the result as an improper fraction.

8. Convert 2435 m to km and express the result as mixed fraction.

9. What should be added to 25.5 to get 50?

10. Add the following:
    20.02 and 2.002

11. Alok purchased 1 kg 200 g potatoes, 250 g dhania, 5 kg 300 g onion, 500 g palak and 2 kg 600 g tomatoes. Find the total weight of his purchases in kilograms.

12. Energy content of different foods are as follows:

Food	Energy Content per kg.
Wheat	3.2 Joules
Rice	5.3 Joules
Potatoes (Cooked)	3.7 joules
Milk	3.0 Joules

Which food provides the least energy and which provides the maximum?

Express the least energy as a fraction of the maximum energy.

13. Round off 20.83 to nearest tenths.

14. Round off 75.195 to nearest hundredths.

HOTS Questions :

1. Subtract the sum of 13.05 and 21.12 from 39.93.

2. How much is the sum of 36.63 and 112.36 greater than their differenc?

3. The maximum temperature of Delhi on Sunday was 34.7°C. On Monday, it increased by 3.2°C and on Tuedsay, it was 5.3°C less than that on Monday. What was the temperature on Tuesday?

3 EXERCISE

Single Option Correct :

DIRECTIONS : *This section contains multiple choice questions. Each question has 4 choices (a), (b), (c) and (d) out of which ONLY ONE is correct.*

1. The expanded form of 31.005 is

(a) $3 \times 10 + 1 \times 1 + \dfrac{5}{100}$

(b) $3 \times 10 + 1 \times 1 + \dfrac{5}{1000}$

(c) $3 \times 100 + 1 \times 10 + \dfrac{5}{1000}$

(d) $3 + 1 \times 100 + \dfrac{5}{1000}$

2. Ravi bought some medicines for ₹ 495.75 and gave the chemist a 1000- rupee note. What amount did the chemist return ?

(a) ₹ 500.75   (b) ₹ 504.50

(c) ₹ 500.25   (d) ₹ 504.25

3. The sum of two numbers is 31.021. The other number will be ________, if one of them is 11.56.

(a) 19.461   (b) 17.461

(c) 18.641   (d) 19.561

4. The sum of 47.027 and 109.01 is

(a) 156.037   (b) 154.031

(c) 156.038   (d) 154.038

5. On the number line, the decimal number 3.7 is exactly between which one of the following numbers?

(a) 1 and 2   (b) 3 and 4

(c) 4 and 5   (d) 5 and 6

6. Riya spent ₹ 34.60 on purchasing a basket. How much money is left if she had ₹100?

(a) ₹ 65.40   (b) ₹ 10.50

(c) ₹ 65.10   (d) ₹ 50.75

7. The place value of underlined digit in number 49.6̲7̲

(a) 6 ones   (b) 6 tenths

(c) 6 hundredths   (d) None of these

8. The lowest term of 0.668 is :

(a) $\dfrac{267}{250}$ (b) $\dfrac{167}{250}$

(c) $\dfrac{250}{167}$ (d) None of these

9. 1.008 and 1.800 are

(a) like decimal   (b) equal decimal

(c) unlike decimal   (d) none

10. Sum of 1.2 + 0.23 + 0.02 will give :

(a) 1.63   (b) 1.45

(c) 1.47   (d) 2.23

11. On taking out 59.2 gm sugar from 70 gm :

(a) 10.8 gm   (b) 1.08 gm

(c) 0.108 gm   (d) 108 gm

12. ₹ 12.50 spent from ₹ 50 will leave :
(a) ₹ 37.50 (b) ₹ 26.50
(c) ₹ 16.50 (d) ₹ 36.50

More Than One Option Correct :

DIRECTIONS : *This section contains multiple choice questions. Each question has 4 choices (a), (b), (c) and (d) out of which ONE or MORE may be correct.*

1. Which of the following are not like decimals?
(a) 5.5, 5.05, 5.005, 5.50
(b) 5.5, 0.55, 5.55, 5.555
(c) 5.5, 6.6, 7.7, 8.8
(d) 0.5, 0.56, 0.567, 0.5678

2. 2.66 + 1.88 is equal to

(a) 4.54 (b) $45\dfrac{4}{10}$

(c) $\dfrac{454}{100}$ (d) 0.454.

3. 0.55 in fractions is equal to

(a) $\dfrac{55}{100}$ (b) $\dfrac{11}{20}$

(c) $\dfrac{5}{20}$ (d) None.

4. 13 m 6 cm in metres is written as
(a) 13.06 (b) 13.6

(c) $13\dfrac{6}{10}$ (d) $13\dfrac{6}{100}$

5. Fractional form of decimal 0.005 is

(a) $\dfrac{5}{1000}$ (b) $\dfrac{5}{100}$

(c) $\dfrac{1}{200}$ (d) $\dfrac{1}{2000}$

6. The place value of 3 in 16.534 is

(a) 0.003 (b) $\dfrac{3}{100}$

(c) $\dfrac{3}{1000}$ (d) 0.03

7. 0.7499 lies between
(a) 0.7 and 0.74 (b) 0.73 and 0.79
(c) 0.749 and 0.75 (d) 0.74992 and 0.75

Assertion & Reason :

DIRECTIONS : *Each of these questions contains an Assertion followed by Reason. Read them carefully and answer the question on the basis of following options. You have to select the one that best describes the two statements.*

(a) If both **Assertion** and **Reason** are correct and **Reason** is the correct explanation of **Assertion**.
(b) If both **Assertion** and **Reason** are correct but **Reason** is not the correct explanation of assertion.
(c) If **Assertion** is correct but **Reason** is incorrect.
(d) If **Assertion** is incorrect but **Reason** is correct.

1. **Assertion:** Expressing 249 m into km is 249000 km.

Reason: 1 m = $\dfrac{1}{1000}$ km

2. **Assertion:** The number 211.902 is expressed in expanded form as $2 \times 100 \times 1 \times 10 \times 1 + 9 \times \dfrac{1}{10} \times 2 \times \dfrac{1}{100}$.

Reason: As we go from left to right, the multiplying factor becomes $\dfrac{1}{10}$ of the previous factor.

3. **Assertion:** 0.3, 0.30, 0.300 are the equivalent decimals.

Reason : Number of zero at the end of decimal number change the value of the number.

Passage Based Questions :

DIRECTIONS : *Study the given passage(s) and answer the following questions.*

PASSAGE-I

To change a decimal numeral to a common fraction, express the decimal as a fraction with denominator 10, 100, 1000 and then reduce it to its lowest term.

1. The sum of 67.25, 5.5, 9.85 in fraction form is

   (a) $\dfrac{826}{100}$ (b) $\dfrac{826}{10}$

   (c) 826   (d) $\dfrac{820}{100}$

2. Amit bought a comic book for ₹ 45.60 and a magazine for ₹ 70.00. What is the total amount spent by Amit (Express in lowest fractional form).

   (a) $\dfrac{102}{5}$ (b) $\dfrac{156}{2}$

   (c) $\dfrac{578}{5}$ (d) $\dfrac{1156}{5}$

3. Convert 19.07 kg in grams.

   (a) 19070 g   (b) $\dfrac{1907}{10}$ g

   (c) 1907 g   (d) None of these

PASSAGE-II

A squash ball weighs 3400 mg, a cricket ball weighs 45 g, a basketball weighs 0.65 kg and a football weighs 3 kg.

4. Which sports ball is heavier in weight?
   (a) Cricket ball   (b) Football
   (c) Squash ball   (d) Basketball

5. What is the weight (in kg) of basketball and football?
   (a) 0.365 kg   (b) 3.65 kg
   (c) 365 kg   (d) 3 kg

6. What is the total weight of all the balls in gram?
   (a) 3729 g   (b) 3.729 g
   (c) 3729000 g   (d) 0.3729 g

Integer Type Questions :

DIRECTIONS : *Answer the following questions. The answer to each of the question is a single digit integer, ranging from 0 to 9.*

1. Ravi bought 5 m 20 cm cloth for his trousers and 2m 80 cm for his shirt. Find the total length of cloth bought by Ravi.

2. Ravi had ₹ 18.50. He bought one ice-cream for ₹ 11-50. How much money does he have now?

3. Radhika bought 3 kg 400 g of apples and 2 kg 600 g of grapes and she put them in a bag. If the bag already had 3 kg of oranges, what is the weight of the fruits in the bag now?

4. What is the decimal part of the sum if we add 8.3 and 5.6?

5. What is the whole number part in sum of 3 + 0.4 + 0.01 + 0.001?

6. What is the tenth place value if we add 13.5 and 1.57?

Multiple Matching Question :

DIRECTIONS : *Following question has four statements (A, B, C and D) given in Column-I and five statements (p, q, r, s, t) in Column-II. Any given statement in Column-I can have correct matching with one or more statement(s) given in Column-II.*

1. Match the following

Column -I	Column -II
(A) Sundaram bought a toothpaste for ₹ 18.75, soap for ₹ 6 and shoe polish for ₹ 12.50. He gave a fifty rupee note to the shopkeeper. Find the money he got back.	(p) 17.34
(B) Shweta travelled 12 km 220 m by bus, 8 km 485 m by car and the rest 760 m she walked. How much distance did she travel in all ?	(q) 64.375
(C) Subtract 34.76 from 52.1	(r) 12.75
(D) Simplify : $77.7 - 7.555 - 5.77$	(s) 21.465
	(t) $10 + 7 + \dfrac{3}{10} + \dfrac{1}{25}$

SOLUTIONS

Brief Explanations of Selected Questions

1 EXERCISE

Fill in the Blanks :

1. 9.26 2. $16\frac{1}{4}$ or $\frac{65}{4}$ 3. 0.28
4. 14.28 5. 6.08 6. 0.33
7. 0.001 km 8. 7.015 kg 9. 2.005 *l*.
10. 2.05 m

True / False :

1. F 2. T 3. T 4. F
5. F 6. T 7. F 8. T
9. T 10. F

Match the Columns :

1. (A) → (s); (B) → (p); (C) → (q); (D) → (r)

A : 1.8 + 16.3 + 72.985 = 01.800
16.300
72.985
91.085

B : 27.091 – 32.05 + 19.05

= 27.091 +19.05 – 32.05

27.091 + 19.05 = 27.091
19.050
46.141

46.141 – 32.05 = 46.141
32.050
14.091

C : 0.5 + 12.56 + 0.003 = 00.500
+12.560
+00.003
13.063

D : Decimal forms of $\frac{7}{100}$, $\frac{124}{1000}$ and $\frac{1956}{100}$ are 0.07, 0.124 and 19.56 respectively.

Their sum = 00.070
+00.124
+19.560
19.754

Very Short Answer Questions:

1. (i) 4 thousandths (ii) 7 tenths
(iii) 5 hundredths (iv) 9 hundredths

2. (i) $5+\frac{6}{10}+\frac{8}{100}$

(ii) $30 + 4 + \frac{0}{10}+\frac{3}{100}$

(iii) $700 + 30 + 2 + \frac{6}{10}$

(iv) $50 + 3 + \frac{0}{10}+\frac{0}{100}+\frac{3}{1000}$

(v) $\frac{8}{10}+\frac{9}{100}$

3. 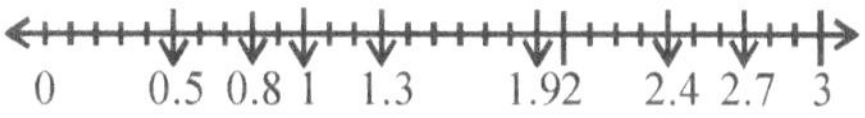

4. (i), (iv), (v)
5. (i) 3.600 4.380 9.008
(ii) 0.40 2.10 3.86
(iii) 81.29 17.90 0.60
6. (i) 0.5 (ii) equal
(iii) 2 (iv) equal
(v) 1.1 (vi) 3.20
7. (i) 0.4 0.43 0.52 0.81
(ii) 0.9 1.32 2.183 5.62
(iii) 4.80 4.83 14.6 14.63
(iv) 17.211 17.341 205.03 205.1
(v) 76.5 82.61 332.192 332.446
8. (i) 79.9 79.09 7.9 7.6
(ii) 158.8 15.88 15.80 15
(iii) 0.68 0.63 0.601 0.6
(iv) 19.25 1.108 0.38 0.25
9. (i) 50.05 rupees (ii) 20.1 cm
(iii) 45.82 cm (iv) 5.454 km

(v)   3.092 kg   (vi) 21.12 rupees

(vii) 13.1 cm   (viii) 1 m 42 cm

(ix) 3.060 km   (x)   520 g

10. (i)   73.84   (ii)   346.095

      (iii) 508.26   (iv) 19.618

      (v)   0.793   (vi) 10.007

Short Answer Questions :

1.   We have:

(i) $\dfrac{7}{20} = \dfrac{7 \times 5}{20 \times 5} = \dfrac{35}{100} = 0.35.$

(ii) $\dfrac{9}{25} = \dfrac{9 \times 4}{25 \times 4} = \dfrac{36}{100} = 0.36.$

(iii) $\dfrac{8}{125} = \dfrac{8 \times 8}{125 \times 8} = \dfrac{64}{1000} = 0.064.$

(iv) $\dfrac{121}{250} = \dfrac{121 \times 4}{250 \times 4} = \dfrac{484}{1000} = 0.484.$

2.   (i) $6.75 = \dfrac{\overset{27}{\cancel{675}}}{\underset{4}{\cancel{100}}} = \dfrac{27}{4} = 6\dfrac{3}{4}$

     (ii) $924.275 = \dfrac{924275}{1000} = \dfrac{36971}{40} = 924\dfrac{11}{40}$

3. $65.251 + 32.72 + 4.9 + 22.64 = 125.511$

4.   Converting the given decimals into like decimals, we get $27.80 + 46.00 + 175.09 + 685.70 = 934.59$

5.   Converting the given decimals into like decimals, we get
$73.00 - 28.65 = 44.35$

6.   The required decimal number
$= 91 - 74.5 = 16.5$

7.   The required decimal number
$= 7.3 - 0.862 = 6.438$

8.   Given weights are 500 g, 2 kg, 1.99 kg, 9999 mg

$500\ g = \dfrac{500}{1000}\ kg = 0.5\ kg$

$9999\ mg = \dfrac{9999}{1000}\ g = 9.999\ g = \dfrac{9.999}{1000}\ kg$
$= 0.009999\ kg$

Weights arranged in ascending order are
0.009999 kg, 0.5 kg, 1.99 kg, 2 kg.

$\therefore$ 9999 mg, 500 g, 1.99 kg, 2 kg.

9. $298\ cm = \dfrac{298}{100}\ m = 2.98\ m$

Difference between 4m and 2.98 m
$= 4\ m - 2.98\ m = 1.02\ m$

10. $4\ cm = \dfrac{4}{100}\ m = 0.04\ m$

$94\ mm = \dfrac{94}{10}\ cm = 9.4\ cm = \dfrac{9.4}{100}\ m = 0.094\ m$

The required sum
$= 7\ m + 0.04\ m + 0.094\ m = 7.134\ m$

$$\begin{array}{r} 7.000 \\ 0.040 \\ +\ 0.094 \\ \hline 7.134 \end{array}$$

Long Answer Questions :

1.

Cost of a book	=	₹ 165.35
Cost of a pen	=	₹ 72.00
Cost of a notebook	=	₹ 14.85
Total cost	=	₹ 252.20

Total money to be paid by Ramesh = ₹ 252.20

2.   We have,

Total amount of money = 0.45

Amount spent of toffees = ₹ 5.30

$$\begin{array}{r} 7.45 \\ -\ 5.30 \\ \hline 2.15 \end{array}$$

$\therefore$ Balance amount of money = ₹ 7.45 − ₹ 5.30
$= ₹ 2.15$

3.   Converting the given decimals into like decimals, and adding and subtracting as shown alongside, the given expression
$= 53.50 - 34.68 + 64.75 - 28.90$
$= (53.50 + 64.75) - (34.68 + 28.90)$
$= 118.25 - 63.58 = 54.67.$

4.   Total length of string = 15.34 m

Length of one piece = 8.26 m

Length of other piece $= (15.34 - 8.26)\ m = 7.08$

5.   0.8 kg or 800 gm

6.   10.250 km

2 EXERCISE

Text-Book Exercise :

1. (i) 5 hundreds + 3 tens + 8 ones + 1 tenth

$$= 5 \times 100 + 3 \times 10 + 8 \times 1 + 1 \times \frac{1}{10}$$

$$= 500 + 30 + 8 + \frac{1}{10} = 538 + \frac{1}{10} = 538.1$$

(ii) 2 hundreds + 7 tens + 3 ones + 4 tenths

$$= 2 \times 100 + 7 \times 10 + 3 \times 1 + 4 \times \frac{1}{10}$$

$$= 200 + 70 + 3 + \frac{4}{10}$$

$$= 273 + \frac{4}{10} = 273.4$$

2. (i) 19.4

$$\because \quad 19.4 = 1 \times 10 + 9 \times 1 + 4 \times \frac{1}{10}$$

$\therefore$ We have,

Tens	Ones	Tenths
(10)	(7)	$(\frac{1}{10})$
1	9	4

(ii) 0.3

$$\because \quad 0.3 = 0 + \frac{3}{10}$$

$\therefore$ We have,

Tens	Ones	Tenths
(10)	(1)	$(\frac{1}{10})$
0	0	3

3. (i) $\dfrac{5}{10} = 0.5$

(ii) $3 + \dfrac{7}{10} = 3 + 0.7 = 3.7$

(iii) $200 + 60 + 5 + \dfrac{1}{10} = 265 + 0.1 = 265.1$

(iv) $\dfrac{88}{10} = 8.8$

(v) $4\dfrac{2}{10} = 4 + \dfrac{2}{10} = 4.2$

4. (i) Length of Ramesh's notebook = 9 cm 5 mm

But 1 mm = $\dfrac{1}{10}$ cm

$$\therefore \ 5 \text{ mm} = 5 \times \frac{1}{10} \text{ cm} = \frac{5}{10} \text{ cm} = 0.5 \text{ cm}$$

Now 9 cm 5 mm = 9.5 cm

Thus, the length of the notebook = 9.5 cm

(ii) $\because \quad$ 1 mm = $\dfrac{1}{10}$ cm

$$\therefore \quad 65 \text{ mm} = 65 \times \frac{1}{10} \text{ cm} = 6.5 \text{ cm}$$

5. (i) 0.8 :

0.8 lies between 0 and 1 and 1 is nearer to 0.8.

(ii) 5.1 :

5.1 lies between 5 and 6 and 5 is nearer to 5.1.

(iii) 2.6 :

2.6 lies between 2 and 3 and 3 is nearer to 2.6.

(iv) 6.4 :

6.4 lies between 6 and 7 and 6 is nearer to 6.4.

(v) 9.1 :

9.1 lies between 9 and 10 and 9 is nearer to 9.1.

(vi) 4.9 :

4.9 lies between 4 and 5 and 5 is nearer to 4.9.

6. (i) We have, $0.60 = \dfrac{60}{100} = \dfrac{3}{5}$

(ii) We have, $0.05 = \dfrac{5}{100} = \dfrac{1}{20}$

(iii) We have, $0.18 = \dfrac{18}{100} = \dfrac{9}{50}$

(iv) We have, $0.125 = \dfrac{125}{1000} = \dfrac{1}{8}$

(v) We have, 0.066

$$= \dfrac{66}{1000} = \dfrac{66 \div 2}{1000 \div 2} = \dfrac{33}{500}$$

7. (i) 2 rupees 5 paise:

   2 rupees + 5 paise $\left[\because 100\,\text{paise} = ₹\,1 \atop \therefore 1\,\text{paise} = ₹\,\dfrac{1}{100}\right]$
   $= (2 + 0.05)$ rupees
   $= ₹\,2.05$

   2 rupees 50 paise:

   2 rupees + 50 paise $\left[\because 100\,\text{paise} = ₹\,1 \atop \therefore 1\,\text{paise} = ₹\,\dfrac{1}{100}\right]$
   $= (2 + 0.50)$ rupees
   $= ₹\,2.50$

   (ii) 20 rupees 7 paise = 20 rupees + 7 paise
   $= ₹\,20 + ₹\,0.07$
   $= ₹\,20.07$

   21 rupees 75 paise
   21 rupees + 75 paise

   $= 21 + 75 \times \dfrac{1}{100}$ rupees

   $= 21 + \dfrac{75}{100}$ rupees

   $= ₹\,[21 + 0.75]$
   $= ₹\,21.75$

8. Yes, we can change the given 'metres' into kilometres.

   $52\text{ m} = 52 \times \dfrac{1}{1000}\text{ km}\ [\because 1\text{ m} = \dfrac{1}{1000}\text{ km}]$

   $= 0.052\text{ km}$

   $340\text{ m} = 340 \times \dfrac{1}{1000}\text{ km} = 0.340\text{ km}$

   $2008\text{ m} = 2008 \times \dfrac{1}{1000}\text{ km} = 2.008\text{ km}$

9. Distance covered:
   by bus = 15 km 268 m
   by car = 7 km 7 m
   on foot = 500 m
   ∴ Total distance covered
   $= (15\text{ km }268\text{ m}) + (7\text{ km }7\text{ m}) + 500\text{ m}$
   $= (15\text{ km} + 268\text{ m}) + (7\text{ km} + 7\text{ m})$
   $\qquad\qquad\qquad + (0\text{ km} + 500\text{ m})$

   $$= \left(15\text{ km} + \dfrac{268}{1000}\text{ km}\right) + \left(7\text{ km} + \dfrac{7}{1000}\text{ km}\right)$$
   $$+ \left(0\text{ km} + \dfrac{500}{1000}\text{ km}\right)$$

   $= (15 + 0.268)\text{ km} + (7 + 0.007)\text{ km}$
   $\qquad\qquad\qquad + (0.500)\text{ km}$
   $= 15.268\text{ km} + 7.007\text{ km} + 0.500\text{ km}$
   $= 22.775\text{ km}$
   Thus, the required distance = 22.775 km.

10. Total distance to be travelled = 20 km 50 m
    Distance travelled by bus = 10 km 200 m
    Remaining distance to be travelled by auto
    $= 20\text{ km }50\text{m} - 10\text{ km} + 200\text{ m}$
    $= (20\text{ km} + 50\text{ m}) - (10\text{ km} + 200\text{ m})$
    $= (20 + .050)\text{ km} - (10 + .200)\text{ km}$
    $= 20.050\text{ km} - 10.200\text{ km} = 9.850\text{ km}$
    Thus, the distance travelled by auto = 9.850 km

Exemplar Questions :

1. 12.104, 12.122, 12.142, 12.214, 12.401

2. 3.4   3. $\dfrac{41}{1000}$ 4. $6\dfrac{3}{100}$

5. 5.201 kg.   6. ₹ 20.09, ₹ $20\dfrac{9}{100}$

7. 15.37 m, $\dfrac{1537}{100}$ m   8. 2.435 km, $2\dfrac{87}{200}$ km

9. 24.5   10. 22.022   11. 9.850 kg

12. Milk, Rice, $\dfrac{30}{53}$ 13. 20.8   14. 75.20

HOTS Questions :

1. Sum of 13.05 and 21.12 = 33.17
   Now, the difference of 33.17 and 39.93 = 5.76

2. Sum of 36.63 and 112.36:
   Difference of 36.63 and 112.36
   ∵ $148.99 - 75.73 = 73.26$
   ∴ The sum of the given numbers is greater than their difference by 73.26.

3. Temperature on Sunday = 34.7°C
   Increase in temperature on Monday = 3.2°C
   ∴ Temperature on Monday
   $\qquad = (34.7 + 3.2)°C = 37.9°C$
   Decrease in temperature on Tuesday = 5.3°C
   ∴ Temperature on Tuesday
   $\qquad = (37.9 - 5.3)°C = 32.6°C$

3 EXERCISE

Single Option Correct :

1. **(b)** $31.005 = 3 \times 10 + 1 \times 1 + \dfrac{5}{1000}$

2. **(d)** Total money = ₹1000
   Ravi gave to chemist = ₹495.75
   Amount the chemist retuned =
   $$\begin{array}{r} 1000.00 \\ -\ 495.75 \\ \hline ₹\ 504.25 \end{array}$$

3. **(a)** let other number be x.
   $x + 11.56 = 31.021$
   $x = 31.021 - 11.56$
   $= 19.461$

4. **(a)** sum = 156.037

5. **(b)**

6. **(a)** Riya spent = ₹ 34.60
   Money left with her =
   $$\begin{array}{r} ₹\ 100.00 \\ ₹\ \ \ 34.60 \\ \hline ₹\ \ \ 65.40 \end{array}$$

7. **(b)**　　8. **(b)**　　9. **(a)**
10. **(b)**　　11. **(a)**　　12. **(a)**

More Than One Option Correct :

1. **(a, b, d)**　2. **(a, c)**　3. **(a, b)**
4. **(a, d)**　　5. **(a, c)**　6. **(b, d)**
7. **(b, c)**

Assertion & Reason :

1. **(d)** As 249 m = 0.249 km
   Assertion: incorrect; **Reason:** correct

2. **(d)** As, $211.902 = 2 \times 100 + 1 \times 10 + 1 + 9 \times$
   $\dfrac{1}{10} + 2 \times \dfrac{1}{1000}$
   Assertion: incorrect; **Reason:** correct

3. **(c)** Addition of zero at the end of decimal number does not change the value of the number.
   Assertion: correct; **Reason:** incorrect

Passage Based Questions :

1. **(b)** As 67.25 + 5.5 + 9.85 = 67.25 + 5.50 + 9.85 = 82.6

   In fraction form, $82.6 = \dfrac{826}{10}$

2. **(c)** Total amount spent by Amit = ₹ 115.60
   Fractional form of 115.60
   $$= \dfrac{11560}{100} = \dfrac{1156}{10}$$
   In lowest form, $= \dfrac{578}{5}$

3. **(a)** We have, 19.07 kg $= \dfrac{1907}{100}$ kg
   As 1 kg = 1000 g
   $$19.07 \text{ kg} = \left(\dfrac{1907}{100} \times 1000 \right) \text{g} = 19070 \text{ g}$$

4. **(c)** Converting all quantites into g
   Weight of a squash ball = 34000 mg
   Weight of a squash ball in grams
   $$= \dfrac{34000}{1000} \text{ g} = 34 \text{ g}$$
   Weight of a cricket ball = 45 g
   Weight of a basketball = 0.65 × 1000 g
   $= 650$ g
   Weight of a football = 3 × 1000 g = 3000 g
   ∴　$34 < 45 < 650 < 3000$
   ∴　The weight of football is the heaviest.

5. **(b)** Total weight of a basketball and football
   $= 0.65 + 3.00 = 3.65$ kg

6. **(a)** Total weight of balls
   $= 34 + 45 + 650 + 3000$ g $= 3729$ g

Integer Type Questions :

1. **(8)** Length of cloth for trousers
   = 5 m 20 cm = 5.20 m
   Length of cloth for shirt
   = 2 m 80 cm = 2.80 m
   ∴ Total length of cloth
   = 5.20 m + 2.80 m = 8 m

2. **(6)** Amount with Ravi = ₹ 18.50
   Cost of ice-cream = ₹ 11.50
   Balance money with Ravi
   = ₹ 18.50 − ₹ 11.50
   We have:
   $$\begin{array}{r} 18.50 \\ -\ 11.50 \\ \hline 06.00 \end{array}$$
   Thus, Ravi has ₹ 6 now.

3.   **(9)**   Weight of apples = 3 kg 400 g = 3.400 kg
Weight of grapes = 2 kg 600 g = 2.600 kg
Weight of oranges = 3 kg = 3.000 kg
Total weight fruits = [Weight of apples] +
[Weight of grapes] + [Weight of oranges]
= 3.400 kg + 2.600 kg + 3.000 kg

$$\begin{array}{r} 3.400 \\ +\ 2.600 \\ +\ 3.000 \\ \hline 9.000 \end{array}$$

Thus, the total weight of the fruits in the bag is 9 kg.

4.   **(9)**   Adding 8.3 and 5.6, we get
$8.3 + 5.6 = 13.9$
$\therefore$ The decimal part is 9.

5.   **(3)** $3 + 0.04 + 0.01 + 0.001$
Put zeroes in 3, 0.4, 0.01 to make three decimal places
i.e., 3.000, 0.400, 0.010, 0.001
$\therefore$ $3.000 + 0.400 + 0.010 + 0.001 = 3.411$
$\therefore$ The whole number part in 3.411 is 3.

6.   **(0)** $13.5 + 1.57 = 13.50 + 1.57 = 15.07$
So, the tenths place value is 0.

Multiple Matching Question :

1.   (A) $\to$ (r); (B) $\to$ (s); (C) $\to$ (p, t); (D) $\to$ (q)

(A)   Cost of the toothpaste   =   ₹ 18.75
Cost of the sopa   =   ₹ 6.00
Cost of the shoe polish   =   ₹ 12.50

Total expenditure   =   ₹ 37.25

Money he got back = 50 – 37.25 = ₹ 12.75

(B)   Distance travelled by bus
= 12 km 220 m = 12.220 km
Distance travelled by car 8 km 485 m
= 8.485 km
Therefore, total distance travelled is
= 12.220 km + 8.485 km + 0.760 km
= 21.465 km
Hence, Shweta travelled 21.465 km in all.

(C)   Converting the given decimals into like decimals, each having 2 places of decimal, we get 34.76 and 52.10.
writing them in column form and subtracting, we get:

$$\begin{array}{r} 52.10 \\ -\ 34.76 \\ \hline 17.34 \end{array}$$

Hence, $(52.1 - 34.76) = 17.34$

(D) $77.7 - 7.555 - 5.77$
$= 70.145 - 5.77 = 64.375$

Chapter 9

Data Handling

DATA

The word **data** means information in the form of numerical figures.

For example : The marks obtained by 10 students of a class in a monthly test are given below :

36, 21, 43, 24, 16, 25, 28, 32, 45, 41

We call these marks as data.

RAW DATA

Data obtained in original form is known as **raw data**. Data given in above example is raw data.

ARRAY

Arranging the data in an ascending or a descending order is called an **array**.

TABULATION OF DATA

Arranging the data in the form of a table is called as **tabulation** or presentation of a data.

OBSERVATIONS

Each numerical figure in a data is called an **observation**.

FREQUENCY OF AN OBSERVATION

The number of times a particular observation occurs is called its **frequency**.

For example: Marks obtained by 10 students in a class are

15, 20, 25, 18, 22, 24, 25, 17, 25, 16

In the above given data, 25 marks are obtained by three students. So, frequency of data 25 is 3.

RANGE

Difference between the highest and the lowest value of the data is called the **'range'**. In above example,

Maximum marks obtained = 25

Minimum marks obtained = 15

Thus, Range = 25 – 15 = 10

TALLY MARKS

A **tally mark** is the symbolic representation of occurrence of an observation in a particular table. The symbol used is '|'.

> **NOTE :** If the observation has frequency 5, then the tally marks are represented as ||||.

ORGANISATION OF DATA

After collection of data, it needs to be recorded and organised in a tabular form. Let us learn it with the help of given illustration.

ILLUSTRATION : 1

The total number of children in 20 families of a locality are given below:

$$2, 2, 3, 2, 1, 3, 3, 2, 2, 1, 2, 2, 3, 1, 2, 1, 1, 3, 2, 2$$

Represent this information in a frequency distribution table.

SOLUTION :

Arranging the data in ascending order we get :

1, 1, 1, 1, 1, 2, 2, 2, 2, 2, 2, 2, 2, 2, 2, 3, 3, 3, 3, 3.

No. of children	Tally marks	No. of families
1	卌	5
2	卌 卌	10
3	卌	5
	Total	20

PICTOGRAPH

Pictograph is a way of representating data through pictures or symbols. It helps us to understand and analyse data at a glance.

Interpretation of a pictograph

Interpretation of a pictograph means drawing some conclusions from it. The first step in interpretation of a pictograph is to know what it represents or what is the information given by it. We also see the picture symbol and find what it represents. It is also important to know the number of units represented by one picture symbol.

ILLUSTRATION : 2

The number of bulbs sold in a shop on different days of the week are :

Scale: = 6 bulbs

 = 3 bulbs

Days	Number of bulbs Sold
Monday	
Tuesday	
Wednesday	
Thursday	
Friday	
Saturday	

Observe the pictograph and answer the following questions:

(i) How many bulbs were sold on Tuesday?

(ii) How many bulbs were sold on Friday?

(iii) If one bulb cost ₹ 20, find the shopkeeper's earning on Wednesday?

SOLUTION :

(i) Since 1 bulb represents 6 bulbs. So,
     $2 \times 6 = 12$ bulbs were sold on Tuesday

(ii) On Friday, $3\dfrac{1}{2}$ bulbs means $6 \times 3 + \dfrac{1}{2} \times 6 = 18 + 3 = 21$ bulbs were sold.

(iii) On Wednesday, $2\dfrac{1}{2}$ bulbs were sold

     i.e. $2 \times 6 + 6 \times \dfrac{1}{2} = 12 + 3 = 15$ bulbs
     As cost of 1 bulb = ₹ 20
     $\Rightarrow$ Cost of 15 bulbs = $15 \times$ ₹ 20 = ₹ 300

Representation of Pictograph

To draw or represent a pictograph, we use pictures or symbols to indicate appropriate units.

ILLUSTRATION : 3

There are 2000 students in a school and Mr. Roy, the principal, wants to know the mode of travelling used by most of the students.
Information on modes of travelling of the students was collected.

Mode of travelling	Number of students
On foot	300
Bicycle	200
Scooter	300
School bus	700
Public bus	300
Car	200

SOLUTION :

The pictograph for the given data is shown below :

Mode of travelling	Number of students
On foot	🚶📚 🚶📚 🚶📚
Bicycle	📚 📚
Scooter	📚 📚 📚
School bus	📚 📚 📚 📚 📚 📚 📚
Public bus	📚 📚 📚
Car	📚 📚

📚 stands for 100 students

BAR GRAPH

A bar graph is a pictorial representation of data by a number of bars (rectangles) of uniform width created horizontally or vertically with equal spacing between them.

Properties of Bar Graph:

- Bars may be either vertical or horizontal, we often use vertical bars as they give a better look.
- The height (or length) of the bar indicates the value of the data.
- Width of the bar always remains equal but height (or length) changes according to the data.
- Bars are equally spaced.
- Bars may be shaded to make them attractive.
- Bar graphs are useful for visual comparison of the given data.

Reading and Interpretation of a Bar Graph.

By observing a bar graph we can understand what kind of data it represents and draw certain conclusions from it. This is known as interpretation of the bar graph.

ILLUSTRATION : 4

Observe the bar graph given here. Answer the following questions:
(i)   What information is provided by the bar graph?
(ii) Which is the most popular game?
(iii) What is the number of students playing football?
(iv) What fraction of the total number of students play table tennis ?

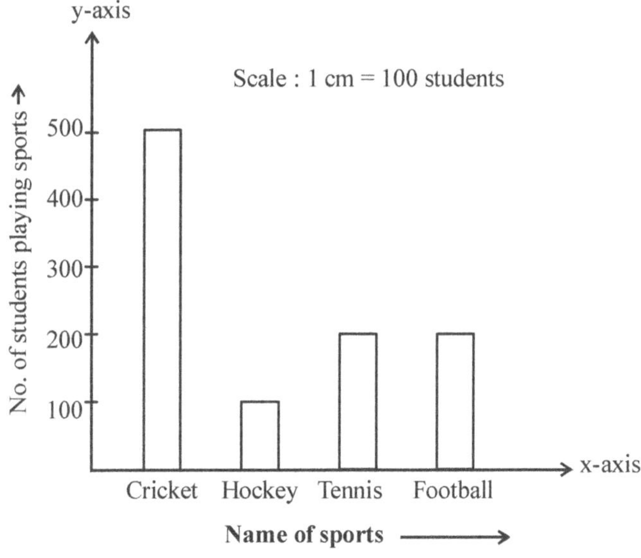

SOLUTION :
(i)   The graph represents the kind of games popular with 1000 students of a school.
(ii) The most popular game is cricket.
(iii) The number of students playing football is 200.

(iv) The fraction of students playing tennis is $\dfrac{200}{1000} = \dfrac{2}{10} = \dfrac{1}{5}$

Drawing a Bar graph

Now you can read a bar graph and interpret it. Let us now construct bar graphs by taking following illustration.

The table below shows the monthly expenditure of a family:

Education	Rent	Food	Clothing	Conveyance	Savings
₹ 900	₹ 2000	₹ 3200	₹ 500	₹ 800	₹ 600

Represent the data in the form of a bar graph.

SOLUTION :

Step I : Draw the horizontal and vertical axes. Write 'items' along the horizontal axis and 'expenditure' along the vertical axis.

Step II : Choose the widths of the bars leaving equal spaces between them on the horizontal axis.

Step III : Choose a convenient scale to represent expenditure on the vertical axis.
Let 1 unit represents ₹ 400.

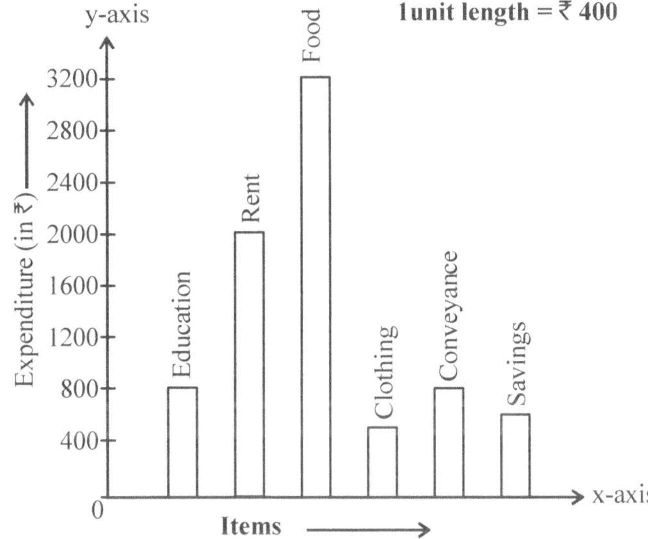

$$₹ 900 = 2\frac{1}{4} \text{ units}$$

$$₹ 2000 = 5 \text{ units}$$

$$₹ 3200 = 8 \text{ units}$$

$$₹ 500 = 1\frac{1}{4} \text{ units}$$

$$₹ 800 = 2 \text{ units}$$

$$₹ 600 = 1\frac{1}{2} \text{ units}$$

CONCEPT MAP

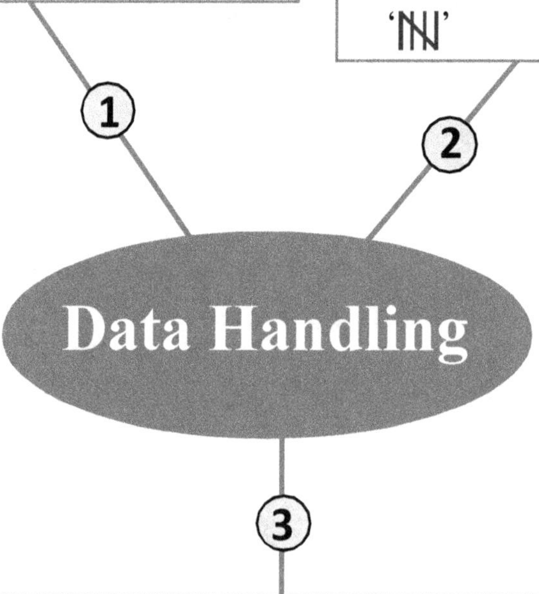

Data
A collection of numbers to give some information is called data.
Raw data- The data collected by a person himself for his own use, is called raw data.
Tabulation of data
Data can be arranged in tabular form to make it easy to understand.
Tabulation of data can be done using tally marks. Counting of data is done in a group of five which is represented by
Data Handling
1
2
3
Different types of graphs
Data can be represented by pictograph using pictures.
Bar graph is another and better way of representing data by a number of rectangular bars having a uniform width with equal spacing between them.

MISCELLANEOUS
SOLVED EXAMPLES

1. **The following pictograph shows the number of balls bought by children from a shop on different days.**
   Read the pictograph and answer the following:
   (i) **On which day, did the shopkeeper sell most balls?**
   (ii) **On which day, did the shopkeeper sell 20 balls?**
   (iii) **On which day, did the shopkeeper sell no balls?**

Day	No. of balls
Monday	◉ ◉ ◉
Tuesday	◉ ◉
Wednesday	◉
Thursday	
Friday	◉ ◉ ◉ ◉
Saturday	◉
Sunday	◉ ◉ ◉ ◉ ◉
One ◉ represents 5 balls	

Sol. (i) The shopkeeper sold most balls on Sunday (25 balls).

   (ii) The shopkeeper sold 20 balls on Friday.

   (iii) The shopkeeper didn't sell any ball on Thursday.

2. **The following are the details of number of people who visited the Appu Ghar on different weekdays. Draw a pictograph to represent it.**

Day	Number of People
Monday	425
Tuesday	350
Wednesday	200
Thursday	525
Friday	600
Saturday	450
Sunday	875

Sol. Let us assume the following symbols.

1 ☖ represents 100 people.

1 ☖ represents 50 people.

1 ☖ represent 25 people.

Now, we draw the required pictograph as follows:

Day	No. of People
Monday	☖☖☖☖☖
Tuesday	☖☖☖☖
Wednesday	☖☖
Thursday	☖☖☖☖☖☖
Friday	☖☖☖☖☖☖
Saturday	☖☖☖☖☖
Sunday	☖☖☖☖☖☖☖☖☖

3. **A die is a cube where six numbers are marked with numbers (or dots) from 1 to 6. One number on each face. The result obtained in 30 throws are 5, 4, 3, 2, 1, 1, 2, 5, 4, 6, 6, 6, 3, 2, 1, 4, 3, 2, 1, 5, 6, 5, 2, 1, 3, 1, 2, 3, 4, 5. Prepare a frequency distribution table.**

Sol. The frequency distribution table is as shown.

Scores	Tally marks	Frequency
1	𝍱 I	6
2	𝍱 I	6
3	𝍱	5
4	IIII	4
5	𝍱	5
6	IIII	4
	Total	30

4. Given below is a bar graph showing the heights of six mountain peaks.

Read the above bar diagram and answer the following questions:

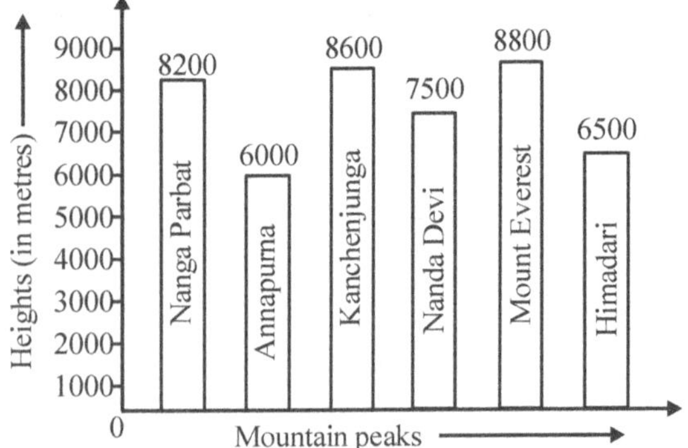

(i) Which is the highest peak and what is its height?

(ii) What is the ratio of the heights of highest and lowest peaks?

(iii) What is the ascending order of the heights of the peaks?

(iv) Which peak is second highest and what is its height?

Sol. (i) Mount Everest is the highest peak and its height is 8800 m.

(ii) Height of the highest peak = 8800 m.
Height of the lowest peak = 6000 m.

$$\text{Required Ratio} = \frac{8800}{6000} = \frac{22}{15} = 22:15.$$

(iii) The heights of the given peaks in ascending order are:

6000 m < 6500 m < 7500 m < 8200 m < 8600 < 8800 m.

So, the peaks in ascending order of their heights are:

Annapurna, Himadari, Nanda Devi, Nanga Parbat, Kanchenjunga and Mount Everest.

(iv) The height of Kanchenjunga is next to that of Mount Everest.

So, the second highest peak is Kanchenjunga and its height is 8600 m.

5. The table shows the number of buses added after every ten years in a city during 1950-2000.

Years	Number of buses added
1950	500
1960	1000
1970	1500
1980	2500
1990	3500
2000	6000

Draw a bar graph to represent the above data, taking 1 division = 500 buses.

Sol.

Number of buses added after every ten years in a city

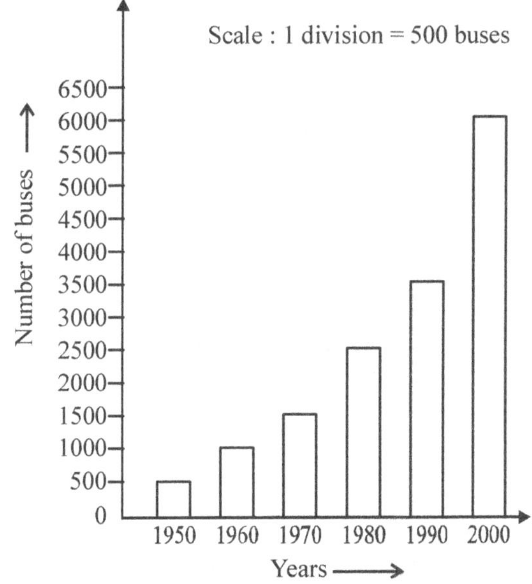

1 EXERCISE

Fill in the Blanks :

DIRECTIONS : *Complete the following statements with an appropriate word / term to be filled in the blank space(s).*

1. The number of times a particular observation occurs is called is __________.
2. Presentation of an information in form of picture is known as __________.
3. A __________ is a collection of numbers gathered to give some meaningful information.
4. The data can be arranged in a tabular form using __________ marks.
5. In a bar graph, bars of __________ width can be drawn horizontally or vertically with __________ spacing between them.
6. In a pictograph, if a symbol  represents 20 flowers in a basket, then 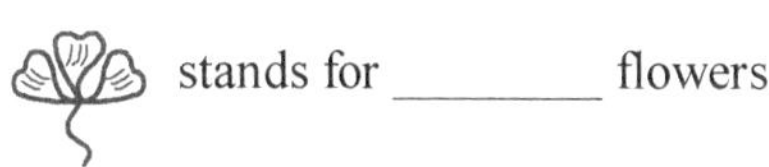 stands for __________ flowers.
7. On the scale of 1 unit length = 10 crore, the bar of length 6 units will represent __________ crore and of __________ units will represent 75 crore.
8. Data presented in original form is called __________.
9. The number of times an observation in data is repeated is called its __________.

True / False :

DIRECTIONS : *Read the following statements and write your answer as true or false.*

1. In a bar graph, bars of uniform width are drawn vertically only.
2. ||||| denotes 4 entries in tally marks.
3. The representation of an information through graph is called a pictograph.
4. In a bar graph, each bar represents only one value of the numerical data.
5. In a bar graph, the gap between two consecutive bars must be the same.
6. If ◖◗◖◗ represents 120 balls, then ◖ represents 60 balls.

Match the Columns :

DIRECTIONS : *Each question contains statements given in two columns which have to be matched. Statements (A, B, C, D) in column-I have to be matched with statements (p, q, r, s) in column-II.*

1. Read the bar graph and match the following.

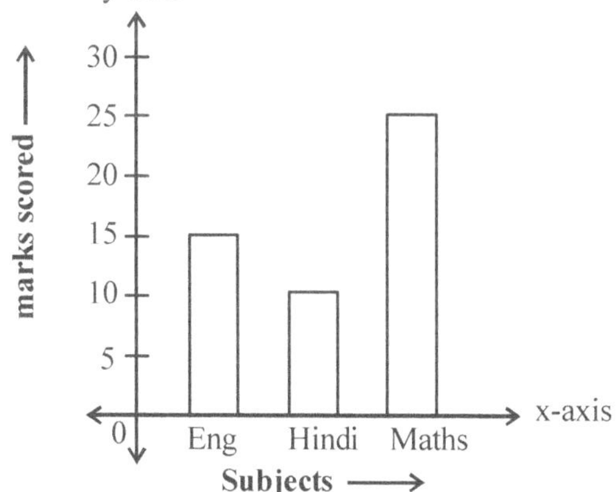

Column-I	Column-II
A. The horizontal line in the graph is called	(p) Maths
B. The vertical line in the graph is called	(q) Hindi
C. Highest marks are scored in the subject	(r) x-axis
D. Least marks scored in the subject	(s) y-axis

Very Short Answer Questions:

DIRECTIONS : *Give answer in one word or one sentence.*

1. Rakesh rolls a die 20 times and records the number shown on the top face as shown below:
   1, 3, 5, 6, 6, 3, 5, 4, 1, 6
   2, 5, 3, 4, 6, 1, 6, 4, 3, 1
   (i) Which appears minimum number of times?
   (ii) Which appears maximum number of times?

2. Given below shows the marks obtained by 15 students of a class in a test.
   26, 39, 21, 25, 30, 28, 22, 19, 20, 43, 6, 17, 18, 20, 40
   If the student who got less than 20 marks is declared to be fail, then how many students are pass?

3. Students of a class were tested to find their pulse rate. The follwoing figures were obtained for the number of beats per minute.
   70, 60, 70, 68, 67, 62, 71, 71, 59, 73, 73, 60, 60, 62, 62, 68, 70, 70, 70, 74, 69
   How many students are there whose pulse rate is more than 60 per minute?

4. The following is a list of size of shoes of 8 students of class VI : 5, 6, 5, 4, 5, 4, 6 and 4. If the shoe size less than 5 is observed for girls, how many girls are there in the list ?

5. If △ represents 150 pillars, what does △ △ △ △ represents?

6. The marks (out of 10) obtained by 28 students in a Mathematics test are listed as below:
   8, 1, 2, 6, 5, 5, 5, 0, 1, 9, 7, 8, 0, 5, 8, 3, 0, 8, 10, 10, 3, 4, 8, 7, 8, 9, 2, 0
   The number of students who obtained marks more than or equal to 5 is________.

7. If ☒☒☒☒☒ represents 50 icecreams, then how will you represent 35 ice-creams?

Short Answer Questions :

DIRECTIONS : *Give answer in 2-3 sentences.*

1. The total number of children in 20 families of a locality are given below.
   2, 2, 3, 2, 1, 3, 3, 2, 2, 1, 2, 2, 3, 1, 2, 1, 1, 3, 2, 2.
   Represent this information in a frequency distribution table.

2. The pictograph shows the rainfall in some cities during a certain year.

Agra	☂ ☂ ☂ ☂
Kolkata	☂ ☂ ☂ ☂ ☂ ☂ ☂
Mumbai	☂ ☂ ☂ ☂ ☂ ☂ ☂ ☂ ☂
Delhi	☂ ☂ ☂ ☂ ☂
Chennai	☂ ☂ ☂ ☂ ☂ ☂

One ☂ represents 10 cm.
Now answer the following questions:
(i) Find the rainfall in cm in the follwoing cities:
   (a) Agra
   (b) Mumbai
   (c) Chennai
(ii) How many more cm of rainfall fell in Mumbai city than in Delhi?

3. Read the pictograph given below and answer the following questions (sales of fan on different days of a week) :

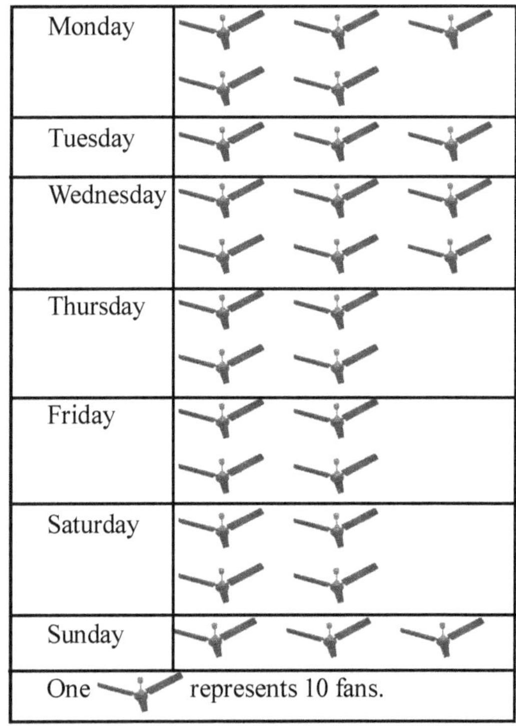

Monday	
Tuesday	
Wednesday	
Thursday	
Friday	
Saturday	
Sunday	
One	represents 10 fans.

(i) How many fans were sold on Monday?

(ii) On which day the minimum number of fans were sold?

(iii) On which day the maximum number of fans were sold?

(iv) Find the total number of fans sold during the week.

4. Read the given bar graph which shows the number of students who participated in an annual function hold during 2001-2007.

(i) How many students participated in 2004?

(ii) How many students participated in 2006?

(iii) How many more students participated in 2005 as compared to 2003?

(iv) In which year, was the participation by the students the minimum? How many students were there?

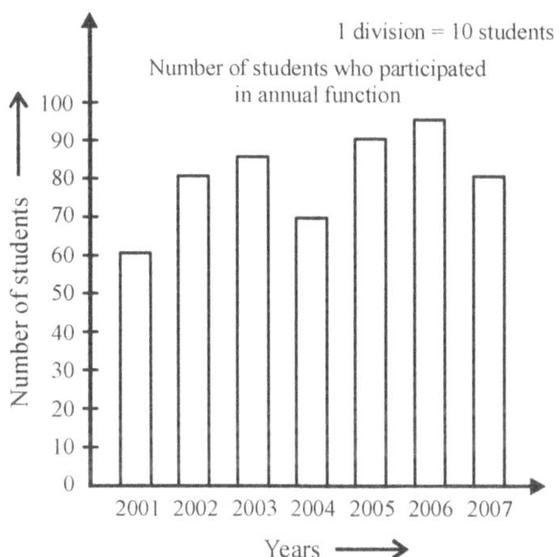

5. Read the following bar graph. It shows us the profit earned by the Government companies of a State in different years.

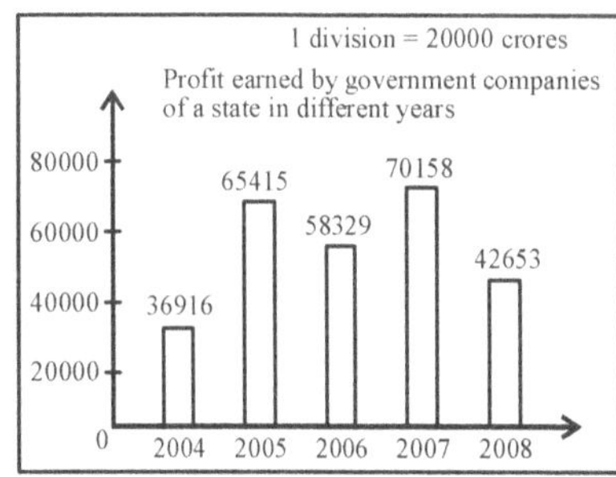

(i) What was the profit earned in 2004 ?

(ii) What was the profit earned in 2007 ?

(iii) Arrange the profit earned in different years in ascending order.

6. Read the following graph and answer the questions given below:

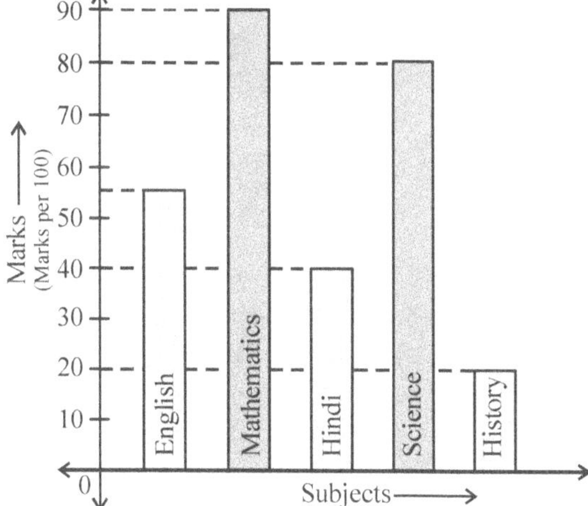

(i) At what subject is the student sharp?

(ii) In which subject is the student poor ?

(iii) What are the average marks obtained by the student?

(iv) What is the percentage obtained by the student?

(v) What is the ratio of the highest marks to the lowest marks obtained by the student ?

7. Following are the choices of games of 40 students of Class VI.

Football, cricket, football, kho-kho, hockey, cricket, hockey, kho-kho, tennis, tennis, cricket, football, football, hockey, kho-kho, football, cricket, tennis, football, hockey, kho-kho, football, cricket, cricket, football, hockey, hockey, kho-kho, tennis, football, hockey, cricket, football, hockey, cricket, football, kho-kho, football, cricket, hockey, football.

(i) Arrange the choices of games in a table using tally marks and choose the most popular game?

(ii) Which game is liked by most of the students?

(iii) Which game is liked by minimum number of students?

8. The bar graph given below shows the number of hours that Aman worked per week in a month.

Number of hours worked by Aman
per week in a month

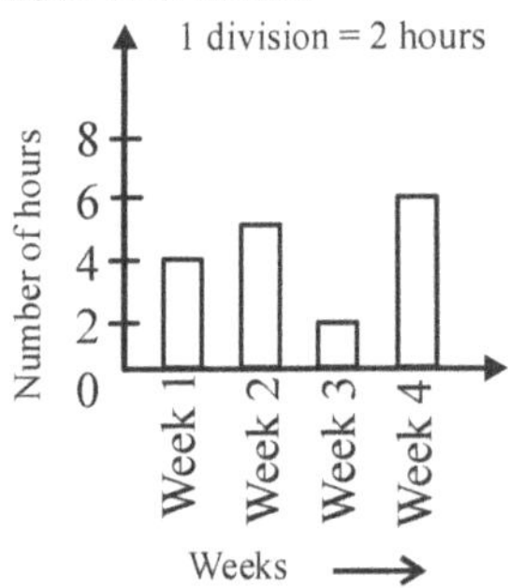

(i) In which week did Aman work for maximum number of hours?
(ii) How much did Aman work in week 2?
(iii) Find the total number of hours worked by Aman in a month.
(iv) How many more hours did Aman work in week 1 as compared to week 3?

Long Answer Questions :

DIRECTIONS : *Give answer in four to five sentences.*

1. The number of cricket bats sold by a shop during a week are given below.

Day	Monday	Tuesday	Wednesday	Thursday	Friday	Saturday
No. of bats sold	20	12	24	32	8	16

Draw a pictograph.

2. The total number of school buses of five different schools in a city is given in table.

Name of School	Number of buses
Happy	30
K.P.S. School	45
Max School	40
Hans School	25
D.S.C school	35

Answer the following questions.

(i) How many symbols represent the number of school buses of Max School?
(ii) Which school has the maximum number of school buses?
(iii) What is the difference between the number of school buses of K.P.S. and Hans School?
(iv) Arrange the schools in the increasing order of their number of buses.

3. The total number of students in class XII of a city, who got admission in Medical College in the last six years, is given below.

Year	Number of students
1995	1500
1996	2000
1997	2500
1998	3000
1999	3500
2000	4000

Draw a pictograph using a symbol to represent 500 students and answer the following questions.

(i) How many symbols represent the number of students in the year 1998?
(ii) How many symbols represent the number of students in the year 1995?
(iii) In which year maximum number of students got admission in medical college?
(iv) In which year the least number of students got admission in medical college?

4. The sale of shirts in a garment shop on various days of a week are as follows:

Monday	Tuesday	Wednesday	Thursday	Friday	Saturday
75	100	125	100	75	50

Draw a pictograph to represent the given information.

5. The number of stools in five rooms of a school are given below:

Room number	I	II	III	IV	V
Number of stools	30	40	60	50	20

Taking the scale ≡ 10 stools, draw the pictograph.

6. The following table shows the heights of 5 trees in meters. Represent it in the form of a bar graph.

Tree	Coconut	Mango	Eucalyptus	Neem	Palm
Height (in metre)	85	50	90	55	65

7. The table shows the monthly expenditure of a company.

Type of expenditure	Amount of expenditure (in lakhs)
Employee salary	80
Refreshment	10
Transport	30
Electricity	10
Miscellaneous	15

Represent the above data by a bar graph, taking 1 division = 10 lakh rupees.

8. The following are the number of students admitted in a school in different classes:

Classes	VI	VII	VIII	IX	X	XI	XII
No. of Students	20	26	30	34	24	32	34

Draw the bar graph to represent the above information.

9. The data given below shows the average rainfall in Cherrapunji, from June to November of a certain year:

Month	June	July	Aug.	Sept.	Oct.	Nov.
Rainfall (in cm)	30	35	25	20	15	15

Draw a bar graph to represent this information.

10. A survey of 120 school students was done to find which activity they prefer to do in their free time:

Preferred Activity	Number of Students
Playing	45
Reading story books	30
Watching TV	20
Listening to music	10
Painting	15

Draw a bar graph to represent the above data taking scale of 1 unit length = 5 students.
Which activity is preferred by most of the students other than playing?

2 EXERCISE

1. Following is the choice of sweets of 30 students of Class VI.
Ladoo, Barfi, Ladoo, Jalebi, Ladoo, Rasgulla, Jalebi, Ladoo, Barfi, Rasgulla, Ladoo, Jalebi, Jalebi, Rasgulla, Ladoo, Rasgulla, jalebi, Ladoo, Rasgulla, Ladoo, Ladoo, Barfi, Rasgulla, Rasgulla, Jalebi, Rasgulla, Ladoo, Rasgulla, Jalebi, Ladoo.
   (i) Arrange the names of sweets in a table using tally marks.
   (ii) Which sweet is preferred by most of the students?

2. Catherine thraw a dice 40 times and noted the number appearing each time as shown below:

1	3	5	6	6	3	5	4	1	6
2	5	3	4	6	1	5	5	6	1
1	2	2	3	5	2	4	5	5	6
5	1	6	2	3	5	2	4	1	5

Make a table and enter the data using tally marks. Find the number that appeared:
   (i) The minimum number of times
   (ii) The maximum number of times
   (iii) Find those numbers that appear an equal number of times.

3. Following pictograph shows the number of tractors in five villages.

Village	Number of tractors
Village A	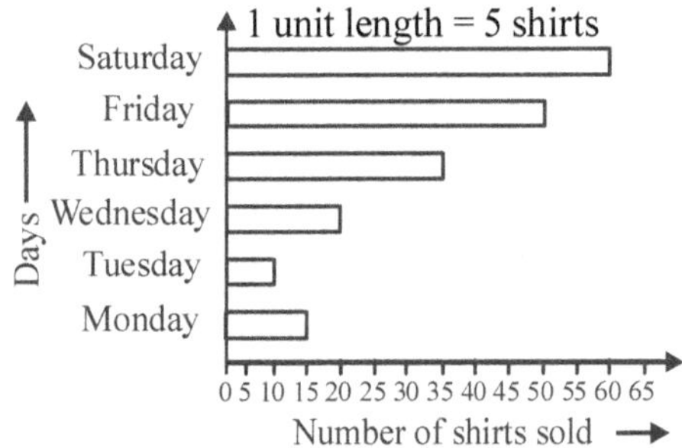
Village B	
Village C	
Village D	
Village E	

shows 1 tractor

Observe the pictograph and answer the following questions.
(i) Which village has the minimum number of tractors?
(ii) Which village has the maximum number of tractors?
(iii) How many more tractors village C has as compared to village B?
(iv) What is the total number of tractors in all the five villages?

4. Total number of students of a school in different years is shown in the following table.

Year	Number of students
1996	400
1998	535
2000	472
2002	600
2004	623

(i) Prepare a pictograph of student using one symbol to represent 100 students and answer the follwong questions:
   (a) How many symbols represent total number of students in the year 2002?
   (b) How many symbols represent total number of students for the year 1998?
(ii) Prepare another pictograph of students using any other symbol each representing 50 students. Which pictograph do you find more informative?

5. Observe the bar graph which is showing the sale of shirts in a ready-made shop from Monday to Saturday.

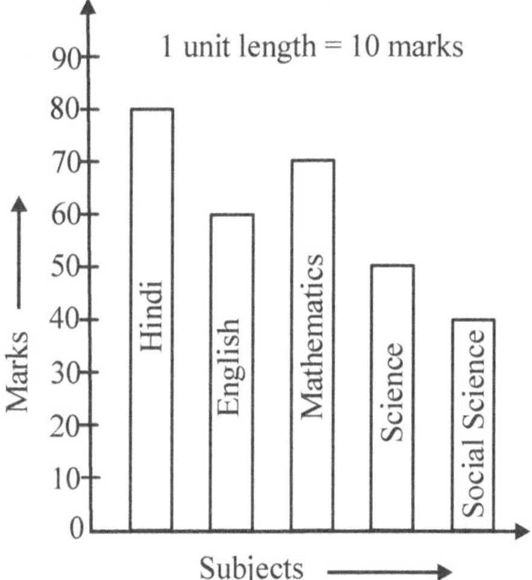

Now, answer the following questions:
(i) What information does the above bar graph give?
(ii) What is the scale chosen on the horizontal line representing number of shirts?
(iii) On which day were the maximum number of shirts sold? How many shirts were sold on that day?
(iv) On which day were the minimum number of shirts sold?
(v) How many shirts were sold on Thursday?

6. Observe this bar graph which shows the marks obtained by Aziz in half-yearly examination in different subjects.
Answer the given questions.
(i) What information does the bar graph give?
(ii) Name the subject in which Aziz scored maximum marks.
(iii) Name the subject in which he has scored minimum marks.
(iv) State the name of the subjects and marks obtained in each of them.

7. Following table shows the number of bicycles manufactured in a factory during the years 1998 – 2000. Illustrate this data using a bar graph. Choose a scale of your choice.

Year	Number of bicycles manufactured
1998	800
1999	600
2000	900
2001	1100
2002	1200

(i) In which year were the maximum number of bicycles manufactured?

(ii) In which year were the minimum number of bicycles manufactured?

Exemplar Questions :

1. Thirty students were interviewed to find out what they want to be in future. Their responses are listed as below:

   doctor, engineer, doctor, pilot, officer, doctor, engineer, doctor, pilot, officer, pilot, engineer, officer, pilot, doctor, engineer, pilot, officer, doctor, officer, doctor, pilot, engineer, doctor, pilot, officer, doctor, pilot, doctor, engineer

   Arrange the data in a table using tally marks.

2. Students of Class VI in a school were given a task to count the number of articles made of different materials in the school. The information collected by them is represented as follows.

Material used	Articles ⊞ = 20 articles
Wood	⊞ ⊟
Glass	⊞
Metal	⊞ ⊞⊞
Rubber	⊞ ▢
Plastic	⊞ ⊟

   Observe the pictograph and answer the following questions:

   (i) Which material is used in maximum number of articles?

   (ii) Which material is used in minimum number of articles?

   (iii) Which material is used in exactly half the number of articles as those made up of metal?

   (iv) What is the total number of articles counted by the students?

3. The following pictograph depicts the information about the areas in sqkm (to nearest hundred) of some districts of Chhattisgarh State:

District	Area (in km²) ◎ = 1000 sqkm
Raigarh	◎◎◎◎◎◎◎◎
Rajnandgaon	◎◎◎◎◎◎◎
Koria	◎◎◎◎◎◎
Mahasamund	◎◎◎◎◎
Kabirdham	◎◎◎◎
Jashpur	◎◎◎◎◎◎◎

(i) What is the area of Koria district?

(ii) Which two districts have the same area?

(iii) How many districts have area more than 5000 square kilometres?

4. The following graph gives the information about the number of railway tickets sold for different cities on a railway ticket counter between 6.00 am to 10.00 am. Read the bar graph and answer the following questions.

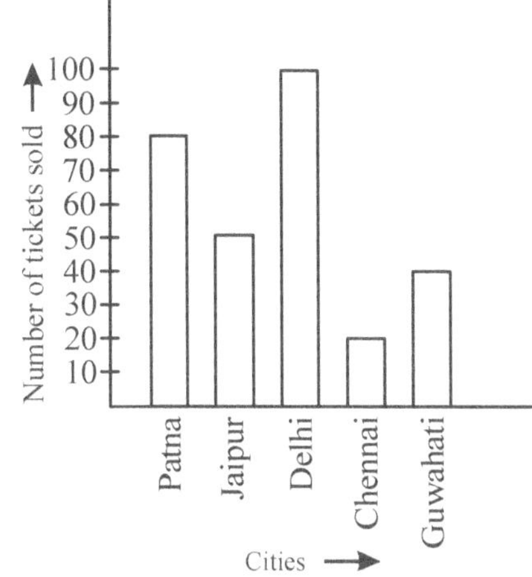

(i) How many tickets were sold in all?

(ii) For which city were the maximum number of tickets sold?

(iii) For which city were the minimum number of tickets sold?

(iv) Name the cities for which the number of tickets sold is more than 20.

5. The bar graph given below represents the circulation of newspapers in different languages in a town. Study the bar graph and answer the following questions:

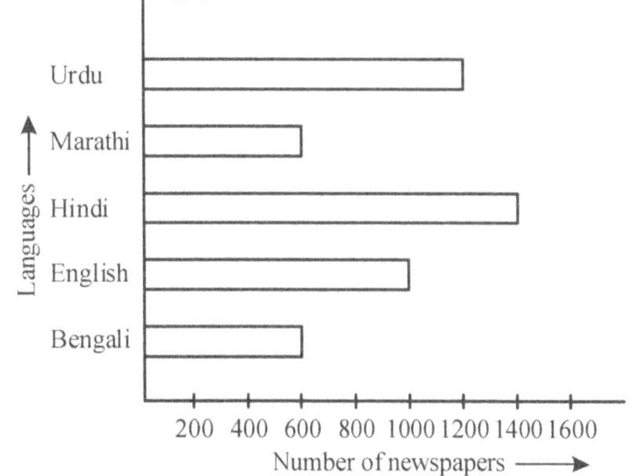

   (i) What is the circulation of English newspaper?

   (ii) Name the two languages in which circulation of newspaper is the same.

   (iii) By how much is the circulation of newspaper in Hindi more than the newspaper in Bengali?

6. The following table gives the number of vehicles passing through a toll gate, every hour from 8.00 am. to 1.00 pm:

Time Interval	8.00 to 9.00	9.00 to 10.00	10.00 to 11.00	11.00 to 12.00	12.00 to 1.00
Number of vehicles	250	450	300	250	150

Draw a bar graph representing the above data.

7. In a botanical garden, the number of different types of plants are found as follows:

Type of the plant	Number of plants
Herb	50
Shrub	60
Creeper	20
Climber	45
Tree	95

Draw a bar graph to represent the above information and answer the following questions:

   (i) Which type of plant is maximum in number in the garden?

   (ii) Which type of plant is minimum in number in the garden?

3 EXERCISE

Single Option Correct :

DIRECTIONS : *This section contains multiple choice questions. Each question has 4 choices (a), (b), (c) and (d) out of which ONLY ONE is correct.*

1. One ◯ represents 5 balloons then number of symbols to be drawn to represent 60 balloons is
  (a) 5   (b) 60
  (c) 10   (d) 12

2. Frequency of 4 in the data 4, 3, 2, 3, 4, 5, 6, 2, 1 is
  (a) 1   (b) 2
  (c) 3   (d) 0

3. If ☆ shows 5 chocolates ⋏ represents
  (a) 1 chocolate   (b) 2 chocolates
  (c) 3 chocolates   (d) 4 chocolates

4. When it become tedious to represent data by pictograph we go to represent data by
  (a) Bar graph   (b) Line graph
  (c) Tally marks   (d) None of these

5. The height of bar indicates the _______ of data.
  (a) Value   (b) Space
  (c) Width   (d) None of these

6. Width of bars always remain equal but _______ changes according to value.
  (a) Space   (b) Height
  (c) Both (a) & (b) (d) None of these

7. To draw a bar graph it is necessary to make a
  (a) Unit   (b) Scale
  (c) Axis   (d) None of these

8. Bar graph may be
  (a) Horizontal or vertical
  (b) Negative or positive
  (c) Both (a) and (b)
  (d) None of these

9. Using tally marks, which one of the following represents the number five?
  (a) | | | | | (b) √ √ √ √ √
  (c) 卌| (d) 卌

10. Representation of data in tabular form is done by using _____.
  (a) Bar graph   (b) Frequency
  (c) Tally marks   (d) None of these

11. In a survey of 12 families, each family is found to have the following number of children.
3, 1, 4, 1, 2, 2, 3, 1, 2, 2, 3, 3
Number of families with 2 children is equal to number of families with ______.
   (a) 1 child
   (b) 3 children
   (c) 4 children
   (d) None of these

12. Data collected from secondary sources like internet, magazines etc. Is called ______.
   (a) Secondary Data
   (b) Primary Data
   (c) Tally marks
   (d) Frequency

13. Production of cars in a factory in different years is shown here.

Year	1990	1991	1992	1993	1994
No.of Cars	1000	1500	2000	2400	3000

The ratio of production in the year 1990 to 1994 is ______.
   (a) 1 : 3
   (b) 1 : 2
   (c) 2 : 3
   (d) 2 : 1

14. Using tally marks, which one of the following represents the number eight?

   (a) ⦅||||⦆ |||
   (b) ﬀ ﬀ
   (c) ﬀﬀ ||
   (d) ﬀﬀ |||

Assertion & Reason :

DIRECTIONS : *Each of these questions contains an Assertion followed by Reason. Read them carefully and answer the question on the basis of following options. You have to select the one that best describes the two statements.*

(a) If both **Assertion** and **Reason** are **correct** and Reason is the **correct explanation** of Assertion.

(b) If both **Assertion** and **Reason** are correct, but Reason is **not the correct explanation** of Assertion.

(c) If **Assertion** is **correct** but **Reason** is **incorrect**.

(d) If **Assertion** is **incorrect** but **Reason** is **correct**.

1. **Assertion:** Consider the marks scored by 10 students in a test.
10, 9, 9, 8, 2, 8, 2, 8, 8, 7
The frequency of 8 in the data is 4.
   Reason: 8 occurs 4 times in the data. So, its frequency is 4.

2. The number of two-wheelers owned by each of 45 families are listed below.

No. of two-wheelers	Tally marks
0	||||
1	ﬀﬀ ﬀﬀ ﬀﬀ |
2	ﬀﬀ ﬀﬀ |||
3	ﬀﬀ ||||
4	|||

Assertion: The number of families having 2 two-wheelers is 13.

Reason: 13 is represented as ﬀﬀ |||.

Passage Based Questions :

DIRECTIONS : *Study the given passage(s) and answer the following questions.*

PASSAGE-I

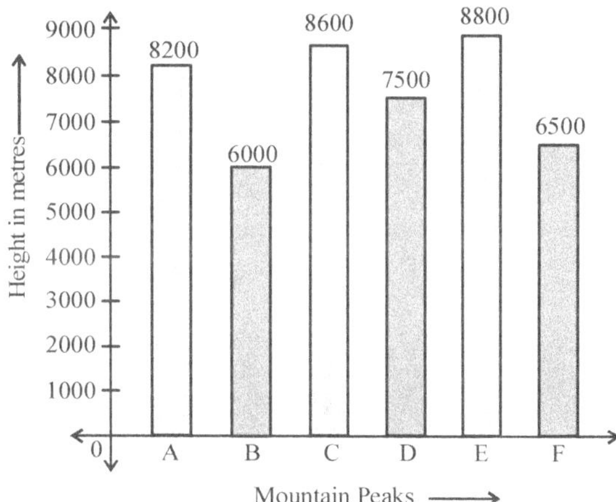

Read the above diagram and answer the following:

1. Which is the highest peak?
   (a) A
   (b) E
   (c) C
   (d) B

2. Write the ratio of the heights of highest peak and the lowest peak.
   (a) 22 : 15
   (b) 15 : 22
   (c) 20 : 13
   (d) 13 : 22

3. Which peak is second highest?
   (a) B
   (b) A
   (c) C
   (d) E

4. When the heights of the given peaks are written in ascending order, then what is the average of the middle two peaks?
   (a) 7950 m   (b) 7560 m
   (c) 7650 m   (d) 7850 m

PASSAGE-II

The pictograph given below shows how many letters were collected from a post box on each of the days of a certain week.

Monday	⊠ ⊠ ⊠ ⊠ ⊠ ⊠ ⊠
Tuesday	⊠ ⊠ ⊠ ⊠ ⊠
Wednesday	⊠ ⊠ ⊠ ⊠
Thursday	⊠ ⊠ ⊠ ⊠ ⊠ ⊠
Friday	⊠ ⊠ ⊠ ⊠ ⊠ ⊠ ⊠ ⊠
Saturday	⊠ ⊠ ⊠
	⊠ = 10 letters

Answer the following questions.

5. On which day were the minimum number of letters collected?
   (a) Tuesday   (b) Wednesday
   (c) Friday   (d) Saturday

6. What are the total number of letters collected from the post box over the whole week?
   (a) 300   (b) 330
   (c) 350   (d) 420

7. How many more letters were collected on Friday than on Wednesday?
   (a) 20   (b) 30
   (c) 40   (d) 50

8. How many less letters were collected on Wednesday than on Tuesday?
   (a) 10   (b) 20
   (c) 30   (d) 40

Integer Type Questions :

DIRECTIONS : *Answer the following questions. The answer to each of the question is a single digit integer, ranging from 0 to 9.*

1. If ⋈ represent 2 toffees, then ⋈ ⋈ ⋈ represents how many toffees?

2. Which number does ⩕⩕ || represent?

3. The frequency of 3 in the data 1, 1, 2, 2, 3, 3, 4, 4, 2, 2, 3, is ______ .

4. If ☺ represents 2 persons, then ☺☺☺☺ represents ______ persons.

5. If ☺ ☺ ☺ = 18 students, then ☺ represents how many students?

6. If ⌂⌂⌂⌂⌂ represents 15 ice creams, then how many ice creams ⌂ ⌂ ⌂ represents?

Multiple Matching Question :

DIRECTIONS : *Following question has four statements (A, B, C and D) given in Column-I and five statements (p, q, r, s, t) in Column-II. Any given statement in Column-I can have correct matching with one or more statement(s) given in Column-II.*

1. The following bar graph shows the number of houses (out of 100) in a town using different types of fuels for cooking.

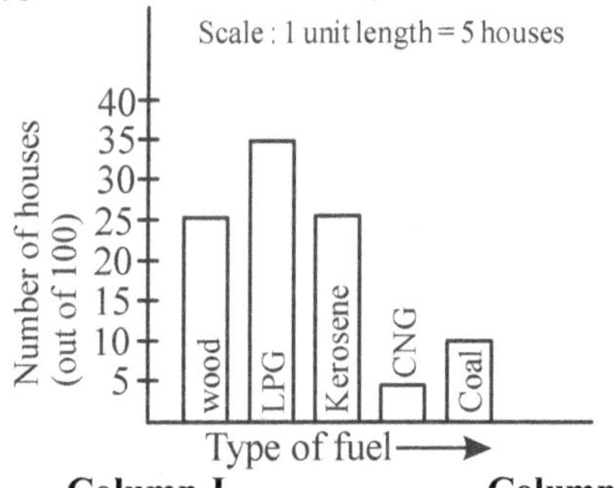

Column-I	Column-II
(A) Fuel which is used in maximum number of houses	(p) C N G
(B) Number of houses using coal as fuel are	(q) Wood
(C) Fuel used in 25 houses	(r) L P G
(D) Fuel which is used in minimum number of houses is	(s) 10
	(t) Kerosene

SOLUTIONS

Brief Explanations of Selected Questions

1 EXERCISE

Fill in the Blanks :

1. frequency
2. pictograph
3. data
4. tally
5. uniform, equal
6. 60
7. 60, 7.5
8. Raw data
9. Frequency

True / False :

1. False : In a bar graph, bars of uniform width can be drawn vertically or horizontally.
2. False : ⼁⼁⼁⼁ denotes 5 entries in tally marks.
3. False : The representation of an information through graph is called bar graph.
4. True
5. True
6. False : represents $\dfrac{120}{4} = 30$ balls.

Match the Columns :

1. (A) → (r); (B) → (s); (C) → (p); (D) → (q)

Very Short Answer Questions:

1. (i) 2 appers once
   (ii) 6 appears 5 times
2. Number of students who pass the test = 11.
3. Number of students whose pulse rate is more than 60 per minute = 17.
4. Number of girls in the list = 3.
5. As △ = 150 pillars

   ∴ △ △ △ ◁ $= 3 \times 150 + \dfrac{150}{2} = 525$ pillars.
6. 17
7.

Short Answer Questions :

1.

No. of children	Tally marks	No. of families
1	⼁⼁⼁⼁	5
2	⼁⼁⼁⼁ ⼁⼁⼁⼁	10
3	⼁⼁⼁⼁	5
	Total	20

2. (i) (a) Agra 4 × 10 = 40 cm
      (b) Mumbai 9 × 10 = 90 cm
      (c) Chennai 6 × 10 = 60 cm
   (ii) Mumbai 90 cm
      Delhi = 5 × 10 = 50 cm
      40 cm more rainfall fell in Mumbai
3. (i) 50 fans
   (ii) Friday and Sunday
   (iii) Wednesday
   (iv) 290 fans (50 + 40 + 60 + 40 + 30 + 40 + 30)
4. (i) 70   (ii) 95
   (iii) 5   (iv) 2001, 60
5. (i) ₹ 36916 crores
   (ii) ₹ 70158 crores
   (iii) 36916 crores < 42653 crores < 58329 crores < 65415 crores < 70158 crores.
6. (i) Mathematics
   (ii) History
   (iii) Total marks

   $$= 55 + 90 + 40 + 80 + 20 = 285$$

   ∴ Average $= \dfrac{285}{5} = 57$

   (iv) Percentage $= \dfrac{285}{500} \times 100 = 57\%$

   (v) Highest marks = 90
   Lowest marks = 20
   Ratio = 90 : 20
   $= 9 : 2$

7.

Games	Tally marks	Number of Students
Football	𝍩𝍩𝍩 |||	13
Cricket	𝍩 ||||	9
Kho-Kho	𝍩		6
Hockey	𝍩 |||	8
Tennis	||||	4

   (i)   Football   (ii)   Football   (iii)   Tennis

8.   (i)   Week 4   (ii)   5 hours
      (iii)   17 hours   (iv)   2 hours

Long Answer Questions :

1.   Scale:  ≡ 4 bats sold

   Now, we may draw the pictograph, as shown below.

Day	No. of bats sold
Monday	
Tuesday	
Wednesday	
Thursday	
Friday	
Saturday	

2.   (i)   8
      (ii)   K.P.S. School
      (iii)   20
      (iv)   Hans School < Happy School < D.S.C School < Max School < K.P.S. School

3.   (i)   6   (ii)   3
      (iii)   2000   (iv)   1995

4.   Let the symbol represents 25 shirts.

∴ The pictograph can be drawn easily as shown below:

Day	Number of Shirts sold
Monday	
Tuesday	
Wednesday	
Thursday	
Friday	
Saturday	

5.   Do it yourself.

6.   Bar graph showing the height of some trees.

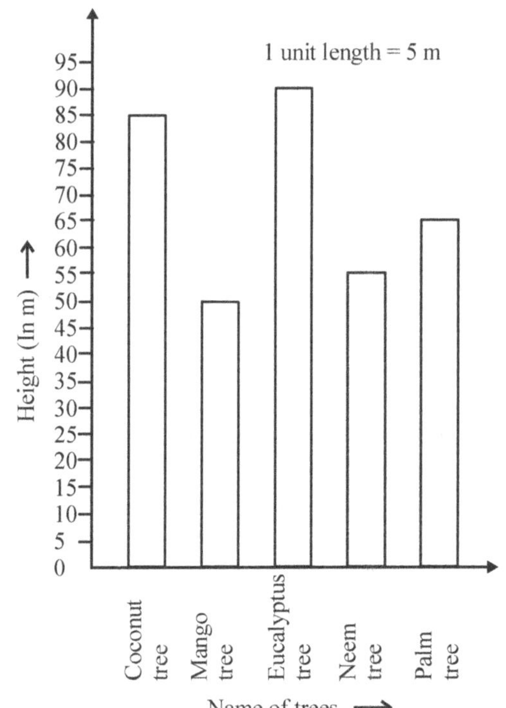

7.

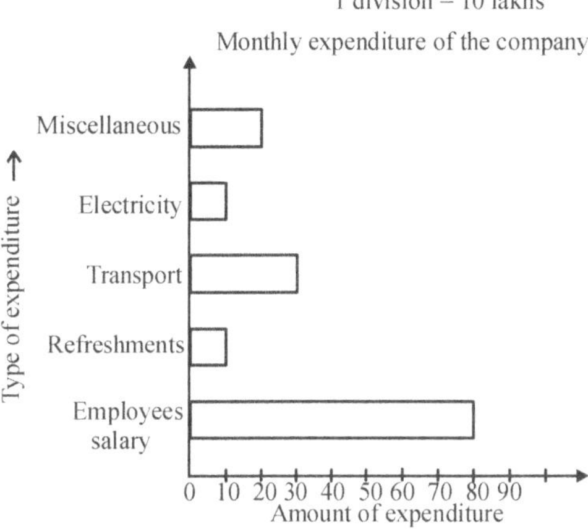

8.

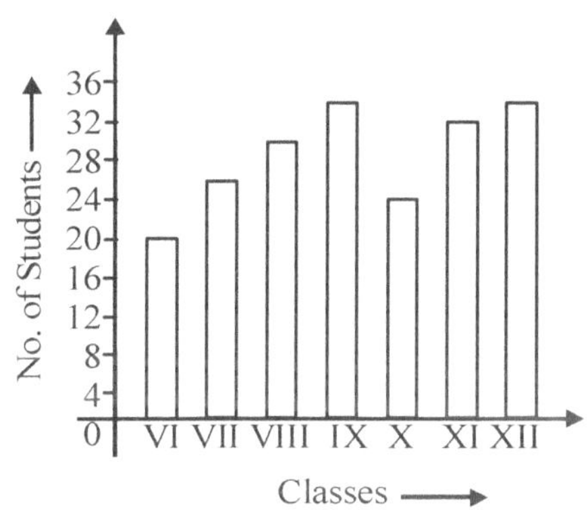

9.

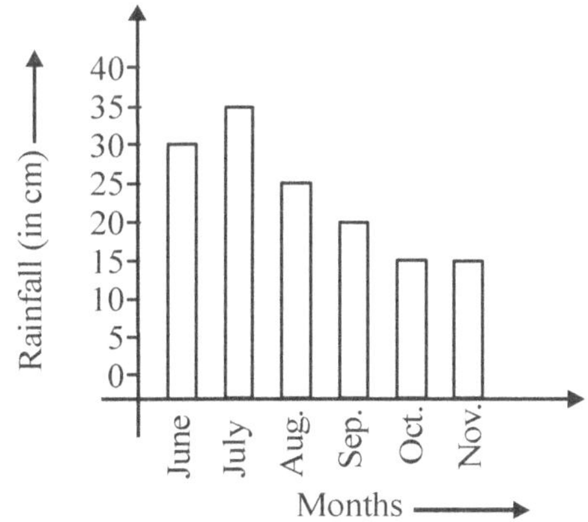

10. Do it yourself.

Text-Book Exercise :

1. (i) We have the following table:

Sweets	Tally Marks	Numbers of students
Ladoo	৸৸ I	11
Barfi	III	3
Jalebi	৸৸ II	7
Rasgulla	৸৸ IIII	9
Total		30

(ii) From the table, we can say that Ladoo in preferred by most of the students.

2.

Number	Tally marks	Number of times
1	৸৸ II	7
2	৸৸ I	6
3	৸৸	5
4	IIII	4
5	৸৸৸৸ I	11
6	৸৸ II	7

From the table we find that:
(i) The number 4 appeared minimum number of times.
(ii) The number 5 appeared maximum number of times.
(iii) The number 1 and 6 appear for the same number of times.

3. Observing the pictograph, we have
(i) Village D has the minimum number of tractors.
(ii) Village C has the maximum number of tractors.
(iii) ∵ $8 - 5 = 3$
∴ Village C has 3 tractors more as compared to village B.
(iv) ∵ $6 + 5 + 8 + 3 + 6 = 28$
∴ 28 tractors are there in all five villages.

4. (i) We have the following pictograph using
�ّ = 100 students.

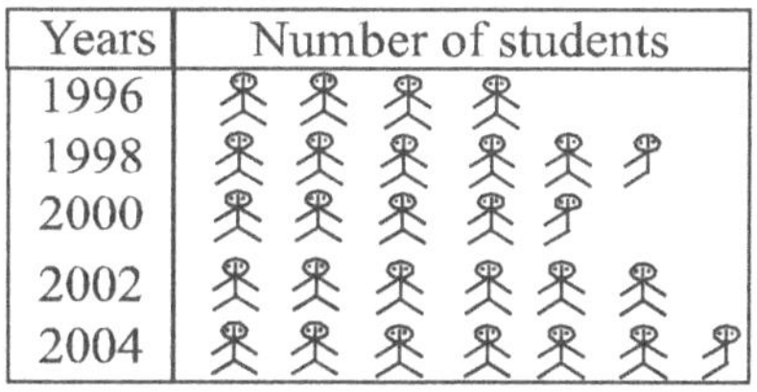

Years	Number of students
1996	☻ ☻ ☻ ☻
1998	☻ ☻ ☻ ☻ ☻ ☻
2000	☻ ☻ ☻ ☻ ☻
2002	☻ ☻ ☻ ☻ ☻ ☻
2004	☻ ☻ ☻ ☻ ☻ ☻ ☻

(a) In the year 2002, total number of students are represented by 6 symbols.

(b) In the year 1998, the total number of students are represented by 5 complete symbols and one incomplete symbol (equivalent to 535 students).

(ii) By taking 🧍 = 50, we prepare another pictograph as shown below:

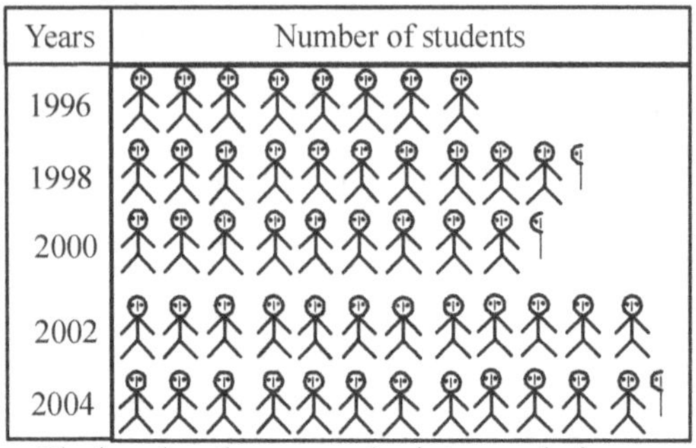

Years	Number of students
1996	(8 symbols)
1998	(10½ symbols)
2000	(9½ symbols)
2002	(11 symbols)
2004	(11½ symbols)

Obviously, the second pictograph is more informative.

5. (i) This bar graph gives the number of shirts sold from Monday to Saturday.
   (ii) Scale on the horizontal line is 1 unit = 5 shirts.
   (iii) Maximum number of shirts were sold on Saturday. 60 shirts were sold.
   (iv) Tuesday   (v) 35 shirts

6. (i) This bar graph represents the marks obtained by Aziz in different subjects.
   (ii) Maximum marks is obtained in Hindi.
   (iii) Minimum marks is obtained in Social Science.
   (iv) Subjectwise marks are:
   Hindi: 80; English: 60; Mathematics: 70; Science: 50; Social Science: 40

7.

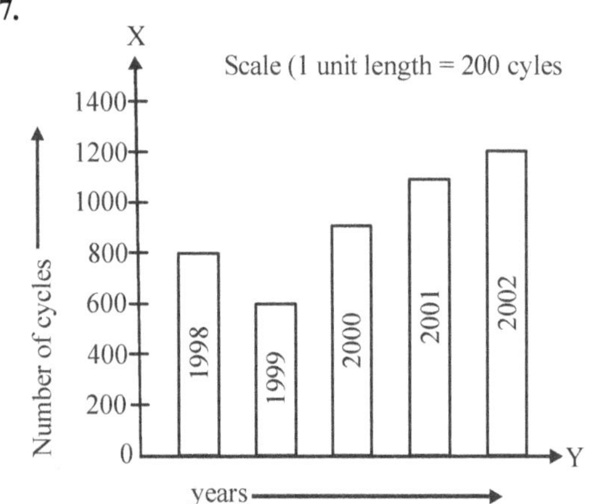

From the bar graph, we have:
(i) The maximum number of cycles were manufactured in 2002.
(ii) The minimum bumber of cycles were manufactured in 1999.

Exemplar Questions :

1.

Responses	Tally Marks	Number of Responses
Doctor	 卌 卌	10
Engineer	卌 I	6
Pilot	卌 III	8
Officer	卌 I	6

2. (i) Metal   (ii) Glass
   (iii) Rubber   (iv) 160

3. (i) 6000 sq. km (ii) Raigarh and Jashpur
   (iii) 4

4. (i) 295   (ii) Delhi   (iii) Chennai
   (iv) Patna, Jaipur, Delhi, Guwahati

5. (i) 1000   (ii) Marathi and Bengali
   (iii) 800

6.

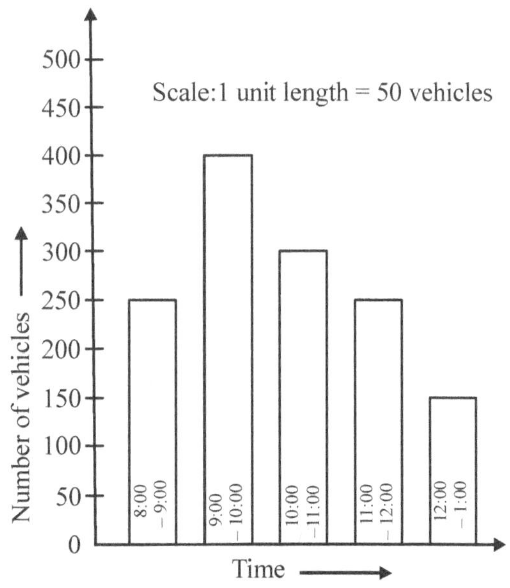

7.

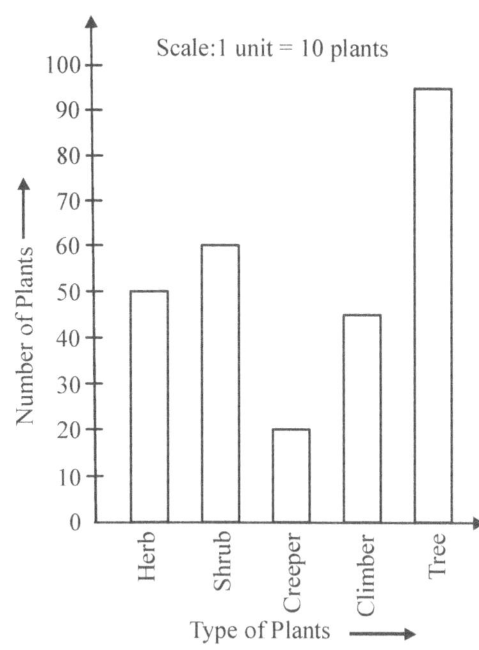

(i) Tree (ii) Creeper

3 EXERCISE

Single Option Correct :

1. (d) $60 \div 5 = 12$ **2.** (b) 2

3. (c)   **4.** (a)   **5.** (a)

6. (b)   **7.** (b)   **8.** (a)

9. (d)   **10.** (c)

11. (b)

No. of children	Tally marks	No. of families
1					3
2						4
3						4
4			1
Total		12

Number of familes with 2 children = 4
= number of families with 3 children.

12. (a)

13. (a) Production in the year 1990 = 1000
Production in the year 1994 = 3000

$\therefore$ Required ratio $= \dfrac{1000}{3000} = \dfrac{1}{3}$ i.e.; 1 : 3

14. (d) 8 can be represented as ||||| |||.

Assertion & Reason :

1. (a) Assertion: True, Reason: True and Reason is the correct explanation of Assertion.

2. (c) ||||| ||||| ||| represents 13.
So, number of families having 2 two-wheelers is 13.
Assertion: True, Reason: False

Passage Based Questions :

1. (b) E is the highest peak.

2. (a) Height of highest peak = 8800 m
Height of lowest peak = 6000 m
Ratio = 8800 : 6000 = 22 : 15

3. (c) Second highest peak is C.

4. (d) The ascending order of heights is,
6000 m < 6500 m < 7500 m < 8200 m
< 8600 m < 8800 m.
The two middle peaks are 7500 m, 8200 m.

$\text{Average} = \dfrac{7500 + 8200}{2} = \dfrac{15700}{2} = 7850\,\text{m}$

5. (d) Saturday   **6.** (b) 330

7. (c) 40   **8.** (a) 10

Integer Type Questions :

1. (6) ◁▷◁ ◁▷◁ = 3 × 2 = 6 toffees.

2. (7)

3. (3) Since 3 occurs 3 times, therefore its frequency is 3.

4. (8)

5. (6) ☺ = $\dfrac{18}{3}$ = 6 students

6. (9) ⌂ = $\dfrac{15}{5}$ = 3 ice creams

$\therefore$ ⌂ ⌂ ⌂ = 3 × 3 = 9 ice creams.

Multiple Matching Question :

1. (A) → (r); (B) → (s); (C) → (q, t); (D) → (p)

Chapter 10

Mensuration

PERIMETER

If you were to start from a place, go around a figure and come back to the same point, then you would have covered some distance. This distance is knwon as perimeter.

So, we say that

Perimeter is the distance around a closed figure when we go along the figure once.

or

The sum of lengths of all the sides of a closed figure is known as perimeter

or

Perimeter is the distance covered in making one complete revolution along the boundary of the closed figure.

ILLUSTRATION : 1

Find the perimeter of the following figures :

(i) 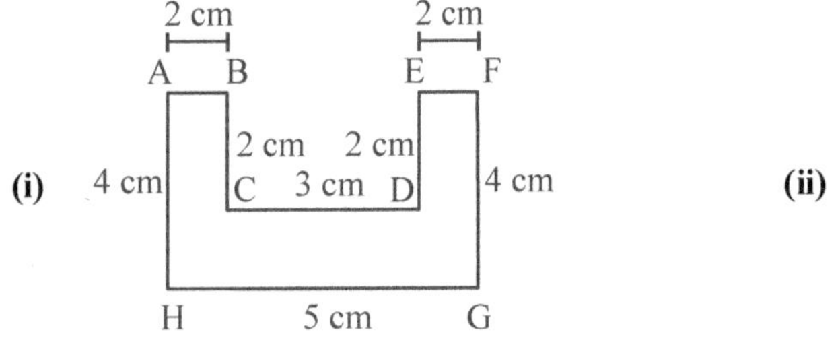 (ii) 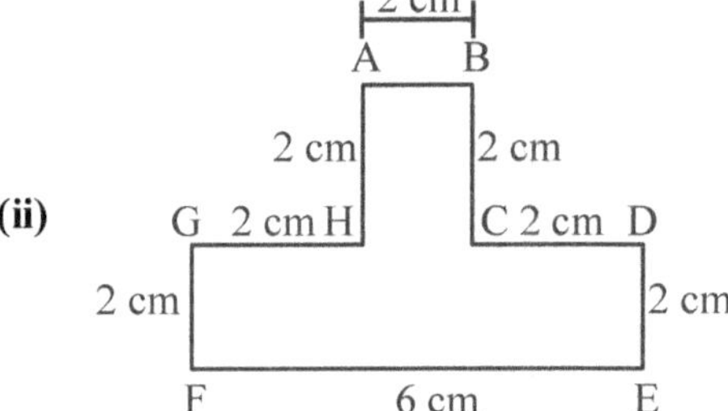

SOLUTION :

(i)   Perimeter of fig (ABCDEFGH) = AB + BC + CD + DE + EF + FG + GH + HA
$$= 2 + 2 + 3 + 2 + 2 + 4 + 5 + 4 = 24 \text{ cm}$$

(ii)   Perimeter of fig (ABCDEFGH) = AB + BC + CD + DE + EF + FG + GH + HA
$$= 2 + 2 + 2 + 2 + 6 + 2 + 2 + 2 = 20 \text{ cm}$$

PERIMETER OF A RECTANGLE

In a rectangle, the opposite sides are equal. consider a rectangle ABCD, where l and b are its length and breadth respectively.

∴   Perimeter = AB + BC + CD + DA

$$\ell + b + \ell + b = 2\ell + 2b = 2(l + b) \text{ units}$$

By the above formula, other formulas can be drawn
Perimeter = 2 (length + breadth)

or $\boxed{\dfrac{\text{Perimeter}}{2} = \text{Length} - \text{Breadth}}$ or $\boxed{\dfrac{\text{Perimeter}}{2} - \text{Length} = \text{Breadth}}$

or $\boxed{\dfrac{\text{Perimeter}}{2} - \text{Breadth} = \text{Length}}$

ILLUSTRATION : 2

Find the breadth of a rectangle whose perimeter is 50 m and length is 15 m.

SOLUTION :

We have, perimeter = 50 m and Length = 15 m

$$\text{Breadth} = \dfrac{\text{perimeter}}{2} - \text{length}$$

$$= \dfrac{50}{2} - 15 = 25 - 15$$

or $\qquad\qquad = 10 \text{ m}$

ILLUSTRATION : 3

An athlete takes 5 rounds of a rectangular field, 30 m long and 10 m wide. Find the total distance covered by him.

SOLUTION :

Length of field = 30 m
Breadth of field = 10 m
Perimeter of field = 2 (Length + Breadth)
$\qquad\qquad\qquad\quad = 2 (30 + 10)$
$\qquad\qquad\qquad\quad = 2 \times 40$
$\qquad\qquad\qquad\quad = 80 \text{ m}$
So, distance covered by athlete in one round = 80 m
Therefore distance covered in 5 rounds = 80 × 5 = 400 m
So, total distance covered by athlete is 400 m.

PERIMETER OF REGULAR SHAPES

A polygon in which all sides are of equal length and measure of each angle is same is called a regular polygon.
Square, equilateral triangle, regular hexagon, etc. are regular polygons.
Perimeter of a regular polygon = n × length of a side

$\Rightarrow$ Length of a side of regular polygon $= \dfrac{1}{n} \times$ Perimeter of regular polygon

Perimeter of a Square

A square is a rectangle having all its sides equal.
∴ Perimeter of a square $= 2 \text{ (side + side)}$
$\qquad\qquad\qquad\qquad\quad = 2 \times 2 \text{ side} = 4 \times \text{side}$
$\qquad\qquad\qquad\qquad\quad = 4\,l \text{ where } l \text{ is the side of square.}$

Also, side of a square $= \dfrac{\text{Perimeter}}{4}$

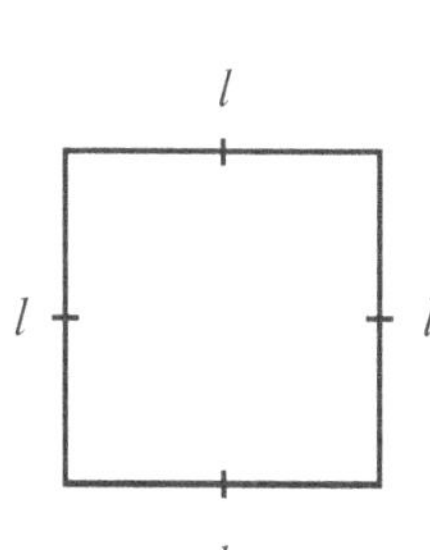

Perimeter of an equilateral triangle

Let each side of the equilateral triangle be l.

Then, its perimeter, $p = l + l + l$

$$= 3l \text{ or } 3 \times \text{side}$$

As, Perimeter of a square $= 4 \times$ side

Perimeter of an equilateral triangle $= 3 \times$ side

Then we can say that

Perimeter of a regular pentagon $= 5 \times$ side of a pentagon

Perimeter of a regular hexagon $= 6 \times$ side of a hexagon

Perimeter of a regular heptagon $= 7 \times$ side of a heptagon

Perimeter of a regular octagon $= 8 \times$ side of an octagon

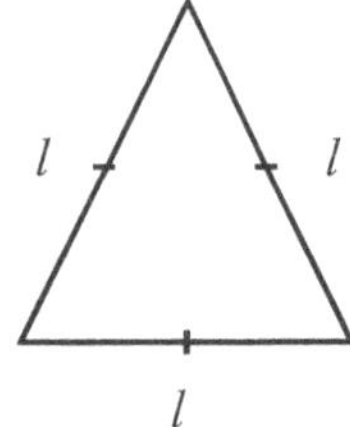

ILLUSTRATION : 4

Find the cost of fencing a square park of side 60 m at the rate of ₹ 10 per meter.

SOLUTION :

We have,

Side of square park = 60 m

Perimeter of the park = 4 × side = 4 × 60 = 240 m

Therefore, Cost of fencing the park = 240 × ₹ 10 = ₹ 2400

ILLUSTRATION : 5

Geeta runs around a square park of side 40 m. Her friend runs around a rectangular park of length 25 m and breadth 12 m. Who covers more distance by how much?

SOLUTION :

Square side = 40 m

Perimeter of square = 4 × side = 4 × 40 = 160 m

Length of rectangular park = 25 m

Breadth of rectangular park = 12 m

Perimeter of rectangle = 2 (length + breadth)

$$= 2 (25 + 12) = 2 \times 37 = 74 \text{ m}$$

So, Geeta runs around square park of perimeter 160 m, while her friend runs around rectangular park of perimeter 74 m.

Therefore, Geeta covers more distance than her friend by 160 m – 74 m i.e. 86 m.

TO FIND THE AREA OF A FIGURE USING A GRAPH

We can find the area of regular and irregular figures by using a graph or squared paper. To find the area, first we draw the figure on the graph paper covering as many squares as possible.

For finding the area by using squared paper, we have to follow the following steps :

(i)   Count the number of complete squares of unit length enclosed by the figure.

(ii)   Count the number of those squares whose more than half parts are enclosed by the figure.

(iii) Count the number of those squares whose exact half parts are enclosed by the figure and divide the number by 2.

(iv) Leave those squares whose less than half parts are enclosed by the figure.

(v)   Add all the steps (i), (ii), and (iii) to obtain the area.

$\therefore$ Area of the figure = Number of complete squares + Number of more than half squares $+ \dfrac{1}{2}$

(Number of half squares)

or $A = c + m + \dfrac{1}{2}h$

Where A = Area,   c = complete squares,

       m = more than half squares   h = half squares.

ILLUSTRATION : 6

Calculate the area of the given irregular figure.

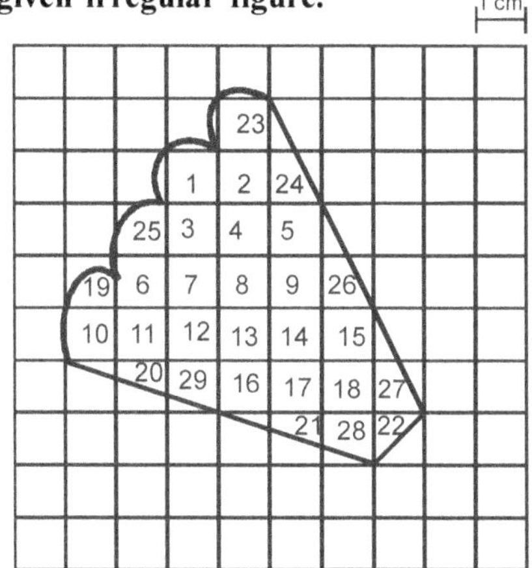

SOLUTION :

Number of complete squares = 18
Number of half-squares = 4
Number of more than half suares = 7

$$\therefore \text{Area} = c + m + \frac{1}{2}h = 18 + 7 + \left(\frac{1}{2} \times 4\right) = 27 \text{ sq. cm (approx.)}$$

AREA OF RECTANGLE AND SQUARE

Counting the squares is not a very efficient way to determine the area of some figures such as rectangle and square. There is a better way-
1. Area of rectangle = length × breadth
2. Area of square = side × side

ILLUSTRATION : 7

Find the area of a cloth in square meter whose length is 3 m and width is 1 m 50 cm.

SOLUTION :

$$50 \text{ cm} = \frac{50}{100} = 0.5 \text{ m} \qquad\qquad [\because 100 \text{ cm} = 1 \text{ m}]$$

Length of cloth = 3 m
Breadth of cloth = 1m 50 cm = 1m + 0.5 m = 1.5 m
Area of cloth = Length × Breadth = 1.5 × 3 = 4.5 m^2.

ILLUSTRATION : 8

The perimeter of rectangle and square are same. If the length and breadth of rectangle are 45 cm and 15 cm. respectively, find which shape has greater area and by how much?

SOLUTION :

Length of rectangle = 45 cm
Breadth of rectangle = 15 cm.
Perimeter of rectangle = 2 (length + breadth)
             = 2 (45 + 15) = 2 × 60 = 120 cm.
So, perimeter of square = 120 cm.

$$\text{Hence, side of square} = \frac{\text{Perimeter}}{4} = \frac{120}{4} = 30 \text{ cm.}$$

So, area of square = side^2 = 30 × 30 = 900 cm^2
Also area of rectangle = length × breadth = 45 × 15 = 675 cm^2
Thus, square has greater area by (900 − 675) sq. cm = 225sq. cm.

CONCEPT MAP

Mensuration

Perimeter

- The total length of boundary enclosing the figure is called perimeter of the figure.

(1)

Area

- The amount of surface enclosed within its bounding lines.

(2)

Square

- It is a quadrilateral with all sides are equal and all angles are 90°.
- If the square has side 'a', then, Perimeter of square
  $$= 4 \times a$$
  Area of square $= a \times a$

(3)

(4)

Rectangle

- It is a quadrilateral with opposite sides are equal and all angles are 90°.
- If the rectangle has length 'l' and breadth 'b', then. Perimeter of rectangle
  $$= 2\,(l + b)$$
  Area of rectangle
  $$= l \times b$$
- A square is a rectangle, but a rectangle is not a square.

MISCELLANEOUS
SOLVED EXAMPLES

1. A rectangular piece of lawn is 55 m wide. and 98 m long. Find the length of the fence around it.

Sol. The length of the fence around the lawn will be equal to the perimeter of the lawn which is rectangular in shape.

Perimeter of a rectangle $= 2(l + b)$
length l $= 98$ m
breadth b $= 55$ m

So, perimeter $= 2(l + b) = 2(98 + 55)$
$= 2 \times 153 = 306$ m

2. Find the perimeter of the following figures.

(a)

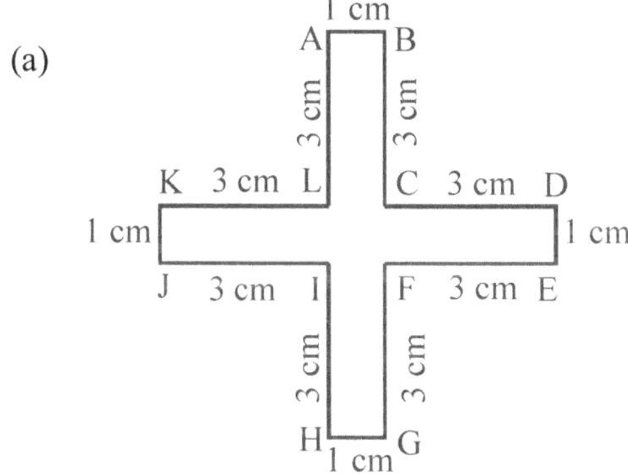

(b)

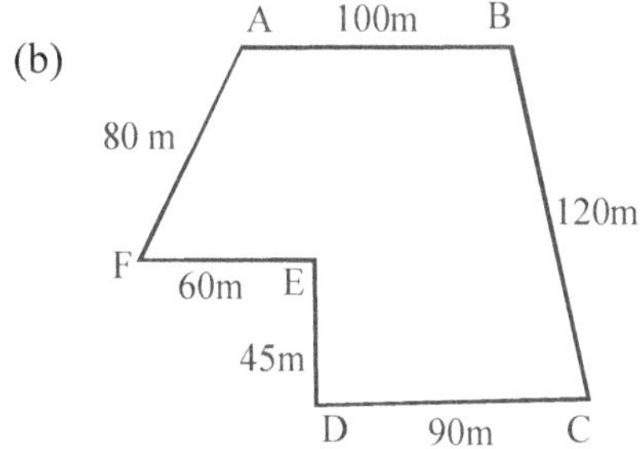

Sol. (a) Perimeter $= AB + BC + CD + DE + EF + FG + GH + HI + IJ + JK + KL + LA$
$= 1 + 3 + 3 + 1 + 3 + 3 + 1 + 3 + 3 + 1 + 3 + 3$
$= 28$ cm

(b) Perimeter $= FA + AB + BC + CD + DE + EF$
$= 80m + 100m + 120m + 90m + 45m + 60m$
$= 495m$

3. The length and breadth of a field are 35.5m and 24.5m, respectively. Find the cost of fencing the field at the rate of ₹15 per metre.

Sol. The portion which is to be fenced = perimeter of the field

perimeter $= 2(l + b)$
$= 2(35.5 + 24.5)$ m
$= 2 \times 60$ m $= 120$ m

Cost of fencing $= 15 \times 120 = ₹1800$

4. Find the area of each of the following figures by counting the number of squares enclosed. Take each square as 1 cm².

(i)

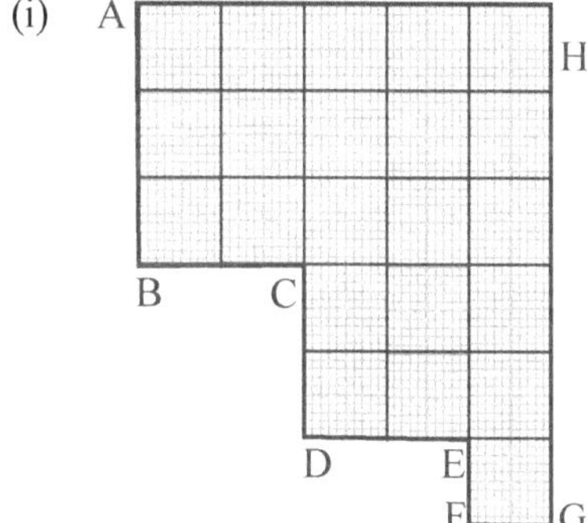

(ii)

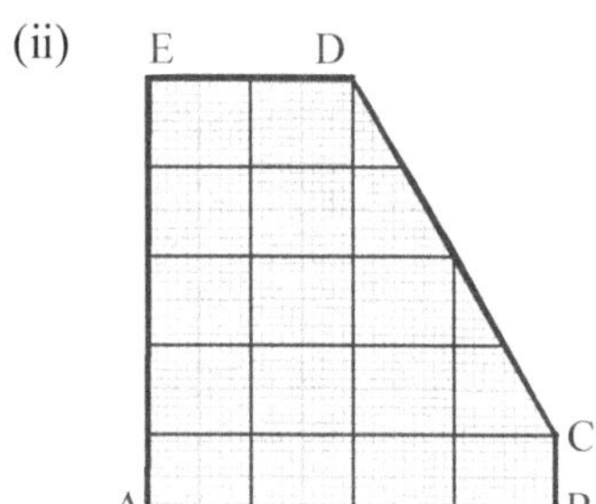

Sol. (i) Number of complete squares enclosed $= 22$
Number of more than half squares enclosed
$= 0$

$\therefore$ Number of half squares enclosed $= 0$

Area of (ABCDEFGH)

$$= 22 + 0 + \frac{1}{2}(0)$$
$$= (22 + 0 + 0)\ \text{cm}^2 = 22\ \text{cm}^2$$

(ii) Number of complete squares enclosed
$= 14$

Number of more than half squares enclosed
$= 2$

$\therefore$ Number of half squares enclosed $= 0$

Area of (ABCDE)

$$= 14 + 2 + \left(0 \times \frac{1}{2}\right)$$
$$= 14 + 2 + 0 = 16\ \text{cm}^2$$

5. **Find the perimeter of a regular hexagon having each side equal to 6.5 cm.**

Sol. Length of each side of the given hexagon
$= 6.5$ cm.

$\therefore$ Perimeter of the hexagon
$$= (6 \times 6.5)\ \text{cm} = 39\ \text{cm}.$$

6. **Find the area and perimeter of a rectangular plot of land whose length and breadth are 28.5 m and 20 m respectively.**

Sol. Here, length $= 28.5$ m and breadth $= 20$m.

$\therefore$ Area of the plot $=$ (length $\times$ breadth) sq units
$$= (28.5 \times 20)\ \text{m}^2$$
$$= \left(\frac{285}{10} \times 20\right)\text{m}^2 = 570\ \text{m}^2.$$

Perimeter of the plot $= 2 \times$ [length $+$ breadth]
$$= 2 \times [28.5 \times 20]\text{m}$$
$$= [2 \times 48.5]\ \text{m}$$
$$= \left(2 \times \frac{485}{10}\right)\text{m} = 97\text{m}.$$

7. **A room is 15m long and 8 m wide. Its floor is to be covered with rectangular tiles, each measuring 20 cm by 8 cm.**

Find (i) how many tiles will be required;
       (ii) the cost of these tiles at ₹16 per tile.

Sol. Length of the room $= 15$ m $= 1500$ cm.

Breadth of the room $= 8$ m $= 800$ cm.

Area of the room $= (1500 \times 800)\ \text{cm}^2$.

Length of each tile $= 20$ cm.

Breadth of each tile $= 8$ cm

Area of each tile $= (20 \times 8)\ \text{cm}^2$

(i) Number of tiles required

$$= \frac{\text{Area of the room}}{\text{Area of each tile}}$$

$$= \left(\frac{1500 \times 800}{20 \times 8}\right) = 7500.$$

(ii) Cost of these tiles
$$= ₹(7500 \times 16) = ₹120000.$$

8. **How many envelopes can be made out of a sheet of paper 125 cm by 85 cm supposing each envelope requires a piece of paper of size 17 cm by 5 cm?**

Sol. Area of the sheet $= (125 \times 85)\text{cm}^2$

Area of the paper required for one envelope
$$= (17 \times 5)\ \text{cm}^2$$

No. of envelopes

$$= \frac{\text{Area of the sheet}}{\text{Area of piece of paper required for 1 envelope}}$$

$\therefore$ No. of envelopes $= \dfrac{125 \times 85}{17 \times 5} = 25 \times 5 = 125$

9. **A rectangular garden is 105 m by 75 m. How many rounds of this garden will a boy make if he runs 3600 m?**

Sol. Distance covered in 1 round
$$= \text{Perimeter of field}$$
$$= 2(105 + 75)$$
$$= 2 \times 180 = 360\ \text{m}$$

No. of rounds $= \dfrac{\text{Total distance covered}}{\text{Distance covered in a round}}$

$$= \frac{3600}{360} = 10$$

Hence, a boy will make 10 rounds to cover 3600 m.

10. **A rope is 30 cm long. What will be the length of each side, if the rope is used in form of**

(i)   **an equilateral triangle ?**

(ii)   **a square ?**

(iii) **a regular hexagon ?**

Sol. Since length of rope in 30 cm long, so

(i)   Side of an equilateral triangle

$$= \frac{\text{perimeter}}{3} = \frac{30}{3} = 10\ \text{cm}$$

(ii)   Side of a square

$$= \frac{\text{perimeter}}{4} = \frac{30}{4} = 7.5\ \text{cm}$$

(iii) Side of A regular hexagon

$$= \frac{\text{perimeter}}{6} = \frac{30}{6} = 5 \text{ cm}$$

11. **Find the area of given shape.**

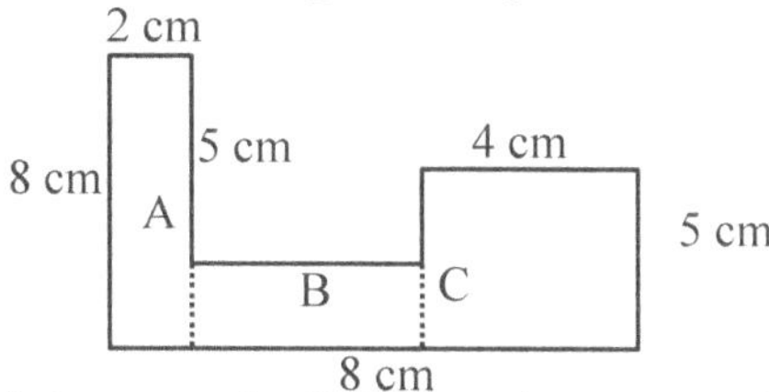

Sol. This figure can be divide into three rectangles, marked A, B and C.

Area of rectangle A = (8×2) cm^2 = 16 cm^2

Area of rectangle B = (3×2) cm^2 = 6 cm^2

Area of rectangle C = (4×5) cm^2 = 20 cm^2

Total area = $(16 + 6 + 20)$ cm^2 = 42 cm^2

12. **Find the perimeter of a rectangle, whose area is 750 cm^2 and its breadth is 15 cm.**

Sol. Area of rectangle = 750 cm^2

Breadth of rectangle = 15 cm

So, length of rectangle

$$= \frac{\text{Area}}{\text{Breadth}} = \frac{750}{15} = 50 \text{ cm}$$

Perimeter of rectangle = 2 (length + breadth)

$$= 2 \,(50 + 15)$$
$$= 2 \times 65 \Rightarrow 130 \text{ cm}$$

13. **What will happen to the area of a square if its side is**

(i) **halved** **(ii)** **doubled** **(iii) tripled**

Sol. Let the side of square is a Then

Area = A = a $\times$ a cm^2 ...(i)

(i) When the side is halved, then,

Side of new square = $\dfrac{a}{2}$ cm

A_1 = Area of new square

$$= \frac{a}{2} \times \frac{a}{2} \text{ cm}^2 = \frac{a \times a}{4} \text{ cm}^2$$

$$= \frac{1}{4} \times a \times a \text{ cm}^2 = \frac{A}{4} \quad \text{[Using (i)]}$$

Thus, if the side is halved, then area becomes one–fourth

(ii) When the side is doubled, then

Side of new square = 2a cm

A_2 = Area of new square = 2a $\times$ 2a cm^2

= 4 (a $\times$ a) cm^2 = 4A [Using (i)]

Thus, if the side is doubled, then area becomes 4 times.

(iii) When the side is tripled, then,

side of new square = 3a cm

A_3 = Area of new square

$$= 3a \times 3a \text{ cm}^2$$
$$= 9 \,(a \times a) \text{ cm}^2$$
$$= 9A \text{ cm}^2$$

[Using (i)]

Thus, if the side is tripled, then area becomes 9 times.

1 EXERCISE

Fill in the Blanks :

DIRECTIONS : *Complete the following statements with an appropriate word / term to be filled in the blank space(s).*

1. Perimeter of a triangle with sides 4.5cm, 6.02 cm and 5.38cm is ________.

2. The amount of surface enclosed by a closed plane figure is called its ____________.

3. The perimeter of a square is ____________ times the length of the side.

4. ____________ is expressed in square units.

5. The distance covered by a farmer around a field of 120m length and 80m width is ________ .

6. Perimeter of a square = ____________ × side.

7. Area of a rectangle = (______) × (______).

8. Area of a square = ____________ .

True / False :

DIRECTIONS : *Read the following statements and write your answer as true or false.*

1. Geeta wants to raise a boundary wall around her house, For this, she must find the area of the land of her house.

2. A person preparing a track to conduct sports must find the perimeter of the sports ground.

3. If length of a rectangle is halved and breadth is doubled then the area of the rectangle obtained remains same.

4. Area of a square is doubled if the side of the square is doubled.

5. To find the cost of a frame of a picture, we need to find the perimeter of the picture.

6. Perimeter of a regular octagon of side 6 cm is 36 cm.

7. If length and breadth of the rectangle are not expressed in the same unit, then first we should convert them to the same unit.

8. The perimeter of square whose area is 25 cm^2 is 20 cm.

9. The breadth of a rectangle of area 24 cm^2 and length 8 cm is 6 cm .

10. If we need to find the cost a levelling a square playground, we need to find its perimeter.

11. The perimeter of regular septagon = 7 × side

Match the Columns :

DIRECTIONS : *Each question contains statements given in two columns which have to be matched. Statements (A, B, C, D) in column-I have to be matched with statements (p, q, r, s) in column-II.*

1.

Column-I (Shapes)	Column-II (Perimeter)
(A) 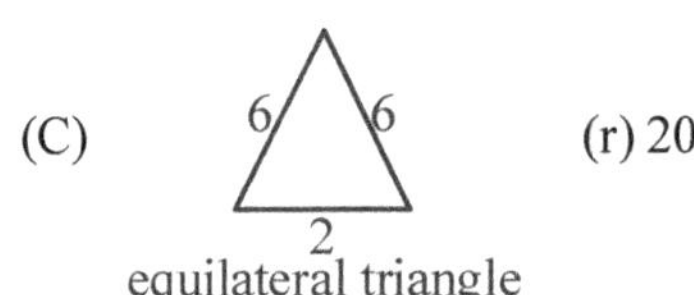 rectangle	(p) 10
(B) square	(q) 22
(C) equilateral triangle	(r) 20
(D) 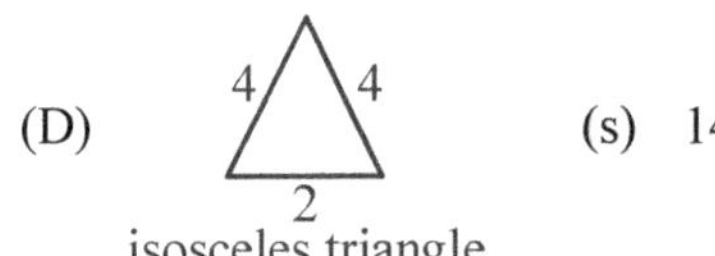 isosceles triangle	(s) 14

Very Short Answer Questions:

DIRECTIONS : *Give answer in one word or one sentence.*

1. A playground which is 250 m long and 20 m broad is to be fenced with wire. How much wire is needed?

2. If the length and breadth of a rectangle are doubled then its perimeter is

3. Find the perimeter of following figures

(i)
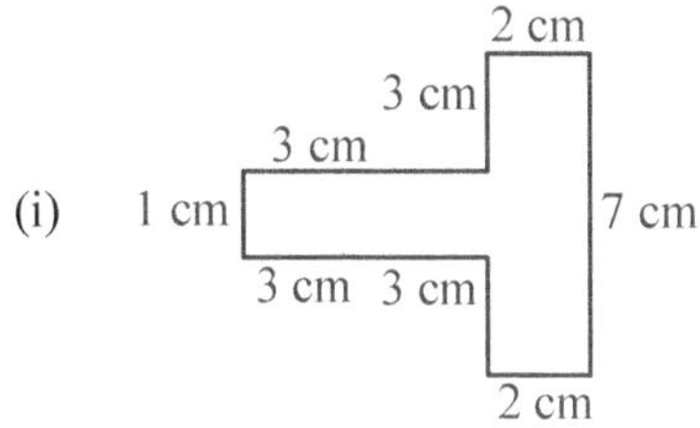

(ii)
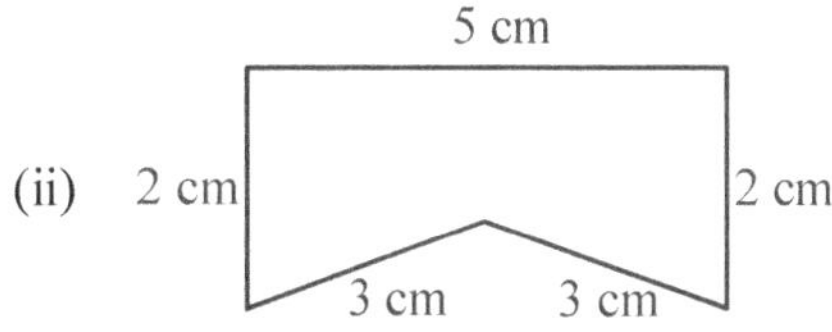

(iii)
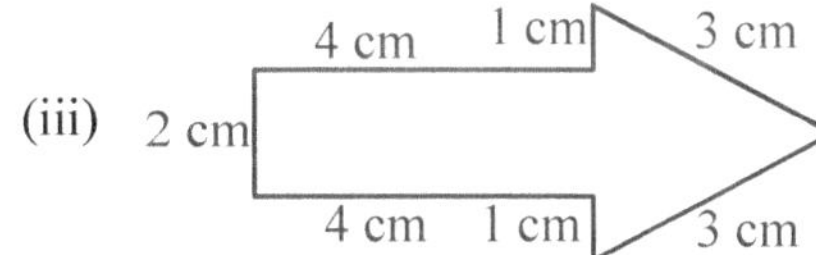

(iv)
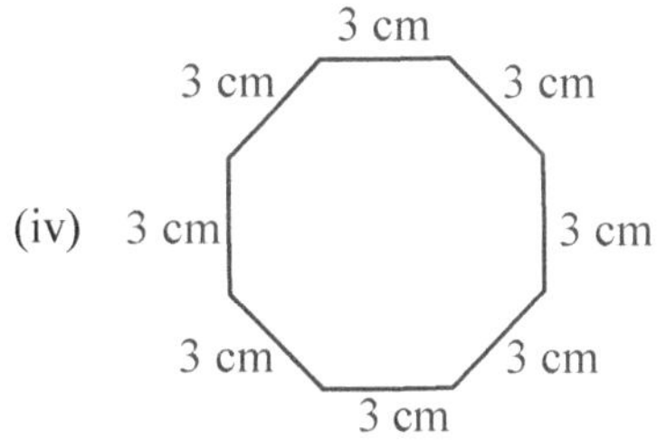

4. Find the perimeter of rectangle whose length and breadth are :
   (i) Length = 11 cm   Breadth = 8 cm
   (ii) Length = 7.5 cm   Breadth = 4.5 cm

5. Find the breadth of rectangle whose perimeter and length are
   (i) Perimeter = 360 cm   Length = 100 cm
   (ii) Perimeter = 220 cm   Length = 60 cm

6. Find the perimeter of a square, whose sides are :
   (i) 4. 8 m   (ii) 3.6 m

7. Find the perimeter of :
   (i) a regular pentagon of side 4.8 m
   (ii) a regular octagon of side 3.3 m
   (iii) a regular decagon of side 5.2 m

8. Find the area of following figures, taking area of each square as 1 cm^2

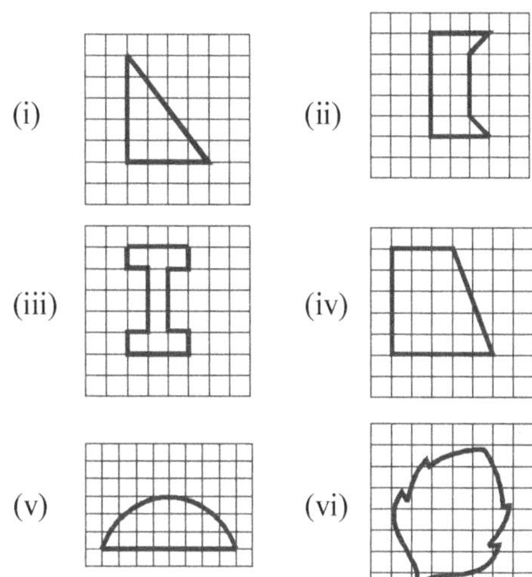

9. Find the area of rectangle whose :
   (i) Length = 6 cm   (ii) Length = 5 cm
       Breadth = 3 cm   Breadth = 2 cm

10. Find the area of square whose side is :
    (i) 5 cm   (ii) 4.5 cm   (iii) 2.4 cm

Short Answer Questions :

DIRECTIONS : *Give answer in 2-3 sentences.*

1. Following is the arrangement of various rooms in house. Find the perimeter of floor of each room.

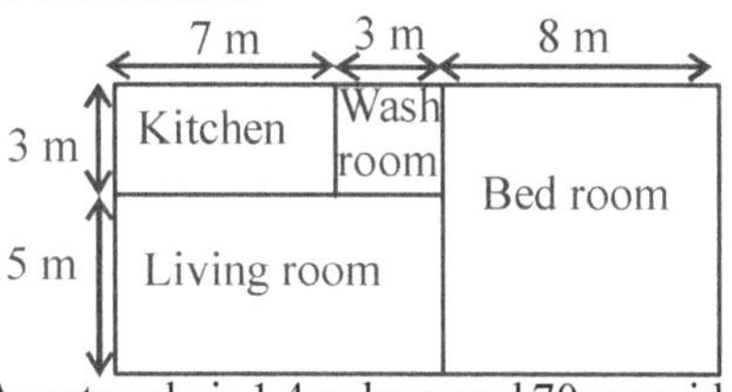

2. A rectangle is 1.4 m long and 70 cm wide. Find its area.
   (i) in m^2 (ii) in cm^2

3. Side of a square measures 60 cm. Find its area in
   (i) m^2 (ii) cm^2

4. The side of a square is 100 cm. Find its area and perimeter.

5. The area of rectangle is 64 cm^2 and its breadth is 4cm. Find the length and perimeter of rectangle.

6. The top of a table measures 4 m 50 cm and 2 m 40 cm. Find its area in square meters.

7. The length of a rectangle is thrice its breadth. If the perimeter of the rectangle is 1 m 28 cm, find the length and the breadth of the rectangle.

8. Find the area of a square whose perimeter is 80 m.

9. Find the cost of cultivating an agricultural land of length 49 m 50 cm and breadth 40 m 50 cm at the rate of ₹ 5 per sq metre.

10. Two sides of a triangle are 12 cm and 14 cm. The perimeter of the triangle is 36 cm. What is the third side?

Long Answer Questions :

DIRECTIONS : *Give answer in four to five sentences.*

1. A boy walks around a rectangular field of length 40 m and breadth 20 m in the morning and a girl walks around a square field at the same time. If the total distance covered by the boy in 5 rounds is equal to that covered by the girl in 6 rounds, find the side of the square.

2. A rectangular lawn 12 m long and 7 m wide has path 2 m wide all around it from outside. Find the area of the path around the lawn.

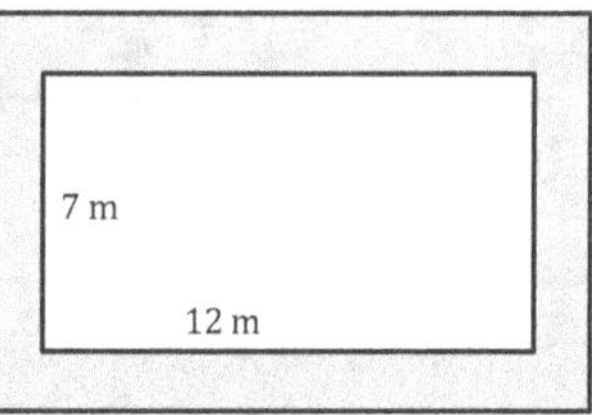

3. The side of a square tile is 10 cm. How many tiles can be fixed on one side of a wall which is 2.5 m long and 2 m high?

4. The area of a rectangle with length 14 cm is 112 sq. cm. Find its perimeter.

5. How many square tiles of side 30 cm will be required to fit in a rectangular hall of length 15 metres and breadth 12 metres?

6. Sketch of a plot is given. Its dimensions are as follows, BCDE is a rectangle. BC = 6 cm, CD = 4 m, CO = 3 m, OD = 5 m.
Calculate the cost of fencing the plot at the rate of ₹ 18 per metre.

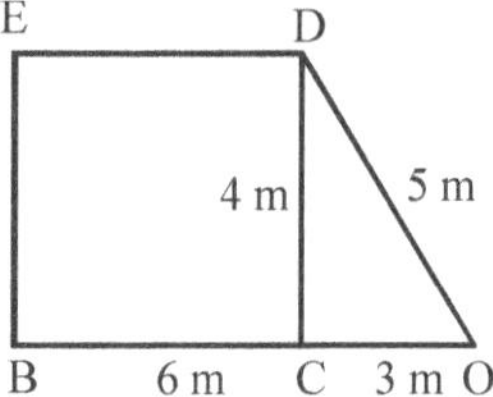

7. The difference between the length and breadth of a rectangle is 23 m. If the perimeter is 206 m, then find the area.

8. On a wall of dimensions 10.5 m long and 8.5 m wide, a square shaped wall poster is stuck at the centre whose measure is 2.5 m. If the remaining part of the wall to be painted with pink colour costing ₹ 12 per sq m, then find the amount to be spent.

2 EXERCISE

Text-Book Exercise :

1. What is the length of the wooden strip required to frame a photograph of length and breadth 32 cm and 21 cm respectively ?

2. A rectangular piece of land measures 0.7 km by 0.5 km. Each side is to be fenced with 4 rows of wires. What is the length of the wire needed?

3. Find the perimeter of each of the following shapes:
   (i) A triangle of sides 3 cm, 4 cm and 5 cm.
   (ii) An equilateral triangle of side 9 cm.
   (iii) An isosceles triangle with equal sides 8 cm each and third side 6 cm.

4. The perimeter of regular pentagon is 100 cm. How long is its each side?

5. A piece of string is 30 cm long. What will be the length of each side if the string is used to form:
   (i) a square ?
   (ii) an equilateral triangle ?
   (iii) a regular hexagon?

6. Find the cost of fencing a square park of side 250 m at the rate of ₹ 20 per metre.

7. Find the cost of fencing a rectangular park of length 175 m and breadth 125 m at the rate of ₹ 12 per metre.

8. The area of a rectangular garden 50 m long is 300 sq. m. Find the width of the garden.

9. What is the cost of tiling a rectangular plot of land 500 m long and 200 m wide at the rate of ₹ 8 per hundred sq. m?

10. A room is 4 m long and 3 m 50 cm wide. How many square metres of carpet is needed to cover the floor of the room?

11. Five square flower beds each of sides 1 m are dug on a piece of land 5 m long and 4 m wide. What is the area of the remaining part of the land?

12. Split the following shapes into rectangles and find their areas. (The measures are given in centimetres.)

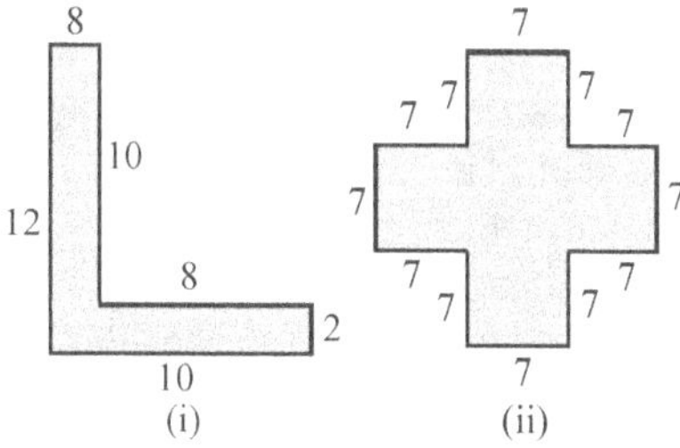

13. How many tiles whose length and breadth are 12 cm and 5 cm respectively will be needed to fit in a rectangular region whose length and breadth are respectively:
   (i) 100 cm and 144 cm
   (ii) 70 cm and 36 cm

Exemplar Questions :

1. Four regular hexagons are drawn so as to form the design as shown in figure. If the perimeter of the design is 28 cm, find the length of each side of the hexagon.

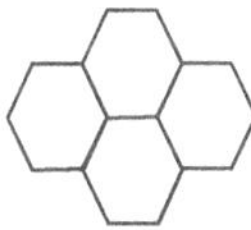

2. There is a rectangular lawn 10 m long and 4m wide in front of *Meena's house*. It is fenced along the two smaller sides and one longer side leaving a gap of 1m for the entrance. Find the length of fencing.

3. Tahir measured the distance around a square field as 200 rods (lathi). Later he found that the length of this rod was 140 cm. Find the side of this field in metres.

4. In figure all triangles are equilateral and AB = 8 units. Other triangles have been formed by taking the mid points of the sides. What is the perimeter of the figure?

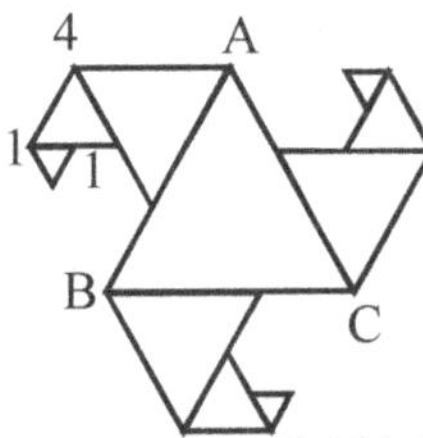

5. Length of a rectangular field is 250 m and width is 150 m. Anuradha runs around this field 3 times. How far did she run? How many times she should run around the field to cover a distance of 4 km?

6. In an exhibition hall, there are 24 display boards each of length 1 m 50 cm and breadth 1 m. There is a 100 m long aluminium strip, which is used to frame these boards. How many boards will be framed using this strip? Find also the length of the aluminium strip required for the remaining boards.

7. A rectangular path of 60 m length and 3 m width is covered by square tiles of side 25 cm. How many tiles will there be in one row along its width? How many such rows will be there? Find the number of tiles used to make this path?

8. How many square slabs each with side 90 cm are needed to cover a floor of area 81 sq m.

9. Amita wants to make rectangular cards measuring 8 cm × 5cm. She has a square chart paper of side 60 cm. How many complete cards can she make from this chart? What area of the chart paper will be left?

10. A magazine charges ₹ 300 per 10 sqcm area for advertising. A company decided to order a half page advertisment. If each page of the magazine is 15 cm × 24 cm, what amount will the company has to pay for it?

11. A wire is cut into several small pieces. Each of the small pieces is bent into a square of side 2 cm. If the total area of the small squares is 28 square cm, what was the original length of the wire?

12. The area of each square on a chess board is 4 sqcm. Find the area of the board.
    (i) At the beginning of game when all the chess men are put on the board, write area of the squares left unoccupied.
    (ii) Find the area of the squares occupied by chess men.

1. What is the length of outer boundary of the park shown in Fig.? What will be the total cost of fencing it at the rate of ₹ 20 per metre? There is a rectangular flower bed in the center of the park. Find the cost of measuring the flower bed at the rate of ₹ 50 per square metre.

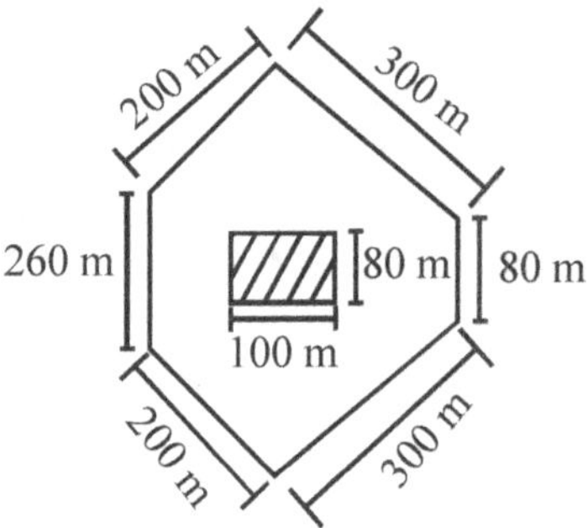

2. Find all the possible dimensions (in natural numbers) of a rectangle with an area of 36 sqcm, and find their perimeters.

3. What is the area of each small square in the figure if the area of entire figure is 96 sqcm. Find the perimeter of the figure.

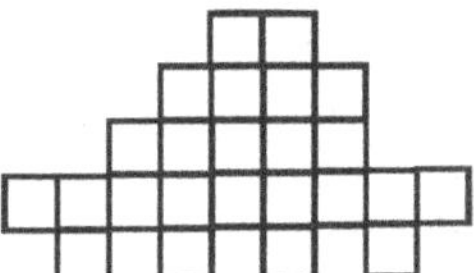

4. A hall measure 6 m long, 4 m wide and 2½ m height. Then find the cost of painting the walls and ceiling at ₹ 30 per m^2.

3 EXERCISE

Single Option Correct :

DIRECTIONS : *This section contains multiple choice questions. Each question has 4 choices (a), (b), (c) and (d) out of which ONLY ONE is correct.*

1. Length and breadth of a rectangle are 3.2 m and 150 cm. Then the area is
  (a) 48 sq cm   (b) 4.8 cm
  (c) 4.8 sq m   (d) 48 cm

2. Area of the shaded region is

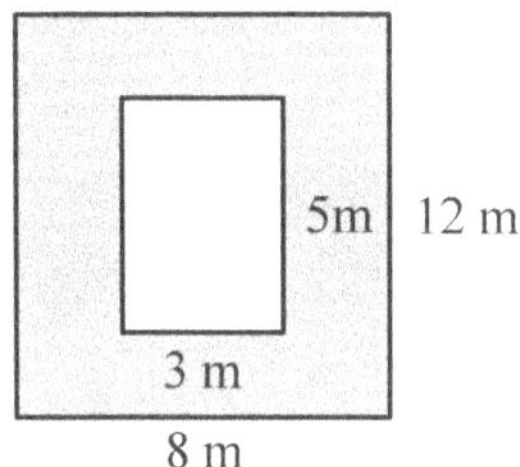

  (a) 96 sq. m   (b) 15 sq. m
  (c) 81 sq. m   (d) 111 sq. m

3. Find the area of the figure shown below.

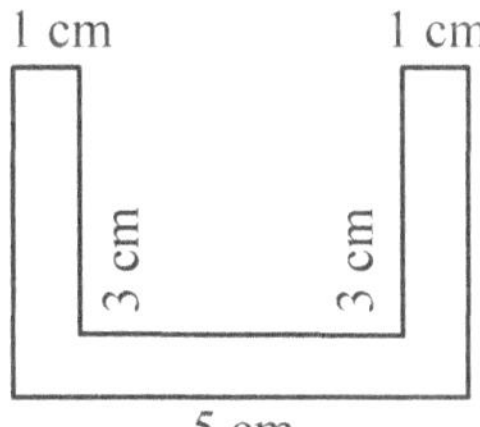

  (a) 9 sq. cm   (b) 10 sq. cm
  (c) 11 sq. cm   (d) 15 sq. cm

4. The side of a square is 10 cm. How many times will the new perimeter become if the side of the square is doubled?
  (a) 2 times   (b) 4 times
  (c) 6 times   (d) 8 times

5. In Fig. which of the following is a regular polygon? All have equal side except (i)

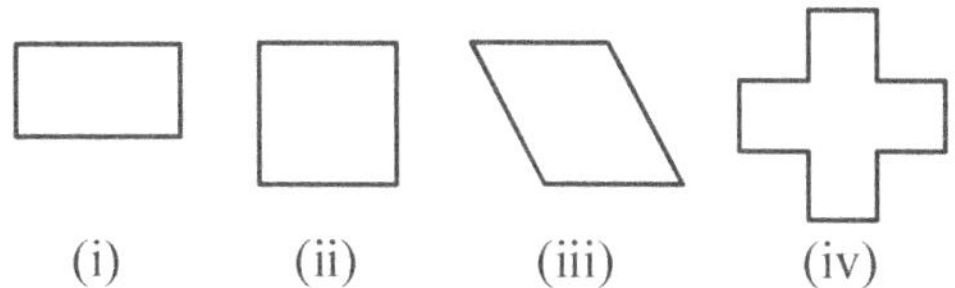

  (a) (i)   (b) (ii)
  (c) (iii)   (d) (iv)

6. The breadth of a rectangle is 19 cm. Its length is 3 times longer than its breadth. Find the area of the rectangle.
  (a) 152 cm^2 (b) 418 cm^2
  (c) 1083 cm^2 (d) 1140 cm^2

7. What is the total area of the 2 identical squares shown below?

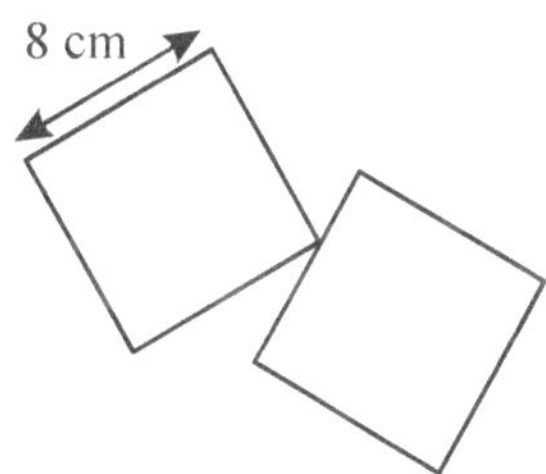

  (a) 32 cm^2 (b) 64 cm^2
  (c) 128 cm^2 (d) 135 cm^2

8. Area is measured in
  (a) sq units   (b) cm units
  (c) metre   (d) cubic units

9. The length of a rectangle is two times its breadth and the area of rectangle is 98 sq. units. The length of the rectangle is
  (a) 7   (b) 14
  (c) 8   (d) 16

10. Venu jogged round a rectangular field 4 times. If the rectangular field was 135 m long and 78 m wide, how far did Venu jog?

(a) 426 m   (b) 852 m
(c) 1278 m   (d) 1704 m

11. A rectangular garden is 105 m by 75 m. How many rounds of this garden will a boy make if he runs 3600 m?
(a) 12   (b) 20
(c) 10   (d) 8

More than One Option Correct :

DIRECTIONS : *This section contains multiple choice questions. Each question has 4 choices (a), (b), (c) and (d) out of which ONLY ONE is correct.*

1. The area of a rectangle is 630 cm^2 and its length is 35 cm. Find the perimeter of the rectangle.
(a) 53 cm   (b) 106 cm
(c) 1 m 6 cm   (d) 1 m 60 cm

2. Find the perimeter of a rectangle of length 2m and breadth 95 cm.
(a) 59 m   (b) 590 cm
(c) 5 m 9 cm   (d) 5 m 90 cm

3. The total cost of flooring a room at ₹10.50 per sq metre is ₹ 840. If the breadth of the room is 8 m, find its length.
(a) 20 m   (b) 200 cm
(c) 10 m   (d) 1000 cm

4. Find the area of a square window which is 1 m 20 cm wide.
(a) 14.4 m^2 (b) 144000 cm^2
(c) 1.44 m^2 (d) 14400 cm^2

5. Find the side of an equilateral triangle whose perimeter is 72 cm.
(a) 24 cm   (b) 240 mm
(c) 18 cm   (d) 180 mm

Assertion & Reason :

DIRECTIONS : *Each of these questions contains an Assertion followed by Reason. Read them carefully and answer the question on the basis of following options. You have to select the one that best describes the two statements.*

(a) If both **Assertion** and **Reason** are **correct** and Reason is the **correct explanation** of Assertion.

(b) If both **Assertion** and **Reason** are correct, but Reason is **not the correct explanation** of Assertion.

(c) If **Assertion** is **correct** but **Reason** is **incorrect**.

(d) If **Assertion** is **incorrect** but **Reason** is **correct**.

1. **Assertion :** If a square has a length of 4 cm, then its perimeter is 8 cm.
Reason : Perimeter of a square is given by the summation of all of its sides.

2. **Assertion**: Breadth of the rectangle whose perimeter 160 cm and length 16 cm is 10 cm.
Reason: Perimeter of a rectangle
$$= 2 \text{ (length + breadth)}$$

Passage Based Questions :

DIRECTIONS : *Study the given passage(s) and answer the following questions.*

PASSAGE - I

The figure below is made up of a square and 2 rectangles. Study the figure carefully and answer the following questions.

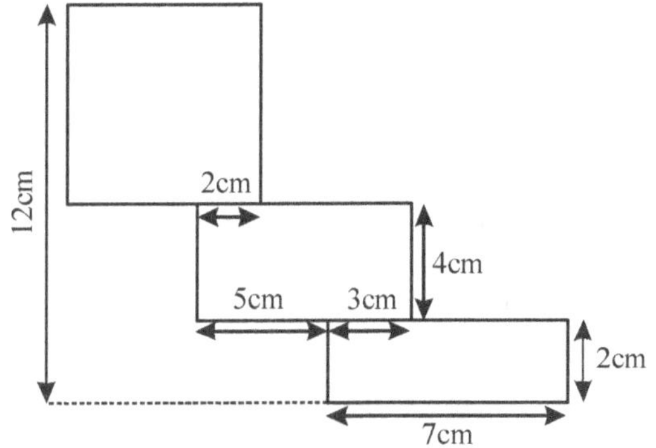

1. The perimeter of the figure is ___________ cm.
(a) 56   (b) 58
(c) 62   (d) 66

2. The sum of the areas of the two rectangles is bigger than the area of the square by .... cm^2.
(a) 10   (b) 14
(c) 32   (d) 36

PASSAGE - II

Area of a rectangle = L × B
Perimeter of a rectangle = 2 (L + B) Where L and B are the length and breadth of the rectangle respectively.

3. The area of a rectangle whose length 20 cm and breadth 15 cm is
(a) 105 cm^2 (b) 300 cm^2
(c) 35 cm^2 (d) 30 cm^2

4. The breadth of a rectanlge of length 4 m and area 8.4 m^2 is
(a) 2.1 m   (b) 1.2 m
(c) 4.2 m^2 (d) 2.1 m^2

5. Find the area of a rectanlgular park whose perimeter is 300 m and breadth is 50 m?
(a) 500 m^2 (b) 100 m
(c) 5000 m^2 (d) 1000 m^2

Integer Type Questions :

DIRECTIONS : *Answer the following questions. The answer to each of the question is a single digit integer, ranging from 0 to 9.*

1. When the perimeter and area of a square are numerically equal, then the numerical value of its side is

2. The perimeter of a rectangle is 36 cm. The measure of its length and breadth are natural numbers. How many such rectangles are possible ?

3. What is the length of a rectangle (in m), if its area is 2m^2 and breadth is $\dfrac{1}{2}$ m?

4. What is the length of sides (in cm), if perimeter of a regular octagon is 40 cm?

5. An area of rectangular floor with dimensions 90 cm and 40 cm is to be paved with square tiles of side 20 cm. How many such tiles will be required?

Multiple Matching Question :

DIRECTIONS : *Following question has four statements (A, B, C and D) given in Column-I and six statements (p, q, r, s, t, u) in Column-II. Any given statement in Column-I can have correct matching with one or more statement(s) given in Column-II.*

1.

	Column - I	Column - II
(A)	Area of rectangular park whose length and breadth are 28.5 and 20 m respechvely.	(p) 28.2 cm
(B)	Perimeter of rectangle whose length and breadth are 2m 25 cm and 1 m 50 cm respectively	(q) 0.282 m
(C)	Perimeter of an equilateral m^2 triangle of side 9.4 cm	(r) 570
(D)	Area of a square of side 1.4 m	(s) 1.96 m^2
		(t) 750 cm
		(u) 7.50 m

SOLUTIONS

Brief Explanations of Selected Questions

1 EXERCISE

Fill in the Blanks :

1. 15.9 cm.

2. Area

3. The perimeter of a square having side a is 4a.

4. Area

5. $120 + 80 + 120 + 80 = 400$ m

6. 4

7. length, breadth

8. (side)^2

True / False :

1.	F	2.	T	3.	T	4.	F	5.	T
6.	F	7.	T	8.	T			9.	F
10.	F	11.	T						

Match the Columns :

1. (A) → (q), (B) → (r), (C) → (s), (D) → (p)

Very Short Answer Questions:

1. The required length of the wire
   $$= \text{Perimeter of the rectangle}$$
   $$= 2 \text{ (length + breadth)}$$
   $$= 2 \ (250 + 20) = 540 \text{ m.}$$

2. Let the initial length and breadth be l and b respectively.

   So, the initial perimeter $= 2 \ (l + b)$

   The final perimeter
   $$= 2 \ (2l + 2b) = 4 \ (l + b)$$

   Now, $\dfrac{\text{Final perimeter}}{\text{Initial perimeter}} = \dfrac{4(l+b)}{2(l+b)} = 2$.

3. (i)   24 cm   (ii)   15 cm
   (iii) 18 cm   (iv)   24 cm

4. (i)   38 cm   (ii)   24 cm

5. (i)   80 cm   (ii)   50 cm
6. (i)   19.2 m   (ii)   14.4 m
7. (i)   24 m   (ii)   26.4 m
   (iii) 52 m
8. (i)   10 cm^2 (ii)   11 cm^2
   (iii) 9 cm^2 (iv)   22 cm^2

   (v)   18 cm^2 (vi) $15\frac{1}{2}$ cm^2

9. (i)   18 cm^2 (ii)   10 cm^2
10. (i) 25 cm^2 (ii)   20.25 cm^2
    (iii) 5.76 cm

Short Answer Questions :

1. Kitchen $= 20$ m, washroom $= 12$ m, bedroom $= 32$ cm, Living room $= 30$ cm

2. (i)   0.98 m^2 (ii)   9800 cm^2
3. (i)   0.36 m^2 (ii)   3600 cm^2
4. 1 m^2, 4 m
5. 16 cm; 40 cm
6. 10.8 m^2

7. Let the breadth of the rectangle be b cm. Then, its length is $3b$ cm. Hence, the perimeter of the rectangle $= 2 \times$ (length + breadth)
   $$= 2 \times (3b + b) \text{ cm} = 2 \times 4b \text{ cm} = 8b \text{ cm}$$
   Given that perimeter $= 1$ m 28 cm $= 128$ cm
   $$\therefore \quad 8b = 128 \Rightarrow b = \frac{128}{8} = 16$$
   Hence the required breadth $= 16$ cm and length
   $$= 16 \text{ cm} \times 3 = 48 \text{ cm.}$$

8. The side of the square
   $$= \frac{\text{Perimeter}}{4} = \frac{80 \text{ m}}{4} = 20 \text{ m}$$
   The required area of the square
   $$= 20 \text{ m} \times 20 \text{ m} = 400 \text{ m}^2$$

9. The area of the land
   $$= 49 \text{ m } 50 \text{ cm} \times 40\text{m } 50 \text{ cm}$$
   $$= 49.5 \text{ m} \times 40.5 \text{ m} = 2004.75 \text{ m}^2$$
   $\therefore$ The required cost
   $$= ₹ \ 5 \times 2004.75 = ₹ \ 10023.75$$

10. Let a be the third side of $\triangle ABC$ (say).
So, perimeter = AB + BC + CA
or 36 cm = 12 cm + a + 14 cm
or 36 cm = 26 cm + a
or a = 36 cm – 26 cm = 10 cm
Hence, the third side of the triangle is 10 cm.

Long Answer Questions :

1. The perimeter of the rectangular field
= 2 × (length + breadth)
= 2 × (40 + 20) m = 2 × 60 m = 120 m
∴ In 1 round, the girl covers a distance of $4a$ metres.
In 5 rounds, the boy covers a distance
of 120 m × 5 = 600 m.
Let a metres be the side of the square.
Then, the perimeter of the square = $4a$ metres.
In 1 round, the girl covers a distance of $4a$ metres.
∴ In 6 round, the girl covers a distance
of $(4a × 6)$ m = $24a$ metres.
∴ By the condition of the problem, we have
$24a = 600$

$\Rightarrow a = \dfrac{600}{24} = 25$ m

Hence, the required side of the square is 25 m.

2. Length of outer rectangle
= 12 + 2 + 2 = 16 m
Breadth of outer rectangle
= 7 + 2 + 2 = 11 m
Area of outer rectangle
= 16 × 11 = 176 sq.m
Area of inner rectangle
= 12 × 7 = 84 sq. cm
Area of path 176 – 84 = 92 sq. m

3. Area of the wall
= 250 × 200 = 50,000 sq cm

Area of the tile = 10 × 10 = 100 sq. cm

Number of tiles required

$= \dfrac{50000}{100} = 500$

4. Breadth of rectangle = $\dfrac{\text{Area}}{\text{Length}}$

$= \dfrac{112}{14} = 8$ cm

Perimeter of rectangle = 2(L + B)
= 2(14 + 8) = 2 × 22 = 44 cm

5. Area of tile = 30 × 30 sq. cm
= 900 sq. cm
Area of hall = 15 × 12 sq. m
= 15 × 12 × 10000 sq. cm

No. of tiles = $\dfrac{\text{Area of hall}}{\text{Area of tile}}$

$= \dfrac{15×12×10000}{900} = 2000$

6. Perimeter of field
= EB + BD + CO + OD + DE
= 4 + 6 + 3 + 5 + 6 = 24 m
Cost of fencing the plot = 24 × 18
= ₹ 432

7. Let breadth = x.
Length = x + 23.
Perimeter = 206 m.
2 (x + 23 + x) = 206
∴ 2x + 23 = 103
x = 40
Area = 1 × b = 63 × 40 = 2520 m².

8. Area of the poster = 2.5 × 2.5 = 6.25
Area of the wall = 10.5 × 8.5 = 89.25
Area of remaining part
= 89.25 – 6.25 = 83.00 sq. m
Amount = 83 × 12 = ₹ 996

2 EXERCISE

Text-Book Exercise :

1. Length of the frame = 32 cm
Breadth of the frame = 21 cm
∴ Perimeter of the frame = 2 [length + breadth]
= 2 (32 cm + 21 cm)
= 2 (53 cm) = 106 cm
∴ Length of the wooden strip required = 106 cm

2. 0.7 km by 0.5 km means,
Length = 0.7 km and breadth = 0.5 km

$\therefore$ Perimeter of the rectangular piece of land
$= 2$ (length + breadth)
$\qquad = 2$ (0.7 km + 0.5 km)
$\qquad = 2$ (1.2 km) $= 2.4$ km
$\therefore$ Length of wire fencing for 1 row $= 2.4$ km
Length of wire fencing for 4 rows $= 4 \times 2.4$ km
$\qquad\qquad = 9.6$ km

3. (i) Sides of the triangle are: 3 cm, 4 cm, 5 cm
$\qquad \therefore$ Perimeter $=$ sum of the sides
$\qquad\qquad = 3$ cm $+ 4$ cm $+ 5$ cm
$\qquad\qquad = 12$ cm

(ii) Length of each side $= 9$ cm
$\qquad \therefore$ Perimeter of an equilateral triangle
$\qquad\qquad = 3 \times$ length of one side
$\qquad \therefore$ Perimeter of the given equilateral triangle $= 3 \times 9$ cm $= 27$ cm

(iii) Perimeter of triangle $= (8 + 8 + 6)$ cm
$\qquad\qquad = 22$ cm

4. Perimeter of a regular pentagon $= 100$ cm
$\because$ Perimeter $= 5 \times$ length of one side
$\therefore 5 \times$ Length of one side $= 100$ cm

$\therefore$ Length of one side $= \dfrac{100 \text{ cm}}{5}$

$\qquad\qquad = 20$ cm

5. Length of the given string $= 30$ cm
(i) $\therefore$ The string is in the form of a square and perimeter of a square $= 4 \times$ side

$\therefore$ Side $= \dfrac{30 \text{ cm}}{4} = 7.5$ cm

$\therefore$ Length of each side $= 7.5$ cm

(ii) The string is in the form of an equilateral triangle
Perimeter $= 3 \times$ length of one side $= 30$ cm

length of one side $= \dfrac{30 \text{ cm}}{3} = 10$ cm

(iii) String is in the form of a regular hexagon and perimeter of a regular hexagon
$= 6 \times$ length of one side
$\therefore 6 \times$ length of one side $= 30$ cm

or length of one side $= \dfrac{30 \text{ cm}}{6} = 5$ cm

6. Side of the park $= 250$ m
$\because$ The park is in the form of a square.
$\therefore$ Perimeter $= 4 \times$ length of one side
$\qquad\qquad = 4 \times 250$ m $= 1000$ m
$\because$ Rate of fencing $= ₹20$ per meter

$\therefore$ Cost of fencing $= ₹20 \times 1000$
$\qquad\qquad = ₹20,000$

7. Length of the park $= 175$ m
Breadth of the park $= 125$ m
Park is in the form of a rectangle.
Perimeter of a rectangle $= 2 \times$ [length + breadth]
$\therefore$ Perimeter of the given park
$\qquad = 2 \times$ [175 m $+ 125$ m]
$\qquad = 2 \times 300$ m $= 600$ m
Rate of fencing $= ₹12$ per metre
$\therefore$ Cost of fencing $= ₹ 12 \times 600$
$\qquad\qquad = ₹ 7200$

8. Area of the rectangular garden $= 300$ sq. m
Length of the rectangular garden $= 50$

$\therefore$ Breadth of the garden $= \dfrac{\text{Area}}{\text{Length}}$

$\qquad = \dfrac{300 \text{ sq. m}}{50 \text{ m}} = 6$ m

9. Length of the rectangular plot $= 500$ m
Breadth of the rectangular plot $= 200$ m
$\therefore$ Area of the plot $=$ length $\times$ breadth
$\qquad\qquad = 500$ m $\times 200$ m
$\qquad\qquad = 100000$ sq. m
Cost of tiling for 100 sq. m area $= ₹ 8$

$\therefore$ Total cost of tiling the plot $= ₹ \dfrac{100000}{100} \times 8$

$\qquad\qquad = ₹ 1000 \times 8$
$\qquad\qquad = ₹ 8000$

10. Length of the room $= 4$ m
$\qquad\qquad = 400$ cm
Breadth of the room $= 3$ cm 50 cm
$\qquad\qquad = 350$ cm
$\therefore$ Area of the floor of the room
$\qquad =$ length $\times$ breadth
$\qquad\qquad = 400$ cm $\times 350$ cm
$\qquad\qquad = 140000$ sq. cm

$\qquad = \dfrac{140000}{100 \times 100} = 14$ sq. m

Thus, 14 sq. m of carpet is required to cover the floor of the room.

11. Length of the piece of land $= 5$ m
Breadth of the piece of land $= 4$ cm
$\therefore$ Area of the piece of land $=$ length $\times$ breadth
$\qquad\qquad = 5$ m $\times 4$ m
$\qquad\qquad = 20$ sq. m

Area of a square flower bed
$$= \text{side} \times \text{side} = 1 \text{ m} \times 1 \text{ m}$$
$$= 1 \text{ sq. m}$$
$\therefore$ Area of 5 square flower beds
$$= 5 \times 1 \text{ sq. m} = 5 \text{ sq.m}$$
$\therefore$ Area of the remaining part
$$= 20 \text{ sq. m} - 5 \text{ sq. m} = 15 \text{ sq. m}$$

12. (i)

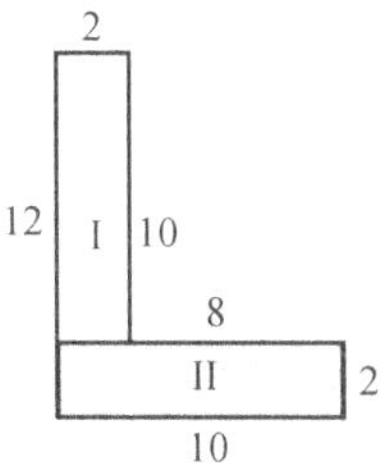

Splitting the given figure into rectangles we have,
Area of rectangle I = length $\times$ breadth
$$= 10 \text{ cm} \times 2 \text{ cm} = 20 \text{ sq.m}$$
Area of rectangle II = length $\times$ breadth
$$= 10 \text{ cm} \times 2 \text{ cm}$$
$$= 20 \text{ sq. cm}$$
$\therefore$ Total area of the figure
$$= 20 \text{ sq. cm} + 20 \text{ sq. cm}$$
$$= 40 \text{ sq. cm}$$

(ii)

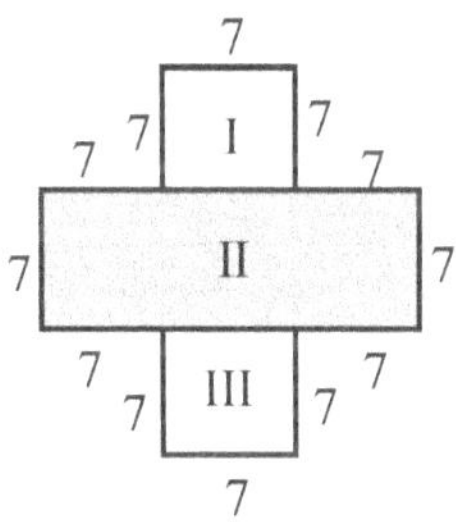

Area of square I = 7 cm $\times$ 7cm
$$= 49 \text{ sq. cm}$$
Area of rectangle II
$$= (7 + 7 + 7) \text{ cm} \times 7 \text{ cm}$$
$$= 21 \text{ cm} \times 7 \text{ cm}$$
$$= 147 \text{ sq.m}$$
Area of square III
$$= 7 \text{ cm} \times 7 \text{ cm}$$
$$= 49 \text{ sq. cm}$$
$\therefore$ Total area of the given figure
$$= \text{Area of I} + \text{Area of II} + \text{Area of III}$$
$$= 49 \text{ sq. cm} + 147 \text{ sq. cm} + 49 \text{ sq. cm}$$
$$= 245 \text{ sq. cm}$$

13. Area of the rectangular tile = 12 cm $\times$ 5 cm
$$= 60 \text{ sq. cm}$$
(i) Area of the rectangular region
$$= \text{length} \times \text{breadth}$$
$$= 100 \text{ cm} \times 144 \text{ cm}$$
$$= 14400 \text{ sq. cm}$$
$\therefore$ Number of tiles required to cover area of 14400 sq. cm
$$= \frac{\text{Area of the region}}{\text{Area of a tile}} = \frac{14400}{60} = 240 \text{ tiles}$$
(ii) Area of the rectangular region
$$= \text{length} \times \text{breadth}$$
$$= 70 \text{ cm} \times 36 \text{ cm} = 2520 \text{ sq. cm}$$
Area of a tile = 60 sq. cm
$\therefore$ Number of tiles required
$$= \frac{\text{Area of the region}}{\text{Area of a tile}} = \frac{2520}{60} = 42 \text{ tiles}$$

Exemplar Questions :

1. Perimeter of the design = 28 cm
Since all are regular hexagons, therefore all sides are of equal length.
$\therefore$ length of side = 28 $\div$ 14 = 2 cm
2. The length of fence = (10 + 4 + 4) – 1 = 17 m
3. The distance around a square field = 200 rods

Side of the field = $\dfrac{200}{4}$ = 50 rods

The length of a rod = 140 cm
$\therefore$ The length of 50 rods = (50 $\times$ 140)cm

$$= 7000 \text{ cm} = \frac{7000}{100} \text{ m} = 70 \text{ m}$$

4. The perimeter of the figure

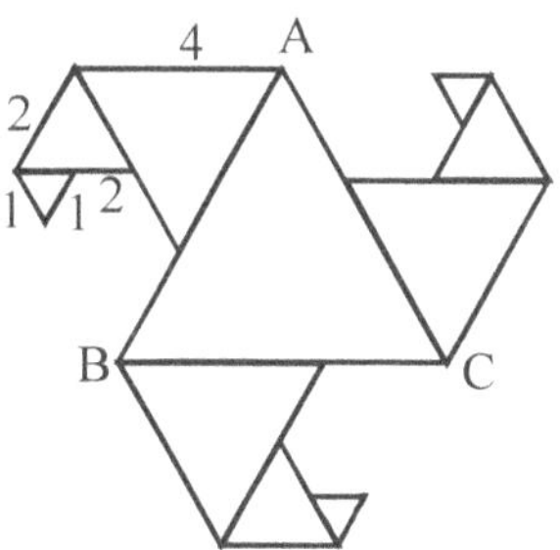

$$= (4 + 2 + 1 + 1 + 1 + 2 + 4) + (4 + 2 + 1 + 1 +$$
$$1 + 2 + 4) + (4 + 2 + 1 + 1 + 1 + 2 + 4)$$
$$= 45 \text{ cm}$$

5. Perimeter of rectangular field = 2 (250 + 150)

= 800 m

She covers distance in 3 rounds = 3 × 800 m

= 2400 m

Distance covered in 1 round = 800 m

Total distance covered = 4 km = 4000 m

No. of rounds to cover 4 km = 4000 ÷ 800 = 5

6. Length = 1 m 50 cm = 1.5 m, Breadth = 1m

Perimeter of a display board = 2 (1.5 + 1) = 5 m

Total length of aluminium strip = 100 m.

No. of boards can be framed = $\dfrac{100}{5}$ = 20

No. of remaining boards = 24 – 20 = 4

The length of strip required = 4 × 5 m = 20 m

7. No. of tiles along its width = 3 m ÷ 25 cm

= $\dfrac{300\,cm}{25\,cm}$ = 12

No. of rows of tiles = 60 m ÷ 25 cm

= $\dfrac{6000\,cm}{25\,cm}$ = 240

No. of tiles used = $\dfrac{6000 \times 300}{25 \times 25}$ = 2880

8. Area of floor = 81sqm = 81 × 10000

= 810000 sq. cm

Area of square slab = 90 × 90 = 8100 sq.cm

No. of square slabs = $\dfrac{810000}{8100}$ = 100

9. When we divide 60 by 8, we get 7 as quotient and 4 as reminder.

and when we divide 60 by 5 we get 12 as quotient.

∴ We can cut off 7(60 ÷ 8) lengths and 12(60 ÷ 5) width of complete cards.

[As shown in the figure]

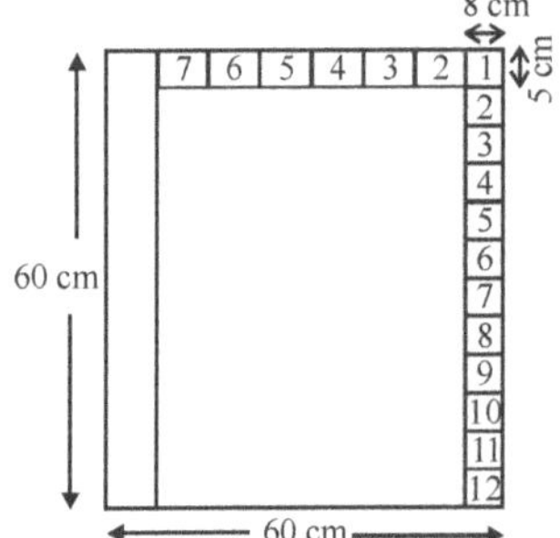

∴ No. of complete cards can be cut off from 60 cm × 60 cm chaart paper = 7 × 12 = 84.

Area of 1 card = 8 × 5 = 40 sq. cm

Area of 84 cards = 84 × 40 = 3360 sq.cm.

Total area of chart paper = 60 × 60

= 3600 sq.cm

Area of chart paper left = 3600 – 3360

= 240 sq.cm

10. Area of a page of magazine = 15 × 24

= 360 sq.cm

Area covered by half page advertisment = $\dfrac{360}{2}$

= 180 sq.cm

Amount paid for 10 sq.cm area = ₹ 300

Amount paid for 1 sq.cm area = $\dfrac{300}{10}$ = ₹ 30

Amount paid for 180 sq.cm area = 30 × 180

= ₹ 5400

11. Side of a square = 2 cm

∴ Area of a square = 2 × 2 = 4 sq.cm.

Total area of small squares = 28 sq.cm.

∴ No. of small squares = 28 ÷ 4 = 7

Perimeter of each square = 4 × 2 cm = 8 cm

∴ Primeter of 7 squares = 7 × 8 = 56 cm.

12. Area of each square on a chess board = 4 sq.cm

Number of chess men = 32

Total number of squares = 8 × 8 = 64.

Total area of squares = 4 × 64 = 256 sq.cm.

(i) Number of square unoccupied

= 64 – 32 = 32

∴ Area of squares left unoccupied

= 4 × 32 = 128 sq.cm

(ii) ∴ Area of squares occupied

= 256 – 128

[From part (i)]

= 128 sq.cm.

HOTS Questions :

1. Length of outer boundary of park

= (200 + 300 + 80 + 300 + 200 + 260) m

= 1340 m

Total cost of fencing = ₹ (20 × 1340) = ₹ 26800

Area of rectangular flower bed

= (100 × 80) sqm = 8000 sqm

Cost of manuring = ₹ (50 × 8000) = ₹ 400000

2. Let land B be length and breadth of rectangle.

Then L × B = 36

We have to find the pairs of natural numbers whose product is 36.

$\therefore$ These number are (1, 36), (2, 18), (3, 12), (4, 9), (6, 6).

Perimeters of rectangles with these dimensions are 2 (1 + 36), 2(2 + 18), 2(3 + 12), 2(4 + 9), 2(6 + 6)

i.e. 74cm, 40 cm, 30 cm, 26 cm, 24 cm.

3. Area of all squares = 96 sqcm

   Number of squares = 24

   $\therefore$ Area of a square = 96 ÷ 24 = 4 sqcm

   Let the side of the square be x cm

   $\Rightarrow$ $x \times x = 4$ sqcm = 2×2

   $\Rightarrow$ $x = 2$ cm

   $\therefore$ Perimeter of figure = $2 \times 34 = 68$ cm

4. Area of fair walls = $2(l + b) \times h$

   $$= 2(6 + 4) \times \frac{5}{2} = 2 \times 10 \times \frac{5}{2} = 50 \text{ m}^2$$

   Area of ceiling = length × breadth

   $\qquad = 6 \times 4 = 24 \text{ m}^2$

   Total area to be painted = 50 + 24

   $\qquad = 74 \text{ m}^2$

   Cost of painting at 1 m^2 = ₹ 30

   $\therefore$ Cost of painting at 74 m^2 = 74×30

   $\qquad\qquad\qquad = $ ₹ 2220

3 EXERCISE

Single Option Correct :

1. **(c)** $l = 3.2$ m.

   b = 150 cm = 1.5 m.

   $l \times$ b = $3.2 \times 1.5 = 4.80$ sq. m.

2. **(c)** $12 \times 8 - 5 \times 3$

   $96 - 15 = 81$ sq m.

3. **(c)**

Area of whole figure = Area of rectangle ABIJ + Area of rectangle BCDE + Area of rectangle HEFG.

$\qquad = 3 \times 1 + 5 \times 1 + 3 \times 1 = 11$ sq. cm.

4. **(a)**   5. **(b)**   6. **(c)**   7. **(c)**

8. **(a)** Area is measured in square units.

9. **(b)** Let breadth of rectangle be x.

   Then, breadth of rectangle = $2x$.

   Area of rectangle = L × B = $2x^2$

   Given $2x^2 = 98$

   $x^2 = 49$

   $x = 7$

   Length of rectangle = $2x = 2 \times 7$

   $\qquad\qquad\qquad\qquad = 14$ units.

10. **(d)**

11. **(c)** Distance moved in 1 round

    $\qquad\qquad = $ Perimeter of field

    $\qquad\qquad = 2(105 + 75)$

    $\qquad\qquad = 2 \times 180 = 360$ m

    No. of rounds

    $$= \frac{\text{Total distance moved}}{\text{Distance moved in a round}}$$

    $$= \frac{3600}{360} = 10$$

More Than One Option Correct :

1. **(b, c)** Area = 630 cm^2 and length = 35 cm.

   $$\text{Breadth of the rectangle} = \frac{\text{area in cm}^2}{\text{length in cm}}$$

   $$= \frac{630 \text{ cm}^2}{35 \text{ cm}} = \left(\frac{630}{35}\right) \text{ cm} = 18 \text{ cm}.$$

   Perimeter of the rectangle

   $\qquad = [2 \times (\text{Length} + \text{Breadth})]$ units

   $\qquad = [2 \times (35 + 18)]$ cm = (2×53) cm

   $\qquad = 106$ cm

   $\qquad = 1$ m 6 cm.

2. **(b, d)** Length = 2m = 2×100 cm = 200 cm

   $\qquad\qquad\qquad\qquad [\because 100$ cm = 1 m]

   Breadth = 95 cm

   $\therefore$ perimeter of the rectangle

   $\qquad = 2 \times (\text{length} + \text{breadth})$

$= 2 \times (200 \text{ cm} + 95 \text{ cm})$

$= 2 \times 295 \text{ cm} = 590 \text{ cm} = 5 \text{ m } 90 \text{ cm}$

Hence, the required perimeter of the rectangle

$= 5 \text{m } 90 \text{ cm}.$

3. **(c, d)** The area of the floor

$$= \frac{\text{Total cost}}{\text{Cost per sq m}} = \frac{840}{10.50} \text{ m}^2 = 80 \text{ m}^2$$

Breadth $= 8$ m

$$\therefore \quad \text{Length} = \frac{\text{Area}}{\text{Breadth}} = \frac{80}{8} \text{ m} = 10 \text{ m}$$

Hence, the required length $= 10$ m

$= 1000$ cm.

4. **(c, d)** Since the window is a square, its length and width are same, i.e. 1 m 20 cm and 1.2 m.

Area of square $=$ side $\times$ side

$= 1.2 \text{ m} \times 1.2 \text{ m}$

$= 1.44 \text{ m}^2 = 1.44 \times 10000 = 14400 \text{ cm}^2$

5. **(a, b)** Perimeter of an equilateral triangle $= 3 \times$ length of a side

Therefore length of a side $= \dfrac{\text{perimeter}}{3}$

$$= \frac{72 \text{ cm}}{3} = 24 \text{ cm} = 240 \text{ mm}$$

Assertion & Reason :

1. **(d)** Perimeter of the square

$= 4 + 4 + 4 + 4 = 16$ cm

Assertion: incorrect; **Reason**: correct

2. **(d)** Perimeter $= 160$ cm

Length $= 16$ cm

Perimeter $= 2$ (length + Breadth)

$\Rightarrow \quad 160 = 2(16 + \text{Breadth})$

$\Rightarrow \quad 80 - 16 = \text{Breadth}$

$\Rightarrow \quad \text{Breadth} = 64$ cm

Assertion: incorrect; **Reason**: correct

Passage Based Questions :

1. **(a)**   **2.** **(a)**

3. **(b)** Length of rectangle $= 20$ cm

Breadth of rectangle $= 15$ cm

Area $= L \times B = 20 \times 15 = 300 \text{ cm}^2$

4. **(a)** Area of rectangle $= L \times B$

$\Rightarrow \quad 8.4 = 4 \times B$

$\Rightarrow \quad B = \dfrac{8.4}{4} = 2.1$ m

5. **(c)** Perimeter of the rectangular park

$= 300$ m

Breadth $= 50$ m

$\Rightarrow \quad$ Perimeter $= 2 (L + B)$

$\Rightarrow \quad 300 = 2(50 + L)$

$\Rightarrow \quad 150 = 50 + L$

$\Rightarrow \quad L = 100$ m

Area $=$ Length $\times$ Breadth $= 100 \times 50$

$= 5000 \text{ m}^2$

Integer Type Questions :

1. **(c)** Side $\times$ Side $= 4 \times$ side

$\therefore$ side $= 4$

2. **(d)** Let L and B be length and breadth of rectangle.

Then, $2 (L + B) = 36$

$$L + B = \frac{36}{2} = 18$$

We have to find number of pairs of natural numbers whose sum is 18. These are (1, 17) (2, 16) (3, 15) (4, 14) (5, 13) (6, 12) (7, 11) (8, 10) (9, 9)

Which are 9 in number.

3. **(4)** Area of rectangle $= 2\text{m}^2$

$\Rightarrow \quad$ Length $\times$ Breadth $= 2$

$\Rightarrow \quad$ Length $\times \dfrac{1}{2} = 2$

$\Rightarrow \quad$ Length $= 4$ m

4. **(5)** Length of side of octagon $= \dfrac{40}{8} = 5$ cm

5. **(9)** Number of tiles

$$= \frac{\text{Area of rectangular floor}}{\text{Area of a square}} = \frac{90 \times 40}{20 \times 20}$$

$$= \frac{3600}{400} = 9$$

Multiple Matching Question :

1. $(A) \rightarrow (r); (B) \rightarrow (t, u); (C) \rightarrow (p, q); (D) \rightarrow (s)$

Chapter 11

Algebra

CONSTANTS

A symbol having fixed numerical value is called a **constant**. Thus, the number 3, –3, $\frac{7}{4}$, 100, etc. represent constants, as they have fixed value.

VARIABLES (OR LITERALS)

A symbol which takes on various numerical values is called a **variable**. These are represented by small English letters

For example: a, b, x, y etc.

MATCHSTICK PATTERNS

Look at the matchstick pattern.

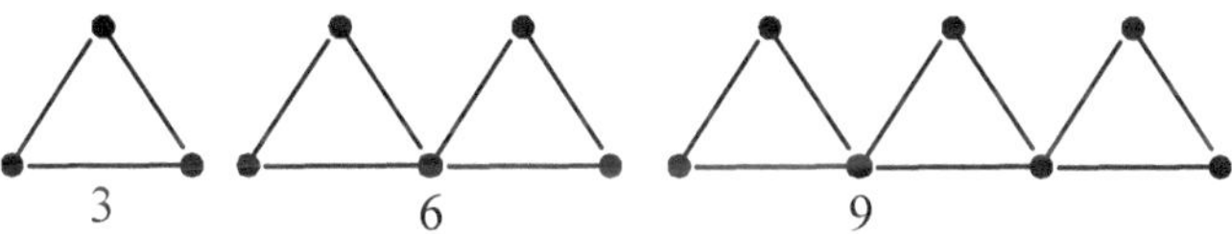

Let us make a table:

No. of triangles	1	2	3	4	5	.....
No. of matchsticks	3	6	9	12	15	.....

From the table, we can make a rule :

$$\boxed{\text{No. of matchsticks} = 3 \times \text{No. of triangles}}$$

Let us represent the number of triangles by 'n'

Thus, $\boxed{\text{No. of matchsticks} = 3 \times n}$

You see while making and using these rules, we made use of variables. These variables can be added, subtracted, multiplied or divided by given number. This is how an algebraic expression born.

RULES FOR GEOMETRY

We have already learnt about the perimeter of an equilateral triangle, square and rectangle. Here, we will deduce them in the form of a common rule.

(i) If an equilateral triangle has side 'a',

Then perimeter of an equilateral triangle = sum of the lengths of its sides.

= a + a + a = 3a units

(ii) If a square has side 'a', then perimeter of a square = sum of the lengths of its sides

$$= a + a + a + a = 4a \text{ units}$$

(iii) If a rectangle has length 'ℓ' and breadth 'b',

then perimeter of a rectangle = sum of the lengths of its sides

$$= \ell + b + \ell + b = 2\ell + 2b = 2(\ell + b)$$

RULES FOR ARITHMETIC

In arithmetic, we have learnt the properties of whole numbers. We have verified the properties by taking examples then generalised the result by taking the numbers as a, b, c, etc.

(i) **Commutativity of addition of two numbers :** Let a and b are two variables which can take any numerical value, then $a + b = b + a$

(ii) **Associative property of addition of numbers :** Let a, b, c are three variables which can take any numerical value, then

$a + (b + c) = (a + b) + c = (a + c) + b$ i.e., we can add three numbers in any order.

(iii) **Commutativity of multiplication of numbers :** When we multiply two numbers, their order does not matter, this property is known as commutativity of numbers. Let a and b are any two numbers which can take any numerical value, then $a \times b = b \times a$.

(iv) **Associativity of multiplication of numbers :** Let a, b, c are three variables which can take any numerical value, then.

$a \times (b \times c) = (a \times b) \times c = (a \times c) \times b$.

(v) **Distributivity of numbers over addition (or subtraction) :** By using variables, a, b and c, we can write this property in a general and concise way as

$a \times (b \pm c) = a \times b \pm a \times c$

ALGEBRAIC EXPRESSIONS

Algebraic expressions are formed by variables and numbers. These are connected by any or all four basic operations of addition, subtraction, multiplication and division *e.g.*

$$3t, \; 3x - y, \; 4a + 2b, \; 2a + r - 3, \text{ etc.}$$

Each part of the algebraic expression along with its sign (+ or –) is known as term.

Algebraic expressions	No. of terms	Terms
$3x$	1	$3x$
$4a + 2b$	2	$4a, 2b$
$2a + 3b - 7$	3	$2a, 3b, -7$
$\dfrac{4x}{3} + 5 - 6y$	3	$\dfrac{4x}{3}, 5, -6y$

Let us learn how algebraic expressions are formed. Some examples are as follows :

	Statement	**Expression**
1.	3 added to a	$3 + a$
2.	6 subtracted from x	$x - 6$
3.	Half of a number x added to one fourth of a number y	$\dfrac{x}{2} + \dfrac{y}{4}$
4.	5 subtracted from the sum of a and b	$(a + b) - 5$
5.	9 added to the product of c and d	$(c \times d) + 9$
6.	Product of 3 and a divided by 7	$\dfrac{3 \times a}{7}$

> **NOTE :** $3a$ and $3 + a$ are two different algebraic expression $3a$ means 3 is multiplied by a and $3 + a$ means 3 is added to a.

USE OF ALGEBRAIC EXPRESSION IN DAILY LIFE

Algebra is very useful in daily life situations. Some situations are as follows :

Situation	Variable years	Expression
1. Sonu scored 20 marks more than Rita	Let Rita's marks be a	Sonu's marks = $a + 20$
2. Age of Runjhun 4 years ago.	Let Runjhun's present age be x years	Four years ago Runjhun's age was = $(x - 4)$ years
3. Speed of train is 30 km/hr more than the speed of car	Let car's speed be s km/h	Train's speed = $(s + 30)$ km/h
4. Cost of 1 kg tea is ₹ 10 less than cost of 2 kg rice.	Let cost of 2 kg rice be ₹ r	Cost of 1 kg tea = ₹ $(r - 10)$
5. Surbhi is twice as tall as Kavita	Let Kavita's height be h	Surbhi's height = $2 \times h$
6. Ansh's father's age is 10 years more than twice the age of Ansh.	Let age of Ansh be y years	Ansh's father's age = $2y + 10$

ILLUSTRATION : 1

Write an algebraic expression for the following:
(a) 5 added to a
(b) 3 subtracted from b
(c) 9 subtracted from the product of 2 and x
(d) 2 added to one fourth of y

SOLUTION :

(a) $a + 5$ (b) $b - 3$ (b) $2x - 9$ (d) $\dfrac{y}{4} + 2$

ILLUSTRATION : 2

The product of 5 and a, divided by the twice of the sum of two number x and y.

SOLUTION :

Product of 5 and $a = 5a$
Sum of x and $y = x + y$
Twice the sum of x and $y = 2(x + y)$

Thus, algebraic expression $= \dfrac{5a}{2(x + y)}$

EQUATION

An equation is a mathematical statement where two expressions are equal

For example : $x + 6 = 16$

It has an equal sign (=) between the two algebraic expression sides. These two sides are known as left hand side (LHS) and Right hand side (RHS). The equation says that the value of the left hand side (LHS) is equal to the value of right hand side (RHS). If LHS and RHS of a expression is not equal then, it is not an equation such as $3x > 12$, then it is not an equation.

Solution of an equation

When a number is substituted for the variable in an equation, it makes LHS = RHS. Then the number is called a **solution or root** of the equation. There are 2 methods to find the solution of an equation.

1. Trial and error method

This method involves substituton of different numbers in the place of the variable till the left hand side becomes equal to the right hand side.

Consider $x + 6 = 16$

We will substitute differrent values of the variable and check the values of LHS and RHS. The value which makes LHS and RHS equal is the solution of equation.

x	8	9	10	11
x + 6	14	15	16	17

At $x = 10$, L.H.S. = R.H.S.

$\therefore x = 10$ is the solution of the equation.

2. Transposition

This is a more systematic approach to solve equations.

Rules for transposition

(i)   We can add the same number to both the sides of an equation.
(ii)   We can subtract the same number from both the sides of an equation.
(iii)   We can multiply both the sides of an equation by the same non-zero number.
(iv)   We can divide both the sides of an equation by the same non-zero number.

Consider $x + 6 = 16$

Subtract 6 from both sides.

$$x + 6 - 6 = 16 - 6$$
$$\Rightarrow x = 10$$

ILLUSTRATION : 3

Solve the following equations :

(a) $a - 4 = 9$ (b) $3x = 27$ (c) $\dfrac{x}{5} = 2$

SOLUTION :

(a) $a - 4 = 9$

Add 4 to both sides.

$a - 4 + 4 = 9 + 4$

$\Rightarrow a = 13$

(b) $3x = 27$

Divide both sides by 3

$$\frac{3x}{3} = \frac{27}{3}$$

$\Rightarrow x = 9$

(c) $\dfrac{x}{5} = 2$

Multiply both sides by 5

$$\frac{x \times 5}{5} = 2 \times 5$$

$\Rightarrow x = 10$

CONCEPT MAP

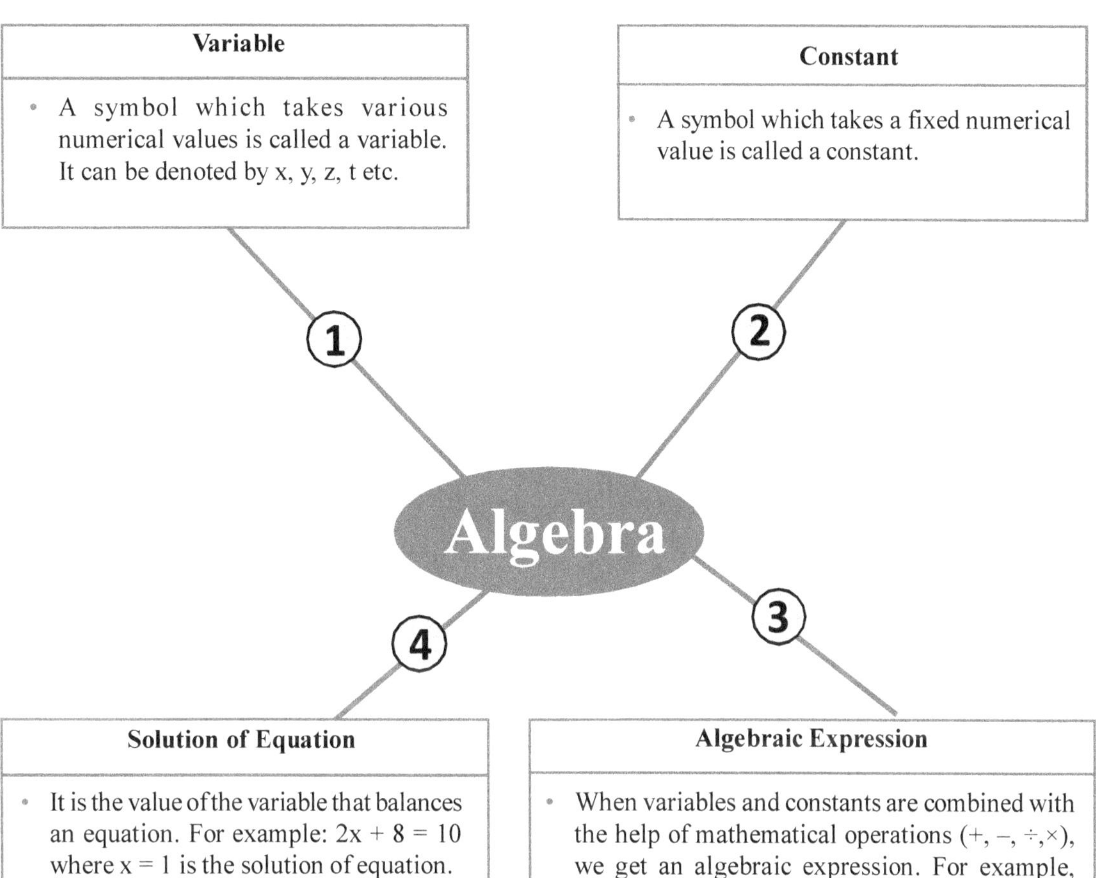

Variable
A symbol which takes various numerical values is called a variable. It can be denoted by x, y, z, t etc.
Constant
A symbol which takes a fixed numerical value is called a constant.
1
2
Algebra
4
3
Solution of Equation
It is the value of the variable that balances an equation. For example: 2x + 8 = 10 where x = 1 is the solution of equation.
Algebraic Expression
When variables and constants are combined with the help of mathematical operations (+, −, ÷, ×), we get an algebraic expression. For example, 3x + 7, 2y + 3 etc.

MISCELLANEOUS
SOLVED EXAMPLES

1. Find out the pattern for the shape ' ⬡ ' through matchsticks.

Sol. 1. ⬡   2. ⬡⬡

3. ⬡⬡⬡   4. ⬡⬡⬡⬡

Observe the following:
1st shape contains $6 = 1 \times 5 + 1$ matchsticks
2nd shape contains $11 = 2 \times 5 + 1$ matchsticks
3rd shape contains $16 = 3 \times 5 + 1$ matchsticks
4th shape contains $21 = 4 \times 5 + 1$ matchsticks
So, we can say that the nth shape will contain $5n + 1$ matchsticks.

2. Write the following using numbers, literals and signs of basic operations:
   (i) 3 more than a number x
   (ii) y less than 6
   (iii) One-third of the sum of x and y
   (iv) 5 less than the quotient of x by y
   (v) The quotient of x by y added to the product of x and y
   (vi) 7 taken away from the sum of x and y

Sol. (i) $x + 3$ (ii) $6 - y$ (iii) $\dfrac{1}{3}(x + y)$

(iv) $\dfrac{x}{y} - 5$ (v) $xy + \dfrac{x}{y}$ (vi) $x + y - 7$

3. Sheena is 10 years older than her sister Pihu. Write an expression for Sheena's age.

Sol. Let Pihu's age be x years.
∴ Sheena's age $= x + 10$ years

4. Express the share of each person if x rupees were distributed equally among six people.

Sol. Amount of money to be distributed $= ₹\,x$
Number of persons $= 6$
Each person's share $= \dfrac{x}{6}$

5. Find the solution of the equation $3x = 18$ by trial-and-error method.

Sol. We think of an integer which when multiplied by 3 gives 18. We show the calculations in a tabular form as shown below.

x	L.H.S.	R.H.S.	Conclusion
1	$3 \times 1 = 3$	18	L.H.S. ≠ R.H.S
2	$3 \times 2 = 6$	18	L.H.S. ≠ R.H.S
3	$3 \times 3 = 9$	18	L.H.S. ≠ R.H.S
4	$3 \times 4 = 12$	18	L.H.S. ≠ R.H.S
5	$3 \times 5 = 15$	18	L.H.S. ≠ R.H.S
6	$3 \times 6 = 18$	18	L.H.S. = R.H.S

Hence, the required solution is $x = 6$.

6. Solve: $\dfrac{3y+5}{4} = 2.$

Sol. $\dfrac{3y+5}{4} = 2$
⇒ $3y + 5 = 8$ [multiplying each side by 4]
⇒ $3y = 8 - 5$ [By transposition]
⇒ $3y = 3$ ⇒ $y = 1$
[Dividing each side by 3]
∴ $y = 1$ is the required solution.

7. Solve: $3(x + 3) - 2(x - 1) = 5(x - 5)$. Check the result.

Sol. $3(x + 3) - 2(x - 1) = 5(x - 5)$
⇒ $3x + 9 - 2x + 2 = 5x - 25$
[removing parentheses]
⇒ $x + 11 = 5x - 25$ ⇒ $x - 5x = -25 - 11$
[transposing $5x$ to LHS and 11 to RHS]
⇒ $-4x = -36$
⇒ $x = 9$ [dividing both sidex by -4]
∴ $x = 9$ is the solution of the given equation.
Checking:
Substituting $x = 9$ in the given equation, we get
LHS $= 3(9 + 3) - 2(9 - 1) = (3 \times 12 - 2 \times 8)$
$= 36 - 16 = 20.$
RHS $= 5(9 - 5) = 5 \times 4 = 20.$
∴ LHS = RHS, when $x = 9$.

8. Raghu's father is thrice as old as Raghu. If father's age is 60 years, what is Raghu's age?

Sol. Let the Raghu's age be y years.
Father's age $= 60$ years $=$ thrice of Raghu's age.
So, $60 = 3y$
or $3y = 60$
or $y = \dfrac{60}{3} = 20$
∴ Raghu's age is 20 years.

9. The length of a rectangular field is twice its breadth. If the perimeter of the field is 228 metres, find the dimensions of the field.

Sol. Let the breadth of the field be x metres. Then, its length $= 2x$ metres.
∴ perimeter of the field $= 2(\text{length} + \text{breadth})$
$= 2(2x + x)$ metres $= 6x$ metres.
So, $6x = 228$
⇒ $x = \dfrac{228}{6}$ [dividing both sides by 6]
⇒ $x = 38.$
Hence, breadth of the field $= 38$ metres, and length of the field $= (2 \times 38)$ metres $= 76$ metres.

1 EXERCISE

Fill in the Blanks :

DIRECTIONS : *Complete the following statements with an appropriate word / term to be filled in the blank space(s).*

1. x metres = _______ centimetres
2. If I spend f from ₹100, the money left with me is ₹_______.
3. The solution of the equation $3x + 4 = -20$ is _______.
4. The number of days in w weeks is _______.
5. The two digit number whose tens digit is 't' and units digit is 'u' is _______ .
6. If the present age of Ramandeep is n years, then her age after 7 years will be _______ .
7. An auto rickshaw charges ₹ 10 for first kilometre then ₹ 8 for each such subsequent kilometre. The total charge (in ₹) for d kilometres is _______.
8. 'x exceeds y by 7' can be expressed as _______.
9. Annual salary at ₹r per month along with a festival bonus of ₹ 2000 is _______.
10. '8 more than three times the number x' can be written as _______ .

True / False :

DIRECTIONS : *Read the following statements and write your answer as true or false.*

1. The equations $x + 1 = 0$ and $2x + 2 = 0$ have the same solution.
2. t minutes are equal to 60t seconds.
3. The difference between the ages of two sisters Leela and Yamini is a variable.
4. In an equation, the LHS is equal to the RHS.
5. 'One third of a number added to itself gives 8', can be expressed as $\dfrac{x}{3} + 8 = x$

6. $a = 3$ is a solution of the equation $2a - 1 = 5$
7. $x = 5$ is the solution of the equation $3x + 2 = 20$
8. $x = \dfrac{2}{3}$ is a solution of $2x + 5 = 8$.

Match the Columns :

DIRECTIONS : *Each question contains statements given in two columns which have to be matched. Statements (A, B, C, D) in column-I have to be matched with statements (p, q, r, s) in column-II.*

1.

	Column-I	Column-II
(A)	When 6 is subtracted from four times a number, the result is 54. The number is	(p) 144
(B)	The difference between a number and its three-fourth is 35. The one-fourth of that number is...........	(q) 25
(C)	The sum of one-half, one-third and one-fourth of a number exceeds the number by 12. The number is	(r) 15
(D)	A number exceeds its one-fifth by 20. The number is..........	(s) 35

Very Short Answer Questions:

DIRECTIONS : *Give answer in one word or one sentence.*

1. Express the following in algebraic expression.
   (i) x increased by 6.
   (ii) m decreased by 7.

(iii) The product of *a* and *b* added to their sum.

(iv) Quotient of *a* and 3.

(v) Sum of a and b divided by 9.

(vi) 4 less than the quotient of *a* by *b*.

2. Write a rule which represents the formation of following figures and number of matchsticks used in their formation.

(i) 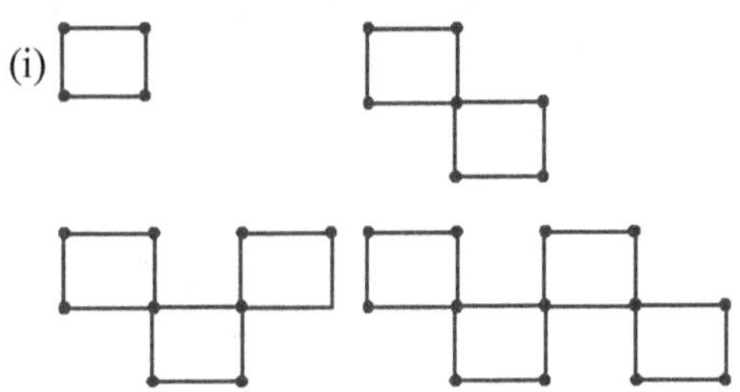

(ii) 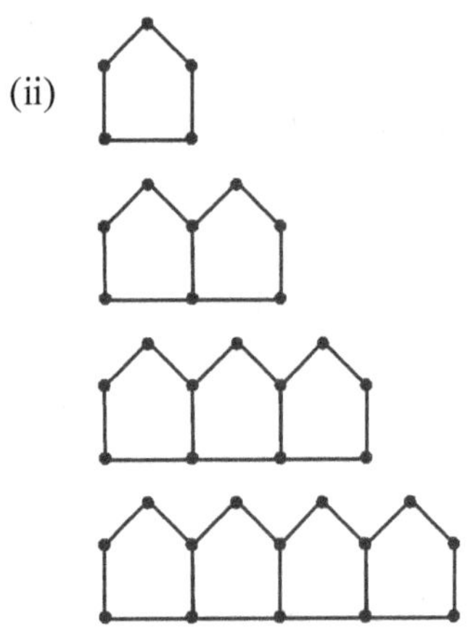

3. Which of the following are algebraic expression?

(i) $25 - 2r$

(ii) $3 \times 4 (5 + 9)$

(iii) $11a + 6$

(iv) $3 + \dfrac{x}{5}$

(v) $-2m + 6$

(vi) $4x + 3 - 2n$

(vii) $2n - 1$

(viii) $4 \times 5 + 7 \times 6 + 10$

4. Write the algebraic expressions for the following :

(i) Three times the difference of 15 and *x*.

(ii) Product of *x* and 14 added to 6.

(iii) One third of *y* subtracted from 10 less than *x*.

(iv) One fifth of *x* added to 5 times of *y*.

(v) *a* is subtracted from the quotient of *b* by 4.

(vi) 20 less than thrice the sum of *a* and *b*.

(vii) Multiply the sum of *x* and *y* by 2 and divide the product by *z*.

(viii) Twice the difference of 15 and *a*.

5. Write the statement for the given expressions.

(i) $2a - 4$

(ii) $y \div 8$

(iii) $-9z$

(iv) $\dfrac{2x}{3}$

(v) $\dfrac{a}{2} + 2$

6. Which of the following are equations? Also find out the variables used in them.

(i) $8 = a + 5$

(ii) $x - 3 < 11$

(iii) $3 > 10y + y$

(iv) $(t - 3) > 5$

(v) $y - 7 = 7$

(vi) $\dfrac{p}{3} = 4$

(vii) $15 = 3m$

(viii) $5y - 2 = 13$

(ix) $\dfrac{5t}{3} < 9$

(x) $\dfrac{7q}{3} > 8$

7. Write a rule to show the relationship between two variables in each of the following tables:

(i)

x	5	10	15	20
y	15	30	45	60

(ii)

a	1	2	3	4
b	4	7	10	13

8. Express the perimeter of following figures

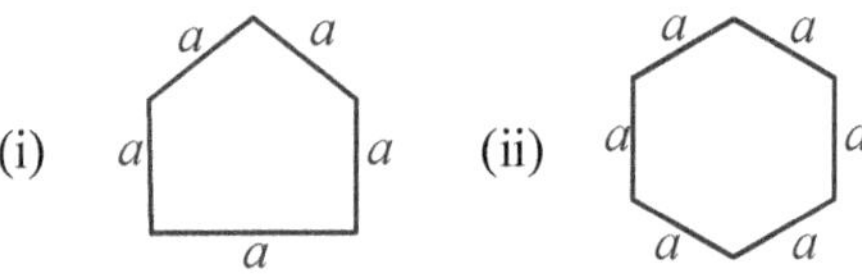

(i) *a* ... (ii) *a* ...

9. The length of a rectangular park is 4 m less than three times of its breadth (*b*). Write an expression for length (ℓ).

10. Find the total distance covered by Rita in *y* steps if in each step she covers *x* cm?

DIRECTIONS : *Give answer in 2-3 sentences.*

1. Ram's age is *y* years. Find algebraic expression for each statement.

(i) Ram's age 3 years ago.

(ii) Ram's age 5 years hence.

  (iii) Ram's father's age, if he is 4 times of what Ram's age will be 5 years from now.

  (iv) Ram's mother's age who is 5 years more than 3 times of Ram's age.

2. Complete the table:

S.No.	Equations	Value of variable	Equations satisfed Yes/No
(i)	$y + 2 = 7$	$y = 5$	
(ii)	$10 - a = 3$	$a = 6$	
(iii)	$3 - x = 5$	$x = -\dfrac{1}{8}$	
(iv)	$\dfrac{x}{3} = 12$	$x = 36$	
(v)	$7y + 4 = 15$	$y = 1$	
(vi)	$9 - 8y = 1$	$y = 0$	
(vii)	$4\ell = 32$	$\ell = 5$	
(viii)	$9 + 2x = -11$	$x = -10$	
(ix)	$\dfrac{z}{10} = 80$	$z = 810$	
(x)	$\dfrac{m}{4} = 4$	$m = 1$	

3. Complete the table by inspection and find the correct solution to the given equation:

  (i) $a + 6 = 11$

a	2	3	4	5	6	7	8
$a + 6$							

  (ii) $\dfrac{3y}{18} = 2$

y	2	4	6	8	10	12	14	16
$3y/18$								

4. Solve the following equations with the help of transposition.

  (i) $a + 5 = 15$ (ii) $2x + 6 = 10$

  (iii) $\dfrac{q}{2} = 7$ (iv) $\dfrac{q}{2} + 5 = 7$

  (v) $4y = 28$ (vi) $5x - 10 = 15$

5. Complete the following tables with the help of given formula.

  (i) $y = 3x + 2$

x	6	8	10	12
y				

  (ii) $p = q - 3$

p	9	8	7	6
q				

6. Verify the distributive property of multiplication for the following: 5, 3, 6

7. Solve the equation $3x - 5 = 7 - x$ by the trial-and error method.

8. Determine if 3 is the root of the equation $5x - 10 = 5$.

9. Solve the equation: $x - 23 = -3x + 5$.

10. Solve: $\dfrac{5x}{3} + 2 = x + 4$.

Long Answer Questions :

DIRECTIONS : *Give answer in four to five sentences.*

1. Solve: $3x + 5 = 13 - x$. Check the result.

2. Find two numbers such that one of them exceeds the other by 9 and their sum is 81.

3. A piece of rope x metres long is cut into 4 equal parts;

  (i) What is the length of each part?

  (ii) If the length of each part is 3 metres, find the length of the whole piece.

4. The total number of students in a school is 1260. If the number of girls is 52 more than that of the boys, find the number of boys in the school. Also, find the number of girls.

5. Solve the equation $\dfrac{3x}{5} - \dfrac{8}{3} = \dfrac{2x}{15} + \dfrac{2}{15}$ and hence verify the solution.

6. Solve: $3(5x - 2) - 4(x + 4) = 7(x - 1) + 1$.

2 EXERCISE

Text-Book Exercise :

1. A bird flies 1 kilometre in one minute. Can you express the distance covered by the bird in terms of its flying time in minutes? (Use t for flying time in minutes.)

2. Radha is drawing a dot rangoli (a beautiful pattern of lines joining dots with chalk powder). She has 9 dots in a row. How many dots will her rangoli have for r rows? How many dots are there if there are 8 rows? If there are 10 rows?

3. Oranges are to be transferred from larger boxes into smaller boxes. When a large box is emptied, the oranges from it fill two smaller boxes and still 10 oranges remain outside. If the number of oranges in a small box are taken to be x, what is the number of oranges in the larger box?

4. A cube is a three-dimensional figure as shown in figure. It has six faces and all of them are identical squares. The length of an edge of the cube is given by l. Find the formula for the total length of the edges of a cube.

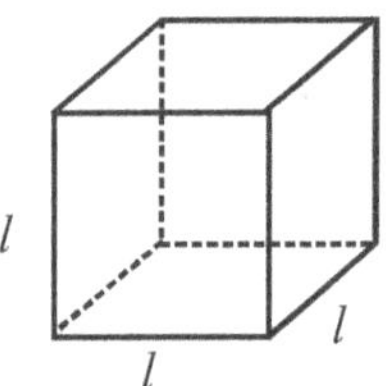

5. The diameter of a circle is a line which joins two points on the circle and also passes through the center of the circle. (In the adjoining figure, AB is a diameter of the circle; C is its center.) Express the diameter of the circle (d) in terms of its radius (r).

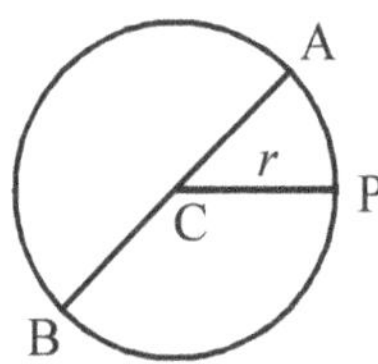

6. Make up as many expressions with numbers (no variables) as you can from three numbers 5, 7 and 8. Every number should be used not more than once. Use only addition, subtraction and multiplication.

   Hint: Three possible expressions are $5 + (8 - 7)$, $5 - (8 - 7)$, $(5 \times 8) + 7$; make the other expressions.

7. Give expressions in the following cases.
   (i) 11 added to 2m
   (ii) 11 subtracted from 2m
   (iii) 5 times y to which 3 is added
   (iv) 5 times y from which 3 is subtracted
   (v) y is multiplied by -8
   (vi) y is multiplied by -8 and then 5 is added to the result
   (vii) y is multiplied by 5 and the result is subtracted from 16
   (viii) y is multiplied by -5 and the result is added to 16.

8. Answer the following:
   (i) Take Sarita's present age to be y years
       (a) What will be her age 5 years from now?
       (b) What was her age 3 years back?
       (c) Sarita's grandfather is 6 times her age. What is the age of her grandfather?
       (d) Grandmother is 2 years younger than grandfather. What is grandmother's age?
       (e) Sarita's father 's age is 5 years more than 3 times Sarita's age. What is her father's age?
   (ii) The length of a rectangular hall is 4 metres less than 3 times the breadth of the hall. What is the length, if the breadth is b metres?
   (iii) A rectangular box has height h cm. Its length is 5 times the height and breadth is 10 cm less than the length. Express the length and the breadth of the box in terms of the height.
   (iv) Meena, Beena and Leena are climbing the steps to the hill top. Meena is at step s, Beena is 8 steps ahead and Leena 7 steps

behind. Where are Beena and Meena? The total number of steps to the hill top is 10 less than 4 times what Meena has reached. Express the total number of steps using s.

(v) A bus travels at v km per hour. It is going from Daspur to Beespur. After the bus has travelled 5 hours, Beespur is still 20 km away. What is the distance from Daspur to Beespur? Express is using v.

9. (i) Complete the table and by inspection of the table find the solution to the equation $m + 10 = 16$.

m	1	2	3	4	5	6	7	8	9	10	–	–	–
m + 10	–	–	–	–	–	–	–	–	–	–	–	–	–

(ii) Complete the table and by inspection of the table, find the solution to the equation $5t = 35$.

t	3	4	5	6	7	8	9	10	11	–	–	–	–	–
5t	–	–	–	–	–	–	–	–	–	–	–	–	–	–

Exemplar Questions :

1. Convert the following expressions into statements in ordinary language.

(i) Leela contributed ₹ y towards the Prime Minister's Relief Fund. Leela is now left with ₹ $(y + 10000)$.

(ii) The maximum temperature on a day in Delhi was $p°$C. The minimum temperature was $(p - 10°)$C.

(iii) John planted t plants last year. His friend Jay planted $2t + 10$ plants that year.

(iv) The number of students dropping out of school last year was m. Number of students dropping out of school this year is $m - 30$.

(v) Price of petrol was ₹ p per litre last month. price of petrol now is ₹ $(p - 5)$ per litre.

(vi) The number of girls enrolled in a school last year was g. The number of girls enrolled this year in the school is $3g - 10$.

2. Translate each of the following statements into an equation:

(i) The perimeter (p) of an equilateral triangle is three times of its side (a).

(ii) The diameter (d) of a circle is twice its radius (r).

(iii) The selling price (s) of an item is equal to the sum of the cost price (c) of an item and the profit (p) earned.

(iv) Amount (a) is equal to the sum of principal (p) and interest (i).

3. If m is a whole number less than 5, complete the table and by inspection of the table, find the solution of the equation $2m - 5 = - 1$:

m					
2m – 5					

4. A class with p students has planned a picnic. ₹ 50 per student is collected, out of which ₹ 1800 is paid in advance for transport. How much money is left with them to spend on other items?

5. In a village, there are 8 water tanks to collect rain water. On a particular day, x litres of rain water is collected per tank. If 100 litres of water was already there in one of the tanks, what is the total amount of water in the tanks on that day?

6. Perimeter of a rectangle is found by using the formula $P = 2 (l + w)$, where l and w are respectively the length and breadth of the rectangle. Write the rule that is expressed by this formula in words.

7. On my last birthday, I weighed 40 kg. If I put on m kg of weight after a year, what is my present weight?

8. Sunita is half the age of her mother Geeta. Find their ages
(i) after 4 years? (ii) before 3 years?

HOTS Questions :

1. Find two consecutive even numbers such that seven times the first exceeds five times the second by 54.

2. Find the value of the expression $3ab - 4a + 5$, if $a = 4$ and $b = 2$.

3. If $x = 1$, $y = 2$, $z = 5$, then find the value of $3x - 2y + 4z$.

4. The number 6 when added to a product of the number k and 4, results in 50. Which equations represents the relation? Also find the value for k.

5. The length of a box is 16 cm more than twice its width. If the width is y cm, what is its length in terms of y. Find out the area of the box when $y = 1$ cm?

6. The average age of Kiran, Ravi and Naveen is 11 years. Kiran is older than Naveen by 8 years, Naveen is younger than Ravi by 4 years. What will be the age of Kiran after 3 years?

3 EXERCISE

Single Option Correct :

DIRECTIONS : *This section contains multiple choice questions. Each question has 4 choices (a), (b), (c) and (d) out of which ONLY ONE is correct.*

1. The breadth of a rectangle is x m. Its length is three times the breadth. The area will be
(a) $3x - x$
(b) $3x + x$
(c) $3x \times x$
(d) $\dfrac{3x}{x}$

2. A boy earns ₹ x in a week and spends ₹y in a week. His savings for the week are
(a) ₹ $(x + y)$
(b) ₹ $(x - y)$
(c) ₹$\dfrac{x}{y}$
(d) ₹ $x \times y$

3. Cost of one pen is ₹ a, then cost of 15 pens is
(a) $15a$
(b) $\dfrac{a}{15}$
(c) $a + 15$
(d) $a - 15$

4. The solution of $\dfrac{2x+1}{3x-1} = \dfrac{3}{2}$ is
(a) $x = 1$
(b) $x = -1$
(c) $x = 2$
(d) $x = -3$

5. Which of the following equation has $x = 2$ as a solution?
(a) $x + 2 = 5$
(b) $x - 2 = 0$
(c) $2x + 1 = 0$
(d) $x + 3 = 6$

6. $10 - x$ means
(a) 10 is subtracted x times
(b) x is subtracted 10 times
(c) x is subtracted from 10
(d) 10 is subtracted from x

7. The sum of two numbers is 19 and one of the numbers is one more than twice the other. Represent this statement in the form of an equation using variable x.

(a) $x\,(2x + 1) = 19$
(b) $x + (2x + 1) = 19$
(c) $x + (2x - 1) = 19$
(d) $x \div (2x - 1) = 19$

8. Solve : $\dfrac{2x - 7}{4} = \dfrac{5x + 2}{3}$

(a) $-\dfrac{29}{14}$
(b) -3
(c) 15
(d) $\dfrac{15}{7}$

9. Atul's father was born on January 1, 1960 and Atul was born on January 1, 1984. On what date did his father became 3 times his age ?

(a) January 1, 1960
(b) January 1, 1990
(c) January 1, 1992
(d) January 1, 1990

10. $\dfrac{4}{2} = 2$ denotes a
(a) numerical equation
(b) algebraic expression
(c) equation with a variable
(d) false statement

11. The algebraic expression for the statement: 'Product of x and a subtracted from the product of b and y'.
(a) $ax - by$
(b) $x + a - by$
(c) $by - ax$
(d) $xa - b - y$

More Than One Option Correct :

DIRECTIONS : *This section contains multiple choice questions. Each question has 4 choices (a), (b), (c) and (d) out of which ONE or MORE may be correct.*

1. Which of these is/are algebraic expressions?
(a) $4 \times 3 - 2$
(b) $4y - 3$
(c) $3P$
(d) $5m + 3$

2. Which of the following equations have a solution in integers?

(a) $x + 1 = 1$ (b) $x - 1 = 3$

(c) $2x + 1 = 6$ (d) $1 - x = 5$

3. If $a = 3, b = 5, c = b - a$, then which of the following expressions do not represent 10 ?

(a) $(a + c) \times b$ (b) $(a + b) - c$

(c) $(b + c) + a$ (d) $(a - b) + c$

4. In algebra, letters may stand for

(a) known quantities

(b) unknown quantities

(c) fixed numbers

(d) variable

5. For any two integers x and y, which of the following show commutative law?

(a) $x + y = y + x$ (b) $x + y > x$

(c) $x - y = y - x$ (d) $x \times y = y \times x$

6. Which of the following is/are an equation?

(a) $x + 7 = 5$ (b) $2y + 3 = 7$

(c) $2p < 10$ (d) $12x$

Assertion & Reason :

DIRECTIONS : *Each of these questions contains an Assertion followed by Reason. Read them carefully and answer the question on the basis of following options. You have to select the one that best describes the two statements.*

(a) If both **Assertion** and **Reason** are **correct** and Reason is the **correct explanation** of Assertion.

(b) If both **Assertion** and **Reason** are correct, but Reason is **not the correct explanation** of Assertion.

(c) If **Assertion** is **correct** but **Reason** is **incorrect**.

(d) If **Assertion** is **incorrect** but **Reason** is **correct**.

1. **Assertion :** x = 2 is a solution of the equation 2 − x = 4.

Reason : x = −2 satisfies the equation 2 − x = 4.

2. **Assertion :** In the equation.

$7p - 12 = 2$, the variable is p.

Reason : p is the unknown that varies.

Passage Based Questions :

DIRECTIONS : *Study the given passage(s) and answer the following questions.*

PASSAGE-I

Rahul's mother's age is 5 years less than four times his age.

1. Write an algebraic expression for the given situation (using 'x' as variable).

(a) $5 - 4x$ (b) $4x + 5$

(c) $4x - 5$ (d) $4(x + 5)$

2. Five years from now, what will be the age of Rahul's mother?

(a) $4x + 5$ years   (b) $4x + 10$ years

(c) $10x - 5$ years   (d) $4x$ years

3. What is his mother's age if his present age is 11 years old?

(a) 44 years   (b) 39 years

(c) 49 years   (d) 45 years

PASSAGE-II

The length of a rectangular hall is 4 metres less than 3 times the breadth of the hall.

4. What is the length of hall if breadth is b metres?

(a) $b - 4$ (b) $3b - 4$

(c) $4 - 3b$ (d) $3b$

5. The expression for the perimeter of rectangular hall in terms of 'b' will be

(a) $4b - 4$ (b) $4b$

(c) $2(4b - 4)$ (d) $2(b + 4)$

6. Perimeter of rectangular hall if breadth is 8 metres, is

(a) 32 metres   (b) 28 metres

(c) 64 metres   (d) 56 metres

Integer Type Questions :

DIRECTIONS : *Answer the following questions. The answer to each of the question is a single digit integer, ranging from 0 to 9.*

1. What is the reciprocal of $\dfrac{1}{a - 3b}$ when $b = \dfrac{a}{3}$?

2. $x - 4 = -2$ has a solution

3. 5 more than a number equals 10. Find the number

4. If $\dfrac{1}{3}x + 5 = 8$, then x = ?

5. Solve the following equation and find the value of variable 'x' in $7x - 4 = 10$

Multiple Matching Question :

DIRECTIONS : *Following question has four statements (A, B, C and D) given in Column-I and five statements (p, q, r, s, t) in Column-II. Any given statement in Column-I can have correct matching with one or more statement(s) given in Column-II.*

1. **Column-I**   **Column-II**

(A) A number y divides 8 gives 4 can be written as   (p) 8

(B) Three-fourth of a number is added to 8 gives 17 can be written as   (q) 56

(C) Number to be added on L.H.S of equation $y - 8 = 6$ to find the   (r) $\dfrac{3}{4}x + 8 = 17$
     value of 'y' is

(D) Half of a number is added to 18 then the sum is 46, the number is   (s) $\dfrac{8}{y} = 4$

                                                                                   (t) $\dfrac{3}{4}p + 8 = 17$

SOLUTIONS

Brief Explanations of Selected Questions

1 EXERCISE

Fill in the Blanks :

1. $100x$ 2. $100-f$ 3. -8 4. $7w$
5. $10t+u$ 6. $n+7$ 7. $8d+2$ 8. $x=y+7$
9. $12r+2000$ 10. $3x+8$

True / False :

1. T 2. T 3. F 4. T
5. F 6. T 7. F 8. F

Match the Columns :

1. (A) $\to$ (r); (B) $\to$ (s); (C) $\to$ (p); (D) $\to$ (q)
   (A) $4x - 6 = 54 \Rightarrow 4x = 60 \Rightarrow x = 15$

   (B) $x - \dfrac{3}{4}x = 35 \Rightarrow \dfrac{x}{4} = 35 \Rightarrow x = 35 \times 4$

   $\therefore$ Required number $= \dfrac{35 \times 4}{4} = 35$

   (C) $\dfrac{x}{2} + \dfrac{x}{3} + \dfrac{x}{4} = x + 12$
   $\Rightarrow 6x + 4x + 3x = 12\,(x + 12)$
   $\Rightarrow 13x - 12x = 144$
   $\Rightarrow x = 144$

   (D) $x = \dfrac{x}{5} + 20 \Rightarrow 4x = 100 \Rightarrow x = 25$

Very Short Answer Questions:

1. (i) $x + 6$ (ii) $m - 7$

   (iii) $a \times b + (a + b)$ (iv) $a \div 3$ or $\dfrac{a}{3}$

   (v) $\dfrac{a+b}{9}$ (vi) $\dfrac{a}{b} - 4$

2. (i)

No. of squares (x)	1	2	3	4
No. of match sticks (y)	4	8	12	16
	(4×1)	(4×2)	(4×3)	(4×4)

$\Rightarrow y = 4x$

(ii)

No. of pentagons (x)	1	2	3	4
No. of match sticks (y)	5	9	13	17
	$(4 \times 1 +1)$	$(4 \times 2 +1)$	$(4 \times 3 +1)$	$(4 \times 4 +1)$

$\Rightarrow y = 4x + 1$

3. (i) Yes (ii) No
   (iii) Yes (iv) Yes
   (v) Yes (vi) Yes
   (vii) Yes (viii) No

4. (i) $3\,(15 - x)$ (ii) $14x + 6$

   (iii) $(x - 10) - \dfrac{y}{3}$ (iv) $\dfrac{x}{5} + 5y$

   (v) $\left(\dfrac{b}{4}\right) - a$ (vi) $3(a + b) - 20$

   (vii) $\dfrac{(x + y) \times 2}{z}$ (viii) $2\,(15 - a)$

5. (i) Four subtracted from the product of 2 and a.
   (ii) y divided by 8.
   (iii) z multiplied by -9.
   (iv) Twice of x is divided by 3.
   (v) Half of a is added to 2.

6. (i) Yes, variable 'a' (ii) No
   (iii) No (iv) No
   (v) Yes, variable 'y' (vi) Yes, variable 'p'
   (vii) Yes, variable 'm' (viii) Yes, variable 'y'
   (ix) No (x) No

7. (i) $y = 3x$ (ii) $b = a \times 3 + 1$

8. (i) $5a$ (ii) $6a$

9. $\ell = (3b - 4)m$

10. xy cm.

Short Answer Questions :

1. (i) $y - 3$ years (ii) $y + 5$ years
   (iii) $4\,(y + 5)$ years (iv) $3y + 5$ years.

2. (i) Yes (ii) No
   (iii) No (iv) Yes
   (v) No (vi) Yes
   (vii) No (viii) Yes
   (ix) No (x) No

3.   (i)   5   (ii)   12

4.   (i)   10   (ii)   2

      (iii) 14   (iv)   4

      (v)   7   (vi)   5

5.   (i)

x	6	8	10	12
y	20	26	32	38

    (ii)

p	9	8	7	6
q	12	11	10	9

6.   We have $5 \times (3 + 6) = 5 \times 9 = 45$

$$5 \times (3 + 6) = (5 \times 3) + (5 \times 6)$$
$$= 15 + 30 = 45$$

Hence, the distributive property of multiplication is verified,

i.e., $5 \times (3 + 6) = 5 \times 3 + 5 \times 6$.

7.

x	LHS	RHS
1	$3 \times 1 - 5 = -2$	$7 - 1 = 6$
2	$3 \times 2 - 5 = 1$	$7 - 2 = 5$
3	$3 \times 3 - 5 = 4$	$7 - 3 = 4$

$\therefore$ $x = 3$ is the solution of the given equation.

8.   Substitute 3 for the unknown x in the equation

$$5x - 10 = 5 \text{ (given)}$$
$$5(3) - 10 = 5$$
$$15 - 10 = 5$$
$$5 = 5$$

Hence, 3 is the root of the equation $5x - 10 = 5$.

9. $x - 23 = -3x + 5$

$\Rightarrow$ $x + 3x = 5 + 23$

      [Transposing $-3x$ to L.H.S. and -23 to R.H.S.]

$\Rightarrow$ $4x = 28$

$\Rightarrow$ $\dfrac{4x}{4} = \dfrac{28}{4}$ [Dividing both sides by 4]

$\Rightarrow$ $x = 7$ which is the required solution.

10. $\dfrac{5x}{3} + 2 = x + 4$

$\Rightarrow$ $\dfrac{5x}{3} - x = 4 - 2$ [By transposition]

$\Rightarrow$ $\dfrac{5x}{3} - x = 2$

$\Rightarrow$ $5x - 3x = 6$ [Multiplying each term by 3]

$\Rightarrow$ $2x = 6$

$\Rightarrow$ $x = 3$ [Dividing each side by 2]

$\therefore$ $x = 3$ is the required solution.

1. $3x + 5 = 13 - x$

$\Rightarrow$ $3x + x = 13 - 5$

     [transposing $-x$ to LHS and $+5$ to RHS]

$\Rightarrow$ $4x = 8$

$\Rightarrow$ $\dfrac{4x}{4} = \dfrac{8}{4}$ [dividing both sides by 4]

$\Rightarrow$ $x = 2$.

Check Substituting $x = 2$ in the given equation, we get

LHS $= 3 \times 2 + 5 = 11$ and RHS $= 13 - 2 = 11$.

$\therefore$ LHS = RHS, when $x = 2$.

2.   Let the smaller number be x.

Then, the other number $= (x + 9)$.

$\therefore$ $x + (x + 9) = 81 \Rightarrow$ $2x + 9 = 81$

$\Rightarrow$ $2x = 81 - 9$ [on transposing 9 to RHS]

$\Rightarrow$ $2x = 72$

$\Rightarrow$ $x = 36$ [dividing both sides by 2].

Hence, one number $= 36$,

and the other number $= (36 + 9) = 45$.

3.   Length of each part $= \dfrac{x}{4}$ metres

According to the question, $\dfrac{x}{4} = 3$

$\Rightarrow$ $x = 3 \times 4$ $\Rightarrow$ $x = 12$.

Hence the length of the whole piece is 12 metres.

4.   Let the number of boys in the school be x.

Number of girls in the school $= x + 52$

The total number of students in the school

         $= 1260$

$\therefore$ $x + x + 52 = 1260$

$\Rightarrow$ $2x + 52 = 1260$

$\Rightarrow$ $2x = 1260 - 52$

$\Rightarrow$ $2x = 1208$

$\Rightarrow$ $x = 604$

$\therefore$ Number of boys $= 604$

      Number of girls $= 604 + 52 = 656$.

5. $\dfrac{3x}{5} - \dfrac{8}{3} = \dfrac{2x}{15} + \dfrac{2}{15}$

$\Rightarrow$ $\dfrac{3x}{5} - \dfrac{2x}{15} = \dfrac{8}{3} + \dfrac{2}{15}$

$\Rightarrow$ $\dfrac{9x - 2x}{15} = \dfrac{40 + 2}{15}$

$\Rightarrow$ $\dfrac{7x}{15} = \dfrac{42}{15}$

$\Rightarrow \quad 7x = 42$ [Multiplying both sides by 15]

$\Rightarrow \quad x = 6$, which is the required solution.

Verification:

Substituting $x = 6$ on both sides of the equation, we get

$$\text{L.H.S.} = \frac{3 \times 6}{5} - \frac{8}{3} = \frac{18}{5} - \frac{8}{3} = \frac{54 - 40}{15} = \frac{14}{15}$$

and

$$\text{R.H.S.} = \frac{2 \times 6}{15} + \frac{2}{15} = \frac{12}{15} + \frac{2}{15} = \frac{12 + 2}{15} = \frac{14}{15}$$

$\therefore \quad$ L.H.S. = R.H.S.

6. $3(5x - 2) - 4(x + 4) = 7(x - 1) + 1$

$\Rightarrow \quad 15x - 6 - 4x - 16 = 7x - 7 + 1$

$\Rightarrow \quad 11x - 22 = 7x - 6$

$\Rightarrow \quad 11x - 7x = -6 + 22$ [By transposition]

$\Rightarrow \quad 4x = 16$

$\Rightarrow \quad x = 4$ [On dividing each side by 4]

Verification:

Putting $x = 4$ in the given equation, we get:

L.H.S. = $3 (5 \times 4 - 2) - 4(4 + 4)$

$= 3(20 - 2) - 4 \times 8 = 3 \times 18 - 4 \times 8 = 54 - 32 = 22$.

R.H.S. = $7 (4 - 1) + 1 = 7 \times 3 + 1 = 21 + 1 = 22$.

$\therefore \quad$ L.H.S. = R.H.S.

2 EXERCISE

Text-Book Exercise :

1. $\because \quad$ The flying time is represented by 't'.

Distance covered in one minute = 1 km

$\therefore \quad$ Distance covered, when

$t = 1$, is 1 km or 1×1 km = $1 \times t$ km

$t = 2$, is 2 km or 1×2 km = $1 \times t$ km

$t = 3$, is 3 km or 1×3 km = $1 \times t$ km

Thus, distance covered in 't' minutes = t km.

2. Number of rows are given by 'r'.

$\because \quad$ Number of dots in a row are 9.

$\therefore \quad$ Total number of dots:

For $r = 1$ is 9 or $9 \times 1 = 9 \times r$

For $r = 2$ is 18 or $9 \times 2 = 9 \times r$

For $r = 3$ is 27 or $9 \times 3 = 9 \times r$

Thus, the total number of dots is given by 9r.

Now, For $r = 8$, we have $9 \times 8 = 72$ dots.

For $r = 10$, we have $9 \times 10 = 90$ dots.

3. Number of oranges in a bigger box = 2 × [Number of orange in a small box] + 10

$$[\because 10 \text{ oranges remain outside}]$$

Since, x represents the number of oranges in the smaller box

$\therefore$ Number of oranges in a big box = $2x + 10$

4. A cube has six identical faces.

It has 12 edges.

Each edge has equal length.

$\therefore \quad$ Total length of edges = $12 \times l$ or $12l$

5. Radius = r and diameter = d

Since, diameter of a circle is double the radius.

$\therefore \quad$ Diameter $= 2 \times$ radius

or $\quad d = 2 \times r$ or $d = 2r$

6. (i) $5 + (7 + 8)$ (ii) $7 \times 5 + 8$

(iii) $(8 - 5) \times 7$ (iv) $(7 - 5) \times 8$

(v) $(5 \times 7) - 8$ (vi) $(8 \times 7) + 5$

(vii) $8 - 5 + 7$ (viii) $(8 - 7) + 5$, etc.

7. (i) $2m + 11$ (ii) $2m - 11$

(iii) $5y + 3$ (iv) $5y - 3$

(v) $-8y$ (vi) $-8y + 5$

(vii) $16 - 5y$ (viii) $16 + (-5y)$

8. (i) (a) [Present age of Sarita] + 5 years

$= (y + 5)$ years

(b) [Present age of Sarita] – 3 years

$= (y - 3)$ years

(c) [Present age of Sarita] × 6 = 6y years

(d) [Present age of grandfather] – 2

$= (6y - 2)$ years

(e) [Sarita's present age] × 3 + 5 years

$= (3y + 5)$ years

(ii) $\because \quad$ Breadth = b cm

$\therefore \quad$ Length = 3 (Breadth) – 4 cm

$= 3b - 4$ metres/h

(iii) Height of the box = h cm

$\therefore \quad$ Length of the box

$= 5 \times$ height= $5h$ cm

Breadth of the box

$= $ (Length – 10) cm

$= (5h - 10)$ cm

(iv) $\because \quad$ Meena is at 's' step

$\therefore \quad$ Beena's position = $(8 + s)$ steps

Leena's position = $(s - 7)$ steps

Total number of steps to the hill top

$= 4s - 10$

(v) Speed of the bus = v km/hr

Distance travelled in 5 hours

$= 5 \times v$ km = $5v$ km

$\therefore$ Distance between Daspur to Beespur

$= (5v + 20)$ km

9. (i)

m	1	2	3	4	5	6	7	8	9	10	...
$m+10$	11	12	13	14	15	16	17	18	19	20	...

$\because$ For $m = 6$, $m + 10 = 16$

$\therefore$ $m = 6$ is the solution to $m + 10 = 16$.

(ii)

t	3	4	5	6	7	8	9	10	11	...
$5t$	15	20	25	30	35	40	45	50	55	...

$\because$ For $t = 7$, $5t = 35$

$\therefore$ $t = 7$ is the solution to $5t = 35$.

Exemplar Questions :

1. (i) Amount left with Leela is ₹ 10,000 more than the amount she contributed towards Prime Minister's Relief fund.

(ii) The difference between maximum and minimum temperature on a day in Delhi was $10°C$.

(iii) Last year Jay planted 10 more plants than twice the number of plants planted by John.

(iv) The number of students dropping out this year is 30 less than the number of students dropped last year.

(v) The price of petrol per liter decreased this month by ₹ 5 than its price last month.

(vi) The number of girls enrolled this year was 10 less than 3 times the girls enrolled last year.

2. (i) $p = 3a$ (ii) $d = 2r$

(iii) $s = c + p$ (iv) $a = p + i$

3.

m		1	2	3	4
$2m - 5$	-5	-3	-1	1	3

Solution is $m = 2$

4. $50p - 1800$

5. $(8x + 100)$L

6. The perimeter of a rectangle is twice the sum of its length and breadth.

7. $(m + 40)$ kg

8. (i) Sunita: $x + 4$, Geeta: $2x + 4$, where x is the present age (in years) of Sunita,

(ii) Sunita: $x - 3$, Geeta: $2x - 3$

1. Let the two consecutive even numbers be

$$x, x + 2$$
$$7x - 5(x + 2) = 54$$
$$7x - 5x - 10 = 54$$
$$2x = 64$$
$$x = 32$$

The required two numbers are 32, 34.

2. We have, $3ab - 4a + 5$ ....(i)

Put a = 4, b = 2 in (i) we get

$3 \times 4 \times 2 - 4 \times 4 + 5$

$= 24 - 16 + 5 = 29 - 16 = 13$

3. We have $3x - 2y + 4z$ ....(i)

Put, $x = 1$, $y = 2$, $z = 5$ in (i), we get

$\Rightarrow$ $3 \times 1 - 2 \times 2 + 4 \times 5$

$= 3 - 4 + 20$

$= -1 + 20 = 19$

4. Product of k and $4 = 4k$

According to question,

$$4k + 6 = 50$$
$\Rightarrow$ $4k = 44$

$\Rightarrow$ $k = 11$

5. Width = y cm then length = $(2y + 16)$ cm

Area of a box = length $\times$ width = $(2y + 16) \times y$

$= (2 \times 1 + 16) \times 1$

$= (2 + 16) \times 1 = 18$ sq. cm

6. Sum of ages of Kiran, Ravi and Naveen

$= 11 \times 3 = 33$

Let Kiran's age be x,

then, Naveen's age $= x - 8$

Ravi's age $= x - 8 + 4$

$= x - 4$

$x + x - 8 + x - 4 = 33$

$3x = 45$

$x = 15$

Kiran's age after 3 years $= x + 3$

$= 15 + 3 = 18$ years

3 EXERCISE

Single Option Correct :

1. (c) **2.** (b) **3.** (a)

4. (a) $\dfrac{2x+1}{3x-1} = \dfrac{3}{2}$

$\Rightarrow \quad 4x + 2 = 9x - 3$

$5x = 5$

$x = 1$

5. (b) **6.** (c)

7. (b) Let one number be x
then other number $= 2x + 1$
According to given condition,
$x + (2x + 1) = 19$

8. (a) $\dfrac{2x-7}{4} = \dfrac{5x+2}{3}$

Cross multiplying we get
$3(2x - 7) = 4(5x + 2)$
$6x - 21 = 20x + 8$
$6x - 20x = 8 + 21$

$$-14x = 29 \Rightarrow x = -\dfrac{29}{14}$$

9. (a) Atul's father was 24 years old when Atul was born.
∴ Difference between Atul and his father's age is always 24 years.
Let Atul be x years when his father became 3 times his age, then
$$3x - x = 24$$
$$2x = 24$$
$$x = 12$$
Atul turned 12 on January 1, 1996

10. (a) **11.** (c) $by - ax$

More Than One Option Correct :

1. (b, c, d) **2.** (a, b, d)
3. (a, b, d)
Given $a = 3$, $b = 5$, $c = b - a = 5 - 3 = 2$
Putting these values, we will evaluate all the expressions
(a) $(a + c) \times b = (3 + 2) \times 5 = 5 \times 5 = 25 \neq 10$
(b) $(a + b) - c = (3 + 5) - 2 = 8 - 2 = 6 \neq 10$
(c) $(b + c) + a = (5 + 2) + 3 = 7 + 3 = 10$
(d) $(a - b) + c = (3 - 5) + 2 = -2 + 2 = 0 \neq 10$

4. (b, d) **5.** (a, d) **6.** (a, b)

Assertion & Reason :

1. (d) **Reason** is correct, but **Assertion** is not correct.
$2 - x = 4$
$x = 2 - 4 = -2$

2. (a) Both **Assertion** and **Reason** are correct.

Passage Based Questions :

1. (c) Let present age of Rahul be 'x' years
∴ Rahul's mother's age $= 4x - 5$

2. (d) Five years now, Rahul's mother's age
$= (4x - 5) + 5 = 4x$ years

3. (b) Rahul's age is 11 years
∴ Mother's age
$= 4x - 5 = 4 \times 11 - 5 = 39$ years

4. (b) breadth $= b$
∴ length $= 3b - 4$

5. (c) Perimeter of hall
$= 2$ (length + breadth)
$= 2 (b + 3b - 4) = 2 (4b - 4)$

6. (d) Perimeter
$= 2 (4b - 4)$
$= 2 (4 \times 8 - 4) = 56$ metres

Integer Type Questions :

1. (0) The reciprocal of $\dfrac{1}{a - 3b} = a - 3b$

$= a - 3 \times \dfrac{a}{3} \quad \left[\because b = \dfrac{a}{3} \right]$

$= a - a = 0$

2. (2)
3. (5)

4. (9) $\dfrac{1}{3} x + 5 = 8$

$\Rightarrow \quad \dfrac{1}{3} x = 3 \Rightarrow \quad x = 9$

5. (2) $7x - 4 = +10$
$\Rightarrow \quad 7x = 10 + 4 \Rightarrow 7x = 14$

$\Rightarrow \quad x = \dfrac{14}{7} \Rightarrow x = 2$

Multiple Matching Question :

1. (A) → (s); (B) → (r, t); (C) → (p); (D) → (q)

Ratio and Proportion

RATIO

If a and b $(b \neq 0)$ are two quantities of the same kind, then the fraction $\dfrac{a}{b}$ is called the ratio of a to b.

- Ratio is denoted by the symbol " : "
- For a ratio, the two quantities must be in the same unit.
- Ratio is expressed in its simplest form cannot be further simplified.

Thus, ratio of a to b is $\dfrac{a}{b}$ and denoted by $a : b$, where 'a' is called antecedent and 'b' is called consequent.

SIMPLEST FORM

When the two terms of a ratio have no common factor other than 1, we say that ratio is in simplest form.
- To reduce a ratio in simplest form, first write ratio as fraction and then divide the numerator and denominator by their H.C.F.

ILLUSTRATION : 1

There are 350 boys and 250 girls in a school. Find the ratio of boys to girls in the simplest form or lowest term.

SOLUTION :

Boys = 350, Girls = 250

Ratio of boys to girls $= \dfrac{350}{250} = \dfrac{350 \div 50}{250 \div 50} = \dfrac{7}{5}$ [$\because$ HCF of 250 and 350 is 50]

or $7 : 5$

NOTE : (i)   Ratio always exists between two quantities of same kind and unit.
(ii)   Ratio, being a fraction have no unit.
(iii)   A ratio does not change if its numerator and denominator are multiplied or divided by a non–zero number.
(iv)   The order of the terms are very important i.e. $7 : 8 \neq 8 : 7$

ILLUSTRATION : 2

The present age of mother is 48 years and that of her daughter is 16 years. Find the ratio of :
(i)   The present age of mother to present age of daughter.
(ii)   The age of mother and daughter after 6 years.
(iii) The age of mother to the age of daughter when daughter was 6 years old.

SOLUTION :

(i) The present age of the mother to the present age of daughter.
Present age of mother = 48 years
Present age of daughter = 16 years

$$\text{Required ratio} = 48 : 16 = \frac{48}{16} = \frac{48 \div 16}{16 \div 16} = \frac{3}{1} = 3 : 1$$

(ii) The age of mother and daughter after 6 years. After 6 years age of mother = 48 + 6 = 54 years.
After 6 years age of daughter = 16 + 6 = 22 years

$$\text{Required ratio} = 54 : 22 = \frac{54}{22} = \frac{54 \div 2}{22 \div 2} = \frac{27}{11} = 27 : 11$$

(iii) The age of mother to the age of the daughter when the daughter was 6 years old.
Daughter was 6 years old 10 years ago
Mother's age 10 years ago = 48 − 10 = 38 years

$$\text{Required ratio} = \frac{38}{6} = \frac{38 \div 2}{6 \div 2} = \frac{19}{3} = 19 : 3$$

ILLUSTRATION : 3

Find the ratio

(i) 4 hrs to 400 minutes　　　　　　　**(ii) 2 dozens to 4 scores**

SOLUTION :

(i) 4 hrs = 4 × 60 = 240 minutes

$$\text{Required ratio} = 240 : 400 = \frac{240}{400} = \frac{240 \div 80}{400 \div 80} = \frac{3}{5} = 3 : 5$$

(ii) 4 scores = 4 × 20 = 80

$$2 \text{ dozens} = 2 \times 12 = 24 \quad \text{Required ratio} = \frac{24}{80} = \frac{24 \div 8}{80 \div 8} = \frac{3}{10} = 3 : 10$$

Equivalent Ratios

A ratio obtained by multiplying or dividing the numerator and denominator by the same number is called an equivalent ratio.

ILLUSTRATION : 4

Find two equivalent ratios of 5 : 9.

SOLUTION :

To find equivalent ratios of 5 : 9, multiply both the terms by 2 and then 3.

$$\therefore \quad \frac{5}{9} = \frac{5 \times 2}{9 \times 2} = \frac{10}{18} = 10 : 18 \text{ and } \frac{5}{9} = \frac{5 \times 3}{9 \times 3} = \frac{15}{27} = 15 : 27$$

Thus, 10 : 18 and 15 : 27 are two equivalent ratios of 5 : 9.

ILLUSTRATION : 5

Fill in the blank box:

$$\frac{14}{21} = \frac{\Box}{3} = \frac{6}{\Box}$$

SOLUTION :

Let $\dfrac{14}{21} = \dfrac{x}{3}$ Then, $21x = 14 \times 3 \Rightarrow x = \dfrac{14 \times 3}{21} = 2$

Again, let $\dfrac{2}{3} = \dfrac{6}{y}$, then, $2y = 6 \times 3 \Rightarrow y = \dfrac{6 \times 3}{2} = 9$ Hence, $\dfrac{14}{21} = \dfrac{\boxed{2}}{3} = \dfrac{6}{\boxed{9}}$

Dividing some quantity in the given ratio

When we have to divide a quantity 'x' in the ratio $p : q$, then two parts are $\dfrac{p}{p+q} \times x$ and $\dfrac{q}{p+q} \times x$.

ILLUSTRATION : 6

Divide ₹ 1250 between Mayank and Ishita in the ratio 3 : 2.

SOLUTION :

Total money = ₹ 1250 and given ratio = 3 : 2. Sum of ratio terms = (3 + 2) = 5.

Mayank's share $= \left(\dfrac{3}{5} of ₹ 1250 \right) = ₹ \left(1250 \times \dfrac{3}{5} \right) = ₹ 750.$

Ishita's share $= \left(\dfrac{2}{5} of ₹ 1250 \right) = ₹ \left(1250 \times \dfrac{2}{5} \right) = ₹ 500.$

ILLUSTRATION : 7

Divide ₹ 1200 among A, B and C in the ratio 2 : 3 : 5.

SOLUTION :

Total money = ₹ 1200
Sum of ratio terms = (2 + 3 + 5) = 10.

A's share $₹ \left(1200 \times \dfrac{2}{10} \right) = ₹ 240.$ B's share $₹ \left(1200 \times \dfrac{3}{10} \right) = ₹ 360.$ C's share $₹ \left(1200 \times \dfrac{5}{10} \right) = ₹ 600.$

COMPARISON OF RATIOS

Suppose we want to compare two given ratios. Then, we express each one of them as a fraction in the simplest form. Now, compare these fractions by making their denominators equal.

ILLUSTRATION : 8

Compare the ratios 9 : 16 and 3 : 4.

SOLUTION :

Here,

$$9 : 16 = \dfrac{9}{16} \text{ and } 3 : 4 = \dfrac{3}{4}.$$

Now, let us compare $\dfrac{9}{16}$ and $\dfrac{3}{4}$. The LCM of 16 and 4 is 16.

Making the denominator of each fraction equal to 16, we have:

$$\frac{9}{16} = \frac{9 \times 1}{16 \times 1} = \frac{9}{16} \text{ and } \frac{3}{4} = \frac{3 \times 4}{4 \times 4} = \frac{12}{16}$$

Clearly, $\frac{12}{16} > \frac{9}{16} \Rightarrow \frac{3}{4} > \frac{9}{16}$ Hence, $3 : 4 > 9 : 16$.

PROPORTION

Proportion is defined as an equality of two ratios,

Four (non-zero) quantities of the same kind a, b, c and d are said to be in proportion if the ratio of a to b is equal to the ratio of c to d

i.e., if $\dfrac{a}{b} = \dfrac{c}{d}$

We can write as $a : b : : c : d$

Here, a, b, c, d are in proportion and are respectively known as first, second, third and fourth term of the given proportion.

Here, the 1st and 4th terms are called the **extreme terms** or **extremes**. The 2nd and 3rd terms are called the **middle terms** or **means**. We can also say, in proportion, Product of extremes = Product of means

If a, b, c, d are in proportion then,

$\dfrac{a}{b} = \dfrac{c}{d}$ or $a \times d = b \times c$

i.e. Product of extremes = Product of means

ILLUSTRATION : 9

Are the numbers 40, 30, 60 and 45 in proportion?

SOLUTION :

Given terms are 40, 30, 60 and 45

Product of extremes = $40 \times 45 = 1800$

Product of means = $30 \times 60 = 1800$

Product of extremes = Product of means

Thus 40, 30, 60 and 45 are in proportion.

Alternate method:

$$\text{Ratio of 40 to 30} = \frac{40}{30} = \frac{4}{3}; \text{ Ratio of 60 to 45} = \frac{60}{45} = \frac{4}{3}$$

Both the ratios are equal. Therefore the numbers are in proportion.

ILLUSTRATION : 10

Radha purchased 14 toffees for ₹35 and Geeta purchased 12 toffees for ₹ 30. Who bought more expensive toffees?

SOLUTION :

Ratio of the number of toffees purchased by Radha to the number of toffees purchased by Geeta: $14 : 12 = 7 : 6$

Ratio of their costs = $35 : 30 = 7 : 6$

Both ratios, $14 : 12$ and $35 : 30$ are equal

Thus, both purchased the toffees for the same price

ILLUSTRATION : 11

Find the value of x in the proportion $5 : 10 : : x : 30$.

SOLUTION :

Product of extremes = Product of means

So, $\quad 5 \times 30 = 10 \times x$ or $x = \dfrac{5 \times 30}{10} \Rightarrow 15$ Thus, $x = 15$

ILLUSTRATION : 12

For every 20 oranges that Raj buys, 4 turns out to be rotten. At this rate, how many rotten oranges will he have if he buys 100 oranges?

SOLUTION :

The ratio of rotten oranges to the oranges bought is 4 : 20.

Let, Raj has x rotten oranges if he buys 100 oranges Therefore, the ratio of rotten oranges to the oranges bought is x : 100.

Then, $\qquad\qquad\qquad 4 : 20 = x : 100$

Now Product of extremes = Product of means

$\Rightarrow 4 \times 100 = 20 \times x \Rightarrow \dfrac{4 \times 100}{20} = x \Rightarrow 20 = x$ or $x = 20$

Thus Raj has 20 rotten oranges if he buys 100 oranges

UNITARY METHOD

The method in which first we find the value of one unit and then the value of required number of units by multiplying the value of one unit with the number of required units.

ILLUSTRATION : 13

A car travels 240 km in 4 hours. How for does it travel in 7 hours?

SOLUTION :

We have,

Distance travelled in 4 hours = 240 km $\therefore$ Distance travelled in 1 hour = $\left(\dfrac{240}{4}\right)$ km = 60 km

Hence, the distance travelled in 7 hours = $(60 \times 7) = 420$ km

ILLUSTRATION : 14

The weight of 72 books is 9 kg.
(i)   What is the weight of 40 such books?
(ii) How many books will weight 4.5 kg?

SOLUTION :

(i)   Weight of 72 books = 9 kg $\Rightarrow$ Weight of 1 book = $\dfrac{9}{72}$ kg

Weight of 40 books = $\dfrac{9}{72} \times 40 = 5$ kg

(ii) 9 kg is the weight of 72 books

$\Rightarrow$ 1 kg is the weight of $\dfrac{72}{9}$ books

$\therefore$ 4.5 kg is the weight of $\dfrac{72}{9} \times 4.5 = 36$ books.

CONCEPT MAP

Ratio
• If a and b (b ≠ 0) are two quantities of the same kind, then the fraction $\dfrac{a}{b}$ is called ratio of a and b. It is denoted by 'a : b' where 'a' is called antecedent and 'b' is called 'consequent'.

Equivalent Ratio
• A ratio obtained by multiplying or dividing the numerator and denominator by the same number is called an equivalent ratio. For example $$= \dfrac{3}{4} = \dfrac{6}{8} = \dfrac{9}{12}$$

① ② ③ ④

Ratio and Proportion

Unitary Method
• The method in which first we find the value of one unit and then the value of required number of units by multiplying the value of one unit with the number of required units.

Proportion
• Four non-zero quantities of the same kind a, b, c and d are said to be in proportion, if the ratio of a to b is equal to the ratio of c to d i.e. $$\dfrac{a}{b} = \dfrac{c}{d} \text{ or } ad = bc$$ We can write as $$a : b :: c : d$$

MISCELLANEOUS
SOLVED EXAMPLES

1. Express each of the following ratios in the simplest form.
  (i) **35 : 49**   (ii) **3 kg 15 g : 450 g**
  (iii) **5 dozen : 6 scores**

Sol. (i) We have $35 : 49 = \dfrac{35}{49} = \dfrac{35 \div 7}{49 \div 7}$

$$= \frac{5}{7} = 5 : 7$$

[Dividing both numerator and denominator by 7, the H.C.F. of 35 and 49]

(ii) We have 3 kg 15 g : 450 g = 3015 g : 450 g

$$= \frac{3015}{450} = \frac{3015 \div 45}{450 \div 45}$$

[Dividing both numerator and denominator by 45, the H.C.F. of 3015 and 450]

$$= \frac{67}{10} = 67 : 10$$

(iii) We have 5 dozen : 6 scores = $5 \times 12 : 6 \times 20$

$$= 60 : 120 = \frac{60}{120} = \frac{60 \div 60}{120 \div 60}$$ [Dividing both

numerator and denominator by 60, the H.C.F. of 60 and 120]

$$= \frac{1}{2} = 1 : 2$$

2. Write the ratio of the following :
  (i) **1 m to 50 cm**   (ii) **500 g to 2 kg**

Sol. (i) Here, two terms are 1 m and 50 cm respectively.

So, we have to express both the terms in the same unit of measurement.

Now, we convert metre into centimetre.

So, 1 m = 100 cm

$\therefore$ Ratio of 1 m to 50 cm

$$= \frac{\overset{2}{\cancel{100\ cm}}}{\underset{1}{\cancel{50\ cm}}} = 2 : 1$$

(ii) Here, we convert 2 kilograms into grams.
So, 2 kg = 2000 g

$$\therefore \quad \text{Ratio} = \frac{\overset{1}{\cancel{500\ g}}}{\underset{4}{\cancel{2000\ g}}} = 1 : 4$$

3. The length and the breadth of a rectangular park are 75 m and 60 m respectively. What is the ratio of the length to the breadth of the park?

Sol. Length of the park = 75 m.
Breadth of the park = 60 m.
$\therefore$ length : breadth = 75 m : 60 m = 75 : 60

$$= \frac{75}{60} = \frac{75 \div 15}{60 \div 15} = \frac{5}{4} = 5 : 4$$

[$\therefore$ HCF of 75 and 60 is 15].
Hence, the required ratio is 5 : 4.

4. Two numbers are in the ratio 7 : 3 and their sum is 600. Find the numbers.

Sol. Let the first number be $7x$ and the second number be $3x$.

Then, their sum $= 7x + 3x = 600$
$$10x = 600$$
$$x = 60$$

The first number $= 7x = 7 (60) = 420$
The second number $= 3x = 3 (60) = 180$

5. Compare the ratios 2 : 5 and 4 : 7.

Sol. We have $2 : 5 = \dfrac{2}{5}$ and $4 : 7 = \dfrac{4}{7}$

The L.C.M. of 5 and 7 = $5 \times 7 = 35$

Now, $\dfrac{2}{5} = \dfrac{2 \times 7}{5 \times 7} = \dfrac{14}{35}$ and $\dfrac{4}{7} = \dfrac{4 \times 5}{7 \times 5} = \dfrac{20}{35}$

Since $20 > 14$, $\therefore \dfrac{20}{35} > \dfrac{14}{35} \Rightarrow \dfrac{4}{7} > \dfrac{2}{5}$

$$\Rightarrow \quad 4 : 7 > 2 : 5$$

6. Find three equivalent ratios of 3 : 4.

Sol. We have :

$$3 : 4 = \frac{3}{4} = \frac{3 \times 2}{4 \times 2} = \frac{3 \times 3}{4 \times 3} = \frac{3 \times 4}{4 \times 4}$$

$$\Rightarrow \quad 3:4 = \frac{3}{4} = \frac{6}{8} = \frac{9}{12} = \frac{12}{16}$$

$\Rightarrow \quad 3:4 = 6:8 = 9:12 = 12:16$

Hence, each one of $6:8$, $9:12$ and $12:16$ is equivalent to $3:4$.

7. Check if 20, 25, 12 and 15 are in proportion.

Sol. If $20, 25, 12$ and 15 are in proportion, then $20:25$ should be equal to $12:15$.

$$\frac{20}{25} = \frac{4}{5} \text{ or } 4:5$$
$$\frac{12}{15} = \frac{4}{5} \text{ or } 4:5$$
equal

Thus $20:25 :: 12:15$

Alternate method :

Product of extremes $= 20 \times 15 = 300$

Product of means $= 25 \times 12 = 300$

Since the product of extremes = Product of means

$\therefore 20, 25, 12$ and 15 are in proportion.

8. The 1st, 3rd and 4th terms of a proportion are 18, 27 and 36 respectively. Find the 2nd term.

Sol. Let the 2nd term of the proportion be x. Then,
$$18:x :: 27:36.$$

Now, product of means = product of extremes.

$$\therefore \quad x \times 27 = 18 \times 36 \Rightarrow x = \frac{18 \times 36}{27} = 24.$$

Hence, the 2nd term of the given proportion is 24.

9. On a map, a length of 4 cm is used to represent a distance of 250 km. If the actual distance between the two places is 6250 km, find the corresponding distance on the map. If the distance between two big cities on the map is 20 cm, find the actual distance between these two cities.

Sol. A distance of 250 km is represented on the map by 4 cm.

$\therefore$ A distance of 1 km is represented on the map by $\dfrac{4}{250}$ cm.

$\therefore$ A distance of 6250 km is represented on the

map by $\left(\dfrac{4}{250} \times 6250\right)$ cm $= 100$ cm.

$\therefore$ The required distance on the map is 100 cm. Again, a distance of 4 cm on the map represent 250 km.

$\therefore$ A distance of 1 cm on the map represents

$\dfrac{250}{4}$ km.

$\therefore$ A distance of 20 cm on the map represents

$\left(\dfrac{250}{4} \times 20\right)$ km $= 1250$ km.

$\therefore$ The required actual distance between the two cities is 1250 km.

10. A rectangular sheet has 3 m length and 200 cm breadth. Find the ratio of:
(a) Its width to its length
(b) Its width to its perimeter.

Sol. Length $(l) = 3$ m $= 3 \times 100 = 300$ cm

Breadth $(b) = 200$ cm

Perimeter $= 2 (\ell + b) = 2 (300 + 200)$
$$= 2 \times 500 = 1000 \text{ cm.}$$

(a) Ratio of its width to its length

$$= \frac{200}{300} = \frac{2}{3} = 2:3$$

(b) Ratio of its width to its perimeter

$$= \frac{200}{1000} = \frac{1}{5} = 1:5$$

11. An office opens at 10 a.m. and closes at 6 p.m. with a lunch interval of 30 minutes. What is the ratio of lunch interval to the total period of the office?

Sol. Total time from 10 a.m. to 6 p.m.
$$= 8 \text{ hrs}$$
$$= 8 \times 60 \text{ minutes} = 480 \text{ minutes}$$

Ratio of the lunch interval to total period

$$= \frac{30 \text{ minutes}}{480 \text{ minutes}} = 1:16$$

1 EXERCISE

Fill in the Blanks :

DIRECTIONS : *Complete the following statements with an appropriate word / term to be filled in the blank space(s).*

1. $8 : 9 = $ _______ $: 36$
2. $15 : $ _______ $= 1 : 7$
3. _______ $: 19 = 27 : 9$
4. $12 : 21 = 8 : $ _______.
5. ₹ $8.30 : $ ₹ $2.15 = $ _______ $: 344$ g
6. 5 boys : 13 boys = 475 cows : _______.
7. $\dfrac{14}{21} = \dfrac{\square}{3} = \dfrac{6}{\square}$
8. 90 cm $: 1.5$ m $= $ _______.
9. If $36 : 81 : : x : 63$, then $x = $ _______.
10. A comparison by _______ is called a radio.
11. In a proportion, the first and the fourth terms are called _______.

True / False :

DIRECTIONS : *Read the following statements and write your answer as true or false.*

1. To find the ratio of two quantities, we must express them in the same units.
2. An equivalent ratio of $2 : 3$ is $18 : 27$.
3. The simplest form of ratio $625 : 225$ is $25 : 10$.
4. If distance travelled by a car in 3 hrs is 120 km then distance travelled by car in 5 hrs is 240 km.
5. Ashish made 42 runs in 6 overs and Anup made 63 runs in 7 overs. Ashish made more runs per over.
6. Akul purchased 10 pens for ₹ 150 and Manish buys 7 pens for ₹ 84. Akul bought cheaper pens.
7. 30, 40, 45, 60 are in proportion.
8. $6 : 8$ and $9 : 12$ are equivalent ratios of $3 : 4$.
9. a dozen : a score $= 5 : 3$.
10. 60 p $: $ ₹ $3 = 1 : 5$.

Match the Columns :

DIRECTIONS : *Each question contains statements given in two columns which have to be matched. Statements (A, B, C, D) in column-I have to be matched with statements (p, q, r, s) in column-II.*

1.

	Column-I	Column-II
(A)	The length and width of a tape are 2 m and 28 cm, ratio of length and breadth is	(p) $5 : 2$
(B)	Ratio of 60 hrs to 600 min is	(q) $6 : 1$
(C)	Simplest form of the ratio $125 : 25$ is	(r) $50 : 7$
(D)	In the word ENGLISH the ratio of number of consonants to number of vowels	(s) $5 : 1$

Very Short Answer Questions :

DIRECTIONS : *Give answer in one word or one sentence.*

1. In the given figure, find the ratio of
   (i) No. of shaded parts to unshaded parts
   (ii) No. of unshaded parts to the total number of parts.

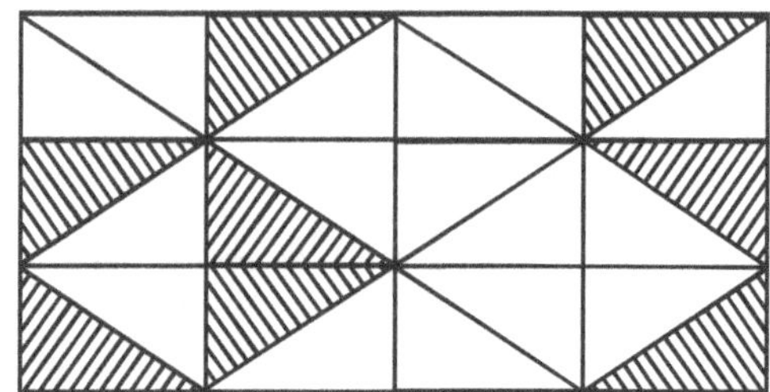

2. Express the following ratios into simplest form
   (i) 240 cm to a metre
   (ii) 40 min to 2 hrs

(iii) 50 paise to 4 rupees
(iv) 4 days to 2 weeks
(v) 500 g to 2kg
(vi) 108 to 360

3. The present ages of Ravi and Tanya are 22 years and 16 years, respectively, Find the ratio of
   (i) Their present ages
   (ii) Ravi's age to the difference of their ages.
   (iii) Ravi's age after 4 years to Tanya's age 3 years ago
   (iv) Ravi's age to that of Tanya's when she was 5 yeras old

4. Radha has 3 white marbles, 4 red marbles and 10 stones find the ratio of marbles to stones.

5. Fill in the blanks with $=$ or $\neq$

   (i) 12 Kg to 15 Kg $\square$ ₹ 28 to ₹ 35

   (ii) 20 to 30 $\square$ ₹ 4 to ₹ 6

   (iii) 60 m to 72 m $\square$ 48 m to 60 m

   (iv) ₹ 4500 to ₹ 5400 $\square$ ₹ 2500 to ₹ 3000

   (v) 2 L to 8 L $\square$ ₹ 3 to ₹ 12

6. What is the ratio of the number of sides of a square to the number of edges of a cube?

7. Neelam's annual income is ₹ 288000. Her annual savings amount to ₹ 36000. what is the ratio of her savings to her expenditure ?

8. I travel 126 km in 3 hours by bus and 315 km in 5 hours by train. Find ratio of speed of the bus and speed of the train.

9. Ashok is 25 years old and Anant is 10 years 6 months old. Find the ratio of the age of Anant to that of Ashok.

10. The length and breadth of a steel tape are 10 m and 2.4 cm, respectively. The ratio of the length to the breadth is

11. Find the ratio of the least prime number to the least composite number.

12. Express the following ratios in the simplest form:
   (i) 55 : 505   (ii) 50 paise : ₹ 10
   (iii) 2 kg 500 g : 3 kg   (iv) 2 h 40 min : 1 day
   (v) 5 l : 10 cm^3 (vi) 2h : 15 s
   (vii) 3 dozen : 4 scores

(viii) ₹ 5.50 : ₹ 15.75
(ix) 200 m : 2 km

Short Answer Questions :

DIRECTIONS : *Give answer in 2-3 sentences.*

1. Show that the numbers 16, 28, 4, 7 form a proportion.

2. If 25, 35, x are in proportion, find the value of x.

3. The ratio of father's age and his son's age is 5 : 2. If the father's age is 50 years, what is his son's age?

4. Find the cost of 15 kg. of sugar if 8 kg. of sugar costs ₹ 88.

5. A bus covers 250 km in 5 hours. How much distances will it cover in 12 hours?

6. Ratio of number of boys to number of girls in a tutorial is 2 : 3. If there are 180 girls, then find the number of boys.

7. Two numbers are in the ratio 5 : 4 and their sum is 162. Find the numbers.

8. In each of the following pairs of ratios, find the ratio which is greater:
   (i) 7 : 11 and 8 : 12
   (ii) 19 : 31 and 3 : 5
   (iii) ₹ 5. 40 : ₹ 3.60 and 3kg : 2 kg 500 g
   (iv) 1 h 30 min : 4 h 30 min and 600 m : 1 km 700 m

9. The ratio of zinc and copper in a brass piece is 13 : 7. How much zinc will be there in 100 kg. of such a piece ?

10. Divide ₹ 40 in the ratio of 3 : 2.

Long Answer Questions :

DIRECTIONS : *Give answer in four to five sentences.*

1. The weight of 72 books is 9 kg.
   (i) What is the weight of 40 such books?
   (ii) How many books will weight 4.5 kg?

2. The ratio of the number of girls to that of boys in a school is 7 : 12. If the number of boys in the school is 1380, find (i) the number of girls in the school and (ii) the total number of students in the school.

3. A woman worker earns ₹ 18000 in 15 months.
   (i) How much does she earn in 7 months?
   (ii) In how many months will she earn ₹ 30000?

4. The weight of 72 books is 9 kg.
   (i) What is the weight of 80 such books?
   (ii) How many such books weight 6 kg?

2 EXERCISE

Text-Book Exercise :

1. Cost of a toffee is 50 paise and cost of a chocolate is ₹ 10. Find the ratio of the cost of a toffee to the cost of a chocolate.

2. Fill in the following blanks:

$$\frac{15}{18} = \frac{\Box}{6} = \frac{10}{\Box} = \frac{\Box}{30}$$

   Are these equivalent ratios?

3. Find the ratio of the following:
   (i) 81 to 108
   (ii) 98 to 63
   (iii) 33 km to 121 km
   (iv) 30 minutes to 45 minutes

4. Find the ratio of the following:
   (i) 30 minutes to 1.5 hours
   (ii) 40 cm to 1.5 m
   (iii) 55 paise to ₹ 1
   (iv) 500 ml to 2 litres

5. Mother wants to divide ₹ 36 between her daughters Shreya and Bhoomika in the ratio of their ages. If age of Shreya is 15 years and age of Bhoomika is 12 years, find how much money Shreya and Bhoomika will get.

6. Present age of father is 42 years and that of his son is 14 years. Find the ratio of
   (i) Present age of father to the present age of son.
   (ii) Age of the father to the age of son, when son was 12 years old.
   (iii) Age of father after 10 years to the age of son after 10 years.
   (iv) Age of father to the age of son when father was 30 years old.

7. Determine if the following are in proportion.
   (i) 15, 45, 40, 120   (ii) 33, 121, 9, 96
   (iii) 24, 28, 36, 48   (iv) 32, 48, 70, 210

8. Determine if the following ratios form a proportion. Also, write the middle terms and extreme terms where the ratios form a proportion.
   (i) 25 cm : 1 m and ₹ 40 : ₹ 160
   (ii) 39 litres : 65 litres and 6 bottles : 10 bottles
   (iii) 2 kg : 80 kg and 25 g : 625 g
   (iv) 200 ml : 2.5 litre and ₹ 4 : ₹ 50

9. If it has rained 276 mm in the last 3 days, how many cm of rain will fall in one full week (7 days)? Assume that the rain continues to fall at the same rate.

10. Cost of 5 kg of wheat is ₹ 30.50.
    (i) What will be the cost of 8 kg of wheat?
    (ii) What quantity of wheat can be purchased in ₹ 61?

11. A car travels 90 km in $2\frac{1}{2}$ hours.
    (i) How much time is required to cover 30 km with the same speed?
    (ii) Find the distance covered in 2 hours with the same speed.

Exemplar Questions :

1. Reshma prepared 18 kg of burfi by mixing khoya with sugar in the ratio of 7 : 2. How much khoya did she use?

2. An office opens at 9 a.m. and closes at 5:30 p.m. with a lunch break of 30 minutes. What is the ratio of lunch break to the total period in the office?

3. The shadow of a 3 m long stick is 4 m long. At the same time of the day, if the shadow of a flagstaff is 24 m long, how tall is the flagstaff ?

4. A recipe calls for 1 cup of milk for every $2\frac{1}{2}$ cups of flour to make a cake that would feed

6 persons. How many cups of both flour and milk will be needed to make a similar cake for 8 persons?

5. In a floral design made from tiles each of dimensions 40 cm by 60 cm (see fig.), find the ratios of:
   (i) the perimeter of shaded portion to the perimeter of the whole design.
   (ii) the area of the shaded portion to the area of the unshaded portion.

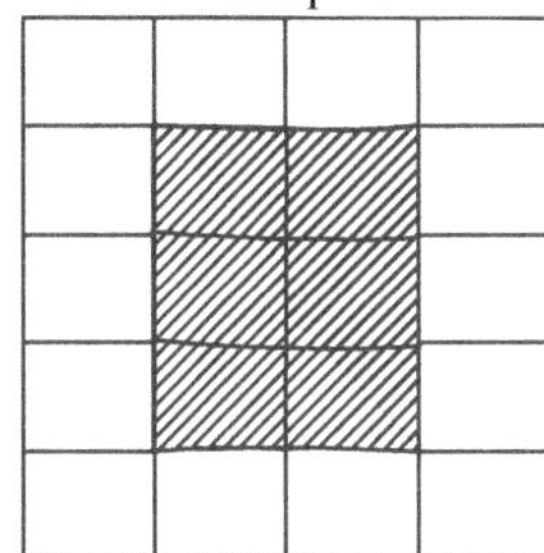

6. The earth rotates 360° about its axis in about 24 hours. By how much degree will it rotate in 2 hours?

7. The quarterly school fee in Kendriya Vidyalaya for Class VI is ₹ 540. What will be the fee for seven months?

8. In an election, the votes cast for two of the candidates were in the ratio 5 : 7. If the successful candidate received 20734 votes, how many votes did his opponent receive?

9. A metal pipe 3 metre long was found to weigh 7.6 kg. What would be the weight of the same kind of 7.8 m long pipe?

10. A recipe for raspberry jelly calls for 5 cups of raspberry juice and $2\dfrac{1}{2}$ cups of sugar. Find the amount of sugar needed for 6 cups of the juice?

HOTS Questions :

1. A tea merchant blends two varieties of tea costing her ₹ 234 and ₹ 130 per kg in the ratio of their costs. If the weight of the mixture is 84 kg, then find the weight of each variety of tea.

2. Length and breadth of the floor of a room are 5m and 3m, respectively. Forty tiles, each with area $\dfrac{1}{16}$ m^2 are used to 'cover the floor partially. Find the ratio of the tiled and the non tiled portion of the floor.

3. A carpenter had a board which measured 3m × 2m. She cut out a rectangular piece of 250cm × 90cm. What is the ratio of the area of cut out piece and the remaining piece?

4. Sunil and Anil together have ₹ 650 in the ratio 8 : 5 respectively. If they both spend ₹ 50 each, then what will be the ratio of the amounts left with them ?

3 EXERCISE

Single Option Correct :

DIRECTIONS : *This section contains multiple choice questions. Each question has 4 choices (a), (b), (c) and (d) out of which ONLY ONE is correct.*

1. The ratio of savings to expenses is 2 : 7. If the expenses are ₹ 3,500, then what was the total income?
   (a) ₹ 7,000   (b) ₹ 5,000
   (c) ₹ 4,500   (d) ₹ 5,500

2. In a box, the ratio of red marbles to blue marbles is 7 : 4. Which of the following could be the total number of marbles in the box?
   (a) 18   (b) 19
   (c) 21   (d) 22

3. On a shelf, books with green cover and that with brown cover are in the ratio 2 : 3. If there are 18 books with green cover, then the number of books with brown cover is
   (a) 12   (b) 24
   (c) 27   (d) 36

4. The ratio of two numbers is a : b. If one of them is x, then other is

(a) $\dfrac{ab}{x}$　　　　(b) $\dfrac{b}{ax}$

(c) $\dfrac{b}{a+b}x$　　　　(d) $\dfrac{bx}{a}$

5. In a cricket coaching camp, 1200 children are trained out of which 900 are selected for various matches. Ratio of non-selected children to the total number of children is
(a) 300 : 120　　　　(b) 4 : 1
(c) 1 : 4　　　　(d) 120 : 300

6. m : 32 : : 4 : 16 value of m is
(a) 16　　　　(b) 8
(c) 4　　　　(d) 2

7. There are 'b' boys and 'g' girls in a class. The ratio of the number of boys to the total number of students in the class is

(a) $\dfrac{b}{b+g}$　　　　(b) $\dfrac{g}{b+g}$

(c) $\dfrac{b}{g}$　　　　(d) $\dfrac{b+g}{b}$

8. 1500 sheets are required to make 100 notebooks. How many sheets will be required to make 12 note books?
(a) 180　　　　(b) 200
(c) 120　　　　(d) 100

9. To make a cup of tea ratio of water to milk is 3 : 1. So to make 4 cups of tea the ratio of water to milk is
(a) 4 : 3 : 1　　　　(b) 12 : 1
(c) 12 : 4　　　　(d) 4 : 12

10. In the word MATHEMATICS the ratio of number of consonants to the number of vowels is
(a) 4 : 7　　　　(b) 7 : 4
(c) 5 : 6　　　　(d) 6 : 5

11. In a quiz programme the ratio of correct answers to incorrect answers is 5 : 2. If 16 incorrect answers are given then the number of correct answers given is
(a) 80　　　　(b) 40
(c) 20　　　　(d) 30

12. Ajay and Vijay start a business investing ₹ 18000 and ₹ 24000 respectively. At the end of the year Ajay receives ₹ 9000 as his share in profit. What was the total profit made?

(a) ₹ 21000　　　　(b) ₹ 24000
(c) ₹ 18000　　　　(d) ₹ 15750

More Than One Option Correct :

DIRECTIONS : *This section contains multiple choice questions. Each question has 4 choices (a), (b), (c) and (d) out of which ONE or MORE may be correct.*

1. Ratio of 60 hrs. to 600 min. is
(a) 3600 : 600　　　　(b) 1 : 6
(c) 6 : 1　　　　(d) 5 : 1

2. The ratio of ₹ 3 and 60 paise is
(a) 1 : 20　　　　(b) 5 : 1
(c) 1 : 2　　　　(d) 20 : 4

3. Ratio of 250 ml to 2 L is
(a) 25 : 200　　　　(b) 8 : 1
(c) 1 : 8　　　　(d) 2 : 1

4. In an office the working hours are 10.30 AM to 5.30 PM and in between 30 minutes are spent on lunch. Find the ratio of office hours to the time spent for lunch.
(a) 420 : 30　　　　(b) 1 : 14
(c) 14 : 1　　　　(d) 30 : 7

5. Equivalent ratio to 3 : 4 are ______ .
(a) 4 : 3　　　　(b) 9 : 12
(c) 2 : 3　　　　(d) 15 : 20

6. Which of the following is an equivalent ratio of 4 : 9?
(a) 8 : 18　　　　(b) 28 : 63
(c) 17 : 13　　　　(d) 16 : 36

Assertion & Reason :

DIRECTIONS : *Each of these questions contains an Assertion followed by Reason. Read them carefully and answer the question on the basis of following options. You have to select the one that best describes the two statements.*

(a) If both **Assertion** and **Reason** are **correct** and **Reason** is the **correct explanation** of **Assertion**.

(b) If both **Assertion** and **Reason** are correct, but **Reason** is **not the correct explanation** of **Assertion**.

(c)   If **Assertion** is **correct** but **Reason** is **incorrect**.

(d)   If **Assertion** is **incorrect** but **Reason** is **correct**.

1.   **Assertion :** $3 : 5 : : 9 : 15$ are equivalent ratios.
        Reason : Both ratios are equal, when simplified.

2.   **Assertion :** If 3, 10, 15, 50 are in proportion, then 3 and 50 are middle terms and 10 and 15 are extreme terms.
        Reason : If a, b, c, d are in proportion then a and d are extreme terms and b and c are middle terms.

3.   **Assertion :** An equality of two ratios is called a proportion.
        Reason : Four quantities a, b, c, d are said to be in proportion if $a : b = c : d$

Passage Based Questions :

DIRECTIONS : *Study the given passage(s) and answer the following questions.*

PASSAGE-I

Prateek runs an ice cream parlour. He earns ₹3500 per month. He is able to save ₹1400 but spends the rest. Find the ratio of

1.   Prateek's income to his expenditure
        (a)   5 : 2   (b)   5 : 3
        (c)   3 : 5   (d)   2 : 5

2.   Prateek's income to his saving.
        (a)   5 : 2   (b)   2 : 5
        (c)   5 : 4   (d)   4 : 5

3.   Prateek's expenditure to his saving.
        (a)   2 : 3   (b)   5 : 3
        (c)   3 : 5   (d)   3 : 2

PASSAGE-II

Read the information given below carefully and answer the questions that follows.

" The ratio of the price of a pencil to the price of an eraser is 5:1"

4.   Which of the following object is more expensive?
        (a)   Eraser
        (b)   Pencil
        (c)   Both
        (d)   None of these

5.   If the price of the pencil is ₹10, can the price of the eraser be ₹ 20?
        (a)   No
        (b)   yes
        (c)   can't say
        (d)   Data is insufficient

6.   If the price of the eraser is ₹ 1, then what will be the price of the pencil ?
        (a)   ₹ 6   (b)   ₹ 4
        (c)   ₹ 5   (d)   ₹ 10

Integer Type Questions :

DIRECTIONS : *Answer the following questions. The answer to each of the question is a single digit integer, ranging from 0 to 9.*

1.   Weight of 45 bags of rice is 900 kg. How many bags of rice have a weight 140 kg?

2.   If $1 : 6 : : x : 18$ then find the value of x.

3.   If the simplest form of the ratio 13 : 65 is 1 : y. What is the value of y?

4.   In a box containing 30 bulbs, 5 are found defective. The ratio of defective to good bulbs is $c : d$. Find the value of $c + d$.

5.   The cost of 8 chocolates is ₹ 56. What will be the cost of 1 chocolates.

Multiple Matching Question :

DIRECTIONS : *Following question has four statements (A, B, C and D) given in Column-I and six statements (p, q, r, s, t, u) in Column-II. Any given statement in Column-I can have correct matching with one or more statement(s) given in Column-II.*

1.   **Match the following.**

Column-I	Column-II
(A) Ratio of 6 days to 2 weeks is	p. 3 : 5
(B) Ratio of 9 km to 18 m is	q. 1 : 4
(C) Ratio of 18 mm to 3 cm is	r. 500 : 1
(D) 3 months to 1 year	s. 3 : 7
	t. 6 : 10
	u. 3 : 12

SOLUTIONS

1 EXERCISE

Fill in the Blanks :

1. 32   2. 105   3. 57   4. 14
5. 1 kg 328 g   6. 1235 cows
7. 2, 9   8. 3 : 5   9. $x = 28$
10. division   11. extremes

True / False :

1. True   2. True   3. False   4. False   5. False
6. False   7 True   8. True   9. False   10. True

Match the Columns :

1. (A) → (r); (B) → (q); (C) → (s); (D) → (p)
   A : length = 2 m = 200 cm
        breadth = 28 cm

   $$\text{Ratio} = 200 : 28 = \frac{200}{28} = \frac{100}{14}$$

   $$= \frac{50}{7} = 50 : 7$$

   B : 60 hrs = 60×60 min. = 3600 min.

   $$\text{Ratio} = \frac{3600}{600} = \frac{6}{1} = 6 : 1$$

   C : $125 : 25 = \frac{125}{25} = \frac{5}{1} = 5 : 1$

   D : Number of consonant = 5
        = (N, G, L, S, H)
        Number of vowels = 2 = (E, I)
        Ratio of no. of consonants to the no. of
        vowels = 5 : 2

Very Short Answer Questions:

1. (i) 1 : 2   (ii) 2 : 3
2. (i) 12 : 5   (ii) 1 : 3
   (iii) 1 : 8   (iv) 2 : 7
   (v) 1 : 4   (vi) 3 : 10
3. (i) 11 : 8   (ii) 11 : 3
   (iii) 2 : 1   (iv) 11 : 5

4. 7 : 10
5. (i) =   (ii) =
   (iii) ≠   (iv) =
   (v) =
6. 1 : 3   7.   1 : 7

8. We know that speed = $\dfrac{\text{Distance}}{\text{Time}}$

   Speed of bus = $\dfrac{126}{3}$ km/h

   Speed of train = $\dfrac{315}{5}$ km/h

   Ratio of speeds = 42 : 63 = 2 : 3

9. Anant's age = 10 years 6 months

   $$= 10 \text{ years } \frac{6}{12} = 10.5 \text{ years}$$

   Ratio of Anant's age and Ashok's age

   $$= 10.5 : 25 = \frac{105}{10 \times 25} = \frac{21}{50}$$

10. 1250 : 3
11. Least prime : Least composite number
    $$= 2 : 4 \text{ or } 1 : 2$$
12. (i) 11 : 101   (ii) 1 : 20   (iii) 5 : 6
    (iv) 1 : 9   (v) 500 : 1   (vi) 480 : 1
    (vii) 9 : 20   (viii) 22 : 63 (ix) 1 : 10

Short Answer Questions :

1. The given trems are 16, 28, 4, 7.
   Product of extremes = 16 × 7 = 112.
   Product of means = 28 × 4 = 112.
   ∴ Product of extremes = Product of means.
   Hence, 16, 28, 4, 7 are in proportion.
2. 25, 35, x are in proportion
   ⇒ 25, 35, 35, x are in proportion
   ⇒ 25 : 35 : : 35 : x
   ⇒ 25 × x = 35 × 35
        [product of extremes = product of means]

$$\Rightarrow \quad x = \frac{35 \times 35}{25} = 49.$$

Hence, $x = 49$.

3. Let the son's age be x years. Then $5 : 2 = 50 : x$

$\therefore 5x = 2 \times 50$

$$\Rightarrow \quad x = \frac{2 \times 50}{5} = 20$$

Hence, the son's age is 20 years.

4. Cost of 8 kg. of sugar = ₹ 88

$$\text{Cost of 1 kg. of sugar} = \frac{88}{8}$$

$$\text{Cost of 15 kg. of sugar} = \frac{88}{8} \times 15$$

$$= ₹ 165$$

5. Distance covered in 5 hours = 250 km.

$$\text{Distance covered in 1 hour} = \frac{250}{5} \text{ km}$$

Distance covered in 12 hour

$$= \frac{250}{5} \times 12 = 600 \text{ km}$$

6. Boys to girls = 2 : 3

Girls = 180

Boys = x

$$\frac{2}{3} = \frac{x}{180}$$

$$x = \frac{2 \times 180}{3} = 120$$

Boys = 120

7. Let the required numbers be $5x$ and $4x$. Then,

$$5x + 4x = 162 \Rightarrow 9x = 162$$

$$\Rightarrow x = \frac{162}{9} = 18.$$

So, the numbers are (5×18) and (4×18), i.e., 90 and 72.

8. (i) $8 : 12$ (ii) $19 : 31$

(iii) ₹ 5.40 : ₹ 3.60

(iv) 600 m : 1 km 700 m

9. Sum of ratios = 13 + 7 = 20

$$\text{Quantity of zinc} = \frac{13}{20} \times 100 = 65 \text{ Kg.}$$

10. Sum of terms of ratio = 3 + 2 = 5.

$$\text{1st part of ₹ 40} = \frac{3}{\cancel{5}} \times \cancel{40}^{8} = ₹ 24.$$

$$\text{2nd part of ₹ 40} = \frac{2}{\cancel{5}} \times \cancel{40}^{8} = ₹ 16.$$

Long Answer Questions :

1. (i) Weight of 72 books = 9 kg

$$\Rightarrow \text{ Weight of 1 book} = \frac{9}{72} \text{ kg}$$

$$\therefore \text{ Weight of 40 books} = \frac{9}{72} \times 40 = 5 \text{ kg}$$

(ii) 9 kg is the weight of 72 books

$$\Rightarrow \quad 1 \text{ kg is the weight of } \frac{72}{9} \text{ books}$$

$$\therefore 4.5 \text{ kg is the weight of } \frac{72}{9} \times 4.5 = 36 \text{ books}$$

2. It is given that ratio of girls to boys = 7 : 12.

(i) Let the number of girls in the school be x. then,

$$7 : 12 = x : 1380$$

$$\Rightarrow \quad 7 : 12 :: x : 1380$$

$$\Rightarrow \quad 12 \times x = 7 \times 1380$$

[$\because$ Product of means = Product of extremes]

$$\Rightarrow \quad x = \frac{7 \times 1380}{12} = 805.$$

$\therefore$ Number of girls in the school = 805.

(ii) Total number of students in the school

$$= (805 + 1380) = 2185.$$

3. (i) We have,

Income for 15 months = ₹ 18000

$$\therefore \text{ Income for 1 month} = ₹ \left(\frac{18000}{15} \right)$$

Hence, income for 7 months

$$= ₹ \left(\frac{18000}{15} \times 7 \right)$$

$$= ₹ (1200 \times 7) = ₹ 8400.$$

Thus, she earns ₹ 8400 in 7 months.

(ii) In this case, the number of months is unknown quantity and the income is the known quantity. So, we proceed as follows:

Number of months required to earn ₹ 18000 = 15

∴ Number of months required to earn

$$₹\,1 = \left(\dfrac{15}{18000}\right)$$

Hence, number of months required to earn

$$= ₹\,30000$$

$$= \left(\dfrac{15}{18000} \times 30000\right) = 25$$

Thus, she will earn ₹ 30000 in 25 months.

4. **(i)** We have,

Weight of 72 books = 9 kg

∴ Weight of 1 book $= \dfrac{9}{72}$ kg

Hence, weight of 80 books

$$= \left(\dfrac{9}{72} \times 80\right) \text{kg} = 10 \text{ kg}$$

Thus, the weight of 80 books is 10 kg.

(ii) Here, weight is the known quantity and the number of books is the unknown quantity. So, we proceed as follows.

The number of books in 9 kg of weight = 72

∴ The number of books in 1 kg weight

$$= \dfrac{72}{9} = 8$$

Hence, the number of books in 6 kg weight = 8 × 6 = 48

Thus, the number of books in 6 kg weight is 48.

2 EXERCISE

1. Cost of chocolate = ₹ 10 = 1000 paise

$$[\because ₹\,1 = 100 \text{ paise}]$$

∴ Ratio $= \dfrac{\text{Cost of toffee}}{\text{Cost of chocolate}}$

$$= \dfrac{50}{1000} = \dfrac{1}{20} = 1:20$$

2. $\dfrac{15}{18} = \dfrac{\square}{6} \Rightarrow 15 \times 6 = \square \times 18$

or $\square = \dfrac{15 \times 6}{18} = 5$

$$\dfrac{15}{18} = \dfrac{10}{\square} \Rightarrow 15 \times \square = 10 \times 18$$

or $\square = \dfrac{10 \times 18}{15} = 12$

$$\dfrac{15}{18} = \dfrac{\square}{30} \Rightarrow 15 \times 30 = 18 \times \square$$

or $\square = \dfrac{15 \times 30}{18} = 25$

Thus, $\dfrac{15}{18} = \dfrac{\boxed{5}}{6} = \dfrac{10}{\boxed{12}} = \dfrac{\boxed{25}}{30}$

$$\therefore \dfrac{15}{18} = \dfrac{5}{6} = \dfrac{10}{12} = \dfrac{25}{30} \left(\text{each} = \dfrac{5}{6}\right)$$

Thus, ratios are equivalent.

3. **(i)** Ratio $= \dfrac{81}{108} = \dfrac{81 \div 27}{108 \div 27} = \dfrac{3}{4} = 3:4$

(ii) Ratio $= \dfrac{98}{63} = \dfrac{98 \div 7}{63 \div 7} = \dfrac{14}{9} = 14:9$

(iii) Ratio $= \dfrac{33\text{km}}{121\text{km}} = \dfrac{33 \div 11}{121 \div 11} = \dfrac{3}{11} = 3:11$

(iv) Ratio $= \dfrac{30\,\text{minutes}}{45\,\text{minutes}} = \dfrac{30 \div 15}{45 \div 15} = \dfrac{2}{3} = 2:3$

4. **(i)** $\dfrac{30\,\text{minutes}}{1.5\,\text{hour}} = \dfrac{30\,\text{minutes}}{90\,\text{minutes}}$

$$\left[\because 1.5 \text{ hour} = \dfrac{15}{10} \times 60 \text{ minutes} = 90 \text{ minutes}\right]$$

$$= \dfrac{30}{90} = \dfrac{30 \div 30}{90 \div 30} = \dfrac{1}{3} = 1:3$$

(ii) Ratio $= \dfrac{40\text{cm}}{1.5\text{m}} = \dfrac{40\text{cm}}{150\text{cm}}$

$$\left[\therefore\ 1m = 100\ cm\ \therefore 1.5\ m = \frac{15}{10} \times 100cm = 150\ cm \right]$$

$$= \frac{40}{150} = \frac{40 \div 10}{150 \div 10} = \frac{4}{15} = 4 : 15$$

(iii) Ratio of 55 paise to ₹ 1 $= \dfrac{55\ paise}{₹\,1}$

$$[\therefore\ ₹\,1 = 100\ paise]$$

$$= \frac{55}{100} = \frac{55 \div 5}{100 \div 5}$$

$$[\therefore\ HCF\ of\ 55\ and\ 100\ is\ 5]$$

$$= \frac{11}{20} = 11 : 20$$

(iv) Ratio of 500 ml to 2 litre

$$= \frac{500\ ml}{2\ litres} \qquad [\because\ 1\ litre = 1000\ ml]$$

$$= \frac{500\ ml}{2000\ ml} = \frac{500}{2000}$$

$$[\because\ HCF\ of\ 500\ and\ 2000\ is\ 500]$$

$$= \frac{500 \div 500}{2000 \div 500} = \frac{1}{4} = 1 : 4$$

5. $\therefore$ Ratio of their ages $= \dfrac{15\ years}{12\ years} = \dfrac{15 \div 3}{12 \div 3} = \dfrac{5}{4}$

Sum of the ratios $= 5 + 4 = 9$

$\therefore$ Shreya's share $= ₹\ \dfrac{5}{9} \times 36 = ₹\ 20$

Bhoomika's share $= ₹\ \dfrac{4}{9} \times 36 = ₹\ 16$

6. (i) $\therefore$ Ratio $= \dfrac{Age\ of\ father}{Age\ of\ son}$

$$= \frac{42\ years}{14\ years} = \frac{42 \div 14}{14 \div 14}$$

$$= \frac{3}{1} = 3 : 1$$

(ii) Obviously when son's age was 12 years (i.e. 2 years ago), then father's age was (42 years – 2 years) = 40 years.

$\therefore$ Ratio of father's age to son's age

$$\frac{40\ years}{12\ years} = \frac{40 \div 4}{12 \div 4} = \frac{10}{3} = 10 : 3$$

(iii) After 10 years

Age of father = 42 years + 10 years = 52 years

Age of son = 14 years + 10 years = 24 years

$\therefore$ Ratio of father's age to son's age

$$= \frac{52\ years}{24\ years} = \frac{52 \div 4}{24 \div 4} = \frac{13}{6} = 13 : 6$$

(iv) $\therefore\ 42 - 30 = 12$

$\therefore$ 12 years age, age of father was $= 30$ years

and 12 years age, age of son was $= 14\ years - 12\ years = 2\ years$

$\therefore$ Ratio of father's age the son's age

$$= \frac{30\ years}{2\ years} = \frac{30 \div 2}{2 \div 2} = \frac{15}{1} = 15 : 1$$

7. (i) Ratio of 15 and 45 = 15 : 45

$$= \frac{15}{45} = \frac{15 \div 15}{45 \div 15} = \frac{1}{3} = 1 : 3$$

$$[\therefore\ HCF\ of\ 15\ and\ 45\ is\ 15]$$

Ratio of 40 and 120 = 40 : 120

$$= \frac{40}{120} = \frac{40 \div 40}{120 \div 40} = \frac{1}{3} = 1 : 3$$

$$[\therefore HCF\ of\ 40\ and\ 120\ is\ 40]$$

$\therefore\ 15 : 45 :: 40 : 120$

(ii) 33, 121, 9, 96

Here, ratio of 33 and 121 = 33 : 121

$$= \frac{33}{121} = \frac{33 \div 11}{121 \div 11} = \frac{3}{11} = 3 : 11$$

Ratio of 9 and 96 = 9 : 96

$$= \frac{9}{96} = \frac{9 \div 3}{96 \div 3} = \frac{3}{32} = 3 : 32$$

Since, $3 : 11 \neq 3 : 32$

$\therefore$ 33, 121, 9 and 96 are not in proportion.

(iii) 24, 28, 36, 48;

$\therefore$ Ratio of 24 and 28 = 24 : 28

$$= \frac{24}{28} = \frac{24 \div 4}{28 \div 4} = \frac{6}{7} = 6 : 7$$

Ratio of 36 and 48 = 36 : 48

$$= \frac{36}{48} = \frac{36 \div 12}{48 \div 12} = \frac{3}{4} = 3 : 4$$

i.e. $6 : 7 \neq 3 : 4$

or $24 : 28 \neq 36 : 48$

$\therefore$ 24, 28, 36 and 48 are not in proportion.

(iv) 32, 48, 70, 210

Ratio of 32 and 48 $= 32 : 48$

$$= \frac{32}{48} = \frac{32 \div 16}{48 \div 16} = \frac{2}{3} = 2 : 3$$

Ratio of 70 and 210 $=$

$$\frac{70}{210} = \frac{70 \div 70}{210 \div 70} = \frac{1}{3} = 1 : 3$$

Since $2 : 3 \neq 1 : 3$

i.e. $32 : 48 \neq 70 : 210$

$\therefore$ 32, 48, 70, 210 are not in proportion.

8. (i) $\dfrac{25\,cm}{1\,m} = \dfrac{25\ cm}{100\ cm} = \dfrac{25 \div 25}{100 \div 25} = \dfrac{1}{4} = 1 : 4$

and $\overline{}40 : \overline{}160 = \dfrac{\overline{}40}{\overline{}160} = \dfrac{40}{160}$

$$= \frac{40 \div 40}{160 \div 40} = \frac{1}{4} = 1 : 4$$

Since, both the ratios are equal,

$\therefore$ They form a proportion.

Now, middle terms are 1m and ₹ 40 and

extreme terms are 25 cm and ₹ 160.

(ii) We have, 39 litres : 65 litres $= \dfrac{39\,litres}{65\,litres}$

$$\frac{39}{65} = \frac{39 \div 13}{65 \div 13} = \frac{3}{5} = 3 : 5$$

and 6 bottles : 10 bottles

$$\frac{6}{10} = \frac{6 \div 2}{10 \div 2} = \frac{3}{5} = 3 : 5$$

Since, both the ratios are equal

$\therefore$ 39 litres : 65 litres : : 6 bottles : 10 bottles

Its middle terms are 65 litres and 6 bottles.

(iii) We have, 2 kg : 80 kg

$$= \frac{2}{80} = \frac{2 \div 2}{80 \div 2} = \frac{1}{40} = 1 : 40$$

and 25 g : 625 g

$$= \frac{25}{625} = \frac{25 \div 25}{625 \div 25} = \frac{1}{25} = 1 : 25$$

Since $1 : 40 \neq 1 : 25$

$\therefore$ The given ratios do not form a proportion.

(iv) 200 ml : 2.5 litres

$$= \frac{200\,ml}{2.5\ litres} = \frac{200\ ml}{2.5 \times 1000\,ml}$$

$$[\therefore\ 1\ litre = 1000\ ml]$$

$$= \frac{200}{2500} = \frac{200 \div 100}{2500 \div 100} = \frac{2}{25} = 2 : 25$$

and ₹ 4 : ₹ 50

$$= \frac{₹\,4}{₹\,50} = \frac{4}{50} = \frac{4 \div 2}{50 \div 2} = \frac{2}{25} = 2 : 25$$

Since the two ratios are equal,

i.e. 200 ml : 2.5 litres $=$ ₹ 4 : ₹ 50

$\therefore$ They form a proportion.

Its middle terms are 2.5 litres and ₹ 4.

Its extreme terms are 200 ml and ₹ 50.

9. $\therefore$ Measure of rainfall in 3 days $= 276$ mm

$\therefore$ Measure of rainfall in 1 day

$$= \frac{276}{3}\ mm = 92\ mm$$

So, measure of rainfall in 7 days $= (92 \times 7)$ mm

$$= 644\ mm$$

10. (i) $\therefore$ Cost of 5 kg of wheat $=$ ₹ 30.50

Cost of 1 kg of wheat $=$ ₹ $\dfrac{30.50}{5}$

$$= ₹\ \frac{30.50}{5} \times \frac{1}{100} = ₹\ \frac{61}{10}$$

So, cost of 8 kg of wheat $= ₹\ \left(\dfrac{61}{10} \times 8 \right)$

$$= ₹\ \frac{488}{100} = ₹\ 48.80$$

(ii) Quantity of wheat that can be purchased

for ₹ $\dfrac{61}{10} = 1$ kg

$\therefore$ Quantity of wheat that can be purchased

for ₹ $1 = \dfrac{1 \times 10}{61}$ kg

So, quantity of wheat that can be purchased

for $₹ 61 = \dfrac{1 \times 10}{61} \times 61$ kg = 10 kg

Thus, (i) Cost of 8 kg of wheat is ₹ 48.80

(ii) 10 kg of wheat can be purchased in ₹ 61.

11. (i) $2\dfrac{1}{2}$ hours $= \dfrac{5}{2}$ hours $= \dfrac{5}{2} \times 60$ minutes

= 150 minutes.

90 km is covered in 150 minutes

Therefore, 1 km can be covered in

$\dfrac{150}{90}$ minutes

Therefore, 30 km can be covered in $\dfrac{150}{90} \times$

30 minutes i.e. 50 minutes

Thus, 30 km can be covered in 50 minutes.

(ii) Distance, covered in $2\dfrac{1}{2}$ hours

(i.e. $\dfrac{5}{2}$ hours) = 90 km

Therefore, distance covered in 1 hours

$= 90 \div \dfrac{5}{2}$ km $= 90 \times \dfrac{2}{5} = 36$ km

Therefore, distance covered in 2 hours

$= 36 \times 2 = 72$ km.

Thus, in 2 hours, distance covered is 72 km.

Exemplar Questions :

1. Total weight of burfi = 18 kg.

Sum of ratios = 7 + 2 = 9

∴ Quantity of khoya $= \left(\dfrac{7}{9} \times 18\right)$ kg = 14 kg

2. Time duration between 9 a.m. and 5.30 p.m.

= 3 hr + 5 hr 30 min.

= 8 hr 30 min.

= 8 × 60 + 30

= 510 min.

The ratio of lunch break to total period in the office = 30 : 510

$= \dfrac{30}{510} = \dfrac{1}{17} = 1 : 17$

3. Let the height of flagstaff be x meter.

$\Rightarrow \dfrac{3}{4} = \dfrac{x}{24} \Rightarrow x = \dfrac{3 \times 24}{4} = 18$

4. Milk needed for cake to serve 6 persons

= 1 cup.

∴ Milk needed for cake to serve 8 persons

$= \dfrac{1}{6} \times 8 = \dfrac{4}{3} = 1\dfrac{1}{3}$ cups

Flour needed for cake to serve 6 persons

$= 2\dfrac{1}{2} = \dfrac{5}{2}$ cups

∴ Flour needed for cake to serve 8 persons

$= \dfrac{5 \times 8}{2 \times 6} = \dfrac{10}{3}$ cups.

Total quantity of flour and milk

$= \dfrac{4}{3} + \dfrac{10}{3} = \dfrac{14}{3} = 4\dfrac{2}{3}$ cups.

5. Dimensions of each tile is 40 cm by 60 cm.

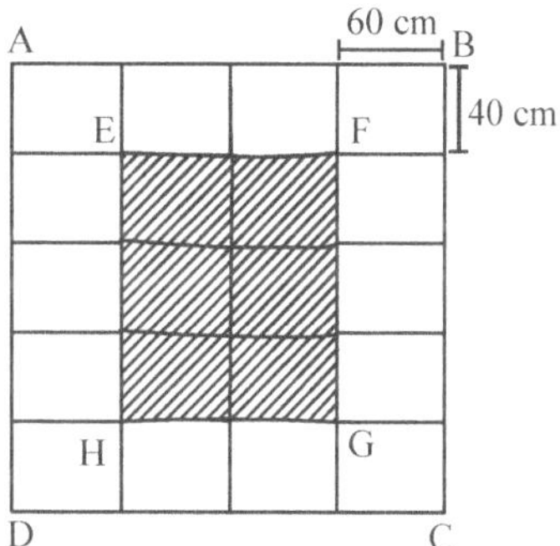

(i) ∴ AB = 4 × 60 cm = 240 cm

BC = 5 × 40 cm = 200 cm

∴ Perimeter of whole design

= 2 (240 + 200) = 880 cm

EF = 2 × 60 cm = 120 cm

FG = 3 × 40 cm = 120 cm

∴ Perimeter of shaded portion

= 2 (120 + 120) = 480

∴ The ratio of the perimeter of shaded portion to the perimeter of the whole design = 480 : 880

= 6 : 11

(ii) Since each tile covers same area and number of tiles covering shaded portion = 6.

Number of tiles covering unshaded portion = 14

$\therefore$ The area of the shaded portion to the area of the unshaded portion

$$= 6 : 14 = 3 : 7$$

6. The earth rotates in 24 hours $= 360°$

The earth rotates in 1 hour $= \dfrac{360°}{24} = 15°$

$\therefore$ The earth rotates in 2 hours $= 2 \times 15° = 30°$

7. The fee for three months $=$ ₹ 540

$\therefore$ The fee for 1 month $=$ ₹ $540 \div 3 =$ ₹ 180

$\therefore$ The fee for 7 months $=$ ₹ $180 \times 7 =$ ₹ 1260

8. Let the opponent receive votes

$\therefore 5 : 7 = x : 20734$

$$\Rightarrow \quad x = \dfrac{5 \times 20734}{7}$$

$$= 5 \times 2962 = 14810$$

9. Let the weight of pipe be x kg

$$\therefore \quad \dfrac{7.6}{3} = \dfrac{x}{7.8}$$

$$\Rightarrow \quad x = \dfrac{7.6 \times 7.8}{3} = 19.76 \text{ kg}$$

10. Let the amount of sugar be x cups.

$$\therefore \quad \dfrac{6}{5} = \dfrac{x}{2\frac{1}{2}}$$

$$\Rightarrow \quad x = \dfrac{6}{5} \times 2\frac{1}{2} = \dfrac{6}{5} \times \dfrac{5}{2} = 3 \text{ cups.}$$

HOTS Questions :

1. The ratio of the cost of two varieties of tea

$$= 130 : 234$$

$$= \dfrac{130}{234} = \dfrac{5}{9} = 5 : 9$$

Sum of ratios $= 5 + 9 = 14$

$\therefore$ The weight of variety – I of tea

$$= 84 \times \dfrac{5}{14} = 6 \times 5 = 30 \text{ kg}$$

The weight of variety – II of tea

$$= 84 \times \dfrac{9}{14} = 6 \times 9 = 54 \text{ kg}$$

2. Area of the floor of room $= 5$ m $\times 3$ m $= 15$ m^2

Area of a tile $= \dfrac{1}{16}$ m^2

$\therefore$ Area of 40 tiles $= \left(40 \times \dfrac{1}{16}\right)$ m$^2 = \dfrac{5}{2}$ m^2

Area of non-tiled portion of the floor

$$= \left(15 - \dfrac{5}{2}\right) \text{m}^2 = \dfrac{25}{2} \text{ m}^2$$

The ratio of the tiled to non tiled portion

$$= \dfrac{5/2}{25/2} = 1 : 5$$

3. Area of the board $= (3 \times 2)$m$^2 = 6$ m^2

Area of cut out piece

$$= \left(\dfrac{250}{100} \times \dfrac{90}{100}\right) \text{m}^2 = 2.25 \text{ m}^2$$

$\therefore$ Area of remaining piece $= (6 - 2.25)$m^2
$$= 3.75 \text{ m}^2$$

$\therefore$ The ratio of the area of cut out piece to remaining piece $= 2.25 : 3.75$

$$= \dfrac{2.25}{3.75} = \dfrac{3}{5} = 3 : 5$$

4. Total amount with Sunil & Anil $=$ ₹ 650

Amount with Sunil $= \dfrac{650 \times 8}{13} =$ ₹ 400

Amount with Anil $= \dfrac{650 \times 5}{13} =$ ₹ 250

When both spend ₹ 50 each the amount left with Sunil and Anil will be ₹ 350 and ₹ 200 respectively.

Ratio $= 350 : 200 = 7 : 4$

3 E X E R C I S E

Single Option Correct :

1. (c) Savings : Expenses $= 2 : 7$

Expenses $= \dfrac{7}{9}$ (2 + 7 Total)

$$\dfrac{7}{9} = 3,500 \qquad \text{(Given)}$$

$$\text{Total Income} = 3{,}500 \div \frac{7}{9}$$

$$= \frac{3500 \times 9}{7} = ₹\ 4{,}500$$

2. **(d)**

3. **(c)**

4. **(d)** Let the required number be y.

$$a : b :: x : y$$

$$a \times y = b \times x$$

$$y = \frac{bx}{a}$$

5. **(c)** $1200 - 900 = 300$ (non -selected)

$$300 : 1200$$

$$1 : 4$$

6. **(b)** $m : 32 :: 4 : 16$

$$m \times 16 = 32 \times 4$$

$$m = \frac{32 \times 4}{16} = 8.$$

7. **(a)**

8. **(a)**

9. **(c)** Water to milk = 3 : 1

4 cups of tea = 12 : 4

10. **(b)** (M T H M T C S) consonants = 7

(A E A I) vowels = 4

con : vow = 7 : 4

11. **(b)** Correct ans : incorrect ans 5 : 2

Incorrect ans = 16

Correct ans = x

$$\frac{5}{2} = \frac{x}{16}$$

$$\frac{5 \times 16}{2} = x$$

$$40 = x$$

12. **(a)** As the investment is for the same period of time, ratio of profits is same as ratio of investments.

$$\therefore\ A : V = 18000 : 24000 = 3 : 4$$

Ajay receives ₹ 9000 as his share in profit.

$$\therefore\ 3 \text{ parts} = 9{,}000$$

$$\therefore\ 4 \text{ parts} = \frac{9000}{3} \times 4 = ₹\ 12000$$

$$\therefore\ \text{Total profit} = 9{,}000 + 12000 = ₹\ 21{,}000$$

1. **(a, c)** $60 \times 60 = 3600$ min : 600 min

$$3600 : 600$$

$$6 : 1$$

2. **(b, d)** ₹ 3 : 60 p = 300 p : 60p = 5 : 1

3. **(a, c)** 2 L = 2000 ml

$$250 : 2000 = \quad 25 : 200 = 1 : 8.$$

4. **(a, c)** Office hours = 10.30 AM to 5.30 PM

$$= 7 \text{ hrs} = 420 \text{ min.}$$

Lunch time = 30 min.

Ratio = 420 : 30 = 14 : 1

5. **(b, d)** As, $\dfrac{3}{4} = \dfrac{3 \times 3}{4 \times 3} = \dfrac{9}{12} = 9 : 12$

and $\dfrac{3 \times 5}{4 \times 5} = \dfrac{15}{20} = 15 : 20$

6. **(a, b, d)**

Clearly, 17 : 13 is not equivalent to 4 : 9.

1. **(a)**

2. **(d)** 3 and 50 are extreme terms and 10 and 15 are middle terms.

Assertion : False, Reason : True

3. **(b)** Both assertion and reason are correct but reason is not correct explanation for assertion.

1. **(b)** Prateek's income = ₹ 3500

His expenditure = ₹ (3500 – 1400) = ₹2100

Ratio of 3500 : 2100 = 5 : 3

2. **(a)** Prateek's income = ₹ 3500

His saving = ₹1400

Ratio = 3500 : 1400 = 5 : 2

3. **(d)** Prateek's expenditure = ₹ 2100

His saving = ₹1400

Ratio = 2100 : 1400 = 3 : 2.

4. **(b)** Pencil is more expensive.

5.   **(a)**   If the price of the pencil is ₹ 10 then price of the eraser will be ₹ 2.

6.   **(c)**   Price of pencil = ₹ 5.

Integer Type Questions :

1.   **(7)** Number of bags of rice which have weight 900 kg = 45

Number of bags of rice which has weight

$$1 \text{ kg} = \frac{45}{900}$$

Number of bags of rice which has weight of 140 kg

$$= \frac{45}{900} \times 140 = 7 \text{ kg}$$

2.   **(3)** If $1 : 6 :: x : 18$

$$\Rightarrow \quad \frac{1}{6} = \frac{x}{18}$$

Clearly, $\dfrac{1 \times 3}{6 \times 3} = \dfrac{3}{18} = \dfrac{x}{18} \Rightarrow x = 3$

3.   **(5)** $13 : 65$ is simplified as

$$\frac{13}{65} = \frac{13 \div 13}{65 \div 13} = \frac{1}{5} = \frac{1}{y}$$

$$\Rightarrow \quad y = 5$$

4.   **(6)** Good bulbs = total bulbs – defected bulbs

$$= 30 - 5 = 25 \text{ bulbs}$$

Ratio of defective to the good bulbs

$$= \frac{5}{25} = \frac{1}{5} = 1 : 5$$

So, $c : d = 1 : 5 \; \therefore \; c + d = 1 + 5 = 6$

5.   **(7)** Cost of 8 chocolates = 56

Cost of 1 chocolates $= \dfrac{56}{8} = ₹ 7$

Multiple Matching Question :

1.   (A) $\rightarrow$ (s); (B) $\rightarrow$ (r); (C) $\rightarrow$ (p, t) ; (D) $\rightarrow$ (q, u)

(A) 2 weeks = (2 × 7) days = 14 days

Ratio of 6 days to 2 weeks $= 6 : 14 = \dfrac{6}{14}$

$$= \frac{3}{7} = 3 : 7$$

(B) 9 km (9 × 1000)m = 9000 m

Ratio of 9 km to 18 m = 9000 : 18

$$= \frac{9000}{18} = \frac{500}{1} = 500 : 1$$

(C) $\therefore 3$ cm = (3 × 10) mm = 30 mm

$\therefore$ Ratio of 18 mm to 3 cm

$$= 18 : 30 = \frac{18}{30} = \frac{3}{5} = 3 : 5 = 6 : 10$$

(D) $\therefore$ 1 year = 12 months

$\therefore$ Ratio of 3 months to 1 year

$$= 3 : 12 = 1 : 4$$

Symmetry

A figure is said to be symmetrical about a line PQ, if it is identical on either side of *l*.

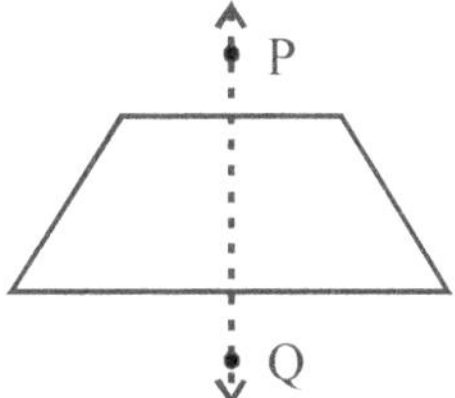

The line which divides the object in exactly two halves is known as **line of symmetry** or **axis of symmetry**. A plane figure through which axis of symmetry can be drawn is said to be a symmetrical figure.

Making of symmetrical figures

Method I. Ink Blot Devils

Take a piece of paper and fold it into two equal halves.
Spill a few drops of ink on one half side.
Press the two halves together and open up the page.
We will find that the resulting figure is symmetric about the folded line (line of symmetry).

Method II. Inked-string Patterns

Take a piece of paper and a small string. Fold the paper into two equal halves. Dip the string in a coloured ink. Arrange the dipped string on one half side. Press the halves together.

The resulting figure is symmetric about the folded line.

On the basis of axis of symmetry. Symmetry can be divided into two types.

(1) **Vertical Line Symmetry :** There are some figures which can be divided into two equal halves by vertical line is known as vertical line symmetry.

  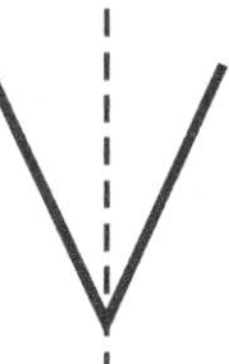

(2) **Horizontal Line Symmetry :** There are some figures which can be divided into two equal halves by a horizontal line is known as horizontal line symmetry.

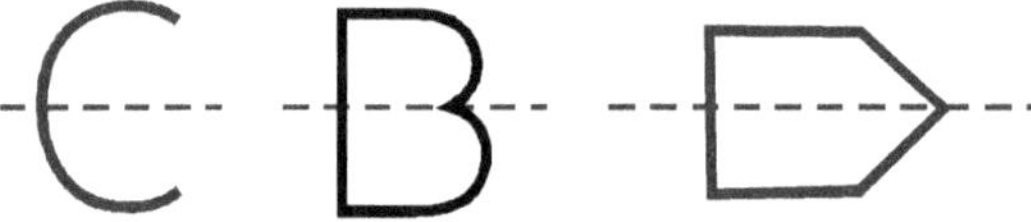

Figures with Two or more Lines of Symmetry

Take a rectangular piece of paper. Fold it vertically into two equal halves. Open it and again fold it into two equal halves horizontally. So, we can fold this paper into half, both lengthwise and breadthwise.

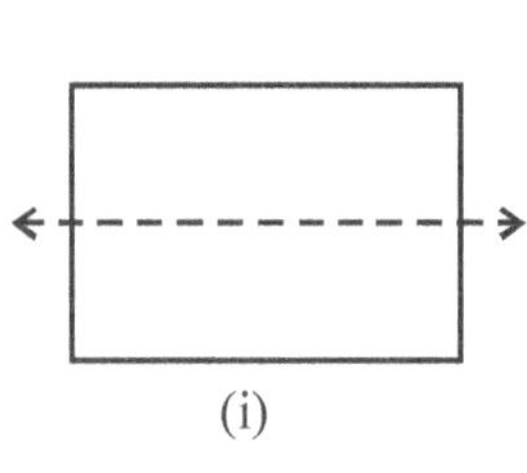

(i)

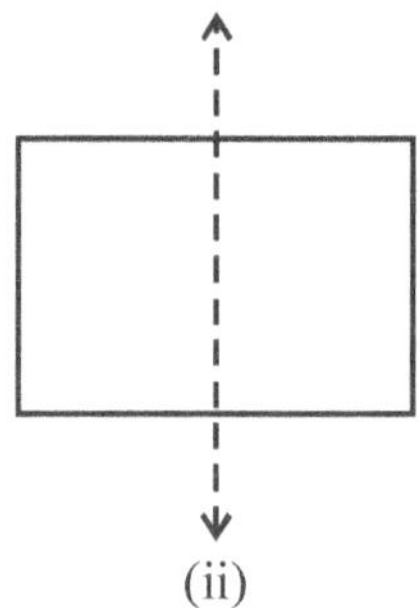

(ii)

Fig. (i) shows the line of symmetry when paper is folded horizontally. Fig (ii) shows the line of symmetry when the paper is folded into half vertically.

Such type of figures have two lines of symmetry.

Symmetrical figures with two lines of symmetry.

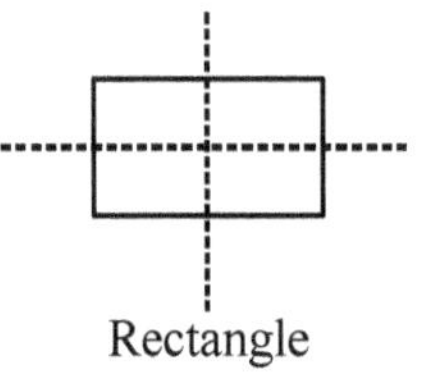

Rectangle

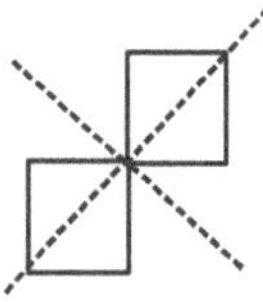

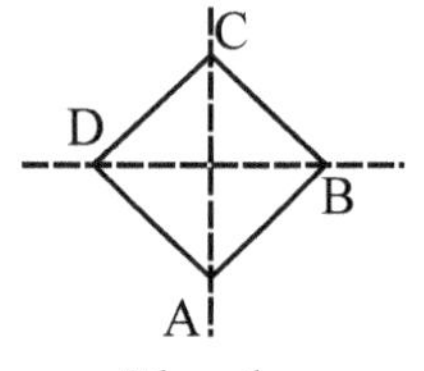

Rhombus

Symmetrical figures with more than two lines of symmetry.
For example

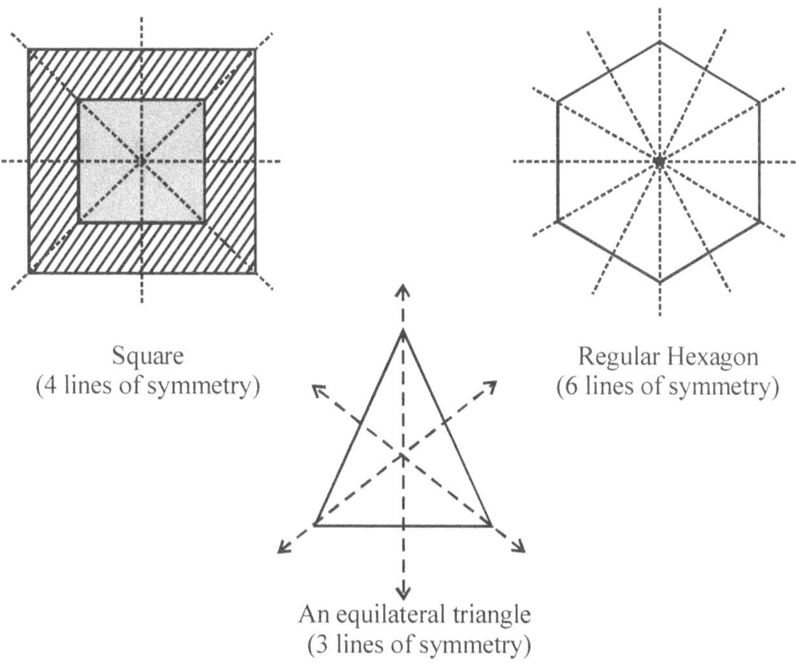

Square
(4 lines of symmetry)

Regular Hexagon
(6 lines of symmetry)

An equilateral triangle
(3 lines of symmetry)

LETTERS OF THE ENGLISH ALPHABET

The following letters are symmetrical about the dotted line (or lines) shown in each case :

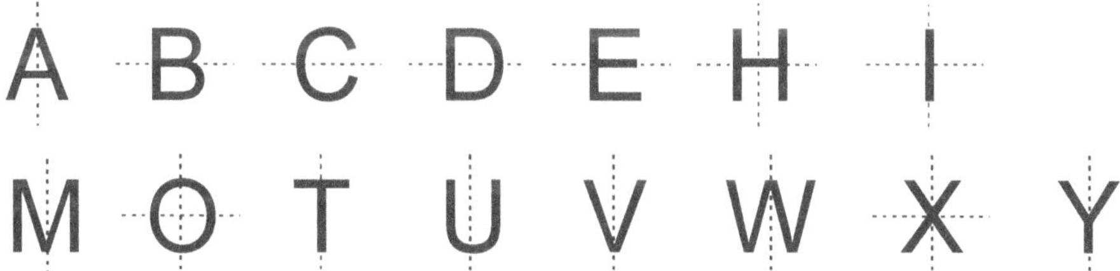

REFLECTION AND SYMMETRY

An object placed in front of a mirror, the object and the image are symmetrical with respect to the mirror line, the mirror line becomes the line of symmetry.

The image is the reflection of the object.

When an object is reflected, there is no change in the lengths and angles of the image. However there is only one difference i.e. the left and the right interchange.

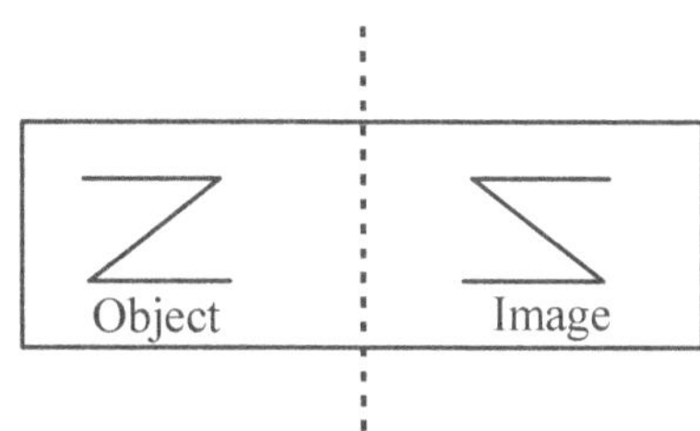

CONCEPT MAP

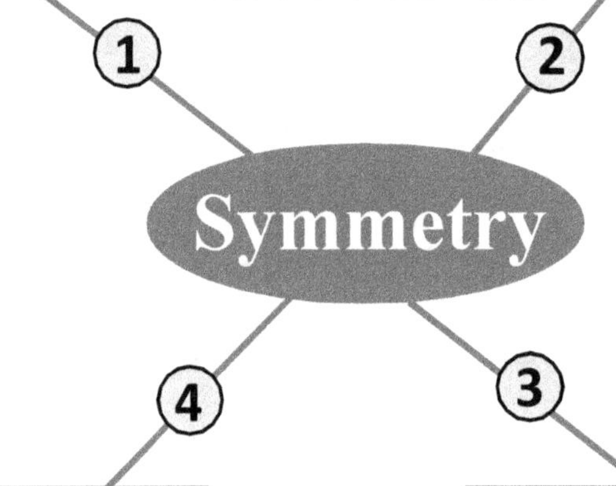

Symmetry

Line of Symmetry
A line which divides a given figure into two identical halves is called the line of symmetry.

Symmetrical Figures
Figures which when folded along a straight line are divided into two identical halves such that one part coincides with the other, are known as symmetrical figures.
A figure may or may not have a line of symmetry or it may have more than one line of symmetry.
A scalene triangle has no line of symmetry.
An isosceles triangle has one line of symmetry.
An equilateral triangle has three lines of symmetry.

Symmetry in Daily Life
Symmetry is applied in everyday life e.g. textile designing, geometrical reasoning, Rangoli etc.

Reflection and Symmetry
An object placed in front of a mirror, the object and image reflected are symmetrical with respect to the mirror line. The mirror line becomes the line of symmetry.

MISCELLANEOUS
SOLVED EXAMPLES

1. Draw the reflection of given shapes taking the dotted line as the mirror line or the line of symmetry.

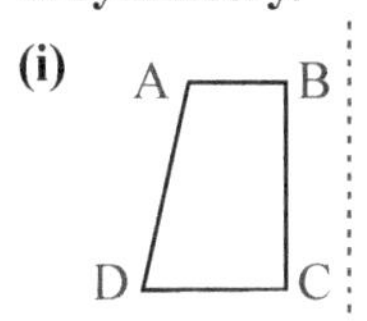

(i)

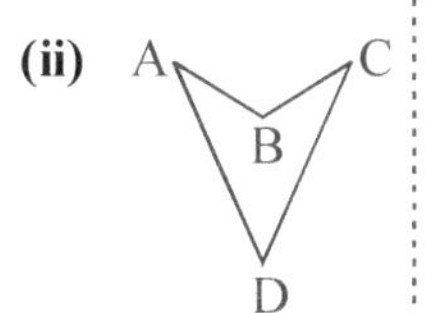

(ii)

Sol. (i) 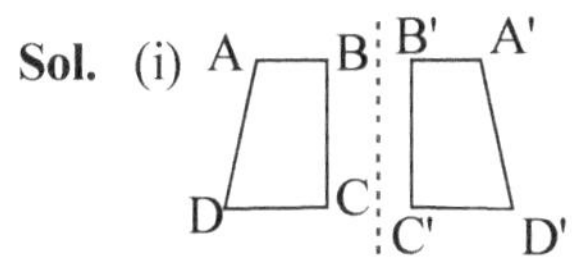 (ii) 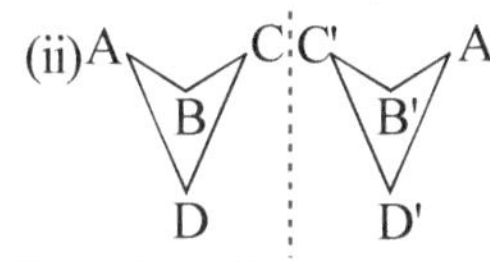

2. Check whether following figures are symmetrical or not. Draw the line of symmetry as well.

(a) 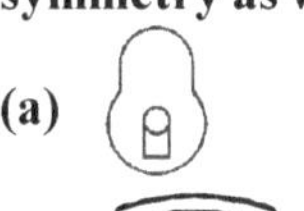 **(b)**  **(c)** 

(d)  **(e)** 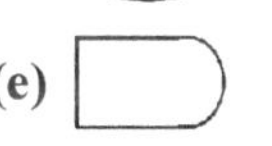 **(f)** 

Sol. (a) 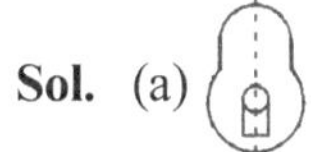 (b) 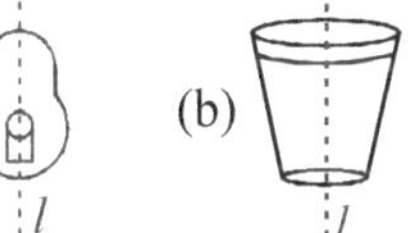 (c) 

(d) 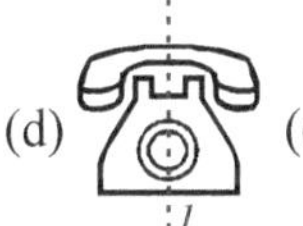 (e) (f) 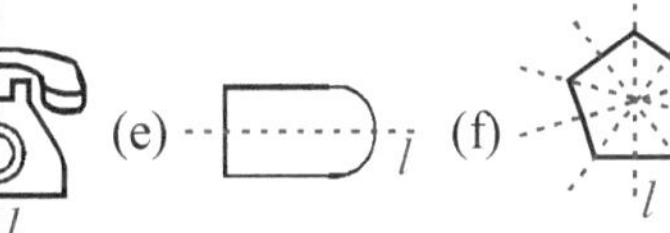

Figures (a), (b), (d), (e), (f), all are symmetrical about the line of symmetry. Figure (c) is not a symmetrical figure, because we cannot find any line of symmetry about which right and left parts are identical and fit to each other.

3. Complete the following figure such that the resulting figure has the two given dotted lines as the lines of symmetry.

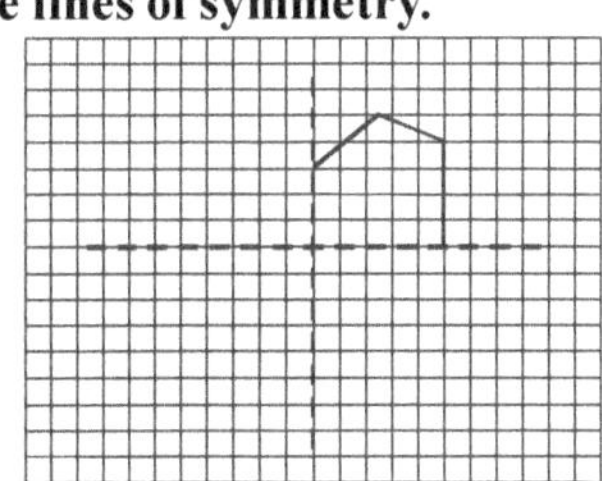

Sol. The resulting figure is shown below.

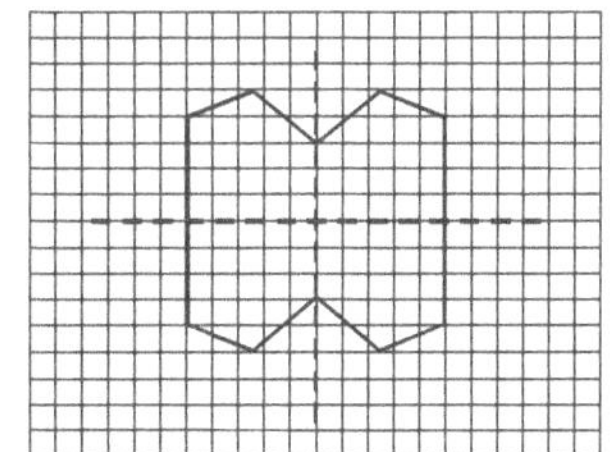

4. Draw the line of symmetry in the following letters:

A B C D E

Sol. A   --B--   --C--   --D--   --E--

5. Draw the mirror image of the given letters, if mirror is placed along the dotted line.

(i) M   **(ii)** P   **(iii)** S

Sol. (i) MM   (ii) Pꟼ   (iii) Sꙅ

6. Copy the following figures and draw all the possible lines of symmetry.

(i)   **(ii)**

(iii)   **(iv)**

Sol. (i) 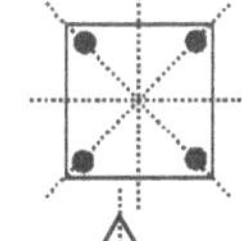 (ii) 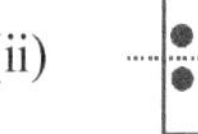

(iii) 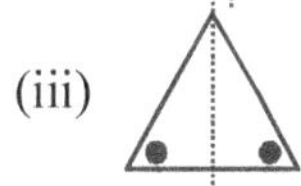 (iv)

7. How many lines of symmetry a square and an equilateral triangle have?

Sol. 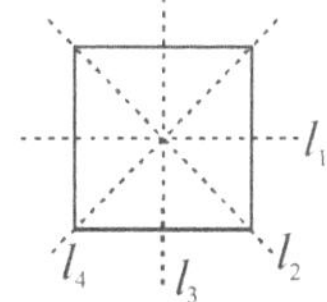

Square   Equilateral Triangle
Four lines of symmetry   Three lines of symmetry

1 EXERCISE

Fill in the Blanks :

DIRECTIONS : *Complete the following statements with an appropriate word / term to be filled in the blank space(s).*

1. The number of lines of symmetry in a picture of Taj Mahal is _______.
2. If an angle of measure 80° is reflected in a line of symmetry, then the reflection is an _______ of measure _______.
3. The digits having only two lines of symmetry are _______ and _______.
4. The digit having only one line of symmetry is _______.
5. The line of symmetry of a line segment is the _______ bisector of the line segment.
6. The number of lines of symmetry in a regular hexagon is _______.
7. A protractor has _______ line/lines of symmetry.
8. A rhombus is symmetrical about _______.
9. A rectangle is symmetrical about the lines joining the _______ of the opposite sides.
10. If a line segment of length 5cm is reflected in a line of symmetry (mirror), then its reflection (image) is a _______ of length _______.
11. Line of symmetry is also known as _______.
12. A figure is known as symmetrical if line of symmetry divides it into two equal _______.

True / False :

DIRECTIONS : *Read the following statements and write your answer as true or false.*

1. A right triangle can have at most one line of symmetry.
2. A kite has two lines of symmetry.
3. A parallelogram has no line of symmetry.
4. A square and a rectangle have the same number of lines of symmetry.
5. A 45°- 45°- 90° set-square and a protractor have the same number of lines of symmetry.
6. A regular octagon has 10 lines of symmetry.
7. The letter F has two lines of symmetry.
8. The letter Z has one line of symmetry.

Match the Columns :

DIRECTIONS : *Each question contains statements given in two columns which have to be matched. Statements (A, B, C, D) in column-I have to be matched with statements (p, q, r, s) in column-II.*

1.

Column-I Characters	Column-II Mirror Image
(A) A	(p) Ꮙ
(B) S	(q) A
(C) 4	(r) Ɛ
(D) 3	(s) Ƨ

Very Short Answer Questions:

DIRECTIONS : *Give answer in one word or one sentence.*

1. Identify the symmetrical figure.

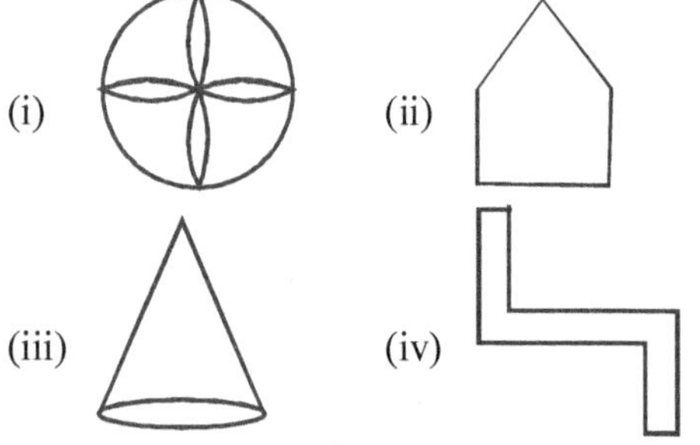

2. How many lines of symmetry can you draw through following figures?

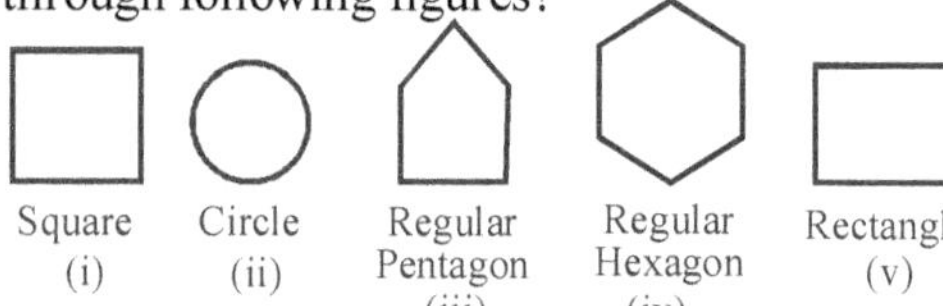

3. Find the letters of English alphabet which have
   (i) Vertical line of symmetry
   (ii) Horizontal line of symmetry
   (iii) Both lines of symmetry
   (iv) No line of symmetry

4. Which of the following are not same after reflection along the mirror line?

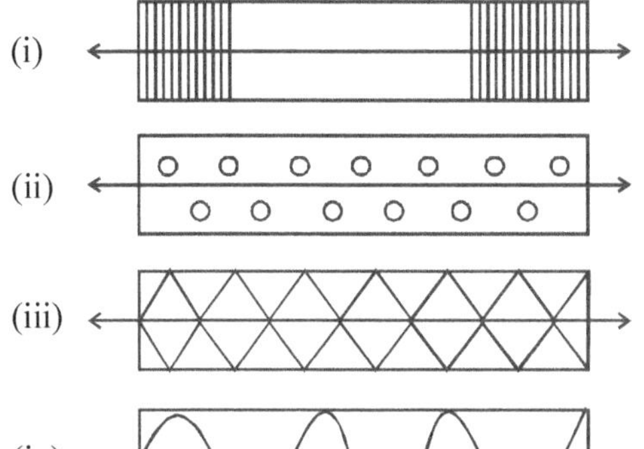

5. In the following figures which one is correct mirror image.

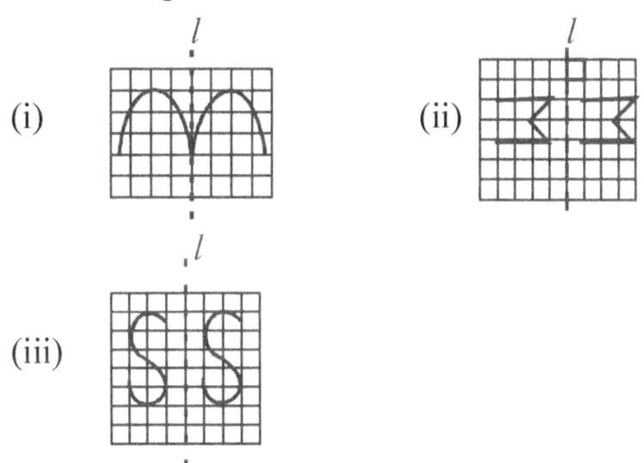

Short Answer Questions :

DIRECTIONS : *Give answer in 2-3 sentences.*

1. Draw the image of each shape if it reflects about line m.

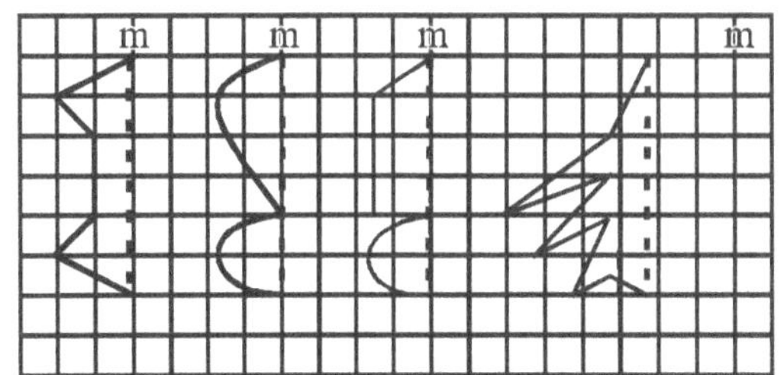

2. Write numbers from 0 to 9 and draw their mirror image. Find which numbers look the same after reflection.

3. Draw the mirror image of the following along the dotted line.

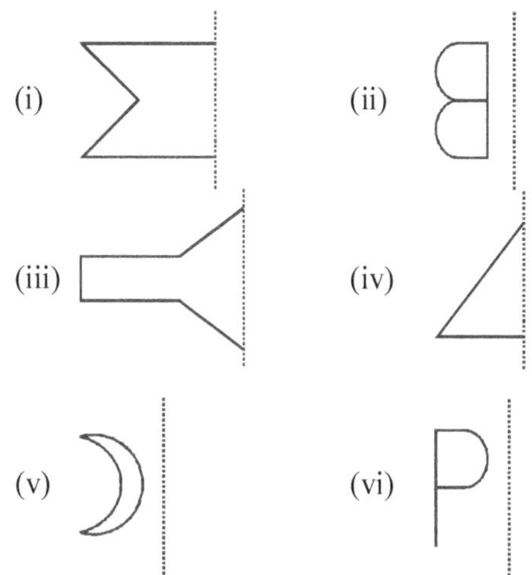

4. Draw the line (or lines) of symmetry of the following shapes and count their number.

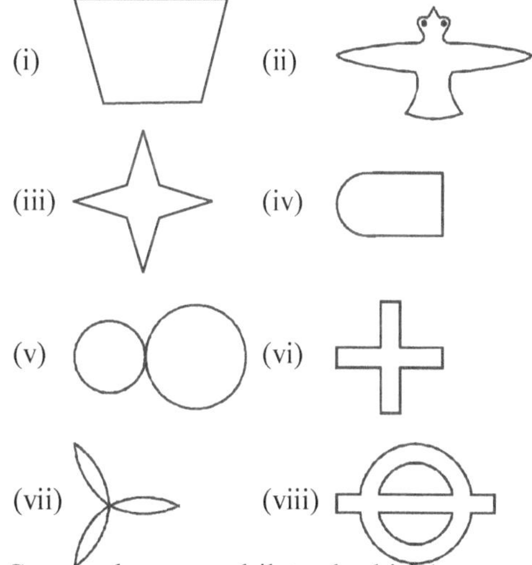

5. Can you draw a quadrilateral, which has -
   (i) only one line of symmetry
   (ii) only two lines of symmetry
   (iii) exactly four lines of symmetry
   (iv) no line of symmetry

6. Name English alphabets which have same mirror image?

2 EXERCISE

Text-Book Exercise :

1. Copy the following on a squared paper. A square paper is what you would have used in your arithmetic notebook in earlier classes. Then complete them such that the dotted line is the line of symmetry.

(i) 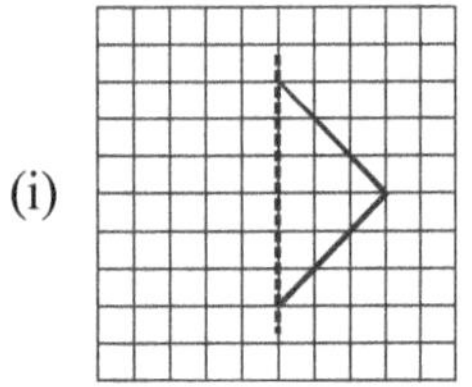   (ii) 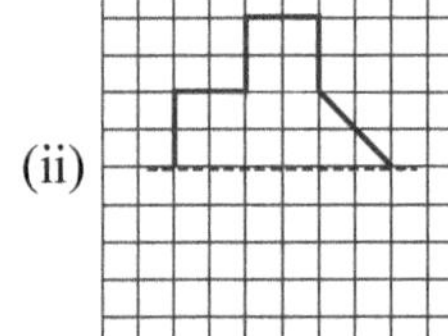

(iii) 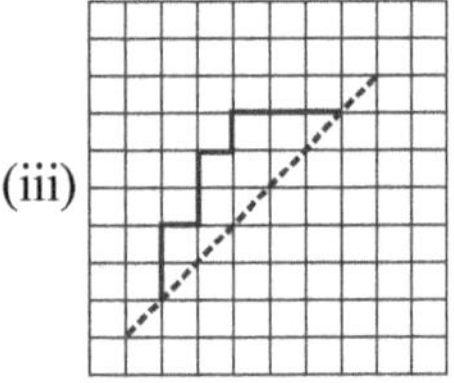   (iv) 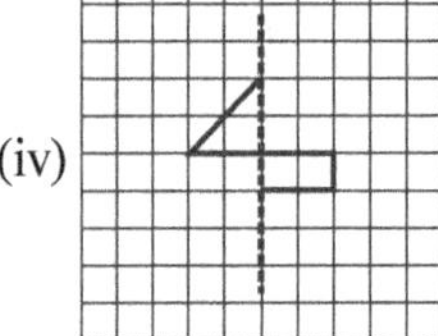

(v) 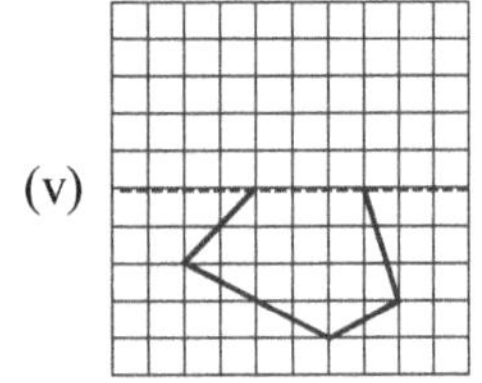   (vi) 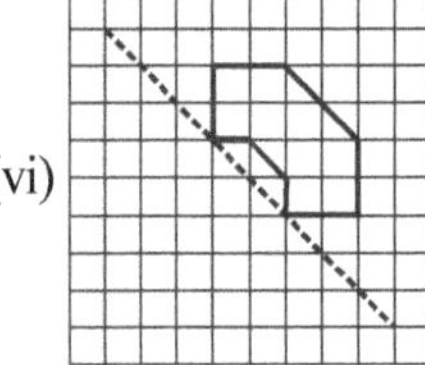

2. Find the number of lines of symmetry for each of the following shapes :

(i)    (ii) 

(iii) 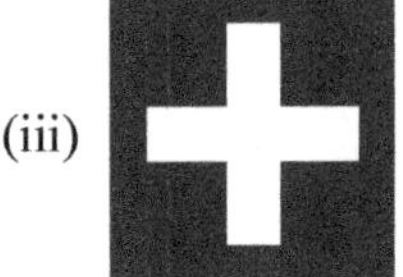   (iv) 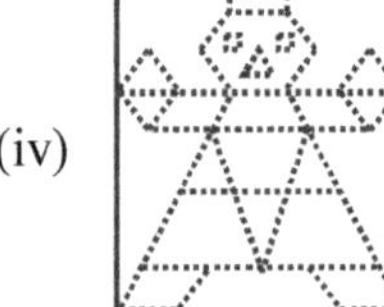

(v) 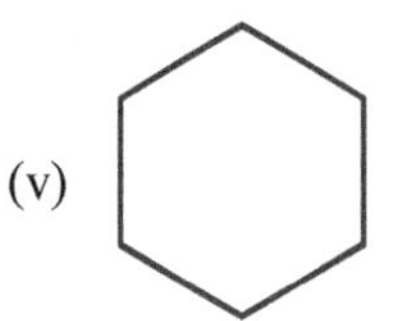   (vi) 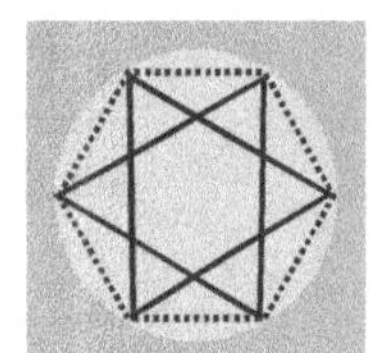

(vii) 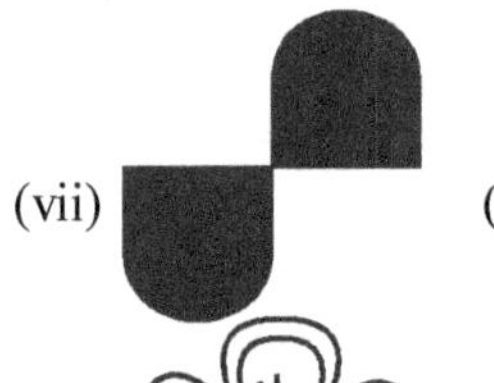   (viii) 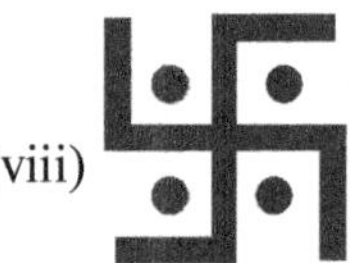

(ix) 

3. Can you draw a triangle which has
   (i)   exactly one line of symmetry
   (ii) exactly two lines of symmetry
   (iii) exactly three lines of symmetry
   (iv) no line of symmetry
   Sketch a rough figure in each case.

4. Trace each figure and draw the lines of symmetry, if any:

(i) 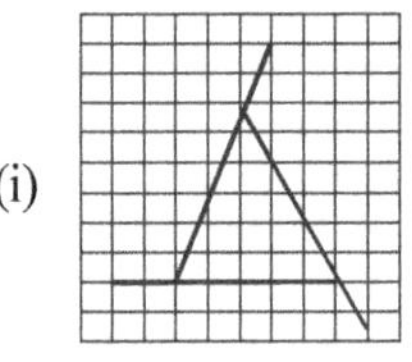   (ii) 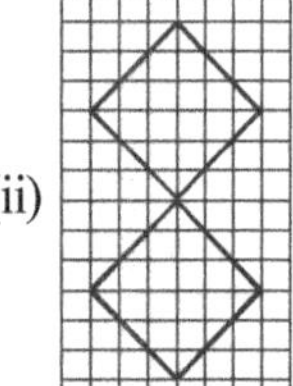

(iii) 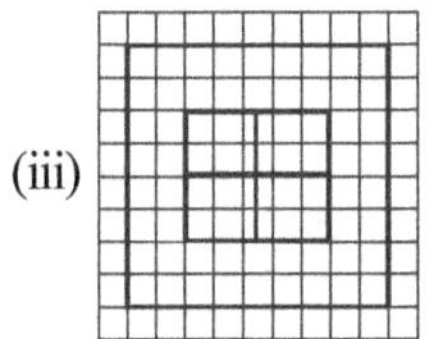   (iv) 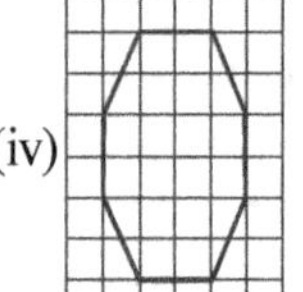

(v) 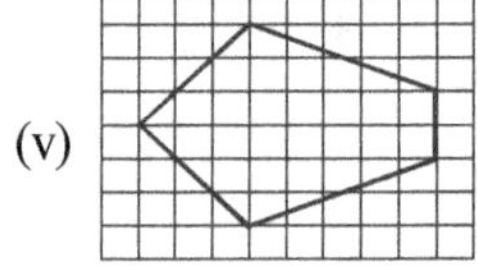   (vi) 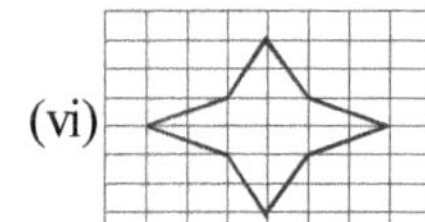

5. Given here are figures of a few folded sheets and designs drawn about the fold. In each case, draw a rough diagram of the complete figure that would be seen when the design is cut-off.

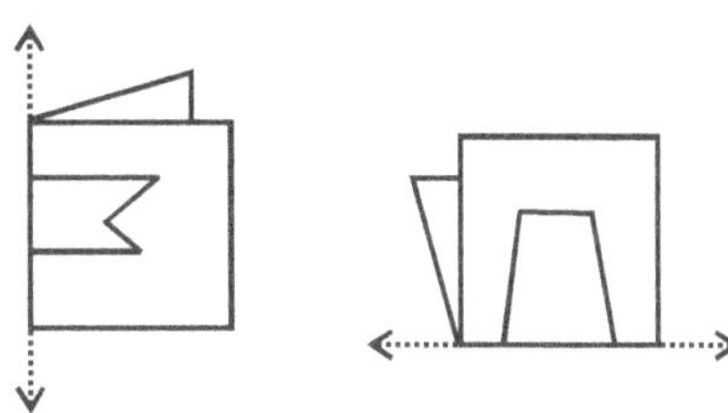

6. Copy the following drawings on squared paper. Complete each one of them such that the resulting figure has two dotted lines as two lines of symmetry.

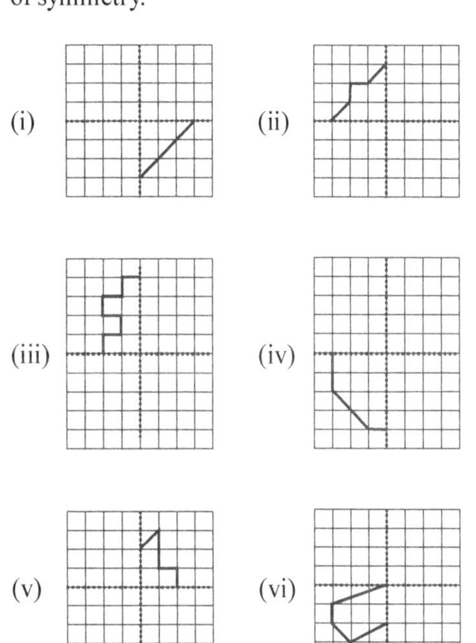

(i) (ii)

(iii) (iv)

(v) (vi)

How did you go about completing the picture ?

Exemplar Questions :

1. Write the letters of the word 'MATHEMATICS' which have no line of symmetry.

2. Write the number of lines of symmetry in each letter of the word 'SYMMETRY'.

3. Open your geometry box. There are some drawing tools. Observe them and complete the following table:

Name of the tool	Number of lines of symmetry
(i) The Ruler	________
(ii) The Divider	________
(iii) The Compasses	________
(iv) The Protactor	________
(v) Triangular piece with two equal sides	________
(vi) Triangular piece with unequal sides	________

4. Complete the figure so that line *l* becomes the line of symmetry of the whole figure.

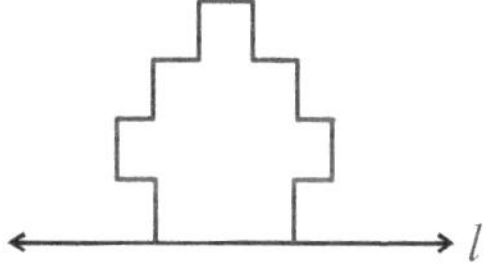

5. Complete figure by taking *l* as the line of symmetry of the whole figure.

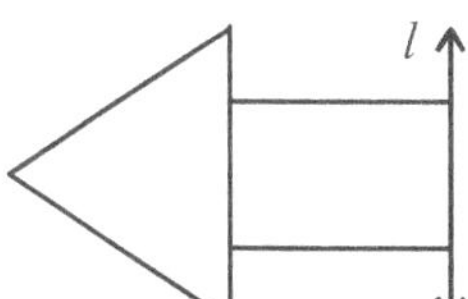

3 EXERCISE

Single Option Correct :

DIRECTIONS : *This section contains multiple choice questions. Each question has 4 choices (a),* (b), (c) and (d) out of which *ONLY ONE is correct.*

1. A figure is said to be symmetrical if-
    (a) It can divide into two equal halves.
    (b) It can divide into three equal parts.
    (c) It can divide into unequal parts.
    (d) None of these

2. Kite is a -
    (a) Symmetrical   (b) Unsymmetrical
    (c) Can't said   (d) None of these

3. Which of the following has an infinite number of lines of symmetry ?
    (a) Equilateral triangle   (b) Isosceles triangle
    (c) Regular hexagon   (d) Circle

4. The object and the image are symmetrical with respect to the
    (a) mirror line   (b) image line
    (c) axis   (d) None of these

5. The number of lines of symmetry in a scalene triangle is
    (a) 0   (b) 1
    (c) 2   (d) 3

6. Which of the following letters does not have the vertical line of symmetry?
    (a) M   (b) H
    (c) E   (d) V

7. The number of lines of symmetry in a 45° - 45° - 90° set-square is
    (a) 0   (b) 1
    (c) 2   (d) 3

8. The number of lines of symmetry in a 30° - 60° - 90° set square is
    (a) 0   (b) 1
    (c) 2   (d) 3

More Than One Option Correct :

DIRECTIONS : *This section contains multiple choice questions. Each question has 4 choices (a), (b), (c) and (d) out of which ONE or MORE may be correct.*

1. Which one of the following figures is symmetrical?

    (a) 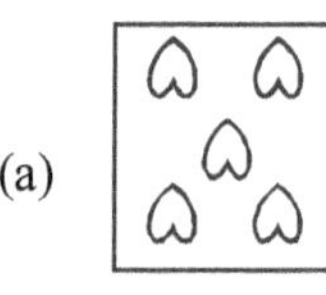   (b) 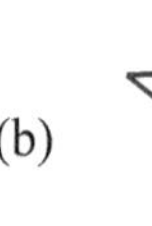

    (c) 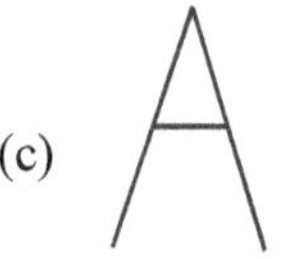   (d) None of these

2. Which of the following letters have line of symmetry?
    (a) E   (b) T
    (c) N   (d) X

3. Which of the following letters does not have any line of symmetry?
    (a) M   (b) S
    (c) N   (d) H

4. Which of the following letters have both horizontal and vertical lines of symmetry?
    (a) X   (b) E
    (c) M   (d) H

5. In the following figures, the figure that is symmetric with respect to any line is:

    (a) 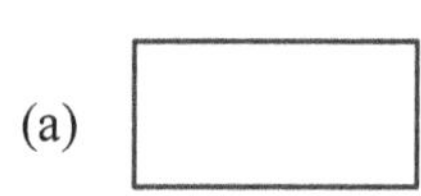   (b) 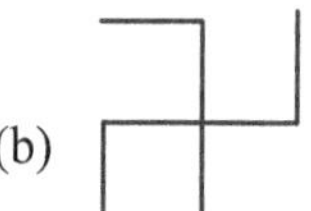

    (c)    (d) 

Passage Based Questions :

DIRECTIONS : *Study the given passage (s) and answer the following questions.*

PASSAGE-I

In our everyday life, we see pictures, leaves of plants, wings of butterflies, blades, etc. All these objects have a property that one half of the object is exactly same in size and shape as the other half. Such objects are called symmetric objects. Thus, A figure is said to be symmetric if on being folded along a line, one part coincides with the other. The line of fold is called the line of symmetry.

1. Which type of line of symmetry divides letter A into two equal halves?
    (a) Vertical line symmetry
    (b) horizontal line symmetry
    (c) Both vertical and horizontal
    (d) Neither vertical nor horizontal

2. Which of the following figure has dotted line as line of symmetry?

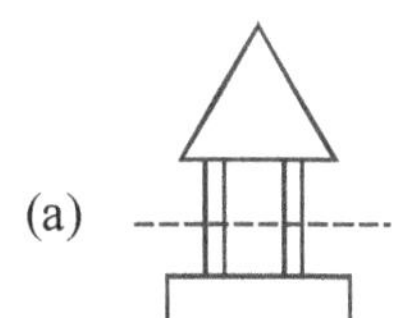
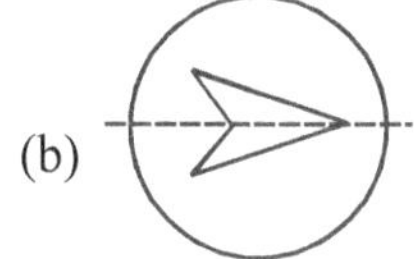

(a)   (b)

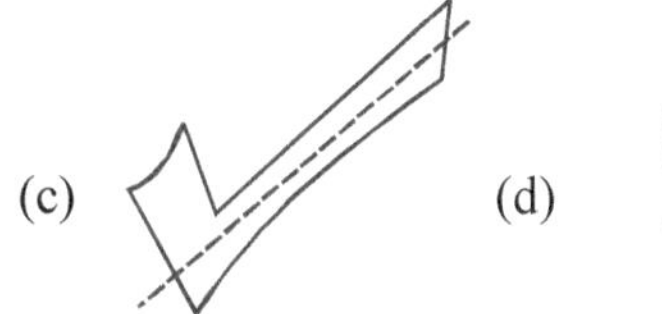

(c)   (d)

3. Which of the following figure has only two lines of symmetry?
    (a) A scalene triangle
    (b) An isosceles triangle
    (c) A rectangle
    (d) An equilateral triangle

Integer Type Questions :

DIRECTIONS : *Answer the following questions. The answer to each of the question is a single digit integer, ranging from 0 to 9.*

1. 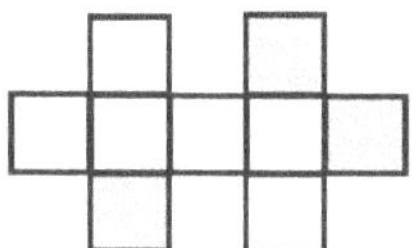 has _________ line of symmetry.

2. How many lines of symmetry scissors have?

3. How many lines of symmetry are there in our National Flag?

4. How many minimum squares must be shaded to make the given figure symmetric?

5. How many lines of symmetry are there in the given figure?

Multiple Matching Question :

DIRECTIONS : *Following question has four statements (A, B, C and D) given in Column-I and five statements (p, q, r, s, t) in Column-II. Any given statement in Column-I can have correct matching with one or more statement(s) given in Column-II.*

1.   **Column-I**   **Column-II**

(A)    (p) Three lines of symmetry

(B) 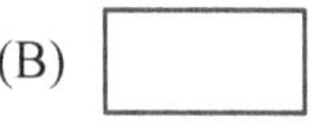   (q) Horizontal line of symmetry

(C)    (r) Vertical line of symmetry

(D) 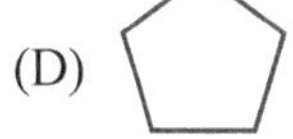   (s) Six lines of symmetry

                                (t) Five lines of symmetry

SOLUTIONS

Brief Explanations of Selected Questions

1 EXERCISE

Fill in the Blanks :

1. One
2. Angle, 80°
3. 0, 8
4. 3
5. perpendicular
6. 6
7. one
8. diagonals
9. mid points
10. Line segment, 5 cm
11. axis of symmetry or mirror line
12. halves

True / False :

1. T
2. F
3. T
4. F
5. T
6. F
7. F
8. F

Match the Columns :

1. (A) → (q); (B) → (s); → (C) → (p); (D) → (r)

Very Short Answer Questions:

1. (i) Yes (ii) Yes (iii) Yes (iv) No
2. (i) Four (ii) Many (iii) One (iv) Six
   (v) Two
3. (i) A, H, I, M, O, T, U, V, W, X, Y
   (ii) B, C, D, E, H, I, K, O, X
   (iii) H, I, O, X
   (iv) F, G, J, L, N, P, Q, R, S, Z
4. (ii), (iv)
5. Only (i) is correct mirror image

Short Answer Questions :

3. 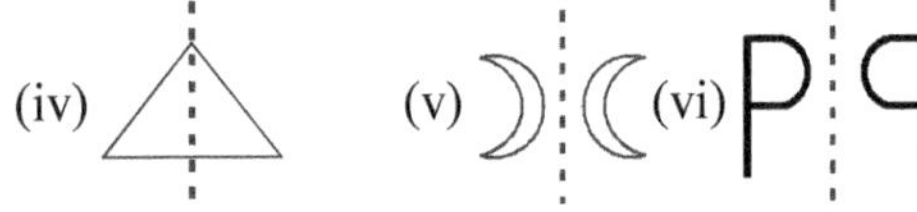

4. (i) 1 (ii) 1 (iii) 4 (iv) 1
   (v) 1 (vi) 4 (vii) 3 (viii) 2
5. (i) Isosceles trapezium
   (ii) Rhombus and rectangle
   (iii) Square

(iv) Parallelogram
6. A, M, H, I, O, U, T, V, W, X, Y

2 EXERCISE

Text-Book Exercise :

1. 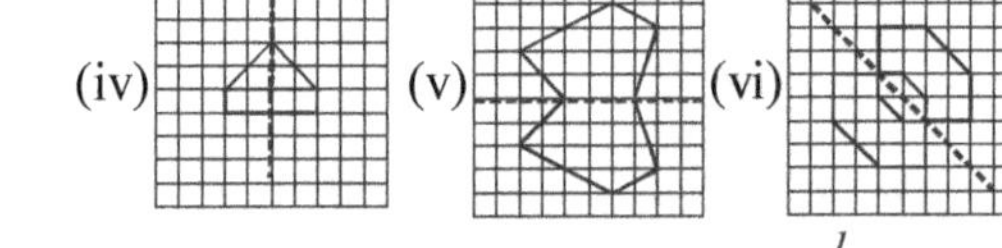
   (i) (ii) (iii)
   (iv) (v) (vi)

2. 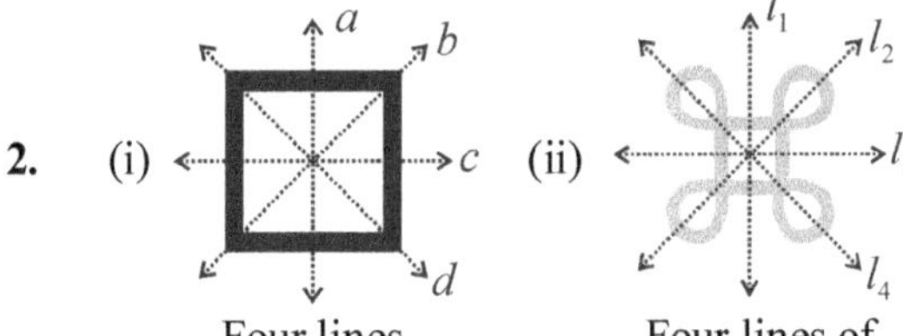

(i) Four lines of symmetry

(ii) Four lines of symmetry

(iii) Four lines of symmetry

(iv) Only one line of symmetry

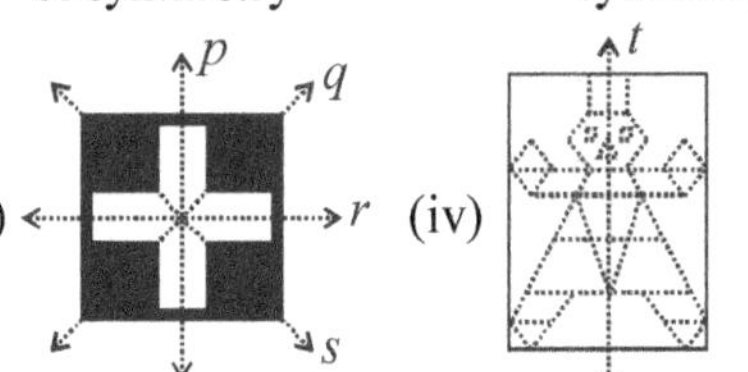

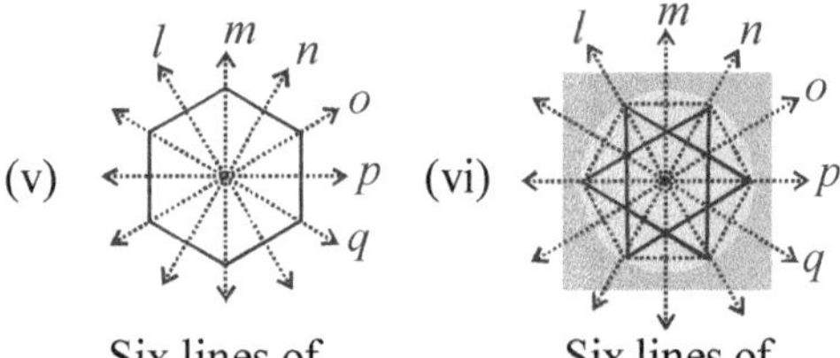

(v) Six lines of symmetry

(vi) Six lines of symmetry

(vii) The given figure is not symmetrical, therefore it has no line of symmetry.

(viii) The given figure is not symmetrical, therefore it has no line of symmetry.

(ix) 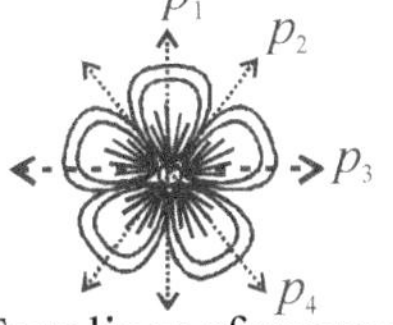

Four lines of symmetry

3. (i) Yes, an isosceles triangle has exactly one line of symmetry 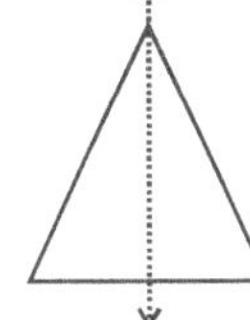

(ii) No, we cannot draw a triangle having exactly two lines of symmetry.

(iii) Yes, an equilateral triangle has exactly three lines of symmetry.

(iv) Yes, a scalene triangle has no line of symmetry.

4. (i) The given figure is not symmetrical and thus, it has no line of symmetry.

(ii) The given figure has two lines of symmetry. 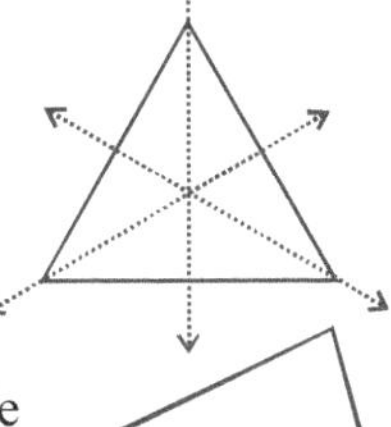

(iii) The given figure has four lines of symmetry

(iv) The given figure has two lines of symmetry 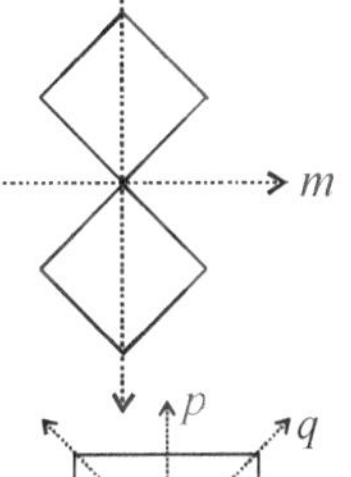

(v) The given figure has one line of symmetry 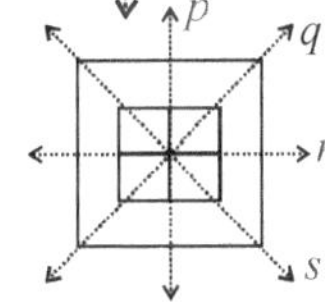

(vi) The given figure has two lines of symmetry 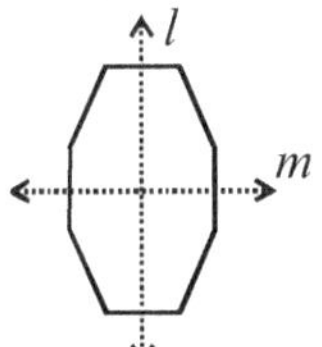

5. 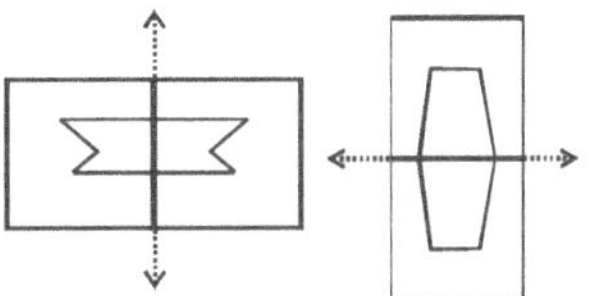

6. Completing the given figures we have:

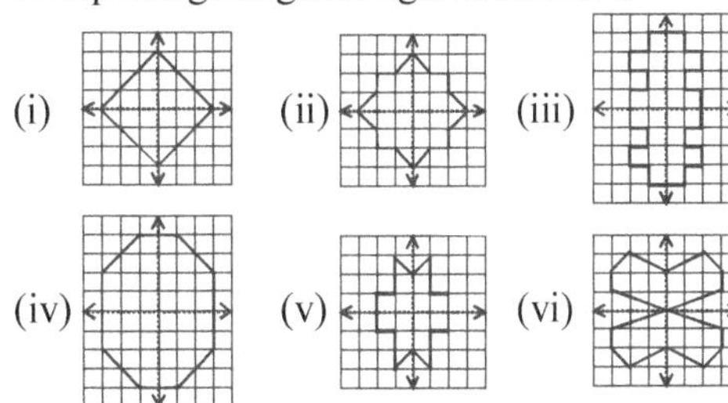

(i) (ii) (iii) (iv) (v) (vi)

1. S

2. S (Zero), Y (One), M (One), E (One), T (One), R (Zero)

3. (i) 2 (ii) 1 (iii) 0 (iv) 1 (v) 1 (vi) 0

4. 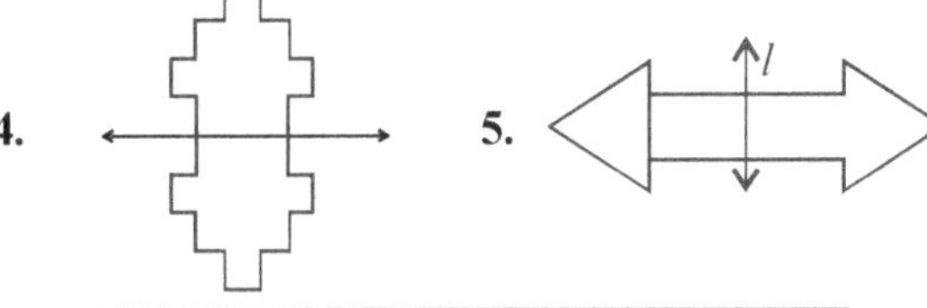   5.

3 EXERCISE

Single Option Correct :

1. (a)   2. (a)   3. (d)   4. (a)
5. (a)   6. (c)   7. (b)   8. (a)

More Than One Option Correct :

1. (a, b, c)   2. (a, b, d)   3. (b, c)
4. (a, d)   5. (a, c, d)

Passage Based Questions :

1. (a) Vertical line symmetry   2. (b)
3. (c) A rectangle

Integer Type Questions :

1. (0)   2. (1)   3. (1)   4. (2) 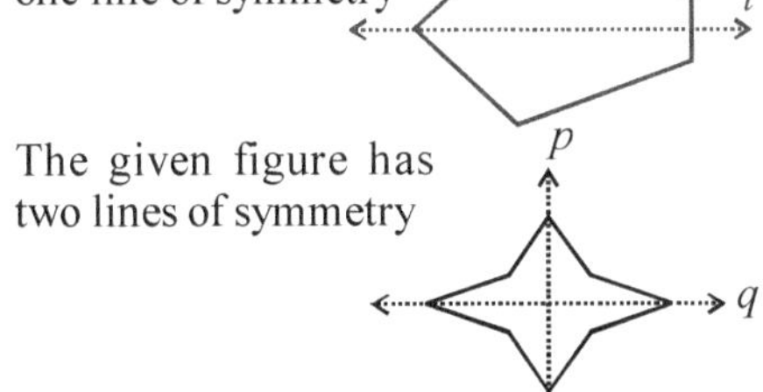

5. (4)   4 lines of symmetry.

Multiple Matching Question :

1. (A) → (p, r); (B) → (q, r); (C) → (q, r, s); (D) → (r, t)

Chapter 14

Practical Geometry

In our daily life we get familiar with various shapes. To draw various shapes we need some instruments. Let us familiarise ourselves with the instruments given in the geometry box.

The process of making figures of given measurements is known as 'construction'. Construction of geometrical figures is done with the help of certain instruments.

RULER

It is widely used to draw and measure line segments.

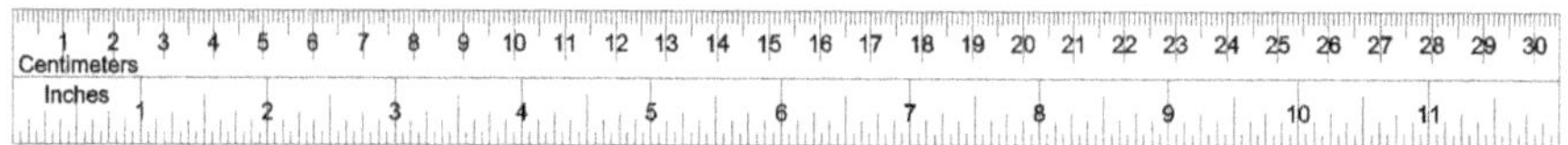

DIVIDER

It is used to compare lengths and angles.

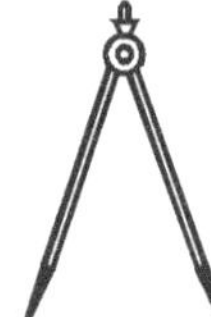

SET SQUARES

There are two types of set squares, one has three angles of measure 45°, 90° and 45° at the vertices while other one has 30°, 90° and 60° angles. These can be used to draw perpendicular and parallel lines.

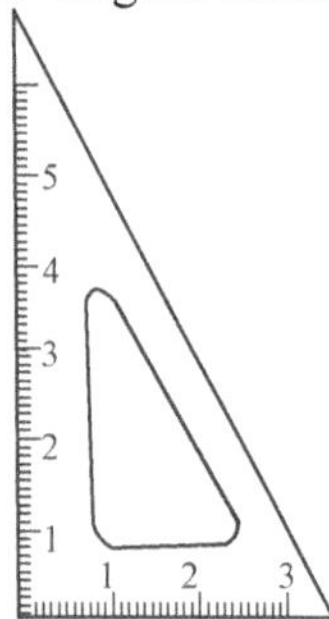

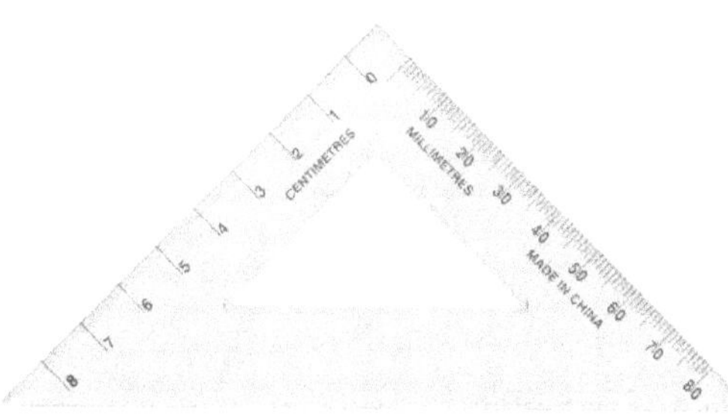

PROTRACTOR

It is semi-circular in (half-circle) shape. It is used to draw and measure the size of an angle in degrees - usually from 0° to 180°.

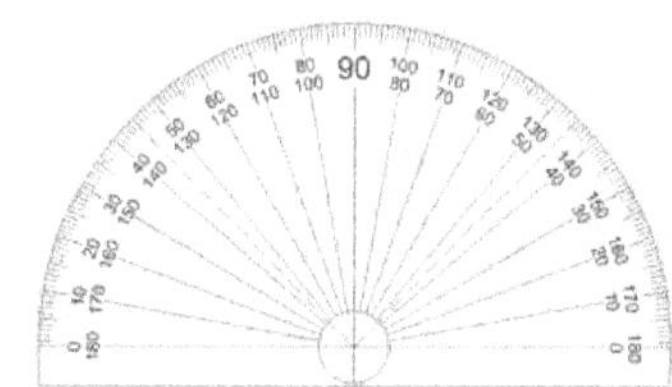

THE CIRCLE

Circle is the set of those points which are at equal distance from a fixed point. The fixed point is called the **centre** of the circle. Let us learn to construct a circle.

Construction of a circle when its radius is known

Let us say we have to construct a circle of given radius 'r' = 8 cm.

Steps of construction :

Step 1 : Open the compass by placing its pointer against initial point of a ruler and opening upto 8 cm.

Step 2 : Mark a point C with a sharp pencil and consider it as centre of the circle.

Step 3 : Place the pointer of the compass on point C.

Step 4 : Turn the compass around the point C, to get the required circle.

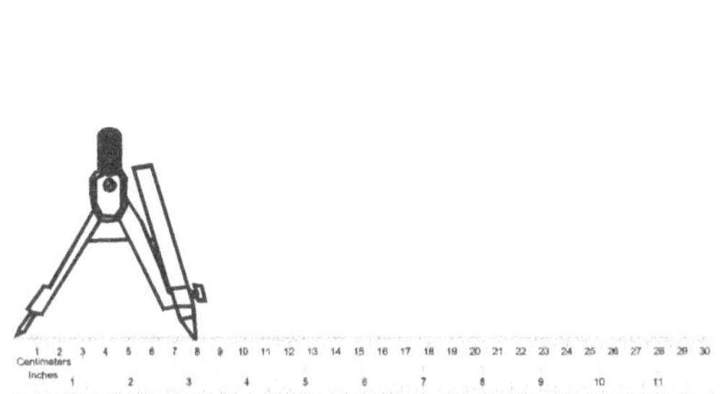
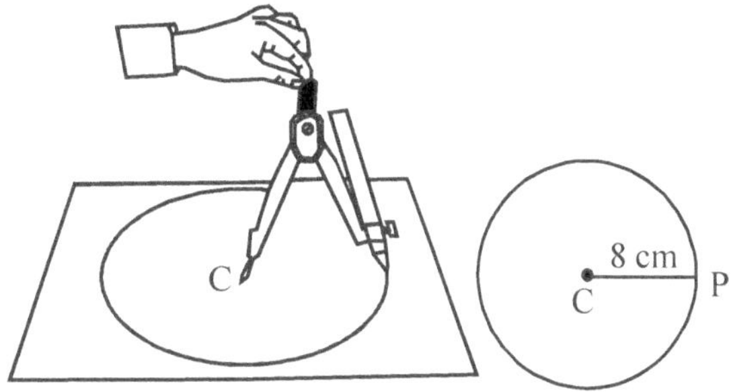

CONCENTRIC CIRCLES

The circles drawn with the same centre but with the different radii are concentric circles. Given figure shows three concentric circles with same centre O and different radii as 2 cm, 3 cm and 4 cm.

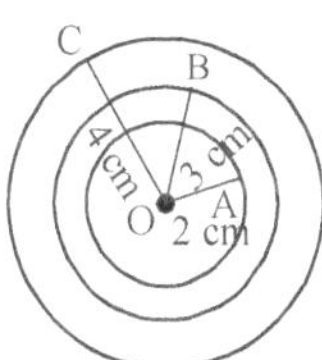

LINE SEGMENT

Line segment is a part of line with two end points. It can be measured by ruler.
Here, PQ is the line segment.

Construction of a Line Segment of a Given length

To draw a line segment of length 3.5 cm (say), using a ruler and compasses, we proceed as follows :

Steps of constructions:

Step 1 : Draw a line l and mark a point P on it, as shown in the figure.

Step 2 : Open the arms of a compass, so that the end-points of the two arms opened equal to 3.5 cm, as shown in the figure.

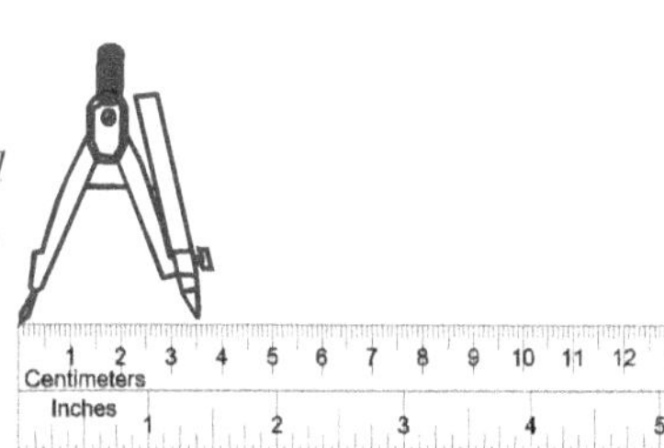

Step 3 : Keeping the opening of the compasses undisturbed, place it along the line *l* such that its metal end coincides with the point P.

Step 4 : Make an arc on the line *l* to cut it at Q.

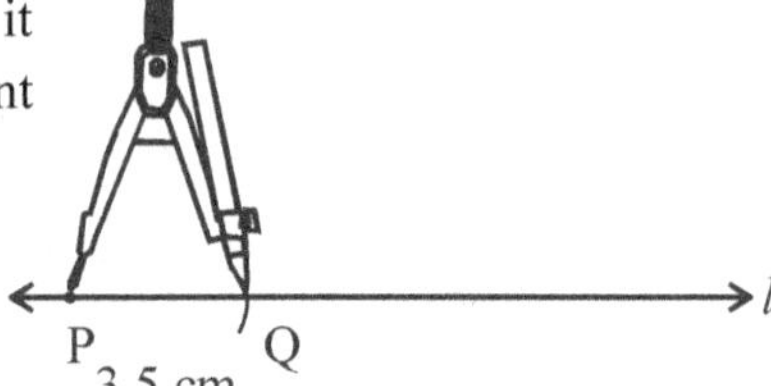

This gives us the required line segment of length 3.5 cm i.e. $\overline{PQ} = 3.5$ cm.

Constructing a copy of a given line Segment, say PQ

Steps of construction :

Step 1 : Put the compass on PQ such that the pointer is on P and the pencil point is on Q. Now, the opening of the compass gives the length of PQ.

Step 2 : Draw any line *l*, mark a point O on it.

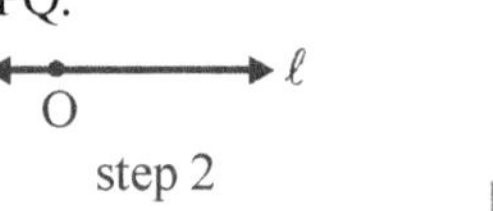

step 2

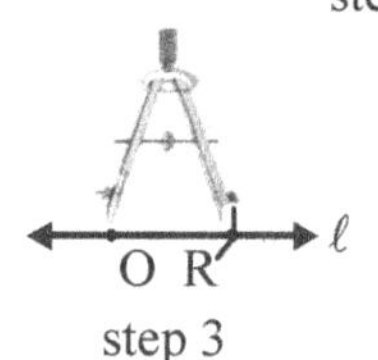

step 1

Step 3 : Put the pointer on O and draw an arc that cuts the line at a point R Thus, OR is the copy of PQ.

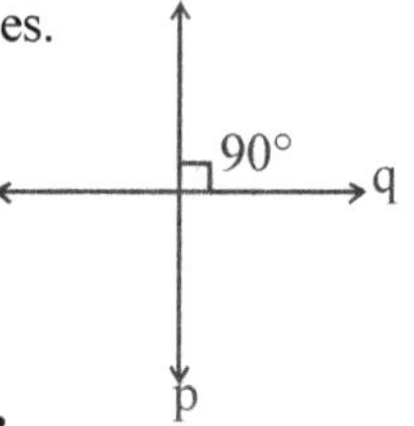

step 3

PERPENDICULAR

The two lines that intersect each other at right angles are known as perpendicular lines. Let us learn to draw perpendicular to a line.

Drawing a perpendicular line to a line through a point on it.

Method I: Using Ruler and a set-square

Let us draw a line segment PQ = 6.5 cm (say) and mark a point R on it such that PR = 4.5 cm (say). Draw a perpendicular to PQ at R.

Steps of construction:

Step 1 : Draw a line segment PQ = 6.5 cm, mark a point R such that PR = 4.5 cm. Place the ruler along the line PQ as shown in figure.

Step 2 : Place the set-square with its shortest side along PQ above the ruler.

Step 3 : Slide the set-square along PQ untill its right angled corner coincides with the given point R.

Step 4 : Holding the set-square, trace the line RS along the edge of the set-square.

Thus, RS is perpendicular on PQ at R, i.e. RS ⊥ PQ

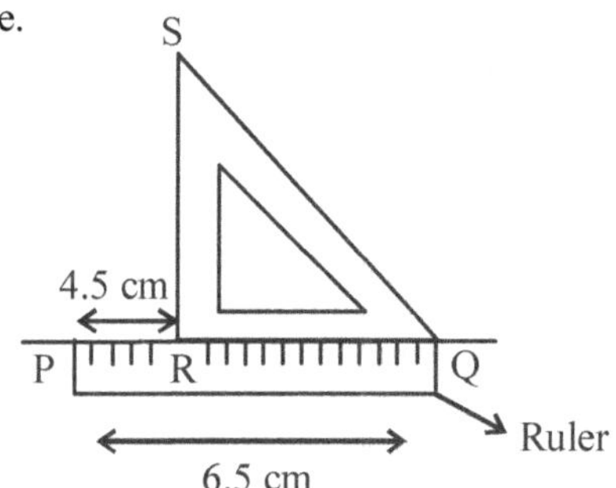

Method II: Using ruler and compasses.

Let us draw a line segment AB = 8 cm (say) and mark a point C on it such that C lies in the mid point of AB i.e. AC = 4 cm draw a perpendicular to it through C.

Steps of construction:

Step 1 :   Draw a line segment AB = 8 cm and mark a point C such that AC = 4 cm. With C as centre and radius less than 4 cm, draw an arc to intersect AB at P and Q.

Step 2 :   Taking P as a centre and radius that should be more than PC, draw an arc on one side of AB.

Step 3 :   Taking Q as a centre and taking the same radius as in step 2, draw another arc to intersect the previous arc at D.

Step 4 :   Draw a line passing through C and D to get CD. CD is the required perpendicular to AB through C.

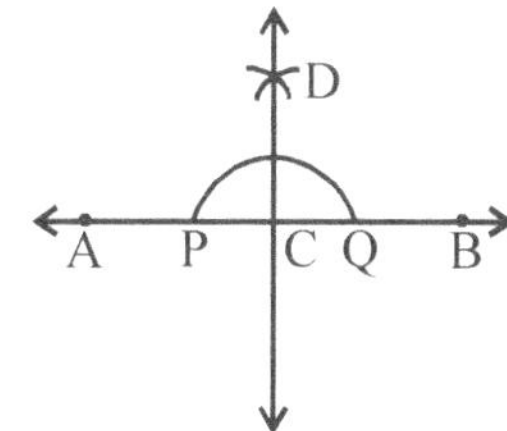

Drawing a perpendicular to a line through a point not on it.

Method I: Using ruler and the set-square

Let us draw a line segment AB = 6 cm. Mark a point C outside AB. Draw a perpendicular to AB through the point C on AB.

Steps of construction:

Step 1 :   Place the set square just below the line AB = 6cm in such a way that one of its sides containing right angle touches the line.

Step 2 :   Place a ruler so that its edge is positioned along the side YZ of the set square.

Step 3 :   Slide the set-square along the ruler until the side XY of the set square passes through the given point C.

Step 4 :   Holding the set-square in the position as shown in the second figure trace the line XY along the edge of the set-square

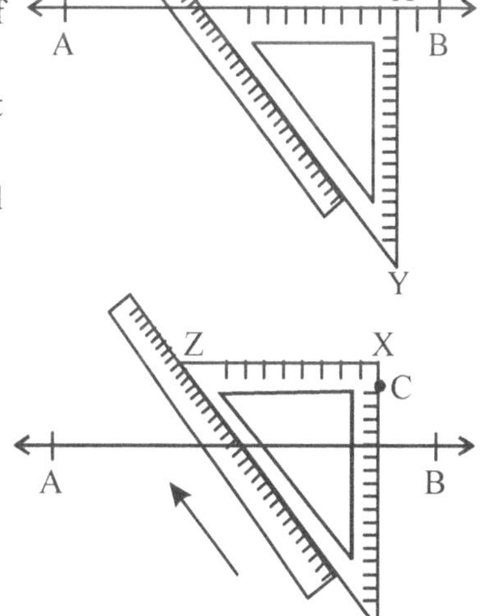

Thus, XY is the perpendicular line to the given line AB passing through the point C.

Method II: Using Ruler and compass

Let us draw a line segment PQ = 7 cm. Mark a point A outside PQ. Draw a perpendicular to PQ through the point A on PQ.

Steps of construction:

Step 1 :   With A as the centre and suitable radius, draw an arc to intersect PQ at S and T respectively.

Step 2 : With S as centre and taking a radius greater than $\dfrac{1}{2}$ ST, draw an arc.

Step 3 : With T as centre and the same radius as in step 2, draw another arc to intersect the previous arc at B.

Step 4 : Draw a line through A and B to obtain line AB.
Thus, AB is the required perpendicular to PQ through the given point A which is located outside PQ.

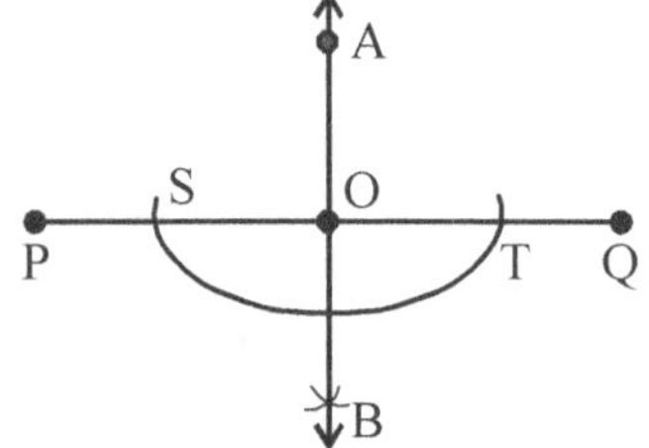

Drawing Perpendicular bisector of a line segment

The perpendicular bisector of a line segment is the line that is perpendicular to the line segment at its mid-point. Let us learn to construct it by two methods:

Method I: Using Transparent Tapes.

Steps of construction:

Step 1 : Draw a line segment MN

Step 2 : Place a strip of a transparent rectangular tape diagonally across MN with the edges of the tape on the end points M and N.

Step 3 : Repeat the above process by placing another tape over M and N just diagonally across the previous one. Thus, two strips cross at A and B.

Step 4 : Join A and B to get AB as the required perpendicular bisectors of MN.

Method II: Using Ruler and Compass

Step 1 : Draw a line segment $\overline{AB}$ of any length.

Step 2 : Using compasses, draw an arc with A as centre and radius, more than half the length of $\overline{AB}$.

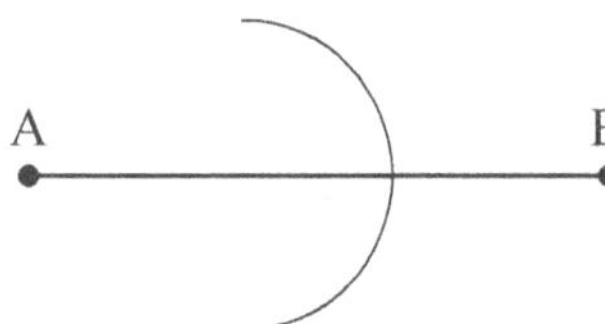

Step 3 : With B as a centre and same radius as in step-2, draw another arc to intersect the previous arc at P and Q.

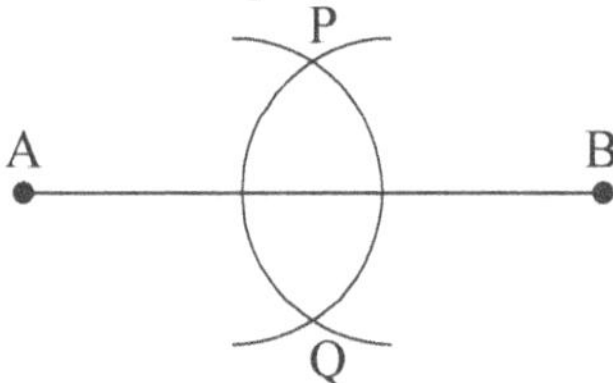

Step 4 : Join P and Q to cut AB at O. This line $\overline{PQ}$ bisects the given line segment $\overline{AB}$ at O i.e. $\overline{AO} = \overline{BO}$.

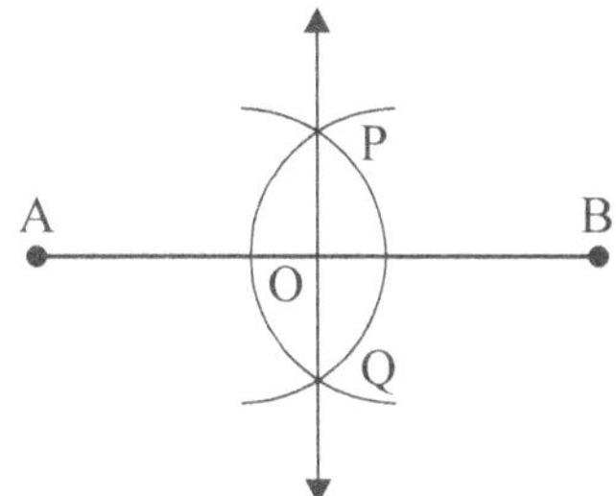

ANGLES

Constructing an angle of a given measure

Suppose we have to construct an angle of 110° (say)

Steps of construction:

Step 1 : Draw a ray OA.

Step 2 : Place the protactor on OA such that its centre coincide with the point O.

Step 3 : Mark a point B on the paper against the mark 110° on the protactor

Step 4 : Remove the protactor and draw OB.
$\angle$AOB = 110° is the required angle.

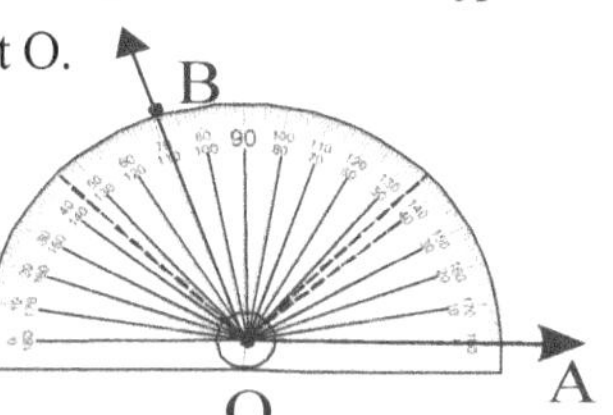

Constructing a copy of an angle of unknown measure

Let us construct an angle equal to $\angle$ABC

Steps of construction:

Step 1 : Draw a ray MN.

Step 2 : With B as a centre and suitable radius, draw an arc intersecting BA and BC at P and Q respectively.

Step 3 : With M as a centre and the same radius as used in step 2, draw an arc to intersect MN at O

Step 4 : With O as centre and radius equal to PQ, draw an arc to intersect the previously drawn arc at to S.

Step 5 : Join O and S and produce it to any point T.
Thus, $\angle$NMT is the required angle.
$\angle$NMT = $\angle$ABC.

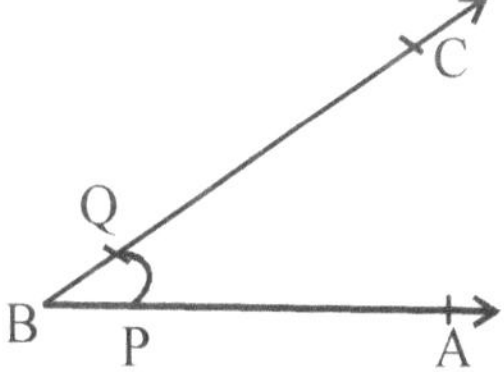

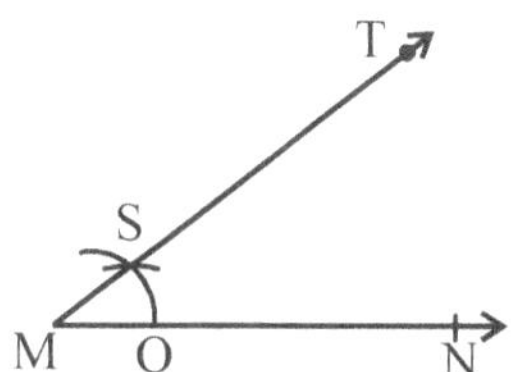

Bisector of an angle

A line which divides a given angle into two equal angles is called its bisector. Let us learn to construct an angle bisector of a given angle

Construct an angle bisector of the given angle

Steps of construction:

Step 1 : With A as centre and suitable radius draw an arc that intersects both arms of $\angle$A at points B and C respectively.

Step 2 : With B as centre, draw (in the interior of ∠A) an arc with radius more than half of BC.

Step 3 : With C as centre and same radius draw another arc that intersects the previous arc at point D.

Step 4 : Join points A and D.

Thus, AD is the bisector of ∠A.

∴ ∠CAD = ∠BAD

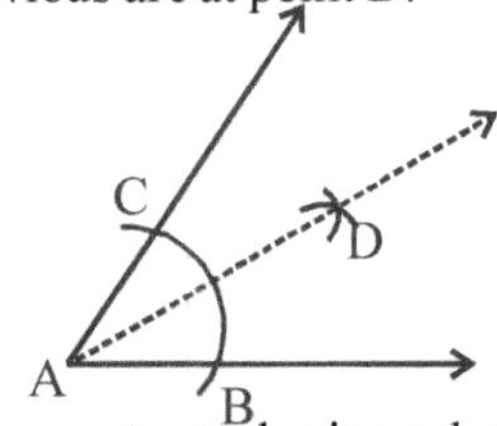

ANGLES OF SPECIAL MEASURES

There are some angles such as 60°, 30°, 120°, 90°, 45°, of special measure that can be constructed using ruler and compasses (without using protractor). Let us learn to draw them.

To construct an angle of 60° using ruler and compass

Steps of construction:

Step 1 : Draw a ray AB.

Step 2 : With A as the centre and a suitable radius draw an arc intersecting AB at C.

Step 3 : With C as the centre and same radius as in step 2, draw another arc intersecting the previous arc at D.

Step 4 : Join AD and extend it to E.

Thus, ∠EAB = 60°

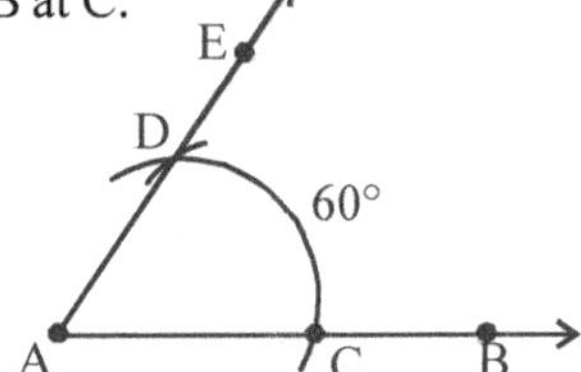

To construct an angle of 30° using ruler and compass.

Steps of construction:

Step 1 : Draw an ∠AOB = 60°

Step 2 : With C as centre, draw an arc with radius more than half of CD.

Step 3 : With D as centre and same radius draw another arc that intersects the previous arc at point E

Step 4 : Join points O and E. OE is the bisector of ∠AOB.

Thus, $\angle AOE = \frac{1}{2} \angle AOB = 30°$ i.e. $\angle AOE = \angle BOE = 30°$

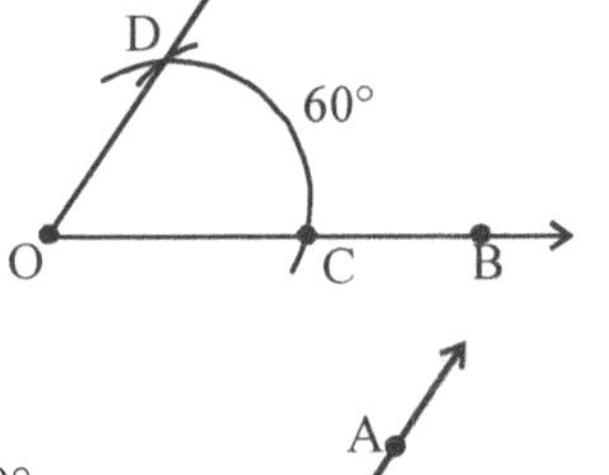

To construct an angle of 120° using ruler and compass.

Steps of construction:

Step 1 : Draw a ray AB.

Step 2 : With A centre and a suitable radius draw an arc intersects AB at C.

Step 3 : With C as the centre and same radius, as in step 2, draw another arc intersecting the previous arc at D.

Step 4 : With D as the centre and same radius, draw another arc intersecting the first arc at E.

Step 5 : Join AE and extend to F.

Step 6 : ∠BAF = 120°

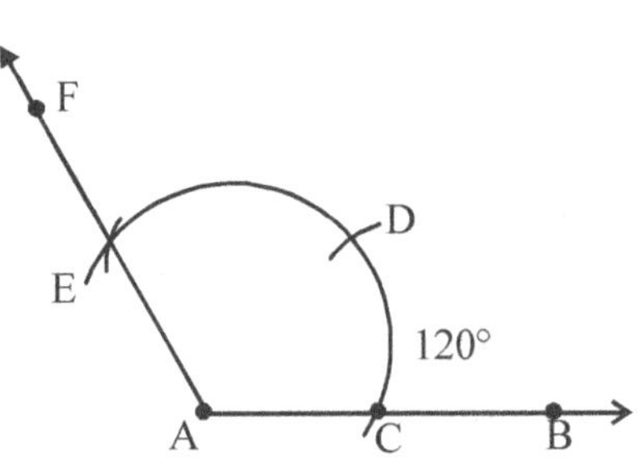

To construct an angle of 90° using ruler and compass

Steps of construction:

Step 1 :   Draw a ray AB

Step 2 :   With A as centre and a suitable radius draw an arc intersecting AB at C.

Step 3 :   With C as the centre and same radius draw another arc that intersects the previous arc at D.

Step 4 :   Taking D as centre and same radius, draw another arc   that intersects same arc at E.

Step 5 :   Now, with D and E as centres and a suitable radius, draw two arcs that intersect each other at F.

Step 6 :   Join AF. Thus, ∠BAF = 90°

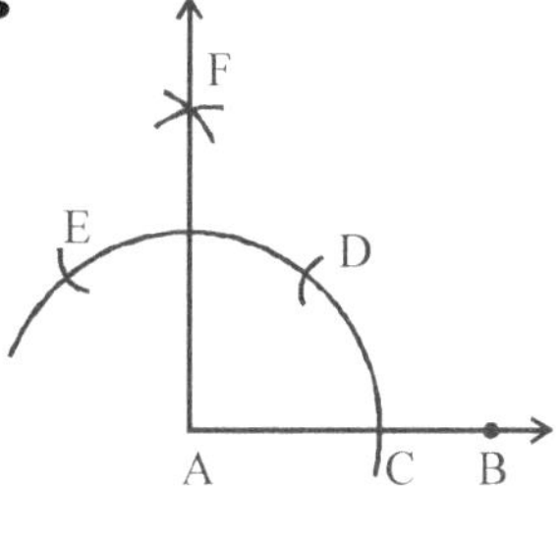

To construct an angle of 45° using ruler and compass

Steps of construction:

Step 1 :   Draw an angle, ∠PQR = 90°

Step 2 :   With A as centre draw an arc with radius more than half of AD.

Step 3 :   With D as centre and same radius draw another arc that intersects the previous arc at point E.

Step 4 :   Join points Q and E.

QE is the bisector of ∠PQR

Thus, $\angle EQR = \dfrac{1}{2} \angle PQR = 45°$

i.e. ∠PQE = ∠EQR = 45°

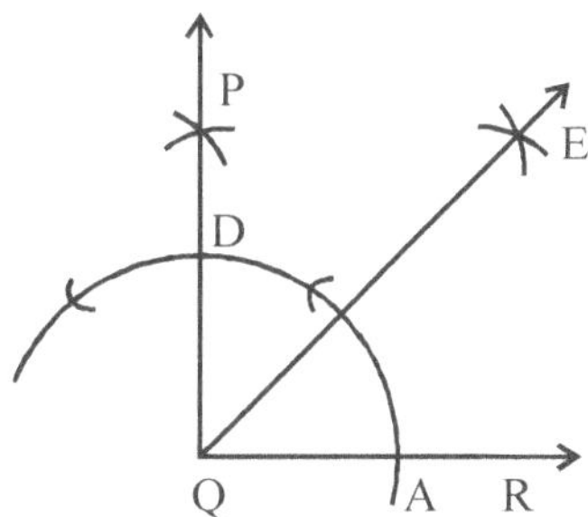

CONCEPT MAP

<table>
<tr>
<td valign="top">

Mathematical Instrument

- While constructing shapes we use some mathematical instruments like, ruler, compasses, divider, set-squares and protractors.

</td>
<td valign="top">

Construction of circle, line segment and perpendicular

- Using mathematical instruments we can construct:
  - (a) A circle, when its radius is known.
  - (b) A line segment of given length.
  - (c) A copy of a line segment.
  - (d) A perpendicular to a line through a point.

</td>
</tr>
</table>

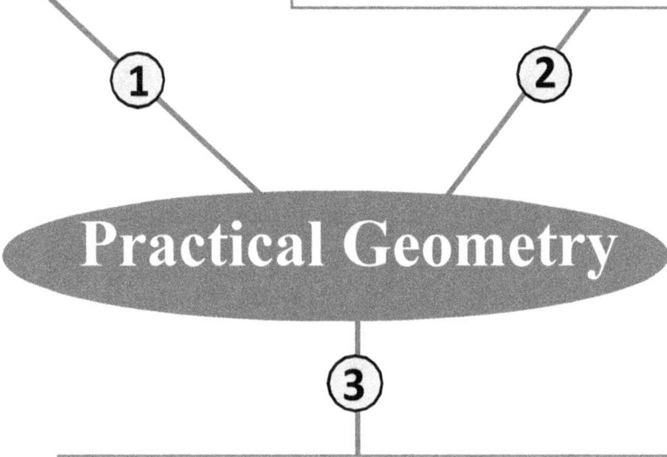

Practical Geometry

Construction of angles

- The Following constructions can also be made:
  - (a) A copy of an angle.
  - (b) Some angle of special measure such as 30°, 60°, 45°, 90° etc.
  - (c) The bisector of an angle.

MISCELLANEOUS
SOLVED EXAMPLES

1.   Draw two circles of radii 3 cm and 4 cm with same centre O.

Sol. Steps of construction

Step 1 :   Open the compasses by putting the pointer on initial point of ruler and opening it upto 4 cm.

Step 2 :   Mark a point O with pencil and consider it as centre of the circle.

Step 3 :   Place the pointer of the compasses on O.

Step 4 :   Turn the compasses around O to get the circle of radius 4 cm.

Step 5 :   With the help of same above steps draw an another circle of radius 3 cm having the same O as centre.

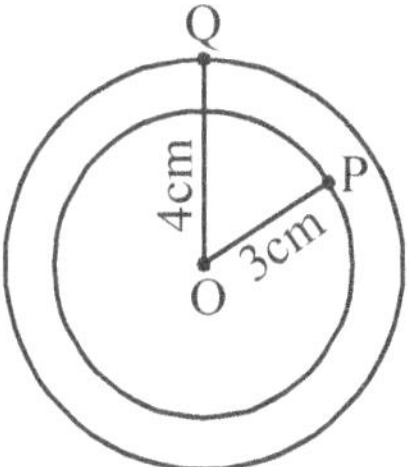

2.   Construct a line segment AC whose length is the sum of the lengths of two given line segments, AB = 3 cm and BC = 4 cm.

Sol. Steps of construction

Step 1 :   Draw a line *l* and mark a point A on it.

Step 2 : Open your compass for radius 3 cm. With A as centre, cut an arc of length 3 cm on the line. Mark the point B where arc cuts the line. Then AB = 3 cm.

Step 3 : Taking B as centre and the radius of 4 cm on your compass, make another arc on line *l* cutting it at another point C. Then AC is the required line segment.

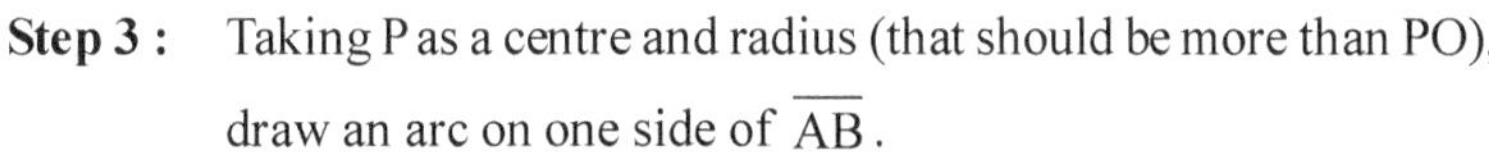

3.   Draw $\overline{AB}$ = 7 cm. Taking a point O on $\overline{AB}$ such that it lies in the mid-point of $\overline{AB}$, draw a perpendicular to it through O.

Sol. Steps of Construction

Step 1 :   Draw a line segment $\overline{AB}$ = 7 cm and mark a point O such that $\overline{AO}$ = 3.5 cm.

Step 2 :   With O as centre and a suitable radius (here we can take 2 cm or 3 cm, but not greater than 3.5 cm), draw an arc to cut AB at P and Q.

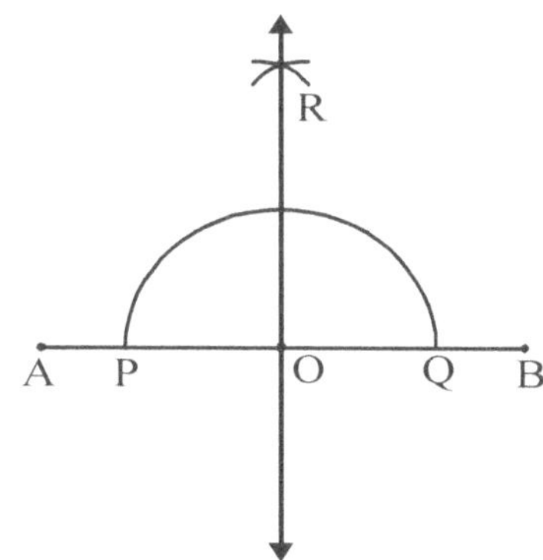

Step 3 :   Taking P as a centre and radius (that should be more than PO), draw an arc on one side of $\overline{AB}$.

Step 4 :   Taking Q as a centre and taking the same radius as in step 3, draw another arc to intersect the previous arc at R.

Step 5 :　Draw a line passing through O and R to get $\overline{OR}$. Now, $\overline{OR}$ is the required perpendicular to $\overline{AB}$ through O.

4.　**Draw a line segment $\overline{PQ} = 7$ cm. Mark a point C outside $\overline{PQ}$. Now Draw a perpendicular to PQ through the point C on PQ, by using set-square.**

Sol.　It is given that PQ = 7 cm.
Take C as any point outside PQ using set squares.
Draw the perpendicular CD on PQ.
Thus, CD $\perp$ PQ.

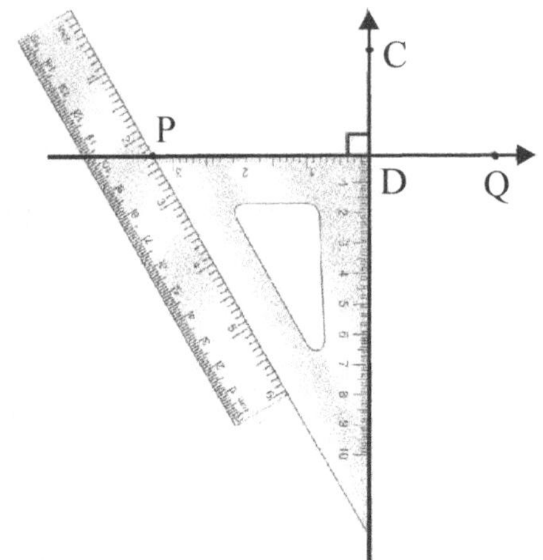

5.　**Draw a line segment of length 10 cm. Using compasses, divide it into four equal parts.**

Sol.　**Step 1:**　Draw a line segment, AB = 10 cm and draw a perpendicular bisector.

Step 2:　In step 1, we have divided $\overline{AB}$ into two equal parts $\overline{AC}$ and $\overline{BC}$.

Similarly, draw the perpendicular bisector of $\overline{AC}$ and $\overline{BC}$ separately.

Now, we have four equal parts $\overline{AB}$ of i.e.

$\overline{AD} = \overline{CD} = \overline{CE} = \overline{BE} = 2.5$ cm

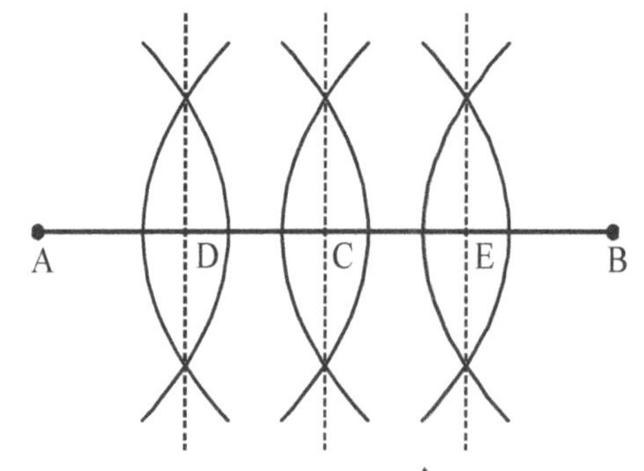

6.　**Construct an angle of 135°.**

Sol.　**Step 1:**　Draw a line AB.

Step 2:　With any point O on line AB as vertex, construct $\angle AOC$ of measure 90°. Then $\angle BOC$ is also of measure 90°.

Step 3:　Bisect $\angle BOC$. Ray OD is the bisector.
Then, $\angle AOD = 90° + 45° = 135°$.

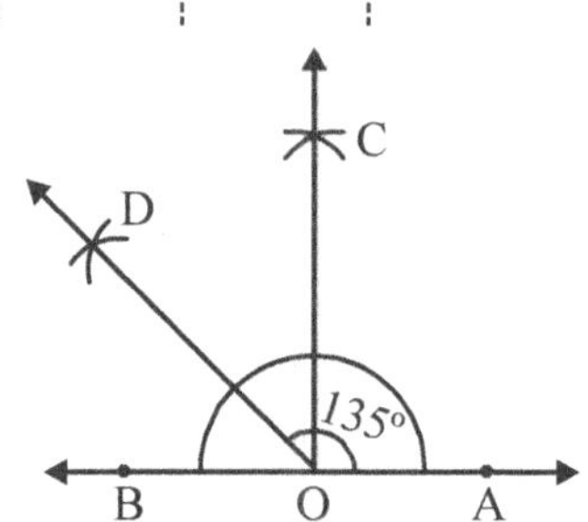

7.　**Construct an angle of 150°.**

Sol.　**Step 1.**　Draw a line AB.

Step 2.　With any vertex O on AB, construct $\angle BOC$ of 120°.

Step 3.　Bisect $\angle AOC$. Let ray OD be the bisector.
Then $\angle BOD = 120° + 30° = 150°$.

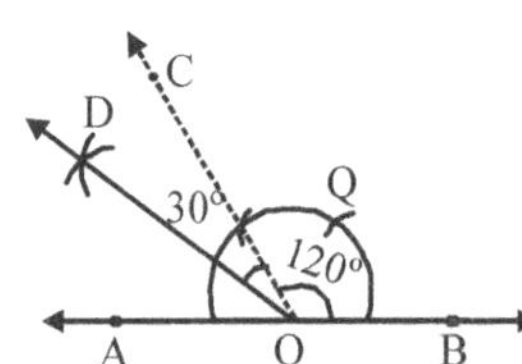

1 EXERCISE

Fill in the Blanks :

DIRECTIONS : *Complete the following statements with an appropriate word / term to be filled in the blank space(s).*

1. _________ is widely used to draw line segments.
2. _________ is used to compare lengths and angles.
3. Compasses is used to mark _________.
4. Set squares are used to draw _________ and _______ lines.
5. Protractor is divided into _________ equal parts.
6. A line which is perpendicular to a line segment at its midpoint is called the _______.
7. Perpendicular bisector can be draw with the help of _______.
8. A perpendicular is at _________ to a given line.

True / False :

DIRECTIONS : *Read the following statements and write your answer as true or false.*

1. Ruler is marked with mm, cm and inches also.
2. Set squares are two types, one has three angles of measure 45°, 90° and 45°. Other one has 30°, 90° and 60° angles.
3. Protractor is used to draw and measure angles.
4. Set square, ruler and compasses are useful for construction of perpendicular.
5. Perpendicular may be drawn from the point which may or may not be on the given line segment.
6. Perpendicular bisector is also known as line of symmetry.
7. Perpendicular bisector divides the given line segment of fixed length into unequal parts.
8. Perpendicular bisector can be drawn with the help of set square and ruler.

Match the Columns :

DIRECTIONS : *Each question contains statements given in two columns which have to be matched. Statements (A, B, C, D, E) in column-I have to be matched with statements (p, q, r, s, t) in column-II.*

1. According to the figure shown below match the column I to column II.

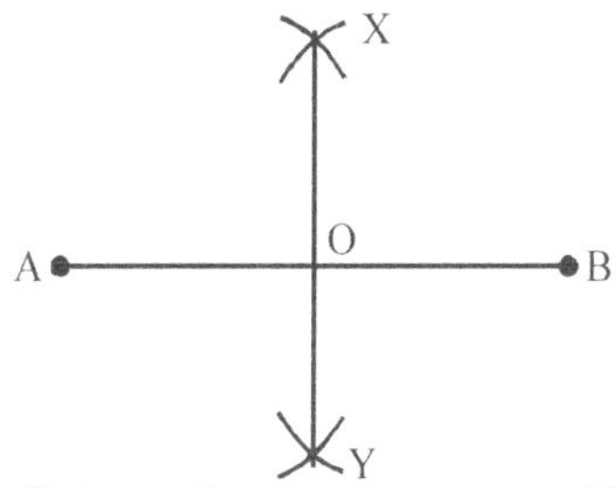

Column-I		Column-II
(A) XY	(p)	90°
(B) ∠AOX is equal to	(q)	OB
(C) ∠AOY is equal to	(r)	Perpendicular bisector
(D) AO is equal to	(s)	∠BOX
(E) ∠AOX and ∠BOX measures	(t)	∠BOY

Very Short Answer Questions:

DIRECTIONS : *Give answer in one word or one sentence.*

1. Construct following line segments with the help of ruler.
   (i)   3.4 cm   (ii) 6.2 cm
   (iii) 8.5 cm
2. Now, draw the above line segment with the help of ruler and compasses.
3. Draw a circle of-
   (i)   radius 5 cm   (ii) radius 4 cm

4. Draw two circles of radii 3 cm and 4 cm with the same centre

5. How many circles can be drawn passing through one given point.

6. With O as the centre, draw three circles of radii 3 cm, 5 cm and 6 cm.

7. If AB = 4.8 cm and CD = 2.8 cm, construct a line segment whose length is AB – CD.

Short Answer Questions :

DIRECTIONS : *Give answer in 2-3 sentences.*

1. Draw a circle of radius 4.4 cm. Mark points A at 4 cm, B at 4.4 cm and C at 5 cm away from the centre of the circle. Name the points that are inside, outside and on the boundary of the circle.

2. Construct the angles equal to the following angles.

(i)

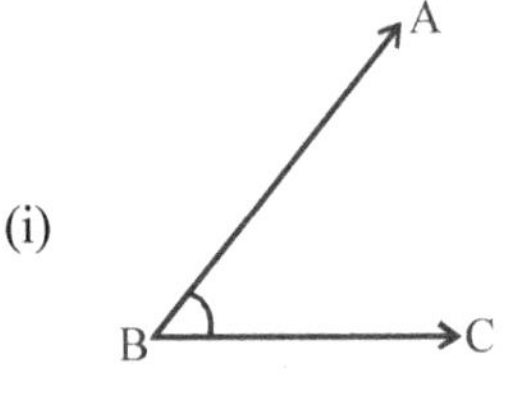

(ii)

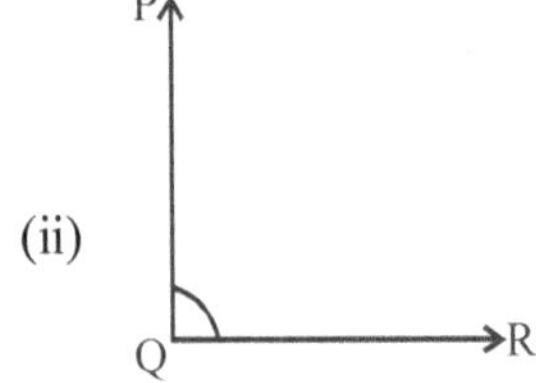

(iii)

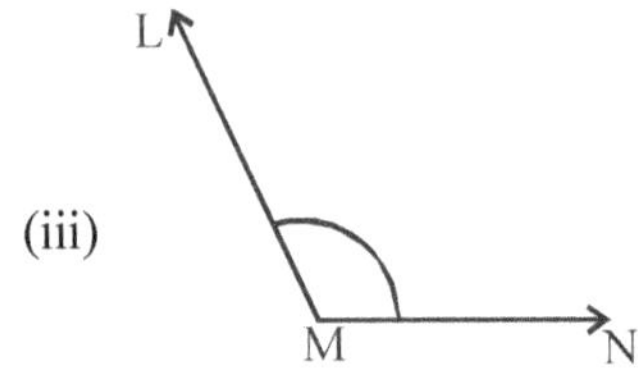

3. Construct $\overline{AB}$ of length 5.8 cm. From A cut off $\overline{AC}$ as 2.5 cm. Now, measure BC with ruler.

4. Draw a circle taking line segment of length 3.4 cm as its diameter.

5. Draw three concentric circles with radii 2 cm, 3 cm and 4 cm.

6. Draw $\overline{AB}$ of length of 8 cm. From this cut off $\overline{AP} = 3$ cm, and $\overline{QB} = 3$ cm . Now find the length of $\overline{PQ}$.

7. Construct an angle of 90° and draw angle bisector of it. Measure the angle so obtained.

Long Answer Questions :

DIRECTIONS : *Give answer in four to five sentences.*

1. Draw a line segment using ruler and compass AB = 3.2 cm. Draw $\overline{PQ}$ such that length of $\overline{PQ}$ is thrice of $\overline{AB}$.

2. Draw a line segment of length 6.6 cm. Bisect it and measure the length of each part.

3. Using a protractor, draw an angle of measure 72°. With this angle as given, draw an angle of measure 36°.

4. Construct an angle of 105° using pair of compasses.

5. Draw $\angle XYZ = 90°$ and divide it into four equal parts. What will be the measure of each angle?

2 EXERCISE

Text-Book Exercise :

1. Let A, B be the centres of two circles of equal radii, draw them so that each one of them passes through the centre of the other. Let them intersect at C and D. Examine whether $\overline{AB}$ and $\overline{CD}$ are at right angles.

2. Given $\overline{AB}$ and of length 3.9 cm, construct $\overline{PQ}$ such that the length of $\overline{PQ}$ is twice that of $\overline{AB}$. Verify by measurement.

Hint: Construct $\overline{PX}$ such that length of $\overline{PX}$ = length of $\overline{AB}$; then cut-off $\overline{XQ}$ such that $\overline{XQ}$ also has the length of $\overline{AB}$.

3. Given $\overline{AB}$ of length 7.3 cm and $\overline{CD}$ of length 3.4 cm, construct a line-segment $\overline{XY}$ such that the length of $\overline{XY}$ is equal to the difference between the lengths of $\overline{AB}$ and $\overline{CD}$. Verify by measurement.

4. Draw the perpendicular bisector of $\overline{XY}$ whose length is 10.3 cm.
  (i) Take any point P on the bisector drawn. Examine whether PX = PY.
  (ii) If M is the midpoint of $\overline{XY}$, what can you say about the length MX and XY?

5. Draw a circle with centre C and radius 3.4 cm. Draw any chord $\overline{AB}$. Construct the perpendicular bisector of $\overline{AB}$ and examine if it passes through C.

6. Draw $\angle POQ$ of measure 75° and find its line of symmetry.

7. Draw an angle of measure 153° and divide it into four equal parts.

Exemplar Questions :

1. Draw a line segment equal to the sum of two line segments given in the figure.

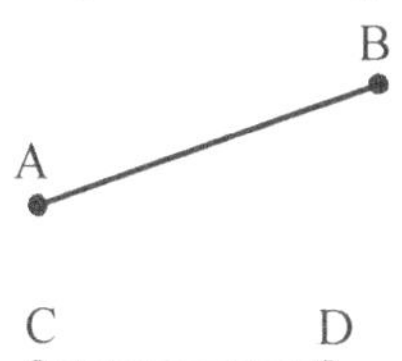

2. Draw an angle equal to the difference of two angles given in the figure.

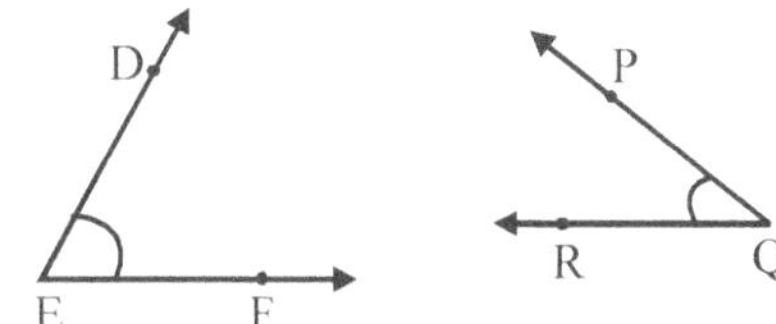

3. Draw an angle of 65° and draw an angle equal to this angle, using ruler and compasses.

4. Copy figure on your notebook and draw a perpendicular to *l* through P, using (i) set squares (ii) protractor (iii) ruler and compasses, How many such perpendiculars are you able to draw?

5. Draw a circle of radius 6 cm using ruler and compasses. Draw one of its diameters. Draw the perpendicular bisector of this diameter. Does this perpendicular bisector contain another diameter of the circle?

6. Draw an angle of 60° using ruler and compasses and divide it into four equal parts. Measure each part.

7. Bisect a straight angle, using ruler and compasses. Measure each part.

8. Draw an angle ABC of measure 45°, using ruler and compasses. Now draw an angle DBA of measure 30°, using ruler and compasses as shown in the figure. What is the measure of $\angle DBC$?

3 EXERCISE

Single Option Correct :

DIRECTIONS : *This section contains multiple choice questions. Each question has 4 choices (a),* (b), (c) and (d) out of which *ONLY ONE is correct.*

1. Two lines are perpendicular if they intersect each other at
   (a) obtuse angle　　(b) right angle
   (c) obtuse angle　　(d) None of these
2. To construct an angle of $30°$, we construct the angle bisector of
   (a) $15°$　　(b) $60°$
   (c) $90°$　　(d) $120°$
3. What measures of angle are marked on protractor?
   (a) $0°$ to $180°$　　(b) $0°$ to $90°$
   (c) $0°$ to $120°$　　(d) None of these
4. What is the smallest unit marked on the scale?
   (a) Inch　　(b) Centimeter
   (c) Millimeter　　(d) None of these
5. The angle bisector of an angle divides an angle into
   (a) Two equal angles
   (b) Two unequal angles
   (c) Infinite equal angles
   (d) None of these
6. Which of the following statement is false?
   (a) Using protractor, angle of any measure between $0°$ and $180°$ can be drawn.
   (b) A line has two end points.
   (c) An angle whose measure is greater than $90°$ is an obtuse angle.
   (d) Two coinciding rays with a common end point form an angle of measure $0°$.
7. Which of the following angles cannot be constructed using ruler and compasses?
   (a) $75°$　　(b) $15°$
   (c) $135°$　　(d) $85°$
8. How many lines can be drawn which are perpendicular to a given line and pass through a point lying on the line?
   (a) one　　(b) two
   (c) three　　(d) infinitely many
9. The triangular shaped instruments in the geometrical box are called ____________.
   (a) Protractor　　(b) Divider
   (c) Compass　　(d) Set-squares
10. The semi-circular shaped instrument (in the geometrical box) is called ____________.
    (a) Protractor　　(b) Divider
    (c) Compass　　(d) Set-squares

More Than One Option Correct :

DIRECTIONS : *This section contains multiple choice questions. Each question has 4 choices (a), (b), (c) and (d) out of which ONE or MORE may be correct.*

1. A geometry box have
   (a) ruler　　(b) compasses
   (c) divider　　(d) None of these
2. Diameter of circle
   (a) touches boundary of circle
   (b) not touches boundary of circle
   (c) passes through centre of the circle
   (d) None of these
3. Perpendicular bisector of a line segment
   (a) is perpendicular to it
   (b) divides it into two equal parts
   (c) make angle of $80°$ on it
   (d) None of these
4. Perpendicular bisector of a chord of a circle
   (a) passes through the centre
   (b) does not passes through centre
   (c) contains diameter of circle
   (d) None of these
5. Perpendicular bisector of two chords of a circle intersect each other.

(a)   at the centre
(b)   at one point in the interior
(c)   at a point in the exterior
(d)   None of these

Assertion & Reason :

DIRECTIONS : *Each of these questions contains an Assertion followed by Reason. Read them carefully and answer the question on the basis of following options. You have to select the one that best describes the two statements.*

(a)   If both **Assertion** and **Reason** are **correct** and Reason is the **correct explanation** of Assertion.

(b)   If both **Assertion** and **Reason** are correct, but Reason is **not the correct explanation** of Assertion.

(c)   If **Assertion** is **correct** but **Reason** is **incorrect**.

(d)   If **Assertion** is **incorrect** but **Reason** is **correct**.

1.   **Assertion:** To construct an angle of 30° we first draw angle of 60° and then bisect it using ruler and pair of compasses.
   Reason: Angle of 30° can be drawn using ruler and pair of compasses.

2.   **Assertion:** Length of line segment can be measured using ruler only.
   Reason: We can construct any line segment using ruler.

Multiple Matching Question :

DIRECTIONS : *Following question has four statements (A, B, C and D) given in Column-I and four statements (p, q, r, s) in Column-II. Any given statement in Column-I can have correct matching with one or more statement(s) given in Column-II.*

1.   **Column - I**   **Column - II**

(A) Bisecting given angle   (p)

(B) Perpendicular lines   (q)

(C) Bisecting given line segment (r)

(D) Concentric circles   (s)

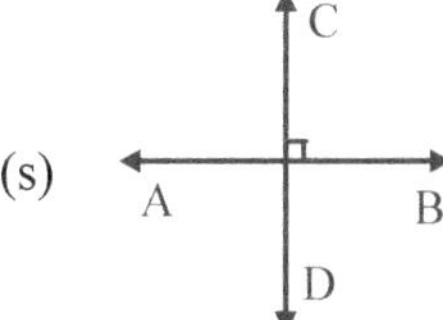

SOLUTIONS

Brief Explanations of Selected Questions

1 EXERCISE

Fill in the Blanks :

1. Ruler
2. Divider
3. equal lengths/arc
4. Perpendicular and parallel
5. 180
6. perpendicular bisetor
7. compasses
8. 90°

True / False :

1. True
2. True
3. True
4. True
5. True
6. True
7. False
8. False

Match the Columns :

1. (A) $\rightarrow$ (r); (B)$\rightarrow$(s); (C) $\rightarrow$ (t); (D) $\rightarrow$ (q); (E)$\rightarrow$(p)

Very Short Answer Questions:

5. Infinitely many

7. Let PQ = AB – CD = 4.8 – 2.8 = 2 cm

   Draw PQ = 2 cm

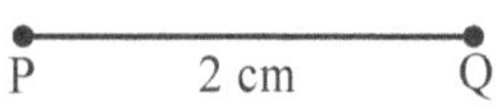

Short Answer Questions :

1. Inside - A, on the circle - B, outside the circle - C

3.

   Now, BC = AB – AC = 5.8 – 2.5 = 3.3 cm.

4. **Steps of construction:**

   Step 1 : Draw a line segment $\overline{AB}$ = 3.4 cm.

   Step 2 : With A as centre and radius more than half of AB, draw a circle C_1.

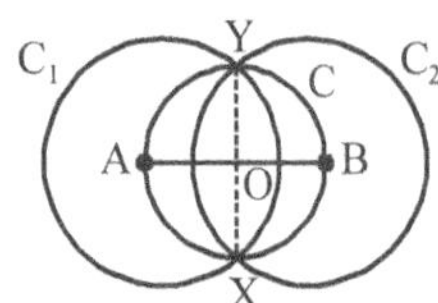

   Step 3 : With the same radius and with B as

---

   centre, draw another circle C_2 using compasses, which cuts the previous cirlce C_1 at X and Y.

   Step 4 : Join $\overline{XY}$. It cuts $\overline{AB}$ at O. Now, O is the mid point of AB.

   Step 5 : Taking O as centre and radius OA (or OB) draw a circle C.

   Step 6 : C is the required circle of diameter 3.4 cm.

5. 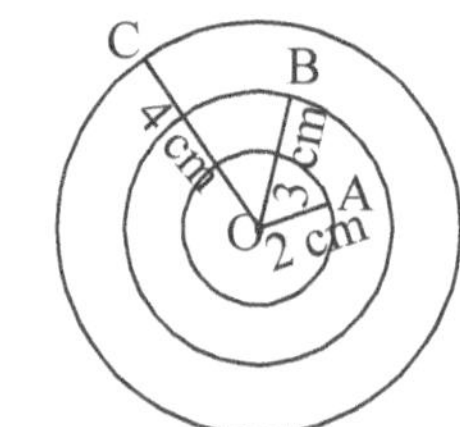

7. **Step 1.** Construct $\angle AOB = 90°$

   Step 2. Draw OC, the bisector of $\angle AOB$.

   The angle $\angle AOC$ so obtained is the angle of measure 45°.

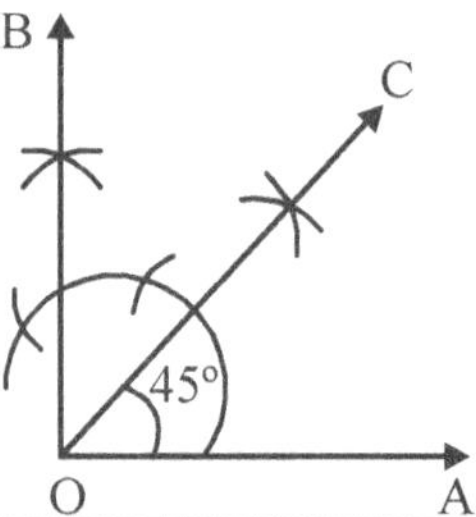

Long Answer Questions :

1. $\overline{PQ}$ = 3(3.2) = 9.6 cm.

   Steps of construction are as follows:

   Step 1 : Draw $\overline{AB}$ = 3.2 cm using ruler as shown.

   Step 2 : Take any line 'ℓ' on paper and mark any point P on it.

   Step 3 : Using ruler and compasses measure length of 9.6 cm.

   Step 4 : Without disturbing the needle of the compasses, from the point P draw an arc which cut the line 'ℓ' at Q as shown.

Step 5 : $\overline{PQ}$ is the required line segment.

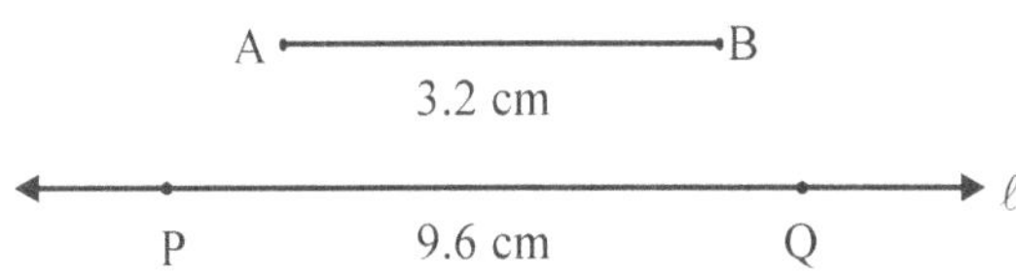

2. Steps of Construction:

Step 1 : Draw a line segment AB = 6.6 cm by using a graduated ruler.

Step 2 : With A as centre and radius more than half of AB, draw arcs, one on each side of AB.

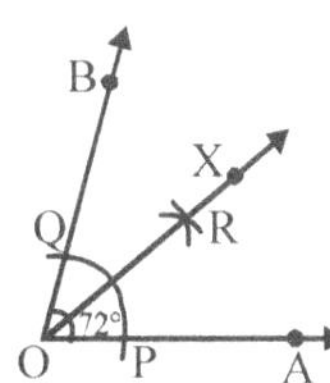

Step 3 : With B as centre and the same radius as in step 2, draw arc cutting the arcs drawn in step 2 at E and F respectively.

Step 4 : Draw the line segment with E and F as end-points. Suppose it meets AB at M. Then, M bisects the line segment AB.

By measuring AM and MB, we find that AM = MB = 3.3 cm.

3. Steps of Construction:

Step 1: Draw a ray OA.

Step 2: With the help of a protractor construct an angle AOB of measure 72°.

Step 3: With centre O and a convenient radius draw an arc cutting sides OA and OB at P and Q respectively.

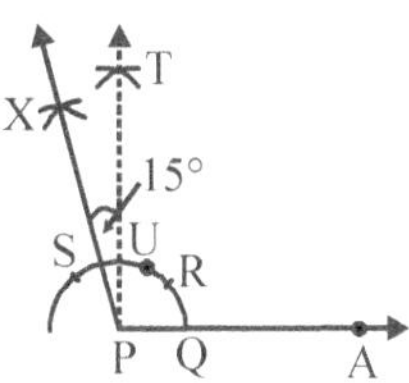

Step 4: With centre P and radius more than $\frac{1}{2}$(PQ), draw an arc.

Step 5: With centre Q and the same radius, as in the previous step, draw another arc intersecting the arc drawn in the previous step at R.

Step 6: Join OR and produce it to form ray OX. The angle ∠AOX so obtained is the required angle of measure 36°.

4. Since 105° = 90° + 15°. So, 105° is constructed by adding 15° to angle of measure 90°.

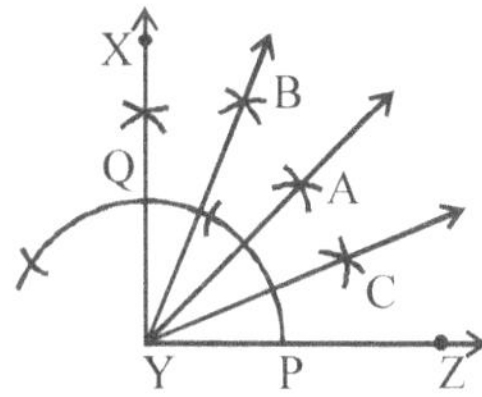

Step 1 : Draw ray PA. With P as a centre draw an arc cutting PA at Q.

Step 2 : Now, without changing radius, draw an arc taking Q as a centre. Both the arcs intersect at R.

Step 3 : Again with R as centre, without changing the radius draw one more arc. Both the arcs intersect at S.

Step 4 : From R and S draw two arcs which intersect at point T.

Step 5 : Join PT to get ∠TPA = 90°.

Step 6 : Now taking S as centre and convenient radius (more then half of length SU) draw an arc.

Step 7 : Again taking U as centre and with the same radius draw an arc intersecting previous arc at X.

Join PX. Now, ∠XPT = 15°.

Therefore, measure ∠XPA = ∠XPT + ∠TPA = 15° + 90° = 105°.

5. Steps of construction:

Step 1 : Draw ∠XYZ = 90° using ruler and compass.

Step 2 : Taking Y as centre draw an arc cutting the arms of angle at P and Q.

Step 3 : Taking P as centre draw an arc of radius more than half of length PQ.

Step 4 : Again taking Q as centre and same radius, draw an arc intersecting previous arc at A. Join AY.

Step 5 : Now, AY bisect ∠XYZ. Therefore ∠XYA = ∠AYZ = 45°.

Step 6 : Now, again bisect the $\angle$XYA and $\angle$AYZ to get four angles namely $\angle$XYB, $\angle$BYA, $\angle$AYC, $\angle$CYZ as shown in the figure.

Now, $\angle$XYB = $\angle$BYA = $\angle$AYC = $\angle$CYZ

$$= \frac{90°}{4} = 22\frac{1}{2}°$$

2 EXERCISE

Text-Book Exercise :

1. yes, the line segments $\overline{AB}$ and $\overline{CD}$ are at right angles.

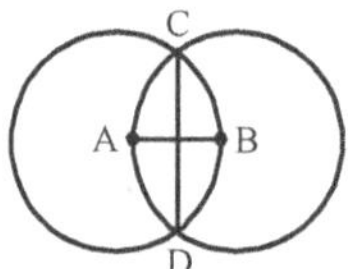

2. **Step I:** Draw a line ℓ.

   Step II: Draw AB = 3.9 cm.

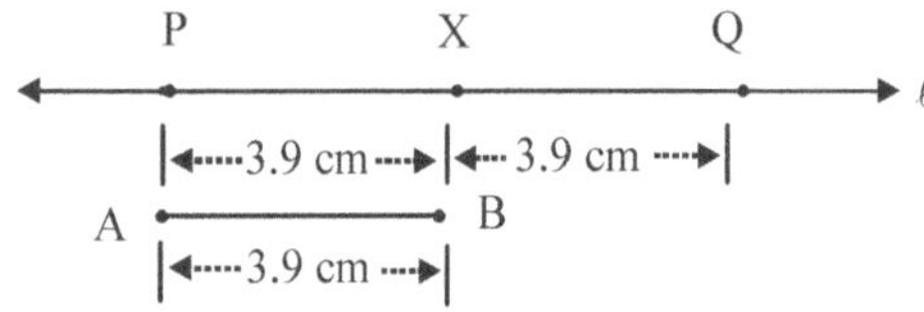

   Step III: From the line-construct $\overline{PX} = \overline{AB}$ (= 3.9 cm).

   Step IV: Next construct $\overline{XQ} = \overline{AB}$ (= 3.9 cm)

   Thus, the lengths of $\overline{PX}$ and $\overline{XQ}$ are added together to make twice the length of AB.

   Verification:

   $$\overline{AB} + \overline{AB} = 3.9 \text{ cm} + 3.9 \text{ cm}$$

   $$2(\overline{AB}) = 7.8 \text{ cm} = \overline{PQ}$$

   Thus, twice of $\overline{AB}$ is equal to $\overline{PQ}$.

3. **Step I:** Draw $\overline{AB}$ = 7.3 cm and $\overline{CD}$ = 3.4 cm.

   Step II: Draw a line ℓ and take a point P on it.

   Step III: Construct $\overline{PR}$ such that length of $\overline{PR}$ = length $\overline{AB}$ (= 7.3 cm).

   A ├────────┤ B C ├────────┤ D
      7.3 cm   3.4 cm

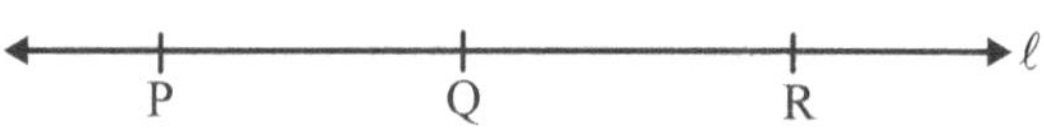

Step IV: Cut-off $\overline{RQ}$ = length of $\overline{CD}$ (= 3.4 cm) such that the length PQ = length of $\overline{AB}$ – length of $\overline{CD}$.

Verification:

$$\overline{PQ} = 3.9 \text{ cm} = 7.3 \text{ cm} - 3.4 \text{ cm} = \overline{AB} - \overline{CD}$$

Thus, we get $\overline{PQ} = \overline{AB} - \overline{CD}$

4. **Step I:** Draw a line-segment $\overline{XY}$ = 10.3 cm

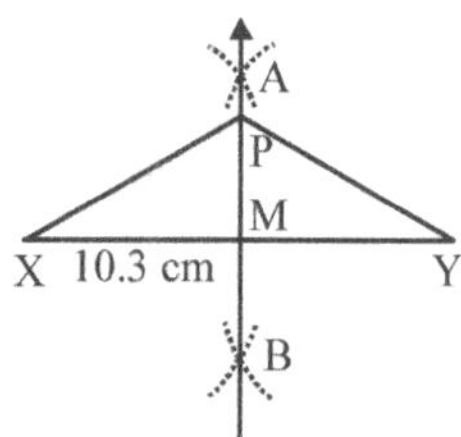

   Step II: With X and Y as centres and radius more than half of XY, draw two arcs which intersect each other at A and B.

   Step III: Join A and B.

   Thus, AB is $\perp$ $\overline{XY}$.

   Step IV: Mark a point 'P' on AB and join PX and PY.

   (a) On measuring $\overline{PX}$ and $\overline{OY}$ (using a divider) we get that $\overline{PX} = \overline{PY}$.

   (b) The midpoint of XY is M. On measuring, we have that

   $$\overline{XM} = \overline{MY} = \frac{1}{2} \text{ XY.}$$

5. **Step I:** Make a point C on a paper.

   Step II: With centre 'C' and radius 3.4 cm, draw a circle.

   Step III: Draw a chord $\overline{AB}$.

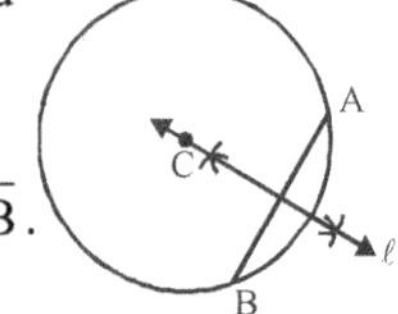

   Step IV: Draw perpendicular bisector of $\overline{AB}$. We find that ℓ (the perpendicular bisector of $\overline{AB}$) passes through the centre of the circle.

6. **Step I:** Construct $\angle$BOQ = 90° and $\angle$AOQ = 60°. Thus, $\angle$BOA = 30°.

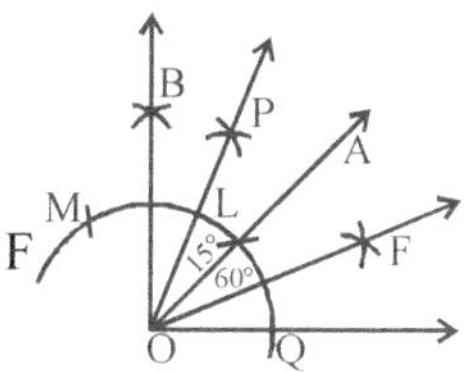

Step II: Draw $\overrightarrow{OP}$, the angle bisector of

$\angle BOA$, such that $\angle AOP = \dfrac{1}{2} \angle BOA$.

or $\quad \angle AOP = \dfrac{1}{2} (30°) = 15°$

Step III: Since $60° + 15° = 75°$

So, $\angle AOQ + \angle AOP = \angle POQ = 75°$

Step IV : With centre Q and L and radius more than half of QL, draw two arcs intersecting at F.

Step V : Join OF, which is the line of symmetry of $\angle$ POQ.

7. Step I : Draw a ray $\overrightarrow{AB}$.

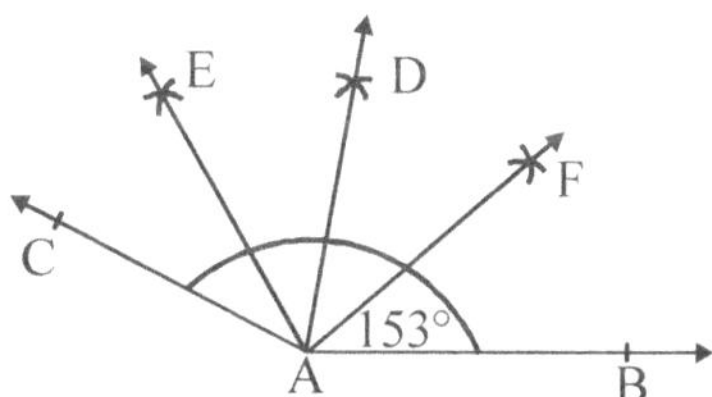

Step II: Using a protractor, construct $\angle BAC = 153°$.

Step III: Draw $\overrightarrow{AD}$, bisector of $\angle BAC$.

Step IV: Again, draw $\overrightarrow{AE}$, bisector of $\angle DAC$.

Step V: Also, draw $\overrightarrow{AF}$, bisector of $\angle BAD$.

Thus, $\overrightarrow{AE}$, $\overrightarrow{AD}$ and $\overrightarrow{AF}$, divide the given $\angle BAC$ into four equal parts.

Exemplar Questions :

1. Step 1: Draw a line l and on it, cut a line segment PQ = AB, using compass.

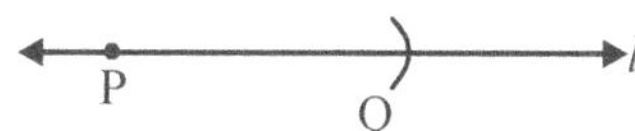

Step 2: With Q as centre and CD as radius, draw an arc to cut a line segment QS = CD on l

Then line segment PS is equal to the sum of AB and CD, i.e., PS = AB + CD

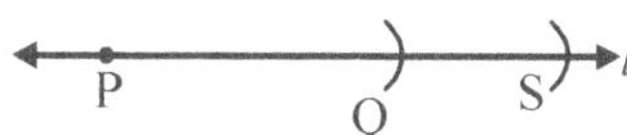

2. Step : Draw an angle ABC equal to $\angle DEF$ (as $\angle DEF > \angle PQR$), using ruler and compasses.

Step 2: With BC as one of the arms, draw an angle SBC equal to $\angle PQR$ such that BS is in the interior of $\angle ABC$. Then, $\angle ABS$ is the required angle which is equal to $\angle DEF - \angle PQR$.

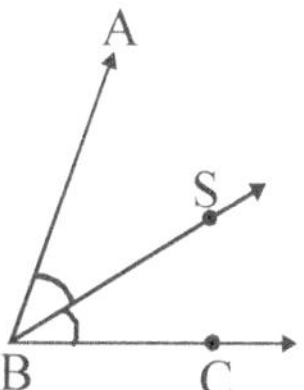

4. One

5. Here, AB is the diameter of circle of radius 6 cm. PQ is the perpendicular bisector of diameter AB. Since it passes through centre, therefore it contains diameter of the circle.

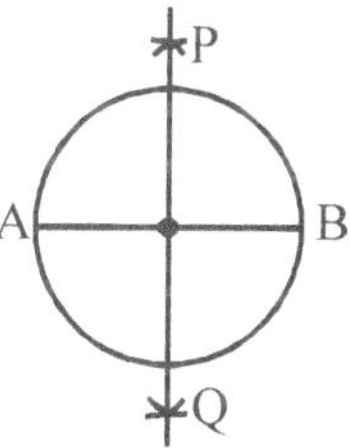

6. Here $\angle AOB = 60°$

OC is the angle bisector of $\angle AOB$ and $\angle BOC = \angle AOC = 30°$

OD is the angle bisector of $\angle BOC$ and OE is the angle bisector of $\angle AOC$.

Therefore, $\angle BOD = \angle COD = 15°$

and $\angle COE = \angle AOE = 15°$

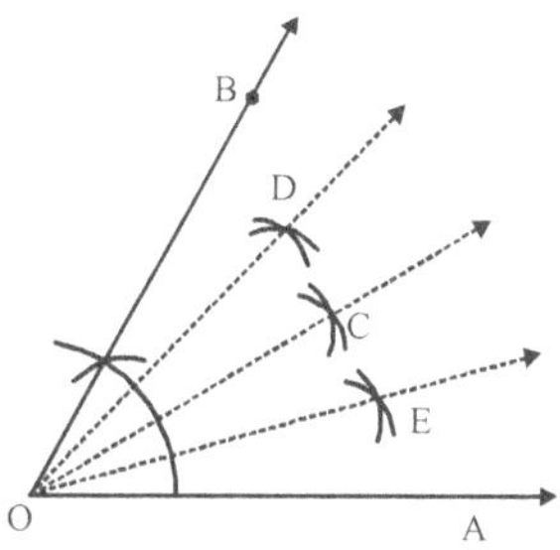

7.

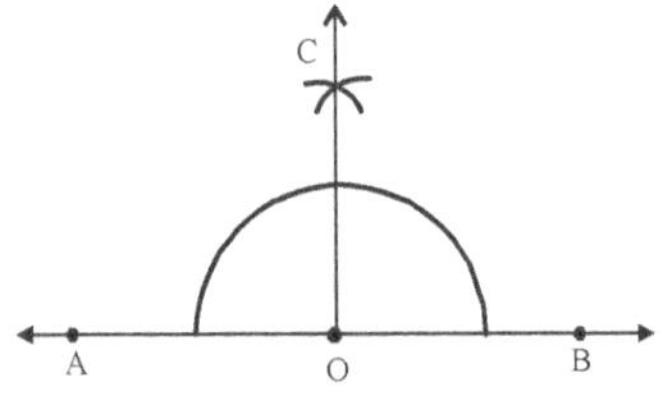

$\angle AOB = 180°$

OC is the angle bisector of $\angle AOB$.

$\angle AOC = \angle BOC = 90°$

8. Construct $\angle ABC = 45°$ and $\angle ABD = 30°$

$\therefore$ Measure of $\angle DBC = \angle ABC + \angle ABD$

$= 45° + 30° = 75°$

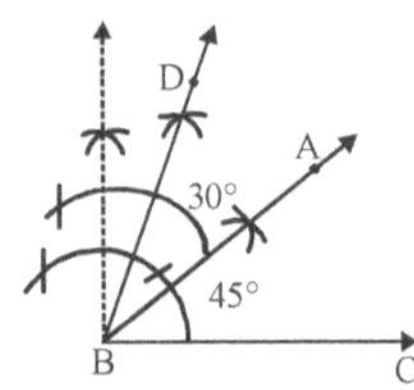

3 EXERCISE

Single Option Correct :

1. **(b)** 2. **(b)** 3. (a) 4. **(c)** 5. **(a)**
6. **(b)** 7. **(d)** 8. (a) one
9. **(d)** Set-squares 10. **(a)** Protractor

More Than One Option Correct :

1. **(a, b, c)** 2. **(a, c)** 3. **(a, b)**
4. **(a, c)** 5. **(a, b)**

Assertion & Reason :

1. **(b)** **Assertion:** True, **Reason:** True but Reason is not the correct explanation of Assertion.

2. **(b)** **Assertion:** True, **Reason:** True but Reason is not the correct explanation of Assertion.

Multiple Matching Question :

1. $(A) \to (p, q); (B) \to (q, s); (C) \to (q); (D) \to (r)$